MW01073553

Law Office Management Series

LAW FIRM ACCOUNTING AND FINANCIAL MANAGEMENT

THIRD EDITION

John P. Quinn
Joseph A. Bailey, Jr.
David E. Gaulin
PriceWaterhouse Coopers LLP

2001
(Date originally published: 1986)

Law Journal Press
105 Madison Avenue
New York, New York 10016
www.lawcatalog.com

00602

Copyright © 1986, 1994, 2001
by NLP IP Company, Law Journal Press,
a division of American Lawyer Media, Inc.,
New York, New York

VISIT OUR WEBSITE AT
www.lawcatalog.com

Library of Congress Cataloging-in-Publication Data
ISBN 1-58852-041-2

Quinn, John P.,
Bailey, Joseph A., Jr.; David E. Gaulin

Law firm accounting:
Third Edition 2001
Bibliography: p.
Includes index
1. Lawyers—United States—Accounting. I. Title.
KF320.A2Q55 1986 657'.834 86-27569

TABLE OF CONTENTS

SECTION I

FUNDAMENTAL ACCOUNTING FOR LAW FIRMS

CHAPTER 1

Financial Reporting Concepts

CHAPTER 2

Cash Basis Financial Statements

CHAPTER 3

Accrual Basis Financial Statements

CHAPTER 4

Revenue and Expenses

CHAPTER 5

Assets and Liabilities

CHAPTER 6

Partners' Accounts

CHAPTER 7

Accounting Controls

SECTION II

FINANCIAL MANAGEMENT CONCEPTS FOR LAW FIRMS

CHAPTER 8

Business Concepts

CHAPTER 9

Management Reporting

CHAPTER 10

Profit Center Accounting

CHAPTER 11

Budgeting

CHAPTER 12

Long-Range Planning

CHAPTER 13

Automated Accounting Records

CHAPTER 14

Organizing The Finance Function

SECTION III

TAX PLANNING AND REPORTING

CHAPTER 15

Tax Information Reporting

CHAPTER 16

Retirement and Pension Plans

CHAPTER 17

Tax Planning

CHAPTER 18

Business Expenses and Fringe Benefits

CHAPTER 19

Law Firm Structures

CHAPTER 20

Global Operations

SECTION IV

ADVANCED ACCOUNTING FOR LAW FIRMS

CHAPTER 21

Risk Management

CHAPTER 22

Financial Modeling

CHAPTER 23

Merger and Acquisition Accounting

CHAPTER 24

Partners' Compensation

CHAPTER 25

Capital Structure and Financing

CHAPTER 26

Pricing Strategies

CHAPTER 27

Uniform Task-Based Management System

CHAPTER 28

Management Information

CHAPTER 29

Property and Equipment Acquisition: The Lease or Buy Decision

Preface

Almost twenty years ago, John P. Quinn, a partner of PricewaterhouseCoopers LLP, realized that there was no reference book that would give a straightforward explanation of law firm accounting and financial reporting practices to law firm partners who were not accountants. Drawing from his extensive experience working with law firms of many sizes, he embarked upon a project to write a reference book that ultimately became the "bible" for those involved in law firm administration.

After more than one year of writing and editing, John's dream was a reality for in 1986 *Law Firm Accounting* was published. It contained seventeen chapters of 286 pages of valuable information that discussed fundamental accounting reports, management accounting reports, and tax accounting reports. John wrote his manuscript with the user in mind, so that a partner, executive director, administrator, chief financial officer or accountant could gain a better understanding of his or her firm's basic financial statements, management financial reports and partnership tax returns. John's foresight gave rise to a reference document that to this day is the most authoritative tool on the subject.

In 1989, I began assisting John with his annual updates to the manuscript by focusing on tax areas. In 1993, J. Christopher Craig joined us as a co-author of accounting and management topics and expanded the book to reflect current accounting pronouncements and to include more management and computer-oriented material.

After John's retirement from a long and distinguished career in public accounting in 1994, Chris and I assumed the co-author responsibilities for the book. That year, we authored a revised edition of the manuscript containing twenty-two chapters and 493 pages with a heavier emphasis on tax and management topics. To recognize the fact that the manuscript covered more than just accounting topics, we changed the book's name to *Law Firm Accounting and Financial Management.* Chris continued as a co-author making valuable cutting-edge contributions to the book, until he resigned from PricewaterhouseCoopers in 1999 to accept a position with a prestigious New York law firm. His legacy, as John's, lives on in this newly revised edition.

This year, I am proud and honored to welcome David E. Gaulin, a PricewaterhouseCoopers Accounting and Business Advisory Services partner, as a co-author. Together, we edited and revised *Law Firm Accounting and Financial Management* so that it contains up-to-date material on topics of interest to law firm partners, administrators and accounting personnel. We expanded the manuscript to twenty-nine chapters containing 825 pages and organized the material into four sections:

Fundamental Accounting for Law Firms. Directed towards the firm's owners and creditors (partners, banks, lessors), this type of financial information is typically found in financial statements focused on the firm's financial position, its assets, liabilities, and equity; upon the firm's results of operations, its revenues, expenses and net income; and upon the firm's accounting controls.

Financial Management Concepts for Law Firms. Designed to facilitate decisions by the firm's management group, this type of financial information contains profitability analysis, profit center accounting, budgeting, and long-range planning that identify the causes and effects of changes in the firm's results of operations. It also incorporates finance functions and using information technology in the financial management context.

Tax Planning and Reporting. Oriented towards optimizing the partners' or shareholders' tax positions, this type of financial information focuses on pension and retirement planning updated for 2001 tax law changes; various tax-planning topics including income recognition, year expenses are deductible, accounting methods, real estate operations, Internet web site development costs, partner profit-sharing arrangements, and multi-state operations; maximizing business expense deductions including travel, meal and entertainment expenses and relocation expenses; providing fringe benefits including *de minimis* benefits, parking and transit pass benefits, and the new employer-provided retirement planning services benefit; choosing various law firm structures including merger considerations; practicing law in the international arena; and partnership reporting requirements including electronic filing.

Advanced Accounting for Law Firms. Focused on advanced accounting and financial considerations for law firm management, this type of financial information addresses managing risk within a law firm, financial modeling, merger and acquisition accounting including strategies and steps for successful mergers, partner compensation alternatives, capital structures and financing, pricing strategies, uniform task-based management systems, management information reports including benchmarking, and property acquisition including the lease or buy analysis.

The book is a logical outgrowth of PricewaterhouseCoopers' broad and extensive experience in providing professional services to law firms and their partners or owners. It distills the thinking of PwC partners and professionals who provide the day-to-day line services to law firms and handle fundamental accounting, financial management, tax planning and reporting and advanced accounting issues relevant to most law firms. Particular credit and thanks is given to John P. Quinn, the original author, and to J. Christopher Craig for his immense contributions while a co-author. Additional credit is given to my partners Jonathan P. Bellis, Robert P. Roche, Richard L. Johnson, Michael Donahue, Elizabeth Case, Thomas Moore, Carl W. Duyck, Greg Falk, and Norman R. Walker. To retired partners John J. McCabe, James F. Rabenhorst, and Michael F. Klein, I say thanks for the technical assistance when it was needed. To other PwC professionals who made or continue to make significant contributions to the relevance and technical accuracy of the financial information contained in this book, I say thank you. Included in this list are, Charles Crawford, Jeffrey Davis, Troy Laws, Glenn S. Fisher, Timothy G. Walsh, Paul Gulbin, Lea Jacovini, Steven S. Moore, Petter Wendel, Elizabeth Plunk, Ada Rousso, W. Brian Williams, Winson W. Tsang, Reni Kopyt, Christine Stafford, and Jasdeep Ahluwalia. Although Charles Crawford is listed among the long list of contributors, I would especially like to single him out for his tireless effort to write and edit material for the book; his significant efforts made this book more than what it would have been without his effort. I am indebted and extremely grateful to Irma Flores, my executive assistant, who spent many overtime hours working with the team to catch our spelling and typing errors and for coordinating with the publisher to make the process run so smoothly. Last, I would like to thank and acknowledge the Law Journal Press for its professionalism in working with PricewaterhouseCoopers to produce this manuscript and particularly for Neil Hirsch who has worked with us every year since the first edition of the book was published. Neil's understanding and patience in the face of deadlines made it easier on everyone to accomplish our missions. Working for Neil and directly with me, I would especially like to thank Ellen Greenblatt for her professionalism in knowing when to apply gentle pressure and for her expertise in recommending ways to communicate better.

Our entire team hopes that we have been faithful to John Quinn's original goal of providing a relevant reference tool to law firm partners and administrators, so that they have a slightly easier time navigating their firms through the challenges presented by the 21st century.

Joseph A. Bailey, Jr.

SECTION I

FUNDAMENTAL ACCOUNTING FOR LAW FIRMS

CHAPTER 1

Financial Reporting Concepts

Chapter Contents

---

§ 1.01 Objectives of Law Firm Financial Statements

The primary objective of law firm financial reporting is to measure the amount of income (or loss) available to distribute to the partners and to communicate information that is useful to management, partners and creditors in making business decisions.

Law firm financial statements are management's representation of the firm's financial position at a particular point in time and its results of operations and cash flows for a particular period of time. Most of the information in law firm financial statements is taken from the firm's accounting records, which generally are organized similar to the components of the firm's financial statements (assets, liabilities, revenues and expenses). Information in the firm's accounting records is data accumulated through a series of processes representing the firm's accounting systems, which may be manual or computerized.

The form and content of law firm financial statements are not static. Financial statements are dynamic and can be affected by the environment and by limitations on the kind of information that periodic financial reporting can provide. For example, available financial information often results from approximations, rather than exact measures, and largely reflects the financial effects of past transactions, rather than present or prospective activities.

The primary focus of readers of law firm financial statements is information about the firm's earnings and partner's capital. Information about cash flow and operational performance also receive considerable attention.

§ 1.02 Basic Financial Statements

For a law firm, as with any other business, there are three basic financial statements that serve as a focal point for all financial reporting. These are the statement of net assets (also referred to as the balance sheet), the statement of revenues and expenses (also referred to as the statement of income), and the statement of cash flows. These statements are based upon the following equations:

Net assets equation	Revenues and expenses equation	Cash flows equation
ASSETS	REVENUE	CASH FLOWS FROM
minus	minus	OPERATING ACTIVITIES
LIABILITIES	EXPENSES	plus
= NET ASSETS	= NET INCOME	CASH FLOWS FROM
		INVESTING ACTIVITIES
		plus
		CASH FLOWS FROM
		FINANCING ACTIVITIES
		= NET INCREASE
		or
		DECREASE IN CASH AND
		CASH EQUIVALENTS

While the form and content of individual financial statements are subject to wide variation, the rationale which underlies their structure is governed by the preceding fundamental equations.

In deciding upon a particular manner in which to present financial statements, management typically selects an approach from a variety of accounting practices. Selecting the appropriate accounting practice will often depend on the facts and circumstances surrounding a particular transaction and the best manner in which to communicate the financial effect of the transaction. Given a choice, an alternative accounting practice which is acceptable can be chosen; however, the wise choice would be to select the accounting practice which is preferable in the circumstances.

Factors influencing the way financial statements are presented include the nature of the entity (e.g., partnership vs. professional corporation), the desired basis of presentation (e.g., accrual basis vs. cash basis), the intended primary audience for the statements (e.g., external vs. internal reports) and the purpose of the statements (e.g., determining net income vs. partners' distributable income).

§ 1.03 Partnership vs. Professional Corporation

The majority of law firms are organized as partnerships. However, some group practice firms have chosen to operate as professional corporations. The form of entity chosen by the firm will influence the form of presentation of certain economic activities in its financial statements including owners' equity, owners' earnings and owners' income tax, as summarized in the following table:

	Form of Presentation	
	Partnership Statements	Professional Corporation Statements
Owners' equity	Partners' capital account	Common stock and paid-in capital
	Partners' current account	Retained earnings
Owners' earnings:	Partners' share of income	Compensation of members Dividend distributions
Owners' income tax:	Taxes are not recorded at the Firm level. Partners are taxed individually on the distributions received from the Partnership.	Firm's income tax provision on corporation's earnings.

Other than the inclusion of an income tax provision in the financial statements of a professional corporation and the resulting effect on the Firm's earnings the financial statements of a professional corporation differ from those of a partnership primarily in form of presentation and not in economic substance.

§ 1.04 Accrual Basis vs. Cash Basis

Law firms typically maintain their accounting records on the cash basis or modified cash basis (sometimes referred to as modified accrual basis) of accounting. Because they are relatively simple methods, they are less burdensome than the accrual method and they put aside the difficult issue of presenting the billable value and eventual collectibility of unbilled professional time in the financial statements. In addition, most firms also prepare their financial statements on the cash basis or modified cash basis because of their similarity to tax based statements. However, a few firms, for various reasons, do prepare their financial statements on the accrual basis because it presents a more realistic (and economic) picture of the firm for the reporting period.

Generally accepted accounting principles (GAAP) are predicated on the accrual basis of accounting. Accrual accounting recognizes revenue and the related assets when earned rather than when received and recognizes expenses when the obligation is incurred rather than when paid.

Financial statements prepared in conformity with GAAP are presumed to provide a better reflection of the firm's economic status than financial statements that are prepared on other bases of accounting. Generally accepted accounting principles represent the conventions, rules and procedures that define accepted accounting practice at a particular time and include not only broad guidelines but also detailed practices and procedures.

Cash basis accounting recognizes revenue when the cash is received and recognizes expenses when the cash is paid. While the cash receipts and disbursements basis of accounting is recognized as a comprehensive basis of accounting other than GAAP, financial statements prepared on this basis are not presented, nor are they intended to be presented, in conformity with generally accepted accounting principles.

The modified cash basis of accounting used by most law firms is a hybrid of the cash basis method. Under this method, certain modifications are made to the cash basis accounts to overcome some of the distortive effects of pure cash basis accounting. These modifications generally incorporate some accrual basis concepts, such as recording client disbursements receivable, and capitalizing and depreciating property and equipment, and recording loans payable. The modifications are usually geared toward achieving symmetry between the basis of accounting that the firm uses for financial reporting purposes and the basis of accounting that the firm expects to use when filing its income tax return.

The method of accounting chosen by the firm will impact the presentation of certain economic resources in the firm's financial statements, including uncollected billed fees, estimated value of unbilled time, accounts payable and accrued expenses, as summarized in the following table:

	Economic resources found in	
	Accrual Basis Statements	Modified Cash Basis Statements
Assets:	Cash	Cash
	Client disbursements receivable	Client disbursements receivable
	Billed fees receivable	n/a
	Estimated value of unbilled time	n/a
	Property and equipment	Property and equipment
Liabilities:	Accounts payable and accrued expenses	n/a
	Benefit Plan Liabilities	n/a
	Loans payable	Loans payable

Some firms maintain their accounting records and prepare their financial statements on the modified cash basis of accounting and maintain additional "memorandum records." These records identify the partners' interests in "memorandum accounts" which, for the most part, represent the value of billed fees receivable and the estimated value of unbilled time, reduced by an estimate of fees that will become uncollectible and in some cases by unpaid accounts payable and accrued expenses.

§ 1.05 External vs. Internal Reports

In recent years, law firms have been responding to increasing requests for financial information from outsiders (such as banks, former partners and the firm's debt holders, if any) and insiders (such as managing committees). These financial reports often include not only historical financial statements but also communications regarding prospective financial information such as management's budgets and financial forecasts. The financial statements and other financial information contained in financial reports furnished to these interested groups has usually been tailored to the needs of the users.

The potential audiences' "need to know" can often dramatically impact the form and content of the financial report, as reflected in the following summary of characteristics found in some typical external and internal law firm reports:

External financial statements of law firms, particularly the larger ones, are often audited by independent accountants to enhance confidence in their reliability.

	Characteristics of	
	External Financial Reports	Internal Financial Reports
Accounting Method:	Modified cash basis	Accrual basis
Focus:	Net Income	Partners' distributable income
Frequency:	Annual/Quarterly	Monthly
Content:	Basic financial statements including the related footnotes	Income statement and operating statistics
Time frame:	Historical	Prospective and retrospective
Corroboration:	Audited	Not audited

Internal financial reports of law firms are typically focused on both historical and prospective events through comparisons to budgets or forecasts. These reports often contain key operating statistics, such as average chargeable hours, billing realization percentages and similar data.

§ 1.06 Net Income vs. Distributable Income

The "bottom line" or focal point of a law firm's financial statements is most often the firm's net income for the year.

For external reporting purposes, the excess of revenues over expenses, which is often referred to as cash or modified cash basis "net income," is the figure focused upon because it represents the results of the firm's operations.

For internal reporting purposes, the partners in most law firms are more interested in how much of this "net income" is available for distribution to the active partners. The key difference between "net income" and "distributable income" is "payments to former partners." Typically these payments are fixed amounts (stated in dollars or percentages) as laid out by the firm's general partnership agreement or arising from contracts with individual former partners. Former partners include partners who have retired from the firm, partners who have withdrawn from the firm, and the estates of deceased partners. These payments represent the former partners' share of the firm's net income recorded subsequent to the termination date and are frequently limited in the aggregate to a set percentage or portion of the firm's net income. In some law firms these payments are nominal and in others the amounts are very significant. Generally, payments are exclusive of repayments of the partner's contributed capital.

When the amounts of payments to former partners are significant or are based on net income and the firm wishes to bridge the gap between external financial reporting focus and internal financial reporting focus, the firm may choose to present "net income," "payments to the former partners," and "partners' distributable income" in its financial statements. When such payments are not based on the firm's net income, they are normally reported as an expense in arriving at net income.

CHAPTER 2

Cash Basis Financial Statements

Chapter Contents

---

§ 2.01 Modified Cash Basis Accounting for Law Firms

Under the cash basis method of accounting, revenue is recognized when cash is received and expenses are recognized when cash is paid. Pure cash basis accounting may produce acceptable financial information over the life cycle of a business; however, it tends to distort a firm's operating results when they are reported on an annual or other periodic basis. Accordingly, most law firms adopt a modified cash basis of accounting to overcome some of these distortive effects. Modifications usually involve the incorporation of some accrual basis concepts. Typical modifications to the cash basis found in law firm financial statements include:

(1) Capitalization and depreciation of property and equipment;
(2) Recognition of receivables resulting from disbursements made on behalf of clients;
(3) Insurance premiums paid in advance;
(4) Accrual of retirement plan contributions payable; and
(5) Recording of loans payable.

Modifications adopted often differ among firms; however, at a minimum most law firms capitalize and depreciate property and equipment.

§ 2.02 Partnership Financial Statements (Modified Cash Basis)

The basic financial statements contained in the annual report of a law firm partnership, using the modified cash basis of accounting, typically include:

(1) Statement of Net Assets;
(2) Statement of Revenues and Expenses;
(3) Statement of Changes in Partners' Accounts;
(4) Statement of Cash Flows; and
(5) Notes to Financial Statements.

To illustrate some typical approaches used in presenting a law firm partnership's modified cash basis financial statements, some examples are set forth in this chapter. The specific content of a particular law firm's financial statements will depend on the facts and circumstances surrounding the firm's activities. Accordingly, financial statements issued by individual law firms may vary from the illustrations presented here.

[1]—Statement of Net Assets

An illustration of a "Statement of Net Assets" for a law firm partnership is presented in Figure 2-A. This statement identifies the partnership's assets and liabilities and reflects partners' equity at a point in time (typically month, quarter or year-end). The illustrative statement separates partners' equity into two components: "partners' capital accounts" and "partners' current accounts." In this context, "partners' capital accounts" represent a permanent infusion of capital by the partners and "partners' current accounts" represent undistributed earnings. Some firms choose to maintain a single account which contains the entire equity of the partnership.

[2]—Statement of Revenues and Expenses and Statement of Changes in Partners' Accounts

Illustrations of the "Statement of Revenues and Expenses" and the "Statement of Changes in Partners' Accounts" are presented in Figure 2-B. These statements present the revenues, expenses and resulting net income for a period of time as well as the changes in partners' equity during the period. The illustration highlights the distinction between "net income" and "distributable income," with the difference between the two attributable to "payments to former partners." As discussed in the previous chapter, when payments to former partners are not based on or limited by the firm's net income, they are normally reported as an expense in arriving at net income.

Figure 2-A. Illustration of a law firm partnership's financial position using the "*modified cash basis*" method of accounting.

ABC PARTNERSHIP
STATEMENT OF NET ASSETS
MODIFIED CASH BASIS OF ACCOUNTING

	Current Year	Prior Year
Current Assets:		
Cash and cash equivalents	$ 5,000,000	$ 4,000,000
Short-term investments	10,000,000	9,000,000
Client disbursements receivable	9,000,000	10,000,000
Advances and deposits	700,000	600,000
Prepaid insurance	300,000	400,000
Total current assets	25,000,000	24,000,000
Property and Equipment, at cost:		
Furniture and equipment	15,000,000	12,000,000
Leasehold improvements	20,000,000	13,000,000
	35,000,000	25,000,000
Less accumulated depreciation and amortization	12,000,000	9,000,000
Net property and equipment	23,000,000	16,000,000
Total assets	48,000,000	40,000,000
Liabilities:		
Accounts Payable	500,000	600,000
Employee payroll withholdings	800,000	100,000
Accrued retirement plan contributions	700,000	300,000
Total current liabilities	2,000,000	1,000,000
Long-term notes payable to bank	20,000,000	15,000,000
Total liabilities	22,000,000	16,000,000
Net assets	$26,000,000	$24,000,000
Net assets represented by:		
Partners' capital accounts	$11,000,000	$10,000,000
Partners' current accounts	15,000,000	14,000,000
	$26,000,000	$24,000,000

Figure 2-B. Illustration of a law firm partnership's results of operations and changes in equity using the "*modified cash basis*" method of accounting.

ABC PARTNERSHIP
STATEMENT OF REVENUES AND EXPENSES
MODIFIED CASH BASIS OF ACCOUNTING

	Current Year	Prior Year
Revenues:		
Professional fees	$195,000,000	$171,000,000
Other services	5,000,000	4,000,000
Interest income	1,000,000	1,000,000
	201,000,000	176,000,000
Expenses:		
Employee compensation	60,000,000	55,000,000
Occupancy costs	20,000,000	15,000,000
Office operating expenses	12,000,000	14,000,000
Professional activities	10,000,000	11,000,000
General business expenses	10,000,000	10,000,000
	112,000,000	105,000,000
Excess of revenues over expenses—Net income	89,000,000	71,000,000
Payments to former partners	4,000,000	3,000,000
Distributable income	$85,000,000	$68,000,000

STATEMENT OF CHANGES IN PARTNERS' ACCOUNTS

	Current Year	Prior Year
Partners' current accounts:		
Balance at beginning of year	$14,000,000	$13,000,000
Distributable income	85,000,000	68,000,000
Payments to active partners	(82,000,000)	(66,000,000)
Transfers to capital accounts	(2,000,000)	(1,000,000)
Balance at end of year	15,000,000	14,000,000
Partners' capital accounts:		
Balance at beginning of year	10,000,000	9,000,000
Capital contributions by partners	2,000,000	1,000,000
Capital withdrawals by partners	(3,000,000)	(1,000,000)
Transfers from current accounts	2,000,000	1,000,000
Balance at end of year	11,000,000	10,000,000
Total partners' accounts	$26,000,000	$24,000,000

[3]—Statement of Cash Flows

The purpose of this statement is to provide information about the cash receipts and cash disbursements of a law firm for the year and indicate whether the cash flows result from operating, investing or financing activities. In most cases cash flows from operating activities result from the day-to-day operations of the firm; cash flows from investing activities result from the purchase of property and equipment; and cash flows from financing activities represent drawings by active partners, payments to former partners, and the receipt and repayment of cash from borrowing arrangements. Preparing a statement of cash flows can be cumbersome and complex. The Financial Accounting Standards Board of the American Institute of Certified Public Accountants has issued Statement of Financial Accounting Standards No. 95, "Statement of Cash Flows" (FAS 95), to address the preparation of the statement of cash flows. FAS 95 and, if necessary, the law firm's independent accountant should be consulted when preparing this statement.

The statement of cash flows can be prepared using either the direct or indirect method. The difference between the two methods relates to the presentation of cash flows from operating activities. Under the direct method, major classes of operating cash receipts and disbursements are shown, such as cash received from clients and cash paid to employees. Additionally, the direct method requires presentation in the statement of cash flows or a footnote, of a reconciliation between net income and cash flows from operations. This reconciliation is performed by adjusting net income for the effects of items that do not affect cash flows, such as depreciation charges on property and equipment. Under the indirect method, the presentation is limited to the reconciliation discussed in the previous sentence which must be in the statement of cash flows.

The selection of either the direct or indirect method for use in the preparation of the statement of cash flows depends on the preference of the management of the law firm.

Statements of revenues and expenses presented on the modified cash basis of accounting essentially reflect operating cash flows. Many law firms using that basis of accounting select the indirect method for presenting cash flows and avoid the redundancy inherent in the direct method.

An illustration of a statement of cash flows using the indirect method for a law firm partnership is presented in Figure 2-C.

Figure 2-C. Illustration of a law firm partnership's cash flows using the indirect method.

ABC PARTNERSHIP
STATEMENT OF CASH FLOWS
MODIFIED CASH BASIS OF ACCOUNTING

	Current Year	Prior Year
Cash flows from operating activities:		
Excess of revenues over expenses -Net income	$89,000,000	$71,000,000
Adjustments to reconcile net income to net cash provided by operating activities		
Depreciation and amortization	3,000,000	2,000,000
Changes in operating assets and liabilities		
Decrease in client disbursements receivable	1,000,000	500,000
Increase (decrease) in other assets and liabilities—net	1,000,000	(1,500,000)
Net cash provided by operating activities	94,000,000	72,000,000
Cash flows from investing activities:		
Expenditures for property and equipment	(10,000,000)	(4,500,000)
Proceeds from the sale of property and equipment	—	1,000,000
Purchase of short-term investments	(3,000,000)	(3,000,000)
Proceeds from the sale of short-term investments	2,000,000	4,000,000
Net cash used in investing activities	(11,000,000)	(2,500,000)
Cash flows from financing activities:		
Proceeds from notes payable to bank	5,000,000	—
Capital withdrawals by partners	(3,000,000)	(1,000,000)
Drawings by active partners	(82,000,000)	(66,000,000)
Payments to former partners	(4,000,000)	(3,000,000)
Capital contributions from partners	2,000,000	1,000,000
Net cash used in financing activities	(82,000,000)	(69,000,000)
Net increase in cash and cash equivalents	1,000,000	500,000
Cash and cash equivalents		
Beginning of year	4,000,000	3,500,000
End of year	$5,000,000	$4,000,000

§ 2.03 Typical Disclosures in Notes to Financial Statements

All information essential for a fair presentation of financial statements should be included in the financial statements. Information and explanations which cannot readily be incorporated in the body of financial statements are included in "notes to the financial statements," which immediately follow the basic financial statements. Consequently, notes to financial statements are considered to be an integral part of the statements.

Typical disclosures found in notes to the financial statements of law firms include:

(1) Brief description of the law firm's operations;

(2) Significant accounting policies (including differences from generally accepted accounting principles);

(3) Billed disbursements, net of allowance for uncollectible amounts;

(4) Fixed assets, net of accumulated depreciation;

(5) Other assets;

(6) Bank or other borrowing arrangements;

(7) Lease commitments;

(8) Commitments to former partners;

(9) Retirement plans; and

(10) Segregated assets belonging to others.

The content of notes to a law firm's financial statements will depend on the activities engaged in by the firm during a given year, the importance of each activity and the usefulness of explaining these activities to the reader of the financial statements. Some illustrations of typical disclosures in notes to financial statements of law firms are presented in this chapter. These illustrations are representative, but they are not all-inclusive.

[1]—Brief Description of the Law Firm's Operations

While most law firms don't follow Generally Accepted Accounting Principles (GAAP), they generally provide these disclosures to the extent relevant. Law Firm financial statements should also include disclosures with respect to the nature of the firm's business (a brief description of their practice and its focus), and the use of estimates in preparation of financial statements.

The description of the firm's business will generally contain information about the legal form, practice areas, client base, and locations where the firm conducts its practice.

Some typical disclosures of a law firm's operational and use of estimates might read as follows:

Business Operations:

"ABC partnership (the "partnership") provides corporate, litigation and tax services to a broad range of domestic and international corporations and other clients. The partnership has offices in New York, Chicago, London and Singapore. A majority of the partnership's revenues are generated by its New York office."

Use of Estimates and significant estimates:

The preparation of financial statements in conformity with accounting principles generally accepted in the United States of America requires management to make estimates and assumptions that affect the reported amounts of assets and liabilities and disclosure of contingent assets and liabilities at the date of the financial statements and the reported amounts of revenues and expenses during the reporting period.

The major areas in which the partnership utilizes estimates include the net realizable value of certain assets. The amounts contained within these financial statements represent management's best estimate of expected outcomes based on available information. However, the partnership recognizes that certain events could occur or fail to occur which would impact the estimates by a material amount in the future.

[2]—Significant Accounting Policies

The objective of disclosing accounting policies is to identify and describe the accounting principles and methods of applying those principles that have a material effect on the determination of a law firm's net assets or net income. This is particularly important when these principles differ from generally accepted accounting principles (GAAP) such as with the modified cash basis of accounting. Principles that are usually disclosed by law firms are those relating to recognition of revenues and expenses, including client disbursements, those describing the allocation of property and equipment costs between current and future periods, and those explaining how income taxes are treated in the firm's financial statements. Some typical disclosures of a law firm's significant accounting policies might include comments, such as the following:

"*Recognition of revenue and expenses*—The partnership's policy is to prepare its financial statements on a modified cash basis, which is a comprehensive basis of accounting other than generally accepted accounting principles. The modified cash basis used by the partnership is comprised of the cash receipts and disbursements basis of accounting modified to include: (1) capitalization and depreciation of leasehold improvements and other property and equipment, (2) deferral and amortization of prepaid insurance, and (3) recording of court costs, registration fees and similar client-related disbursements as assets when paid, and as a reduction of assets when collected.

"The modified cash basis policy followed by the partnership differs from generally accepted accounting principles principally because: (1) fees for professional time and other services are recorded as revenues when received rather than when earned, (2) leasehold improvements are amortized over tax lives which are longer than economic lives, and (3) expenses are recorded when paid rather than when incurred."

"*Depreciation and amortization of property and equipment*—Depreciation of property and equipment is computed on a straight-line basis over periods of five to seven years. Leasehold improvements are amortized on a straight-line basis over the shorter of their estimated tax lives or the remaining ten-year life of the office lease."

"*Taxes*—No provision has been made in the financial statements for federal, state or local income taxes on partnership income since the partners are taxed as individuals. The partnership is subject to unincorporated business tax, commercial rent and occupancy taxes, and various employer taxes which are recorded as paid."

"*Pension costs*—The Partnership records as pension expense the annual actuarially determined contributions to be made to its Retirement Income Plan for eligible partners and employees; accordingly, pension expense does not represent 'net periodic cost' as defined in Statement of Financial Accounting Standards No. 87, and the Partnership does not record any pension assets or liabilities on its statement of net assets."

"*Cash and cash equivalents*—Cash and cash equivalents include cash deposited in demand deposit accounts and highly liquid investments with maturities of less than three months."

[3]—Commitments to Former Partners

Many partnership agreements contain provisions calling for payments to former partners (such as partners who have retired or withdrawn and estates of deceased partners). The modified cash basis of accounting usually results in these amounts being disclosed as commitments at the end of an accounting period. Some partnership agreements call for fixed payments over a specified period of time, which are not based on or limited by net income of the firm. These payments are normally recorded as expenses in arriving at net income. Other agreements call for lifetime benefits and are based on a percentage share of net income. These benefits are generally shown on the statement of revenues and expenses as the difference between net income and distributable income. Typical disclosures of these commitments by a law firm where recipients receive a percentage share of the net income might include comments, such as the following:

> "Under terms of the partnership agreement, the partnership is obligated to make payments to retired partners and the estates of former partners. The timing of such payments, which are reflected in the accompanying financial statements as an allocation of the partnership's net income, depends upon various elections made by the recipients and other factors. Amounts to be distributed are usually based on a percentage of the partnership's net income determined under the modified cash basis of accounting, but are nevertheless limited in the aggregate to 5% of the partnership's net income. During the forthcoming year, it is estimated that payments to former partners will approximate $5,625,000."

[4]—Bank and Other Borrowing Arrangements

Many law firms maintain borrowing arrangements with banks to cover short-term operating needs during the year. These short-term borrowings are sometimes necessitated due to the unevenness of cash collections by the firm or unforeseen expenses. Generally, law firms will repay these short-term borrowings before the firm's year end. Additionally, law firms may enter into long-term borrowing arrangements with banks or other lenders such as insurance companies to finance major purchases of office furniture and fixtures, computer equipment and leasehold improvements. Typical disclosure of a law firm's bank and other borrowing arrangements might include the following:

> "The partnership obtained a 10 year term loan from ABC Bank & Trust (the "Bank") in 20X1 which allows the partnership to borrow up to $20,000,000 for operating needs and to finance expenditures for

property and equipment. The interest rate charged on the term loan is the Bank's prime rate plus 1%. Principal amounts are repayable beginning in 20X6.

"Under the terms of the term loan agreement, the partnership must abide by certain covenants including, among other things, maintaining a minimum number of partners and observing limitations on additional borrowings.

"The partnership also maintains a $2,000,000 line of credit with the Bank which is generally subject to the same covenants as the term loan. The line expires in 20X4. There were no balances outstanding at the end of the current or prior years. Interest rates on borrowings under the line averaged 7% during the current year and 6% during the prior year."

[5]—Lease Commitments

Leases can generally be classified as either "capital" leases or "operating" leases. Capital leases are accounted for as assets and liabilities on the face of financial statements, whereas operating leases are disclosed as commitments in the notes to the financial statements. Lease obligations of law firms usually relate to rental of office space for use by professional and administrative staff, warehouse space for storage of records, and rental of computers and other office equipment. Typical disclosure of lease commitments for rental of office space by a law firm under operating leases might include the following description:

"The partnership is obligated under several leases for office space. Rentals under these leases aggregated $18,500,000 for the current year and $17,900,000 for the prior year. Minimum annual rental commitments (excluding escalations) at the current year-end under all noncancelable leases were:

Year	
20X1	$ 18,900,000
20X2	19,100,000
20X3	19,500,000
20X4	19,500,000
20X5	19,500,000
Thereafter	39,000,000
	$135,500,000

[6]—Retirement Plans[1]

Law firm retirement plans vary from firm to firm. In addition to unfunded arrangements for retired partners, which are often provided for in partnership agreements, law firm retirement plans are generally of two types:

(1) Funded defined *benefit* plans (usually for partners and administrative employees); and
(2) Funded defined *contribution* plans (for partners, associates and administrative employees).

Some typical disclosures of a law firm's retirement plans might include comments, such as the following:

"The partnership has a *defined benefit plan* covering substantially all of its administrative employees. The benefits are based on years of service and the employee's compensation during the last five years of employment. The partnership's funding policy is to contribute annually the maximum amount that can be deducted for federal income tax purposes. Contributions are intended to provide not only for benefits attributed to service to date, but also for those expected to be earned in the future. The firm's contribution to the plan, was $380,000 for the current year, and $400,000 for the prior year. The following table sets forth the plan's funded status as of the end of the current year:

Actuarial present value of benefit obligation:

The weighted-average discount rate and rate of increase in future compensation levels used in determining the actuarial present value of the projected benefit obligation were 7% and 5%, respectively."

"The partnership also has a *defined contribution plan* which provides coverage to partners and associates who have attained age 21, completed 1 year of service and elected to participate in the plan. The partnership's annual contributions to the trustee of the retirement plan are specified percentages of each participant's compensation or share of firm income, limited to a maximum contribution of $10,500 per participant. Partnership contributions on

---

[1] For additional discussion regarding law firm defined benefit and defined contribution plans, see Chapter 16 *infra.*

behalf of associates are charged to firm expense and amounted to $300,000 during the current year and $285,000 during the prior year. Contributions on behalf of partners are considered a distribution of the partners' allocation of net income and charged to the accounts of the respective partners."

The format of this retirement plan note is based, in part, on the concepts contained in Statement of Financial Accounting Standards No. 87, "Employers' Accounting for Pensions" (FAS 87) issued by the Financial Accounting Standards Board. FAS 87 prescribes an employer's accounting for retirement programs and the related financial disclosure in its accrual basis financial statements. While most law firms use the modified cash basis of accounting and therefore would not necessarily be required to follow the guidance set forth in FAS 87, most firms do observe the financial statement disclosure requirements as set forth in FAS 87.

Some law firms may also offer postretirement benefits. These benefits can be divided into two groups:

(1) Postretirement benefits other than pensions such as health care coverage; and

(2) Postemployment benefits such as severance, salary and/or health benefit continuation or disability related benefits.

The extent of postretirement and postemployment benefits will vary from firm to firm. The accounting for these benefits can be complex and detailed. The Financial Accounting Standards Board has issued separate Statements of Financial Accounting Standards to address the accounting and reporting requirements of these benefits on an accrual basis. Statement of Financial Accounting Standards No. 106, "Employers' Accounting for Postretirement Benefits Other Than Pensions" (FAS 106), addresses postretirement benefits. Statement of Financial Accounting Standards No. 112, "Employers' Accounting for Postemployment Benefits" (FAS 112), addresses postemployment benefits. As most law firms use the modified cash basis of accounting, postretirement and postemployment benefits are accounted for on a pay-as-you-go basis and not recorded as a liability in the firm's statement of net assets. However, if significant benefit obligations exist, firms have generally chosen to disclose such information in the notes to their financial statements, similar to FAS 87 with respect to the actuarial present value of accumulated benefit obligations and plan assets. FAS Nos. 106 and 112 should be reviewed, if necessary, with the firm's independent accountant, to determine the proper reporting for these benefits if they are offered by the firm.

[7]—Segregated Assets Belonging to Others

Law firms frequently act as custodians of assets of various types (usually cash) that belong to individuals who are not associated with the firm. These assets often relate to real estate and similar escrowtype deposits. While these assets are not usually included in the firm's basic financial statements, they are often disclosed as supplementary financial information. Typical disclosure in the notes to a law firm's financial statements might include the following explanation:

> "At the end of the current year and at the end of the prior year, cash totalling $1,200,000 and $900,000, respectively, was held for clients and others. Neither the cash balances nor the related liabilities are included in the accompanying financial statements."

§ 2.04 Additional Financial Analysis Schedules

Additional analysis schedules, which are not a required part of the basic financial statements, are nevertheless often contained in a law firm's annual report. Typical additional financial analysis schedules include:

(1) Details of certain current assets (cash, short-term investments, client disbursements receivables);

(2) Details of certain expenses (employee costs, occupancy costs, other operating expenses);

(3) Changes in property and equipment and accumulated depreciation;

(4) Changes in individual partners' accounts (current accounts, capital accounts, former partners' accounts);

(5) Reconciliation of net income with ordinary income reported on U.S. partnership return of income (Form 1065); and

(6) Insurance coverage.

Examples of several of these analyses are presented in subsequent chapters of this book.

The number of additional financial analysis schedules and types and the amount of detail presented therein will vary from firm to firm. Some law firms have reduced the number of these additional financial analysis schedules contained in the law firm's annual report.

§ 2.05 Professional Corporation Financial Statements (Modified Cash Basis)

The basic financial statements contained in the annual report of a law firm professional corporation, which uses the modified cash basis of accounting, typically include:

(1) Statement of Net Assets;
(2) Statement of Revenues and Expenses;
(3) Statement of Changes in Shareholders' Equity;
(4) Statement of Cash Flows; and
(5) Notes to Financial Statements.

Some typical approaches used in presenting a law firm professional corporation's modified cash basis financial statements are illustrated in this chapter.

[1]—Statement of Net Assets

An illustration of a "Statement of Net Assets" for a law firm professional corporation is presented in Figure 2-D. The illustrative statement separates shareholders' equity into three components: "common stock" and "paid-in capital," which represent permanent capital, and "retained earnings," which represents that portion of the professional corporation's cumulative earnings which have not been distributed to shareholders in the form of dividends.

[2]—Statement of Revenues and Expenses and Statement of Changes in Shareholders' Equity

Illustrations of a "Statement of Revenues and Expenses" and a "Statement of Changes in Shareholders' Equity" for a law firm professional corporation are presented in Figure 2-E. The illustration highlights "member compensation" (amounts paid to shareholder members of the corporation) which together with income taxes represent the principal factors differentiating net income of a professional corporation from net income of a partnership. Because taxes are recorded when paid, current year tax payments relate, in part, to income earned in the prior year. Consequently, "income taxes" reflected in the illustrative statement may bear little relationship to income before income taxes.

[3]—Statement of Cash Flows

An illustration of a "Statement of Cash Flows" using the indirect method for a professional corporation is presented in Figure 2-F. Again the principal factor differentiating a professional corporation from a partnership is the manner in which the shareholders'/partners' compensation is reported. With a partnership, partner distributions are treated as a cash flow from financing activities. With a professional corporation, partner compensation is presented as cash flow from operations. Refer to the "Partnership Financial Statements (Modified Cash Basis)" section of this chapter for a discussion of the preparation of a statement of cash flows and the related authoritative guidance.

Figure 2-D. Illustration of a law firm professional corporation's financial position using the "*modified cash basis*" method of accounting.

XYZ PROFESSIONAL CORPORATION
STATEMENT OF NET ASSETS
MODIFIED CASH BASIS

	Current Year	Prior Year
Assets:		
Cash and cash equivalents	$ 9,000,000	$ 7,000,000
Disbursements recoverable from clients	8,000,000	6,000,000
Advances and deposits	1,000,000	1,000,000
Furniture, fixtures and leasehold improvements, at cost less accumulated depreciation and amortization	13,000,000	15,000,000
Total	31,000,000	29,000,000
Liabilities:		
Payroll deductions withheld	4,000,000	3,000,000
Notes payable to bank	2,000,000	4,000,000
Dividends payable	1,000,000	—
Retirement plan contribution payable	8,000,000	7,000,000
Total liabilities	15,000,000	14,000,000
Net assets	$16,000,000	$15,000,000
Shareholders' Equity:		
Common stock	$ 1,000,000	$ 1,000,000
Paid-in capital	12,000,000	12,000,000
Retained earnings	3,000,000	2,000,000
Total shareholders' equity	$16,000,000	$15,000,000

Figure 2-E. Illustration of a law firm professional corporation's results of operations and changes in equity using the "*modified cash basis*" method of accounting.

XYZ PROFESSIONAL CORPORATION
STATEMENT OF REVENUES AND EXPENSES
MODIFIED CASH BASIS

	Current Year	Prior Year
Revenues:		
Fees	$180,000,000	$170,000,000
Other services	5,000,000	4,000,000
Interest income	500,000	500,000
	185,500,000	174,500,000
Expenses:		
Member compensation	72,000,000	69,000,000
Employee compensation	60,000,000	58,000,000
Occupancy costs	21,000,000	16,000,000
Office operating expenses	15,000,000	16,500,000
Professional activities	3,000,000	3,000,000
General business expenses	8,000,000	7,000,000
	179,000,000	169,500,000
Income before income taxes	6,500,000	5,000,000
Income taxes	3,500,000	3,000,000
Excess of income over expenses—Net income	$3,000,000	$2,000,000

STATEMENT OF CHANGES IN SHAREHOLDERS' EQUITY

	Current Year	Prior Year
Retained earnings:		
Balance at beginning of year	$2,000,000	$1,000,000
Net income	3,000,000	2,000,000
Dividends	(2,000,000)	(1,000,000)
Balance at end of year	3,000,000	2,000,000
Common stock	1,000,000	1,000,000
Paid-in capital	12,000,000	12,000,000
Shareholders' equity	$16,000,000	$15,000,000

Figure 2-F. Illustration of a law firm professional corporation's cash flows using the indirect method.

XYZ PROFESSIONAL CORPORATION
STATEMENT OF CASH FLOWS MODIFIED CASH BASIS

	Current Year	Prior Year
Cash flows from operating activities:		
Excess of revenues over expenses-Net income	$3,000,000	$2,000,000
Adjustments to reconcile net income to net cash provided by operating activities		
Depreciation and amortization	3,000,000	2,500,000
Changes in operating assets and liabilities		
(Increase) decrease in disbursements recoverable from clients	(2,000,000)	1,000,000
Increase (decrease) in other assets and liabilities (net)	2,000,000	(1,500,000)
Net cash provided by operating activities	6,000,000	4,000,000
Cash flows from investing activities:		
Expenditures for property and equipment	(1,000,000)	—
Cash flows from financing activities:		
Payments of bank notes	(2,000,000)	(2,000,000)
Dividends paid to shareholders	(1,000,000)	(1,000,000)
Net cash used in financing activities	(3,000,000)	(3,000,000)
Net increase in cash and cash equivalents	2,000,000	1,000,000
Cash and cash equivalents		
Beginning of year	7,000,000	6,000,000
End of year	$9,000,000	$7,000,000

CHAPTER 3

Accrual Basis Financial Statements

Chapter Contents

---

§ 3.01 Accrual Basis Accounting for Law Firms

Under the "accrual basis" method of accounting, revenue is recognized when earned and expenses are recognized when incurred. While the modified cash basis of accounting more closely parallels a partnership's reporting for income tax purposes, the accrual basis of accounting usually provides a better reflection of a law firm's financial status as compared to the modified cash basis of accounting. This is because, during a single accounting period, the accrual basis (1) achieves a better matching of revenue with related costs and (2) provides for a more comprehensive inclusion of all assets and liabilities relevant in determining the partners' or shareholders' equity in the firm.

Because of its comprehensive inclusion of all relevant partnership assets and liabilities, the accrual basis of accounting often is used to calculate law firm partners' interests to determine payments on account of retirement, death, withdrawal or severance at firms where the firm's regular accounting reports are prepared on the modified cash basis of accounting.

Typical economic resources and obligations reflected in law firm accrual basis financial statements, but not reflected in modified cash basis statements, include:

(1) Revenues and related receivables for fees billed but not collected;

(2) Revenues and related work-in-progress assets for the estimated realizable value of unbilled time;

(3) Expenses and related accounts payable and accruals for expenses incurred but not yet paid, including partners and other postretirement or postemployment benefit expenses and related obligations; and

(4) Unincorporated business tax provisions (or corporate income tax provisions) and related liabilities for taxes on income earned but not yet received.

Law firms which adopt the accrual basis of accounting in preparing their financial statements usually adopt this method completely; however, some firms have adopted a hybrid "modified accrual basis accounting" which typically represents a combination of the modified cash basis of accounting together with an accrual of revenues and related receivables for fees billed but not collected.

§ 3.02 Partnership Financial Statements (Accrual Basis)

The basic financial statements of a law firm partnership on the accrual basis of accounting are similar to that of a cash basis and typically include:

(1) Balance Sheet;
(2) Statement of Income;
(3) Statement of Changes in Partners' Accounts;
(4) Statement of Cash Flows; and
(5) Notes to Financial Statements.

To illustrate some typical approaches used in presenting a law firm partnership's accrual basis financial statements, some examples are set forth in this chapter. The specific content of a law firm's financial statements will depend on the facts and circumstances of the firm's activities. Accordingly, financial statements issued by individual law firms may vary from the illustrations presented here.

[1]—Balance Sheet

An illustration of a "Balance Sheet" for a law firm partnership is presented in Figure 3-A. This statement presents the financial position of the partnership based on the assets (principally "fees receivable" and "unbilled fees") and liabilities and the resulting partners' equity on the accrual basis at the end of the year.

[2]—Statement of Income and Statement of Changes in Partners' Accounts

Illustrations of the "Statement of Income" and the "Statement of Changes in Partners' Accounts" are presented in Figure 3-B. These statements present the revenues, expenses and resulting net income on the accrual basis for the year as well as the other changes in partners' equity during the year.

Figure 3-A. Illustration of a law firm partnership's financial position using the "*accrual basis*" method of accounting.

ABC PARTNERSHIP BALANCE SHEET

Assets:	Current Year	Prior Year
Current Assets		
Cash and cash equivalents	$ 5,000,000	$ 4,000,000
Short-term investments	10,000,000	9,000,000
Fees receivable	34,000,000	30,000,000
Unbilled fees (realizable value)	51,000,000	45,000,000
Client disbursements receivable	9,000,000	10,000,000
Advances and deposits	700,000	600,000
Prepaid insurance	300,000	400,000
Total current assets	110,000,000	99,000,000
Property and Equipment, at cost:		
Furniture and equipment	15,000,000	12,000,000
Leasehold improvements	20,000,000	13,000,000
	35,000,000	25,000,000
Less accumulated depreciation and amortization	12,000,000	9,000,000
Net property and equipment	23,000,000	16,000,000
Total assets	$133,000,000	$115,000,000
Liabilities and Partners' Equity:		
Current Liabilities		
Employee payroll withholdings	$1,200,000	$600,000
Accrued retirement plan contributions	800,000	400,000
Other payables and accruals	9,000,000	7,000,000
Total current liabilities	11,000,000	8,000,000
Long-term notes payable to bank	20,000,000	15,000,000
Total liabilities	$ 31,000,000	$ 23,000,000
Partners' Equity		
Partners' capital accounts	$ 11,000,000	$ 10,000,000
Partners' current accounts	91,000,000	82,000,000
Total partners' equity	102,000,000	92,000,000
Total liabilities and partners' equity	$133,000,000	$115,000,000

Figure 3-B. Illustration of a law firm partnership's results of operations and changes in equity using the "*accrual basis*" method of accounting.

ABC PARTNERSHIP STATEMENT OF INCOME

	Current Year	Prior Year
Revenue:		
Professional fees	$205,000,000	$176,000,000
Other services	5,000,000	4,000,000
Interest income	1,000,000	1,000,000
Total revenue	211,000,000	181,000,000
Expenses:		
Employee compensation	61,000,000	55,500,000
Occupancy costs	20,000,000	15,000,000
Office operating expenses	14,000,000	15,000,000
Professional activities	10,000,000	10,500,000
General business expenses	9,000,000	10,000,000
Total expenses	114,000,000	106,000,000
Net income	97,000,000	75,000,000
Payments to former partners	4,000,000	3,000,000
Distributable income	$ 93,000,000	$ 72,000,000

STATEMENT OF CHANGES IN PARTNERS' ACCOUNTS

	Current Year	Prior Year
Partners' current accounts:		
Balance at beginning of year	$ 82,000,000	$ 77,000,000
Distributable income	93,000,000	72,000,000
Payments to active partners	(82,000,000)	(66,000,000)
Transfers to capital accounts	(2,000,000)	(1,000,000)
Balance at end of year	91,000,000	82,000,000
Partners' capital accounts:		
Balance at beginning of year	10,000,000	9,000,000
Capital contributions by partners	2,000,000	1,000,000
Capital withdrawals by partners	(3,000,000)	(1,000,000)
Transfers from current accounts	2,000,000	1,000,000
Balance at end of year	11,000,000	10,000,000
Total partners' accounts	$102,000,000	$ 92,000,000

[3]—Statement of Cash Flows

This statement provides information about the cash receipts and cash disbursements of a law firm for the year and indicates whether the cash flows result from operating, investing or financing activities. Investing activities include the purchase or sale of fixed assets, equity instruments, or other productive assets. Financing activities typically pertain to increases/decreases to partners' capital accounts, and proceeds from or payments relating to debt. All other activities are generally classified as operating activities.

Preparing a statement of cash flows can be cumbersome and complex. The Financial Accounting Standards Board of the American Institute of Certified Public Accountants has issued Statement of Financial Accounting Standards No. 95, "Statement of Cash Flows" (FAS 95), to address the preparation of the statement of cash flows. FAS 95 and, if necessary, the law firm's independent accountant, should be consulted when preparing this statement.

The statement of cash flows can be prepared using either the direct or indirect method. The difference between the two methods relates to the presentation of cash flows from operating activities. Under the direct method, major classes of operating cash receipts and disbursements are shown, such as cash received from clients and cash paid to employees. Additionally, the direct method requires presentation, in the statement of cash flows or a footnote, of a reconciliation between net income and cash flows from operations calculated by adjusting net income for the effect of items that do not affect cash flows, such as depreciation charges on property and equipment. Under the indirect method, the presentation is limited to the reconciliation discussed in the previous sentence which must be in the statement of cash flows.

The selection of either the direct or indirect method to prepare the statement of cash flows depends on the preference of the management of the law firm; however, as set forth in FAS 95, the use of the direct method is encouraged for those firms preparing their financial statements on the accrual basis.

An illustration of a statement of cash flows using the direct method for a law firm partnership is presented in Figure 3-C.

Figure 3-C. Illustration of a law firm partnership's cash flows using the direct method.

ABC PARTNERSHIP
STATEMENT OF CASH FLOWS

	Current Year	Prior Year
Cash flows from operating activities:		
Cash received from clients	$200,000,000	$175,000,000
Cash paid to employees	(60,000,000)	(55,000,000)
Cash paid to operate firm	(46,000,000)	(48,500,000)
Interest paid	(1,000,000)	(500,000)
Interest received	1,000,000	1,000,000
Net cash provided by operating activities	94,000,000	72,000,000
Cash flows from investing activities:		
Expenditures for property and equipment	(10,000,000)	(4,500,000)
Proceeds from the sale of property and equipment		1,000,000
Purchase of investments	(3,000,000)	(3,000,000)
Proceeds from the sale of investments	2,000,000	4,000,000
Net cash used in investing activities	(11,000,000)	(2,500,000)
Cash flows from financing activities:		
Proceeds from notes payable to bank	5,000,000	—
Capital withdrawals by partners	(3,000,000)	(1,000,000)
Drawings by active partners	(82,000,000)	(66,000,000)
Payments to former partners	(4,000,000)	(3,000,000)
Capital contributions from partners	2,000,000	1,000,000
Net cash used in financing activities	(82,000,000)	(69,000,000)
Net increase in cash and cash equivalents	1,000,000	500,000
Cash and cash equivalents		
Beginning of year	4,000,000	3,500,000
End of year	$5,000,000	$4,000,000

(Figure continued on page 3-8)

(Figure continued from page 3-7)

	Current Year	Prior Year
Reconciliation of net income to net cash provided by operating activities:		
Net income	$97,000,000	$75,000,000
Adjustments to reconcile net income to net cash provided by operating activities:		
Depreciation and amortization	3,000,000	2,000,000
(Increase) in fees receivable	(4,000,000)	(2,000,000)
(Increase) in unbilled fees receivable	(6,000,000)	(3,000,000)
Decrease in client disbursements receivable	1,000,000	500,000
Increase in employee payroll withholdings	600,000	500,000
Increase in accrued retirement plan contributions	400,000	—
Increase (decrease) in other payables and accruals	2,000,000	(1,000,000)
Net cash provided by operating activities	$94,000,000	$72,000,000

[4]—Notes to Financial Statements

Generally, the notes to the financial statements and the additional financial analysis schedules of a law firm partnership that prepares its financial statements using the accrual basis of accounting are similar to those of a law firm that prepares its financial statements using the modified cash basis of accounting. One significant difference is that in addition to being disclosed in the notes to the financial statements, under the accrual basis of accounting assets and liabilities relating to defined benefit, postemployment and postretirement plans are also included in the balance sheet.[1]

---

[1] Typical disclosures in the notes to a law firm's financial statements and additional financial analysis schedules are discussed in Chapter 2 *supra*.

§ 3.03 Reconciliation of Accrual Basis Statements with Modified Cash Basis Statements

Those law firms that prepare their internal management financial statements on an accrual basis of accounting, often using estimated values when developing precise figures would be time-consuming, usually continue to prepare their external financial statements on a modified cash basis of accounting. Preparing a formal reconciliation is a useful way to "bridge the gap" between these two types of statements. Adjustments which affect the reconciliation include:

(1) Asset adjustments;
(2) Liability adjustments; and
(3) Equity adjustments.

An illustration of a "Reconciliation of Accrual Basis Statements with Modified Cash Basis Statements" is presented in Figure 3-D.

Figure 3-D. Illustration of the effect on a law firm partnership's financial statements resulting from using different accounting methods.

ABC PARTNERSHIP
RECONCILIATION OF ACCRUAL BASIS STATEMENTS
WITH MODIFIED CASH BASIS STATEMENTS
(Current Year)

	Distributable Partners'	Income Equity
Amounts presented using a "modified cash basis" method of accounting	$85,000,000	$26,000,000
Asset adjustments:		
Fees receivable	4,000,000	34,000,000
Unbilled fees	6,000,000	51,000,000
Liability adjustments:		
Other payables and accruals	(2,000,000)	(9,000,000)
Amounts presented using an "accrual basis" method of accounting	$93,000,000	$102,000,000

[1]—Asset Adjustments

The two most significant and most difficult to determine adjustments which are made to convert modified cash basis statements into accrual basis statements are:

(1) Determining receivables for uncollected fees and estimating the related reserve for uncollectible amounts, and

(2) Determining the value of unbilled time and estimating the related reserve for unrealizable amounts.

Firms that formally determine monthly figures for unbilled time and for fees receivable usually accumulate the necessary financial information through use of a "client accounting system," which is automated in many cases. Estimating reserves for uncollectible receivables and unrealizable time charges are matters of judgment, which are often difficult to make because they depend on the uncertain outcome of future events.

[2]—Liability Adjustments

The standard liability adjustments involve the determination of accounts payable for unpaid bills, usually through the use of a voucher system, and determination of accrued expenses by reference to schedules for unpaid recurring costs such as payrolls, rent, utilities, unfunded retirement plan obligations, employee postemployment and postretirement benefits and similar items.

[3]—Equity Adjustments

In most cases, the only equity adjustment is the net effect of the previously described asset adjustments and liability adjustments. In a few instances, some firms make an additional adjustment reducing partners' current equity and increasing a liability for partners' undistributed earnings (representing the unpaid portion of partners' current year's earnings which will not be paid until the next year). This approach is analogous to the creation of a dividends payable liability for dividends declared but not paid by a corporation.

§ 3.04 Professional Corporation Financial Statements (Accrual Basis)

The basic financial statements contained in the annual report of a law firm professional corporation, which uses the accrual basis of accounting, typically include:

(1) Balance Sheet;
(2) Statement of Income;
(3) Statement of Changes in Shareholders' Equity;
(4) Statement of Cash Flows; and
(5) Notes to Financial Statements.

Some typical approaches used in presenting a law firm professional corporation's accrual basis financial statements are illustrated in this chapter. The specific content of a particular law firm's financial statements will depend on the facts and circumstances surrounding the firm's activities. Accordingly, the financial statements issued by individual law firms may vary from the illustrations presented here.

[1]—Balance Sheet

An illustration of a "Balance Sheet" for a law firm professional corporation is presented in Figure 3-E. The illustrative statement highlights the law firm's two most significant assets ("fees receivable" and "unbilled fees") and its most significant liability ("deferred income taxes payable"). These represent the principal difference between the accrual basis statements and the modified cash basis statements.

[2]—Statement of Income and Statement of Changes in Shareholders' Equity

Illustrations of a "Statement of Income" and a "Statement of Changes in Shareholders' Equity" for a law firm professional corporation are presented in Figure 3-F. With a professional corporation "member compensation" relates to payments to the owners of the corporation (i.e., partners). In a partnership, these amounts would be shown as distributions to partners. The "income tax provision" in the accrual basis illustrative statement bears a direct relationship to "income before taxes." This is unlike the modified cash basis statements where taxes are reported when paid, which usually lags behind the reporting of pre-tax income. Common stock, paid-in capital and retained earnings of a law firm professional corporation represent the capital contributions made by the shareholders (i.e., partners) and undistributed profits left with the firm. This shareholders' equity corresponds to the partners' equity of a partnership.

[3]—Statement of Cash Flows

An illustration of a "Statement of Cash Flows" using the direct method for a professional corporation is presented in Figure 3-G. Again the principal factors differentiating a professional corporation from a partnership are the method in which the shareholders (i.e., partners) are compensated and income taxes. Refer to the "Partnership Financial Statements (Accrual Basis)" section of this chapter for a discussion of the preparation of a statement of cash flows and the related authoritative guidance.

[4]—Notes to Financial Statements

Generally, the notes to the financial statements and additional financial analysis schedules of a law firm professional corporation that prepares its financial statements using the accrual basis of accounting are similar to those of a law firm that prepares its financial statements using the modified cash basis of accounting. One significant difference is that in addition to being disclosed in the notes to the financial statements, under the accrual basis of accounting assets and liabilities relating to defined benefit, postemployment and postretirement plans are also included in the balance sheet. Typical disclosures in the notes to law firms' financial statements and additional financial analysis schedules are discussed in the previous chapter entitled "Cash Basis Financial Statements."

Law firm professional corporations also need to follow the accounting and disclosure requirements of Statement of Financial Accounting Standards No. 109, "Accounting for Income Taxes" (FAS 109). The accounting and disclosure requirements relating to FAS 109 can be cumbersome and complex. Management should consult its accounting and tax advisors regarding the implementation of FAS 109.

Figure 3-E. Illustration of a law firm professional corporation's financial position using the "*accrual basis*" method of accounting.

XYZ PROFESSIONAL CORPORATION
BALANCE SHEET

	Current Year	Prior Year
Assets:		
Cash and cash equivalents	$ 900,000	$ 700,000
Fees receivable, less reserve for uncollectible amounts	3,000,000	2,800,000
Unbilled fees at net realizable value	4,500,000	4,200,000
Disbursements recoverable from clients	800,000	600,000
Advances and deposits	100,000	100,000
Furniture, fixtures and leasehold improvements, at cost less accumulated depreciation and amortization	1,300,000	1,500,000
Total assets	$10,600,000	$9,900,000
Liabilities and Shareholders' Equity:		
Liabilities		
Payroll deductions withheld	$400,000	$300,000
Notes payable to bank	200,000	400,000
Dividends payable	100,000	—
Retirement plan contribution payable	800,000	700,000
Deferred income taxes payable	3,300,000	3,200,000
Other payables and accruals	400,000	300,000
Total liabilities	5,200,000	4,900,000
Shareholders' Equity		
Common stock	100,000	100,000
Paid-in capital	1,200,000	1,200,000
Retained earnings	4,100,000	3,700,000
Total shareholders' equity	5,400,000	5,000,000
Total liabilities and shareholders' equity	$10,600,000	$9,900,000

Figure 3-F. Illustration of a law firm professional corporation's results of operations and changes in equity using the "*accrual basis*" method of accounting.

XYZ PROFESSIONAL CORPORATION
STATEMENT OF INCOME

	Current Year	Prior Year
Revenue:		
Professional fees	$18,500,000	$17,500,000
Other services	500,000	400,000
Interest income	50,000	50,000
	19,050,000	17,950,000
Expenses:		
Member compensation	7,300,000	6,800,000
Employee compensation	6,100,000	5,750,000
Occupancy costs	2,100,000	1,800,000
Office operating expenses	1,600,000	1,700,000
Professional activities	300,000	300,000
General business expenses	600,000	700,000
	18,000,000	17,050,000
Income before income taxes	1,050,000	900,000
Income tax provision	450,000	400,000
Net income	$600,000	$500,000

STATEMENT OF CHANGES IN SHAREHOLDERS EQUITY

	Current Year	Prior Year
Retained earnings:		
Balance of beginning of year	$3,700,000	$3,300,000
Net income	600,000	500,000
Dividends	(200,000)	(100,000)
Balance at end of year	4,100,000	3,700,000
Common stock	100,000	100,000
Paid-in capital	1,200,000	1,200,000
Shareholders' equity	$ 5,400,000	$ 5,000,000

Figure 3-G. Illustration of a law firm professional corporation's cash flows using the direct method.

XYZ PROFESSIONAL CORPORATION
STATEMENT OF CASH FLOWS

	Current Year	Prior Year
Cash flows from operating activities:		
Revenues from clients	$18,500,000	$17,400,000
Compensation paid to members and employees	(13,200,000)	(12,700,000)
Cash paid to operate corporation	(4,350,000)	(3,800,000)
Interest paid	(50,000)	(50,000)
Interest received	50,000	50,000
Income taxes paid	(350,000)	(500,000)
Net cash provided by operating activities	600,000	400,000
Cash flows from investing activities:		
Expenditures for property and equipment	(100,000)	—
Cash flows from financing activities:		
Payments of bank notes	(200,000)	(200,000)
Dividends paid to shareholders	(100,000)	(100,000)
Net cash used in financing activities	(300,000)	(300,000)
Net increase in cash and cash equivalents	200,000	100,000
Cash and cash equivalents		
Beginning of year	700,000	600,000
End of year	$900,000	$700,000

(Figure continued on page 3-16)

(Figure continued from page 3-15)

	Current Year	Prior Year
Reconciliation of net income to net cash provided by operating activities:		
Net income	$600,000	$500,000
Adjustments to reconcile net income to net cash provided by operating activities		
Depreciation and amortization	300,000	250,000
(Increase) in fees receivable	(200,000)	(300,000)
(Increase) in unbilled fees receivable	(300,000)	(200,000)
(Increase) decrease in disbursements recoverable from clients	(200,000)	450,000
Increase in payroll deductions withheld	100,000	50,000
Increase (decrease) in retirement plan contribution payable	100,000	(200,000)
Increase (decrease) in deferred income taxes payable	100,000	(100,000)
Increase (decrease) in other payables and accruals	100,000	(50,000)
Net cash provided by operating activities	$600,000	$400,000

CHAPTER 4

Revenue and Expenses

Chapter Contents

§ 4.01 Net Income of a Law Firm

"Net income" of a law firm consists of fee revenue generated by the firm's professional activities, reduced by compensation costs and operating expenses. Each of these factors is discussed in the sections that follow. Net income also can be described as "Income subject to distribution," Income distributable to active partners" or simply "Distributable income."

§ 4.02 Fee Revenue

The process of determining fee revenue for a law firm involves:

(1) Recording time charges;
(2) Billing clients; and
(3) Collecting fees.

This process is the same whether the firm uses the modified cash basis of accounting or the accrual basis of accounting. However, the fees recorded as revenue in the firm's financial statements will differ for a given period depending on the accounting method chosen. Under the accrual basis, fee revenue represents the realizable value of time charges incurred. Under the modified cash basis, fee revenue represents fees collected. The difference is solely in the timing of revenue recognition.

The following illustrates the difference between accrual basis and modified cash basis fee revenue.

	Current Year	Prior Year
Total time charges incurred during the year at realizable value (accrual basis fee revenue)	$21,000,000	$18,000,000
Billings to clients during the year	$20,400,000	$17,700,000
Cash collected during the year (modified cash basis fee revenue)	$20,000,000	$17,500,000

Each of the three steps involved in determining fee revenue is discussed in more detail in the paragraphs that follow.

[1]—Recording Time Charges

Recording of attorney time charges is the heart of the law firm's business and gives rise to virtually all of its revenue. A reliable system of accumulating time charges is imperative so that the value of the firm's work effort can be billed to clients in the form of fees. Time charge accumulation involves:

(1) Recording chargeable hours by attorneys and by relevant administrative staff involved in providing client services;

(2) Assigning billing rates to each attorney and to each relevant administrative staff member commensurate with their responsibility and experience; and

(3) Multiplying chargeable hours by billing rates to arrive at time charges.

Because of the volume of chargeable hours, the diversity of billing rates used for different attorney and staff levels and the repetitive calculations involved, most law firms find it desirable (often essential) to use computerized systems to calculate and accumulate time charges. Time charge calculation methodology is usually carried out in the following manner:

		Client X		Client Y	
	Hourly Billing Rate	Hours	Time Charges	Hours	Time Charges
Partner A	$600	10	$6,000	20	$12,000
Associate B	$425	20	8,500	40	17,000
Secretary C	$85	5	425	10	850
			$14,925		$29,850

As law firms grow, their time recording systems become more sophisticated. Firm that are organized by practice groups often accumulated fee income by practice group, so that management can effectively determine which groups are making money and which aren't. Likewise, firms with branch offices, especially non-U.S.-based offices, find it very important to be able to track revenue by location so that it can evaluate the profitability of branch locations. By tracking a combination of practice group and location, management can determine if a particular practice group is profitable in a particular location.

This type of tracking also is important for tax purposes because it gives the firm information that is needed in order to apportion its income to the states or countries in which it does business.

[2]—Billing Clients

Billing clients is an often difficult, sometimes tedious, but nevertheless essential task carried out by law firm partners. A law firm's client often sees only two documents generated by the firm. The first is the brief or other document for which the firm was retained to provide its professional services. The second is the firm's bill for rendering these services. Add to this the fact that many clients are "fee sensitive" as they try to control their own costs. i.e., the bill is an important document, which should receive the partner's attention and should be rendered on a timely basis. The collectibility of bills rendered varies inversely with the delay factor involved in issuing the bill. The billing process includes:

(1) Determining the fee to be billed to the client;
(2) Relieving the related time charges from the firm's accounting records; and
(3) Calculating and recording the underrealization (or overrealization) associated with the billing.

In determining the amount of fees to be billed to the client, the partner will take many factors into account, including the value of standard time charges related to carrying out the professional services, special benefits derived by the client from these services, extra efforts and overtime of the staff, efficiencies (or inefficiencies) and other factors. Once the fee is determined, it is matched against the value of time charges incurred to carry out the work. The difference represents a write-up ("overrealization") or write-down ("underrealization") to be recorded in the firm's accounting records, subject to the approval of the firm's partner responsible for billing the client. Billing methodology is usually reflected in the following manner:

	Client X	Client Y
Time Charges accumulated	$7,000	$14,000
Over (Under) Realization	1,000	(2,000)
Bill recorded	$8,000	$12,000

There are many types of billing arrangements that can be negotiated with clients; however, most fall into three general categories:

(1) Billing at the conclusion of the work;
(2) Progress billing; and
(3) Retainers.

Some clients prefer to pay at the conclusion of the work being performed by the firm. Some examples could be billing the client at the conclusion of document preparation in instances such as securities or debt filings with governmental bodies or billing the client when a particular case or matter has concluded such as for services performed in bankruptcy situations.

Progress billing arrangements are probably the most preferable type of billing arrangement as the firm can bill a client at a point in time closer to when the actual services were performed for the client. Progress billing arrangements generally also produce a more even cash flow for the firm.

Retainers are used by clients that want to pay "upfront" for services that the law firm will be providing sometime in the future. Those law firms that follow the modified cash basis of accounting would record the receipt of a retainer from a client as fee revenue. Those law firms following the accrual basis of accounting would record the receipt of a retainer from a client as cash with an offsetting liability on the balance sheet. As services are performed for the client the liability is reduced and fee revenue is recorded.

Some clients prefer detailed itemized bills, setting forth each service rendered in detail, while some clients are satisfied with a brief explanation and other clients will accept tersely worded interim bills at short intervals as long as a detailed cumulative bill is rendered on a quarterly or other periodic basis. Depending on the needs of the majority of its clients, the law firm's billing system should be geared to generate bills in a succinct or detailed format.[1]

[3]—Collecting Fees

In many firms, collecting fees is an automatic process. In other firms, it is a difficult and time-consuming chore. The difference results from the nature of each firm's clients (large publicly traded companies vs. struggling small businesses), the type of services rendered (general corporate or litigation services vs. initial offerings or bankruptcy services), and the time spent by the firm's partners and/or associates in "clearing" the amount of the bill with the client *before* it is rendered. Typically, bills that are rendered at or near the time of service delivery tend to be easier to collect than bills that are issued significantly after the service has been provided.

When a fee is collected it is matched against the fee billed and the difference, if any, is recorded as a "write-off" in the firm's accounting records. Cash collection methodology calculation is usually reflected as follows:

	Client X	Client Y
Fees billed	$8,000	$12,000
Write-off	-0-	(200)
Fees collected	$8,000	$11,800

[1]See Chapter 26 *infra* for a further discussion of client billing practices by law firms.

If the firm follows the modified cash basis of accounting, the "write-off" will have no effect on the firm's financial statements, however; it will be reflected in the firm's fee memo accounts. If the firm follows the accrual basis of accounting the "write-off" should be reflected in the firm's financial statements as an expense.

§ 4.03 Compensation Costs

Compensation costs for law firms fall into three general categories: (1) associates' compensation, (2) administrative staff salaries, and (3) fringe benefits and other employee costs.

[1]—Associates' Compensation

Payroll accounting information relating to associates is often entered into the accounting system with a departmental or practice group designation (such as corporate, litigation, tax) so that annual and monthly departmental payroll summaries can be generated for comparison to departmental budgets. In addition, some firms find it useful to capture, the average compensation of associates by "year graduated from law school." This information is usually gathered in order to assist the law firm's compensation committee in developing annual guidelines for associates' compensation. The grouping by law school class (or by the number of years an associate has been practicing law) usually proves helpful in drawing comparisons with legal profession averages and prior year figures, and in determining an appropriate spread between each group. An example of a table summarizing associates' compensation, ranked by the number of years since the associate graduated from law school, is illustrated below:

Years practicing law	Number of Associates	Aggregate Compensation	Average Compensation
First	30	$2,700,000	$90,000
Second	25	2,375,000	95,000
Third	18	1,800,000	100,000
Fourth	16	1,680,000	105,000
Fifth	8	896,000	112,000
Sixth	3	360,000	120,000
Seventh or more	2	250,000	125,000
	102	$10,061,000	

[2]—Administrative Staff Salaries

The size and content of a law firm's administrative staff will vary depending on the nature of the firm's practice (for example: lawyer intensive work vs. workproduct intensive work). Accounting systems for recording administrative staff salaries usually contain procedures for entering and summarizing payroll costs by department in order to facilitate comparisons to budget. An example of a departmental summary of administrative salaries in a law firm is illustrated below:

Department	Current Year	Prior Year
Secretarial and stenographic	$2,800,000	$2,600,000
Word processing	1,000,000	900,000
Administration	700,000	550,000
Finance	1,700,000	1,400,000
Information Technology	1,000,000	1,000,000
	$7,200,000	$6,450,000

[3]—Fringe Benefits and Other Employee Costs

Certain fringe benefits are statutory; others are optional and vary from firm to firm. Various types of insurance programs (e.g., health insurance, dental insurance, eye-care insurance, life insurance, long-term disability insurance, etc.) often are offered to employees; some of which are paid for by the firm, some partially subsidized by the firm, and others paid for by the employees. Additionally, some firms provide their administrative staff with post-employment benefits such as salary and health benefit continuation, disability related benefits or postretirement benefits such as health care coverage. Generally, fringe benefits are summarized by type for comparison to budgets. A summary of several types of fringe benefit and other employee costs is illustrated below:

	Current Year	Prior Year
Social security taxes	$3,600,000	$3,200,000
Retirement plan expense	1,200,000	900,000
Hospitalization insurance	1,200,000	1,000,000
Disability insurance	400,000	350,000
Major medical insurance	2,200,000	2,000,000
Group life insurance	600,000	500,000
Employment agency fees	450,000	900,000
Cafeteria	850,000	700,000
	$10,500,000	$9,550,000

§ 4.04 Operating Expenses

Operating expenses for law firms generally fall into five broad categories: (1) occupancy costs, (2) office operating expenses, (3) professional activities costs, (4) general business expenses and (5) payments to former partners. Some firms also include a non-operating expense caption for interest income and expense, charitable contributions and payments to former partners. The classification and type of operating expenses will vary from firm to firm.

[1]—Occupancy Costs

For some law firms, occupancy costs include only rent expense. Other firms use a broader definition and include other costs associated with the firm's lease of office space in compiling occupancy costs. Use of the broader definition usually proves to be helpful in drawing comparisons with legal profession averages. Typical components of broadly defined occupancy costs include the following types of expenses:

	Current Year	Prior Year
Rent of office space	$16,000,000	$12,300,000
Electricity and other utilities	1,000,000	900,000
Commercial rent and occupancy taxes	400,000	350,000
Amortization of leasehold improvements	1,000,000	500,000
Storage costs for records	300,000	150,000
	$18,700,000	$14,200,000

[2]—Office Operating Expenses

Some law firms use a narrow definition of office operating expenses and include only the day-to-day expenses involved in running the firm's office in this expense caption. Other firms use a broader definition and include a wide variety of expenses in this caption. Use of the narrow definition usually proves to be helpful in drawing comparisons to legal profession averages. Typical components of narrowly defined office operating expenses include the following types of expenses:

[3]—Professional Activities

For most law firms, the professional activities expense caption usually contains expenses incurred by attorneys, which are related to professional, educational and firm activities. Costs associated with professional activities typically include the following types of expenses:

	Current Year	Prior Year
Rental of office equipment	$4,000,000	5,000,000
Depreciation of office furniture	1,500,000	1,500,000
Computer costs	2,400,000	2,400,000
Office cleaning and supplies	500,000	500,000
Repairs and maintenance of office machines	500,000	1,000,000
Stationery, printing and duplicating supplies	1,500,000	1,500,000
	$10,400,000	$11,900,000

Some firms monitor professional activity costs on a lawyer-by-lawyer basis. This is usually accomplished by coding each relevant expense voucher with an employee identification number at the time it enters the accounting system and subsequently summarizing these expenses by employee number.

[4]—General Business Expenses

General business expenses consist of a wide variety of costs. For each law firm, these costs vary in importance and relevance. Consequently, each firm must select the appropriate expense captions for recording and summarizing the components of its general business expenses and for comparing the accumulated costs to budgets. General business expenses are incurred to carry out firm business, as contrasted with client activities. These expenses include communication costs (telecommunications, postage, express and messengers), library costs (books, periodicals and other reference materials), professional services (actuaries, auditors, computer consultants and retirement plan consultants), insurance (lawyers' professional liability, fire, theft and general liability), interest expenses on loans or notes payable to banks, write-offs of uncollectible client disbursements, charitable contributions and (for partnerships in certain cities) unincorporated business taxes. A typical summary of a law firm's general business expenses might include:

	Current Year	Prior Year
Communication costs	1,500,000	$400,000
Library costs	300,000	280,000
Professional services	650,000	600,000
Insurance	500,000	500,000
Interest expense on notes payable to bank	450,000	525,000
Uncollectible client disbursements	40,000	30,000
Charitable contributions	150,000	125,000
Unincorporated business taxes	250,000	240,000
	$3,840,000	$2,700,000

[5]—Payments to Former Partners

Law firms that make fixed payments that are not based on or limited by the firm's net income to former partners over a specified period of time can record the payments as either operating expenses or non-operating expenses. If the payments are reported as operating expenses, then they are used in calculating the firm's net income. Including these payments as operating expenses, however, can distort the firm's operating income when compared to other firms. Law firms tend to avoid distortions like this. As an alternative (and as a way to distinguish these payments from other true operating expenses), it is becoming more common to report all payments to non-equity partners as non-operating expenses. Accordingly, payments to former partners (whether the payment is fixed or based on a percentage of the firm's net income), former partners' spouses or descendents, contract partners or fixed distribution partners are shown as non-operating expenses. This line appears below the net operating income or net income line. The line immediately below the non-operating expense line can be described as "Income subject to distribution," "Income distributable to active partners" or "Distributable income,"

§ 4.05 Cost Recoveries

In addition to travel expenses, filing fees, court costs and other similar external disbursements to third parties, which the law firm makes on behalf of clients (sometimes referred to as "hard" client disbursements), the law firm incurs additional internal costs on behalf of clients (sometimes referred to as "soft" client disbursements). Typical "soft" costs include:

(1) secretarial and word processing services;
(2) duplicating services;
(3) automated legal research;
(4) communication services (telephone, faxes, e-mail); and
(5) Infrastructure (cost of providing and maintaining access to Internet).

For financial accounting purposes, "hard" costs are normally reported as assets, client disbursements receivable, when paid and a reduction of assets when recovered from clients. As a result, they do not impact revenues, expenses or net income of the firm, unless of course they are subsequently written off as uncollectible. The treatment of "soft" costs varies from firm to firm. Some firms identify all "soft" costs attributable to client service (vs. those attributable to firm activities) and separately itemize these costs on the bills to clients (usually based on an estimated rate). Other firms only identify some of these "soft" costs on bills to clients. Firms also vary as to how they classify the cost recovery of these "soft" costs in their financial statements. Some firms treat these cost recoveries as revenues and classify them along with professional fees in the revenue section of the firm's statement of income. Other firms treat these cost recoveries as cost reductions and classify them as a reduction in the expense section of the firm's statement of income. A third practice is to classify certain cost recoveries (such as secretarial and word processing services) as revenue and classify the other types of cost recoveries as expense reductions. One approach to charging cost recoveries to clients involves the following six-step cost accounting exercise:

(1) Identify *all* costs related to the cost recovery (internal labor costs plus third-party charges, such as machine rentals, supplies and maintenance);
(2) Select an appropriate statistical measure ("time" for secretarial services, communication services and automated legal research services vs. "number of copies" for duplicating services);
(3) Calculate a "standard" cost rate for each type of "soft" cost;

(4) Capture the "time" and "number of copies" statistics attributable to client services (vs. firm activities);

(5) Bill clients for their share of "soft" costs ("time" or "copies" statistic multiplied by related cost rate); and

(6)Reduce total "soft" costs by the cost recovery from clients, leaving the resulting net costs as firm expenses.

It should be noted that the "hard" and "soft" costs may be treated differently from tax purposes. Refer to Chapter 17 for a discussion of tax planning alternatives for "hard" and "soft" costs.

The cost accounting exercise might be calculated in the following manner:

	Duplicating Services
(1) Average monthly costs:	
Salaries and fringe benefits	$100,000
Third party charges	10,000
	$110,000
(2) Average monthly statistics:	
Number of copies	1,100,000
(3) Standard cost rate:	
Cost ÷ statistic	$0.10
(4) Client statistic:	
Client copies	800,000
(5) Client charges:	
Cost rate X statistic	$80,000
(6) Firm expense:	
Total monthly costs	$110,000
Less client charges	<80,000>
Net	$30,000

CHAPTER 5

Assets and Liabilities

Chapter Contents

---

§ 5.01 Net Assets of a Law Firm

The "net assets" of a law firm principally consist of the following assets, reduced by the firm's liabilities, if any:

(1) Cash and short-term investments;
(2) Fees receivable and unbilled fees;
(3) Client disbursements receivable; and
(4) Property and equipment.

Law firms that use the accrual basis of accounting reflect "fees receivable and unbilled fees" in the firm's financial statements. Law firms that use the modified cash basis of accounting reflect "fees receivable and unbilled fees" in memorandum records, which are not a part of the firm's financial statements. The presentation of other assets and liabilities also varies with the method of accounting used; however, the differences are generally less pronounced. Components of significant assets and liabilities are discussed in the sections that follow.

§ 5.02 Fees Receivable and Unbilled Fees

Unbilled fees represent professional and administrative time spent on matters chargeable to clients (priced at appropriate billing rates) that have not, as yet, been billed to clients. For financial statement presentation purposes, unbilled fees are reduced by a reserve for estimated unrealizable amounts. Unbilled fees at the end of a period are comprised as follows:

	Current Year	Prior Year
Unbilled fees (beginning of year)	$ 49,000,000	$ 46,000,000
Time charges incurred	225,000,000	190,000,000
Billing to clients	(204,000,000)	(177,000,000)
Underrealizations	(15,000,000)	(10,000,000)
Gross unbilled fees (end of year)	55,000,000	49,000,000
Reserve for unrealizable amounts	(4,000,000)	(4,000,000)
Net unbilled fees at realizable value	$ 51,000,000	$ 45,000,000

Fees receivable represent fees billed to clients that have not, as yet, been collected in cash. For financial statement purposes, fees receivable are reduced by a reserve for estimated uncollectible amounts. Fees receivable are comprised of the following:

	Current Year	Prior Year
Fees receivable (beginning of year)	$ 34,000,000	$ 33,000,000
Billings to clients	204,000,000	177,000,000
Cash collections	(200,000,000)	(175,000,000)
Write-offs of uncollectible amounts	(1,000,000)	(1,000,000)
Gross fees receivable (end of year)	37,000,000	34,000,000
Reserve for uncollectible amounts	(3,000,000)	(4,000,000)
Net fees receivable	$ 34,000,000	$ 30,000,000

The real challenge in valuing unbilled fees and fees receivable comes from determining the collectibility of the accounts. This is often a difficult and time-consuming task because it involves estimating the impact of several variables. Factors to be taken into account in determining an appropriate reserve for unrealizable and/or uncollectible amounts include:

(1) Relationship - is the relationship with client strong or weak?

(2) History -Does the client have a history of disputing fees?

(3) Service - Was value provided obvious to client or were they more routine in nature?

(4) Staffing -Was the staff an efficient experienced team or was a group of new associates?

The age of unbilled and uncollected amounts often provides a key to collectibility. The older an account gets, the more difficult it becomes to bill and collect full value. Some firms find it useful to calculate reserves for unrealizable and uncollectible fees by first applying a standard percentage (developed from historical trends) to each age group of accounts (a "mechanical" approach) and then adjusting this "mechanical" reserve to take into account known current events relating to specifically identified client situations. Some firms wait several months after the end of the year before calculating their reserves, so that they can take advantage of "hindsight" to the greatest extent possible. While this delay may improve the accuracy of the reserves, it has the detrimental effect of slowing the production of timely financial statements. Reserves are sometimes calculated in the following manner:

			Reserve	
	Recorded Amounts	Historical Rate	Mechanical Calculation	Adjusted for Current Events
Unbilled fees:				
Over 12 months	$ 8,000,000	25%	$2,000,000	$1,000,000
Over 6 months	12,000,000	10%	1,200,000	1,500,000
Under 6 months	30,000,000	3%	900,000	900,000
	$50,000,000		$4,100,000	3,400,000
Fees receivable:				
Over 12 months	$ 1,000,000	50%	$ 500,000	$600,000
Over 6 months	10,000,000		100,000	200,000
Under 6 months	20,000,000	.5%	100,000	100,000
	$ 31,000,000		$ 700,000	$3,400,000

§ 5.03 Client Disbursements Receivable

Client disbursements represent costs incurred by the law firm on behalf of clients. There are two types of client disbursements, (1) "Hard" disbursements (travel, filing fees, and similar third party payments) and (2) "Soft" disbursements (duplicating, word processing and similar service costs).

Law firms follow divergent practices in accounting for client disbursements. Three accounting methods are presently in use:

> (1) "Receivable" method. Under this method, both "hard" and "soft" disbursements are reported as receivables when the costs are incurred and have no effect on the firm's net income.
>
> (2) "Expense" method. Under this method, both "hard" and "soft" disbursements are classified as expenses when the costs are incurred and as revenue or cost reductions when the amounts recovered from clients are recorded. The recovery may be in the same or a later financial reporting period.
>
> (3) "Hybrid" method. Under this method, "hard" disbursements are classified as receivables when incurred and "soft" disbursements are classified as expenses when incurred.

The "hybrid" method appears to be gaining more widespread acceptance by firms that follow the modified cash basis of accounting. Below is an illustration of the effect on a law firm's net assets and net income of using each of these methods (when the firm also utilizes the modified cash basis of accounting):

	"Receivable" Method	"Expense" Method	"Hybrid" Method
Net asset effect (year 1):			
Cash	($9,000,000)	($9,000,000)	($9,000,000)
"Hard" disbursements	5,000,000	—	5,000,000
"Soft" disbursements	4,000,000	—	—
Asset decrease	$ —	($9,000,000)	($4,000,000)
Net asset effect (year 2):			
Cash	$9,000,000	$9,000,000	$9,000,000
"Hard" disbursements	(5,000,000)	—	(5,000,000)
"Soft" disbursements	(4,000,000)	—	—
Asset increase	$ —	$9,000,000	$4,000,000
Net income effect (year 1):			
"Hard" disbursements	$ —	($5,000,000)	$ —
"Soft" disbursements	—	(4,000,000)	(4,000,000)
Income decrease	$ —	($9,000,000)	($4,000,000)
Net income effect (year 2):			
"Hard" disbursements		$5,000,000	$ —
"Soft" disbursements	$ —	4,000,000	4,000,000
Income increase	$ —	$9,000,000	$4,000,000

§ 5.04 Cash and Short-Term Investments

Law firm cash and short-term investment balances are principally affected by: (1) cash collections from clients, (2) borrowings (usually to finance fixed assets), (3) payments of compensation costs and operating expenses, (4) partners' drawings, (5) purchases of property and equipment, and (6) repayment of debt.

The amount of cash and short-term investments a particular firm maintains is really dependent on several factors, including the desired capital structure of the firm. While capital structure is discussed more thoroughly in Chapter 25, certain factors which influence the capital structure for a particular firm include: (1) culture; (2) strategy (both short-term and long-term); (3) anticipated growth plans; (4) anticipated short-term needs (planned office renovations, planned partner retirements, etc.).

§ 5.05 Property and Equipment

Property and equipment of a law firm usually consists of office furniture, computer equipment (if owned or subject to a capitalized lease), office machines and leasehold improvements. In recent years, many law firms have used bank financing to purchase new equipment (particularly computers) and for the construction costs of leasehold improvements in new offices. However, leasing of computer equipment on an operating basis has widespread popularity as well. Typically, property and equipment activity for a law firm can be summarized as follows:

	Balance at Beginning of Year	Additions	Retirements	Balance at End of Year
At cost:				
Furniture and equipment	$12,000,000	$3,100,000	$(100,000)	$15,000,000
Leasehold improvements	13,000,000	7,000,000	—	20,000,000
	25,000,000	10,100,000	(100,000)	35,000,000
Accumulated depreciation and amortization:				
Furniture and equipment	6,000,000	1,100,000	(100,000)	7,000,000
Leasehold improvements	3,000,000	2,000,000	—	5,000,000
	9,000,000	3,100,000	(100,000)	12,000,000
Property and equipment - net	$16,000,000	$7,000,000	$ —	$23,000,000

Practices which are prevalent in many firms include the depreciation of furniture and fixtures under the accelerated cost recovery method using a recovery period of five years, the amortization of leasehold improvements on a straight-line basis over the life of the firm's lease for office space, the elimination of fully depreciated assets from the firm's records and the noncapitalization of minor fixed asset purchases (such as amounts under $500).

§ 5.06 Liabilities

The principal liability of many law firms consists of bank loans, usually to finance office equipment and leasehold improvements. Many firms have no debt at all. Consequently, there is a wide range of debt-to-equity ratios among law firms. A few firms finance part of their working capital through bank loans. This is often counterproductive because it provides cash flow for partner distributions and an "easy out" for partners who do not want to generate cash flow through aggressively seeking to bill and collect old balances of fees due from clients.

Some bank loans to law firms contain no restrictions or covenants. Others contain some restrictions on the use of funds and a series of covenants with which the firm must comply. These covenants sometimes include requirements to maintain a specified level of working capital or partners' equity. The specific level of working capital and partners' equity usually includes the realizable value of the firm's unbilled fees and fees receivable, notwithstanding that these amounts are not included in the firm's financial statements if the statements are prepared on the modified cash basis of accounting. Firms borrowing for the first time, particularly those which use the modified cash basis of accounting, should be careful to determine (1) whether the bank will require that the firm furnish quarterly and/or annual financial statements, (2) the time frame for submission of these financial statements (such as 45 days or 120 days after the end of the period) and (3) the method of accounting to be followed in preparing these financial statements (for example: the firm's *usual method* which is the "modified cash basis" vs. the use of *generally accepted accounting principles* which is the "accrual basis").

Other liabilities reflected in the financial statements of a law firm, if it follows the modified cash basis of accounting, include employee payroll withholdings and accrued retirement contributions. Additional liabilities reflected in the financial statements of a law firm, if it follows the accrual basis of accounting, include accounts payable, accrued expenses, postretirement and postemployment benefits to administrative employees, deferred taxes payable (in the case of professional corporations), and liabilities for unfunded retirement plans.

CHAPTER 6

Partners' Accounts

Chapter Contents

---

§ 6.01 Law Firm Partnership Agreements

Partnership agreements among lawyers range from a handshake and an oral agreement to lengthy complex documents that try to pinpoint every conceivable facet of partnership activity. The agreement among partners is important from a business standpoint because, among other things, it establishes each partner's financial interest in the firm.

When the agreement is committed to writing, it is important that all major business aspects of partnership operations be included in the agreement and that they be defined as carefully as possible. Important business items that should be covered in a law firm partnership agreement include:

(1) Amount of capital to be contributed by each partner initially and annually and the rate of interest, if any, to be paid on the capital account balance;

(2) Participation of each partner in earnings or losses of the firm and the way such earnings may be drawn (the list of units of participation may be a schedule attached to the partnership agreements so that reprinting the whole agreement is not required for changes in units);

(3) Provisions for bonuses, the extent to which any earnings are guaranteed, and any special arrangements to compensate particular partners;

(4) Provisions for mandatory retirement or reduced participation of older partners, for repayment of capital to retired partners, and for pension payments (if any) to retired partners;

(5) Provisions for payments to estates upon death of partners;

(6) Provisions to continue the partnership in the event of withdrawal or severance of a partner for any reason and for the repayment of capital and severance payments (if any);

(7) Limitations on the maximum aggregate amount to be paid annually to all former partners (retired, deceased, severed, withdrawn) as a group;

(8) Procedures for terminating and liquidating the firm and method of liquidating and distributing assets or the proceeds from the sale of assets;

(9) Nature, extent and frequency of financial reports to be prepared and distributed to the partners;

(10) Method of accounting to be followed in preparing the partnership's financial statements and for calculating partners' interests (accrual basis of accounting vs. modified cash basis of accounting);

(11) Nature of expenditures that may be charged to the partnership and a designation of authority for approving expenditures and for writing-off fees and client disbursements;

(12) Extent to which the partnership may enter into unrelated ventures or make investments;

(13) Means by which the firm is managed and the limits of authority delegated to the committee or group charged with the responsibility of operating the firm; and

(14) Rights and duties of partners with respect to voting, meetings, and time devoted to partnership matters.

§ 6.02 Composition of Partners' Accounts

Partners' accounts represent the partners' equity in the net assets of the law firm. Some law firms maintain a single partners' equity account, while others maintain three or more subdivisions of partners' equity because of changes in sharing arrangements or special purpose capital arrangements. Typically, there are two partners' accounts. One account usually represents undistributed earnings (current account) and the other represents the partners' permanent capital contributions (capital account).

Most law firm partnerships seek to achieve an allocation of partners' equity accounts among the partners in the current profit-sharing ratio. Often this is illusory because of new partners phasing-in, older partners phasing-out, special arrangements for laterally hired partners and the dynamics of annual (or more frequent) changes in partner profit-sharing percentages. A practical approach involves establishing a time frame (e.g., five years) within which each partner who is in some transitional phase is expected to have his equity balance brought into line with his profit-sharing ratio. To mitigate temporary imbalances in certain partners' capital accounts, some firms pay interest (or impute interest) annually on balances in partners' capital accounts.

§ 6.03 Allocation of Partners' Income

Partners' income allocation formulas differ from firm to firm. Some allocation formulas are very complex and some are very simple. Some firms strictly allocate cash income resulting from revenue collected and expenses disbursed using the current year's profit-sharing percentages. Some firms allocate income on the basis of each year's historical profit-sharing percentages, which requires identifying revenue collections and expense payments with the year when the fees were generated and the expenses incurred. This often results in a complex, cumbersome, and time-consuming accounting exercise. Other firms take a practical approach and allocate income on the basis of the current year's profit-sharing percentage—except that prior-years' profit-sharing percentages are applied to collections of significant prior-year generated fees (those above a specified dollar limit). For example, assume that a firm has twenty-five partners with the following share allocations:

			Aggregate Profit Percentage	
	Number of Partners	Average Profit-Sharing Percentage	Current Year	Prior Year
Elder partners	5	4%	20%	20%
Prime partners	10	5%	50%	60%
Newer partners	10	3%	30%	20%
	25		100%	100%

Following is an illustration of an allocation of partner income based on these profit-sharing percentages, assuming that the firm (1) used the modified cash basis of accounting, (2) allocated revenue collections based on the year fee income was generated, and (3) allocated all expenses to the current year (amounts are in thousands of dollars):

	Revenue Collected		Expenses disbursed and payments to former partners	Active partners' share of distributable income
	Generated in current year	Generated in prior year		
5 Elder partners	$ 7,600	$ 440	$ (4,640)	$ 3,400
10 Prime partners	19,000	1,320	(11,600)	8,720
10 Newer partners	11,400	440	(6,960)	4,880
	$38,000	$2,200	$(23,200)	$17,000

§ 6.04 Partners' Current Accounts

Partners' current accounts usually represent partnership earnings that have not yet been distributed to the partners. In some firms, a portion of each partner's share of the current year's earnings must be deposited in the partners' capital account. This is reflected as a transfer in the firm's financial statements. The intent of this transfer is to build up the "permanent" capital a partner has invested in the firm. Here is an illustration of activities typically reflected in partners' current accounts (amounts are in thousands of dollars):

	Balance at beginning of period	Distributable income	Payments to active partners	Transfers to capital account	Balance at end of year
5 Elder partners	$ 600	$ 3,400	$ (3,200)	$ (80)	$ 720
10 Prime partners	1,600	8,720	(8,400)	(200)	17,200
10 Newer partners	600	4,880	(2,800)	(120)	560
	$2,800	$17,000	$(16,400)	$(400)	$ 3,000

§ 6.05 Partners' Capital Accounts

Partners' capital accounts usually represent amounts contributed by the partners to finance their share of the partnership's operations. In some law firms, partners' capital contributions are nominal amounts, because the firm is financed principally through bank borrowings. In some law firms, partners' capital contributions are larger, because the partners finance the firm's operations in the entirety. In other law firms, the partners' capital contributions are extremely large, because, in addition to financing the firm's day-to-day operations, the partners are required to deposit additional amounts with the firm in a "reserve" fund which is usually invested in highly liquid investments. Because partners' reserve fund balances are sometimes not proportionate to the partners' profit-sharing percentages, some firms allocate imputed interest to the partners based on average reserve fund balances. The "reserve" fund philosophy is usually practiced by firms that want partner cash distributions to continue at their current level, even when the firm is faced with a sudden short-term downturn in profits.

In addition to requiring that new partners gradually build up their balances in the firm's capital account, some firms provide for a gradual withdrawal of capital by elder partners over a period of years prior to retirement. Some firms repay partners' capital accounts to retired partners in full on the day they retire, and other firms repay partners' capital accounts (usually with interest) over a period of years after retirement. Activity typically reflected in partners' capital accounts is illustrated below (amounts are in thousands of dollars):

	Balance beginning at of period	Capital contributions by partners	Capital withdrawals by partners	Transfers from current accounts	Balance at end of period
5 Elder partners	$1,320		$(600)	$ 80	$800
10 Prime partners	640	160		200	1,000
10 Newer partners	40	240		120	400
	$2,000	$400	$(600)	$400	$2,200

CHAPTER 7

Accounting Controls

Chapter Contents

---

§ 7.01 Internal Accounting Control for Law Firms

For a law firm, as with businesses in general, there are two principal objectives of a system of internal accounting control:

(1) To safeguard the assets of the firm from loss through inadvertent error or purposeful malfeasance; and
(2) To assure the integrity and accuracy of the firm's accounting records and financial reports.

To obtain reasonable assurance that these objectives are achieved, law firm management should identify the points within the firm's accounting system that represent the highest risk of loss of assets or material misstatement of financial information and then design controls to prevent significant losses or errors from occurring. In designing a control system, management usually takes into consideration whether the cost of a particular control is reasonable in terms of the benefit to be achieved. Developing a system of internal accounting control involves two processes:

(1) Devising operating procedures (such as procedures designed to confirm the accuracy of the recording of transactions as they flow through the firm's accounting records) including controls which monitor that the system is operating properly; and
(2) Segregating duties (such as assigning responsibility for the recording of accounts receivable to employees separate from the employees who are responsible for cash receipts).

The firm's systems are focal points for developing procedures segregating duties. There are five principal accounting systems which process transactions for a law firm:

(1) Client accounting system (including cash receipts);
(2) Operating expense system (including accounts payable and cash disbursements);
(3) Payroll accounting system;
(4) Financial reporting system; and
(5) Partners' accounts system.

The first three of these systems represent input to the firm's general ledger accounting system and the last two systems draw significant information from the general ledger accounting system. A flowchart illustrating the integration of these systems is set forth in Figure 7-A.

Figure 7-A. Illustration of the flow of financial information through the accounting records of a law firm.

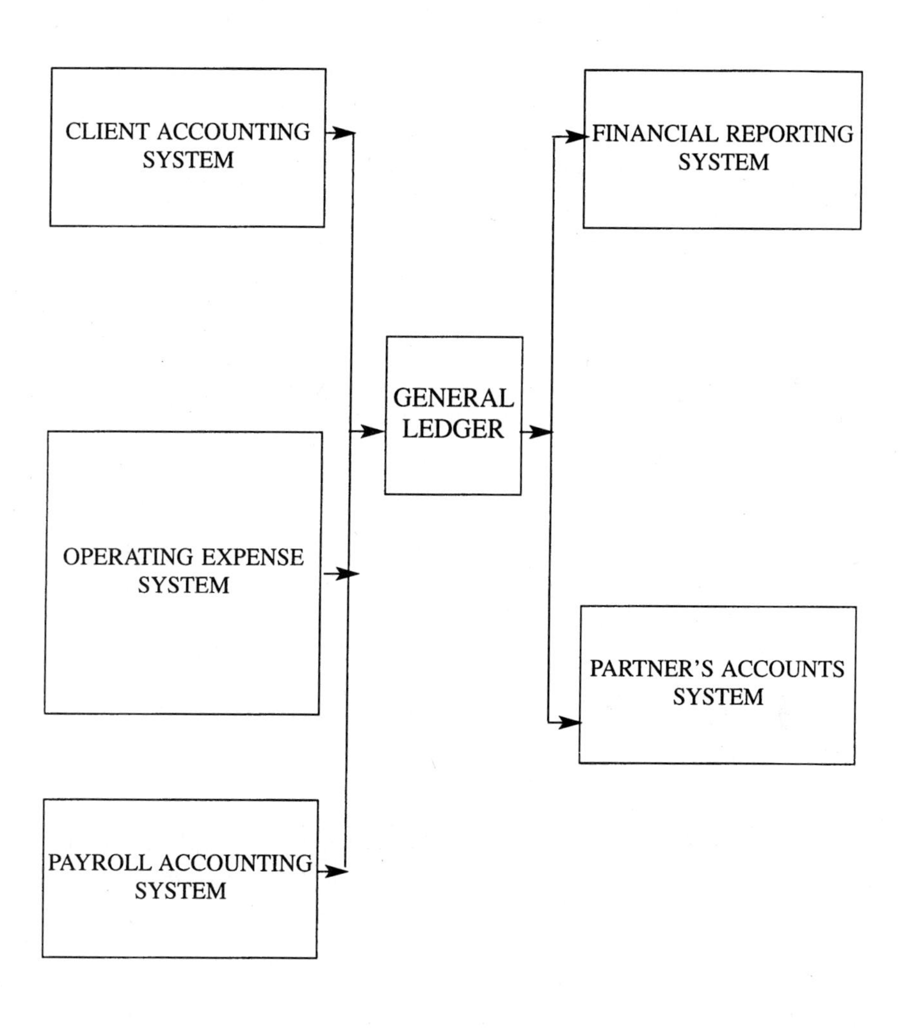

§ 7.02 Client Accounting System and Cash Receipts Controls

At a minimum, there are three key points in a law firm's client accounting system where control procedures should be considered:

(1) Recording of chargeable time;
(2) Billing of fees; and
(3) Collection of cash.

Each of these points is discussed in more detail in the paragraphs that follow.

[1]—Recording of Chargeable Time

The objective of establishing procedures for recording chargeable time is to ensure that *all* professional time that is chargeable and related to a client matter is recorded and that *none* of the time recorded represents duplicate charges. Accurate recording is important to ensure that the proper client is charged. Timely recording is important to ensure that the information is collected and summarized swiftly, so that the engagement partner will have the data necessary to promptly render bills to clients.

Consequently, the firm should have a procedure in place whereby each lawyer (or his or her secretary) and each relevant administrative employee periodically (e.g., daily or weekly) submits a record of his or her chargeable time, identifying the client and matter for each entry. Historically, this has been done by each attorney keeping a diary of matters worked on during that day.

Depending on the type of accounting system used by the firm, the record of time can consist of daily time slips, monthly time sheets, or direct input into a computer. Regardless of who actually enters the information into the reporting system (i.e., executive assistant for an attorney) the person whose time is being reported should review and sign off on the information being reported. The accounting department should also have procedures to ensure that, at the end of each month, an entry has been recorded for each workday by each lawyer. In some firms, the time reporting system checks for entries that appear to be unusual (e.g., less than eight hours or more than twenty-four hours in a particular day). A policy that requires that each lawyer account for at least eight hours each workday (whether chargeable to clients or related to nonchargeable matters) has proven to be a regimen that several firms have successfully used to prevent the inadvertent omission of chargeable hours.

[2]—Billing of Fees

Creating an accurate bill to submit to a client begins with a series of processes and ends with a professional review. The processes include summarizing the time charges for the specific matters, determining the fee to be billed, and recording the resultant under (over) realization. The firm should have a series of procedures to ensure that time charges (hours charged multiplied by billing rates) have been accurately accumulated and calculated. In addition, the amount of the final bill and the under (over) realization should be subject to approval by a partner of the firm. To ensure that all recorded chargeable time is eventually billed and collected, the firm should have a procedure for periodic (e.g., daily or weekly) reconciliation of beginning-of-month and end-of-month unbilled fees and fees receivable balances, taking into account all time recording, billing and collection activity during the period. Such reconciliation might take the following form:

	Unbilled fees	Fees receivable
Balance-beginning of period	$4,080,000	$2,800,000
Time charges	18,750,000	
Billings	(17,000,000)	17,000,000
Collections		(16,700,000)
Write-offs	(1,250,000)	(80,000)
Balance-end of period	$4,580,000	$3,020,000

[3]—Collection of Cash

Misappropriation of cash receipts constitutes the law firm's principal risk in the functioning of its accounting system. Accordingly, the firm should establish control over fees to be received prior to the time at which cash is received. A "fees receivable" control account is the usual method of establishing this control. In order for the control to be effective, the firm's cashier should have no part in the procedures leading up to entries in the fees receivable account to which cash receipts are to be credited. Furthermore, employees responsible for accounts receivable and billing have no access to incoming cash. Incoming receipts should go directly to the cashier. In no event should a client's check be delivered to or made payable to a partner or employee of the firm. In smaller firms, where the division of duties is limited, it may be necessary to establish control at the point of cash receipt (i.e., in the mail room) by having a list of all receipts prepared at that point and by having an employee who has no connection with cash transactions compare the list with entries in the cash receipts book and deposit ticket at a later date.

Many firms have adopted newer cash management systems that allow them to collect cash in lock-boxes, so that there is less cash delivered to the firm. Using a lock-box system also speeds up the processing time of clearing checks, so that law firms have quicker access to cash. The lock-box vendor also gives the law firm a computer tape of the daily receipts, so the law firm can input the tape directly into their cash receipts ledger - again speeding up the processing time. There still are control issues with a lock-box system, it is important to establish procedures to insure that the various functions are segregated.

The most efficient cash-collection system is the use of wire transfers. Using this method, a client simply instructs a bank to wire funds directly from its account to the law firm's. Using wire transfers is faster (and normally more error free) than any other method, but like other systems, it too requires controls.

The Internet has introduced yet another method of cash collection. The benefit of using the Internet is that it is available "24 by 7". As a result, a transaction can be initiated any time and there is a permanent record of each transaction. (This is not to infer that there are no permanent records in other systems. However, in this system, the same record is saved in different computers in different locations throughout the world, so there is always a backup.) Firms send bills to clients through the Internet and require payment through the same means. This increases efficiency and reduces administrative personnel.

[4]—Self-Assessment Checklist

In developing new procedures or in assessing the effectiveness of existing procedures for the firm's client accounting system, law firm management might ask the following questions:

(1) How do we ensure that the input of "hours worked" and "billing rates" are valid and that the calculation of "time charges" (hours x rates) are accurate?

(2) How do we determine that the input of "bills rendered" and "time charges relieved" has been approved by the engagement partner and that calculations of "underrealizations" (time charges minus billings) are accurate?

(3) How are we assured that all "cash collections" received and "fees receivable relieved" have been properly recorded and that "write-offs" (receivables minus collections) are properly approved, accurately calculated and recorded in a timely manner?

(4) Do we have a procedure for reviewing output reports containing the aged "unbilled time charge inventory," the aged "fees receivable" listing, and the cumulative "cash collection" listing in detail by client?

(5) Do we have a procedure for reconciling the change in the balance of "unbilled time charges" and in "fees receivable" at the beginning of the month with that at the end of the month, taking into account all elements of activity during the month (time charges incurred, billings, underrealizations, cash collections, write-offs)?

(6) Are the employees who are responsible for recording and reconciling cash receipts separate from the employees who handle and deposit cash receipts?

[5]—Segregation of Duties Flowchart

A flowchart illustrating one approach used to segregate duties surrounding the flow of cash receipts in a law firm is set forth in Figure 7-B.

Figure 7-B. Illustration outlining an example of segregation of duties for a law firm's cash receipts data flow.

ABC LAW FIRM
CASH RECEIPTS SEGREGATION
OF DUTIES FLOW CHART

	Mail Dep't	Cashier Section	Accounts Receivable Section	General Accounting Section
A. Mail opened. checks restrictively endorsed and listing of incoming remittances furnished to general accounting	A →			→ A
B. Remittances (i.e., checks) forwarded to cashier	B →	→ B		
C. Deposit made and deposit slip (and/or bank statement) forwarded by bank directly to general accounting		C →		→ C
D. Cash receipts recorded and total amount furnished to general accounting		D →		→ D
E. Remittance advices sent to accounts receivable		E →	→ E	
F. Accounts receivable ledgers posted and advice of total credited to accounts receivable control account furnished to general accounting			F →	→ F
G. Comparison made between (A) mail room listing of remittances, (C) deposit slip (and/or bank statement), (D) cash receipts recorded, and (F) credit to accounts receivable control account				G

§ 7.03 Operating Expense System and Cash Disbursement Controls

Cash disbursements of law firms involve payments for three types of activities: operating expenses of the firm, client disbursements, and asset and liability items (e.g., the purchase of property and equipment, repayment of debt, and similar items). There are at least three key points in a law firm's operating expense system where control procedures should be considered:

(1) Approval of expenditures;
(2) Recording of disbursements; and
(3) Authorization of disbursements.

Each of these points is discussed in more detail in the paragraphs that follow.

[1]—Approval of Expenditures

Before a wire transfer of funds is made or a check is drawn by a law firm's business office, a proper "voucher package" (hard or electronic copy) should be prepared and approved. The voucher package can either contain a vendor's original invoice or an expense reimbursement request from a partner or employee of the firm, together with supporting documentation and a description of the business purpose for the expenditure. An expense reimbursement request submitted by one individual in the firm should be approved by someone who is at least one level higher in the firm's organization structure. For example, an associate's expense report would typically be approved by a partner.

[2]—Recording of Disbursements

When disbursements are recorded, it is important to distinguish between disbursements that will be recovered from clients and disbursements that are firm expenses. It is also necessary to identify specific clients and the related matter to be billed for each "client disbursement" and to identify the specific expense classification for each "firm expense." This is particularly important when the firm uses budgets as control tools. Consequently, the firm should have adequate procedures for coding each expense and the account coding should be reviewed by an employee who has sufficient familiarity with the coding system and the firm's operations to ascertain that there is a proper accounting distribution of expenditures.

[3]—Authorization of Disbursements

Diversion of cash disbursements represents the law firm's principal risk in the functioning of its operating expense system. Accordingly, the firm should establish strong controls over check signing and wire transfer authorization. The signature on a check or authorization of a wire transfer is the authority to the bank to disburse funds from the law firm's bank account and the partner (or senior employee) who affixed the authorized signature assumes final responsibility for the propriety of the disbursements. The firm's procedures should enable this individual to assume such responsibility and afford the firm reasonable protection against loss through negligence or fraud. A check signer or individual authorizing a wire transfer should be satisfied that the amount of the check or wire transfer presented to him or her for signature or authorization covers, in the aggregate, the amount of bona fide invoices or services rendered to or assets purchased by the firm; that the assets or services have been satisfactorily received by the firm and are at prices which have been appropriately approved; that payment has not previously been made; that there are no clerical errors in computing the amounts in the vendor's invoices, and that the invoice or transfer has been properly coded so that it will be posted to the correct general ledger account. It is, of course, impossible, except in very small firms, for this individual to perform all of the operations necessary to be completely satisfied on these points, but it is his or her duty to ascertain that the supporting documents bear evidence that these duties have been satisfactorily performed by the employees to whom they have been delegated.

[4]—Self-Assessment Checklist

The following questions might be asked by law firm management in assessing the effectiveness of cash disbursement procedures:

(1) How do we ensure that invoices approved for payment are valid in terms of vendor authenticity, receipt of assets or services, authorized purchase orders, and nonduplication of recurring expenses?

(2) Do we have appropriate procedures for hierarchical approval of lawyers' expense reports, checking of supporting documents, and rebilling of client-related disbursements to clients?

(3) Do we have a procedure for periodically reminding employees and vendors of the firm's "conflicts of interest" policy?

(4) How do we determine that individuals are authorized to sign checks or initiate wire transfers, unused checks and check signature plates are safeguarded, vouchers are canceled, and signed checks are delivered directly to the mailroom?

(5) How are we assured that all disbursements are recorded on a timely basis, all checks and wire transfers are accounted for, and expenses are properly classified?

(6) Do we have a procedure for reviewing the reasonableness of output reports listing "firm expenses" and "client disbursements"?

(7) Do we have appropriate procedures for timely reconciliation of all bank accounts, including examination of canceled checks and correlation of bank deposits with recorded cash receipts and wire transfers with recorded cash disbursements?

(8) Are separate bank accounts maintained for "funds held on behalf of clients and others" and are they subject to relevant partner approval of all deposits and withdrawals?

(9) Are the employees who are responsible for recording and reconciliation of cash disbursements separate from the employees who handle checks and disburse cash?

[5]—Segregation of Duties Flowchart

A flowchart illustrating one approach used to segregate duties surrounding the flow of cash disbursements in a law firm is set forth in Figure 7-C.

Figure 7-C. Illustration outlining an example of segregation of duties for a law firm's cash disbursements data flow.

ABC LAW FIRM
CASH DISBURSEMENTS
SEGREGATION OF DUTIES FLOW CHART

	Cash Disbursements Section	Partner (check signer)	Mail Dep't	General Accounting Section
A. Vendor invoices and supporting documents checked, approved for payment, and forwarded to individuals authorizing the cash disbursement	A →	A		
B. Check or wire transfer authorization prepared and sent to individuals authorizing the cash disbursement	B →	B		
C. Checks or wire transfers recorded and total furnished to general accounting	C →	→	→	C
D. Vendor invoices and supporting documents examined, cancelled and returned to cash disbursements section	D	← D		
E. Checks signed and forwarded to mail department		E →	E	
F. Advice of total amount of checks signed furnished to general accounting		F →	→	F ↓
G. Bank statements and cancelled checks received and forwarded unopened to general accounting department			G →	G ↓
H. Bank reconciliations prepared and reviewed and comparison made between (C) recorded cash disbursements, (F) total of checks signed, and (G) cash withdrawals from banks				H

§ 7.04 Payroll Accounting System Controls

Payrolls of law firms involve payments to two groups; associates and administrative staff. There are at least three key points in a law firm's payroll accounting system where control procedures should be considered:

(1) Payroll authorization;
(2) Payroll distribution; and
(3) Payroll recording.

Each of these points is discussed in more detail in the paragraphs that follow. For purposes of this discussion it is assumed that all payroll functions are being performed in-house. Many law firms engage a service bureau to perform their payroll function.[1]

[1]—Payroll Authorization

To ensure that only valid changes are processed through the payroll system, the law firm should have a procedure requiring that all additions, separations and salary rate changes be authorized. In some firms, the staffing level and range of salary rates are authorized by a committee of partners and the day-to-day changes passing through the system are approved by the firm's Director of Administration or personnel department supervisor.

[2]—Payroll Distribution

In larger firms, it is not always possible for the signer of the payroll checks to know each employee on the payroll. Consequently, where the size of the professional staff and administrative staff warrants, the distribution of payroll checks (electronically or manually) should be carried out by an employee who neither supervises the employees nor takes part in the preparation of payrolls. Undelivered payroll checks and W-2 forms should be returned to the firm's Director of Administration for follow-up. One way to mitigate the control concerns surrounding payroll distribution is to offer employees the ability to have their salary or pay deposited directly in their personal bank account via electronic funds transfer.

[3]—Payroll Recording

Payments to fictitious employees represent the law firm's principal risk in the functioning of its payroll system. Accordingly, it is important

---

[1] See Chapter 13 *infra* for a discussion of payroll service bureau capabilities.

that the firm's payroll procedures be so designed as to give reasonable assurance that names do not appear on the payroll unless they rightfully belong there. This can best be accomplished by a proper division of duties and by so arranging them that each employee engaged in the payroll process acts as a check on the preceding employee. In smaller firms, where the payroll duties may be concentrated in one or two employees, it is incumbent on the partner (or senior employee) who signs the payroll checks to be acquainted with the role of each employee in the firm in order to be better equipped to detect unauthorized changes in the payroll as he or she reviews the payroll checks (or the check reimbursing the payroll bank account) prior to affixing his or her signature. To ensure the validity of the current payroll, some law firms have an employee independent of the payroll function reconcile the current payroll with the prior payroll, taking into account all authorized additions, separations and salary changes. Also, to avoid issues associated with recording payroll (e.g., entries made to the wrong ledger accounts), the payroll journal should be reviewed and posted to the general ledger by a different person than the clerk responsible for the payroll journal.

[4]—Self-Assessment Checklist

The following questions might be asked by law firm management in assessing the effectiveness of payroll accounting procedures:

(1) How do we ensure that payrolls approved for payment are valid in terms of the bona fide existence of employees, employee salary rates, payroll deductions, hours worked (including overtime), and bonuses?

(2) Do we have procedures to ensure that all payrolls are promptly recorded, each payroll is reconciled with the previous payroll, and payroll bank accounts are reconciled promptly?

(3) Do we have procedures for reviewing the reasonableness of departmental payroll reports?

(4) Are the employees who distribute payroll checks and W-2 forms separate from the employees who prepare and record the payroll and from those who supervise the employees on a day-to-day basis?

(5) Are the employees who prepare the payroll and journal entry different from those who review the calculations and post the journal entry to the general ledger?

[5]—Segregation of Duties Flowchart

A flowchart illustrating one approach used to segregate duties surrounding the flow of payroll transactions in a law firm is set forth in Figure 7-D.

Figure 7-D. Illustration outlining an example of segregation of duties for a law firm's payroll system data flow.

ABC LAW FIRM
PAYROLL SEGREGATION
OF DUTIES FLOW CHART

	Supervisors	Payroll Accounting Section	Partner (check signer)	General Accounting Section
A. Additions, separations and salary changes initiated by supervisors, authorized by management, and submitted to payroll accounting	A →	A		
B. Summary of payroll changes furnished to general accounting for review and reconciliation with prior period payroll		B →	→	B ↓
C. Time and attendance date documented by employees, approved by supervisors (if required) and forwarded to payroll accounting	C →	C		↓
D. Payrolls prepared, summarized, earnings records updated and totals furnished to general accounting		D →	→	D ↓
E. Payrolls, checks and direct deposit authorization forwarded for approval and signing		E →	E	↓
F. Signed payroll checks forwarded to general accounting for distribution to employees			F →	F ↓
G. Comparison made between (B) reconciliation with prior period payroll register, (D) current period payroll register, and (F) listing of total payroll				G

§ 7.05 Financial Reporting System Controls

Generally, there are two types of financial reports which typically are issued on a regular basis by law firms. These are as follows:

(1) Partnership financial reports - reports generally issued at the completion of the firm's fiscal year-end and typically on a cash, modified cash or modified accrual basis. These reports are used to provide information to the partners and certain outside parties (i.e., banks, landlords, leasing companies, etc). Financial reports include the four basic statements, namely the statement of net assets (balance sheet), statement of revenue and expenses (income statement), statement of changes in partners' capital accounts and the statement of cash flows.

(2) Management reports these reports are used for managing the firm on a daily basis and typically are issued weekly, monthly or quarterly. In addition, certain firms issue "flash reports" on a daily basis for certain key information (cash received and cash position).

The format of these reports vary depending on the type of information the managing partner and management team need to run the business. Types of information that may be included in this type of a report are as follows: fees earned, cash collected, unbilled time, billed but not collected fees, chargeable hours, expenses, pro-bono work, office-by-office analysis, analysis of the various practice groups and new clients or clients lost, to mention but a few. In addition, the reports typically will compare current period results with the same period last year and provide year-to-date information for both the current and prior years. Additionally, if budgets are prepared, the results typically are compared to the budget and a forecast for remainder of the year may also be provided.

Inaccurate or untimely reports constitute the law firm's principal risks as it relates to the financial reporting system. Accordingly, operating procedures for the firm's accounting department should be clearly delineated. Written procedures, instructions and assignments of duties will prevent duplication of work, overlapping of functions, omission of important functions, misunderstandings and other situations that might result in the preparation of inaccurate financial reports. In smaller firms, where preparation of an accounting procedures manual may be impractical, the details of procedures might be set forth in formal memoranda, which should also show explicit assignment of duties to individual employees. These memoranda can be particularly helpful in instructing new employees or when substitutes are used during an employee's absence.

The following questions might be asked by law firm management in assessing the effectiveness of financial reporting system controls:

(1) Does the firm have an adequate accounting procedures manual?

(2) Does the firm have an organization chart and job descriptions for its accounting department personnel?

(3) Do the partners (and the managing committee) receive periodic financial and statistical reports frequently and promptly enough to be useful?

(4) Are these reports clear and in sufficient detail to be useful, without being cumbersome?

(5) What type of information is necessary to help management better identify issues or concerns on a regular basis?

§ 7.06 Partners' Accounts System Controls

In addition to the law firm's overall partnership financial statements, the firm's accounting system should be able to render reports presenting each partner's interest in the firm's income and equity. Three reports, for which control procedures should be considered, include:

(1) Allocation of partners' income;
(2) Changes in partners' current accounts; and
(3) Changes in partners' capital accounts.

Misclassifying income or payments among partners is the firm's principal risk as it relates to the partners' accounts. Procedures should be established to ensure that the data is processed accurately and is subject to review at a senior level. In smaller firms, where there are no senior accounting department employees who can be assigned to process the partners' accounts, this task may be assumed by the firm's chief financial officer.

In today's environment, computer programs are frequently used to perform the calculations which are needed to derive the partner income and capital account balance. While the use of these programs increases the accuracy of the processing, controls are still necessary to ensure that the correct information is entered, that the data is processed accurately and that the output makes sense in light of the circumstances of the firm.

The following questions might be asked by law firm management in assessing the effectiveness of partners' accounts system controls:

(1) Does the firm have a written partnership agreement that covers all profit sharing and other financial arrangements for *all* present partners of the firm?

(2) Are calculations of the allocation of income among the partners reviewed for reasonableness by a supervisory employee and are they correlated with the terms of the partnership agreement?

(3) Are there adequate controls over data entry?

(4) Is the program used to process the information reliable and has it been tested for accuracy?

(5) Are reports containing details of changes in partners' current accounts and partners' capital accounts reviewed for reasonableness by a supervisory employee and are they correlated with the underlying transaction records (income allocation schedules, cash disbursement record, and other relevant schedules)?

§ 7.07 Information Systems (IS) Controls

Because of the speed and efficiency achievable through automation of accounting systems, most law firms now use computerized information systems to record, process and report the firm's financial activities. Notwithstanding the high degree of accuracy usually built into these systems, they can be tampered with. The law firm's principal risks in the functioning of its automated accounting systems relate to:

(1) Data (e.g., inaccurate data, uncorrected rejected transactions);
(2) Processing (e.g., inaccurate processing, incorrect scheduling of production jobs, unauthorized access to processing functions, data files or programs);
(3) Programming (e.g., inaccurate program changes, unauthorized changes to data files or programs); and
(4) Organization (e.g., lack of segregation of duties).

When automated accounting systems process data, law firm management must evaluate the effectiveness of control procedures in terms of control points that would have been established for manual activities around the computer *and* consider the desirability of establishing additional control procedures in the following areas:

(1) Access controls;
(2) Input controls;
(3) Processing controls;
(4) Segregation of duties; and
(5) Business recovery planning.

A checklist of questions which might be asked by law firm management in assessing the effectiveness of IS controls surrounding the firm's accounting systems is illustrated in Figure 7-E.[1]

---

[1] Chapter 13 contains a more detailed discussion of automated accounting records and a data security appendix.

Figure 7-E. Illustration of a checklist for assessing IS controls over a law firm's accounting system.

ABC LAW FIRM
IS ACCOUNTING CONTROLS CHECKLIST

	ANSWER (Yes or No)
ACCESS CONTROLS:	
—User has access to transaction functions based on job responsibilities?	______
---User access request changes are documented and contain evidence of proper authorization?	______
—User is required to sign on to the system with a user ID and password?	______
—Passwords are masked on the screen, required to be changed periodically, and required to have at least a minimum password length of 6 characters?	______
---User IDs are automatically disabled after a specified number of invalid signon attempts?	______
—Access violation reports are reviewed consistently by management?	______
—Terminated employees have their access immediately removed from the system?	______
---User access assignments are periodically re-evaluated?	______
---Remote access to the system is appropriately secured?	______
—User access to the computer room is restricted to a "need-only" basis?	______
INPUT CONTROLS:	
—User approval of input data independent of data enterer?	______
—User approval of master file changes independent of data enterer?	______
—User review of rejected transactions and timely reentry?	______
—Are control procedures used to ensure the data is entered completely and not duplicated?	______
---Key verification performed?	______
PROCESSING CONTROLS:	
—Independent user reconciliation of output to input?	______
—Independent user reconciliation of opening/closing balances?	______
—User review of output for reasonableness?	______
—Numerical control of negotiable output?	______
—Restricted access to critical output?	______
—Data validation programs used?	______
SEGREGATION OF DUTIES:	
—User approval separate from IS department?	______
—Programmers separate from machine operators?	______
---Programmers have restricted access to production programs and data?	______
—Data security position is separate from end users and programmers and reports directly to senior management?	______
BUSINESS RECOVERY PLANNING:	
---System, program and data files are backed up on a regular basis and recent copies are stored at an offsite location?	______
---A disaster recovery plan has been developed that outlines the actions to be taken to recover the IS systems in the event of a disaster?	______
---A business contingency plan has been developed that outlines the actions to be taken in the event that existing user locations are no longer usable.	______

§ 7.08 Budgetary Control

Most of the previously discussed checks and balances that can be built into a sound internal control system involve procedures and controls that focus on single facets of the law firm's financial activities. In addition to these detailed controls, budgets represent an overall control procedure that can be of significant value to law firm management. This type of control is common with many businesses and with the increase in the size of many law firms today, as a result of recent mergers or acquisitions of other law firms, becomes a relevant and valuable tool for law firms as well. If the firm has taken the time to develop a realistic budget based on reasonable assumptions and expectations, it can be a very valuable management tool when compared to actual results on a regular basis (monthly or quarterly) by helping to identify areas of strengths and weaknesses and provide management the ability to react rather timely to opportunities or concerns.[1] In addition, budgets when compared to actual results can be beneficial in helping management forecast results for the remainder of the year. Accordingly, budgets are an effective high level control for top management.

---

[1] The preparation of budgets are discussed more thoroughly in chapter 11.

§ 7.09 Organization Control

Another important and valuable control to an organization is the creation of a role for the chief administrative officer (CAO) and chief financial officer (CFO). In some large firms, these are two separate roles. In other firms, they are held by the same person and could be a partner of the firm. However, many large or megasize firms use a non-lawyer to fill this role, primarily because of the complexities of the role and time commitment required. Typically, the CAO/CFO reports directly to the administrative partner(s) or the senior partner and is responsible for all administrative (i.e., human resources, facilities, security, technology, etc.) and financial (budgeting, reporting, cash collection, taxes, etc.) aspects of the firm.

In addition to establishing CAO/CFO position(s), many firms today are considering creating a role for an internal audit department. This has become necessary because firms have dramatically increased the size and scope of their organizations over the past several years and many no longer have offices in one or two key cities—rather, they now have offices in many cities or even several countries and establishing consistency of operations and maintaining control become significant challenges. An internal audit department (IAD) can provide valuable assistance in the development of policies and procedures and ensure the consistency of their application throughout all of the firm's offices. They can assist in the implementation of new systems, can provide resources to perform special projects (analysis of practice groups or offices or due diligence of potential acquisition candidates, etc.) and even provide assistance to the external auditors, if any. Just the presence of an IAD can be a valuable control to an organization.

In most organizations, the director of IAD should report to an independent party, typically the audit committee. However, if the firm does not have an audit committee, then the director of IAD should report to either the management committee or the senior partner, rather than his or her boss (CAO/CFO), to ensure impartiality of opinion.

§ 7.10 Insurance

Adequate insurance coverage in a law firm is no less important than similar coverage in any other business. It represents the firm's ultimate protection against business risks, including breakdowns in control procedures, should they occur. Among the more standard types of insurance which should be considered by a law firm are:

(1) Lawyers' professional liability;
(2) Comprehensive general liability;
(3) Business interruption for lost fees and extra expenses;
(4) Fire and extended coverage on building, furniture, equipment, and personal property;
(5) Computer hardware, software and establishment of alternate operating facility;
(6) Comprehensive dishonesty;
(7) Automobile liability and property damage;
(8) Travel accident;
(9) Standard workmen's compensation; and
(10) Standard disability.

Although professional standards are high, an element of risk is always involved when a professional assumes responsibility for client matters. In recognition of this risk, prudent law firms carry lawyers' professional liability insurance policies. A professional liability policy usually carries an aggregate limit of millions of dollars and protects the firm from damages arising from claims of malpractice, negligence, incompetence, and the like. An annual review by the law firm of the adequacy of its insurance coverage is usually useful to ensure that protection against risks continues to be adequate and that deductibles are not substantially lower than necessary, causing payment of excessive premiums. Not only should the policies and coverages be reviewed, but also firms need to consider technological developments and how those may impact the firm's risk profile. For example, some firms today are considering banning the use of cellular phones while driving automobiles and the threat of business interruption for other than natural disasters (e.g., Oklahoma City bombing, World Trade Center attack) should cause firms to reevaluate their existing coverage. To better manage their risk profile, many firms require their employees to maintain minimal amounts of coverage on their automobiles if used as part of carrying out their duties for the firm to help better manage the costs.

SECTION II

FINANCIAL MANAGEMENT CONCEPTS FOR LAW FIRMS

CHAPTER 8

Business Concepts

Chapter Contents

---

§ 8.01 Law Firm Profitability: An Overview

Providing quality professional services to clients is the first and foremost concern of most law firm partners. Earning a suitable income for providing these services, while a secondary consideration, however, cannot be overlooked. A law firm's profitability is usually measured by "average income per equity partner," with equity partner being defined as a partner with ownership interests in the firm who shares in the firm's profits. Average income per equity partner is illustrated in the following example:

	Current Year	Prior Year
Revenue collected	$150,000,000	$140,000,000
Expenses disbursed	100,000,000	92,000,000
Net income	$50,000,000	$48,000,000
Number of equity partners	100	101
Average income per equity partner	$ 500,000	$ 475,000

Three types of factors influence a law firm's profitability: (1) revenue factors, (2) expense factors and (3) leverage of lawyers. As the example demonstrates, a change in one or more of these profitability factors results in an increase or decrease in average income per equity partner. In the example, average equity partner income for the current year increased by $25,000 over the prior year. This increase was caused by the following changes in profitability factors:

	Approximate Increase in:	
	Partnership Net Income	Income Per Equity Partner
Increase in revenue	$10,000,000	$100,000
Increase in expenses	(8,000,000)	(80,000)
Decrease in number of equity partners	—	5,000
Increase in profitability	$ 2,000,000	$ 25,000

The components of each of these types of factors are discussed in the sections that follow.

§ 8.02 Revenue Factors

A law firm's revenue is usually generated almost entirely from providing legal services. Three factors affect the level of fee revenue: (1) chargeable hours; (2) billing rates; and (3) realizations. These factors do not operate in a vacuum. Consequently, an improvement in one factor may be offset, to some extent, by a decline in another factor.

[1]—Chargeable Hours

Chargeable hours represent those hours, spent by the law firm's professional staff and relevant administrative staff, that are directly related to client engagements. The personnel who generate chargeable hours are partners (both equity and non-equity), associates and other classifications of lawyers such as of counsel and senior attorneys, paralegals, and some administrative staff. Because paralegal and administrative staff hours typically represent a very small portion of a law firm's revenue, for ease of demonstration only the lawyer timekeepers are included in the revenue-related examples that follow. Average chargeable hours typically are determined in the following manner:

	Equity Partners	Non-equity Partners	Of Counsel	Associates	Senior Attorneys
Total chargeable hours	190,000	28,125	18,000	320,450	9,125
Number of personnel	100	15	10	170	5
Average chargeable hours	1,900	1,875	1,800	1,885	1,825

Over the past several years, the level of average partner chargeable hours has increased and, in many firms, has overtaken the average chargeable hours of other attorneys. This trend has been driven by the market, with law firm clients increasingly demanding partner time and attention and, at the same time, refusing to pay for what they deem to be the training of the firm's less-experienced lawyers.

[2]—Billing Rates

Billing rates represent the standard hourly fees that a law firm charges for client services provided by each member of its professional staff and by relevant members of its administrative staff. A unique rate (taken from a range of rates) is usually assigned to each individual (or class of individuals). These rates typically are adjusted annually (or more often) to take into account the impact of changed economic and market conditions, including inflation. For example, during the well-documented "associate salary wars" beginning in early 2000 and extending throughout the year, firms were faced with the business decision of whether to raise rates to match the costs of upwardly spiraling associate salaries. Firms that opted not to raise billing rates faced the unattractive alternative of having the increased costs negatively impact firm profitability.

The interaction of billing rates with chargeable hours produces a figure commonly referred to as time charges, as illustrated below:

	Equity Partners	Non-equity Partners	Of Counsel	Associates	Senior Attorneys
Average hourly billing rate	$400	$350	$300	$265	$200
Average chargeable hours	1,900	1,875	1,800	1,885	1,825
Average "time charges"	$760,000	$656,250	$540,000	$499,525	$365,000

It is important to note that law firms increasingly are using alternative billing arrangements, usually due to pressure from clients. The term alternative billing arrangements refers to an economic relationship a law firm has with a client that is not based on the law firm billing the client on an hours-times-rates basis. Such alternatives include arrangements such as fixed fees, value/incentive billing (i.e., billing based on the value of the services rendered or based on a favorable result), stock for services, blended rates (e.g., a single rate used for all time on a matter), volume-based discounts, and contingency fees. The specific terms of such arrangements are highly dependent upon the firm's relationship with the client and their respective expectations for the future.

[3]—Realizations

Realizations represent the dollar amount of standard time charges which are eventually billed and collected by a law firm. Realizations are often expressed in terms of percentages. There are two types of realizations: billing realizations and collection realizations. Billing realizations are the amount (or percentage) of standard time charges which are eventually billed to clients. Collection realizations are the amount (or percentage) of billed fees which are eventually collected. The interaction of time charges with both types of realizations produces fees collected, as illustrated below:

	Equity Partners	Non-equity Partners	Of Counsel	Associates	Senior Attorneys
Average time charges	$760,000	$656,250	$540,000	$499,525	$365,000
Realization rate	85%	88%	88%	85%	92%
Approximate average fees collected	$646,000	$577,500	$475,200	$424,596	$335,800

Law firms that use alternative billing arrangements find it more difficult to measure the traditional billed or collected realizations, because something is missing from the calculation. For example, if a law firm uses an incentive billing arrangement with a client under which the firm bills hours at 75% of standard while the matter is in process, but can retroactively increase the rate to 125% if the matter is successful, then the traditional billing realization percentage or collection realization percentage may be understated when the matter is in process, but inflated when the matter is valued billed. As a result, there is an emerging need for cost accounting-based analyses to measure profitability.

§ 8.03 Expense Factors

The three principal types of expenses incurred by a law firm are: (1) compensation for timekeepers other than equity partners; (2) administrative salaries; and (3) operating expenses. Variations in these expenses are caused by changes in the number of lawyers in the firm, by inflation and by current business events (such as a move to a new office).

[1]—Timekeeper Compensation

Timekeepers other than equity partners include non-equity partners (usually lawyers with the title of partner who have no ownership or profit-sharing interest in the firm), associates, of counsel, senior attorneys, other classifications of lawyer-timekeeper that firms may use, and paralegals. Compensation for these groups typically is determined by reference to current market rates for salaries in the particular geographic market where the timekeepers are based. These rates are usually related to years of experience.

Law firms (or branch offices of firms) compete with the other firms (or branch offices) within their local geographic area for the quantity and quality of lawyers needed to provide the proper level of legal services to their clients. For example, the Los Angeles office of a large New York firm might determine its compensation levels by reference to the current market levels in Los Angeles. As an alternative, national or international law firms normally try to maintain the same compensation matrix for all associates with similar work experience, except possibly for cost-of-living adjustments based on geographic location.

Average compensation of timekeepers other than equity partners is typically organized by category and viewed in the following manner:

	Non-equity partner	Of Counsel	Associates
Aggregate class compensation	$3,750,000	$2,000,000	$29,750,000
Number of personnel	15	10	170
Average compensation of class	$ 250,000	$ 200,000	$ 175,000

Note that the compensation statistics above and other cost metrices below are presented by lawyer timekeepers with no separate classification for costs per paralegal. This is consistent with the revenue-related examples presented earlier in the chapter.

[2]—Administrative Salaries

The number of secretaries and other administrative staff in a law firm is usually based, to some degree, on the number of lawyers employed by the firm. Administrative salaries vary with the market rates of salaries paid by the business community for qualified secretarial and other administrative staff. Generally, administrative compensation is measured in terms of "cost per lawyer," determined in the following manner:

Aggregate administrative salaries	$18,450,000
Number of lawyers	300
Cost per lawyer (for administrative staff)	$ 61,500

In a number of firms, clients are billed for time spent on client matters by secretaries and other relevant administrative staff. In some firms, these billings are classified as revenues (which is the case in the "overview" section of this chapter). In other firms, these billings are treated as cost recoveries that reduce expenses (which is the case in the "calculation components" section of this chapter). In most instances, firms do not charge clients for secretary/word processing time unless the time spent is not deemed to be usual and ordinary or is deemed to be overtime.

[3]—Operating Expenses

Operating expenses for a law firm consist of occupancy costs, office operating expenses, professional activities costs and general business expenses (including for marketing, recruiting, and professional liability insurance). Occupancy costs, which represent the largest single non-salary operating expense of a law firm, tend to rise with the impact of inflation gradually, and then increase substantially when the firm leases additional space or moves to new offices. A law firm's operating expenses are typically measured in terms of "cost per lawyer," determined in the following manner:

Aggregate operating expenses	$47,100,000
Number of lawyers	300
Cost per lawyer (for operating expenses)	$ 157,000

§ 8.04 Leverage of Lawyers

Leverage of lawyers represents the law firm equity partners' ability to provide quality service to clients, in a timely manner, while delegating the bulk of the work to other lawyers for completion. In today's market, with increasing numbers of lawyer classifications (non-equity partners, of counsel, senior attorneys, etc.), the leverage metric firms find most useful is equity partner leverage. Thus, leverage is typically viewed in the following manner.

Number of equity partners	100
Number of other lawyers	200
Ratio of other lawyers to equity partners	2.0 to 1

Partnership income provides an equity partner with (1) compensation to the partner for services as a lawyer, and (2) a return on the partner's capital investment in the firm.

As the number of equity partners in a law firm shrinks, the share of income for each remaining equity partner increases; however, the workload of the remaining equity partners also increases, unless some of their work can be delegated to other lawyers in the firm. The impact on "income per equity partner" of reducing the number of equity partners in a law firm can be seen in the following example:

	Before reduction	After reduction	Increase (decrease)
Partnership net income	$50,000,000	$50,000,000	—
Number of partners	101	100	(1)
Average income per partner	$495,000	$500,000	$5,000

§ 8.05 Components of the Profitability Calculation

A law firm's profitability is determined by the factors previously discussed. Before embarking on a program to improve the firm's profitability, it is worthwhile to look at the components of the profitability calculation to appreciate how these factors interact. A summary of the profitability calculation, showing average income per equity partner and taking into account all of the factors previously discussed, is illustrated below:

	Equity Partners	Non equity Partners	Associates	Other Lawyers
Revenue factors:				
Average chargeable hours	1,900	1,875	1,885	1,808
Average hourly billing rates	$400	$350	$265	$250
Average realizations	85%	88%	85%	92%
Approximate average fees collected	$646,000	$577,500	$424,596	$415,840
Expense factors:				
Average compensation	—	$250,000	$175,000	$175,000
Cost per lawyer for administrative staff	$ 61,500	61,500	61,500	61,500
Cost per lawyer for operating expenses	157,000	157,000	157,000	157,000
Average expenses paid	$218,500	$468,500	$393,500	$393,500
Leverage of lawyers:				
Average profit per lawyer	$427,500	$109,000	$31,096	$21,843
Multiplied by number of lawyers	100	15	170	15
Total profit	$42,750,000	$1,635,000	$5,286,320	$327,645
Divided by number of equity partners	100	100	100	100
Average income per equity partner	$427,500	$16,350	$52,863	$3,276

The result of the profitability calculation can be broken down into two distinct segments:

	Income in the aggregate	Income per partner
Income generated by partners	$42,750,000	$427,500
Income generated by leverage of lawyers	7,250,000	72,500
Net income for partnership	$50,000,000	$ 500,000

Note that the presentation above is intended to demonstrate the interrelation among the revenue and cost factors and the effect of leverage. It is not intended to demonstrate the results of an analysis of profitability by lawyer class, as such an analysis would entail more complex cost-accounting concepts and methodologies.

§ 8.06 Improving Profitability

A law firm can increase profitability by focusing on each factor that influences "average income per equity partner." Illustrated below is an example of a program to improve profitability in a firm of 100 partners:

	Potential approximate increase in:	
	Income in the aggregate	Income per partner
Revenue factors:		
Increase of 2% in average chargeable hours of associates	$1,444,000	$14,440
Increase of 3% in average billing rates of partners	1,938,000	19,380
Decrease of 1% in billing realization	(1,775,000)	(17,750)
Expense factors:		
Increase of 3% in associates' compensation	(1,487,500)	(14,875)
Decrease of 5% in administrative salaries	553,500	5,535
Decrease of 7% in operating expenses	1,413,000	14,130
Leverage of lawyers:		
Decrease by 2% in number of partners	6	5,000
Increase in profitability	$2,086,000	$25,000

Profitability improvement programs tend to be more successful when they concentrate on improving profits through increasing revenue as contrasted with programs that focus attention on reducing expenses. A program that highlights the positive aspects of revenue enhancements, such as increasing chargeable hours, raising billing rates, and improving realizations tends to gain support from within the firm. Programs that focus on the negative aspects of cost reductions, such as reducing personnel, holding back on salary increases, eliminating perquisites and reducing the level of administrative services do not receive as much support.

Improvement in leverage usually can be achieved only as part of a long-term program. Sudden sizable increases in the number of associates may prove to be counterproductive if sufficient client work does not materialize to occupy the new associates' time. Reduction in the number of partners in a firm (through retirement and other programs) must be carefully planned. The above illustration assumes that the law firm had been in operation for a number of years and planned for a net decrease of one partner, resulting from the retirement of three partners and the admission of two partners. Firms that have recently been formed or are in a growth mode should expect to plan for a net increase in the number of partners in each future year. This will dilute income per partner, unless action is taken to counteract this factor by improvements in the other factors that affect profitability.

The metric discussed have been presented thus far at the firm level. It is important to understand that these measures and statistics can be calculated and analyzed at the practice group or office level as well.

CHAPTER 9

Management Reporting

Chapter Contents

---

§ 9.01 Management Reporting for Law Firms

Law firm management reports are usually prepared for use by the firm's managing partner or managing committee. One purpose of management reports is to give the partner or committee information needed to make sound business decisions. Therefore, it is important for these reports to be brief and to contain highlights which focus attention on important matters. Since management's focus varies from firm to firm, the form and content of management reports vary considerably. A typical law firm management report will usually contain some (or all) of the following elements:

(1) Financial highlights and key items;
(2) Actual vs. budgeted results;
(3) Operating statistics;
(4) Financial charts; and
(5) Financial position information.

Law firm management reports often are issued monthly, but should be issued at least quarterly.

§ 9.02 Financial Highlights and Key Items

"How do we improve the firm's profits?" is the typical question in the minds of the readers of law firm management reports. The purpose of the financial "highlights" section of the report is to put forward the key financial and statistical information that summarizes the firm's performance during the current period and compare these results with the firm's financial plan (or budget). Armed with this information, management can focus on those areas where performance did not measure up to the plan and concentrate their attention on solutions designed to improve future performance. An example of a "Financial Highlights" section of a law firm management report is illustrated in Figure 9-A.

Figure 9-A. Illustration of the financial highlights section of a law firm management report.

ABC LAW FIRM FINANCIAL HIGHLIGHTS
($ in thousands)

Current Month			Year-to-date	
Actual	Plan	Results of Operations	Actual	Plan
$10,000	$9,500	—Fee revenue	$119,600	$113,800
$4,000	$3,750	—Net income	$ 51,150	$ 47,500
		Key Operating Statistics		
35,000	33,000	—Chargeable hours	420,000	400,000
92%	90%	—Realization percent	92%	90%
3.8	3.5	—Speed of billing and	3.8	3.5
		collections	2.0	2.1
		—Ratio of other lawyers to equity partners	2.9	2.1
		Financial Position		
		—Partners equity	$41,000	$40,000
		—Debt	$22,000	$20,000
		—Uncollected receivables	$17,000	$15,000
		—Unbilled time	$25,000	$22,500

Firms with multiple offices and practice groups may choose to report some of the financial highlights (such as revenue, chargeable hours, realization, and leverage) not only on a firmwide basis, but also by office and practice group.

§ 9.03 Actual vs. Budgeted Results

A key way to measure a law firm's performance is to compare current operating results with budgets established by the firm at the beginning of the year. These results are usually compared periodically (monthly or quarterly) and cumulatively (for the year-to-date). Operating results for some firms can only be measured on the modified cash basis method of accounting because that is the only information maintained by the firm. The modified cash basis method of accounting is useful for determining cash available for distribution to partners for payment of living expenses and income taxes. However, from a managing-the-business standpoint, measuring results on the accrual basis method of accounting has advantages, since this method measures results as they occur (for example: revenue is based on time charges incurred) and is not subject to the vagaries of cash collections and cash payments.

[1]—Modified Cash Basis Operating Statement

Firms which measure their actual vs. budgeted results on the modified cash basis method of accounting are, in many ways, measuring their cash flow from operations, except that this cash flow has been reduced by the impact of a few modifications, principally depreciation. An example of an operating statement for a law firm which uses the modified cash basis method of accounting is illustrated in Figure 9-B. The illustration compares actual vs. budgeted amounts for the current period and for the year-to-date. Two columns are used to display the information for each time period. If desired, a third column can be added to identify favorable (or unfavorable) variances between actual vs. budgeted amounts.

[2]—Accrual Basis Operating Statement

The accrual basis method of accounting matches revenues earned with the expenses related to earning that revenue. An example of an operating statement for a law firm that uses the accrual basis method of accounting is illustrated in Figure 9-C.

Figure 9-B. Illustration of a law firm partnership's operating statement using the *modified cash basis* method of accounting.

ABC LAW FIRM
OPERATING STATEMENT—MODIFIED CASH BASIS
($ in thousands)

Current Month			Year-to-date	
Actual	Budget	Revenue	Actual	Budget
$9,550	$9,100	—Professional fees	$114,400	$109,000
50	50	—Interest Income	500	600
9,600	9,150		114,900	109,600
		Expenses		
3,400	3,200	—Employee compensation	40,600	37,900
840	840	—Occupancy costs	10,500	10,500
500	500	—Office operating expenses	6,300	5,300
420	470	—Professional activities	5,200	5,200
440	540	—General business expenses	5,400	5,800
5,600	5,550		68,000	64,700
$4,000	$3,600	Excess of revenue over expenses	$ 46,900	$ 44,900

Figure 9-C. Illustration of a law firm partnership's operating statement using the *accrual basis* method of accounting.

ABC LAW FIRM
OPERATING STATEMENT—ACCRUAL BASIS
($ in thousands)

Current Month			Year-to-date	
Actual	Budget	Revenue	Actual	Budget
$9,960	$9,490	—Professional fees	$119,600	$113,800
50	50	—Interest Income	500	500
10,010	9,540		120,100	114,300
		Expenses		
3,400	3,200	—Employee compensation	40,600	37,900
840	840	—Occupancy costs	10,500	10,500
550	500	—Office operating expenses	6,850	6,300
470	470	—Professional activities	5,200	5,800
450	540	—General business expenses	5,800	6,300
5,710	5,550		68,950	66,800
$4,300	$3,990	Net income	$ 51,150	$ 47,500

[3]—Conversion of Modified Cash Basis Statement to Accrual Basis Statement

Some law firms maintain their accounting records and issue their external financial reports on the modified cash basis method of accounting, but choose to prepare their management reports using the accrual basis method of accounting. These firms convert their modified cash basis financial information to accrual basis information through the use of memorandum records. These memorandum records typically capture certain accrual basis information such as uncollected billed fees, realizable value of unbilled time and liability accruals. An example of an operating statement for a law firm which converts from the modified cash basis method of accounting to the accrual basis method of accounting is illustrated in Figure 9-D.

Figure 9-D. Illustration of a law firm partnership's operating statement converted from the *modified cash basis* of accounting to the *accrual basis* of accounting.

ABC LAW FIRM
OPERATING STATEMENT—MODIFIED CASH
VS. ACCRUAL BASIS
($ in thousands)

	Actual			Budget
	Modified Cash Basis	Memorandum Records	Accrual Basis	
Revenue:				
Professional fees	$114,400	$5,200	$119,600	$113,800
Interest income	500		500	500
	114,900	5,200	120,100	114,300
Expenses:				
Employee compensation	40,600		40,600	37,900
Occupancy costs	10,500		10,500	10,500
Office operating expenses	6,300	550	6,850	6,300
Professional activities	5,200		5,200	5,800
General business expenses	5,400	400	5,800	6,300
	68,000	950	68,950	66,800
Net Income	$46,900	$4,250	$ 51,150	$ 47,500

§ 9.04 Operating Statistics

Law firm operating statistics represent an important management tool. They serve to highlight superior performance and flag below-average results. When properly utilized, key operating statistics can provide law firm management with the key information needed to manage the firm's business. The acronym "RULES" can be used to illustrate the key operating statistics found in law firm management reports:

(1) Realization of billing rates;
(2) Utilization of attorneys;
(3) Leverage of lawyers;
(4) Expense control; and
(5) Speed of billings and collections.

The R, U and S letters of "RULES" represent factors that relate to earning the firm's revenue. Responsibility for generating the firm's revenue rests with the firm's partners. Consequently, it is important to assign this responsibility to specific partners. There is a wide variety of designations used by law firms in assigning responsibilities to partners. Some examples include:

(1) The *billing partner* who is responsible for realization of time charges and speed of billings for designated clients;

(2) The *project partner* who is responsible for overseeing time spent by professional personnel on specific client matters; and

(3) The *engagement partner, or relationship partner,* is responsible for maintaining client relations and for generating business from designated clients. He or she also is the "go to" partner for important client-initiated communications.

In recognition of the assigned responsibility concept, many firms choose to present revenue-related operating statistics in a format that focuses on each partner's responsibility. This gives the management group the ability to assess each partner's "business" performance (as contrasted with the partner's "professional" performance).

Each type of operating statistic as illustrated by "RULES" is discussed in more detail in the following paragraphs.

[1]—Realization of Billing Rates

Increasing attorneys' chargeable hours or increasing attorneys' billing rates will not produce additional revenue for the firm, unless these increases can be realized when bills are rendered. Over realization of standard time charges occurs when the billing partner concludes that a premium should be billed to the client for a particular matter, due to the unique nature of the service rendered, the overtime efforts of the staff, or for some other appropriate reason. For example, during the robust economic conditions of the late 1990s through most of the year 2000, many of the well-known firms were able to achieve over realization of rates, either on complex transactional work or on critical litigation for their clients. This situation contributed to the financial growth and success experienced during that time period, particularly by the large and/or prominent firms.

Under realization of standard time charges occurs when the billing partner concludes that a discount should be applied to a client's bill for a particular matter, due to staff inefficiencies, a misunderstanding regarding the undertaking, or for some other appropriate reason. Additionally, under realizations may occur due to fee pressures placed on a law firm by its clients.

Law firm profitability is particularly sensitive to increases and decreases in realizations because they directly affect profit on a dollar-for-dollar basis. Consequently, the management group in many law firms closely monitors realization statistics and, in some cases, takes these statistics into account (along with many other factors) when determining partner compensation and client retention or acceptance. An example of one type of law firm billing realization report is presented in Figure 9-E.

Figure 9-E. Partial illustration of a law firm partnership's billing realization report.

ABC LAW FIRM
BILLING REALIZATION REPORT

Billing Attorney	Current month			Year-to-date		
	Billings	Realization over(under)	Percent	Billings	Realization over(under)	Percent
Partner A	$400,000	$ 80,000	125%	$3,000,000	$30,000	111%
Partner B	50,000	(5,000)	90%	800,000	(50,000)	94%
Partner C	125,000	—	100%	1,200,000	(50,000)	96%
↓						
Total	$8,000,000	$(250,000)	97%	$100,000,000	$(8,000,000)	93%

Realization reports can be prepared not only by partner, as shown above, but also by office or practice group.

[2]—Utilization of Attorneys

The time of professional staff (partners, associates, and other timekeepers) is the law firm's most valuable asset. Utilization of this time in an effective manner (usually by spending it on matters chargeable to clients) generates revenue for the firm. Permitting valuable professional time to be wasted on nonessential non-chargeable matters, or overlooking an opportunity to utilize the "available time" of lawyers, represents lost revenues for the firm. For these reasons, many firms closely monitor the utilization of attorneys. In these firms, reports which highlight overutilization or underutilization of lawyers receive prompt attention by the management group. This often results in strategic decisions to hire, redeploy or separate lawyers.

Historically, average utilization percentages of equity partners was lower than that of other lawyers as the equity partners focused on maintaining client relationships and winning new work, while the other lawyers tended to concentrate on utilization and productivity. Over the past several years, however, there has been increasing demand among law firm clients for partner time, instead of less-experienced and less-qualified associates. This trend, combined with increasing client reluctance to pay for what they consider to be training of the less-qualified lawyers, has contributed to a general increase in the levels of average partner chargeable hours. In some cases, partner productivity levels, as measured by chargeable hours, have overtaken those of associates and other lawyers.

Figure 9-F is an example of one type of law firm utilization report. The illustration focuses only on chargeable hours. If the law firm wants to monitor non-chargeable time, a column or separate page can be added to the existing report to accumulate the relevant hours.

Figure 9-F. Partial illustration of a law firm partnership's utilization report for attorneys.

ABC LAW FIRM
ATTORNEY UTILIZATION REPORT

	Current-month hours			Year-to-date hours		
Attorney	Chargeable	Target	Variance	Chargeable	Target	Variance
—Partner A	145	150	(5)	1,600	1,650	(50)
—Partner B	160	150	10	1,800	1,650	150
—Partner C	80	75	5	800	825	(25)
↓						
—Associate X	180	155	25	1,725	1,705	25
—Associate Y	140	155	(15)	1,700	1,705	(5)
—Associate Z	150	155	(5)	1,675	1,705	(30)
↓						
Total	35,000	33,000	2,000	420,000	400,000	20,000

As in the case of realization, utilization can also be measured by office or practice group in addition to by individual lawyer.

[3]—Leverage of Lawyers

In some law firms (usually smaller firms), partners tend to do most of the client work. These firms employ very few associates. In other firms (usually larger firms), partners tend to delegate substantial segments of work to one or more associates. Traditionally, "leverage" has been determined by the ratio of associates to partners in the firm. However, with the increasing use of other categories of lawyers (non-equity partner, of counsel, senior attorneys, etc.), leverage typically is measured by the ratio of all lawyers other than equity partners to equity partners. Thus, an increase in the number of non-equity partners, associates, or senior attorneys, or a decrease in the number of equity partners results in higher "leverage." Average equity partner income will increase when leverage increases, as long as utilization of associates results in sufficient billable time to cover the direct and indirect costs of employing the associates.

Leverage is usually compared with historical trends, budgets and industry averages. An example of a law firm leverage of lawyers report is presented in Figure 9-G. This summary report can be expanded to include statistics for each of the firm's departments or office locations, if desired.

Figure 9-G. Illustration of a law firm partnership's leverage of lawyers report.

ABC LAW FIRM
LEVERAGE OF LAWYERS REPORT

	Prior Year Actual	Current Year Actual	Budget	Industry Average (Hypothetical)
Number of lawyers:				
Equity Partners	101	100	103	—
Other lawyers	205	200	215	—
Ratio of other lawyers to equity partners	2.0	2.0	2.1	2.1

[4]—Expense Control

Control of expenses is key to the continued profitability of a law firm. Generally, expenses incurred by a law firm can be placed into two broad categories: compensation costs and operating expenses.

[a]—Compensation Costs

Monitoring compensation costs involves three levels of comparison: aggregate compensation, number of personnel, and average compensation by employee category. There are four general categories of employees in a law firm: lawyers other than equity partners, legal assistants (paralegals), secretaries and other administrative personnel. These employees are of two types: (1) those who charge time to clients and (2) those who do not. In all law firms, the lawyers and legal assistants charge time to clients. In some firms, secretaries and certain administrative employees also charge time to clients and in other firms, they do not. An example of a law firm compensation costs report is presented in Figure 9-H. The report illustrated is a summary report. It could be expanded to provide details by department, practice group, location or more specific employee classifications, if the law firm chooses to monitor costs in greater detail.

[b]—Operating Expenses

In a law firm, few expenses are "fixed." Expenses are usually "variable" (for example: professional activities costs) or "semi-variable" (for example: occupancy costs). These expenses tend to vary either directly or indirectly with the number of lawyers in the firm. For this reason, operating expenses are often monitored against budgets and measured against industry averages in terms of "cost per lawyer."

An example of a law firm operating expense report is presented in Figure 9-I. The summary report illustrated could be expanded to accommodate comparisons of more detailed classifications of expenses, if the law firm chose to monitor these expenses in greater detail.

Figure 9-H. Illustration of a law firm partnership's compensation costs report.

ABC LAW FIRM
COMPENSATION COSTS REPORT

	Actual	Budget
Aggregate Compensation:		
Non-equity Partners	$3,750,000	$3,700,000
Associates	29,750,000	29,000,000
Of Counsel	2,000,000	2,100,000
Senior Attorneys	625,000	525,000
Legal Assistants	1,750,000	1,725,000
Secretaries	6,175,000	6,100,000
Other Administrative	6,841,250	6,800,000
	$50,891,250	$49,950,000
Employee Count:		
Non-equity Partners	15	14
Associates	170	165
Of Counsel	10	11
Senior Attorneys	5	3
Legal Assistants	35	34
Secretaries	130	128
Other Administrative	180	178
	545	533
Average Compensation:		
Non-equity Partners	$250,000	$264,500
Associates	175,000	176,000
Of Counsel	200,000	191,000
Senior Attorneys	125,000	175,000
Legal Assistants	50,000	50,500
Secretaries	47,500	47,500
Other Administrative	38,000	38,000
	$885,500	$942,500
Ratio of Staff to Lawyers (assuming 100 equity partners):		
Legal Assistants	0.12	0.12
Secretaries	0.43	0.44
Administrative	0.60	0.61
	1.15	1.17

Figure 9-I. Illustration of a law firm partnership's operating expense report.

ABC LAW FIRM
OPERATING EXPENSES REPORT

	Aggregate Expenses		Cost per lawyer		
Type of expense	Actual	Budget	Actual	Budget	Industry Average (Hypothetical)
Occupancy costs	$15,000,000	$15,000,000	$50,000	$51,000	$49,000
Office operating expenses	9,250,000	9,000,000	30,833	30,600	30,500
Professional activities	6,000,000	6,100,000	20,000	20,700	19,500
General business expenses	7,500,000	7,300,000	25,000	24,800	24,500
	$37,750,000	$37,400,000	$125,833	$127,100	$123,500

[5]—Speed of Billings and Collections

Cash does not become available for distribution to law firm partners unless and until bills are rendered to and collected from clients. Law firm partners appropriately focus their primary attention on providing quality service to clients. They focus secondary attention on issuing and collecting bills.

Many reasons have been advanced for the general slowness in bill rendering by law firms. These reasons include the historical reluctance by partners to "press" bills upon clients, billing systems that are not up-to-date, client matters that can only be billed upon completion of the engagement and many others. Some firms historically have resisted any acceleration in the speed with which bills are rendered. A few of these firms generate such a substantial cash flow that delays in billing and collections might be ignored. However, for the vast majority of firms, prompt billing and collection practices are necessary, particularly where the firm either incurs high interest costs to borrow money or requires additional contributed capital from its partners to finance uncollected and unbilled client fees.

There may be valid reasons why some part of a firm's investment in client services cannot be billed on a timely basis. Nevertheless, there is one particularly important reason for the management group to pursue timely billing and collection. That reason relates to the unfortunate reciprocal effect that monitoring billing realizations can have on the speed of collections. When a firm only monitors billing realizations, there is a disincentive to prompt billing because slow billing delays the recognition of under realizations. Consequently, a firm that monitors realizations should also monitor speed of billings. This enables management to view the complete picture of the firm's (and each partner's) billing performance.

One type of law firm speed of billings and collections report is presented in Figure 9-J. Speed of billings and collections has been determined for purposes of this illustration in the following manner:

A- Uncollected fees receivable	$17,000,000
B- Unbilled time charges	25,000,000
C- Investment in client services (A + B)	$42,000,000
D- Monthly average time charges	$12,500,000
E- Speed of billings and collections in months (C ÷ D)	3.4

Figure 9-J. Partial illustration of a law firm partnership's speed of billings and collections report.

ABC LAW FIRM
SPEED OF BILLINGS AND COLLECTIONS REPORT

	Investment in client services				
Billing Attorney	Uncollected "fees receivable"	Unbilled "time charges"	Total	Monthly average "time charges"	Speed of billings
Partner A	$170,000	$250,000	$420,000	$140,000	3.0
Partner B	145,000	275,000	420,000	100,000	4.2
Partner C	207,000	300,000	507,000	130,000	3.9
↓					
Total	$17,000,000	$25,000,000	$42,000,000	$12,500,000	3.4

The "speed of billings and collections factor" represents the average number of months it takes from the date time charges are incurred until the date cash is eventually collected. There are other ways to express this calculation (such as dividing the investment by monthly average "billings" or by "collections"). There are other titles which can be applied to the factor (such as "number of months investment in client services" or "turnover factor" or "billing lag factor"). However, the important consideration is not the methodology nor the title chosen, it is the consistency with which the particular method is used in drawing comparisons that is paramount. Using today's powerful computers and sophisticated software, management should be able to review a "speed of billings and collections" report at their convenience. Generally, the review would be done at least one per week, except near year-end when it might be done daily.

§ 9.05 Financial Charts

One purpose of management reports is to focus management's attention on important financial matters. This is usually accomplished by presenting tables of figures in the reports and through the use of a highlights section at the front of the report. Very often the tables and highlights do not provide sufficient emphasis on the most important points in the report. Graphs may be added to the report to illuminate some of the key points. Line graphs are used most frequently in reports for law firm management groups; however, there is no reason why bar graphs or pie charts could not be used effectively in specific presentations. Graphs have been used to present a variety of law firm statistics, such as:

(1) Partner income trends;
(2) Revenue trends;
(3) Expense trends; and
(4) Leverage trends.

The partnership's net income is usually the focal point of most readers of the firm's financial statements. Trends in this important figure usually serve as a key indicator of the firm's health, growth and stability. An equally important figure is the firm's "average income per partner." This identifies the trend in individual partners' earnings. This trend may be quite different from the trend in aggregate earnings for several reasons, such as instances when average partner income has been diluted as a result of the admission of new partners.

Figure 9-K is an example of graphs that depict partner income trends in a law firm. The trends illustrated are based on the following information:

	Year 1	Year 2	Year 3	Budget
Net income of the partnership	$9,000,000	$9,000,000	$10,000,000	$9,600,000
Average number of partners	40	45	40	40
Average income per partner	$ 225,000	$ 200,000	$ 250,000	$ 240,000

This illustration is designed to compare the firm's historical trends with its budget. If the firm chose to compare historical trends with industry averages or with firm goals, the "budget" figure could be replaced by a "target" figure in the table and in the graph.

Figure 9-K. Illustration of a law firm partnership's income trends.

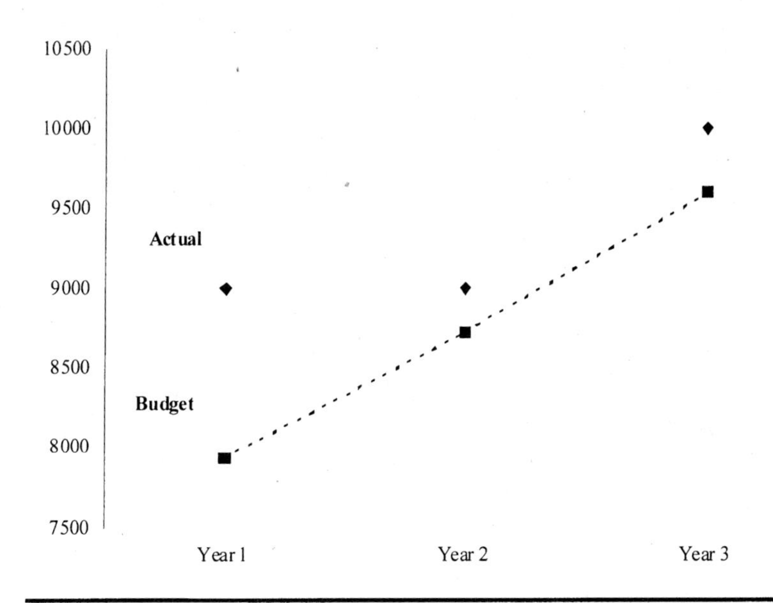

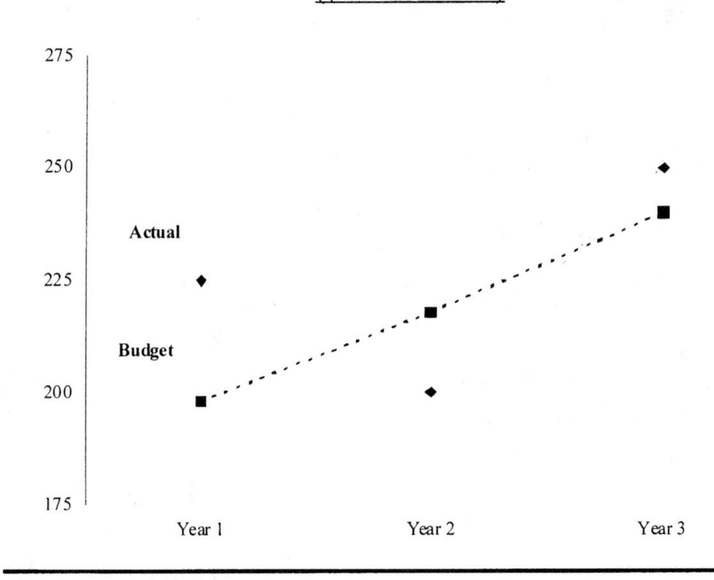

§ 9.06 Financial Position Information

Since most management reports focus on operating results, financial position information is not usually prominently featured. It is often relegated to the back of the report. Typical financial position information contained in management reports includes:

(1) A condensed statement of net assets and
(2) An aged summary of fees receivable and unbilled fees.

[1]—Condensed Statement of Net Assets

Some firms combine (a) the information contained in their accounting records, which is recorded using the modified cash basis method of accounting, with (b) memorandum records, which capture certain accrual basis information such as uncollected billed fees, realizable value of unbilled time, and liability accounts. This will produce (c) accrual basis statements of net assets for management reporting purposes. An example of a condensed statement of net assets containing all of these elements is illustrated in Figure 9-L.

Figure 9-L. Illustration of a law firm partnership's condensed statement of net assets that has been converted from the *modified cash basis* method of accounting to the *accrual basis* method of accounting.

ABC LAW FIRM
CONDENSED STATEMENT OF NET ASSETS
($ in thousands)

	Actual			Budget
	Modified Cash Basis	Memorandum Records	Accrual Basis	
Cash and investments	$1,500		$ 1,500	$ 1,500
Fees receivable		$3,400	3,400	3,000
Unbilled fees		5,100	5,100	4,500
Other current assets	1,000		1,000	1,000
Fixed assets	2,300		2,300	2,000
Total assets	4,800	8,500	13,300	12,000
Less - liabilities	2,200	900	3,100	3,000
Net assets	$2,600	$7,600	$10,200	$ 9,000

[2]—Aged Summary of Fees Receivable and Unbilled Fees

Fees receivable and unbilled fees usually represent a law firm's most significant asset. The aggregate amount and age of these assets usually have an important bearing on the law firm's near-term cash flow. Consequently, it is important that these assets be closely monitored. Management reports typically contain a summary aging report of fees receivable and unbilled fees. In those cases where reserves have been established, the report identifies the relevant reserves for uncollectible amounts. An example of an aging summary is illustrated in Figure 9-M. The illustration contains only three aging periods. This can be expanded to include additional time periods, if the law firm wants to monitor aging in more depth.

In addition to the summary aging report furnished to the management group, in most firms more detailed additional information is furnished to billing partners. Each billing partner normally receives a monthly aging analysis of fees receivable that pertain to his assigned clients. The partner also usually receives a monthly aging analysis (or at least a client-by-client analysis) of unbilled time charges that pertain to his assigned clients (often referred to as work-in-progress).

Figure 9-M. Illustration of a law firm partnership's aged summary of fees receivable and unbilled fees.

ABC LAW FIRM
AGED SUMMARY OF
FEES RECEIVABLE AND UNBILLED FEES
($ in thousands)

	Fees Receivable		Unbilled Fees	
	Current Year	Prior Year	Current Year	Prior Year
Age				
Over 12 months	$ 300	$ 200	$ 200	$ 400
Over 6 months	400	300	300	300
Under 6 months	3,000	2,700	5,000	4,300
Total	3,700	3,200	5,500	5,000
Less - reserve for estimated uncollected amounts	300	200	400	500
Net realizable value	$3,400	$3,000	$5,100	$4,500

CHAPTER 10

Profit Center Accounting

Chapter Contents

10.01 Profit Center Accounting for Law Firms

Profit center accounting is used by law firms to develop meaningful financial information to assist management in making strategic decisions in areas such as:

(1) Client retention;
(2) Equity partners' compensation;
(3) Expansion or contraction of practice in specific areas of law; and
(4) Opening or closing branch offices.

The broad-based nature of these objectives, plus the need for timely information, usually make it unnecessary for the firm to develop an overly detailed cost accounting system. It is important, though, to create an efficient, clear, concise and logical accounting model. Such a model normally consists of a series of spreadsheets which present and summarize the results of the profit center accounting calculations. Developing the accounting model involves three steps:

(1) Cost allocation;
(2) Fee classification; and
(3) Profit determination.

Each of these steps will be discussed in the sections that follow. The illustrations contained in this chapter assume that costs are recorded in the year incurred and fee revenues are recorded in the year earned, thus achieving a matching of costs with related revenues. Law firms that use the cash basis method of accounting will have to supplement their cash basis records with memorandum records to adjust for the impact of unbilled and uncollected fees, in order to achieve the appropriate matching of costs with related revenues.

§ 10.02 Cost Allocation

A law firm must consider four broad categories of costs (and imputed costs) when developing procedures for cost allocation:

(1) Imputed equity partner compensation;
(2) Other timekeepers' compensation (other than equity partners);
(3) Support costs; and
(4) Non-chargeable activities costs.

Some of the problems inherent in developing allocation procedures for each of these categories of costs and some possible practical solutions are discussed in the paragraphs that follow.

[1]—Imputed Equity Partner Compensation

Equity partner time is normally an essential and important part of each client engagement. Equity partners share in the profits of the firm; consequently, their time is not listed as a cost in the financial records of a typical law firm partnership. Yet, in order to measure the true profitability of a client engagement, the impact of partners' time must be considered. (Note that in a firm that has chosen the Professional Corporation form of entity, shareholder compensation would represent a cost; thus, the exercise of imputing equity partner compensation would not be necessary).

To achieve this goal, imputed costs can be developed (e.g., either by reference to (a) notional compensation levels paid to client service attorneys with similar years of experience to the equity partner or group of equity partners in question, or (b) compensation paid to comparable executives) and ascribed to equity partner compensation. Imputed compensation amounts can be developed for each equity partner, for subsets of equity partners, or for all equity partners as a general class, depending on how precise the firm wants to be in allocating costs. These imputed costs can then be apportioned based on equity partner hours worked on each matter.

[2]—Other Timekeepers' Compensation

Compensation of timekeepers other than equity partners usually represents the least complicated cost allocation process since time spent by most of these timekeepers is ordinarily related to client engagements. A typical method of allocating these costs involves (1) the determination of an hourly cost factor and (2) the use of such cost factor to apportion individual timekeeper's compensation costs to each assigned client engagement and to each relevant non-chargeable activity (usually based on hours worked on each matter, and hours devoted to non-chargeable activities, respectively).

Hourly cost factors are typically calculated by dividing the aggregate compensation of each timekeeper class (non-equity partner, associate, paralegal, etc.) by the firm's annual standard level of chargeable hours for the class. The resulting number represents the average cost to the firm of one hour of client work performed by a member of the particular staff class. Hourly cost factors can be calculated for each individual timekeeper, for subsets of staff classes, or for staff classes as a whole.

[3]—Support Costs

Support costs include the salaries of administrative employees, occupancy costs and other operating expenses. There are a variety of cost allocation methodologies that can be used to apportion these overhead expenses. A practical approach is to allocate these expenses based on the allocation of hours charged by the firm's lawyers to client engagements and nonchargeable activities.

[4]—Non-chargeable Activities Costs

An integral part of the procedures for allocating the three costs previously discussed is a partial allocation of such costs to non-chargeable activities. These include activities such as firm management and administration, recruiting, and practice development. These costs are not directly related to client engagements. They are, however, a necessary part of the firm's practice and so are indirectly related to client engagements. Consequently, in order to achieve full cost allocation, these indirect costs should be allocated to client engagements. A practical approach for allocating these costs involves an apportionment based on lawyers' hours charged to individual client engagements versus total client engagements.

[5]—Cost Allocation Calculations

Examples of condensed cost allocation calculations, for a law firm which has three principal clients, are illustrated in Figure 10-A ("percentage" method) and Figure 10-B ("cost-per-hour" method). The cost allocations illustrated, which are based on broad concepts, consist of three steps:

Step I—Identify and summarize lawyers' hours.
Step II—Develop an allocation statistic.
Step III—Allocate costs based on the statistic.

Figure 10-A. Illustration of a condensed cost allocation exercise for a law firm, using the "percentage" method, which allocates support costs based on the percentages of time recorded against clients and non-chargeable activities, and allocates the costs associated with non-chargeable activities based on the percentage of chargeable hours charged to the firm's clients.

ABC LAW FIRM
ALLOCATION OF COSTS BY CLIENT ENGAGEMENT
($ in thousands)
PERCENTAGE METHOD

			Client Engagements		
	Total	Non-chargeable Activities	Client X	Client Y	Client Z
I. HOURS					
(1) Partner hours	66,000	6,000	30,000	20,000	10,000
(2) Associates' hours	118,000	10,000	50,000	40,000	18,000
(3) Lawyers' hours	184,000	16,000	80,000	60,000	28,000
(4) Lawyers' chargeable hours	168,000	—	80,000	60,000	28,000
II. PERCENTAGES					
(1) Partner hours	100%	10%	45%	30%	15%
(2) Associates' hours	100%	8%	42%	34%	16%
(3) Lawyers' hours	100%	9%	43%	33%	15%
(4) Lawyers' Chargeable hours	100%	—	48%	36%	16%
III. COSTS (in thousands)					
(1) Imputed partner compensation	$ 7,000	$ 700	$ 3,150	$ 2,100	$ 1,050
(2) Associates' compensation	3,000	240	1,260	1,020	480
(3) Support costs	8,000	720	3,440	2,640	1,200
(4) Non-chargeable activities costs	—	(1,660)	797	598	265
	$18,000	—	$ 8,647	$ 6,358	$ 2,995

Figure 10-B. Illustration of a condensed cost allocation exercise for a law firm, using the "cost-per-hour" method.

ABC LAW FIRM
ALLOCATION OF COSTS BY CLIENT ENGAGEMENT
($ in thousands)
COST-PER-HOUR METHOD

			Client Engagements		
	Total	Non-chargeable Activities	Client X	Client Y	Client Z
I. HOURS					
(1) Partner hours	66,000	6,000	30,000	20,000	10,000
(2) Associates' hours	118,000	10,000	50,000	40,000	18,000
(3) Lawyers' hours	184,000	16,000	80,000	60,000	28,000
(4) Lawyers' chargeable hours	168,000	—	80,000	60,000	28,000
II. COST-PER-HOUR					
(1) Partner	$106				
(2) Associates	$ 25				
(3) Support activities	$ 43				
(4) Non-chargeable activities	$ 10				
III. COSTS (in thousands)					
(1) Imputed partner compensation	$ 6,996	$ 636	$ 3,180	$ 2,120	$ 1,060
(2) Associates' compensation	2,590	250	1,250	1,000	450
(3) Support costs	7,912	688	3,440	2,580	1,204
(4) Non-chargeable activities cost	—	(1,680)	800	600	280
	$ 17,858	(106)	$ 8,670	$ 6,300	$ 2,994

[6]—Using the Percentage Method and Cost-per-Hour Method

Firms are increasingly turning to profit-center accounting as a critical tool in producing information for effective management reporting. Thus, as in the corporate world where business units are operated as distinct profit centers, cost attribution and allocation approaches have become increasingly important. Figure 10-A above, with its "percentage method" approach, is an appropriate method for calculating profit-center results at the end of a fiscal year, when actual hours worked (both chargeable and non-chargeable) and final compensation figures-including bonuses-are readily available. However, this method would not be appropriate for periodic reporting during a year (e.g., monthly or quarterly) due to the unevenness of workloads throughout the year and the uncertainty of potential bonus amounts. For example, if working hours are typically lower during the summer months-due to vacations and other time off-than in other times of the year, then costs allocated to client engagements during that period would likely be overstated when using the percentage method.

A practical approach for periodic profit-center accounting throughout the year is the "standard costing method," which is shown in Figure 10-B above. With its "cost-per-hour" methodology, the standard costing system allows for the application of costs to profit centers only to the extent that hours have been worked; therefore, the risk of overstating or understating costs in a monthly or quarterly period is minimized. Then, at the end of the year, final profit-center costs can be determined by the percentage method, as discussed above. Next, cost-per-hour figures can be calculated for the subsequent year for input into the standard-costing model based on the percentage method results and adjusted for anticipated changes in associate bonuses or other unusual events (good or bad). Another benefit of this approach is the ability to gauge profit-center performance versus prior years' interim results throughout the year.

§ 10.03 Fee Classification

There are four ways of classifying fees in the context of developing procedures for profit center accounting:

(1) By client;
(2) By client partner;
(3) By area of law (including by particular practice group or broad department); and
(4) By office location.

Some law firms classify fees at the start of the accounting process. This is done by incorporating classification information in the code number that is assigned to each client matter. At the end of the accounting process, this information can then be summarized using a computer program. Other law firms collect this information using a time-consuming manual process, whereby fee information is analyzed after it has been processed.

An example of a condensed classification of fees summary for a law firm is illustrated in Figure 10-C.

Figure 10-C. Illustration of a condensed fee classification summary for a law firm.

ABC LAW FIRM
CLASSIFICATION OF FEES SUMMARY
($ in thousands)

		Client Partner		
	Total	Partner A	Partner B	Partner C
FEES CLASSIFIED BY CLIENT PARTNER				
Client X	$10,000	$10,000		
Client Y	6,000		$6,000	
Client Z	3,000		3,000	
	$19,000	$10,000	$9,000	—

		Area of Law		
	Total	Corporate	Litigation	Estates
FEES CLASSIFIED BY AREA OF LAW				
Client X	$10,000	$2,000	$8,000	
Client Y	6,000	5,000		$1,000
Client Z	3,000		3,000	
	$19,000	$7,000	$11,000	$1,000

		Office Location		
	Total	New York	Washington	Los Angeles
FEES CLASSIFIED BY OFFICE LOCATION				
Client X	$10,000	$8,000	$2,000	
Client Y	6,000	4,000		$2,000
Client Z	3,000		3,000	
	$19,000	$12,000	$5,000	$2,000

§ 10.04 Profit Determination

Once a law firm has developed reasonable procedures for cost allocation and fee classification, the results of these calculations can be easily assembled in profit centers to determine "profit by client" and grouped to determine "profit by client partner."

Some law firms collect cost information by office location or by area of law. In firms that do not collect costs in this manner, the methodology used to allocate costs among the firm's clients can be used to allocate costs among the firm's office locations and among the areas of law practiced by the firm. These allocated costs and the related fees can be summarized in profit centers to determine "profit by area of law" and "profit by office location."

A condensed summary of this profit center information is illustrated in Figure 10-D.

Figure 10-D. Illustration of a condensed profit center accounting report for a law firm.

ABC LAW FIRM
PROFIT CENTER ACCOUNTING REPORT
($ in thousands)

		Client		
	Total	Client X	Client Y	Client Z
Profit by client				
Fee revenues	$19,000	$10,000	$ 6,000	$3,000
Costs	18,000	8,647	6,358	2,995
Profit	$ 1,000	$ 1,353	$ (358)	$ 5

		Client Partner		
	Total	Partner A	Partner B	Partner C
Profit by client partner				
Fee revenues	$19,000	$10,000	$ 9,000	—
Costs	18,000	8,647	9,353	—
Profit	$ 1,000	$ 1,353	$ (353)	—

		Area of Law		
	Total	Corporate	Litigation	Estates
Profit by area of law				
Fee revenues	$19,000	$ 7,000	$11,000	$1,000
Costs	18,000	7,027	9,913	1,060
Profit	$ 1,000	$ (27)	$ 1,087	$ (60)

		Office Location		
	Total	New York	Washington	Los Angeles
Profit by office location				
Fee revenues	$19,000	$12,000	$5,000	$2,000
Costs	18,000	11,157	4,724	2,119
Profit	$1,000	$843	$276	$ (119)

§ 10.05 Analyzing the Results

Figure 10-D presents an illustration of financial information, analyzing four aspects of the law firm's practice. The results of this profit center accounting report should be related to each of the purposes for which it was developed. For example, the results of the illustration could be correlated with the report's four purposes in the following manner:

(1) *Client retention.* The results indicate that work for client X is very profitable, whereas work for client Y is unprofitable, and work for client Z is marginal. The message for management is that it should investigate the reasons why client Y work and client Z work is not profitable and determine whether they should be retained as clients, assuming more profitable replacement work could be obtained.

(2) *Partners' compensation.* The results indicate that work for partner A's clients was very profitable while work for partner B's clients resulted in a loss. Management may wish to (a) reward partner A, (b) investigate the reasons for poor profit performance on the part of partner B's clients before setting his compensation, and (c) determine partner C's compensation in a manner unrelated to client profitability because, while he worked on several client engagements, he was not designated as the billing partner for any of them.

(3) *Practice strategy.* The results indicate litigation work is very profitable for this firm, whereas estate work and corporate work are marginal. The firm may consider expanding its litigation work and/or contracting its corporate and estate work.

(4) *Office location strategy.* The results indicate that this firm's New York and Washington offices are profitable, whereas its Los Angeles office operates at a loss. The firm may consider closing its Los Angeles office unless the purpose of its existence is connected to the profitability of the firm's other offices.

It is important to note that, although profit center accounting results provide useful input into the decision making process, other firm strategy factors need to be considered before any action is taken. For example, it is possible that the results being analyzed represent an anomaly in a consistent trend, or that the numbers are a result of the firm's entering a new practice or opening a new office. It is critical to identify the underlying factors that contribute to the final results.

CHAPTER 11

Budgeting

Chapter Contents

---

§ 11.01 Budgeting for Law Firms

To manage its affairs successfully, a law firm should prepare a budget at the start of each year and, depending on the size of the firm, should monitor and adjust the budget periodically throughout the year. Large and megasize firms find that having a "living" budget that is updated periodically (i.e., monthly, quarterly or semiannually) allows management to make "mid-course corrections" to eliminate surprises or large variations that occur when budgets are prepared and never changed. In developing a formal budget, management must:

(1) Project fees;
(2) Estimate personnel costs; and
(3) Estimate operating expenses.

There are two approaches management can take when preparing a budget. A budget can be based on management's knowledge and perception of the firm's potential client activities and nonchargeable activities for the forthcoming year. Or, management can seek input from the firm's partners for use in developing fee projections and from the firm's administrative supervisors for use in estimating expenses. This latter approach is the more successful way to budget.

§ 11.02 Projecting Fees

Projecting fee revenue for the coming year involves: (1) developing an estimate of the level of work (recurring and nonrecurring matters) for existing clients during the upcoming year, and (2) making an assessment of the level of new work which will be generated by new clients during the next year.

The level of fees for existing clients can be assessed by asking the partners: (a) to estimate the hours of professional time and the level of professional staff which they anticipate for the forthcoming year, and (b) to estimate the expected realization rates on each client engagement. These estimates can be developed by partner at the practice group level as part of the annual practice planning process, with results from all practice groups then being aggregated to arrive at firm-wide numbers. This productivity information can be supplemented with management's estimate of billing rates for the forthcoming year, the combination of which will elicit an estimate of fees for existing clients for the coming year.

An estimate of fees for new clients involves the same variables as an estimate of fees for existing clients. These variables are hours, rates and realizations. Hours are assessed based on partners' subjective judgments. Consequently, hours estimated for new client work are rarely precise. Such an assessment of hours for new client work is based on factors that affect the firm's ability to expand its practice. These include the current economic environment, the firm's strategic plans for expansion or contraction of work in each area of law, the amount of new business development effort, the firm's capacity for absorbing new work, competitive pressures, and past patterns of new work generated annually by the firm.

Figure 11-A illustrates a summary worksheet for projecting fee revenues.

Figure 11-A. Illustration of a summary worksheet for projecting a law firm's fee revenue.

ABC LAW FIRM
SUMMARY WORKSHEET FOR PROJECTING FEES

	Current Year (Actual)			Next Year (Estimated)		
Clients	Hours	Average Rate	Fees	Hours	Average Rate	Fees
X	10,000	$250	$2,500,000	12,000	$260	$ 3,120,000
Y	25,000	$210	5,250,000	15,000	$220	3,300,000
Z	3,000	$290	870,000	—	—	—
	.	.	.	.	.	.
	.	.	.	.	.	.
	.	.	.	.	.	.
Total time charges	607,000		161,290,000	478,000		130,100,000
Under-realizations		7%	(11,290,000)		8%	(10,425,000)
Existing clients' fees			150,000,000	478,000		119,675,000
New clients' fees	—	—	—	151,000	$275	41,525,000
Total fees			$150,000,000	629,000		$161,200,000

§ 11.03 Estimating Personnel Costs

Budgeting for personnel costs requires management to estimate three types of costs:

(1) Compensation (of timekeepers other than equity partners);
(2) Administrative staff salaries; and
(3) Fringe benefits and other employee costs.

The estimation process for each of these costs will be discussed in the paragraphs that follow.

[1]—Timekeepers' Compensation

Estimating compensation of all timekeepers other than equity partners requires: (a) a determination of the number of timekeepers that the firm desires to maintain, and (b) a determination of the compensation level for each timekeeper. The firm must first project the aggregate level of lawyers' chargeable hours for the subsequent year and the portion attributable to equity partners. It can then derive an estimate of chargeable hours for the other classes of timekeepers and the number of legal staff required to carry the workload. Timekeeper compensation levels for the forthcoming year are often determined by a committee of partners who establish a range of compensation for each class of legal staff based on level of experience. Specific compensation amounts are then determined for each timekeeper in each class. A summary of the results of this process is illustrated below for the associate class:

	Average Compensation			
Experience Level	Current Year	Next Year	Number	Aggregate Compensation
Senior associates	$160,000	$165,000	50	$ 8,250,000
Experienced associates	135,000	140,000	90	12,600,000
New associate	110,000	115,000	30	3,450,000
				$24,300,000

[2]—Administrative Staff Salaries

Estimating administrative staff salaries requires: (a) a determination of staffing levels for each administrative department based on the needs of the firm and number of its lawyers; (b) a determination of each administrative staff member's salary; and (c) a determination of total costs that will be recovered by billing relevant secretarial, word processing, and possibly other administrative time to clients. A summary of the results of this process is illustrated below:

($ in thousands)

Department	Current Year (Actual)	Next Year (Estimate)
Administrative management	1,100	1,200
Finance and data processing	500	500
Human resources	300	300
Information systems	1,300	1,400
Library/reference materials	1,900	2,000
Marketing	500	550
Professional staff recruiting	450	550
Secretarial and word processing (net)	$10,600	$11,000
Other administrative staff	2,350	2,500
	$19,000	$20,000

[3]—Fringe Benefits and Other Employee Costs

Estimating fringe benefits requires: (a) a determination of the number of associate lawyers and administrative staff eligible for each fringe benefit, and (b) a determination of the level of fringe benefits to be offered by the firm during the forthcoming year and the cost per employee for each benefit. A summary of the results of this process is illustrated below:

($ in thousands)

	Current Year (Actual)	Next Year (Estimate)
Social security taxes	$2,500	$2,750
Retirement plan expense	700	750
Insurance and other programs	2,200	2,400
	$5,400	$5,900

§ 11.04 Estimating Operating Expenses

In order to budget operating expenses, four types of costs must be estimated:

(1) Occupancy costs;
(2) Office operating expenses;
(3) Professional activities; and
(4) General business expenses.

The estimation process for each of these costs will be discussed in the paragraphs that follow.

[1]—Occupancy Costs

When estimating occupancy costs, the firm must: (a) determine its space requirements for the forthcoming year, (b) determine the cost per square foot for this space, and (c) determine peripheral costs (i.e., electricity and other utilities, commercial rent and occupancy taxes, and amortization of leasehold improvements). The firm's space requirements are usually directly related to the number of lawyers and administrative staff working in the firm's offices. A summary of the results of this process is illustrated below:

($ in thousands)

	Current Year (Actual)	Next Year (Estimate)
Rent of office space	$10,600	$10,700
Amortization of leasehold improvements	1,000	1,200
Other occupancy costs	1,000	1,100
	$12,600	$13,000

[2]—Office Operating Expenses

Estimating office operating expenses requires (a) a determination of the firm's anticipated usage level for office equipment and supplies, and (b) an assessment of the extent of cost recoveries to be achieved by billing clients directly for equipment usage (such as duplicating services). A summary of the results of this process is illustrated below:

($ in thousands)

	Current Year (Actual)	Next Year (Estimate)
Office equipment and supplies (net)	$5,500	$5,600
Depreciation of office furniture	500	550
Repairs and maintenance	500	450
	$6,500	$6,600

[3]—Professional Activities

When assessing professional activities expenses, the firm must: (a) determine the number of lawyers needed in the forthcoming year, and (b) determine the level of professional activities costs to be reimbursed to each attorney. A summary of the results of this process is illustrated below:

($ in thousands)

	Current Year (Actual)	Next Year (Estimate)
Professional dues and continuing education	$ 850	$ 900
Prospective client entertainment	650	600
Travel on firm business	1,000	950
	$2,500	$2,450

[4]—General Business Expenses

When estimating general business expenses, the firm must: (a) determine the anticipated operating level for the firm's support services (e.g., telephone, library, messengers, reprographics, etc.); (b) determine the extent of cost recoveries to be achieved by billing support services to clients directly; (c) determine the firm's anticipated use of outside services (e.g., professional services, marketing and public relations, insurance, interest expense on loans, and charitable contributions); and (d) calculate an estimate for the firm's local franchise or business taxes (e.g., New York City unincorporated business tax, Philadelphia net profits tax, Philadelphia business privilege tax, etc). A summary of the results of this process is illustrated below:

($ in thousands)

	Current Year (Actual)	Next Year (Estimate)
Marketing and public relations	$2,300	$ 2,500
Professional recruiting	1,300	1,500
Professional liability insurance	1,000	1,100
Other insurance and taxes	750	950
Communications	1,600	1,750
Library/Reference materials	1,350	1,400
Professional services	1,200	1,300
	$9,500	$10,500

This is also an appropriate category in which to capture estimated costs related to temporary help (i.e., non-payroll staff) and the costs of any outsourced or sub-contracted administrative functions.

§ 11.05 Responsibility Accounting

Responsibility accounting requires the firm to: (a) assign to individuals within the organization the responsibility for achieving financial targets (such as a certain level of revenue or a budgeted level of expense), and (b) produce financial reports which compare actual financial results with budgeted amounts. This comparison should highlight the performance of those who are responsible for achieving financial targets for specific types of revenues or expenses. Responsibility accounting takes on more meaning if those who are held responsible for meeting budgets are actively involved in developing the budgets. These individuals should have the ability and authority to take the necessary action to affect the revenue and/or expenses for which they are held accountable.

In a smaller law firm, responsibility accounting normally is done by the managing partner and his or her team. In larger firms, however, responsibility accounting can descend several levels in the organization. For example, a large or megasize firm with multiple branch offices may delegate responsibility accounting to the managing partner of each practice office, so that revenue and expenses are monitored closely at a local level. This is particularly true for firms with offices in other countries where local costs may be unique (e.g., mandatory firm-provided lunches for staff, firm-provided automobiles for partners, or special benefits for support staff or associates in some countries) and require the scrutiny and authorization of a local managing partner. Depending on the size of the branch office, the local managing partner may delegate responsibility accounting to one or more leaders within the office.

Responsibility accounting reports can be developed by using (1) the functional approach, or (2) the profit-center approach.

[1]—Functional Approach

If a law firm is not departmentalized, responsibility accounting could be assigned along functional lines, in the following manner:

[a]—Fees

Each partner could be assigned target levels of fees for existing clients based on his/her client billing responsibilities, with another level of fee responsibility for the practice group leader. The firm's practice development committee could assume responsibility for achieving target revenues for new client engagements.

[b]—Personnel Costs

The firm's compensation committee could be responsible for monitoring the costs of compensation of timekeepers other than equity partners. The responsibility for monitoring administrative staff salaries could be assigned to the heads of the firm's various administrative departments.

[c]—Occupancy Costs

The firm's executive director, director of facilities, or director of administration position could be assigned the responsibility for monitoring these costs.

[d]—Office Operating Expenses

These expenses could be assigned to the firm's office manager for monitoring.

[e]—Professional Activities

The firm could establish a special committee of partners to monitor these costs, or this responsibility could be assigned to the firm's finance committee.

[f]—General Business Expenses

Communication, professional recruiting, marketing, and library costs could be monitored by the department heads of these administrative departments. Monitoring of other general business expenses could be assigned to the firm's executive director or chief financial officer.

Figure 11-B illustrates a summary page of a responsibility accounting report for a law firm that uses a functional approach.

Figure 11-B. Illustration of a summary page of a responsibility accounting report for a law firm that assigns responsibilities along functional lines.

ABC LAW FIRM
SUMMARY RESPONSIBILITY ACCOUNTING
REPORT FUNCTIONAL APPROACH

($ in thousands)

	Budget	Actual	Variance
Fee Revenues:			
Existing clients	$120,900	$128,000	$7,100
New clients	40,300	38,000	(2,300)
	161,200	166,000	4,800
Personnel Costs:			
Timekeepers' compensation (other than equity partners)	48,750	49,000	250
Administrative staff salaries	20,000	20,000	—
Fringe benefits and other employee costs	5,900	6,000	100
	74,650	75,000	350
Operating Expenses:			
Occupancy costs	13,000	13,000	—
Office operating expenses	6,600	7,000	400
Professional activities	2,450	2,500	500
General business expenses	10,500	11,000	
	32,550	33,500	950
Net income	$ 54,000	$ 57,500	$3,500

[2]—Profit-Center Approach

If a law firm is departmentalized, it may have a system of profit-center accounting which produces detailed profit and loss statements for each professional department (such as corporate, litigation and estate departments), with support and overhead costs being allocated to the professional departments.[1] If so, the prime responsibility for achieving budgets for each type of revenue or expense which is allocated to each professional department should be assigned to

[1] See §10.02 for more information on cost allocation.

each respective department head using the profit-center approach. The department heads, in turn, can make each billing partner responsible for monitoring individual clients or groups of clients within the department.

Figure 11-C illustrates a summary page of a responsibility accounting report for a law firm that uses a profit-center approach.

Figure 11-C. Illustration of a summary page of a responsibility accounting report for a law firm that assigns responsibilities along profit-center lines.

ABC LAW FIRM SUMMARY
RESPONSIBILITY ACCOUNTING REPORT
PROFIT-CENTER APPROACH

($ in thousands)

	Budget	Actual	Variance
Fee Revenues:			
Litigation department	$ 97,000	$101,000	$4,000
Corporate department	59,000	60,000	1,000
Estates department	5,200	5,000	(200)
	161,200	166,000	4,800
Costs and expenses:			
Litigation department	57,000	58,000	1,000
Corporate department	46,500	47,000	500
Estates department	3,700	3,500	(200)
	107,200	108,500	1,300
Net Income:			
Litigation department	40,000	43,000	3,000
Corporate department	12,500	13,000	500
Estates department	1,500	1,500	—
	$ 54,000	$ 57,500	$3,500

It is typical for firms to use a combination of both approaches, with the professional staff (primarily the practice leaders) having responsibility for the revenue targets and the appropriate administrative staff (primarily administrative department heads) having responsibility for the costs in their respective departments.

11.06 Unit Cost Comparison

A comparison of budgeted costs with actual costs provides management with useful information about aggregate variances from the firm's plan. However, it does not identify the cause of an increase or decrease in costs. This is best accomplished through a cost analysis. Costs are either (a) fixed, (b) variable or (c) semivariable. The cause of an increase in fixed costs can be explained through a direct review of the facts. Before exploring the cause of an increase in variable or semivariable costs, management must first determine whether the cause is related to: (a) a variation in volume (e.g., the number of lawyers), or (b) a variation in unit costs. For example, assume the following facts about a hypothetical law firm:

	Budget	Actual	Variance
Operating Costs (excluding timekeeper compensation)	$58,450,000	$59,500,000	$1,050,000
Number of Lawyers	305	300	(5)
Cost per Lawyer	$ 191,639	$ 198,333	$ 6,694

If we also assume (for purposes of the example only) that all operating costs are variable, the cause of the aggregate increase in costs can be analyzed into two components, as follows:

	Increase (Decrease)
Variance due to decrease in number of lawyers ($191,639 x 5)	($958,195)
Variance due to increase in unit cost per lawyer ($6,694 x 300)	2,008,200
Aggregate increase in costs	$1,050,000

For purposes of analyzing variances between budgeted and actual costs, some law firms have found it useful to calculate and summarize unit cost information. Once the unit costs have been determined, management can use this information to assist in the search for the underlying causes of increases and decreases in variable and semivariable costs. Figure 11-D illustrates an example of a unit cost comparison for a law firm. The example illustrates two types of unit costs:

(1) Cost per lawyer and
(2) Cost per chargeable hour.

Figure 11-D. Illustration of a unit cost comparison for a law firm.

ABC LAW FIRM
COMPARISON OF UNIT COSTS
BUDGET VS. ACTUAL

	Budget	Actual	Variance
OPERATING COSTS:			
(Excluding Timekeepers' Compensation)			
Administrative salaries	$20,000,000	$20,000,000	$ —
Fringe benefit costs	5,900,000	6,000,000	100,000
Occupancy costs	13,000,000	13,000,000	—
Office operating expenses	6,600,000	7,000,00	400,000
Professional activities	2,450,000	2,500,000	50,000
General business expenses	10,500,000	11,000,000	500,000
	$58,450,000	$59,500,000	$1,050,000
STATISTIC:			
Number of lawyers	305	300	(5)
COST PER LAWYER:			
Administrative salaries	$65,574	$66,667	$1,093
Fringe benefit costs	19,344	20,000	656
Occupancy costs	42,623	43,333	710
Office operating expenses	21,639	23,333	1,694
Professional activities	8,033	8,333	301
General business expenses	34,426	36,667	2,240
	$191,639	$198,333	$6,694
STATISTIC:			
Chargeable hours	629,000	634,000	5,000
COST PER CHARGEABLE HOUR:			
Administrative salaries	$31.80	$31.55	$(.25)
Fringe benefit costs	9.38	9.46	.08
Occupancy costs	20.67	20.50	(.16)
Office operating expenses	10.49	11.04	.55
Professional activities	3.90	3.94	.05
General business expenses	16.69	17.35	.66
	$92.93	$93.84	$.93

§ 11.07 Cash Requirements Budgeting

A law firm can prepare an operating budget, which focuses on the firm's projected net income. In addition, the firm can prepare a more comprehensive cash requirements budget, which includes the results of the operating budget as one component and takes into account the timing of the firm's major cash expenditures. Cash requirements budgets have taken on greater importance recently as the legal market and professional has become increasingly competitive, with many firms opting to fund both geographic and practice area expansion. In such an environment, these budgets provide a valuable tools in managing debt levels and maintaining positive banking relationships. Cash requirements budgets are ordinarily prepared on a monthly or quarterly basis. The typical components of a cash requirements budget for a law firm are:

(1) Equity partner distributions;
(2) Property and equipment purchases, including technology investments;
(3) Cash provided by operations;
(4) Bank loans; and
(5) Cash balances.

The estimation process for each of these components will be discussed in the paragraphs that follow.

[1]—Equity Partner Distributions

When estimating equity partner distributions the firm must: (a) estimate the firm's profits for the year, (b) determine the monthly cash drawings to be provided to each equity partner, and (c) select a month (or months) during which the balance of the profits in excess of the monthly drawings will be paid. Most firms are conservative in setting the monthly drawings to avoid a situation where aggregate drawings might exceed firm profits, resulting in equity partners being asked to repay excess drawings to the firm.

[2]—Property and Equipment Purchases

Estimating property and equipment purchases requires: (a) a determination of the firm's anticipated needs for leasehold improvements, computer equipment and office furniture, and (b) an estimate of the cost and timing of these purchases.

[3]—Cash Provided by Operations

Cash provided by operations flows from the results of the operating budget. It represents net income in the operating budget, exclusive of the deduction for depreciation expense, which does not affect cash. When estimating cash provided by operations the firm must: (a) determine the flow of fee revenue by month (understanding that fee collections in the last quarter of a firm's fiscal year can compose a significant portion of the annual cash basis revenue), and (b) determine the flow of expenses by month (expenses are ordinarily paid systematically from month-to-month).

[4]—Bank Loans

Projecting bank loans requires: (a) a determination of long-term financing needs (e.g., to finance the purchase of property and equipment), and (b) a determination of the amount of short-term loans or lines of credit needed to finance seasonal business needs (i.e., delays in billings and collections, usually during the earlier months of a firm's fiscal year).

[5]—Cash Balances

When estimating cash balances, the firm must determine a minimum level of working cash that must be available at all times to operate the firm's business effectively on a day-to-day basis, allowing for the fact that cash collections can be uneven and unpredictable.

Figure 11-E illustrates an example of quarterly cash requirements budget for a law firm. The example illustrates: (a) fairly level partner distributions, (b) mid-year purchases of property and equipment, (c) cash from operations "bunched" in the last quarter based on the firm's fee collection history, and (d) bank loans geared to finance the shortfall between the firm's cash requirements and its cash provided by operations, while maintaining a minimum working cash balance (which rises slightly from the beginning to the end of the year).

Figure 11-E. Illustration of quarterly cash requirements budget for a law firm.

ABC LAW FIRM
CASH REQUIREMENTS BUDGET
($ in thousands)

	Year	1st Quarter	2nd Quarter	3rd Quarter	4th Quarter
CASH REQUIREMENTS:					
Partner distributions	$(50,000)	$(10,000)	$(10,000)	$(10,000)	$(20,000)
Property and equipment purchases	(9,000)	(1,000)	(2,000)	(2,500)	(3,500)
	(59,000)	(11,000)	(12,000)	(12,500)	(23,500)
SOURCES OF CASH:					
Cash from operations	53,000	8,500	9,000	9,500	26,000
Bank loans	6,500	2,600	3,150	3,100	(2,350)
	59,500	11,100	12,150	12,600	23,650
CASH BALANCE:					
Increase	500	100	150	100	150
Beginning of period	1,000	1,000	1,100	1,250	1,350
End of period	$ 1,500	$ 1,100	$ 1,250	$ 1,350	$ 1,500

CHAPTER 12

Long-Range Planning

Chapter Contents

---

§ 12.01 Long-Range Planning for Law Firms

In business as in life, success typically does not just happen. Much planning and preparation are necessary. The same is true for successful law firms. The objective of strategic planning is to properly position the firm for the long term by evaluating many factors including (1) the culture of the firm, (2) the wants and needs of the partners, (3) the economy, (4) the industry and developments in areas that impact law and business (i.e., political, social, technological, etc.). As many firms expand their traditional areas of expertise and geographic reach, the legal marketplace has become progressively more competitive. As a result, many firms are developing strategic plans to help them remain competitive in today's increasingly intense environment. To properly plan for the future, law firm management must study the possible scenarios that may come about as a result of an action taken today. This can be achieved by creating a multi-year financial projection based on assumptions about future events. Creating a financial projection requires the development of a:

(1) Strategic Plan;
(2) Staffing Plan;
(3) Operating Plan; and
(4) Capital Financing Plan.

The latter three should be formulated in a coordinated manner to support the firm's strategy.

Each of these four components will be discussed in detail in the following sections.[1]

---

[1] For additional information regarding long-range planning, see Chapter 22 *infra*, entitled "Financial Modeling."

§ 12.02 The Strategic Plan

Strategy is a careful plan for gaining and sustaining a competitive advantage in the marketplace, tactics, i.e., specific actions to be undertaken to carry out the plan, must be developed. A law firm must analyze two important business dimensions when developing the firm's strategic plan: (1) market identification and (2) growth focus. These steps build the foundation for the firm's long-range plan.

[1]—Market Identification

The potential market for a law firm's services can be viewed from three perspectives:

(1) Expansion of existing services to broader client base within existing geographic market(s).
(2) Diversification of services to include additional areas of law (e.g., banking litigation, insurance, etc).
(3) Geographic dispersion of services by opening or acquiring additional branch offices (domestically or internationally).

The firm's assessment of each potential market segment can be accomplished by focusing on key questions, such as:

(1) Is there a high level of client demand (existing or potential) for a new service or a new location?
(2) Is there a competitive reason for locating an office in a certain location?
(3) Will the new service or new location generate an adequate level of recurring work?
(4) Will the new service or new location provide work that will be viewed as challenging by existing associates and recruits?
(5) Does the new service or new location offer a reasonable return on the expected investment (i.e., acquisition or opening of a new office in a foreign location)?

These questions should be studied within the context of the firm's existing practice mix, its geographic coverage, and its industry and client focus.

[2]—Growth Focus

Once the firm has identified and assessed the potential market for its services, from both a geographic and type of law-practiced basis, it should make a careful selection of those services and those locations that offer the best potential for sustained growth. For example, a firm might consider the following elements of a strategic plan (assuming that its past operations were confined to corporate services rendered solely in New York):

(1) Expand corporate services;
(2) Expand the size of the New York office;
(3) Diversify to include litigation services;
(4) Diversify to include tax services;
(5) Open a Washington office; and
(6) Open an office in London and Singapore.

For ease of demonstration purposes, these proposed actions must be reduced to an overall estimated growth rate in terms of lawyers' productive time (for example: 6%).

§ 12.03 The Staffing Plan

The firm must assess personnel needs, whether the strategic plan calls for growth or contraction in the practice. This requires the development of a staffing plan. The plan projects the need for two distinct groups of personnel: (1) lawyers and (2) support staff. Factors to be considered in developing projections for each group of personnel are discussed below.

[1]—Lawyer Projections

In determining the need for lawyers and their levels of experience, the firm should consider the following factors for each year of the plan:

(1) Desired growth rate, in terms of number of attorneys;
(2) Desired ratio of all non-equity partner lawyers to equity partners;
(3) Anticipated rate of equity partner retirements and withdrawals;
(4) Number of years to equity partnership admission;
(5) Number of lawyers admitted to the partnership;
(6) Anticipated rate of lawyer attrition; and
(7) Required number of new lawyers to be hired.

The staffing plan lists the present lawyer complement for the first year of the projection and projects the number of attorneys required for subsequent years, taking into account the preceding factors. The plan presumes that the number of attorneys in each staff classification will be advanced to the next staff level in the following year. For example, here is a staffing plan together with the assumptions underlying its preparation:

	20X2	20X3	20X4
Experience Level			
Equity partners:			
More than 10 years	7	9	11
5 to 10 years	10	10	10
Under 5 years	8	8	7
	25	27	28
Other lawyers:			
More than 6 years	5	10	11
2 to 6 years	35	35	35
Under 2 years	10	8	11
	50	53	57
	75	80	85

Assumptions:

-Growth rate	:	6%
-Ratio of other lawyers to equity partners	:	2 to 1
-Equity partner retirements	:	None
-Average years to equity partnership admission	:	7
Non-equity partner lawyer attrition	:	10%

[2]—Support Staff Projections

One way to develop a plan for support staff is to assume that the firm's present percentage relationship between support staff and lawyers will continue as the firm grows. If this assumption is reasonable the staffing plan for support personnel, which is based upon the preceding projection of lawyers, would be:

	20X2	20X3	20X4
Secretaries (.60 per lawyer)	45	48	51
Administrative staff (.50 per lawyer)	37	40	43
	82	88	94

§ 12.04 The Operating Plan

Once the firm has determined a strategy and projected the number of personnel required to carry out the mission, it is time to convert these decisions into an operating plan. To form an operating plan the firm must make:

(1) Revenue projections;
(2) Cost projections;
- ➢ Compensation
- ➢ Occupancy
- ➢ Office (including technology)
- ➢ Other

(3) Net income forecasts based on these projections.

The operating plan should be developed for periods of one-to-five years. Examples in this chapter focus only on a three-year plan.

[1]—Revenue Projections

Projecting revenues requires the firm to estimate fees for each year of the operating plan. This estimate can be developed using several approaches. The estimate could be made by applying individual growth rates to the current-year's fee revenue for each practice area, office, geographic region or a combination of these. Another approach is to calculate billable fees as a function of lawyers' billable hours based on the staffing plan, which has built-in growth rates. This latter approach allows the firm to correlate professional fee projections with professional compensation expense projections. To use this approach the firm must develop assumptions for:

(1) Billable hours for each professional class;
(2) Billing rates for each professional class;
(3) Firmwide billing realization factor; and
(4) Firmwide bad debt factor.

Figure 12-A illustrates an abbreviated example of revenue projections for a law firm. For ease of demonstration, the table assumes only two staff classes: equity partners and associates. However, in reality most firms have many classes of associates (based on years of experience with the firm, time in grade, or years out of law school) and it is not uncommon for a firm to have two different levels of partners (equity and salaried). This illustration assumes that fees were earned, billed, and collected in the same year. In practice, fees earned in the last few months of the year are often billed and collected in the subsequent year. To adjust for this, a firm-wide speed-of-billings and collections factor can be introduced into the fee projection calculation. Also, fee projections in the illustration are based on average billing rates for all partners and all associates. In practice, the projection should be developed using billing rates for each professional class.

Figure 12-A. Illustration of an abbreviated example of revenue projections for a law firm.

ABC LAW FIRM
REVENUE PROJECTIONS

	20X2	20X3	20X4
ASSUMPTIONS			
A-Staff count			
Equity partners	25	27	28
Associates	50	53	57
B-Billable hours:			
Partners (1,500 per year)	37,500	40,500	42,000
Associates (1,800 per year)	90,000	95,400	102,600
C-Billing rates (average):			
Partners	$300	$305	$310
Associates	$175	$180	$185
D-Billing realization factor	90%	90%	90%
E-Bad debt factor	98%	98%	98%
PROJECTIONS			
F-Billable Fees (B x C)	$27,000,000	$29,524,500	$32,001,000
G-Realizable Fees (F x D)	$24,300,000	$26,572,050	$28,800,900
H-Collectible Fees (G x E)	$23,814,000	$26,040,609	$28,224,882

[2]—Compensation Cost Projections

To project compensation costs, the firm must estimate (a) timekeepers' compensation (for all timekeepers other than equity partners), (b) support staff salaries, and (c) fringe benefit costs. They can be assessed in the following way:

(1) Timekeepers' compensation: Calculated as a function of the previously determined staffing plan, an estimate of salaries for each timekeeper level in the first year, and an assumed inflation index for subsequent years;

(2) Support staff salaries: Calculated as a function of the previously determined staffing plan, an estimate of salaries for secretaries and other administrative staff, and an assumed inflation index;

(3) Fringe benefits: Calculated using the current year's percentage relationship between fringe benefits and compensation, assuming no major changes in the future in the firm's fringe benefit program.

Figure 12-B illustrates an abbreviated example of compensation cost projections for a law firm, with the simplifying assumption of associates being the only timekeeper class other than equity partners.

Figure 12-B. Illustration of an abbreviated example of compensation cost projections for a law firm.

ABC LAW FIRM
COMPENSATION COST PROJECTIONS

	20X2	20X3	20X4
ASSUMPTIONS			
A-Staff count:			
Associates	50	53	57
Secretaries	45	48	51
Administrative Staff	37	40	43
B-Inflation index	—	5%	5%
C-Average compensation:			
Associates	$100,000	$105,000	$110,250
Secretaries	$ 50,000	$ 52,500	$ 55,125
Administrative Staff	$ 30,000	$ 31,500	$ 33,075
D-Fringe benefit factor	15%	15%	15%
PROJECTIONS			
E-Total compensation (A x C):			
Associates	$5,000,000	$5,565,000	$6,284,250
Secretaries	2,250,000	2,520,000	2,811,375
Administrative Staff	1,110,000	1,260,000	1,422,225
Total compensation projection	8,360,000	9,345,000	10,517,850
F-Total fringe benefits (E x D)	1,254,500	1,401,750	1,577,677
	$9,614,000	$10,746,750	$12,095,527

[3]—Operating Expense Projections

To project operating expenses, the firm must estimate: (a) occupancy costs, (b) office operating expenses, (c) professional activities, and (d) general business expenses. One way to project these costs is to separate occupancy costs from all other operating expenses and then make the following two calculations:

[a]—Occupancy Costs

Calculated as a function of the number of attorneys previously determined in the staffing plan, the number of square feet of required space for each attorney, the cost per square foot of office space and an inflation index. This assessment assumes that additional office space can be leased on a flexible basis. In practice, additional assumptions should be factored into the calculations to accommodate typical leasing patterns, such as the leasing of space in increments.

[b]—Other Operating Expenses

Calculated as a function of cost per attorney, based on historical patterns in the first year and an assumed inflation index for subsequent years.

Figure 12-C illustrates an abbreviated example of operating expense projections for a law firm.

Figure 12-C. Illustration of an abbreviated example of operating expense projections for a law firm.

ABC LAW FIRM
OPERATING EXPENSE PROJECTIONS

	20X2	20X3	20X4
ASSUMPTIONS			
A-Number of attorneys	75	80	85
B-Space per attorney (sq. ft.)	800	800	800
C-Inflation index	—	5%	5%
D-Occupancy cost per square foot	$30	$32	$33
E-Per lawyer costs:			
Office operating expenses	$20,000	$21,000	$22,000
Professional activities	$7,500	$7,875	$8,268
General business expenses	$12,500	$13,125	$13,781
PROJECTIONS			
F-Occupancy costs (A x B x D)	$1,800,000	$2,048,000	$2,244,000
G-Other operating expenses (A x E):			
Office operating expenses	1,500,000	1,680,000	1,870,000
Professional activities	562,500	630,000	702,780
General business expenses	937,500	1,050,000	1,171,385
Total operating cost projection	$4,800,000	$5,408,000	$5,988,165

[4]—Net Income Projections

To project net income, the firm must compile the results of the several projections, which represent the component parts of the income statement, including (a) revenue projections, (b) compensation cost projections and (c) operating expense projections. An abbreviated example of net income projections is illustrated in Figure 12-D.

Figure 12-D. Illustration of an abbreviated example of net income projections for a law firm. (Assuming a modest billing rate increase.)

ABC LAW FIRM
NET INCOME PROJECTIONS
BEFORE PROFIT IMPROVEMENT PROGRAM

	20X2	20X3	20X4
KEY ASSUMPTIONS			
A-Number of attorneys	75	80	85
B-Billing rate increase	—	3%	3%
C-Expense inflation factor	—	5%	5%
PROJECTIONS			
D-Revenue (Fig. 12-A)	$23,814,000	$26,040,609	$28,224,882
E-Compensation costs (Fig. 12-B)	(9,614,000)	(10,746,750)	(12,095,527)
F-Operating expenses (Fig. 12-C)	(4,800,000)	(5,408,000)	(5,988,165)
Net income	$ 9,400,000	$ 9,885,859	$10,141,190
Equity partners	25	27	28
Income per equity partner	$376,000	$366,142	$362,185

While the illustration in Figure 12-D presents a favorable trend in revenue and net income, it also presents an unfavorable trend in income per equity partner. This illustration is only a preliminary outline of an operating plan. After management has determined the projected results (which in this case are flat), a plan of action to improve profits can be developed. For example, management may decide on an increase in billing rates, which is higher than the 3% projected in the preliminary outline. Management also may decide to plan for higher associate utilization by decreasing the partner/staff ratio, requiring partners to spend more time on billable vs. administrative functions, significant cost reductions, slow-down in partner admissions, or other variations. As each variation is developed, revised calculations are required to determine how these variations will affect projected net income. This iterative process is why it is advantageous to set up the assumptions and plan parameters using spreadsheet software, in order to generate projections for multiple "what if" scenarios. Once management has reviewed the various scenarios and decided upon an appropriate plan of action, the Operating Plan can be finalized.

Figure 12-E ("Net Income Projections—*After* Profit Improvement Program") illustrates the result of adopting a plan of action.

Figure 12-E. Illustration of an abbreviated example of net income projections for a law firm. (Assuming a billing rate increase keeping pace with inflation).

ABC LAW FIRM
NET INCOME PROJECTIONS
AFTER PROFIT IMPROVEMENT PROGRAM

	20X2	20X3	20X4
KEY ASSUMPTIONS			
A-Number of attorneys	75	80	85
B-Billing rate increase	—	5%	5%
C-Expense inflation factor	—	5%	5%
PROJECTIONS			
D-Revenue	$23,814,000	$30,311,100	$33,661,800
E-Compensation costs	(9,614,000)	(10,746,750)	(12,095,527)
F-Operating expenses	(4,800,000)	(5,408,000)	(5,988,165)
Net income	$ 9,400,000	$14,156,350	$15,578,108
Equity partners	25	27	28
Income per equity partner	$376,000	$524,309	$556,361

It is based on the same assumptions as Figure 12-D ("Net Income Projections—*Before* Profit Improvement Program"), except that billing rates are assumed to increase at a faster pace. Figure 12-E assumes that billing rates will increase at 5% annually (to keep pace with the rate of inflation assumption applied to expenses). This contrasts with the modest 3% annual billing rate increase assumed in Figure 12-D. The impact of adopting this one-step plan of action can be seen through the following summary which compares the firm's projected income per partner "Before" vs. "After" application of the profit improvement program:

	Projected Income Per Partner		
	Before Profit Improvement Program	After Profit Improvement Program	
Year	(Fig. 12-D)	(Fig. 12-E)	Increase
20X2	$376,000	$16,376,460	—
20X3	366,142	524,309	$158,167
20X4	362,185	556,361	194,176
Cumulative	$1,104,327	$1,456,670	$352,343

§ 12.05 The Capital Financing Plan

The last step a law firm must take in its long-range planning is to develop a capital financing plan, which includes determining: (1) how the firm's operations will be financed (debt vs. equity), and (2) the timing for the distribution of cash flow to the firm's partners.

[1]—Debt vs. Equity Financing

Historically, most law firms financed their operations entirely with partner capital. Some firms still do; however, in recent years with that dramatic increase in spending needed to make the technological improvements (e.g., computers, networks, telephone systems, etc.) within a law firm, many firms have decided to finance their equipment through bank loans (or capital leases which are substantially the same thing). In addition, some firms have entered into loan agreements to finance expansion plans or refurbish office space. Because of cash flow concerns, some firms have also financed part of their working capital with bank loans.

While debt does provide a ready source of capital and has many advantages, it also usually has certain stipulations that reduce the flexibility of the firm to a certain extent. These are in the form of debt covenants and typically require the firm to maintain a certain level of working capital, limit merger opportunities without bank consent, and limit the amount of capital leases a firm may enter into. Also, bank agreements frequently require the debtors to provide the bank with certain financial reports on a monthly, quarterly and yearly basis and cause management to make certain representations to the bank on a periodic basis. Prior to entering into a debt agreement, a firm should explore all the advantages and disadvantages and decide if acquiring the debt makes sense for it.

Figure 12-F summarizes the net assets of a law firm that uses the accrual basis method of accounting. It also illustrates three ways a law firm can finance its operations:

- Scenario 1: Assets are totally financed by partners' equity.
- Scenario 2: Property and equipment are financed with bank loans; working capital is financed with partners' equity.
- Scenario 3: Property and equipment and a portion of working capital are financed with bank loans; the remainder of working capital is financed with partners' equity.

The illustration in Figure 12-F contrasts the relationship of bank loans to partners' equity for each of the approaches to financing, through the use of a debt-to-equity ratio. A high ratio (or highly leveraged position) signals a dependency on bank financing for survival. The approach outlined in Scenario 2 is the approach chosen by many firms because it provides for bank financing of long-term assets (i.e., fixed assets) and equity partner financing of short-term assets (i.e., unbilled and uncollected fees).[1]

Figure 12-F. Illustration of alternative approaches to financing a law firm's assets.

ABC LAW FIRM
COMPARISON OF ALTERATIVE
FINANCING APPROACHES

	Scenario 1	Scenario 2	Scenario 3
Net Assets to be financed:			
Unbilled and uncollected fees	$ 8,500,000	$ 8,500,000	$ 8,500,000
Other current assets	2,500,000	2,500,000	2,500,000
Property and equipment	2,100,000	2,100,000	2,100,000
Payables	(1,100,000)	(1,100,000)	(1,100,000)
Net assets	$12,000,000	$12,000,000	$12,000,000
Financing vehicle:			
Bank loans	—	$ 2,000,000	$ 7,000,000
Partners' equity	$12,000,000	10,000,000	5,000,000
Total financing	$12,000,000	$12,000,000	$12,000,000
Ratio of debt to equity	0 to 1	0.2 to 1	1.4 to 1

[2]—Equity Partners' Distributions

The distribution of cash flow to the firm's equity partners is dependent on (a) the firm's operating plan, (b) the firm's plans to acquire property and equipment, and (c) the firm's capital financing plan. A cash flow projection is the typical method used to present this information. One way to make this projection is to use the following calculations:

(1) Results of operations: Calculated based on the firm's previously determined operating plan adjusted to add-back non-cash items (such as depreciation).

(2) Property and equipment acquisitions: Calculated based on the firm's plans for expansion or contraction.

---

[1] For an in-depth discussion of capital financing see Chapter 25 *infra.*

(3) Capital financing: Calculated with the assumption that property and equipment will be financed with bank loans and working capital will be financed with equity partners' equity.

Figure 12-G illustrates an abbreviated example of a cash flow projection for a law firm.

Figure 12-G. Illustration of an abbreviated cash flow projection for a law firm.

ABC LAW FIRM
CASH FLOW PROJECTION

	20X2	20X3	20X4
Planned Source of Cash:			
Net income from operations (Fig. 12-D)	$ 9,400,000	$ 9,885,859	$10,141,190
Add back-Depreciation	220,000	343,000	447,000
	9,620,000	10,228,859	10,588,190
Proceeds of borrowings	400,000	600,000	1,000,000
Cash balance-beginning of period	1,200,000	1,100,000	1,300,000
	11,220,000	16,928,859	12,888,190
Planned Use of Cash:			
Property and equipment purchases	400,000	600,000	1,000,000
Payments to former partners	400,000	450,000	500,000
Cash balance to be maintained for working capital requirements	1,100,000	1,300,000	1,500,000
	1,900,000	2,350,000	3,000,000
Planned cash distributions to equity partners	$ 9,320,000	$ 9,578,859	$ 9,888,190

CHAPTER 13

Automated Accounting Records

Chapter Contents

[iv] Storage
[v] Disposal

---

§ 13.01 Use of Information Technology by Law Firms

Practically all law firms rely on automation. Today, information technology is used for data input, data processing, data storage and data output. As a result, technology is now used to carry out numerous "back office" repetitious tasks as well as support the lawyers on a daily basis. Since speed and efficiency are the principal advantages of using computers, automation is particularly helpful in tasks where large volumes of data must be handled. Law firms use information technology for a variety of functions, including:

(1) *Data processing* of accounting and statistical information;
(2) *Word processing* in the preparation of letters and reports; and
(3) *Data retrieval* of legal research information and litigation documents.

Law firms have a variety of computers and software to chose from. Sometimes, software restricts what hardware a firm can buy, because it might only work on certain computers. Large and megasize firms might develop their own software, or, more commonly they license law-firm-specific applications that are modified to meet their individual needs. Smaller firms generally will use less sophisticated software, but even that software is more advanced then the old manual systems. It also is common to use different computer systems for different applications, such as general ledger, payroll, conflict testing, etc. Almost all law firms use electronic spreadsheet programs for law firm financial information. The computer systems that are most frequently automated for the processing of law firm accounting information include:

(1) Client Accounting System;
(2) Payroll Accounting System;
(3) Accounts Payable System;
(4) General Ledger Accounting and Budget Reporting System;
(5) Management Information Technology;
(6) Partners' Accounts System; and
(7) Auxiliary Systems.

Each of these systems is discussed in more detail in later sections of this chapter.

§ 13.02 Automation Strategy

Because of the strategic importance of information technology and the sizable investment involved, many law firms form a technology committee to oversee plans to automate major segments of the firm's operations or upgrade previously automated operations. The typical composition of these automation oversight committees includes three to five partners and the firm's Administrator. Automation oversight consists of three phases:

(1) Defining the firm's information technology requirements;
(2) Selecting the proper computer "software" and "hardware"; and
(3) Implementing the automation plan.

Each phase will be discussed in the paragraphs that follow.

[1]—Defining the Firm's Requirements

One approach to defining the firm's information technology requirements focuses on the following four factors:

[a]—Objectives

This involves an overall assessment of the key reasons why the firm wishes to automate a particular facet of its operations. In many cases, the automation strategy directly supports or links to a firm's overall business strategy. For example, the firm may wish to speed up its billing and collection cycle in order to improve cash flow. (It is important to always keep the key objectives in mind as the automation project proceeds, in order to avoid the expense of irrelevant expansion at later stages of the project.)

[b]—Expectations

It is recommended that the firm's lawyers (partners and associates), or a sample group, be debriefed to determine what output they expect from the automation project. For example, they may expect the computer to produce draft bills. (It is essential to convey to the lawyers, as early as possible in the process, a clear statement of what the automation project is expected to achieve *and* what it will not achieve. This will avoid unrealistic expectations.)

[c]—Economics

This involves assessing the size of the investment that the firm would be required to make in order to achieve the automation objective and determining whether it would be economically feasible for the firm to undertake this commitment. In order to make this determination, the firm would have to project the estimated total cost of the project less any estimated cost savings.

[d]—Facts

A fourth factor involves assembling facts and statistics with the assistance of the firm's administrative staff. Of particular importance is information that would hinder a smooth, swift, and successful completion of the automation project. Information to be gathered should include a description of the firm's existing manual or automated system which is being replaced, statistics on the volume of transactions processed, and an organization chart of the personnel involved in processing the data. This process also includes identifying the key data that is "input" into the system, the key "output" reports which flow from the system, and the purpose of each output report. (Obtaining a clear understanding of the purpose of each output report is particularly important in defining the firm's automation requirements.)

Once the objectives of the proposed automation project have been articulated, the lawyers' expectations clarified, the economics assessed, and the facts relevant to completion of the project identified, a clear statement, or goal, of the firm's automation requirements can be prepared.

[2]—Selecting the Proper Computer Software and Hardware

There are four steps involved in selecting appropriate computer software and hardware for an automation project. They are:

[a]—Requesting Vendor Proposals

The first step requires either (a) the inviting of one or more vendors to the firm's offices to make a presentation of their automation capabilities, or (b) the furnishing of a selected list of vendors with a formal Request For Proposal ("RFP"). The latter defines the firm's automation requirements and requests vendors to express the qualifications of their systems in response to a series of specific automation requirements. The RFP approach has the advantage of forcing the vendors to focus on the firm's requirements rather than merely on the features of their systems. This is helpful in making explicit specific instances where a particular vendor cannot meet a requirement or when meeting a requirement could be costly. Information typically solicited from vendors includes descriptions of:

(1) System Features and Functions;
(2) Processing Capabilities;

(3) Report Capabilities;
(4) Cost Information;
(5) Hardware Requirements and Configuration;
(6) Conversion Plan; and
(7) Vendor Support and User Training.

[b]—Evaluating Proposals

Developing an array of the firm's key automation requirements, together with comparative information identifying each vendor's ability to satisfy each requirement, is the next step. Once this information is obtained, the strengths and weaknesses of each vendor's proposal then can be identified and summarized. An evaluation of each proposal can then be completed and the vendors can be ranked in priority order, based on their expressed or proven capability to achieve the firm's automation objectives.

[c]—Choosing the Vendor

Once the vendors have been ranked, it is important to consider the practical capabilities of the top vendor candidates. The probe might consist of contacting other law firms who are presently using the vendor's systems and inquiring into their degree of satisfaction and/or site visits to observe the vendor's systems in operation. After the probes have been completed, the firm can choose the vendor which is most suited to its needs based on these results, the theoretical rankings, and the firm's cost considerations.

[d]—Contract Negotiations

This involves discussing with the vendor the arrangements for purchasing the computer hardware and software and reducing the terms to a written contract. In some cases, the hardware purchase may involve a third party. In other cases, the software vendor may serve as the agent for the hardware vendor. The contract negotiation should clarify the parties' obligations and responsibilities including warranties for both hardware and software. Key items to be spelled out in the contract are:

(1) Modifications to meet the firm's requirements;
(2) Installation and testing arrangements;
(3) Documentation and training to be provided;
(4) Control and security features;
(5) Software licensing provision;
(6) Ongoing maintenance arrangements;
(7) Warranty; and
(8) Price.

Once the requests for proposals have been solicited, received, and evaluated, and the firm has made its choice of vendor and negotiated a contract, the project can proceed to the implementation stage.

[3]—Implementing the Automation Plan

Implementing an automation plan consists of three separate tasks:

[a]—Hardware Installation

Once the computer equipment has been selected and purchased (or leased), it must be delivered to the firm's offices, assigned to an appropriate room (temperature-controlled in some instances), interfaced with electrical connections and tested to ensure that the equipment is operational. An important consideration is that the equipment be delivered on time and in good working order. Installation of a distributed system, such as a local area network (LAN), may require special wiring specification or modification to existing wiring capacities. These special requirements should have been identified during the proposal evaluation process.

[b]—System Conversion

System conversion usually poses the most difficult and time-consuming problems in implementing an automation plan and, therefore, should be carefully planned and supervised. The firm's existing records must be transferred from the old system (manual or automated) to the new system, current transactions must be processed and new reports must be printed. The conversion can be swift and efficient or it can be slow and cumbersome, based on the facts and circumstances surrounding the conversion. In many situations, the introduction of new software with enhanced processing features and functions will change the manner in which a business process (such as accounts payable) is performed. This "re-engineering" of the business process impacts both the automated and manual activities during system conversion. Situations which tend to slow down the conversion process include (a) coding and entering data from a manual format into a computer acceptable format, (b) reformatting data to accommodate the requirements of the new system, (c) documenting systems and procedures which were not previously formalized, (d) testing processing routines (including parallel processing using both the old and new systems and comparing output for consistency), and (e) identifying and checking key input controls, processing controls and output controls. It is prudent to maintain parallel processing for about two months, or until such time as the quality of the output of the new system is equal to or better than the quality of the output from the old system. For example, the firm may wish to test several monthly closings or a quarterly close before final cutover from the old process to the new process.

[c]—User Training

This involves training the firm's personnel to operate the new system. It should include formal instruction and on-the-job training of the firm's administrative staff by the vendor's personnel. The vendor should also supply the firm's personnel with operating manuals.

Once the hardware has been installed, the system converted, and the operators trained, the firm can begin operating the new system.

§ 13.03 Client Accounting System

The client accounting system is the heart of a law firm's financial operations, because it processes the firm's revenue stream. Large volumes of data are handled by this system. Because of its importance, capacity and uniqueness, the client accounting system is usually the first system that a law firm automates and the first system that it upgrades.

Virtually all law firms have automated their client accounting system. The only variable is the size of the computer that it runs on. Generally, the software vendor advises on the size needs of a law firm and often programs its software to work more efficiently on certain types of computers. As in most purchase decisions, the choice of software and hardware often comes down to the cost and features of one system compared to another. Firms have to consider growth, expansion, modifications, and maintain issues when deciding what software and hardware to purchase.

When a law firm is evaluating what to buy or how to automate or upgrade their existing accounting system, three factors have the most relevance:

(1) System Functions (the system's purpose and how it operates);

(2) System Features (specific tasks which the system can execute); and

(3) Report Capabilities (specific reports which the system can generate).

Each factor will be discussed in the following paragraphs.

[1]—System Functions

The client accounting system records, processes, and reports fees and disbursements chargeable to client matters, bills rendered, and client payments received. Functions typically included in a law firm's automated client accounting system are:

(1) Recording attorney chargeable hours;

(2) Maintaining client matter descriptions and attorney bill rates in files;

(3) Calculating attorney time charges;

(4) Interfacing with client disbursement system;

(5) Billing fees related to client matters, including write-offs and write-downs ("underrealizations").

(6) Recording cash receipts from clients;

(7) Reporting monthly time charges, client disbursements, billings and fee collections sorted by client and by engagement partner;

(8) Reporting cumulative unbilled time charges, fees receivable and client disbursements aged by time period and sorted by client and by engagement partner; and

(9) Providing data for the firm's Management Information System.

A flowchart presenting an example of a law firm's automated client accounting system is illustrated in Figure 13-A.

Figure 13-A. Illustration outlining an example of a flowchart for a law firm's automated client accounting system.

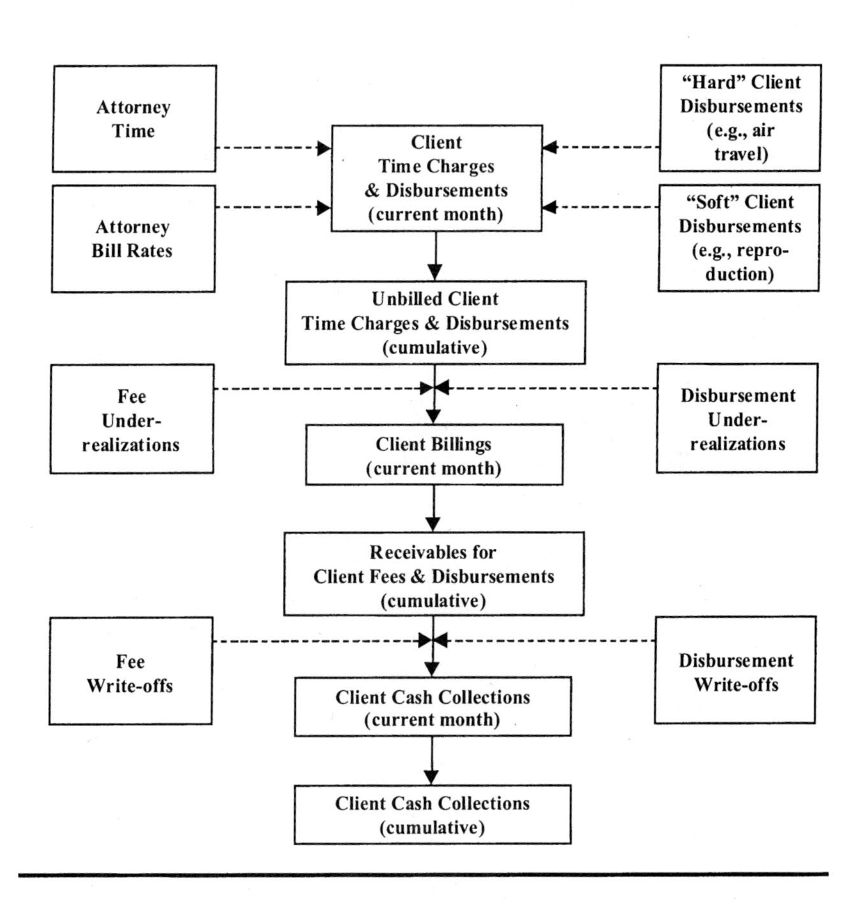

[2]—System Features

A client accounting system can be basic or comprehensive, depending on the firm's objectives in using the system. If the main concerns are to compile, process, and report billing and collection information, a basic system will suffice. If the firm wishes to have the system generate draft bills, analyze fees by department, or carry out a multitude of other tasks, a more comprehensive system will be needed. Many software packages will carry out a wide variety of tasks, but usually these are tasks which have been requested in the past by a number of law firms and are rather general in nature. If the firm has objectives for which standard software is not available, many vendors are willing to customize or modify software to meet the firm's requirements, though the firm should recognize that this undertaking could be costly, time-consuming, and error prone. While it is impractical to recite all of the tasks that could be carried out by a client accounting system, listed below are some examples of features that have been incorporated into a number of automated law firm systems:

(1) Input, verify, and edit time and disbursements daily;

(2) Input, store, and edit narrative descriptions accompanying time and disbursement entries for use in billing;

(3) Accept time data from optical scanning devices or other mechanical devices to eliminate the need for key entry of data;

(4) Accept direct data entry for disbursements from automated recording devices for photocopy, telephone, and mailroom charges without manual keying;

(5) Store a minimum number of billing rates for each attorney;

(6) Specify value-based billing rates for particular client matters;

(7) Designate a billing frequency for each client matter and automatically prepare billing memoranda at this frequency;

(8) Prepare detailed billing memoranda through a specified date, including disbursements summarized by category and unbilled time summarized by lawyer and secretary;

(9) Write-off or transfer time and disbursements given proper authorization;

(10) Generate client bills automatically and on demand in a variety of formats;

(11) Flag a client or matter to restrict charging additional time and disbursements upon preparation of a final billing;

(12) Prepare reminder statements automatically for all outstanding receivables;

(13) Accept partial payments against bills;

(14) Maintain a history of billing and collection activity by client and matter;

(15) Provide on-line inquiry into client files;

(16) Control access to data input and reports by user name and password; and

(17) Interface automatically with the general ledger system.

[3]—Report Capabilities

Many automated client accounting systems are capable of generating a wide variety of reports. A system typically generates a series of standard reports and can be programmed to generate an additional series of tailored reports. If the tailored reporting requirements will be extensive, the cost of additional programming, system features, and system capacity to generate these reports should be explored in advance of an undertaking to develop the reports. Some examples of reports that have been generated by a number of automated law firm client accounting systems are listed below:

[a]—Transaction Activity Reports

[i]—Transaction Registers

Lists of daily transaction entries (with summary totals) for: hours, time charges, client disbursements, bills, write-offs, cash receipts, transfers, and corrections.

[ii]—Missing Diary Reports (i.e., Time Sheets)

Lists of missing diaries for lawyers and other timekeepers who have not accounted for every working day or a specified minimum number of hours per working day.

[iii]—Posting to General Ledger

List of entries to the general ledger (or memorandum ledger) for time charges, billing, cash receipts, and relief of work-in-progress and accounts receivable.

[b]—File Maintenance Reports

[i]—Report of Client and Matter Information

Details of all additions, deletions or changes to client and matter information.

[ii]—Report of Lawyer and Other Timekeepers Information

Details of all additions, deletions or changes to lawyer and other timekeepers information.

[c]—Work-In-Progress Reports

[i]—Work-In-Progress Ledger Detail

Details of unbilled hours and time charges by attorney and other timekeepers and unbilled disbursements for each client matter.

[ii]—Billing Partner Work-In-Progress Summary

List of unbilled time charges and disbursements for all matters assigned to each billing partner, with client totals and billing partner total.

[iii]—Billing Partner Work-In-Progress Aging

List of unbilled balances for each matter assigned to a billing partner group by specified aging periods.

[d]—Billing Reports

[i]—Billing Memorandum

Details of all unbilled hours, time charges, and disbursements for a client matter.

[ii]—Draft and Final Bills

A *pro forma* bill for a particular client and matter and the billing value of any time and disbursement associated with that matter.

[iii]—Billing Partner Billing Activity

List of bills issued by each billing partner during a specified time period, with client totals and billing partner total.

[iv]—Client Billing History

List of all bills rendered to a client containing bill date, amount billed, write-offs, amount collected and amount uncollected.

[v]—Statement of Unpaid Bill Notice

Automatically generated reminder notices to be sent to clients with outstanding bills for more than a predefined number of days.

[e]—Receivable Reports

[i]—Billing Partner Uncollected Bills Summary

List of all uncollected bills issued by each billing partner, with client totals and billing partner total.

[ii]—Billing Partner Uncollected Bills Aging

List of uncollected bills issued by each billing partner grouped by specified aging periods.

[f]—Cash Receipts Reports

[i]—Daily Cash Receipts Journal

Details of cash receipts for a specific date.

[ii]—Monthly Cash Receipts Summary

List of all cash receipts for the month.

[iii]—Statement of Fee Income

Details of cash receipts and their application to fees, client disbursements or other accounts with client totals and billing partner totals.

[g]—Practice Management Reports

[i]—Client Investment Summary

Summary for each client of total value of unbilled time, accounts receivable and disbursements.

[ii]—Summary Aging of Work-In-Progress

Summary of unbilled work assigned to each billing partner grouped by specified aging periods.

[iii]—Summary Aging of Accounts Receivable

Summary of uncollected bills assigned to each billing partner grouped by specified aging periods.

[iv]—Billing Realization Report

Summary of billings by each billing attorney for the current month and year-to-date indicating dollars billed, dollars relieved from work-in-progress, variance and realization percentages.

[v]—Staff Utilization Report

Summary of chargeable hours and nonchargeable hours for each attorney for the current month and year-to-date with a comparison indicating actual chargeable hours, planned chargeable hours and variance.

[vi]—Fee Analysis Report

Summary of fees by client, by area of law, by office location, by client partner and by lawyer responsible for originating the work.

A representative computer-generated report ("Work-In-Progress Ledger Detail") is illustrated in Figure 13-B.

Figure 13-B. Illustration of an example of a computer generated work-in-progress ledger for a law firm client matter.

ABC LAW FIRM
WORK-IN-PROGRESS LEDGER DETAIL

Billing Partner: #050 Partner A Client: #001 XYZ Business Matter: #05 EFG Litigation

		Current Month			Year-to-date		
Code	Name	Hours	Billing Value	Disburse-ments	Hours	Billing Value	Disburse-ments
050	Partner A	10	$3,500		50	$17,500	
120	Associate B	15	3,000		75	15,000	
330	Secretary C	5	350		25	1,750	
991	Telephone			$ 75			$ 375
992	Reproduction			25			125
	Total Charges	30	6,850	100	150	34,250	500
	Billing to date				(60)	(7,000)	(200)
	Underrealization					(200)	
Unbilled		30	$6,850	$100	90	$27,080	$ 300

§ 13.04 Payroll Accounting System

Payroll costs are a law firm's single most important expense, often representing more than one-half of a law firm's operating expenses. Consequently, it is essential that each law firm have an effective and efficient payroll system. Because the processing of payroll data for law firms involves many tasks that are similar to the processing of this data for businesses in general, a sizable number of law firms outsource this function. There are two factors to be considered by a law firm that has decided to automate its payroll accounting system: (1) system functions and (2) outsourcing to payroll processor. Each factor will be discussed in the following paragraphs.

[1]—System Functions

The payroll system generates salary and wage payments for the law firm's employees, computes payroll tax withholdings, and provides the firm's accounting reports for compensation expenses. Functions typically included in a law firm's automated payroll system are:

(1) Maintenance of employee names, personnel data and pay rates in files;

(2) Acceptance of input from employee time reports (on-line or through batch input);

(3) Verification and editing of input (daily or weekly);

(4) Calculation of employees' salaries;

(5) Computation of applicable withholding taxes and voluntary deductions;

(6) Calculation of individual employees' retirement plan credits;

(7) Printing payroll checks or direct deposit of net pay into employees' bank accounts via electronic funds transfer;

(8) Reporting of payroll tax information to appropriate government jurisdictions;

(9) Generation of payroll reports and record; and

(10) Interface with general ledger.

Figure 13-C illustrates an example of a flowchart for a law firm's automated payroll accounting system.

Figure 13-C. Illustration outlining an example of a flowchart for a law firm's automated payroll accounting system.

ABC LAW FIRM
PAYROLL ACCOUNTING SYSTEM FLOWCHART

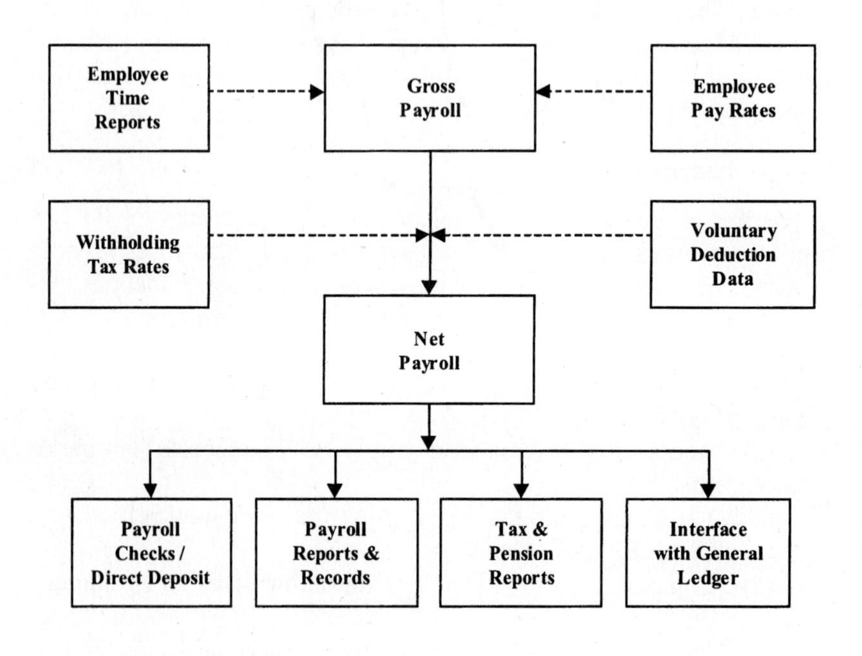

[2]—Outsourcing to Payroll Processor

When a law firm decides to outsource its payroll function, it should consider the following:

(1) Employee payroll reporting capabilities (e.g., payroll register, year-to-date earnings record);

(2) Functional payroll expense reporting capabilities (e.g., compensation by class of employee, by department, by branch office);

(3) Regulatory agency reporting capabilities (e.g., withholding tax reports, retirement information reports, voluntary deduction reports);

(4) Flexibility to accommodate a variety of production dates (e.g., printing payroll checks semimonthly for associates vs. biweekly for administrative employees);

(5) Turnaround time (i.e., from the date employee time is entered until the date payroll reports and checks are issued); and

(6) Cash disbursing capabilities (i.e., payroll check preparation or interaction with bank for direct deposit of employees' paychecks via electronic funds transfer).

§ 13.05 Accounts Payable System

The accounts payable system processes the firm's cash disbursements (other than payroll costs). Three factors deserve consideration when a law firm decides to automate this system: (1) system functions; (2) system features; and (3) report capabilities. Each factor will be discussed in the following paragraphs.

[1]—System Functions

The accounts payable system records, processes and reports cash disbursements chargeable to firm expense, asset purchases, client disbursements and partner distributions. Functions typically included in a law firm's automated accounts payable system are:

(1) Maintenance of records of open vendor invoices and preparation of monthly aging of accounts payable;
(2) Maintenance and updating of vendor files;
(3) Preparation of cash disbursements record (i.e., "check register");
(4) Preparation of vendor checks/electronic funds transfer;
(5) Preparation of reports that will be used in managing expenditures;
(6) Preparation of outstanding check lists for bank reconciliations; and
(7)Projection of cash requirements.

Figure 13-D presents an example of a flowchart for a law firm's automated accounts payable system.

Figure 13-D. Illustration outlining an example of a flowchart for a law firm's automated accounts payable accounting system.

ABC LAW FIRM
ACCOUNTS PAYABLE SYSTEM FLOWCHART

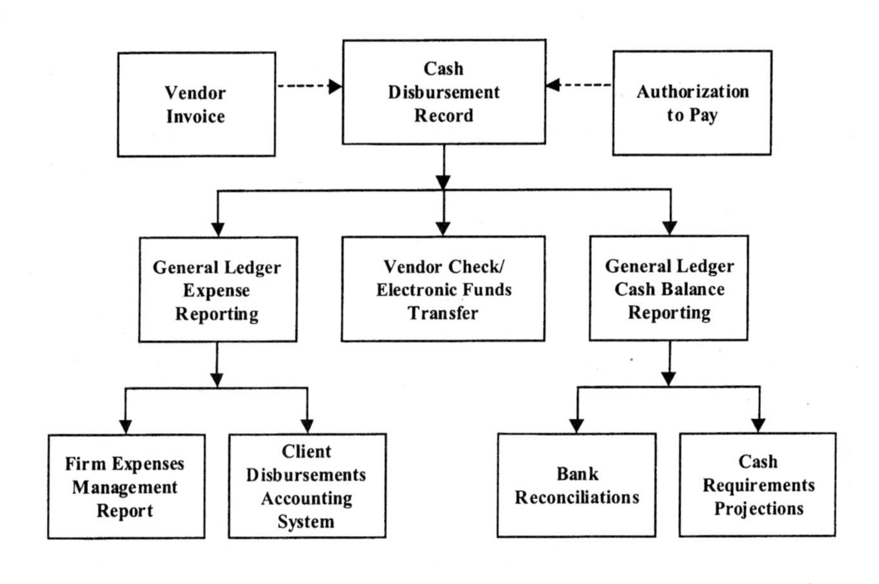

[2]—System Features

Examples of features that have been incorporated into some law firm automated accounts payable systems include:

(1) Accepting input from remote locations or from the Internet

(2) Editing of disbursements;

(3) Maintaining and inquiring as to current vendor information and payment history;

(4) Preparing checks automatically on an invoice due-date basis or on request at a specified date;

(5) Allowing direct payment to vendors via electronic funds transfer;

(6) Producing vendor information, check registers, and cash requirements in both detail and summary format; and

(7) Interfacing directly between the general ledger accounting system and accounts payable subledger.

[3]—Report Capabilities

Reports that have been generated by a number of automated law firm accounts payable systems include:

(1) Vendor maintenance report—Reflects all changes to the vendor master file;

(2) Voucher register—Reports all vouchers entered into the system;

(3) Check register—Reports all checks prepared during the period;

(4) Accounts payable distribution—Reports disbursements by general ledger account number;

(5) Operating expense report—Reports firm expenses by department number and by office location number;

(6) Client disbursement report—Reports client disbursements by client matter number;

(7) Accounts payable aging—Detail report of open invoices by vendor;

(8) Cash requirements report—Report of open invoices due within specified time intervals for cash planning purposes; and

(9) Check reconciliation journal—Detailed listing of checks that have cleared versus those that are still outstanding, for use in preparing bank reconciliations.

§ 13.06 General Ledger Accounting and Budget Reporting System

The general ledger accounting and budget reporting system is at the center of a law firm's operations. It receives input from the firm's other key accounting systems (client accounting system, payroll subledger and accounts payable subledger) and produces the firm's financial statements and budget comparisons as output.

There are three important factors to be considered by a law firm that decides to automate its general ledger accounting and budget reporting system. They are: (1) system functions; (2) system features; and (3) report capabilities. Each factor will be discussed in the following paragraphs.

[1]—System Functions

The general ledger accounting system accounts for all assets, liabilities, capital accounts, receipts, disbursements and partner distributions of the firm. This system encompasses the books of original entry, the general ledger and the firm's monthly financial statements and budget comparison reports. Functions typically included in a law firm's automated general ledger accounting system are:

(1) Recording input from the firm's books of original entry (i.e., cash receipts, cash disbursements, payroll and general journals);

(2) Providing control of accounting transactions generated by the firm;

(3) Providing a summarized record of account balances;

(4) Accepting budget data required for use in reporting comparisons;

(5) Maintaining a history of prior year's data for comparison purposes; and

(6) Providing timely financial statements and appropriate analyses and summaries.

Figure 13-E illustrates an example of a flowchart for a law firm's automated general ledger accounting and budget reporting system.

Figure 13-E. Illustration outlining an example of a flowchart for a law firm's automated general ledger accounting and budget reporting system.

ABC LAW FIRM
GENERAL LEDGER ACCOUNTING
AND BUDGET REPORTINGS SYSTEM FLOWCHART

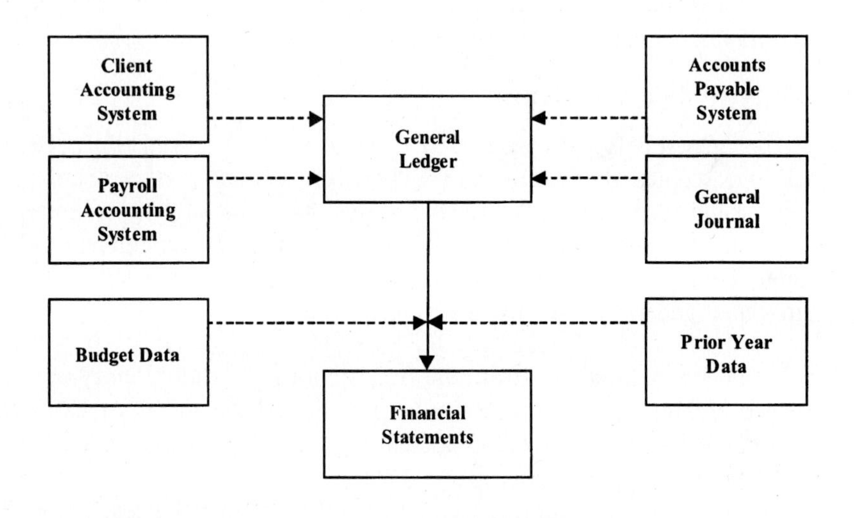

[2]—System Features

Features that have been incorporated into some law firm automated general ledger accounting and budget reporting systems and are considered desirable by other firms include:

(1) Edit and update chart of accounts;

(2) Interface the general ledger automatically with subsystems—specifically client accounting, payroll and accounts payable;

(3) Input, validate and edit journal entries;

(4) Produce a weekly cash report that includes cash receipts, cash disbursements and daily cash balances in bank accounts;

(5) Maintain and report financial data by responsible departments and by offices; and

(6) Maintain financial information on both a cash basis and an accrual basis.

[3]—Report Capabilities

Reports that have been generated by a number of automated law firm general ledger accounting and budget reporting systems include:

(1) Transaction Activity and File Maintenance Reports:
- Chart of Accounts
- Transaction Registers
- Journal entries processed (detail and summary)

(2) Ledger reports:
- General Ledger (detail and consolidated)
- General Ledger trial balance
- Subsidiary ledgers

(3) Financial reports:
- Statement of revenues and expenses
- Statement of cash flows
- Budget report
- Statement of firm expenses
- Summary comparison of receipts and expenses
- Statement of net assets

§ 13.07 Management Information Technology

The management information technology generates periodic or on-request financial and statistical reports by interfacing with the firm's other reporting systems (i.e., general ledger, client accounting). The purpose of these reports is to identify key features of financial performance so that the firm's management committee may:

(1) Monitor the financial strength of the firm;

(2) Anticipate problems or opportunities and determine appropriate corrective action;

(3) Plan distributions and investments;

(4) Evaluate the contribution of individual partners and associates; and

(5) Determine the effectiveness of the firm's policies for increasing profitability.

There are two factors to be considered when a law firm automates this system: (1) system functions and (2) report capabilities. Each factor will be discussed in the following paragraphs.

[1]—System Functions

The law firm's management information technology typically involves two stages: (a) the assembly of data from other sources into a report, and (b) the preparation of a summary page containing highlights. Financial and statistical reports produced by the law firm's automated management information technology are drawn from data contained principally in two of the firm's accounting systems (client accounting system and general ledger accounting system) and from the firm's statistical records.

Figure 13-F illustrates an example of a flowchart for a law firm's automated management information technology.

Figure 13-F. Illustration outlining an example of a flowchart for a law firm's automated management information technology.

ABC LAW FIRM
MANAGEMENT INFORMATION TECHNOLOGY FLOWCHART

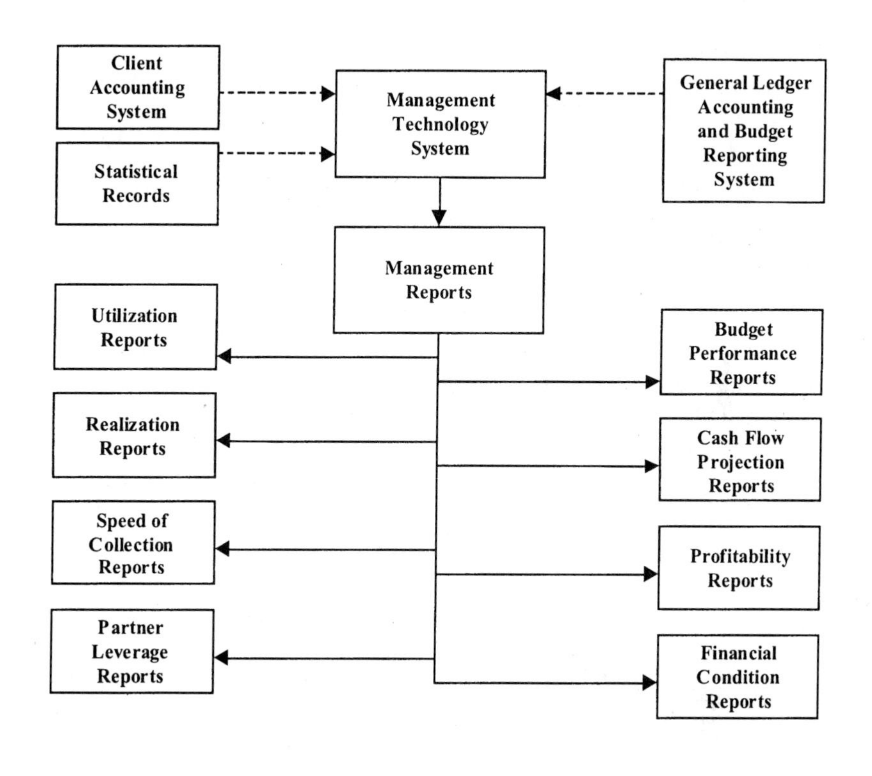

[2]—Report Capabilities

Reports that have been generated by some automated law firm management information technology and the source of the data contained in these reports are:

[a]—Reports Generated by the Client Accounting System

[i]—Utilization Reports

A compilation of the number of hours each lawyer and other timekeeper has charged to client matters in the current month and year-to-date, compared to a standard.

[ii]—Realization Reports

The dollar value at which time and disbursements were billed, compared to their value at full bill rates, on each client matter and on all client matters managed by each partner, and the difference stated in dollars and as a percentage of full bill rates.

[iii]—Speed of Billing and Collection Reports

The investment in unbilled time and disbursements and uncollected billings by client matter and by billing partner, together with a turnover rate.

[iv]—Leverage Reports

The ratio in which associates and paralegals are used, relative to partners, on each matter, and the number of attorney and paralegal hours managed by each partner.

[b]—Reports Generated by the General Ledger Accounting and Budget Reporting System

[i]—Budget Performance Reports

These reports provide a monthly comparison of budget vs. actual performance for revenue and major expense categories.

[ii]—Cash Flow Projection Reports

Cash flow projection reports contain a forecast of monthly cash availability and are used to plan periodic partner distributions and determine appropriate investments.

[iii]—Profitability Reports

These are a series of reports designed to present an analysis of the firm's profitability by client, by client partner, by area of law, and by office location.

[iv]—Financial Condition Reports

The financial condition reports contain a condensed summary of the firm's balance sheet, often prepared on a quarterly basis.[1]

---

[1] Examples of typical management information reports are contained in the "management reporting," Chapter 9 of this book.

§ 13.08 Partners' Accounts System

The partners' accounts system is the law firm's most sensitive system. While the law firm's other accounting systems affect the partners collectively as members of the partnership, the financial information generated by this system affects each of the partners individually. Due to the sensitive nature of the partners' profit sharing information contained in this system access to it generally is restricted and passwords are used to insure security.

Two factors should be considered by a law firm that has decided to automate its partners' accounts system: (1) system functions and (2) computer system capabilities. Each factor will be discussed in the following paragraphs.

[1]—System Functions

The partners' accounts system records, processes, and reports the allocation of partnership income among the firm's individual partners and the changes in the partnership capital accounts of the individual partners. Functions typically included in a law firm's automated partners' accounts system are:

(1) Maintenance of partners' names and income-sharing percentages in files;

(2) Interface with the general ledger system for input of partnership earnings data;

(3) Calculation of each partners' share of the partnership's earnings;

(4) Recording of payments to or on behalf of the individual partners;

(5) Recording of capital contributions from the individual partners;

(6) Reporting of the individual partner's cumulative current account balances (i.e., undistributed earnings) and capital account balances;

(7) Reconciliation of book income vs. taxable income for the individual partners; and

(8) Reporting of the individual partner's financial information for tax form Schedule K-1.

Figure 13-G illustrates an example of a flowchart for a law firm's automated partners' accounts system.

Figure 13-G. Illustration outlining an example of a flowchart for a law firm's automated partners' account system.

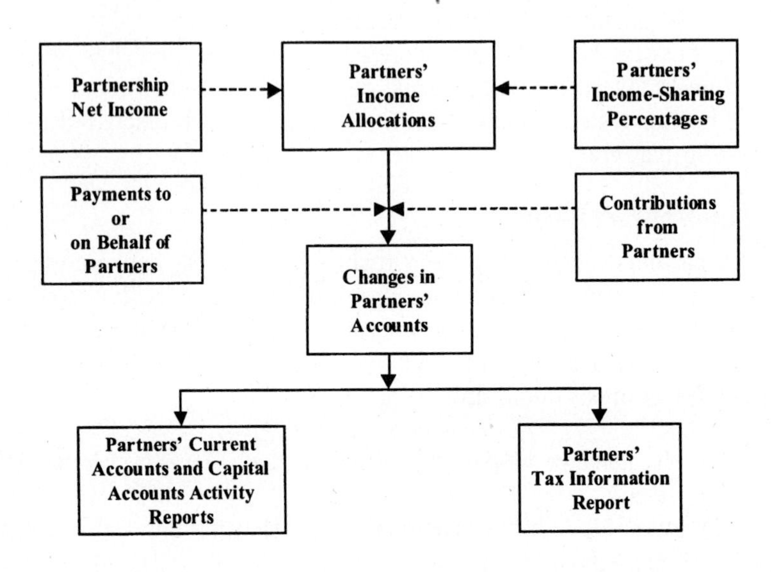

[2]—Computer System Capabilities

In selecting computer hardware and software to automate the processing of the firm's partners' accounts system, the following considerations should be taken into account:

(1) Flexibility to accommodate a variety of income allocation methods (e.g., percentage partners vs. fixed-income partners vs. retired partners with formula allocations);

(2) Report capabilities (i.e., summary of balances and activity, detail by partner, detail by type of activity); and

(3) Data Security.

§ 13.09 Auxiliary Systems

Some law firms process significant volumes of auxiliary financial data, in addition to their regular financial activities. Most of the time, these auxiliary activities are processed using personal computers in the accounting department and commercially available software or electronic spreadsheet programs. Auxiliary activities most frequently automated are:

(1) Property and equipment records;
(2) Retirement plans; and
(3) Trust, estate and other segregated assets held for others.

Some of the matters to consider when selecting a system to process data for each of these activities are discussed in the following paragraphs.

[1]—Property and Equipment Records

Property and equipment records represent subsidiary analyses of activity flowing through the property and equipment control accounts in the firm's general ledger. An automated system for processing property and equipment records should be capable of satisfying each of three objectives. The system should:

(1) Inventory in detail and summary, on a periodic basis, property and equipment and depreciation reserve balances by type of asset, by location and by year of acquisition;

(2) Calculate depreciation, amortization and gain or loss on disposition for each asset under a variety of depreciation methods; and

(3) Report property and equipment activity, quarterly and annually, detailing additions, retirements, transfers and balances for each class of property and equipment and related depreciation reserve.

[2]—Retirement Plans

Retirement plans' financial records are not part of the firm's general ledger accounting records; however, they do interact with these records through the transfer of retirement contributions from the firm to the plans. The firm's accounting department or human resources department normally is responsible for maintaining these records. Recordkeeping for retirement records should be capable of satisfying each of these objectives:

(1) Control over investment transactions;
(2) Control over contributions received; and
(3) Control over benefits paid.

[3]—Trust, Estate and Other Segregated Assets Held for Others

Financial records for trust, estate and other segregated assets held for others are not part of the firm's general ledger accounting records. However, because some of the firm's partners act as executors or trustees of estates and trusts, the firm's estate and trust department may become responsible for maintaining relevant financial records. In addition, when the firm acts as custodian of cash or other assets related to real estate and similar escrow type deposit arrangements, the firm's accounting department often becomes responsible for maintaining relevant financial records. Recordkeeping for trust, estate and other segregated assets held for others has three principal objectives. An automated system for processing these records should be capable of satisfying each of these objectives:

(1) Inventory in detail and summary, on a periodic basis, of all assets held in custody, indicating name of depositor, dollar amount deposited, type of asset, custodian and responsible partner;
(2) Calculation of income earned on each asset under a variety of formulas; and
(3) Report of receipts, payments and investment activity (monthly, annually and for the term of the engagement).

§ 13.10 Data Security

A law firm processes significant volumes of information, including sensitive partnership financial data and confidential client communications. When this information is processed using automated accounting systems or automated word processing systems, the firm must take additional security precautions to prevent unauthorized access to and unauthorized processing of this data. The more law firms use personal computers as a standard tool to process sensitive firm and client information, the issues of data security and integrity become critically important. Data security is complicated because much of a firm's critical or sensitive information is stored on small computers that are easily stolen. Factor in the ability to download sensitive information onto disks or the ability of someone outside of the firm from breaking into a firm's computer via a modem and the data security and integrity become paramount. Unless data security is adequate, the firm is at risk for: (a) potential diversion of assets to unauthorized employees or outsiders, and (b) potential embarrassment to the firm's partners or clients due to inappropriate or premature disclosure of confidential partnership financial information or confidential client activities (such as takeovers).

Data security risks can be minimized through the use of three types of controls:

(1) Access controls;
(2) Procedural controls; and
(3) Management controls.

Each type of control will be discussed in the following paragraphs.

[1]—Access Controls

Access controls, which are designed to prevent unauthorized use of the firm's computer systems, can be divided into four categories:

[a]—Physical Security Controls (Computer Room Access)

This limits the number of people having physical access to the firm's main computer room to computer operations personnel and enforces this decision through the controlled use of computer room access devices.

[b]—Workstation Security Controls (In-House Personnel Access)

Password control procedures can be used to determine both the authenticity of the user and the user's authorization to access specific programs and data. This is particularly important when there is wide on-line access to the firm's systems by a large class of users.

[c]—Communication Security Controls (Outside Interaction Access)

This involves, among other things, verification that the sending or receiving computer is valid, the operator is authorized to transmit or receive, and the transmission is appropriate for the identified work station and operator. Procedures may include a disconnect by the firm and a callback to the workstation.

[d]—Preventive Security

This can be accomplished by creating a data security environment that is preventive rather than diagnostic (i.e., active, not passive). For example, when an unauthorized user attempts to access the system, the "preventive" approach has the system go into extended dialogue with the perpetrator and alerts the firm's computer operator to the problem. The "diagnostic" approach merely reports the unauthorized attempt and notes the time. Another example of the "preventive" approach is the periodic review by management of individual user profiles for usability and appropriate access.

[e]—Security Software

Several computer vendors have developed sophisticated security software packages. Any law firm concerned with computer security that has branch offices or interacts with clients through the firm's intranet or through the Internet will use sophisticated security software. Using this software will lessen the vulnerability to "hackers" and others seeking to breach the firm's security, but it may not prevent it entirely. Computer security must be monitored constantly not only for "hackers," but also for "viruses" that often are attached to computer files and infect a computer when it is connected to the Internet or when a file is read in from a disk. The cost of security systems varies based on the level of security a law firm wants to maintain.

[2]—Procedural Controls

Access controls alone are not sufficient to assure the effectiveness of a law firm's data security program. The firm must also institute a series of operating procedures to augment and implement the access controls on a day-to-day basis. Three procedures are particularly relevant:

[a]—Written Data Security Policies

By communicating the firm's expectations regarding the safeguarding of data to the firm's employees, management can improve security consciousness. To be effective, the communication should be in writing, because written policies are often useful in reducing those computer security violations caused by employees who did not understand the consequences of their acts. The policies should include statements about computer viruses and the use of licensed software. The policy memo should be initially furnished to all employees and subsequently furnished to new employees. An annual reminder notice should be considered. Employees should formally indicate their understanding and acceptance of these policies and procedures through signature of a data security policy statement.

[b]—Password Procedures

It is advisable to periodically change passwords and enforce password confidentiality policies (for example: not allowing a computer technician to access to a person's password). Passwords should be long enough to require a large permutation to crack it. For example, a password might be at least six digits long and be a combination of alpha and numeric characters. It is also sensible to exercise control over user identification codes and to promptly delete user codes for terminated employees.

[c]—Violations Reporting Procedures

This involves recording, monitoring and reporting unauthorized attempts to access the system, misuses of passwords, and unauthorized activity by employees. The firm should designate an individual to formally follow-up all reports of data security breaches. Periodically, it is wise to test the procedures in place by engaging professional consultants to try to break into a law firm's computer system.

[3]—Management Controls

Management's attitude toward data security usually creates the environment that determines the seriousness with which employees treat data security procedures. Management's interest in data security can be demonstrated in three ways:

[a]—Organization Structure

Management must ensure an adequate segregation of duties within the data processing function (for example: assigning responsibility for the crosschecking of one employee's work to another employee or to a supervisor.) It also involves assigning responsibility for overseeing the data security function to an independent senior employee with a reporting line to top management.

[b]—Risk Profiles

On a periodic basis, senior management should assess the firm's vulnerability to data security breaches. Installation of a new computer system, involvement by the firm in particularly sensitive work, or a merger with another firm with significant computer-dependent activities often signal the desirability of updating the firm's profile of its data security risks.

[c]—Business Recovery Planning

Management should have a disaster recovery and business resumption plan in place to ensure that the firm continues to operate after an unforeseen disaster such as a fire, power failure, or a terrorist act. Such a plan would include the availability of backup systems and storage of financial and management data offsite. As part of some law firm contingency or disaster plans, arrangements are made with other landlords, clients, or service providers (i.e., accountants) to temporarily use office space for a limited period of time while the disaster can be dealt with. Most firms will maintain computer systems in another city to allow the firm to have access to its client files during a period when it can not use its existing space. Another option (although not a good one from a security point-of-view) is to allow attorneys to work at home during disasters. No matter which option is chosen, the focus should be on the ability to continue working on client matters during disasters. Firms that have not had disaster recovery plans quickly develop them after a disaster occurs such as the World Trade Center terrorist attack.

13.11 Data Security Appendix

Information is a valuable asset to law firms. As a result, all law firm partners and employees are responsible for protecting firm and client information. To accomplish this, proper safeguards are needed to protect information from accidental or intentional unauthorized modification, destruction and disclosure.

Law firm information processing resources should be used only for designated business purposes. These resources should not be used for such purposes as personal benefit, entertainment or amusement. Policies, standards and guidelines are needed to protect information assets stored on distributed computing platforms (i.e., personal computers), and provide a framework for the continued development of these rules as the law firm information processing environment changes.

The policies, standards and guidelines should apply to all law firm offices operating worldwide. These policies, standards and guidelines also apply to any person who accesses information through computers or networks. The security procedures addressed in this Appendix apply to all partners, employees, vendors and contractors involved in data processing services at the law firm.

In the event a combination of circumstances creates doubt as to which requirement applies, the most rigorous security protection method should be used, subject to the review of the firm's management.

[1]—Data Security Policy Background

The purposes of data security policies, standards and guidelines is to ensure that *due care* is exercised in protecting a law firm's computing systems and data. *Due care* is defined as the cost-effective protection of information at a level appropriate to its value. The value of the information can be quantified as the risk to the firm if the information were lost or compromised. The remainder of this Appendix provides some tools to help quantify the value of information and describes the methods used to develop specific action steps to achieve data security policy objectives.

[a]—Glossary of Terms

The following terms of reference are used in this Appendix:

[i]—Policy

A broad statement of principle that presents management's position for each defined control area. Policies are interpreted and supported by standards, guidelines and procedures. Policies are intended to be long-term and guide the development of rules to address specific situations. Standards, guidelines and procedures address short-term issues or clarifications and should be periodically updated to respond to those situations that not specifically addressed in the long-term policies.

[ii]—Standard

A rule that specifies a particular course of action or response to a given situation. Standards are mandatory directives to carry out management's policies and are used to measure compliance with policies.

[iii]—Guideline

A statement that recommends or suggests conduct in a specific situation. Guidelines are essentially recommendations to consider when assessing the particular level of security needed for each information system. They are to be followed unless there is a documented and approved reason to exclude them.

[iv]—Procedure

Documents a plan of action for how a standard or guideline will be implemented in a given part of the organization. Procedures may be developed by division, at the local level or by specific system, under the direction of the system owner. The law firm's security officers or risk management partner(s) are responsible for reviewing and approving procedures to ensure that they fully support the firm's information security policies, standards and guidelines.

[v]—Information Technology

The computers, communications facilities, networks, data and information that may be stored, processed, retrieved or transmitted by them, including programs, specifications and procedures for their operation, use and maintenance.

[vi]—Availability

The characteristic of data, information and information technology being accessible and usable on a timely basis in the required manner.

[vii]—Confidentiality

The characteristic of data and information being disclosed only to authorized persons, entities and processes with a right to know at authorized times and in an authorized manner.

[viii]—Integrity

The characteristic of data and information being accurate and complete and the preservation of accuracy and completeness.

[b]—Managerial and Staff Responsibilities

The protection of all information system resources, such as computer systems hardware, application and systems software, data, documentation, and personnel, is a fundamental responsibility of law firm management. Often, a law firm will assign the immediate responsibility for this area to a risk management partner. Ultimately, all partners and department heads are directly responsible for ensuring that all employees and contractors are aware of their obligation to safeguard both firm and client information. Managers are also responsible for carrying out information security procedures as set forth in the various policies, standards, and guidelines. All individuals, whether partners, employees or contractors, should familiarize themselves with the information security policies, standards, and guidelines and conscientiously support their enforcement. A person should be designated at each law firm site to be responsible for ensuring that security standards are enforced. This information security officer should monitor security violations and direct corrective action. Every new employee of the firm, regardless of job function, should acknowledge in writing that he or she has read and understands the firm's policies regarding data security. At the discretion of the firm's management, an annual statement should be issued to every employee that requires each person to verify that he or she has complied with the data security policies.

[c]—Definition of Roles

The following roles are suggested for law firms:

[i]—Information Security Officers

In law firm locations where information processing systems exist as separate computer processing sites (e.g., LANs, locally owned applications on centralized systems) or are located in locations where security cannot be effectively managed centrally, an information security officer should be appointed to help administer the security function.

[ii]—Information Security Advisory Committee

An information security advisory committee provides the security officers with policy direction and support for the information security function. The committee should be comprised of representatives from each of the firm's domestic and international offices. The committee should establish and approve changes to the information security policies, standards, and guidelines and review the implementation of these policies on a regular basis, at least semiannually).

[iii]—Information Technology Owners

The owner of an information technology is the person who is responsible for maintaining the information that is processed on the system. Law firm information processed by a computer system should have a designated owner.

The owner should:

- Classify the sensitivity and criticality of the information system according to the levels described in this appendix;
- Acknowledge/approve system administrators for the systems;
- Specify controls for their use and communicate the control requirements to both the custodians and the users. The owner should ensure that business continuity plans can recover information technology on a timely basis in case of disaster.

[iv]—System Administrator

The system administrator is the person designated by the information technology owner to administer information services and/or maintain physical control of data or application software. Examples of system administrators would be managers of applications such as electronic mail or the accounting systems.

The system administrators should:

- Authorize requests for application access to systems;
- Implement the controls specified by the owners of the information;
- Provide physical and procedural safeguards for the transfer of information;
- Manage access rules; and
- Develop, implement, and test all business continuity plans as specified by the owner.

[v]—Users

Users of information technology are those individuals who have received permission from the owner to access the owner's information. All individuals must demonstrate a business need to access the desired information in order for access to be granted. Users are expected to:

- Use the system for authorized business purposes only;
- Comply with law firm security policies, standards and guidelines as well as any procedures specified by the information owner; and
- Participate in the testing of business continuity plans, as necessary.

[vi]—Compliance Monitor

A compliance monitor is the group or person that is responsible for monitoring compliance with the policies, standards and guidelines contained in this entire discussion. Law firm management should determine when a compliance monitor will perform an independent review of selected systems' security schemes. In larger firms, an internal function may perform this function. Management may also determine whether the review can be performed adequately by an internal audit group or whether the review should be performed by a technically qualified third party. At the conclusion of the review, the compliance monitor should report the results to the appropriate parties. The compliance monitor is also responsible for making recommendations for improvements to the overall internal control structure.

[d]—Statement of Information Processing Responsibilities

Following is an example statement that should be signed by all partners and employees of a law firm.

(1) Take appropriate actions to ensure that the firm's information technology resources in your area are protected from accidents, tampering and unauthorized use or modification. Use of the firm's computers and related computer resources is restricted to business purposes authorized or permitted by firm management.

(2) The law firm, with a vested interest in maintaining the integrity of all information, must be particularly sensitive to copyrighted information. Do not copy software purchased or developed for use in connection with personal computers. This software is proprietary and cannot be copied without the permission of its legal owner or license from the developer. Follow all terms and conditions of the software licenses and copyright laws.

(3) Handle all information stored on a computer or downloaded to portable media such as diskettes and hard copies with appropriate care to prevent unauthorized disclosure of the information.

(4) Protect your passwords as follows:

- Your password is your own. Keep it secret and never disclose or share it with anyone.

- Make your passwords at least six characters in length and change your password every sixty days. In most cases, the system will automatically prompt each user for these requirements. However, you are ultimately responsible for your password and you should change it whenever you feel that it may have been compromised. When choosing a password, select one that cannot be easily guessed by someone else (e.g., months, first names, constant word with rotating numbers).

(5) Report to your supervisor any possible or actual security violations that come to your attention. The supervisor is then responsible for bringing the issue to the attention of the firm's information security officer.

[e]—Risk Analysis

A law firm should perform a periodic, formal risk analysis of information system resources to reassess security vulnerability and the effectiveness of existing controls. The frequency of evaluations depends on the frequency of major changes to the application or systems environment. At a minimum, each application or database should be reviewed annually by the designated data owner and a report must be presented to the management. The respective information security officers are then responsible for ensuring that the appropriate changes are made to the computerized information technology. In performing a formal risk assessment, the owners will evaluate each of the following parameters:

[i]—Loss-Fraud

Potential for financial loss from unauthorized disclosure of information as a result of either willful or accidental modification of information. This risk is magnified if confidential client information is willfully or negligently disclosed. For example, sealed trial records may be unintentionally disclosed to the public if proper safeguards are not in place.

[ii]—Direct Value

The value of the information measured by the firm's direct expense required for its creation, storage, and manipulation.

[iii]—Operational Impact

The extent to which the loss of the information or its integrity affects management decisions, system operations, or business functions.

The effect also includes the costs of correcting mistakes so that they do not recur and the costs of recreating the information.

[iv]—Competitive Value

The value of the information to competitors, including the amount of income, business, or market share that could be lost if they obtained the information. The competitive value also can be viewed as the competitor's ability to keep data more secure than one's own law firm.

[v]—Compliance Impact

The extent to which regulatory agencies or governing bodies mandate retention of the information and its integrity.

[f]—Information Sensitivity

Information technology owners may wish to consider classifying all designated sensitive firm information as confidential/restricted or confidential. This process should be completed for all new system development projects and be performed for existing systems. Information should be classified according to the most sensitive detail it includes. Information stored in several media formats (either hardcopy or electronic) will have the same level of classification. Suggested classifications include:

[i]—Confidential/Restricted

This assignment is for critical information of the highest sensitivity that, if revealed, could cause irreparable damage to the firm's image or financial stability. Examples of this type of information may include data that relate to clients. Access to such information must be strictly limited and controlled at all times by access control software or other equivalent means. Data classified "Confidential/Restricted" should not be left unprotected and, as a result, will require the highest level of protection. The level of disclosure of this data will be determined by the owner.

[ii]—Confidential

This assignment is for sensitive information that, if revealed, could have a potential financial impact or expose the company to fraud. Access to such information should be limited to those who require it to perform their job function or have a valid business need. Data classified as "Confidential" must be protected by access control software or other means whenever feasible. The level of disclosure of this data should be on a need-to-know basis by the owner.

[iii]—Public/Non-critical

This assignment is for information that is considered non-confidential, but will be treated as proprietary. Appropriate protection should be defined by the owner.

[g]—Network Privacy

As previously stated, firm computers should be used only for valid business reasons. The information contained on networks is, therefore, the responsibility of management. The activity and content of user information on computer networks is within the scope of review by management. To maintain the privacy of employees, the company networks should not be used for personal and/or private information unrelated to job functions. Each employee is expected to avoid accessing areas on networks for which they do not have a valid business need. While networks are intended to share information, it is each user's responsibility to exercise judgment over the information they access. Consider the contents of electronic mail (e-mail) messages to be the same as formal, written memoranda. When composing e-mail messages, comply with all personnel policies regarding the use of inappropriate language. Messages containing language that is in violation of Human Resources policies should not be tolerated. Be aware that electronic messages are periodically backed up by automated devices and that messages, although deleted from electronic mail files, still exist until the backup medium is erased.

[h]—Backup/Storage Determination

Law firms depend on certain information to be available in order to conduct business. Information availability standards rank how information is required for daily operations.

[i]—Essential

Information technology data or functions that, if unavailable, would completely interrupt business from functioning (i.e., the process cannot be performed manually). Data classified as *essential* will be backed up daily and stored in a suitable off-site location. Consideration will be made between the system administrators and system owners as to whether incremental backups will occur between daily backups.

[ii]—Critical

Information technology data or functions that could be performed manually for a limited period of time without noticeable impact on the firm's operations. Data classified *critical* will be backed up daily and stored in a suitable off-site location.

[iii]—Normal

Information technology data or functions that, if unavailable, pose no disruption of service. Data classified *normal* will be backed up periodically, as determined jointly by the system owner and system administrators, and periodically removed to a secure location.

[2]—Data Security Standards

[a]—Physical Security

This section addresses the protection of, and physical access to, distributed computing facilities. These facilities include computer rooms, network control centers and other related areas.

In general, physically secure each (non-laptop) component of the data processing equipment including computers, peripherals, terminals, controllers and other related equipment. Adhere to all local, state and national electrical and fire codes, as well as other appropriate codes and insurance requirements.

[i]—Access to Computing Facilities Standards

- Prevent unauthorized access to host computer equipment (i.e., servers, processors, communications equipment, etc.) through the use of locked rooms and/or pass-code protection.
- Where technically possible, provide a log of successful and unsuccessful access attempts using access control devices.
- Require written approval for and assign a liaison to non-employees who need access to the computer room. These people may include vendors, service and maintenance personnel. These accesses should be logged and retained for at least one year.
- Lock and alarm doors not normally used for access to restricted areas. Combinations or key locks protecting doors should be changed periodically and, at the discretion of management, when an employee having access is terminated.
- For large computer rooms (more than ten servers), consider restricting access through electronic access control systems using encoded badges.
- As part of a periodic third-party review of access controls, management should commission the reviewer (either the Audit Department or external auditor) to review automated access control audit trails and visitor logs for appropriateness.
- Provide adequate building security (e.g., guards and/or alarmed doors) to protect the entire facility (in addition to computer room security) during off-hour periods.

[ii]—Component Protection Standards

- Protect computer room components that may be located outside the computer room from unauthorized access. These components may include routers, modems and telecommunications equipment. The appropriate protection will be determined by the security officer. Examples include using password protection on equipment and maintaining components in locked closets.
- Do not post signs on wiring closets, telephone rooms and other equipment components that attract the attention of unauthorized individuals.

[iii]—Computer Room Safety Standards

- Prohibit food or drink in the computer room at anytime.
- Store trash in appropriate containers and empty them periodically (i.e., at least daily). Do not allow trash to spill onto floors or equipment.
- Store sensitive waste paper in burn bags or in containers to be shredded.
- Store fluids, cleaning supplies, and other liquids in containers away from equipment.
- Keep computer room facilities clean of dust and debris. Ensure exits and aisles remain unobstructed at all times.
- Provide flashlights in all computer room facilities.

[iv]—Fire Protection

- Prohibit smoking in the computer room. Prohibit cooking equipment, including coffeepots, within the computer room.
- Equip all computer room facilities with adequate smoke and fire detection devices. Install these devices in such a manner so that they are easily identifiable and readable. Place smoke detectors in all critical support facilities including electrical, telephone, emergency generator, air conditioning, and similar areas.
- Provide the computer room facilities with fire suppression equipment recommended by the local fire regulations for electrical equipment. For smaller computer rooms, hand-held fire extinguishers will be used. For larger computer rooms the security officers of these locations should consider implementing a fire suppression system, based upon an analysis of the criticality of the information processed at that location.
- Ensure procedures exist for facilities management to monitor and test fire suppression system test equipment at least every six months. Document test results. Install fire extinguishers in easily accessible locations.

- Train all computer room personnel in the use of any automatic fire suppression systems, the use of portable fire extinguishers, and in the proper response to smoke and fire alarms.
- Store flammable supplies outside of computer room areas.

[v]—Water Protection Standards

- Equip computer room facilities with covers to protect equipment. Make plastic sheeting readily available to protect equipment and paper supplies from falling water.
- Locate computer room equipment away from water pipes to minimize the potential for water damage.
- Train all computer room personnel to respond to any threat of water damage or leakage.

[vi]—Air Conditioning and Electrical Systems

- Provide backup ventilation plans in the event that air conditioning systems in the computer rooms fail. Backup ventilation procedures should be part of the firm's disaster recovery plan in the case of a power outage.
- Protect computer room electrical systems from electrical problems (e.g., power surges, spikes) that could cause an equipment malfunction or failure.
- Organize computer equipment in a manner that will protect them from malfunction or abuse. If there is a chance that environmental controls cannot always be maintained, initiate procedures to monitor temperature and humidity where computer room equipment is located to prevent the equipment from damage and loss of data.
- Train all computer room personnel to monitor existing environmental controls.
- Locate electrical distribution control panels in a secure area and clearly label them.
- For large installations, require authorization for the removal of equipment from the computer room.
- Maintain storage media containing data (disks, tapes etc.) in a secure location that prevents access by persons who do not have responsibility for their custody.
- Transport and dispose of hard-copy reports in a manner consistent with the sensitivity of the information printed on them.
- Erase both file allocation tables and the actual data files from storage media before selling, reassigning or discarding so that erased data cannot be recovered using sophisticated hardware and software tools.

- Transport sensitive data by using previously approved and bonded delivery services.
- Protect on-site magnetic media in a fireproof vault or safe rated to protect against the effects of heat and fire.

[vii]—Backup of Data Storage

- The system administrator should develop off-site backup rotation and retention schedules for each processing site that reflects the risk assessment of the information being stored. Since backups are generally performed by physical computer platform, the system administrator should be responsible for developing a schedule for each one.
- Perform daily backups of all data that is classified as Confidential/Restricted. Store the backups off-site at least once per day if the data is classified as critical. Otherwise, remove the backups to an information security officer-approved offsite location weekly.
- Business recovery planning for law firms is a necessary process that must be undertaken to ensure restoration of the firm's critical legal and administrative services following a disaster. It should be a firm-wide, organized and supported effort to protect the firm, its physical property and its unique informational assets.
- Finance department business recovery plans should provide for the identification and restoration of critical accounting functions, such as payroll, client billing and work in process. The recovery plan must include tasks and responsibilities for resumption of those critical accounting functions, as well as detailed documentation of the systems and procedures required to support those functions following a disaster.

The process of developing a business recovery plan for the firm should generally follow the structure outlined below:

- Confirm objectives and scope of the business recovery planning project with senior firm management.
- Create appropriate project structure and recovery team(s) organization.
- Gather appropriate project structure and recovery team(s) organization.
- Gather all relevant documents and information to assist in the process.
- Perform a threat assessment to identify risks to the firm, their likelihood of occurrence and their estimated impact on the firm. Where possible, implement control measures to reduce the probability or magnitude of any threat category.

- Perform a business impact to identify those legal and administrative functions that are most critical to the firm's continuity.
- Recommend a recovery strategy from available alternatives.
- Document business recovery plans and distribute them to recovery team members.
- Establish plan maintenance and testing procedures to ensure the plan stays current and viable.
- Conduct a periodic review of the business recovery plan, preferably through an independent audit.

[b]—Personnel Security

This section addresses how data security controls are integrated into the hiring, employment and termination of employees. This is one of the most critical areas of data security since employees are ultimately responsible for controlling the dissemination of confidential information.

Ensure that the firm provides the training to encourage adherence to company policies and procedures. Upon termination of employment or changes in responsibilities, the firm will take measures to assure that the access controls have been changed to reflect the changes in responsibilities.

[i]—Prior to Employment

- The human resources department should subject employees to pre-employment screening, which includes background investigations, as determined by management and the human resources director.
- Ensure that all employees receive a copy of the data security policies and acknowledge in writing that they understand their responsibilities as stated in the document.

[ii]—During Employment

- Consider any employee's chronic problems adhering to security policies and standards during the performance evaluation process.
- Assign a liaison for each consultant who is responsible for ensuring that they comply with all data security policies.
- Provide training to employees upon changes in security policies or procedures.

[iii]—Transfer or Termination

- Human resources should immediately notify the information security officer upon the resignation or termination of employees.

- Revoke all IDs and passwords upon termination or resignation of employees and revoke or modify access upon transfer of responsibilities.
- For situations where users with access to highly sensitive information are terminated, the employee's supervisor should be responsible for directly coordinating with the system administrator or other appropriate supervisor to remove the user's access rights.
- Require that all PCs, keys, ID cards, software, data, documentation, manuals, etc. are returned to the employee's direct supervisor or Human Resources, as appropriate.
- Upon termination of an employee, inspect all materials that an employee wishes to remove from the premises.
- Establish proper procedures for the removal of employees terminated for a cause. Depending on the nature of the termination, the former employees will be subject to varying levels of observation and escort.

[c]—Information Security

This section addresses programmed access security surrounding computer systems data, files, programs or transactions. The application of this ("logical") access security will help to reduce unauthorized access to, or alteration of, data.

Protect all information from unauthorized modification, disclosure or destruction and assure that the system is accurate, trusted and available. Determine the appropriate level of access control features to protect the information in each application by performing an application risk analysis. Restrict access to computer systems to those people who need the information for their business function.

[i]—User Identification Code

- Where technically possible, establish user IDs that become inoperative after a 90-day period of inactivity.
- Where technically possible, disable default user IDs shipped with software. Otherwise, ensure that the passwords are changed in accordance with the password change policies.
- Identify each user with a unique user identification code ("User ID") to distinguish that user from other users when accessing networks or applications. System administrators can assign the same user ID to different networks/applications, as long as the shared user ID belongs to a single user.
- Do not issue user IDs without documented authorization. System administrators may use a request from a user, supervisor or system owner through the firm's e-mail as acceptable documentation.

However, system administrators are still responsible for determining that the authorization request is appropriate. Additionally, ensure that the request is supported by a documented business need.

- Do not provide shared user IDs to multiple users where it is technically feasible to provide individual IDs. In situations where a shared ID is required, other than inquiry-only access, document the reason and users who have been granted the right to use this ID and password.
- The system owner should approve user IDs based on a documented business need and job function.
- Ensure that user IDs conform to the firm's naming conventions.
- User management must formally notify the security officer of changes in the employee's job function in order to ensure that access privileges are appropriately maintained.
- Require that user management or Human Resources formally notify the security officer of extended absences (e.g., long-term sick leave, temporary transfers, etc.) in order to ensure that computer access is temporarily revoked.
- For contract employees and consultants, consider creating an ID expiration date that coincides with the conclusion of the contracted project.

[ii]—Password Management

- Require that passwords remain confidential and are not shared, posted or otherwise divulged in any manner.
- Ensure security software enforces password changes once every sixty days.
- Require that security software disables and revokes passwords following three unsuccessful log-on attempts.
- Require passwords to be at least six alphanumeric characters in length for all users.
- Require that security software does not allow the reuse of passwords for five generations or more.
- Do not include passwords in batch log-on sequences. Exceptions to this standard should be brought to the attention of management. The system administrator responsible for these log-ons should change the encoded password at least every six months.
- Require that files containing passwords are one-way encrypted.
- Require passwords to be entered in non-display fields.
- Set the initial passwords, issued by the system administrator, to be valid for two log-ons only.

- Require security software to enforce a password change following the initial log-on.
- Disable or change default passwords shipped with software.
- Disallow group passwords so that individual accountability can be maintained. See the User Identification Code section for information on shared user IDs.
- Encourage users to create passwords that will prohibit easy guessing (i.e., passwords such as spouse's first name, favorite team, etc.).
- Consider the use of intelligent authentication devices such as smartcards for remote access for applications determined to be confidential/restricted.

[iii]—Device Identification

- The physical component and, where possible, the location of the logical access request should be identified to the system being accessed. Devices may include terminals, lines, communication nodes, controllers, remote processors and personal computers.
- Catalog hardwire communication lines (e.g., network lines, telephone lines, etc.) and make them uniquely identifiable to the system being accessed to facilitate the discovery of wiretaps.

[iv]—Application Software

- Restrict access to application resources to authorized users. Protect all access to application system resources by assigning individual user rights.
- Define authorization to modify data or execute commands, transactions or programs, or other access to production data on a need-to-know basis by job function.
- To obtain or change access privileges, a representative of the user department should complete and sign a form that requests the specific access privileges and submit the documentation to the system administrator. The system administrator will then submit the form to the appropriate application owner who will approve or deny the request. The system administrator will then make the necessary changes to the access privileges for approved requests.
- Maintain appropriate segregation of duties related to application systems.
- Protect application-level access control tables and profiles (i.e., the lists maintained within a computer application that contain access authorizations) from unauthorized access. Generally, the system administrators should be the only people with access to these functions.

• Use standard naming conventions for similar files and require that application developers conform to these conventions.

• Require that all non-scheduled (i.e., special or ad hoc) requests for access to production data are authorized by the security officer or system owner.

• A review cycle of each application should be determined and performed by Internal Audit or an appropriate third party. These reviews may include a review of application software logs and monitoring reports for appropriateness, on a periodic basis.

• Where technically feasible, secure access to highly sensitive processing functions (e.g., check processing, artist information, etc.) by limiting the terminals from which these functions can be executed and physically and/or logically restricting these terminals. Secure these terminals by physical (e.g., keyboard locks) and/or logical (access control software) means when unattended.

[v]—System Software

• The system administrators should restrict access to programs or utilities that can dynamically alter data (e.g., programs that circumvent the standard access, through an application program, to data files) to those people who demonstrate an urgent business need. The system administrators should notify the system owners of this activity.

• Restrict access to operating system software, commands and sensitive utilities to those individuals who require access to perform their job functions.

• Each system administrator should be responsible for maintaining a record of essential programs and data files. The system administrator must control changes to these files, following approval by owners.

• Provide protection to the system-level security tables. For systems that contain information that has been classified as confidential/restricted, the appropriate system administrators will determine the need for encryption of these access control tables.

• Where technically feasible, and after review with the application owner, have the system time-out on-line terminals after thirty minutes of inactivity.

[vi]—Security Software

• Where possible, each system administrator should follow established data security procedures. Specific procedures and settings have been developed for each platform-server, e-mail, mainframe, PC, etc.

• Other operating systems, network software or application software should be evaluated by the MIS departments. The MIS departments should commission control procedures to be developed and documented for those systems that are determined to have a significant impact on the control environment.

• Report security breaches in a timely manner based on the severity of the incident and the nature of the data involved.

• For applications that have been determined to contain *confidential/restricted* information, and where the system or application software permits, the system administrator will produce security log reports, investigate access violations and resolve the violations periodically, as determined by the system owner.

• The system administrator or information security officer is responsible for summarizing and reporting data security violations to the owners on a timely basis.

[d]—Network Security

This section addresses security policies and standards related to data networking resources. If all computing resources are interconnected through a firm-wide enterprise network (i.e., intranet), this level of connectivity presents significant risks to the firm. Therefore, it is important that an adequate level of security exists over the entire data network.

The firm should provide network security resources at a level that is appropriate for the nature of the data transmitted. In order to determine what level of security is appropriate, the system administrators should perform a risk analysis on the data transmitted every time the nature of the data changes significantly, for example, when a new system is implemented. The system administrators should ensure that access to data transmissions is restricted to authorized personnel internally and should control the flow of data between the private network and external, public networks through the use of network firewalls.

[i]—Data Communication Security

• Secure data networks through the use of an appropriate combination of controls including, but not limited to, message authentication, message validation, message logging, message acknowledgment, message reconciliation, terminal validation or data encryption.

• Encrypt information that is classified as confidential/restricted while passing through the network using encryption software or hardware.

- Classify all encryption hardware, software, and keys as confidential and essential.
- Owners should ensure the protection of any data encryption keys entrusted to them. Owners should not print out private keys and should password-protect user IDs in e-mail that contain each user's e-mail encryption key(s).
- The system administrators of those systems that use data encryption should periodically inform users of the importance of maintaining keys including making them aware that once the key is lost, the data cannot be recovered.
- The system or network communications administrators should ensure that encryption hardware and software complies with all the applicable governmental regulations concerning the import and export of encryption technology.
- The network administrators should approve and maintain records of all computer hardware attached to the local network backbones. Where applicable, the administrators should ensure that the equipment complies with the firm's standard configurations and vendors.

[ii]—Network Connectivity

- Restrict access to network screen capture and/or local system control utilities. These utilities are installed on local PCs and are intended for use by the help desk to assist end users in resolving problems. The access to the utilities should be limited to authorized help desk personnel. They should be used only after the help desk has informed the user of this capability and has received permission from the user (each time) to use them.
- Where feasible, locations that require more than five modems should use centralized modem banks attached to a dedicated modem/communications server. Direct all incoming calls to the Local Area Network from these modem servers to the operating system specifically designated for remote use.
- For non-public information, require that all equipment that provides dial-in capability to the network positively identify the user through a log-in sequence before allowing access. This can be accomplished through the communications software itself or by a combination of routing the user directly to a specific application and/or operating system and using its log-in routine.
- Do not distribute telephone numbers for dial-in devices to anyone other than people who have a demonstrated business need to use them. Maintain lists of users with remote access and change the access numbers periodically, notifying each authorized user of the changes in advance of the number change.

- Telecommunications administrators should consider the use of different exchanges for data lines from the published exchanges the voice communications, depending on the technical feasibility of this option at each location.
- The use of personal communications equipment (modems, ISDN cards, etc.) attached directly to personal computers with remote control software should be strictly controlled by the local network administrators. Before users can attach hardware and install remote control communications software (software that allows a remote user to dial into a PC attached to the network and issue commands from it as if it were attached to the network itself), the local network administrators should review the requests and determine if adequate procedures can be created to protect the network.
- For users who remotely access systems that contain information that is considered to be confidential/restricted, consider employing authentication technologies such as smartcards.
- Where applicable, change all network equipment default passwords (e.g., routers) when installed.

[iii]—Network Operations

- The network administrators, where feasible, should use access control lists on routers.
- Do not display a greeting on any external network connections until the user is authenticated through a sign-on sequence that requires a unique user ID and password.
- Display a message on all external network connections warning potential users that unauthorized use is prohibited.
- Require software that performs unattended file transfer to or from other systems to authenticate the origin and destination file names as well as any user submitting the request unless the information being transferred is classified as *Public*.

[iv]—Component Security Standards

- The network administrators should ensure that all network components are uniquely identifiable and restricted for their intended business function. This includes protection for all vulnerable points in the network.
- The network administrators should consider using automated tools to monitor the integrity of network operations and provide alerts of unusual activity.
- The network administrators should ensure that procedures exist to authenticate callers to all network devices that can be remotely initialized or configured through dial-in mechanisms.

• Physically secure all network and server equipment including LAN-servers, bridges, routers, multiplexors, or front-end processors from unauthorized access by placing them in locked rooms or closets.

• Require approval from the information security officer for all direct, dedicated network connections to entities outside the firm.

• Locate all cable and line facilities for both voice and data in secured areas. If the lines cannot be secured, the telecommunications manager must document the reasons and submit them to the appropriate security officer.

[v]—Network Access

• The network administrators should require that the host operating system validates each user prior to allowing network access. Once verified, users will automatically be directed to applications for which they have been authorized.

• Isolate all hosts that run applications or contain data that are non-public behind a firewall from public external networks. A firewall is a collection of components placed between the private network and public networks (e.g., the Internet, network, etc.).

• All traffic from inside the firm to external networks, and vice-versa, must pass through a gateway (or firewall) that does not serve as a general purpose host and therefore does not require features that weaken security (e.g., log-in, etc.).

• Note: Certain e-mail servers have a certification process that provides a sufficient gateway mechanism and therefore a separate gateway server is not required.

• Only authorized traffic, as defined by the system owner, should be allowed to pass.

• The firewall itself should be immune to penetration.

• The specifications for the firewall should conform to the firm's standards.

[vi]—Internet Connectivity Standards

• The system administrator for the Internet server should ensure that anonymous file transfers into systems are disallowed.

• Internet connections should be used only for valid business purposes. As such, any information posted to discussion groups bearing a firm address should reflect only firm positions. Information transferred from a firm address should be treated with the same standards as information on firm letterhead.

• Designate a technically appropriate person (with adequate Internet experience) to be responsible for maintaining Internet access. This individual should review Internet news groups or other appropriate forums to be aware of new security weaknesses/threats and should coordinate any necessary changes to Internet connectivity on a timely basis.

[e]—Software Development

This section addresses the security issues surrounding the development of new applications and the maintenance of existing applications. When performing application changes, it is essential to consider the protection of computing resources. As part of this consideration, an analysis of the security features required by the changes to application software should be performed and evaluate the impact that software changes will have on the existing security.

Compliance with the firm's application development methodology is important. This methodology recognizes the importance of security planning during each phase of development or maintenance. The methodology requires that the development team assess the sensitivity and availability of the application and data and create access controls that are appropriate for each independently controlled system.

[i]—Project Planning

- To initiate a project, the developer should obtain authorization from the local owner or other appropriate individual.
- Require that all requests for system development or maintenance are supported by a documented and approved business need.
- Perform a formal risk analysis (i.e., sensitivity and availability) as part of the project-planning phase. Ensure that the results are a primary consideration when determining the feasibility and security requirements of the project.
- Require that systems that will contain information designated as *Confidential/Restricted* are approved by the System Owners before they are moved onto a production server.

[ii]—System Design

- Design all systems and applications with security as a major objective, including those systems with high sensitivity or availability requirements.
- The design teams are responsible for determining the appropriateness of security requirements for all major system components (including hardware, software and communications) before the system is implemented.

• The system design specifications should identify security features and their implementation requirements in the pre-implementation process, based upon an assessment by the system owners of the sensitivity of the information processed. The features specified (or absence of security) should be submitted to the information system owners for review and approval.

• If security is built into the application, the design team should isolate security-related code and data (e.g., profiles and tables) from application modules and clearly document all interactions with the rest of the system.

• The design team should consider including logging and monitoring facilities in new application programs. Examples include logging of critical transactions and user activity. The design should determine a level of activity logging consistent with the sensitivity of the information being processed, as determined by the application system risk assessment forms.

• Programmatically restrict the display of menu options or processing functions for which the individual is not authorized to perform.

• Provide protection to the system-level access control tables.

• Prohibit the development or installation of software (e.g., user exits) that has the capability to bypass security systems or routines. If an exception to this standard is needed, management must approve and document the exception.

• Consider that all cooperative applications perform persistent verification between the client and the server application when communicating through remote. Periodic verification subjects each request to authorization checks on the client.

• For remotely accessed programs, do not identify the network as belonging to the firm until the software authenticates the user. Additionally, do not display any welcome messages other than a message that requests a valid user identification code and password.

• Discourage the development of independent security routines as part of any application system when centralized, well-controlled security routines are available.

• If all or part of the software is written by contract programmers or software houses, negotiate a contract specifying that the law firm owns all copyrights to the software, including source code, and that the vendor is not allowed to use any of the code in applications done for other customers or clients.

[iii]—System Installation

The system development team is responsible for executing the following standards, unless noted otherwise:

- As appropriate, review security features with the information system owners prior to system installation.
- Identify, document and test all security features prior to installation and use.
- Prior to implementation, require that all systems use the logical access controls specified in the program development plan. These are provided by the application package or operating system.
- Prior to implementation, ensure that security is understood by the appropriate system administrators and security officers. Do not allow access to systems until security administration functions are in place.

[iv]—Testing

The person responsible for user acceptance testing should be responsible for the following:

- Ensure that appropriate measures are taken during system testing so that sensitive information is not disclosed.
- Perform testing of security features and controls as part of the system testing.
- Maintain separation of the test environment from the production environment at all times.
- Perform testing using copies of production data. Consider parallel or acceptance-using in cooperation with the information system owners.
- Use naming standards to distinguish between test and production jobs, data and programs.
- Maintain access controls over test results if the information is non-public.

[v]—Maintenance Request

- The development team must obtain authorization from the data owner for all application program maintenance requests.
- In addition to the appropriate approvals and authorizations, the requestor should provide a documented business reason for maintenance requests.
- All requests for program moves between the test and production environments should include documented authorization from the system owner.
- At the discretion of the system owners, changes to applications that process information that has been designated as

confidential/restricted should be reviewed by a group independent of the design team (e.g., internal or external auditors). They should review the adequacy of controls prior to and following implementation.

[vi]—Development Resources

- Consider data processing resources under development (e.g., programs, files and documentation) to be assets of the firm and provide protection to them, as would be applicable to the finished product.
- A firm network administrator should be assigned to the development team. This is to ensure that information used during the design, implementation or testing is not compromised on the development and test systems.
- All developers should adhere to package software license agreements and copyright laws. Copy package software products in accordance with license agreements (e.g., a backup copy for protection).
- The use of copy protection bypass software should be prohibited by any firm employee. If problems occur with master copies of software, the situation should be resolved directly with the vendor or authorized vendor representative.
- Programs written by employees or contractors in the performance of their job for the firm will remain the property of the firm. Do not distribute these programs without appropriate documented authorization.
- Do not copy products licensed to run on a specific computer or at a particular site onto another computer or another site without written authorization from the vendor.
- It is recommended that a review of the contract be performed to ensure the terms of the contract are clearly defined.

[vii]—Software Evaluation

- The firm should evaluate prospective packaged software for the software's ability to provide adequate security safeguards against unauthorized use or modification of data.
- It is recommended that contracts for packaged software purchase/lease contracts be reviewed to ensure that contract provisions are adequate to meet the demands of the firm (e.g., adequate site-license provisions).
- For critical software vendors, consider the use of third-party escrow services to maintain access to source code in the event of the vendors failure to support the product.

[f]—PC Security

This section addresses the security standards needed to protect information stored on personal computers (PCs). The term PC will encompass all end-user workstations including desktop systems and portable computers.

Firms should provide access controls that are appropriate for the nature of the data stored on the PCs. They should consider access controls for each storage media where data is resident (e.g., hard disk, floppy disk, file server or other network devices).

[i]—Acquisition

- All PC hardware and software requests should follow the firm's purchasing procedures.
- Obtain PC hardware and software from standard vendors, when available, based on approved technical standards, where they exist.

[ii]—Off-Site Usage Standards

- Unauthorized removal of company PCs is considered theft.
- Non-portable PCs should be removed from company premises only if there is appropriate authorization from the system administrators.
- Portable PCs and electronic devices (Laptops, PDAs, etc.) should be issued to individuals who will acknowledge, in writing, their responsibility for them and the information that they contain. For large sites, portable computers should be issued passes that can be verified, as deemed appropriate, on leaving the premises.
- Power-on passwords are strongly encouraged on portable PCs. The security officers may determine, at their discretion, to require the use of power-on passwords for portable computers issued from their locations.
- Portable PCs that have passwords included in the batch log-on sequence are required to have power-on passwords. Exceptions to this rule can only be granted by the management.
- Do not use personally owned PC equipment and programs on company premises to access data networks unless the configurations have been approved by the system administrators.

[iii]—Ownership of Software

- Before distributing proprietary software that is owned by the firm to a third party, obtain authorization from the system owner.

• The information technology department should consider, in consultation with the system owners, creating a plan to periodically review the activity of outside personnel who use firm networks (i.e., contractors, service bureaus).

[iv]—Purchased Software

• All users should observe PC software license agreements and copyright laws.

• Copies of software should only be made in accordance with license agreements (e.g., backup copies).

• License software to the company, not to individuals.

• Where technically feasible, the network administrators should consider periodically using automated software inspection utilities. These products, which are run from the server, can survey the software on PCs attached to the network and alert network administrators of potential violations of license agreements and copyright laws.

[v]—Data Backup/Recovery

• The network administrators are responsible for ensuring that backups of software on the servers are performed, and that off-site storage procedures are followed.

• Where possible, the system administrators should backup all affected PC system/application software before system upgrades or maintenance occurs.

• The network administrators should prepare a retention schedule for PC backups of programs, data and electronic mail messages. They should use the conventions established in this manual for classifying the *criticality* of data processed. If backups are performed at the server or host level, the backup schedule of the most critical application should determine the backup frequency of the server.

• The system or network administrators should ensure that the backups are executed according to the schedule and that the backup tapes are deleted according to the schedule.

[vi]—On-Line Access

• Instruct employees who access external information services (e.g., the Internet, bulletin boards, on-line services, etc.) that they should use the services only for valid business purposes.

• Restrict vendors' remote access to the network, based on the sensitivity of the information resident on the network. If the vendor requires remote access to the network, limit the vendors' access to the network to a specific segment.

[vii]—Virus Prevention

- Install virus scanners and/or detection programs as part of the start-up process on PCs. Update the programs regularly to scan for new strains of viruses. Where it has been determined that virus scanners cannot be used, the system administrators should be responsible for documenting the reasons and developing a strategy to migrate to configurations that can support virus filters.
- Install only standard/approved products obtained from authorized suppliers onto PCs.
- Use virus filters and/or detection programs prior to installing any software on a PC.
- If a virus is suspected, disconnect the PC from the network immediately, notify the information security officer and remove the virus prior to any re-connection to network services.
- If public domain or mass distributed programs (e.g., printer drivers) are required for a valid business need, obtain the software from a reputable source such as a vendor bulletin board. While the software must still be scanned for viruses, this reduces the likelihood that the software is infected.

[viii]—File Server Access

- Limit the physical access to file servers to individuals with a documented business need for such access (e.g., LAN administrator).
- The LAN administrator should utilize LAN security features as specified in the firm's data security procedures. These include the following:
- Require identification and authentication of individuals attempting file server access.
- Record and review unsuccessful file server access attempts.

[ix]—Dial-in Access

- Each user who desires dial-in access to the firm's networks must apply for access to the appropriate LAN administrator. Authorization should be granted by the administrator if there is a demonstrated business need for it and the approved request should remain on file with the LAN administrator.
- The LAN administrators should configure the network to require all users to identify and authenticate themselves prior to gaining dial-in access to the network.
- The LAN administrators are responsible for maintaining a list of authorized dial-in users.

[g]—Third-Party Services

This section addresses the standards for controlling the use of outside data processing services. These types of services include the processing of production systems that cannot be done internally (third-party service bureaus such as payroll processing), applications development consulting and information services. A primary consideration when evaluating an outside vendor will be the adequate protection of corporate assets.

At a minimum, the firm should subject vendors to the same access restrictions to which an internal user would be subject. Further consideration will be made that confidential information cannot be controlled once it is distributed outside of the firm. As a result, restrict vendors to the information they require to complete the contracted work and require them to formally acknowledge their responsibility for confidentiality through a written statement.

[i]—Vendor Selection

- For large projects or for vendors who access *Confidential/Restricted* information, ensure that appropriate information is obtained regarding the control structure of vendors performing critical data processing functions. Ensure that the contractor is bound contractually to uphold the firm's data security policies.
- Depending on the sensitivity and criticality of the services or data provided, the firm should consider commissioning or requesting a review of the service-providers internal control structure.
- Vendor business continuity plans must be evaluated to ensure that they correspond to the firm's processing requirements.
- The firm should consider requesting background information that may include financial statements or customer referrals on unknown vendors.

[ii]—Service Contracts

- The manager responsible for contracts with outside data processing services should specify security requirements and potential actions to be taken for violations in the contracts.
- Do not sign contracts with vendors who have violated firm security policies.
- Ensure that contracts require vendors to sign nondisclosure arrangements and/or confidentiality agreements. All vendor personnel should be informed in a written statement of the importance of data processing security. Each vendor employee should sign a nondisclosure agreement, which should be kept on file.
- The information security officer should maintain records which outline security problems that have occurred with vendors.

- The vendor should be responsible for immediately informing the firm of any security breaches, including unauthorized access to or compromise of firm data or resources.
- Any firm employee who is aware of security violations by vendors should report them to firm management.
- Define the ownership of software developed by outside personnel (i.e., contractors) in the contract agreement.

[iii]—Consultants/Contractors

- The firm manager responsible for hiring contractors should be responsible for requiring them to read and sign a non-disclosure agreement. This manager should also be responsible for including security provisions in the contract.
- All contracts with outside contractors should provide that all programs and related products developed by contractors and staff for the firm may not be copied, distributed or otherwise used by outside organizations without documented authorization from the appropriate management unless other contractual arrangements are expressly agreed upon.

[h]—Information in Hard Copy

This section addresses the standards for security over hard copy documents. The standards cover labeling, copying, distribution, storage, and disposal of documentation that is deemed to be sensitive.

The firm should provide security over hard copy documentation in a manner consistent with the protection over automated information stored on the firm's computers.

[i]—Labeling

- Where technically feasible, clearly mark reports containing confidential or restricted information on every page.
- Confidential or restricted microfiche should be secured as are all other sensitive hard copy documents.
- Where technically feasible, all pages of confidential reports must be numbered (e.g., page 1 of 2).

[ii]—Copying

- The system owners should be responsible for controlling the initial distribution of system-generated reports. The authorized recipients of restricted reports are responsible for controlling the further distribution of these reports. They should provide copies only to users who have a valid firm business need for them.

[iii]—Distribution

- Restricted or sensitive documents should be placed in confidential envelopes and sealed with the name of the intended recipient clearly marked.
- Consider hand delivery for extremely sensitive information, where practical.
- Confidential information should be sent via some form of registered mail in order to track its distribution.

[iv]—Storage

- Restricted information should be adequately secured in archive facilities.
- When not in use, confidential information should be stored in locked drawers or cabinets that are accessible only by authorized individuals.

[v]—Disposal

- Confidential or restricted information must be shredded before discarding.
- Microfiche must be shredded finely to ensure that information cannot be recovered after it has been discarded.

CHAPTER 14

Organizing The Finance Function

Chapter Contents

---

§ 14.01 Organization Structure of Law Firms

A law firm's organization structure is often representative of the partners' operating philosophy. Some firms have a "concentrated" management structure, whereby an executive partner runs the firm in an autocratic manner. While this management style may get the job done efficiently, it does not always satisfy the majority view. Other firms have a "diffused" management structure that operates in a very democratic fashion, whereby a vote of a majority of the partners is usually necessary for decision making. This often results in delays in resolving matters, both important and routine. Many firms have adopted a third approach, an "organized" management structure, which is a hybrid of the "concentrated" and the "diffused" structures. It involves the democratic election of an executive committee to operate the firm and the selection by that committee of an executive partner to lead the firm. Beginning in the late 1980s, law firms that participated in the growth and merger boom focused more on efficient business operation and structure by adopting a management style that more closely resembles corporate America. In that structure, the executive committee or executive board essentially ran the firm and allowed partners to focus more on client matters and less on administration or management functions. The firm culture and structure of the partnership usually sets the tone for the type of organization structure adopted by all of the firm's administrative functions, including the finance function, which carries out the firm's accounting and financial activities. A law firm's size also has a bearing on the organization structure of its administrative functions. Thus, a smaller firm has fewer personnel and, therefore, less flexibility in developing a multi-level organizational structure. Trends in the way a law firm processes its financial transactions also affect organization structure, over time. For example, the expanded use of technology, integrated back-office systems (e.g., time and billing system, general ledger system, fixed asset depreciation system), and off-site work station considerations have expanded the role of the law firm's finance and administrative functions.

In the sections that follow, two issues of importance to organizing a law firm's finance function will be explored. They include:

(1) Determining the structure of the organization, which involves focusing on the lines of reporting from the firm's chief financial officer to the firm's partners *and* the lines of reporting from the accounting supervisors and the branch managers to the chief financial officer; and

(2) Defining the duties of personnel, including the duties of the chief financial officer *and* the duties of each of the finance function supervisors.

For purposes of this discussion, the law firm's leader will be referred to as the "managing partner." It is recognized that various other titles, such as "chairman," "executive partner," and "senior partner," have been used by some firms to designate their leader.

§ 14.02 Organization Charts—Law Firm Administrative Functions

In some law firms (usually smaller firms without an executive director), the chief financial officer usually reports directly to the firm's managing partner. In other law firms (usually larger firms), while the chief financial officer also reports to the firm's managing partner, the line of reporting usually passes through an executive director and/or a partner committee. For purposes of this discussion, law firms have been divided into four categories related to size:

(1) Small firms (under 25 lawyers);
(2) Medium firms (25 to 100 lawyers);
(3) Large firms (100 to 300 lawyers); and
(4) Megasize firms (over 300 lawyers).

The lines of reporting to the partners by law firm administrative functions for each size firm will be discussed in the following paragraphs.

[1]—Small Law Firms

In small law firms, the managing partner often carries out many of the firm's financial and administrative functions. Typically, there are two people who handle administrative functions and report to the managing partner - an accounting manager and an office manager. The managing partner typically delegates responsibility for routine accounting tasks to an accounting manager and routine office services tasks to an office manager. Figure 14-A provides a sample organization chart for the administrative functions of a small law firm.

Figure 14-A. Illustration of an example of an organization chart for the administrative functions of a small law firm (less than 25 lawyers).

SMALL LAW FIRM
ORGANIZATION CHART—ADMINISTRATIVE FUNCTIONS

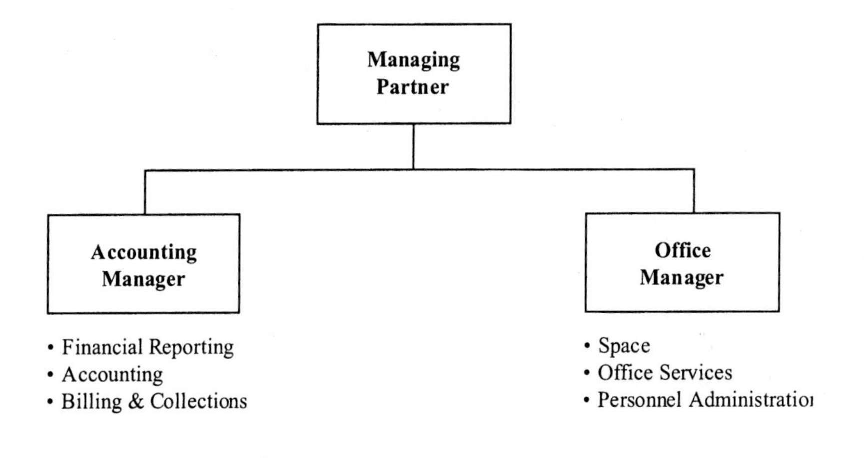

[2]—Medium Law Firms

In medium law firms, the managing partner often carries out some administrative functions, however, two additional partners typically assist in carrying out more time-consuming administrative functions. Financial responsibility is delegated to a financial partner, while office administration tasks are delegated to an administrative partner. These two partners are usually practice partners who are busy servicing clients and consequently carry out their administrative tasks on a part-time basis. The financial partner typically has strong competencies in corporate or accounting matters, while the administrative partner is someone who generally has a natural inclination for administration and leadership. In this scenario, it would be common for the firm's controller and information technology managers to report to the financial partner. The medium law firm's office manager and human resources supervisor typically report to the administrative partner. Figure 14-B shows an example of an organization chart for the administrative functions of a medium law firm.

Figure 14-B. Illustration of an example of an organization chart for the administrative functions of a medium law firm (25 to 100 lawyers).

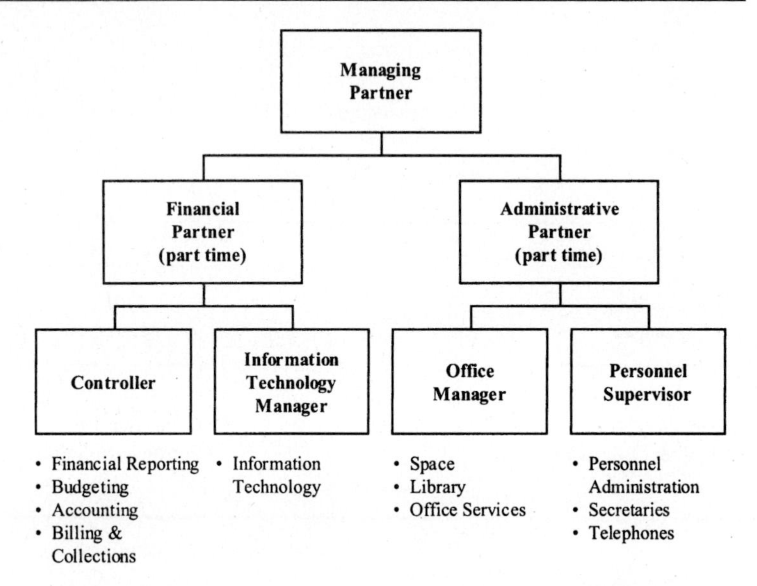

[3]—Large Law Firms

In large law firms, the managing partner often focuses on leadership activities such as practice development and strategic planning while an executive committee manages the firm. This executive committee often delegates the responsibility for day-to-day administrative functions to an executive director or to subcommittees that report directly to the full executive committee. The executive director is usually a business executive (not a lawyer) who occupies a partner-equivalent position in the firm. Key competencies of the executive director would include developed management skills, significant interpersonal and communication skills, and financial prowess. All non-legal positions usually report to the executive director. This includes the firm's controller, information technology manager, office services manager, and human resources manager. Figure 14-C illustrates an example of an organization chart for the administrative functions of a large law firm.

Figure 14-C. Illustration of an example of an organization chart for the administrative functions of a large law firm (100 to 300 lawyers).

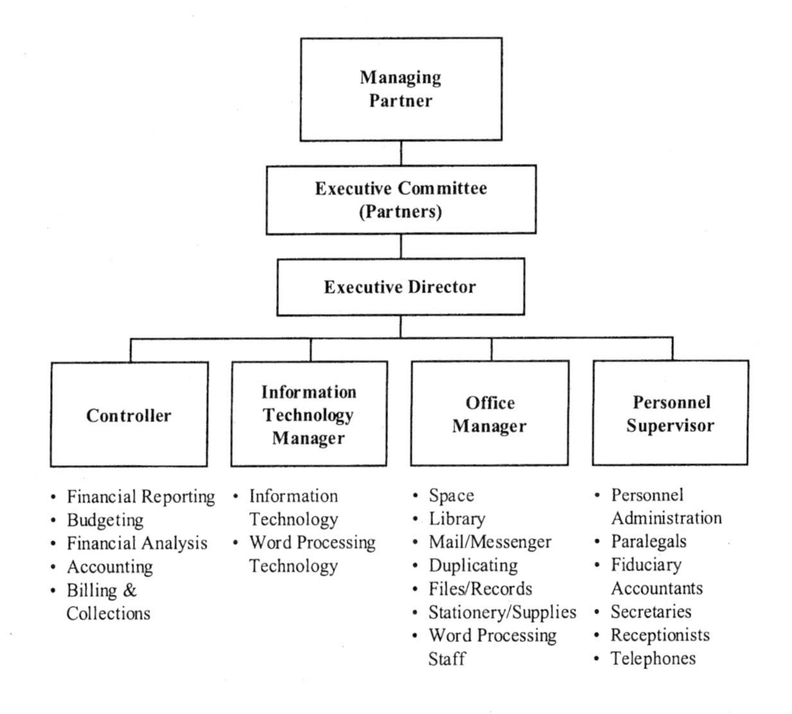

[4]—Megasize Law Firms

The megasize law firm differs from the large firm in that there is yet another committee layer added above the director of finance. The managing partner often exclusively focuses on leadership activities such as merger and acquisition opportunities or addressing the more significant inter-firm client-service issues, while the executive committee focuses on policy decisions and appoints a finance committee and an administrative committee to oversee the firm's respective financial and administrative activities. Sheer size alone usually requires that these responsibilities be divided between two committees. The finance committee typically delegates responsibilities for day-to-day financial activities to a director of finance (the equivalent of a corporate vice president of finance). The firm's controller and its information technology manager usually report to the director of finance. In some megasize law firms, a director of technology reports directly to the finance committee and often has dotted line responsibility to the director of finance. The administrative committee typically delegates responsibility for day-to-day administrative activities to a director of administration (the equivalent of a corporate vice president of operations). The firm's office services manager and its human resources manager usually report to the director of administration. It is not uncommon in megasize law firms that a director of human resources position exists with that person reporting directly to the administrative committee and often has a dotted-line reporting responsibility to the director of administration. Figure 14-D illustrates an example of an organization chart for the administrative functions of a megasize law firm.

The preceding discussion focuses on several examples of how law firms have structured their administrative functions. These examples are not all-inclusive. Certain aspects of law firm administrative functions are continually evolving. For example, firms that depend heavily on information technology in all facets of their operations often expand the role and importance of their information systems function. In some of these firms the information technology manager reports to both the director of finance (for information systems activities) and the director of administration (for word processing and data retrieval activities). In other firms, a new position, "director of information technology," has been created to acknowledge the significant role that technology plays in the firm and the responsibility associated with the function. In these firms, the director of information technology position is on a par with the director of administration and the director of finance, with all three positions reporting to partner committees (i.e., information technology committee, administrative committee, and finance committee).

Figure 14-D. Illustration of an example of an organization chart for the administrative functions of a megasize law firm (over 300 lawyers).

MEGASIZE LAW FIRM
ORGANIZATION CHART—ADMINISTRATIVE FUNCTIONS

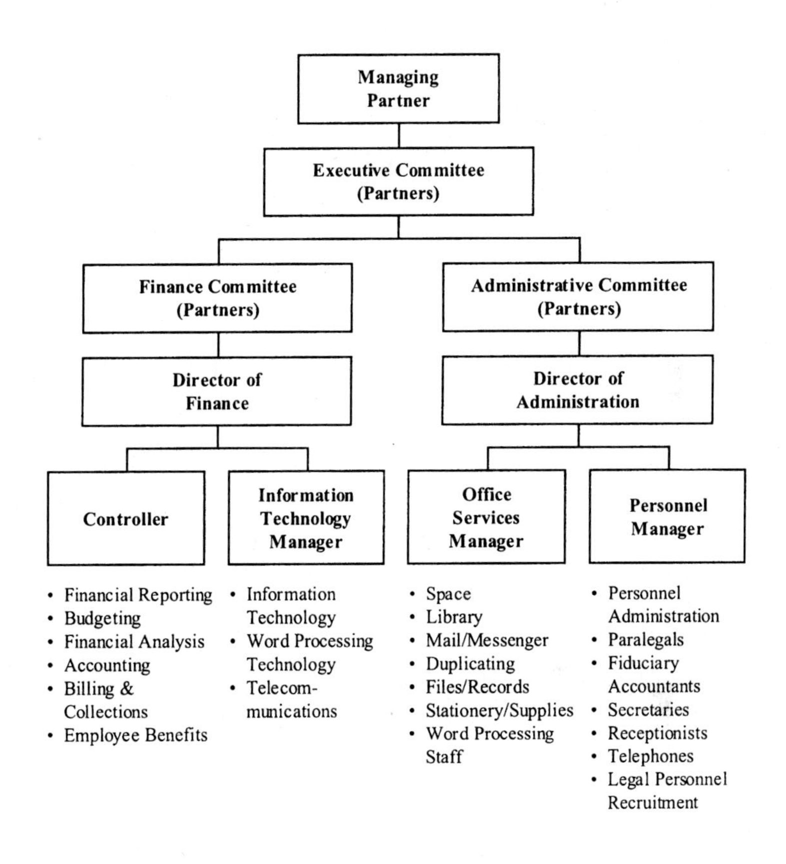

§ 14.03 Organization Charts—Law Firm Finance Function

The size and skill of a law firm's finance function usually varies directly with the size of the firm. As a firm grows, the volume and complexity of its financial activities multiply. This calls for more sophisticated systems, procedures and controls, together with personnel having the knowledge and experience to operate effectively and efficiently in a more complex environment. The title for a law firm's chief financial officer will usually vary with the skill required for the position. Typical titles include:

- Accounting manager (small firms)
- Controller (medium/large firms)
- Director of finance (megasize firms)

The structure of the finance function of each size firm is discussed in the following paragraphs.

[1]—Small Law Firms

In small law firms, where financial activities are typically uncomplicated and volume is relatively modest, an accounting manager ordinarily oversees the finance function. Typically, an accounting manager has some experience in law firm accounting and may have had some public or private accounting or finance background. The accounting manager is usually assisted by a general ledger bookkeeper who posts the books of original entry and ledgers, and by a billing and collections clerk. Figure 14-E illustrates an example of an organization chart for the finance function of a small law firm.

Figure 14-E. Illustration of an example of an organization chart for the finance function of a small law firm (less than 25 lawyers).

SMALL LAW FIRM
ORGANIZATION CHART—FINANCE FUNCTION

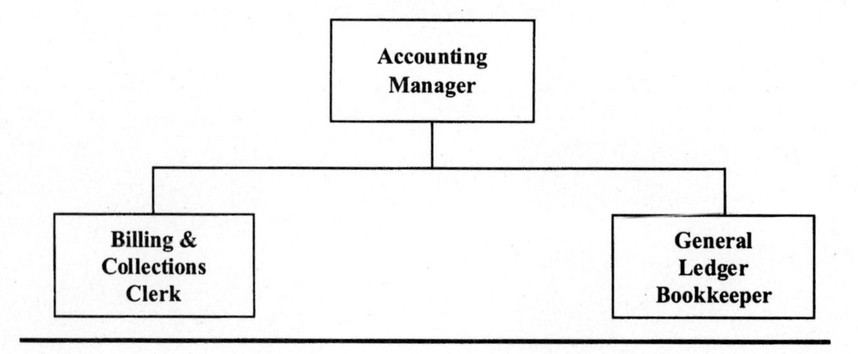

[2]—Medium Law Firms

In medium law firms, where the volume of financial activities is large enough to require the establishment of systems, procedures, and supervision, a controller ordinarily oversees the finance function. Typically, a controller will have had previous public or private accounting experience or may have been a controller or accounting manager at a smaller firm.

Two groups usually report to the controller: first, a general ledger group (general ledger accountant, payroll clerk, cashier and accounts payable clerk), and second, a billing and collections group (a supervisor and several clerks). Figure 14-F illustrates and example of an organization chart for the function of a medium law firm.

Figure 14-F. Illustration of an example of an organization chart for the finance function of a medium law firm (25 to 100 lawyers).

MEDIUM LAW FIRM
ORGANIZATION CHART—FINANCE FUNCTION

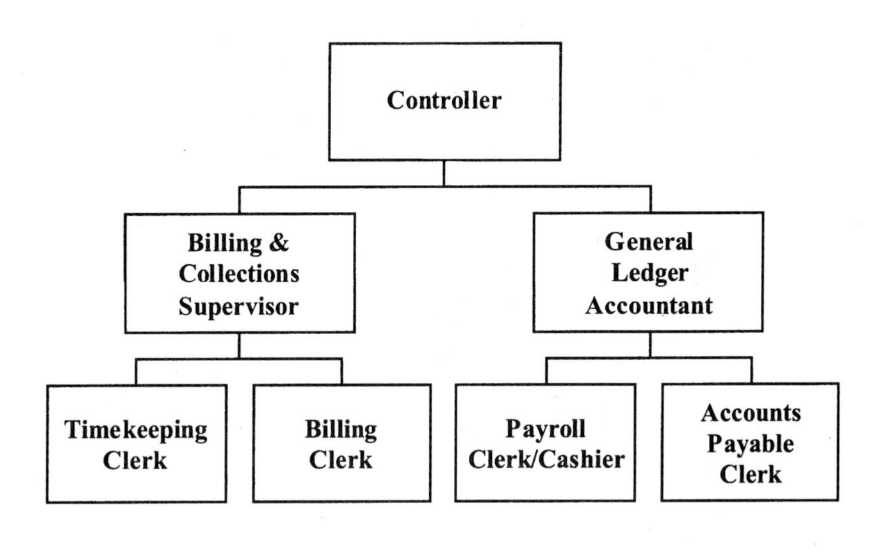

[3]—Large Law Firms

In large law firms, where the sizable volume of financial activities demands sophisticated systems and a large staff of accountants and clerks, a controller ordinarily oversees the finance function. The controller is typically assisted by a series of intermediate supervisors (or section heads):

(1) Billing and collections supervisor;
(2) Payroll supervisor;
(3) Accounts payable supervisor;
(4) Cashier supervisor;
(5) Financial reporting accountant;
(6) General ledger accountant; and
(7) Partners' accounts accountant.

Each section head supervises several clerks who carry out the accounting-related tasks, through interfaced back-office systems.

Figure 14-G illustrates an example of an organization chart for the finance function of a large law firm.

Figure 14-G. Illustration of an example of an organization chart for the finance function of a large law firm (100 to 300 lawyers).

LARGE LAW FIRM
ORGANIZATION CHART—FINANCE FUNCTION

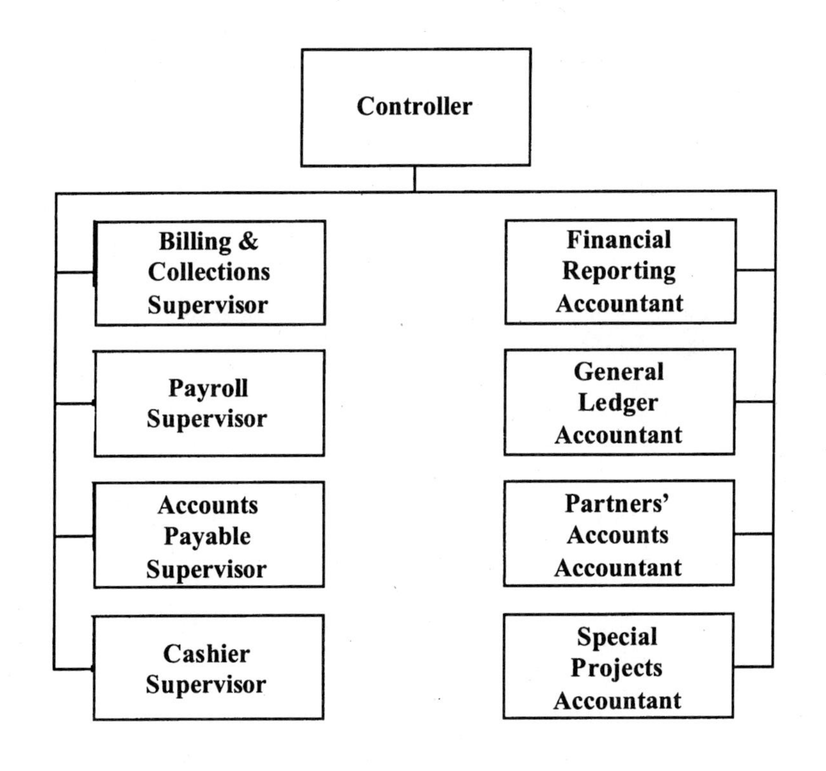

[4]—Megasize Law Firms

In megasize law firms, where the sizable volume of financial activities and the complexities of branch office oversight require a high degree of automation and a financial staff with a high level of knowledge and experience, a director of finance ordinarily oversees the finance function. Usually reporting to the director of finance are: (a) a controller who oversees the firm's accounting activities and (b) an information technology manager who oversees the firm's technology operations. (When the preponderance of the firm's technology -is oriented toward nonfinancial activities, the line of reporting for the information technology manager will usually be outside the finance function.) If the volume of the firm's financial activities is sufficient to warrant it, the controller may choose to divide the accounting department into two groups:

[a]—Accounting Operations

An assistant controller for operations is ordinarily placed in charge of this group. Supervisors for (1) billing and collections, (2) payroll, (3) accounts payable, and (4) cashier sections usually report to this assistant controller. Depending on the volume and complexity of the function, the person responsible for the function could be on the same level as the controller (as opposed to the controller's assistant). In that case, the person might report directly to the director of finance.

[b]—Financial Reporting

An assistant controller for reports is ordinarily placed in charge of this group, which is responsible for (1) financial reporting, (2) general ledger, (3) partners' accounts and (4) special projects (e.g., budgets, employee benefits, bank reconciliations).

Figure 14-H illustrates an example of an organization chart for the finance function of a megasize law firm.

Figure 14-H. Illustration of an example of an organization chart for the finance function of a megasize law firm (over 300 lawyers).

MEGASIZE LAW FIRM
ORGANIZATION CHART—FINANCE FUNCTION

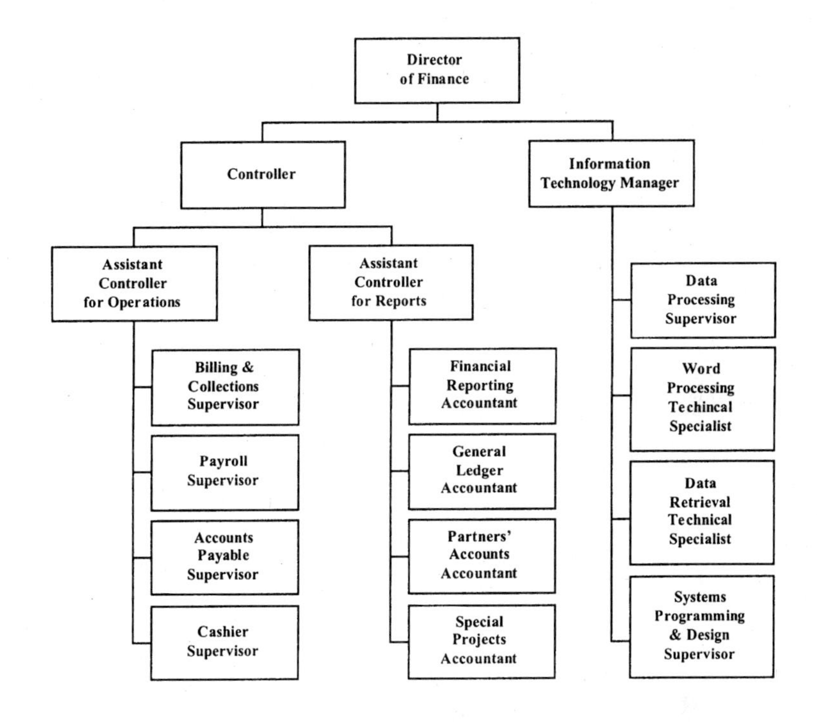

§ 14.04 Branch Office Coordination

Large and megasize law firms often have one or more branch offices in other cities and locations around the world. The firm's executive director (or director of finance), located in the firm's main office, is typically responsible (directly or indirectly) for the financial activities carried out at both the main office and the branch offices. Coordination of activities between the main office and the branch offices can become a formidable task if the firm has a significant number of branches and if the branches are sizable in relation to the main office.

To achieve branch office coordination, firms have used different approaches:

(1) Centralized approach,
(2) Decentralized approach, and
(3) Combination approach

Each of these approaches will be discussed in the following paragraphs.

[1]—Centralized Approach

Law firms that take a "centralized approach" to branch office coordination are usually those firms which are: (1) highly organized, (2) led by an autocratic managing partner and (3) governed by a strong executive committee. Under the centralized approach, each branch office's administrative and financial functions report: (1) directly to the firm's executive director in the main office and (2) indirectly (i.e., in an advisory capacity) to the partner in charge of the branch office.

In addition to a centralized organization structure, the centralized approach to branch office coordination includes centralizing the following:

[a]—Technology Systems

It is possible to centralize billing, collection, disbursement, and payroll functions of all branches, by having a single computer process all financial data at the main office. Each branch is usually permitted the use of a small imprest bank account for the payment of routine disbursements.

[b]—Procedures

This involves either (1) the branch batching all time entries, checks received, checks drawn, and payroll changes for delivery to the main office for input into transaction systems or (2) the branch entering transactions remotely to the main office's back-office systems via a secure communications network.

[c]—Controls

Centralization can be further accomplished by establishing a uniform system of internal accounting controls, organizationally and procedurally, at all branches. These controls usually focus on the separation of duties of employees involved in the recording of transactions and the custodianship of assets, before their transmission to the main office. It also includes procedures surrounding the periodic reimbursement by the main office of disbursements made by the branch office from its imprest bank account. Typically, the main office will not reimburse the branch office unless all disbursements are properly documented as to purpose, supported by invoices or other appropriate documentation, and properly approved by a partner.

[d]—Reports

It is advisable to use standard forms for accumulating financial data by all branches for transmission to the main office and to use uniform financial reports for the transmission of branch office financial results from the main office to the partners in charge of the branch offices.

[2]—Decentralized Approach

Law firms that take a "decentralized approach" to branch office coordination are usually those firms which: (1) are democratically organized, (2) encourage local autonomy to promote practice development, (3) have a history of mergers and (4) have branch offices which are sizable in comparison to the main office. Under the decentralized approach, each branch office manager reports: (1) directly to the partner in charge of the branch office and (2) indirectly (i.e., in an advisory capacity) to the firm's Executive Director in the main office.

In addition to a decentralized organization structure, the decentralized approach to branch office coordination includes decentralized (and sometimes different): (1) accounting systems, (2) accounting procedures, (3) internal accounting controls and (4) financial reports. This approach typically places the burden of coordination on the shoulders of the firm's Executive Director and its Controller. They are faced with two challenges: (1) to ensure that the firm's financial objectives are met; notwithstanding the differences in the branches' systems, procedures, and controls, and (2) to ensure that consistent consolidated financial reports are presented to the firm's partners, notwithstanding the differences in the branches' financial reporting formats.

[3]—Comparison of Centralized vs. Decentralized Approach

Figure 14-I provides an example of an organization chart illustrating a comparison of the centralized vs. the decentralized approach to branch office coordination.

Figure 14-I. Illustration of examples of law firm organization charts comparing a centralized administration approach with a decentralized administration approach.

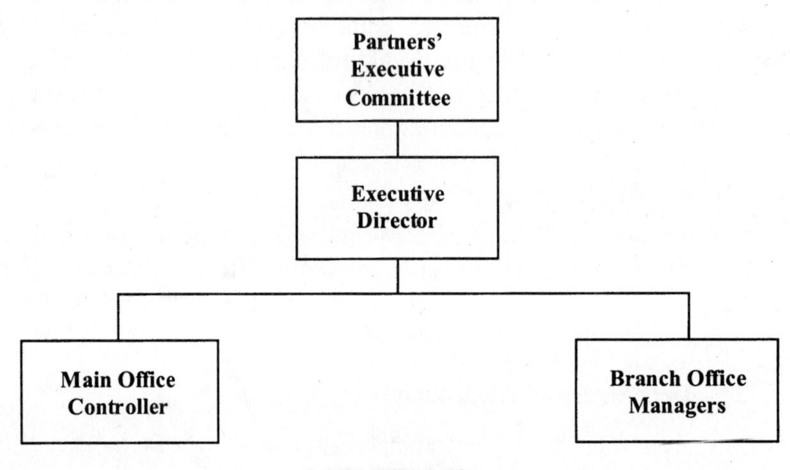

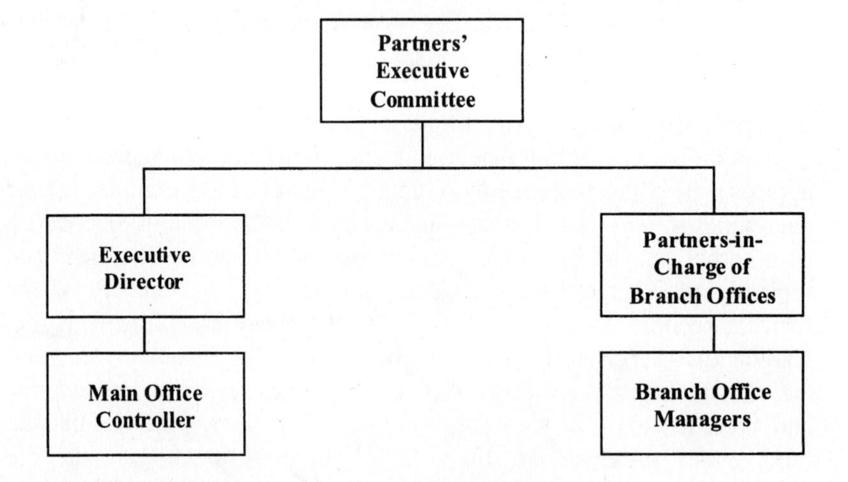

[4]—Combination Approach

Law firms that use either the centralized approach or the decentralized approach often grow to the realization that neither approach can be used effectively in all situations. Firms with established, large non-US offices realize that they need a certain amount of autonomy locally, but also need central reporting for management to make good business decisions. Offices that generate a measurable or material part of a firm's revenue often adopt a combination approach so that the offices can be managed locally with local accounts for supervisory or regulatory purposes, and global reporting and overall control for financial and strategic purposes. Offices that do not materially effect a firm's revenue can operate under either approach, depending on what makes sense under the circumstances. Firms also found that a combination approach encourages development of individual management skills in branch offices, while affording the home office the control it needs to effectively manage the firm.

§ 14.05 Responsibilities of the Chief Financial Officer

Depending on the size of the firm, it may have a chief financial officer or a director of finance. When both functions are present in the same firm, the director of finance normally reports to the chief financial officer. For purposes of this section, references are to the duties of chief financial officer of a law firm and often include the responsibility for three functions:

(1) Controller function;
(2) Treasury function; and
(3) Office automation function.

Some examples of the duties of the chief financial officer of a megasize law firm have been listed in the following paragraphs. This list is representative but not all-inclusive or mandatory. The content of each law firm's list of duties for its chief financial officer will depend upon the firm's size, the complexity of its operations, the firm's management structure, the willingness of the partners to delegate responsibilities to an administrative employee, and the qualifications of the individual currently assigned as chief financial officer. Generally, a chief financial officer will retain the treasury function responsibility but will delegate the controller function responsibility to the firm's director of finance or controller and delegate the office automation function responsibility to the firm's information technology manager.

In order to be comprehensive, the following list focuses on the duties of the chief financial officer of a megasize law firm. In small, medium, and large law firms, some of these duties are assumed by the firm's financial partner or managing partner.

[1]—Controller Responsibilities

These responsibilities include:

(1) Providing overall direction and supervision of the general accounting and client accounting operations;

(2) Controlling and supervising preparation of the partnership's financial books, payrolls, and records;

(3) Ensuring that effective systems and procedures for accounting and financial reporting are developed and maintained;

(4) Coordinating the flow of financial information between the partners and internal/external financial and accounting functions;

(5) Directing the timely submission of all federal, local, and state tax reports;

(6) Developing cost accounting studies to determine appropriate charge-out rates or administrative services rendered to clients, such as reproduction, messengers, and similar services; and

(7) Presenting accurate management information in a timely and reliable manner (e.g., submits monthly financial statements and reports on the firm's operations to the management committee.)

[2]—Treasury Responsibilities

These responsibilities include:

(1) Directing the maintenance of an effective system of internal controls to assure proper delegation of responsibilities and appropriate checks and balances within the firm's financial and accounting functions;

(2) Ensuring that effective systems and procedures for financial planning and budgeting are developed and maintained;

(3) Supervising the preparation of financial plans, projections, and budgets for the firm;

(4) Controlling and accounting for all capital expenditures authorized by the firm;

(5) Authorizing operating expenditures for ordinary and necessary expenses provided within the annual budget. Submits request for expenditures in excess of the approved budget for an expense category to the managing partner (or finance committee chairman) for review and approval;

(6) Monitoring the firm's cash position. Submits guidelines to the management committee (or finance committee) for the temporary investment of excess cash balances and for short-term bank borrowings. Invests cash balances and borrows funds to meet working capital needs within established policy guidelines; and

(7) Assessing trends in the firm's income and expenses, identifying targets of opportunity for increasing profitability, and bringing these to the attention of the management committee. (Examples might include excessive investments in unbilled time and disbursements or past-due accounts receivable.)

[3]—Office Automation Responsibilities

These responsibilities include:

(1) Supervising the procurement and design of the firm's computerized information systems (hardware and software);

(2) Overseeing the management, operation, and maintenance of the firm's data processing, word processing, and data retrieval systems, including equipment and application programs; and

(3) Preparing strategic plans and strategies for developing and integrating new or improved automated systems within the firm.

The preceding discussion identifies all office automation functions as being the responsibility of the chief financial officer of a megasize law firm. In practice, this is only one type of organization structure. Other structures include: (a) the director of administration being responsible for all office automation functions, (b) the duties are split, with the director of finance being responsible for data processing and the director of administration handling word processing and data retrieval and (c) a director of information technology reporting directly to the partners' automation committee. Very often the responsibility for office automation activities is delegated to the individual with the most experience and knowledge in this area, irrespective of the individual's title in the firm.

§ 14.06 Key Tasks of Finance Function Supervisors

Finance function supervisors (with the exception of the information technology supervisor) usually report directly to the law firm's controller. For purposes of supervision, the accounting department typically is divided into functional sections, each composed of one or more employees. The workflow in each section is under the direction of a supervisor. A megasize law firm usually engages several finance function supervisors. Some typical positions include:

(1) Billing and collections supervisor;
(2) Payroll supervisor;
(3) Accounts payable supervisor;
(4) Cashier supervisor;
(5) Financial reporting supervisor;
(6) General ledger supervisor;
(7) Partners' accounts supervisor;
(8) Special projects supervisor; and
(9) Information systems supervisor.

Key tasks assigned to staff in each section under the direction of finance function supervisors will depend on many factors, including the size of the firm, complexity of its systems, and the level of experience and knowledge of the individuals assigned to the positions. The main purposes of each supervisory position and some examples of key tasks carried out by staff under the direction of each supervisor are listed in the following paragraphs. The tasks identified in these lists are representative, but they are neither all-inclusive nor mandatory. Additionally, these tasks may be performed manually or with the aid of automated systems. The supervisor positions and tasks include:

[1]—Billing and Collections Supervisor

The main purposes of this position are: (1) to maintain accurate and complete time accumulation and billing records, (2) to ensure that all bills to be rendered are properly prepared, approved, and processed by controlling input to and output from the client accounting system and (3) to assist partners in collection of fees in a timely manner. Some key tasks carried out under the direction of the billing and collections supervisor are:

- Monitoring the submission of lawyer time;
- Issuing a list of those lawyers delinquent in the reporting of their chargeable time;
- Preparing information for client bills for input into the client accounting system;

- Reviewing completed work-in-progress ledgers and accounts receivable ledgers for completeness and accuracy and arranging for distribution to relevant attorneys;
- Reconciling daily activity reports with changes in unbilled time and uncollected receivables;
- Reconciling monthly trial balances of work-in-process ledgers and fees receivable ledgers with control accounts;
- Providing attorneys with requested detail on status of unbilled time and disbursements, bills rendered and remittances received; and
- Providing information and follow-up on overdue bills to attorneys, as requested.

[2]—Payroll Supervisor

The main purposes of this position are: (1) to maintain accurate and complete payroll accounting records, (2) to ensure timely preparation and distribution of payroll checks, (3) to be responsible for filing various mandatory reports, such as W-2 forms and long-term disability reports, and (4) to coordinate with the human resource or benefits department to provide payroll information for benefit purposes and to key in to the payroll system withholding deductions for health insurance, 401(k) deductions, life insurance, etc. Some key tasks carried out under the direction of the payroll supervisor are:

- Receiving, controlling and submitting payroll information concerning additions, changes and terminations for input into the payroll system;
- Reviewing the completed payroll register, payroll expense distribution, payroll checks and direct deposit authorization for completeness and accuracy;
- Arranging for the signing and distribution of payroll checks or direct deposit of net pay into employees' bank accounts (if this function is done in-house, checks are normally signed by a signature machine);
- Reconciling the totals in the payroll register to the total input data;
- Reconciling the current payroll register with the prior payroll register, taking into account additions, changes and terminations; and
- Preparing and filing various payroll compliance reports such as withholding tax returns, W-2 forms, and long-term disability reports.

Instead of maintaining their own payroll departments, many firms opt to outsource the payroll functions to companies that specialize in payroll processing. Payroll companies are equipped to handle payroll for employees working in most states and prepare all of the required tax or accounting forms needed to substantiate payroll. Outsourcing often saves law firms money and allows them to reduce the number of support staff without effecting the periodic payroll deadlines. When the payroll function is outsourced, the payroll supervisor acts as a liaison with the payroll company.

[3]—Accounts Payable Supervisor

The main purposes of this position are: (1) to maintain accurate and complete cash disbursement records, (2) to ensure that all vendors' invoices and lawyers' expense reimbursement requests are properly approved, controlled, and processed for payment and (3) to be responsible for the timely preparation of checks drawn or wire transfers made to pay for the firm's expenditures and its client disbursements. Some key tasks carried out under the direction of the accounts payable supervisor are:

- Receiving, controlling and submitting approved vendors' invoices and lawyers' expense reimbursement requests for input into the accounts payable system;
- Updating the vendor masterfile with approved changes;
- Reviewing completed cash payments register, firm expense listing, client disbursements listing (i.e., input into the client accounting system), vendors' checks, lawyers' expense reimbursement checks, and wire transfer authorizations for completeness and accuracy;
- Arranging for signing and mailing of checks and authorization of wire transfers;
- Reconciling firm expenses listing and client disbursements listing with total of cash payments register;
- Handling vendor inquiries; and
- Preparing a vendor changes report highlighting changes in the status of the firm's vendors for review by management.

[4]—Cashier Supervisor

The main purposes of this position are: (1) to maintain accurate and complete cash receipt records, (2) to ensure that all cash received (principally checks) is properly recorded and deposited on a daily basis and (3) to be responsible for the compilation of financial data (identifying client and matter) to be entered into the firm's client accounting system to reflect the collection of outstanding bills. Some key tasks carried out under the direction of the Cashier Supervisor are:

- Receiving, controlling and depositing checks received from clients;
- Preparing, controlling and submitting remittance advices for input into the client accounting system;
- Reviewing completed cash receipts register and client collections listing for completeness and accuracy; and
- Providing information on status of client cash collections to attorneys, as requested.

In large and megasize firms, computers have modified the responsibilities of a cashier supervisor, to a point that many of these firms no longer have such a position. Firms that use lock boxes in banks are given computer files that account for daily receipts, so general accounting personnel often handle this function. The Internet has introduced a new means to collect cash from clients through electronic transfers. Here again, this function is often integrated into the job responsibilities of a member of the accounting department.

[5]—Financial Reporting Supervisor

The main purpose of this position is to supervise the accurate and complete preparation of: (1) financial reports to be furnished to the firm's managing partner, executive committee, and the partners in general, (2) financial reports to be furnished to external sources, such as banks and (3) reports to be furnished to tax authorities. Some key tasks carried out under the direction of the financial reporting supervisor are:

- Receiving, controlling and submitting financial statement source data for input into the management information system;
- Receiving, controlling and submitting management report source data (i.e., output from the client accounting system and selected data from statistical records) for input into the management information system;
- Reviewing completed financial statements and management reports (e.g., utilization reports, realization reports, speed of collection reports, leverage reports) for accuracy and completeness;
- Reconciling financial statements and management reports to underlying supporting records such as general ledger trial balance; and

- Furnishing appropriate financial reports to management, partners, banks and taxing authorities.

[6]—General Ledger Supervisor

The main purposes of this positions are: (1) to maintain accurate and complete general ledger accounting records, (2) to prepare monthly and quarterly trial balances and (3) to provide data to the financial reporting supervisor for preparation of financial statements. Some key tasks carried out under the direction of the general ledger supervisor are:

- Receiving, controlling and submitting general ledger source data (i.e., cash receipts, cash payments, payroll and general journal entries) for input into the general ledger accounting system;
- Maintaining a complete chart of accounts for classifying all accounting transactions;
- Reviewing completed general ledger and trial balance for completeness and accuracy;
- Reconciling balances in general ledger control accounts with balances in subsidiary ledgers (e.g., client disbursements, lawyer expense advances, property and equipment); and
- Handling inquiries from management concerning balances in key accounts (e.g., cash, property and equipment, bank loans).

[7]—Partners' Accounts Supervisor

The main purposes of this position are: (1) to maintain accurate and complete accounting records of the individual partners' current accounts and capital accounts, (2) to ensure that schedules allocating income among the partners are calculated accurately and are in compliance with the partnership agreement and other approved formulas and (3) to be responsible for the preparation of reports to be furnished to current and former partners which set forth their financial interests in the firm. Some key tasks carried out under the direction of the partners' accounts supervisor are:

- Receiving, controlling and submitting partners' accounts source data (i.e., partnership net income, partners' income-sharing percentages, payments to or on behalf of partners), for input (or download from the general ledger accounting system) into partners' accounts spreadsheets maintained on a microcomputer;

- Reviewing completed partners' accounts activity reports for completeness and accuracy (particularly the partners' income allocation calculator); and
- Handling inquiries from partners concerning changes in balances in individual partner's accounts.

[8]—Special Projects Supervisor

The main purpose of this position is to supervise nonroutine finance functions as directed by the firm's chief financial officer. Special projects often include: (1) preparation of financial plans, projections, and budgets, (2) strategic planning and profitability analysis, (3) accounting for partnership retirement plans, employee pension and benefit plans, and insurance programs, and (4) internal audit type activities (unless this function reports directly to the audit committee), such as operational audits of branch offices, review of bank reconciliations, and similar activities. Some key tasks carried out under the direction of the special projects supervisor are:

- Receiving, controlling and submitting special project data (e.g., budget and financial planning data, retirement plan data, insurance data, branch office data) for input into the budget reporting system or spreadsheet program maintained on a microcomputer;
- Reviewing special project reports (e.g., budget reports, retirement plan reports) for completeness and accuracy;
- Reconciling bank account balances and branch office control account balances; and
- Providing management with financial reports on budgets and financial plans, retirement plans, insurance programs and results of internal audit type activities.

[9]—Information Technology Supervisor

The main purposes of this position are: (1) to oversee the operation of information technology in the processing of the firm's general ledger and client accounting activities throughout the world, (2) evaluating and implementing technology that will allow the firm and its attorneys to be more efficient, (3) implementing technology that will allow electronic communication and transfer of documents with clients, and (4) to support the firm's automation committee in planning for future uses of technology.

Some key tasks carried out under the direction of the information technology supervisor are:

- Identifying, procuring, implementing and maintaining information systems hardware, software and communications that support the firm's business objectives;
- Maintaining a reliable information systems hardware and software environment;
- Supporting an effective flow of work into and out of the information systems;
- Implementing security procedures to protect confidential financial data through control of physical and logical access to computer resources; and
- Developing and maintaining a business recovery plan.

SECTION III

TAX PLANNING AND REPORTING

CHAPTER 15

Tax Information Reporting

Chapter Contents

---

§ 15.01 Law Firm Partnership or Corporate Tax Returns

Generally, law firms operating as partnerships or S Corporations are not taxed by the federal government as separate entities. Instead, each partner or owner files an income tax return (either individual or corporate in the case of a professional corporation) and includes his or her share of the law firm's income in that return.

The type of tax return to be filed by the firm depends on how it is organized (e.g., as a partnership, a limited liability company, a limited liability partnership, an S corporation or a regular C corporation). Most law firms are organized as partnerships and, as such, are required to file a U.S. Partnership Return of Income (Form 1065) together with a Schedule K-1 for each partner. Likewise, limited liability partnerships always file partnership returns. Limited Liability Companies that have two or more members, however, can follow the federal law allowing them to file partnership returns, except those operating in Texas where they are required to file as corporations. A law firm operating as an S corporation must file a Form 1120S and issue a special Schedule K-1 (unique to Form 1120S) to each partner. If a law firm is organized as a regular C corporation, it files a Form 1120. Owners of C corporations are taxed only on income distributions, not on their entire share of current profits like partners in a partnership, because tax also is levied at the corporate level.

Since most law firms operate as partnerships, this chapter will focus on the reporting requirements unique to partnerships (remember that limited liability companies with two or more members are treated as partnerships for federal income tax purposes).

The share of partnership income each partner reports on his or her individual income tax return (or corporate return when the partner is a Professional Corporation) generally corresponds to the income reported on the partnership's Schedule K. The firm communicates tax information to individual partners by furnishing each partner with a copy of his or her Schedule K-1 of Form 1065. This schedule includes each partner's share of the partnership's income, as well as each partner's allocated share of certain deductions and credits, tax preference items and other significant data.

Developing partnership tax information for a law firm involves four steps:

(1) Identifying partners' taxable income by type;

(2) Reconciling book income with taxable income;

(3) Preparing the U.S. Partnership Return of Income (Form 1065); and

(4) Preparing each partner's Schedule K-1.

Each of these steps will be discussed in more detail in succeeding sections of this chapter.

Before discussing the development of partnership information, it is relevant to discuss comparatively recent legislation affecting the Internal Revenue Service and the way that some law firms will have to file partnership returns in the future.

[1]—Restructuring the IRS

For decades it seems, it was popular for some people to engage in IRS-bashing. Many believed that the IRS had too much power and was abusing the power they had. In 1998, Congress led the way to sweeping IRS reform by passing the Internal Revenue Service Restructuring and Reform Act of 1998 ("the Act").[1] The law is multi-faceted and will affect the basic structure of the IRS and the way taxpayers, including law firms, deal with the IRS.

Structurally, the IRS will change from a three-tier geographic structure (i.e., national office, regional offices, and district offices) to an organizational structure that focuses on operating units serving particular groups of taxpayers with similar needs (e.g., small businesses, large businesses, not-for-profits, etc.). Included in the plan is a Taxpayer Advocate's Office that will have an independent appeals function and have more latitude to provide assistance to taxpayers. The plan will prohibit the type of unofficial communication that existed in the past between appeals officers and other IRS employees to the extent that those communications appeared to compromise the independence of the appeals function.

The most dramatic change caused by the Act will be the shifting of the burden of proof from the taxpayer to the IRS. Lawyers know that in non-tax matters, the defendant was innocent until proven guilty. That axiom was reversed when it came to tax matters. The Act shifts the burden of proof to the IRS in court proceedings if the taxpayer introduces creditable evidence, cooperates with the IRS, and meets certain record-keeping and substantiation requirements. However, corporations, trusts, and partnerships whose net worth exceeds $7 million cannot shift the burden of proof to the IRS.

State tax laws are unaffected by the federal legislation, so while the burden of proof shifts to the IRS at the federal level, it remains on the taxpayer at the state or local level.

Except for a wave of IRS exams precipitated by the Market Segment Specialization Program on Attorneys,[2] most law firms have not been bothered by IRS examiners combing their the law firm's books and records. One reason for ignoring law firm partnerships was the conflict between the examination division which did all the field work and the regional processing center that processed the adjustment. Since audit adjustments could be processed only by the regional processing center

---

[1] Pub. L. No. 105-206.

[2] Department of the Treasury, Internal Revenue Service Training 3149-102 (Rev. 6-94) TPDS 83183A.

(which then got credit for the adjustment), the IRS field audit supervisor has a dilemma; do the field work and generate a tax adjustment for which his or her team got no credit, or ignore a possible audit target because of a suspicion that an adjustment was possible. Most supervisors opted not to audit so that the revenue per agent evaluation criteria was not effected.

There is growing recognition that the IRS restructuring effort may lead to audits of law firm partnerships, because there is no longer the conflict between the field supervisor doing the work and the regional office getting the credit. Now the same team can initiate the audit, bring in specialists and process the adjustments, thereby giving credit to the team that did the work.

It should be noted that law firms operating as corporations were not effected by the jurisdictional work verses credit issue because an agent could propose an adjustment for a corporation and process the adjustment, thereby keeping the credit in the group.

[2]—Electronic Filing

Like most taxpayers, law firm partnerships historically have filed paper copies of their federal Partnership Returns of Income (i.e., Form 1065) with the Internal Revenue Service. Other taxpayers that file a large number of documents have been required by the IRS to file many of those documents using magnetic media.[3] Congress felt that if some taxpayers could use magnetic media filing, then there was no reason to exempt large partnerships (i.e., those with more than 100 partners) from the same requirement. To facilitate integration of partnership information into existing data systems and to ensure its integrity (i.e., no data entry errors), Congress changed the law requiring that partnerships with more than 100 partners had to file Form 1065 and Schedules K-1 using magnetic media.[4] Initially, the effective date of this legislation was for tax years *ending* on or after December 31, 1997. However, legislative history of the Act provided that the effective date should have been for tax years *beginning* on or after December 31, 1997. The Tax Technical Corrections Act of 1997 corrected the inconsistency so that the law was effective for tax years beginning on or after December 31, 1997.

Based on the amended Internal Revenue Code section, a calendar year-end law firm with more than 100 partners should have filed its 1998 partnership return and K-1s using magnetic media. Fortunately,

---

[3] See General Explanation of Tax Legislation Enacted in 1997 (i.e., Joint Committee Blue Book), page 367.

[4] Taxpayer Relief Act of 1997, P.L. 105-34 amending IRC § 6011(e).

the IRS announced that this requirement would not be mandated until it issued regulations implementing the new magnetic-media-filing requirements. On October 22, 1998, the IRS issued proposed regulations, but indicated that it would give a one-year reprieve to large partnerships, so that they did not have to file 1998 returns on magnetic media. The clear inference from the proposed regulations was that large partnerships would have to file on magnetic media for taxable years ending on or after December 31, 1999, and that the IRS would most likely choose "electronic filing" as the only permissible form of magnetic media available to large partnerships. This did not come as any surprise because several months prior to the issuance of the proposed regulations Congress mandated the use of "electronic filing" to make processing returns more efficient.[5] As the new deadline approached, however, there was concern expressed by many taxpayers and practitioners that not enough information had been communicated to allow large partnerships to prepare for the new filing requirement. Realizing partnership community concerns regarding computer systems and programming changes, the IRS again postponed the effective date. This time, the IRS said that it was waiting for Treasury to issue final regulations before it would implement the new filing requirement. Final regulations were adopted on November 10, 1999 and, as a result, large partnerships with taxable years ending on or after December 31, 2000 must file their federal returns electronically. The same rule applies to large partnerships with foreign addresses for tax years ending before January 1, 2001. Although there are limited exemptions from electronic filing, they are difficult to obtain.

Law firms with more than one hundred partners know they are required to adopt the new electronic filing format. For some law firm partnerships, however, it may not be so obvious. For example, if a partnership had more than 100 partners, it is required to file electronically regardless of whether a partner was a partner for the entire year or whether the partnership had over 100 partners on any particular day in the partnership year.[6] The following examples highlight this requirement:

Example 1: ABC Law Firm Partnership is a general partnership. On January 1, 200X it had 90 equity partners and 5 contract partners. On March 15, 200X it admitted 10 new equity partners and on

[5] Internal Revenue Service Restructuring and Reform Act of 1998, P.L. 105-206 adding new IRC § 6011(f).

[6] Treas. Reg. § 301.6011-3(d)(5); 26 C.F.R. § 301.6011-3(d)(5).

September 29, 200X, 10 equity partners retired. On December 31, 200X ABC had 95 partners. However, since ABC had 105 partners over the course of taxable year 200X, it is required to file electronically.

Example 2: ABC Law Firm Partnership is a general partnership. On January 1, 200X it had 90 equity partners and 5 contract partners. No new partners were admitted during 200X and none retired. However, one of ABC's partners, DE, is a partnership with 50 partners. DE is one partner, regardless of the number of partners DE has. Therefore, ABC has 100 partners and is not required to file its 200X partnership return electronically.

At first glance the general requirement seems quite clear — if a law firm has more than 100 partners it must file its federal Form 1065 electronically. For those firms that have less than 100 partners, more analysis is necessary. As discussed later in this chapter, law firms are increasingly relying on guaranteed payment arrangements to admit contract partners. Not everyone agrees, however, that these so called "contract partners" are actually partners for tax purposes. Whether a contract partner qualifies as a partner for purposes of electronic filing depends on all of the facts and circumstances and should be determined on a case-by-case basis. The IRS, however, probably will look to the actual number of K-1s as the deciding factor. If a law firm has more than 100 K-1s attached to its tax return, regardless of classification (i.e., equity partner or contract partner), it will be required to file its return electronically or subject itself to penalties.

Law firms that are required to file their returns electronically, and fail to do so, are subject to failure to file information return penalties at a rate of $50 per Schedule K-1, up to a maximum of $250,000.[7]

Although the electronic rules are mandatory only for large partnerships, the IRS has stated that it would accept electronically filed returns for partnerships with less than one hundred partners. At this point, a smaller firm can elect to file electronically. In the future, it remains to be seen if the IRS will lower the bar and require partnerships with less than one hundred partners to file electronically.

While it might be obvious which law firms are required to file electronically based on size, it is not quite so obvious what has to be filed electronically. For the most part, only approved federal forms need to be filed electronically. This includes pages one through four

---

[7] Treas. Reg. § 301.6011-3(c); 26 C.F.R. § 301.6011-3(c).

of Form 1065, Schedule K, Schedule K-1 for each partner, and many other government forms (e.g., Form 4797 for sale of business property, Form 4562 for depreciation and amortization, Schedule D for capital gains and losses, etc.) Other parts of the return which are prepared on non-government forms (i.e., white paper schedules which detail other assets, other liabilities, etc.) cannot be filed electronically and must be filed in paper form. Presumably, the IRS will combine those parts of the return that are filed electronically with those that are filed in paper form. It is anticipated that the IRS will add additional forms to the electronic filing list as it becomes more proficient with electronic filing for partnerships.

Once a determination has been made that a law firm partnership is required to file its return electronically, a decision needs to be made how it is going to comply with the final regulation. The first question that a firm might ask is who is going to actually transmit the return electronically? There are three groups that the IRS may qualify to transmit Form 1065. They are:

- The law firm itself — the law firm can create electronic return data (i.e., Form 1065, Schedules K-1 and related forms and schedules) through commercially available tax software. It is the responsibility of the firm to ensure that the return data is transmitted to the IRS.
- The return preparer or originator (typically a public accounting firm) — the return originator can work with the law firm to collect the return data and transmit such data to the IRS on behalf of the law firm.
- The transmitter — a firm, organization or individual who receives return data and transmits such data to the IRS.

Participants who expect to file electronic returns with the IRS must file Form 9041, Application for Electronic Filing of Business and Employee Benefit Plan Returns, with the Austin Service Center at least sixty calendar days prior to transmission of tax return data. Upon verification of Form 9041, the IRS will assign an Electronic Transmitter Identification Number ("ETIN") and a temporary password to each registered participant. This will enable participants to start testing, which is mandatory and should be done at least sixty calendar days prior to transmission. Using the sixty-day advanced period as a benchmark, law firm partnerships that intend to file their own partnership returns electronically should allow sufficient lead time internally to establish processing procedures and to complete the necessary test files. The time required to complete internal matters should be added to the mandatory sixty-day window to calculate the lead time needed to be capable of filing electronically.

If a law firm uses a third-party transmitter to file its return, the law firm is not required to file Form 9041 with the IRS.

Once a law firm files Form 9041, receives verification, and successfully completes transmission of the test package, it is ready to transmit live 1065 data. In conjunction with the transmission of the 1065 data, the electronic tax return also must be properly executed. Form 8453-P, U.S. Partnership Declaration and Signature for Electronic Filing, serves as the required signature document for the electronically filed tax return. It is the paper part of the return that transmits other tax forms and supporting documentation that could not be filed electronically. Examples of some documents that will be attached to the paper part of the return are:

(1) Forms and schedules not required by the IRS;

(2) Forms and schedules not approved by the IRS; or

(3) Forms and schedules that are required to be attached to the electronically filed return but require separate signatures (e.g., Form 5713, International Boycott Report).

As with most other government regulations, there are always exceptions to the general rule. Generally, the following partnership tax returns are excluded from filing electronically:

(1) Amended returns;

(2) Fiscal year returns ending any month after August 31st of the current tax year;

(3) Delinquent returns (except returns covered by an extension of time to file, which was submitted to the service center where the paper return would have been filed);

(4) Short period returns;

(5) Returns with foreign addresses (not required for tax years ending before January 1, 2001);

(6) Nominee returns;

(7) Returns with any dollar amount greater than $99,999,999,999; and

(8) Returns for inactive partnerships with no income on pages 1, 2, 3 and 4 of Form 1065.

Presently, states do not require partnerships to file Form 1065 electronically. However, several states have initiated projects to investigate electronic filing and are expected to have computer systems comparable to the IRS's in the next few years.

Although the original purpose of implementing electronic filing was to integrate data systems and to prevent data-entry errors, the successful implementation of this program will have a profound impact on partners' everywhere. The IRS will now have partner K-1 information available in a format that will allow cross-referencing to a partner's electronically filed Form 1040. As a result, it will be significantly easier for the IRS to perform materiality checks on certain items such as unreimbursed business expenses, which are typically deducted from a partner's ordinary income. The IRS will have a much easier time identifying non-filers by cross checking K-1s to the data file of those filed tax returns. Once a partner's name and EIN (or ITIN) are entered into a database, a simple query will confirm if that partner filed an individual tax return.

§ 15.02 Reconciliation of Book Net Income with Ordinary Income for Tax Purposes

The first steps in reconciling book net income to ordinary income for tax purposes are to determine what income is taxable, what expenses are deductible, and what items have to be reported separately to the partners.

Identifying net book income normally is not difficult, because law firms generally maintain their books and records and prepare their financial statements using the modified cash basis method of accounting. However, because of unique reporting conventions required for income tax reporting purposes, certain adjustments must be made to conform "book net income" to "ordinary income" for tax purposes on Form 1065. These adjustments can be categorized into (1) nontaxable income and nondeductible expenses, (2) timing differences in reporting, and (3) separately accounted for items.

[1]—Nontaxable Income and Nondeductible Expenses

Items of income or expense that flow through book net income but will never be taxable or deductible for federal income tax purposes are referred to as "permanent differences." As a general rule, law firms have very few permanent differences. Although an item is a permanent difference for federal income tax purposes, it may not be for state tax purposes.

There are two types of permanent differences:

[a]—Nontaxable Income

The Internal Revenue Code provides that certain items of income are nontaxable (e.g., interest income on certain municipal bonds). To the extent that this income is included in book net income, it must be excluded in arriving at ordinary income for tax purposes. Income excluded for federal income tax purposes may be a tax preference item for alternative minimum tax purposes and taxable for state income tax purposes.

[b]—Nondeductible Expenses

The Internal Revenue Code also provides that certain items of expenses are not deductible for tax purposes (e.g., partners' life insurance premiums, partners' annual physicals, partners' parking, disallowed business meal and entertainment expenses, penalties or fines, and club dues). To the extent that these expenses were deducted in determining book net income, they must be added back to arrive at ordinary income for tax purposes. These items need to be re-evaluated for state income tax purposes (e.g., a few states allow a full deduction—no limitation—for ordinary and necessary meal and entertainment expenses).

[2]—Timing Differences in Reporting

A timing difference is an item of income or expense that will be reflected in book net income and ordinary income in different taxable years. Unlike permanent differences that never reverse, timing differences reverse over some period of time—often in the following year and sometimes over many years.

Conceptually, there are four categories of timing differences: (1) income included in the tax return, but not on the books; (2) expenses on the books, but not deducted on the tax return; (3) income on the books, not on the return; and (4) expenses on the return, not on the books.

Some typical timing differences are depreciation or amortization of property, contributions to defined contribution or defined benefit plans, valuation reserves, prepaid items (income or expense items), capitalized interest under Internal Revenue Code Section 263A, Subpart F income, and differences in accounting methods (e.g., opening adjustments from changing an accounting method for tax purposes).

[3]—Separately Stated Items

The third step in reconciling book net income to ordinary income for a partnership is to identify items of income and expense that Congress mandated must be reported directly to the partners.[1]

Except for guaranteed payments which are specifically allocated, these separately stated items are apportioned to each partner based on the partner's profit sharing percentage. A law firm partnership reports separately stated items to each partner on a Schedule K-1.

[a]—Rental Income or Loss

Generally, income or loss from real estate and other rental activities is excluded from "ordinary income" in order to isolate items which may be subject to "passive activity" limitations. Tax rules limit the amount of losses that a partner may claim from passive activities. Generally, losses from passive activities can be offset only against income from passive activities, not against law firm services income or portfolio income. A rental activity is considered to be a passive activity, unless the material participation in a real estate business requirement is met.

---

[1] IRC § 702(a); 26 U.S.C. § 702(a).

In the case of a law firm partnership, a passive activity is any activity in which the partnership does not participate on a regular, continuous, and substantial basis. For example, a law firm invests in another partnership which owns and leases office space in a city where the law firm does not have an office. However, based on the law firm's particular facts and circumstances, a rental activity that is insubstantial to the practice of law may be considered an "appropriate economic unit" and, therefore, income or loss from the rental activity may be combined with income from the practice of law. For example, subleasing some of a law firm's unused office space in the building where the firm has its office may be "insubstantial" and, therefore, not reportable as a passive activity.

Each partner is expected to report this income or loss (subject to the relevant limitations) on his or her individual income tax return. (Professional Corporation partners report this income or loss on a corporate tax return.)

[b]—Portfolio Income and Investment Interest Expense

For tax reporting purposes, (1) "portfolio income" arising from interest, dividends, and royalties, (2) deductions related to portfolio income, and (3) interest expense on investment debts are excluded from ordinary income in order to isolate items which are affected by the "investment interest" limitations. Included in portfolio income is interest earned on overnight deposits of working capital. However, interest earned on accounts receivable is not portfolio income. Each partner is expected to report this income and expense (subject to the relevant limitations) on his or her individual income tax return. (Professional Corporation partners report this income or loss on a corporate tax return.)

[c]—Capital or Section 1231 Gains or Losses

Income or loss from the disposition of marketable securities or from the disposition of property used in the business (e.g., sale of leasehold improvements or furniture and fixtures) are typical items excluded from ordinary income under the auspices of capital or Section 1231 gains or losses. Gain or loss is determined by deducting the tax basis of the asset (representing cost less accumulated depreciation or amortization) from the sales price for the asset.

The Tax Relief Act of 1997 made important changes to the capital gain rules by applying different tax rates depending on how long an asset was held and when it was sold. In retrospect, the rules were considered too complicated because they created three categories of capital assets and required more analysis and calculations to determine what tax rate applied to each sale. The rules particularly created havoc with mutual funds that declared mid-year and year-end dividends.

Recognizing the complexity that they created and wishing to lower the overall capital gains rates, Congress changed the law during 1998 to retroactively eliminate the eighteen-month holding period and replaced it with the historic twelve-month holding period. The new twelve-month period applies for tax years ending after 1997 for non-corporate taxpayers. The maximum capital gain rate for most people is now 20%. For taxable years beginning after December 31, 2000 a special 18% capital gains tax rate applies to sales of most assets held more than five years. There are special rules associated with capital gains and different rates (e.g., 8%, 10%, 28%) apply depending on the type of property sold and the tax bracket of a person for the year in which the sale takes place.

Each equity partner's share of these gains or losses is reported separately on each partner's Schedule K-1 either as long-term or short-term capital gain or loss or as Section 1231 gains or losses. Depending on its source, each percentage partner is expected to report this income on either Schedule D or on Form 4797 of his or her individual income tax return. (Professional Corporation partners report this income on either Schedule D or a corporate Form 4797.)

[d]—Guaranteed Payments to Partners

Guaranteed payments for a law firm partnership represent amounts paid to one or more of its partners for services rendered or for the use of capital if the payments are determined without regard to partnership income. Fixed payments of this type are often made by a law firm partnership to: (a) former partners or spouses of former partners under a retirement arrangement, (b) newly admitted partners for the initial year during which their share of fees collected is minimal, (c) fixed distribution partners who do not have a percentage interest in the firm, or (d) partners receiving premium compensation while temporarily assigned to foreign offices.

As law firms face growth challenges, they increasingly use guaranteed payment arrangements to compensate partners. Guaranteed payment arrangements allow law firms to admit lateral partners or individuals with unique specialties without the complexities of making them full equity partners. This is normally done with the understanding that if a person "proves" himself or herself during a trial period, then the firm will consider the person for full-equity status after the evaluation period ends. The evaluation period is important because it does not bind the firm as much as admitting a lateral equity partner might and it quantifies how much the firm is willing to have at risk economically while the person is evaluated for full-equity status. In the case of a person who brings a unique specialty to the firm, but is not regarded as qualified for full-equity status, using the guaranteed payment option allows a "win win" situation. The individual is held out as a partner to clients and is treated the same way as full-equity partners (except for sharing a percentage of firm profits) and the firm adds a specialty practice to its arsenal of available legal services. From a pragmatic perspective, admitting a person under a properly structured guaranteed payment agreement allows the firm to "terminate" the person at the end of an evaluation period or if the person does not meet the expectations of the firm.

There is a saying that you can only slice a pie so many ways. In the context of law firm profits, the saying means that distributable profits can only be split so many ways. Unless, of course, a law firm agreement considers two types of partners: equity partners and guaranteed payment partners. Using guaranteed payments allows a firm to alter the split of firm profits so that each group is compensated differently while at the same time holding them all out to the public as "partners."

Not everyone agrees, however, that a person receiving a guaranteed payment is a partner for tax purposes. Some argue that only one who shares profits or losses or has an economic risk can be a true partner. Anyone else, they argue, is an employee, *albeit* a highly paid employee, no matter the title.

The Internal Revenue Code defines "partner" as "a member of the partnership."[2] The question then is, what is a member? The answer depends on the facts and circumstances. The Supreme Court said that a partnership is created, "when persons join together their money, goods, labor, or skill for the purpose of carrying on a trade, business, or profession and where there is community of interest in the profits and losses."[3] In a later decision, the Supreme Court emphasized the importance of the intent of the parties "to join together in the present conduct" of business.[4]

Law firms demonstrate their intent to have guaranteed payment partners in various ways. Some firms modify their partnership agreements to provide for different classes of partners, so that guaranteed partners are formally acknowledged as partners. Other firms pass on making changes to the partnership agreement (assuming there is a written partnership agreement) and simply create the alternative classification.

---

[2] IRC § 761(b); 26 U.S.C. § 761(b).

[3] Commissioner v. Tower, 327 U.S. 280, 66 S.Ct. 532, 90 L.Ed. 670 (1946) and Commissioner v. Culbertson, 337 U.S. 733, 69 S.Ct. 1210, 93 L.Ed. 1659 (1949).

[4] *Commissioner v. Culbertson, supra.*

Some firms do not intend that persons receiving guaranteed payments be considered partners. These firms might designate a person as a partner solely to enhance a person's reputation and to aid in attracting new clients. They conclude that since the person receives only a guaranteed payment and does not share in profits, he or she is not a partner, but is an employee. If the firm subjects the guaranteed payment to the normal payroll taxes, then it is demonstrating its intention to classify the recipient as an employee and not as a partner. This principle was demonstrated in a case involving two individuals who were held out to the public as partners, but treated as employees by the firm. The firm paid their employment taxes, paid their medical and vacation benefits, and did not allow them to participate in partner meetings. The individuals had federal and state taxes withheld from their paychecks and never claimed any benefits otherwise associated with partners. The court held that these "special partners" were employees and not partners.[5]

Title then is not a determinant. Some factors that point to the intent are:

- Does the person make a capital contribution of any amount?
- Does the person share profits in any way?
- Does the person have a vote on partnership matters?
- Does the person sign a partnership agreement?
- Does the firm announce to clients the admission of the person as a partner?
- Does the guaranteed payment agreement document an understanding between the firm and the individual that he or she will be considered a partner?
- Does the person pay his or her own self-employment taxes?
- Are FICA and FUTA taxes withheld by the firm?
- Does the firm include the person in a list of partners in its federal, state and local tax returns?
- Does the person enjoy partner attributes (i.e., partner office, partner retirement plans, partner health or benefit plans, luncheon or country clubs, etc.)?
- Does the person have the authority to accept new clients, to make billing decisions, or to bind the firm?
- Is the person liable for partnership liabilities or losses?

[5] Matter of Ladas and Perry, N.Y. City Tax App. Trib. No TAT(H) 98-19(UB), Feb. 24, 2000.

Given the wide range of variables, there is no clear and accepted answer to when a person receiving a guaranteed payment is a partner for tax purposes. Generally, state law does not control the classification of an entity for federal tax purposes.[6] State law, however, can be a factor in the determination of whether a person is a partner for federal tax purposes. For New York State tax purposes, a person was considered to be a partner when he reported his compensation on his federal tax return as partnership income, the firm did not withhold any payroll taxes, and he paid his own social security taxes.[7] He was considered to be a partner even though he was not required to contribute to the firm's capital, had no interest in the partnership assets, did not participate in partnership decisions as to management, did not receive a share of profits, and was not liable for partnership losses. However, when a person signed an agreement which admitted him to a New York law firm as a partner and provided that in addition to a guaranteed payment he would share in the excess profits of the Washington, D.C. office, the person was not considered to be a partner for New York State purposes because the firm reported his compensation as a salary in its partnership return.[8] This despite the fact that the individual paid his own self-employment taxes.

Often, if a firm holds out a person to the public (i.e., to clients) as a partner and treats the person like a partner internally (e.g., issues a Schedule K-1), then those are signs that the person is closer to the partner attributes than to the employee attributes. The issuance of a Schedule K-1 is not controlling either as demonstrated in a case involving a Texas partner who California determined not to be a partner, even though he was issued a federal K-1.[9] In the final analysis, the determination of whether a person receiving a guaranteed payment is a partner depends on the particular facts and circumstances and cannot be distilled into a comprehensive checklist.

Guaranteed payments are deducted in the year paid on Form 1065 by a partnership in arriving at ordinary income and are reported separately to each recipient partner. However, a partner receiving a guaranteed payment does not necessarily receive a share of ordinary income. In a sense, a partner, for a myriad of reasons, agrees to accept a guaranteed payment instead of a share of ordinary income. Guaranteed payment

---

[6] Commissioner v. Tower, 327 260, 66 S.Ct. 532, 90 L.Ed. 670 (1946) and Commissioner v. W.O. Culbertson, Sr., 337 U.S. 733, 69 S.Ct. 1210, 93 L.Ed. 1659 (1949).

[7] In the Matter of James H. Heller v. New York State Tax Commission, 116 A.D.2d 901, 498 N.Y.S.2d 211 (A.D. 3d Dept. 1986).

[8] Petition of Walter Pozen, 79-80 NY-TAXRPTR-TB ¶ 98-130 (1979).

[9] Charles C. Frederiksen, SBOE No., 98-A-0162, Jan 7, 1999.

agreements should be negotiated by the partner and the law firm and should be documented *prior* to the effective date of the agreement (e.g., a calendar year law firm should negotiate guaranteed payment agreements prior to the beginning of the applicable year). Federal and state tax implications associated with guaranteed payments should be understood prior to entering into a guaranteed payment agreement.

In addition to the types of guaranteed payments identified previously, amounts paid by the firm on behalf of the partners for personal expenses are guaranteed payments if the amounts are taken as a deduction on Form 1065. (e.g., health insurance premiums, fees paid to prepare individual income tax returns, health club fees, annual physical examinations, foreign housing allowances, cost of living allowances, etc.)

Each partner must report guaranteed payments as income on his or her individual income tax return. (Professional Corporation partners report this income on a corporate tax return.) Some of the items classified as guaranteed payments also may give rise to deductions on a partner's personal income tax return (e.g., fees to prepare a personal income tax return, health insurance premiums, and foreign housing allowances.)

[e]—Charitable Contributions

Deductions for charitable contributions made by the firm are not applied as a reduction in determining "ordinary income." Instead, each partner is entitled to take a charitable contribution deduction, subject to formula limitations on the partner's personal income tax return. (Professional Corporation partners report these amounts, subject to formula limitations on a corporate tax return.)

[f]—Section 179 Expense Deduction

Under special circumstances and subject to specific limitations, a law firm partnership can elect to expense tangible property purchased during a year. The election is referred to as a Section 179 expense deduction. If a firm elects this benefit, the Section 179 expense deduction must be allocated to each percentage partner and reported separately on the partner's Schedule K-1. The partner must accumulate all Section 179 expense deductions from whatever source and pass another limitation test before taking the tax advantage on a personal income tax return.

[g]—Other Deductions

The last separately reported item is other deductions. This "catchall" classification includes expenses which are required to be reported separately because they are partner-related items and, as such, are deductible only (subject to appropriate limitations) on a partner's personal income tax return. They are not deducted in arriving at the firm's ordinary income, except to the extent that they are classified as guaranteed payments. Typical items in this category are payments to partner retirement plans (i.e., Keoghs, IRAs, or SEPs), partner health insurance premiums, a partner's share of state taxes paid on composite returns, and fees paid by a firm to prepare a partner's personal income tax return. Each partner must analyze the composition of other deductions reported on the partner's Schedule K-1 to determine the appropriate income tax treatment and how to report the items on an individual or corporate income tax return.

[4]—Ordinary Income

Simply stated, ordinary income is the net income or loss of a partnership exclusive of separately stated items (e.g., guaranteed payments, capital gains or losses, portfolio income, and passive activity income or loss). It is the result of adjusting book net income for income that is taxable, expenses that are deductible, and items that have to be reported separately to each partner. Ordinary income is determined each year by following procedures set forth in the instructions to the U.S. Partnership Return of Income (Form 1065) and by reference to Revenue Procedures and Notices issued by the Internal Revenue Service.

Generally, ordinary income is allocated to partners based on their share of firm profits. Figure 15-A illustrates a law firm partnership's reconciliation of book net income with ordinary income and presents examples of the reconciling adjustments previously discussed.

Figure 15-A. Illustration of a law firm partnership's reconciliation of book net income with ordinary income for tax purposes (Form 1065).

ABC LAW FIRM PARTNERSHIP
RECONCILIATION OF BOOK NET INCOME
WITH ORDINARY INCOME FOR TAX PURPOSES
(FORM 1065)

	Partnership	Partner A
Book net income	$8,900,000	$255,000
Separately stated items:		
Guaranteed payments to partners	(400,000)	—
Gain on disposition of marketable securities	(30,000)	(900)
Charitable contributions	50,000	1,500
Dividend/Interest income	(80,000)	(2,400)
Partner health insurance premiums	100,000	3,000
Nontaxable income and unallowable deductions:		
Tax-exempt interest income	(20,000)	(600)
Partners' life insurance premiums	20,000	600
Disallowed business meal and entertainment expenses	50,000	1,500
Timing differences in reporting:		
Different depreciation accounting methods	(40,000)	(1,200)
Ordinary income for tax purposes	$8,550,000	$256,500

§ 15.03 U.S. Partnership Return of Income (Form 1065)

As with the preparation of any tax return, the preparer of the law firm's U.S. Partnership Return of Income should (a) gather relevant tax information in an orderly manner, (b) seek competent tax advice when important judgments are required, and (c) exercise care in following the instructions to the form.

Five sections of the return are of particular relevance because they report detailed financial information for tax purposes. They are: (1) income and deduction items comprising ordinary income; (2) Partners' Share of Income, Credits, Deductions, etc. (Schedule K); (3) Balance Sheets (Schedule L); (4) Reconciliation of Income per Books With Income per Return (Schedule M-1); and (5) Analysis of Partners' Capital Accounts (Schedule M-2).

[1]—Income and Deduction Items Comprising Ordinary Income

For purposes of reporting income and deduction items on U.S. Partnership Return of Income, it is necessary to conform income and expense items included in the law firm's "Statement of Revenue Collected and Expenses Disbursed" to captions identified on the tax form. Two steps are required:

[a]—Adjustments

As previously mentioned in this chapter, the book income and expense amounts must be adjusted for (1) nontaxable income and nondeductible expenses, (2) timing differences in reporting, and (3) separately stated items.

[b]—Reclassification

The book income and expense amounts must be reclassified using tax return captions. For example, certain expenses (e.g., rent and repairs or maintenance) must be categorized under their own captions on a tax return, whereas these expenses were included in an aggregate functional expense caption (i.e., occupancy costs) for book purposes. Law firms can simplify the reclassification process by conforming the financial statement presentation to the tax return presentation.

Figure 15-B illustrates a worksheet for conforming a law firm partnership's income and expenses from a book reporting format to the tax reporting format outlined in U.S. Partnership Return of Income (Form 1065).

Figure 15-B. Illustration of a worksheet for conforming a law firm partnership's income and expenses from a book reporting format to the tax reporting format outlined in U.S. Partnership Return of Income.

ABC LAW FIRM PARTNERSHIP
WORKSHEET FOR CONFORMING
INCOME AND EXPENSES
BOOK FORMAT TO TAX FORMAT (FORM 1065)
($ in thousands)

	Line Item on Tax Return	Book Format	Adjustments (Fig. 15-A)	Reclassifications	Tax Format
1	Gross receipts or sales	$20,000			$20,000
2	Cost of goods sold				
4	Other partnerships' income				
5	Net farm profit				
6	Net gain (loss) from sale of business property	30	(30)		—
7	Other income				
--	Interest/dividend	100	(100)		—
9	Salaries and wages	(6,000)		680	(5,320)
10	Guaranteed payments to partners		(400)		(400)
11	Repairs and maintenance			(80)	(80)
12	Bad debts	(40)			(40)
13	Rent expense	(2,000)		180	(1,820)
14	Taxes and licenses	(250)			(250)
15	Interest expense (not claimed elsewhere)				
16	Depreciation		(40)	(100)	(140)
17	Depletion				
18	Retirement plans			(110)	(110)
19	Employee benefit programs			(570)	(570)
--	Partners' life and health insurance premiums	(120)	120		—
20	Other deductions	(2,520)		(200)	(2,720)
--	Business meal and entertainment expenses	(250)	50	200	—
--	Charitable contributions	(50)	50		—
22	22 Ordinary income	$8,900	($350)	$0	$8,550

[2]—Partners' Shares of Income, Credits, Deductions, etc. (Schedule K)

Schedule K of Form 1065 is designed to identify the partners' share of income, credits, deductions, etc., that are required to be reported directly to each partner. Schedule K is the summary form that accumulates the separately stated items reported to each partner on Schedule K-1.

A partnership's net income is calculated on the top of page 4 of Form 1065 in the section "Analysis of Net Income (Loss)." Line 1 of that section is the mathematical result of combining certain separately stated items from Schedule K (i.e., the combination of lines 1 through 7 less the sum of lines 8 through 11 and 14a, 17g, and 18b). In theory, the result represents the net income of a partnership, but in practice it might not because Schedule K may include such items as partners' health insurance or retirement payments that are included in line 11 (i.e., other deductions), but were not charged to book income in determining the distributable income of the firm. The same is true of foreign taxes (e.g., French or Japanese taxes) that are assessed against each partner and not charged to net income, but for reporting purposes are reported on line 17g.

Line 2 of the Analysis of Net Income is used to stratify net income by type of partner. The stratification requires significant analysis to break out net income by type of partner. Unfortunately, the form does not consider special situations such as a partner who left the firm in a previous year (i.e., not active), but is receiving a current payment, or a partner who retired and is receiving a guaranteed payment. These types of exceptions are normally entered on line 2a in column (vi).

To verify that Schedule K balances with other parts of Form 1065, ordinary income on line 1 should agree with line 22 of Form 1065 on page 1. Also, net income on line 1 of the Analysis of Net Income should agree with line 9 of Schedule M-1 on page 4.

An illustration of how aggregate partners' income and deductions on Schedule K correlates with individual partner's share of these items on Schedule K-1 is presented in Figure 15-C. Instructions to Schedule K-1 and Revenue Procedures or Notices issued by the Internal Revenue Service identify the type of items to be included under the caption "Other deductions" (line 11). Some items shown as other deductions may not have been deducted by a law firm in computing its income. Those items are reported on line 11 as an accommodation or reminder to a partner that some of these items should be reported on the partner's personal or corporate tax return.

Figure 15-C. Illustration of law firm partners' share of income and deductions reported on Schedule K and Schedule K-1 of U.S. Partnership Return of Income.

ABC LAW FIRM PARTNERSHIP
PARTNERS' SHARE OF INCOME AND DEDUCTIONS
(Form 1065 Tax Return Format)

Line No.	Item on Tax Return	Schedule K (Partnership)	Schedule K-1 (Partnership)
1	Ordinary income (loss)	$8,550,000	$265,500
2	Real estate rental income (loss)		
3	Other rental income(loss)		
4	Portfolio income (loss)	80,000	2,400
--	Dividends/interest	30,000	900
--	Capital Gains	400,000	
5	Guaranteed payments to partners		
6	New gain (loss) under Section 1231		
7	Other income		
8	Charitable contributions	(50,000)	(1,500)
9	Section 179 expense deduction		
10	Deductions related to portfolio income		
11	Other deductions:		
--	Partner health insurance premiums	(100,000)	(3,000)
--	Payments to partners' Keogh plans	(650,000)	(20,000)
17	Foreign taxes paid for partners	(20,000)	(600)

[3]—Balance Sheets (Schedule L)

For purposes of reporting assets, liabilities, and partners' capital items on Form 1065, it is necessary to conform asset, liability, and capital items included in the law firm's "Statement of Net Assets" to captions identified on the tax form. Conforming the book figures to the tax format usually involves some reclassification of the book figures. There are generally no adjustments involved because the amounts shown on the tax form should agree with the partnership books and records, unless a statement is attached explaining any differences. Balance sheets at both the beginning and end of the tax year are required.

Figure 15-D illustrates an example of a law firm partnership's balance sheets compiled using the format outlined in Schedule L of Form 1065.

Figure 15-D. Illustration of a law firm partnership's balance sheet compiled using the format outlined in Schedule L of U.S. Partnership Return of Income.

ABC LAW FIRM PARTNERSHIP
BALANCE SHEETS
(Form 1065 Tax Return Format)

Line	Item on Tax Return	Beginning of Tax Year	End of Tax Year
	Assets		
1	Cash	$ 400,000	$ 500,000
2	Receivables (net)	1,000,000	900,000
3	Inventories		
4	Government obligations		
5	Tax exempt securities	250,000	250,000
6	Other current assets	100,000	100,000
7	Mortgage & real estate loans		
8	Other investments	650,000	750,000
9	Depreciable assets (net)	1,600,000	2,300,000
10	Depletable assets (net)		
11	Land (net)		
12	Intangible assets (net)		
13	Other assets		
14	Total assets	$4,000,000	$4,800,000
	Liabilities and Capital		
15	Accounts payable		
16	Debt payable in less than 1 year	$100,000	$100,000
17	Other current liabilities	100,000	200,000
18	Nonrecourse loans		
19	Debt payable in 1 year or more	1,400,000	1,900,000
20	Other liabilities		
21	Partners' capital accounts	2,400,000	2,600,000
22	Total liabilities & capital	$4,000,000	$4,800,000

[4]—Reconciliation of Income per Books with Income per Return (Schedule M-1)

Schedule M-1 is one of the most important parts of Form 1065, because it gives a law firm an overall mechanism to reconcile "Book net Income" with "Net Income for Tax Purposes." This "macro" approach allows a law firm to have confidence that all differences between book net income and items that are reported to partners (separately or as part of ordinary income) are, in the aggregate, in agreement. Once Schedule M-1 has been completed, a law firm can prepare Schedule K-1s for the partners.

Some of the components of the "Reconciliation of Income Per Books with Income Per Return" previously discussed in this chapter are included in the Schedule M-1 reconciliation. Specifically, nontaxable income and nondeductible expenses are entered on appropriate lines on Schedule M-1. Also, timing differences in reporting income or expenses are entered on Schedule M-1.

In addition to these items, payments made by a law firm on behalf of partners for expenses which were not included in book net income or ordinary income are reported on Schedule M-1. For example, French taxes paid by a firm and charged against partners' draw accounts or capital accounts (and not charged against book income) are entered on line Schedule M-1, line 7.

Likewise, 401(k) contributions paid by a partner or charged against a partner's capital account are entered on Schedule M-1, line 7.

Figure 15-E illustrates an example of a law firm partnership's reconciliation of "book net income" with "theoretical taxable income" using the format outlined in Schedule M-1 of Form 1065.

Figure 15-E. Illustration of a law firm partnership's reconciliation of income per books with income per return using the format outlined in Schedule M-1 of Form 1065.

ABC LAW FIRM PARTNERSHIP
RECONCILIATION OF INCOME PER BOOKS WITH INCOME PER RETURN
(Form 1065 Tax Return Format)

	Line item on Tax Return	Schedule M-1 Partnership	(Reference only) Partner A
1	Net income per books	$8,900,000	$255,000
2	Income on Schedule K, not on books		
3	Guarantee payments		
4	Expenses recorded on books, not on Schedule K:		
	Business meal and entertainment limitation	50,000	1,500
	Partner life insurance	20,000	600
6	Income on books, not on Schedule K:		
	Tax exempt interest	(20,000)	(600)
7	Deductions on Schedule K, not charged to book income:		
	Depreciation timing difference	(40,000)	(1,200)
	Partner Keogh contributions	(650,000)	(20,000)
	Foreign taxes paid on behalf of partners	(20,000)	(600)
9	Income (Analysis of Net Income, line 1) representing aggregate taxable income related to partnership activities	$8,240,000	$234,700

[5]—Analysis of Partners' Capital Accounts (Schedule M-2)

Schedule M-2 of the U.S. Partnership Return of Income shows what caused changes in the partners' capital accounts during the tax year. The amounts shown should agree with the partnership's books and records or a statement should be attached explaining any differences. Line 1, "Balance at beginning of year" and line 9, "Balance at end of year" should agree with the amounts shown on line 21, columns (b) and (d) of Schedule L ("Balance Sheet"). Line 3, "Net income per books" should agree with the amount shown on line 1 of Schedule M-1. The other lines in Schedule M-2 are designed to identify items that change partners' capital accounts but are not reported on other lines of Form 1065 (e.g., line 2 is used to report partners' capital contributions and line 6 is used to report distributions to partners.)

Figure 15-F illustrates an example of a law firm partnership's analysis of partners' capital accounts indicating: (1) changes in all partners' capital accounts (compiled in the format outlined in Schedule M-2 of Form 1065) and (2) changes in each partner's capital account (compiled and referenced in the format outlined in Schedule K-1 of Form 1065).

Figure 15-F. Illustration of a law firm partnership's analysis of partners' capital accounts compiled using the format outlined in Schedule M-2 of U.S. Partnership Return of Income.

ABC LAW FIRM PARTNERSHIP
ANALYSIS OF PARTNERS' CAPITAL ACCOUNTS
(Form 1065 Tax Return Format)

Line Item on Tax Return	Schedule M-2 Partnership	Schedule K-1 Partner A	Column on K-1 Line J
1 Balance at beginning of year	$2,400,000	$ 72,000	(a)
2 Capital contributed during the year	200,000	—	(b)
3 Net Income (per books)	8,900,000	255,000	(c)
4 Other increases	—	—	(c)
6 Distributions:			
a. Cash	(8,500,000)	(249,000)	(d)
Guaranteed payments	(400,000)	—	(d)
b. Property	—	—	(d)
7 Other decreases:			
9 Balance at end of year	$2,600,000	$ 78,000	(e)

§ 15.04 Individual Partner's Share of Income, Credits, Deductions, etc. (Schedule K-1)

Schedule K (Form 1065) is a summary schedule of all the partners' shares of the partnership's income, credits, deductions, etc. Amounts on Schedule K are allocated or apportioned to each partner and reported separately to each partner on a Schedule K-1. Attach a copy of each Schedule K-1 to the Form 1065 that is filed with the IRS, keep a copy of each K-1 with the file copy of the partnership return, and distribute to each partner his or her K-1 to use in preparing individual or P.C. tax returns.

Schedule K-1 contains the following three types of tax accounting information: (1) partner's share of income and deductions, (2) partner's share of items relevant to computation of tax credits, and (3) partner's share of items relevant to other tax computations.

[1]—Partner's Share of Income and Deductions

The first type of tax accounting information appearing on Schedule K-1 identifies the partner's share of specific items of partnership income and deductions. The purpose of identifying these specific items is to facilitate the partner's preparation of his or her individual federal income tax return or, in the case of a corporate partner, the preparation of its corporate income tax return. In addition to identifying the dollar amount of each item, Schedule K-1 also identifies the specific Form 1040 line number or schedule reference where the amount is to be entered on a partner's tax return.

Figure 15-C illustrates an example of a law firm partner's share of income and deductions reported on Schedule K-1 of Form 1065, together with the aggregate of all partners' shares of these items reported on Schedule K.

[2]—Partner's Share of Items Relevant to Computation of Tax Credits

The second type of tax accounting information appearing on Schedule K-1 identifies the partner's share of items which are relevant to the computation of tax credits. These items include:

[a]—Foreign Tax Credits

Income attributable to a foreign office of a U.S. law firm partnership may be subject to tax by a foreign country. Depending on the country, the income may be subject to tax at the partnership level or at the partner level. If branch income is subject to tax at the partnership level (i.e., the firm pays tax on its branch income), the foreign tax is apportioned among equity or percentage partners and is reported on lines 17a through 17h of Schedule K-1.

Of all the lines on Schedule K, lines 17a through 17h are the most demanding because they require details for each country. For example, other than lines 17b and 17e, all of the lines require details as to the specific country from which income was earned, deductions were claimed, and taxes were paid. To comply with the instructions requires attachment of one or more supplemental schedules that break out the sources of income, deductions and credits in enough detail so that each partner can properly complete a personal or corporate tax return. Since this detail is needed only for tax purposes, accumulating the information will challenge even the most efficient accounting departments. Unfortunately, that's what the instructions require.

If a foreign tax is assessed at the partner level (as opposed to be a tax against the firm and then allocated to each partner), each partner sharing in branch income must file a foreign tax return (some countries allow partners to file a composite return) and pay applicable foreign taxes. As an accommodation, a firm's foreign office often pays the foreign taxes on behalf of its U.S. partners. Taxes paid on behalf of partners are charged against each partner's income, distribution account, or capital account and are reported to each partner on Schedule K-1, line 25 as supplemental information.

Only foreign taxes for which a partner is eligible to claim a deduction or a foreign tax credit should be entered on lines 17g or 25. In Japan, for example, there may be Japanese income taxes withheld by clients when they pay a law firm's invoices. Because each partner is allowed a fairly sizable personal exemption in Japan, it is not uncommon that the amount of tax withheld and allocated to each partner exceeds that partner's actual Japanese tax liability. When the tax withheld exceeds the amount due, the excess is refundable the next year. Treasury regulations prohibit claiming a foreign tax credit when it is reasonably certain that the amount paid or withheld will be refunded.[1] In this example, therefore, the excess would not be eligible for a credit, but should be reflected as a receivable.

Using this information a partner should complete Form 1116 to determine his or her foreign tax credit.

[b]—Other Credits

Lines 12a through 12d and 13 of Schedule K-1 are used to report credit for low-income housing credits, credits related to rental real

---

[1] Treas. Reg. § 1.901-2(e)(2)(i); 26 C.F.R. § 1.901-2(e)(2)(i).

estate activities, and other credits. Some of these credits may be subject to limitations on the partner's personal or corporate income tax return.

[3]—Partner's Share of Items Relevant to Other Tax Computations

The third type of tax accounting information appearing on Schedule K-1 identifies the partner's share of items which are relevant to computations that the partner must make when preparing his or her individual income tax return. These items include:

[a]—Investment Interest

Investment interest expense incurred on investment debts must be reported separately to each partner because it is deductible on an individual's personal tax return only to the extent of net investment income. Interest expense incurred by a firm and attributable to a partner is reported on Schedule K-1, lines 14a and 14b(2) while associated investment income is reported on line 14b(1).

[b]—Self-Employment Earnings

A partner's share of ordinary income and guaranteed payments earned as an active partner in a law firm partnership are self-employment income and must be reported to a partner on line 15a of Schedule K-1. In some situations, ordinary income earned by nonresident alien partners is not self-employment income.[2] A partner should include his or her self-employment income earned from the law firm with self-employment income from other sources and compute self-employment tax.

[c]—Adjustments and Tax Preference Items

As a result of certain tax accounting methods adopted by a firm, there may be tax deductions which create tax preference items. The most common tax preference items are accelerated depreciation of real property which was placed in service before 1987 and depreciation adjustment on property placed in service after 1986. These and other preference items are reported to each partner on Schedule K-1, lines 16a though 16e. It is assumed that partners include these items in their computation of alternative minimum taxable income (Form 6251).

---

[2] Treas. Reg. § 1.1402(b)-1(d); 26 C.F.R. § 1.402(b)-1(d).

[d]—Other and Supplemental Information

Lines 18 of Schedule K-1 is used to report each partner's share of optional ten-year write-off of certain tax preferences. Lines 19 and 20 are used to report each partner's share of tax exempt income. Line 21 is used to report each partner's share of nondeductible expenses (e.g., disallowed meal and entertainment expenses, partner's club dues, partner's life insurance premiums, etc.). Lines 22 and 23 analyze distributions to partners with distributions of money and marketable securities reported on line 22 while all other distributions are reported on line 23. Line 24 is used to report detailed breakdown of items entered elsewhere on Schedule K-1 (for example, a detailed analysis of nondeductible items on line 21) or to report each partner's share of supplemental information which a partner needs in order to prepare his or her individual income tax return (for example, a partner's share of municipal income by jurisdiction, the amount of U.S. government interest included in line 4a, Schedule K-1, or foreign tax paid on his or her behalf.

[4]—Schedule K-1 Reporting for a Deceased Partner

Most people have heard the old saying that there are only two certainties in this world: death and taxes. No matter how invincible attorneys think they are, when it's their time, they pass on. Reporting financial information for a deceased partner can be confusing because of the interplay between the IRS requirements and the deceased partner's partnership agreement.

Depending on the provisions in the partnership agreement with respect to the continuation of a deceased partner's interest, a partnership may have to issue more than one Schedule K-1. If a partner's interest in the firm ceases at the date of death, then there is only one Schedule K-1 issued. If, however, an estate or successor in interest carries on after the death, then multiple K-1s have to be issued.

As a result of simplification changes made by the The Tax Relief Act of 1997 simplified the procedures of reporting income for a deceased partner. For partnership years beginning after December 31, 1997, a partnership's year closes with respect to a partner whose interest terminated because of death.[3] This means that the deceased partner's share of partnership income in the year of death is reported for the partner on his or her final Schedule K-1. Likewise, self-employment income, if any, applicable to the partner is reported on the final

---

[3] IRC § 706(c)(2)(A); 26 U.S.C. IRC § 706(c)(2)(A).

Schedule K-1. These rules make reporting a deceased partner's interest in the firm considerably easier than under previous rules, which bifurcated a deceased partner's interest by reflecting income on the estate's K-1 and self-employment income on the decedent's K-1. The current rules are more intuitive because anything that happens while the partner was alive is reported on his or her final K-1.

If a deceased partner's interest continues after death, then a second Schedule K-1 has to be issued to the estate or successor in interest for activity occurring after the date of death. Income, deductions or credits for the reporting period beginning on the day after the partner's death through the end of the partnership's year-end are reported on the second K-1.

§ 15.05 State and Local Income Taxes

When preparing state and local income tax returns for law firm partnerships and law firm partners, three matters deserve attention. They are: (1) type of tax return, (2) taxable income determination, and (3) income tax credits.

[1]—Type of Tax Return

Law firm partnerships are not usually taxed by state or city governments as separate entities. Instead, each partner is taxed on his or her share of partnership income after adjusting for specific modifications required by the taxing jurisdiction. In a few instances, cities (such as New York and Philadelphia) levy an unincorporated business tax or business profits tax on law firm partnerships. Three methods of filing state and city income tax returns exist. They are:

[a]—Individual Tax Returns

Each individual partner (as opposed to a corporate partner) files a personal income tax return in each state or city in which the firm does business and includes his or her share of partnership income adjusted in accordance with the tax laws of the taxing jurisdiction. The partnership files a partnership information return with a schedule identifying each partner's share of income and expense items. This is similar to the filing procedures for the federal return.

[b]—Combined/Composite Tax Returns

Certain states and cities permit a partnership to file a combined or composite income tax return for all nonresident partners. Where a firm obtains permission to file this type of return, it pays the applicable tax on behalf of the nonresident partners who elect to be included in the combined return. Those partners are charged individually for their share of the tax shown on the combined return. Firms that operate in several states and cities find that the filing of combined or composite returns eases the administrative burden of the firm's partners. However, sometimes the trade-off to filing a combined or composite return is that the nonresident partners are not permitted any deductions, exemptions, or credits and must pay tax at the highest marginal tax rate for individuals; a trade-off that is sometimes more expensive than a benefit. To avoid the extra cost, a partner can opt out of filing as part of the combined group and file his or her own nonresident individual income tax return. The firm should consult its professional tax advisor to determine whether the use of combined or composite returns is practical or advisable.

Some states do not provide for the filing of combined or composite returns. Partners must file individual nonresident income tax returns in those states.

Partners who are resident in states in which the firm files a composite return are not allowed to be included in the composite return. They must file their own personal income tax returns. Corporate partners normally are not allowed to be included in composite returns either. Likewise, partners who otherwise had to file as a nonresident in a state (e.g., the partner may be a partner in a real estate venture that has to file in a particular state) are not allowed to be included in a firm's combined return.

[c]—Unincorporated Business Tax Returns

Where an unincorporated business tax is levied on a law firm partnership by a particular city, the firm files a single tax return, pays the tax, and treats it as an expense of the business. Some states require partners to add unincorporated business taxes back to income when computing individual income tax for those particular states. Depending on the type of unincorporated business tax, some states allow a partner to claim a credit on his or her individual state income tax return for unincorporated business taxes paid to another state.

[d]—Personal Property Tax Returns

Some states or cities require a law firm to file personal property tax returns and to pay a tax for the use of personal property in that taxing jurisdiction. The definitions of "personal property" subject to tax and the depreciation methods or lives allowed for personal property tax purposes can differ from those used for federal or state income tax purposes. For example, many states consider computer software—whether custom-designed or "off-the-shelf"—to be intangible property, and therefore, not subject to personal property tax. Care should also be taken in reviewing property included in a personal property tax return, so that tax is paid only on assets still in use.

[e]—Sales and Use Tax Returns

State and local governments are continuing to focus on sales and use tax returns to close budget shortfalls. As the base of items subject to sales or use tax expands, law firms are finding themselves subject to new or increasing taxes. Generally, the practice of law is not subject to sales or use tax; however, supplies law firms consume or services they buy might be. When a law firm pays a sales or use tax, it is a business expense, unless it is associated with the acquisition of personal property, in which case sales tax must be capitalized and depreciated with the basis of the property. Sales and use tax returns may be due in states or cities in which a firm does business, even though it is not required to file a partnership income tax return in that jurisdiction.

[2]—Taxable Income Determination for State Income Tax Purposes

Taxable income for computing state and local income taxes often differs from taxable income for computing federal income taxes. For example, several states do not permit the use of the federal Accelerated Cost Recovery System for computing depreciation or a deduction for guaranteed payments to partners. Most states apportion guaranteed payments based on a partnership's business allocation percentage regardless of where a partner renders professional services. Partners should consult their professional tax advisor for help in identifying and adjusting for these differences when preparing and filing their state and local income tax returns.

The method of apportioning income between states also differs. Most states apportion income based on a standard three-factor formula with sales (service fee income in the case of a law firm) apportioned based on where services are rendered (this method is referred to as the "place of work" method). A growing tendency among state tax jurisdictions is to double weight the sales factors, thereby creating a four-factor formula. If a firm does not file a tax return in a state to which it allocates income, some states require that the sales be "thrown back" to another state. A few jurisdictions ignore the "place of work" sourcing rule and use the "office of assignment" method. Under this method, all services are apportioned to the attorney's assigned office regardless of where services are rendered. In practice, this method is easier to calculate because law firms historically have accounted for service fee income based on the office of assignment method. Problems arise when an attorney is assigned to an office in a state which uses the "office of assignment" method and provides services in a state which uses the "place of work" method. When this happens, both jurisdictions can try to tax the same income.

[3]—Income Tax Credits

Most states allow resident law firm partners a credit for income taxes paid to other states. Generally, this is true even if the resident partner is included in a nonresident composite return in another state. However, because of state-imposed limitations, the credit may not adequately compensate a partner for taxes paid to another state. As a result, it is not unusual for a partner to end up paying tax more than once on the same income. Partners should consult their professional tax advisor to ensure that they maximize the use of state tax credits.

§ 15.06 Foreign Income Tax Returns for Partnership and Partners

There are many reasons why law firms open offices outside of the United States. Two of the most common reasons for opening offices in other countries are that clients demand service in another country or growth plans of the firm anticipate global expansion. Whatever the reason, law firms that decide to open non-U.S.-based offices may face formidable challenges. Some of the challenges include identifying where income is subject to tax, what method of accounting has to be used, how and when to recognize currency fluctuations, and the myriad of tax compliance issues facing the firm and its partners.[1] This section will review the issues relating to tax compliance.

A word of caution to law firms that decide to open foreign offices. Plan the event, don't react to it. When a law firm sends a "pioneer" into a new country to generate new contacts and to begin developing the market it is asking for tax trouble somewhere down the road. What frequently happens is that the pioneer is successful in operating out of a hotel room and eventually decides that he or she needs office space. At some point, the law firm will create a permanent establishment in the country and will be subject to all the local tax filing requirements. Having a permanent establishment can also subject nonresident partners to tax filings in that country. What may happen, as the attorney becomes more successful in generating new business, is that one by one the unattended tax matters will surface. When they do so, unexpected tax problems become a distraction for the lawyer and may create problems for the law firm.

The best approach is to have administrative personnel set up an office in another country by signing a lease for office space, registering with the tax office, obtaining permits, if required, establishing a payroll system, and generally preparing the office for the lawyer. At that time, the office is ready and the lawyer can concentrate on practicing law instead of being distracted by administrative functions that he or she probably is not trained for or very good at. It only takes one bad experience caused by a "pioneer" to teach a law firm that there is a better way.

This section discusses some of the complexities that a law firm may encounter when opening offices outside of the United States. The section gives an overview of some of the tax return compliance

---

[1] Section 17.04 *infra* discusses the non-return issue.

complexities facing a partnership or its partners. It also touches on withholding issues that law firms may face when doing business in foreign countries and value-added taxes that apply in many parts of the world.

[1]—Partnership Returns

In the majority of cases, when a U.S. law firm operates a branch office in a foreign country, net income or expense of that office has to be reported in a tax return for that country. Determining what income to report is one of the first challenges facing a law firm. Some countries do not allow depreciation like the U.S., but instead allow a capital recovery allowance (e.g., the U.K. or Hong Kong). Most European countries require the use of the accrual method of accounting for at least accounts receivable and maybe work-in-process. Beginning with the fiscal year 1999/2000, the U.K. began requiring law firms to include the cost component of work-in-process in the calculation of income. Some expenses may be limited or not deductible in particular countries (e.g., in the U.K. and Russia, entertainment expenses are not deductible).

The form in which a law firm does business is another important factor. Often, operating logistics are easiest if a partnership operates through a branch of the main partnership. Other times, a firm may have to set up an intermediary entity, such as a multinational partnership in the U.K., to allow the firm to admit solicitors as partners. In some countries, the firm is not allowed to operate as a partnership, but must operate as a corporation (e.g., Poland or Turkey). More recently, firms are allowed to operate in some countries only if the firms are owned by lawyers admitted to the bar in those countries (e.g., Hungary, Indonesia, and the Czech Republic). This parochial rule applies even though lawyers only intend to practice U.S. law.

Each of these variables complicates the firm's global tax profile. The more a firm branches into other countries, the more complicated its international tax compliance function becomes. When coupled with different cultures, languages, taxing bureaucracies, and tax forms, law firms find a geometric increase in the number and complexity of tax issues when they operate branch offices in multiple foreign jurisdictions.

From the perspective of who pays the tax, law firms that operate in the U.S. as partnerships can be treated as either transparent entities or taxable entities.

[a]—Transparent Entity

For treaty purposes, a partnership is commonly referred to as a transparent entity, meaning that its income and expenses pass through the entity to its partners who are subject to tax, if any. The U.S. uses the pass-through approach because the firm is not subject to tax directly; rather its partners are allocated a share of income and pay their own taxes. Some countries follow the same flow-through concepts used in the U.S. and determine the applicable tax at the partner level (e.g., Belgium, France, Japan, Australia, or, after self-assessment, England).

[b]—Taxable Entity

Countries that recognize the partnership structure, but not its transparent nature, subject the branch activity to tax (e.g., Hong Kong, Singapore, India, Indonesia, Hungary, Vietnam, Mexico, Russia, the Czech Republic, or, before self-assessment, England). The tax paid by the firm on branch income flows through the firm to each equity partner as a foreign tax paid. Each partner is charged his or her share of the tax and must claim a credit, if any, on a federal personal income tax return.

Countries that do not recognize or authorize the partnership structure may require a law firm to do business as a corporation and to pay corporate tax (e.g., Poland, Brazil or Turkey). Depending on the position the firm has taken in the U.S. with respect to a corporate structure, the tax could be an expense of the firm or a creditable tax for its partners.

Under U.S. tax rules, it is possible to look through the existence of a corporate structure using the check-the-box rules. These rules essentially allow the owner of a corporate structure to elect to treat the entity as a partnership instead of a corporation. The benefit of this election is that a tax paid to a foreign country by a corporation becomes a tax paid by a partnership. Converting the tax in this way allows a partner to claim a direct credit for the tax, subject to other limitations.

[2]—Partner Returns

U.S. partners are used to filing tax returns—probably more than they like filing. Introduce globalization, and the task of filing returns becomes more than some partners want to cope with. In addition to the extra forms included in a federal tax return (e.g., Form 1116 for foreign tax credits), there are complexities of what income has to be reported in which countries, when tax returns are due in other countries, what countries allow credits for taxes paid in other countries, and how is tax paid in other jurisdictions. As daunting as these considerations are to U.S. partners, they are mild compared to a nonresident alien's reaction to the mound of returns he or she has to contend with. Most nonresident aliens have never seen a tax return as complicated as a U.S.

personal income tax return (or nonresident income tax return) and may not be prepared for state tax returns in every state in which the partnership does business. This is one area where owners of a professional service corporation (PC) have an advantage over partners because they only file tax returns where they rendered services, not where the PC has offices.

Taxation of a partner depends on whether the individual is a resident or nonresident of a particular country and whether the U.S. has a treaty with that country. A person can have residency status if he or she is in a country over a specified period of time. The time period varies by country. Some countries tax a resident's worldwide income, unless a treaty provides otherwise (e.g., France, Germany, United States, U.K., or Belgium). Depending on the treaty in force, a person might be subject to tax only on remittance into a country (e.g., England), on 50% of his or her worldwide income (e.g., France), or only on the income actually attributable to sources within a country (e.g., Belgium).

If a person is considered a resident of a country with which the U.S. has a treaty, it is probable that the individual will avoid double tax on the same income. The mechanism to accomplish a single-level tax is through a foreign tax credit allowed on a person's U.S. return. Generally, a foreign tax credit is allowed only to a person filing a U.S. Form 1040. The rules to calculate foreign tax credits are complicated and require information that should be contained on the partners' Schedules K-1.

Countries may tax nonresidents only on branch income to the extent that it was earned in their jurisdiction (e.g., Belgium, France, or Germany). In calculating a nonresident's tax, a country might require "tax with progression," which generally means that the highest tax rates will apply even though income is small (e.g., Belgium).

Determining branch income depends on the laws of each country and whether the U.S. treaty, if any, specifies how branch income is determined. Normally branch income in a developed country is determined based on legal services rendered in the country. So, for example, if only 10% of the legal services were rendered in the U.K., then only 10% of the fee would be allocated to the U.K., regardless of where it was paid. Some developing countries use a method known as "the force of attraction" rule to source income to their countries (e.g., Indonesia, India, and, if no P.E., Spain). Under this method, income is allocated entirely to the country if the payer is a resident of that country. In the example above, if only 10% of the legal services were rendered in Indonesia, but the payer was a resident of Indonesia, then that country would have a right to source 100% of the fee income to tax in Indonesia. Having conflicting sourcing rules like these makes it difficult for law firms to do business because they have to focus on tax issues before immersing themselves in a client's problem. These conflicting rules may also cause a law firm to pay tax on the same income in two different countries.

Some countries make the tax calculations and tax return preparation less painful by allowing nonresident partners to file composite returns in which all the partners are listed and their individual taxes are calculated on one form (e.g., Germany, Belgium, Australia, or, depending on the level of income, England). This method is administratively easier because only one person has to sign the tax return.

[3]—Tax Withholding

Countries use various techniques to insure that income taxes are paid. One tried and tested method is to require tax to be withheld from payments made for legal services. A law firm may be subject to withholding taxes when it does not have a fixed place of business in a country and it has generated revenue in that country. There are situations, however, in which withholding is required even though a law firm has a presence in a country (e.g., India, Indonesia or Brazil). It is more common for countries to withhold only on income earned within their countries, although there are a few countries that use the force of attraction method and withhold on the entire amount, regardless of where the work was done (e.g., Indonesia, Brazil, India, or Spain and Italy if no fixed place of business in the country).

Most law firms like to avoid situations in which tax will be withheld because the withholding rates can be high (e.g., 35%) and, as mentioned, can be applied to gross fees. If a treaty is in effect between the U.S. and the country in which the client is located, withholding might be avoided by obtaining a certification from the IRS (i.e., Form 6166). The purpose of a certification is to attest that the taxpayer has filed an income tax return. Since a partnership is not subject to tax, the certification process means that the IRS has to verify that all of the partners have filed their tax returns and that they are residents in the U.S. As long as all of the partners are physically resident in the U.S., a full certification can be obtained with very little effort.

However, if just one equity partner is not physically resident in the U.S., then potentially only a partial certification will be issued. A partial certification means that the other country will not exempt the entire invoice from withholding.

The certification process becomes more complicated as more partners are assigned to non-U.S. offices, even temporarily. To minimize withholding when there are partners in multiple countries, it might be necessary to use procedures in those countries that are similar to the U.S. certification procedures. Combining certifications from multiple countries into one package can demonstrate that partners are paying taxes in their countries of residence and, thereby, avoid or minimize withholding.

Countries know that corporations in their jurisdictions will be pressured not to withhold taxes. Some countries put the onus on the payer to verify that the payee should not be subject to withholding. The procedure used by these countries is to hold the payer responsible whenever the tax authorities decide that there should have been withholding (e.g., Brazil, Argentina, Italy, Canada or Spain). This harsh consequence effectively forces withholding in all but the clearest situations.

As a general rule, once tax is withheld, a law firm cannot file a tax return to get a refund. Given a situation in which only 10% of the legal services were rendered in a country, but withholding applied to 100% of the bill, the tax might negate the profit margin on the work and make it disadvantageous to do future work in that country.

Another problem caused by withholding is the inability to claim a foreign tax credit for the amount withheld. Under U.S. tax principles, a taxpayer has to make every effort to get a foreign tax refunded before the tax is creditable. It is conceivable that "making every effort" means initiating potentially expensive litigation that may cost a law firm more than the amount of the withheld tax. Unfortunately, if every effort is not made, then the IRS can disallow the foreign tax credit.

[4]—VAT

Many Americans live in states that charge sales taxes when certain items are purchased. In other parts of the world, such as in Europe, value-added taxes or consumption taxes are charged instead of sales taxes. A value-added tax ("VAT") is a tax that follows the item or service. For example, in manufacturing a widget, a VAT would be added to the item during each stage of production. Each person or entity that adds value to the item must add a VAT to the item when that person or entity passes the item on to the next process. When the consumer buys the widget, the VAT is built into its price. The amount that is added to the value of an item becomes payable to the government when the item is sold.

The entity that manufactures the widget also pays VAT when it buys parts to make the widget or when it pays its rent or utilities. The amount it pays is allowed to be reclaimed against the amount it owes to the government.

Depending on the country, VAT may be applied to legal fees. For example, in England, France or Russia, VAT is applied when legal services are rendered. In Belgium or Hungary, however, VAT may apply only if the legal services are rendered by non-Belgian or non-Hungarian lawyers, but does not apply when legal services are rendered by avocats in Belgium or Hungarian-registered lawyers practicing Hungarian law.

It is not always easy to know when VAT applies. Some countries assess VAT (or something like VAT) if the legal service was rendered by a law firm within their countries, regardless of where the client (the consumer) is located. Other countries do not assess VAT when a law firm provides services outside of the country. There are exceptions to that rule if the ultimate consumer (i.e., a subsidiary of the client) is in the same country as the law firm service provider or work is done for the home office of the law firm and then rebilled to a client. It is also possible for countries to require taxpaying entities or businesses to reverse charge VAT if, for example, they receive (i.e., consume) the benefit of legal services rendered in another country.

Suffice it to say that VAT rules vary a great deal throughout the world and are important considerations for law firms. Significant penalties can be assessed if transactions (i.e., billings) are not reported, even though there may be no tax due. Conferring with a VAT specialist is a wise decision that can avoid unexpected problems.

§ 15.07 Changes in Income Tax Rules

Information contained in this chapter is based on the tax rules in effect during calendar year 2001. It is important to remember, however, that tax rules are constantly subject to change. When preparing tax returns, the preparer is encouraged to read the current year's instructions carefully and to consult with a professional tax advisor regarding recent changes in tax laws, proposed tax legislation, and overall tax strategy.

The exhibits contained in Chapter 15 are based on proofs of the 2001 Form 1065, which were published in June 2001. Since the proofs are subject to change, readers should consult with their tax advisors concerning the final versions of the form.

CHAPTER 16

Retirement and Pension Plans

Chapter Contents

---

§ 16.01 Law Firm Retirement Arrangements

Tax law changes and competition for highly qualified lawyers and administrative staff have caused many law firms to focus on their benefit programs (particularly retirement arrangements) in terms of their ability to attract new personnel and to retain existing personnel, including partners. The objectives of a firm's retirement arrangements will have a bearing on the types of programs that the firm ultimately selects.

[1]—Objectives of Retirement Arrangements

Most law firm retirement programs are designed to achieve three broad objectives:

(1) To provide individual personnel within the firm with a degree of financial security during their retirement years.

(2) To create a benefit program that can be used by the firm to recruit and retain top-grade personnel.

(3) To make maximum use of available tax benefits.

In addition, most retirement programs are tailored to achieve specific objectives of the firm's three levels of personnel: (a) partners, (b) associates, and (c) administrative employees. For example, because partners' incomes are often taxed at the highest tax rate, retirement programs which provide tax deferrals are usually of particular interest to them. Associates may focus on the program's portability (i.e., the ease with which accumulated benefits can be transferred from one employer's program to another employer's program, in the event that the associate is not admitted into the partnership). Administrative employees are ordinarily interested in a retirement program's vesting provisions.

[2]—Types of Retirement Arrangements

Law firm retirement arrangements for partners may be funded or unfunded programs or a combination of both. Retirement arrangements for employees generally are required to be funded. When the programs are funded, the relevant assets usually are placed under the control of a trustee. The trustee typically deposits the program's assets with a custodian (often a bank or trust company) for safekeeping.

There are three typical types of retirement arrangements in use by law firms. They are:

[a]—Unfunded Retirement Programs

Payments to retired partners under these programs generally are treated similarly to distributions made to active partners. These payments are considered to be payments out of current income, even though they may be reported on a Schedule K-1 as a guaranteed payment.

[b]—Defined Contribution Plans[1]

Under these plans, specific amounts are contributed to the plan on behalf of and credited to a separate account for each participant. Contributions typically are based on compensation.

[c]—Defined Benefit Plans[2]

Under these plans, benefits ultimately distributable from the plan are based on a pension formula that typically takes into account both compensation and years of service. Contributions to the plan are actuarially determined.

[3]—Limitations on Tax Deductions

For tax-qualified funded plans, the tax deduction limit for plan contributions will depend on the type of retirement plan selected. In the case of defined contribution plans, the deduction is based upon the contribution formula, subject to limitations that apply to the contributions made for any one participant[3] and the sum of the contributions made for all participants.[4] For defined benefit plans, the annual deductible contribution is the actuarially determined amount required to fund the

---

[1] IRC § 414(i); 26 U.S.C. § 414(i).
[2] IRC § 414(j); 26 U.S.C. § 414(j).
[3] IRC § 415(c); 26 U.S.C. § 415(c).
[4] IRC § 404(a)(3); 26 U.S.C. § 404(a)(3).

pension benefits.[5] A separate deduction limit applies to the sum of the contributions made to a defined contribution plan and a defined benefit plan.[6]

Unfunded partner retirement programs are not affected by any special tax deduction limitations.

---

[5] IRC §§ 404(a)(1) and 412; 26 U.S.C. §§ 404(a)(1) and 412.
[6] IRC § 404(a)(7); 26 U.S.C. § 404(a)(7).

§ 16.02 Unfunded Partner Retirement Programs

[1]—In General

Establishing a sound and equitable policy governing the retirement of partners and the amounts to be paid to retired partners is one of the more difficult law firm management problems. This policy deserves careful consideration because it may be vital not only to maintaining harmonious relationships among the partners, but also to providing an incentive for younger partners and promising associates by establishing a means of succession in a planned, orderly manner. The financial arrangement aspects of this policy are particularly important since they will have an impact on (and perhaps determine) the firm's continued financial viability in future years.

Retirement considerations must start with the firm's particular circumstances and should not be unduly influenced by programs developed by other firms. The size of the firm, the nature and financial success of its practice, the ages of the partners and their concept of the firm's obligation with respect to retirement are factors which vary from firm to firm. These factors affect the approach used by a law firm in implementing its retirement policy and the manner in which it determines the retired partners' retirement allowances. Multinational firms need to consider the retirement systems of the countries in which they have offices and how those systems will affect U.S. citizens or non-resident alien partners or employees.

In recent years, there has been less use of unfunded partner retirement plans because they create a potentially heavy burden on newer partners. As partners who are covered by these plans age and retire, the amount paid to them may become a significant percentage of the firm's net income. Most firms limit how much net income can be paid to recipients of unfunded plans and monitor the potential exposure to active partners. When income is high, there is less concern than when income starts falling.

Firms that face potential large unfunded payments are migrating to qualified plans so that active partners basically provide for themselves. By introducing qualified plans and capping or grandfathering existing unfunded plans, firms are able to better protect future profits.

There are three principal approaches used for partner retirement. They may be described as:

[a]—Scale-Down Approach

This approach contemplates a transition period of gradual reduction in activity and profit participation (during which the partner is an "active" partner), with a residual lifetime profit-participation income commencing at the close of the transition period.

[b]—Deferred-Equity Approach

This approach results in a determination of the financial equity of the partner at retirement date (including his or her (a) capital account, (b) share of undistributed profits, and (c) share of unbilled and uncollected fees), and the payment of such equity in installments over a relatively short period of years. This settlement comprises the sole retirement benefit under the deferred-equity approach.

[c]—Retirement-Allowance Approach

Some law firms have no scale-down of income and no concept of an equity payout. These firms simply pay retired partners an annual retirement allowance for life.

Retirement payments during the early years of retirement are usually larger under the deferred-equity approach than under the scale-down approach. However, these payments eventually cease under the deferred-equity approach, whereas they continue for life under the scale-down approach. Often, law firms use a combination of these three approaches in designing partner unfunded retirement plans.

[2]—Plan Features

Basic features which should be included in a sound partner retirement plan include:

(1) A plan concept that is simple, flexible to a degree, and easily understood.

(2) A requirement for some form of mandatory retirement or reduced participation, to place the decision on an impersonal and definitive basis.

(3) An approach that contemplates either a straight-life annuity or aggregate, periodic payments of not less than an amount equal to the partner's interest in the firm's inventory of uncollected and unbilled fees at the partner's retirement date.

(4) A limitation (in terms of a specified percentage of current firm income) on the aggregate amount that may be paid to all retired partners in any one year.

[3]—Methods of Calculation

There are three methods of calculating payments to be made to retired partners. The method used will depend upon the firm's choice of retirement arrangement. The methods are: (1) profit participation arrangements, (2) fixed payment arrangements, and (3) settlement for a share of the firm's inventory.

[a]—Profit Participation Arrangements

Under this method, profit participation would be sizably reduced at retirement date or gradually reduced annually for active partners commencing at a specified age. There is no uniform pattern for the annual steps, but generally the scale-down is made in equal annual reductions, coordinated with the level deemed desirable for periodic lifetime benefits to commence at the close of the transition period. The amount of such lifetime payments would ordinarily reflect some decrease from the retired partner's participation in the last year of transition, but would also depend on the overall profitability of the firm and considerations as to its ability to sustain retirement benefits on a long-term basis. Under this method, the retiring partner is afforded some protection against future inflation, since the amount of the partner's retirement benefit is directly related to the level of firm profits.

[b]—Fixed Payment Arrangements

Under this method, the firm makes fixed dollar payments to the retired partner over the partner's lifetime. Typically, this type of program includes a provision for cost-of-living adjustments. In some firms, the initial fixed benefit amount is adjusted annually for changes in the Bureau of Labor Statistics' cost-of-living index. Some firms use a variation of the fixed payment arrangement by focusing instead on a fixed number of shares or units. Payments under this approach vary each year, because they are determined based on how much a fixed number of units would generate during the measurement period. Some firms' retirement arrangements also provide for surviving spouse benefits at a reduced amount.

[c]—Settlement for Share of the Firm's Inventory

The deferred-equity approach for determining a partner's retirement payments contemplates a retirement benefit arising solely from a partner's interest in the firm's inventory (i.e., unbilled time charges and uncollected fees). Some firms make a continuing accounting for the retired partner's interest in inventory as fee collections (relating to work prior to retirement) are made subsequent to the retirement date. This procedure can become complex because fees must be prorated for work-in-progress at retirement date and an additional accounting effort is needed to identify relevant fees as additional partners retire. This approach results in large amounts of taxable income being attributed to the partner in the first year or two of retirement, which then declines to nominal amounts in subsequent years. Other firms have devised formulas or provided for negotiated amounts that are used in lieu of computing the retired partner's share of inventory. In these cases, the inventory interest is usually paid in equal installments over a period of from three to five years after retirement. This relieves severe demands on the firm's financial resources and also minimizes high income tax rates on this income for the retired partner.

Figure 16-A compares the retirement allowance paid to a hypothetical retired partner under each of the three calculation methods discussed. Payments to the retired partner in Year 1 and in Year 10 are presented. Assumptions underlying the calculation are:

Method A (Profit participation arrangement)—The retired partner receives 10% of the firm's profits.

Method B (Fixed payment arrangement)—The retired partner receives $55,000 per year for life.

Method C (Settlement for share of the firm's inventory)—The retired partner receives 10% of the firm's inventory of $3,000,000 when it is collected (60% in Year 1 and 40% in Year 2).

Figure 16-A. Illustration comparing a hypothetical law firm partner's retirement allowance calculated under three different methods.

ABC LAW FIRM PARTNERSHIP
PARTNER'S RETIREMENT ALLOWANCE
COMPARISON OF THREE CALCULATION METHODS

	Method A (Profit Participation)	Method B (Fixed Payments)	Method C (Inventory Share)
FIRM'S PROFITS:			
Year 1	$500,000	$500,000	$500,000
Year 10	$1,000,000	$1,000,000	$1,000,000
RETIRED PARTNER'S ALLOWANCE:			
Year 1	$50,000	$55,000	$180,000
Year 10	$100,000	$55,000	—

§ 16.03 Defined Contribution Plans

Tax qualified defined contribution plans provide a vehicle for participants to accumulate retirement benefits with three tax advantages. They are:

(1) Contributions to the plans are tax deductible[1] or excludable[2] (subject to limitations which must be coordinated if there is more than one plan).

(2) Investment earnings accumulate tax-free in the plans until distributed.[3]

(3) Potential exists for ultimately withdrawing the accumulated funds (i.e., contributions plus investment earnings) after retirement at an attractively low effective tax rate.

Another advantage of defined contribution plans is that most plans offer participants various investment options. The number and type of investment options will differ from plan to plan and firm to firm. However, most plans offer a variety of investments which range from government bond and blue chip common stock mutual funds, money market funds and guaranteed income contracts to high-yield higher risk mutual funds. Many law firms are increasing the number and sophistication of investment options offered to participants.

Types of defined contribution plans that law firms often use are: (1) profit-sharing plans, (2) money purchase pension plans for partners and administrative employees, and (3) cash or deferred plans [401(k) plans] for partners, associates and administrative employees. A tax qualified plan must not discriminate in favor of "highly-compensated" employees (including partners)[4] in either coverage[5] or contributions[6] and also must cover a minimum number of employees.[7]

Contributions generally are required to be made as a level percentage of compensation for each participant subject to the compensation limit discussed in the next section. Contribution rates may vary, however,

---

[1] I.R.C. §§ 62(a)(6), 404(a)(3) and 404(a)(8); 26 U.S.C. §§ 62(a)(6), 404(a)(3) and 404(a)(8).

[2] I.R.C. § 402(a); 26 U.S.C. § 402(a).

[3] I.R.C. § 501(a); 26 U.S.C. § 501(a).

[4] I.R.C. § 414(q)(1); 26 U.S.C. § 414(q)(1).

[5] I.R.C. § 410(b); 26 U.S.C. § 410(b).

[6] I.R.C. § 401(a)(4); 26 U.S.C. § 401(a)(4).

[7] I.R.C. § 401(a)(26); 26 U.S.C. § 401(a)(26).

when a plan is "integrated" with social security.[8] Also, if certain requirements are met, contributions may vary based on a formula that takes age and service, as well as compensation, into account.[9]

[1]—Profit-Sharing Plans

Many firms have profit-sharing plans which benefit both partners and administrative employees. Associates often are not included in these plans. Under the terms of these plans the firm makes contributions to the plan for the benefit of the participants. Firm contributions, which may be discretionary each year, generally are allocated to participants based on compensation, and are credited to separate accounts for the participants. Tax deductible contributions, for 2001, are limited to 15% of the compensation of the plan participants[10] and, for 2001, the maximum annual aggregate contribution per participant to *all* defined contribution plans of the employer is $35,000 or, if less, 25% of the participant's compensation.[11] For 2002, the aggregate deduction limit is 25% of compensation and the individual limit is the lesser of $40,000 or 100% of compensation.[12] For 2001, only the first $170,000 of a participant's compensation is taken into account under the deductible and individual limits.[13] For 2002, the limitation is $200,000.[14] The $40,000 and $200,000 limits will be automatically increased periodically for inflation.[15]

Employer contributions (and plan earnings allocable thereto) may be subject to deferred vesting. The employee's termination before becoming fully vested will result in a forfeiture that may be allocated to other participants as if a contribution, or may be used to offset otherwise required employer contributions. Generally, a plan participant must be fully vested after completing five years of service.[16] However, full vesting can be delayed for up to seven years if graduated vesting commences at the completion of two years of service.[17]

---

[8] I.R.C. § 401(1)(5)(A); 26 U.S.C. § 401(1)(5)(A).

[9] Treas. Reg. § 1.401(a)(4)-8; 26 C.F.R. § 1.401(a)(4)-8.

[10] I.R.C. § 404(a)(3); 26 U.S.C. § 404(a)(3).

[11] I.R.C. § 415(c)(1); 26 U.S.C. § 415(c)(1).

[12] I.R.C. §§ 404(a)(3)(A)(i)(1), 415(c)(1); 26 U.S.C. as amended by EGTRRA §§ 616(A)(1)(a), 611(B)(1), 632(A)(1).

[13] I.R.C. § 401(a)(17)(A); 26 U.S.C. § 404(a)(17)(A) as amended by EGTRRA §611(c).

[14] I.R.C. §401(a)(17(A); 26 U.S.C. § 401(a)(17)(A) as amended by EGTRRA §611(c).

[15] I.R.C. §§ 401(a)(17)(B), 415(d)(1); 26 U.S.C. §§ 401(a)(17)(B), 415(d)(1), as amended by EGTRRA §611(b)(2)(A), (c).

[16] I.R.C. § 411(a)(2)(A); 26 U.S.C. § 411(A)(2)(A).

[17] I.R.C. § 411(a)(2)(B); 26 U.S.C. § 411(a)(2)(B).

If plan benefits are concentrated in "key employees" (including partners) under a "top heavy plan," plan participants are required to become vested sooner than under the otherwise permitted vesting schedules.[18] Minimum contributions also may be required for "nonkey" participants.[19]

[2]—Money Purchase Pension Plans

Many firms have money purchase pension plans in lieu of, or in addition to, profit-sharing plans. Firm contributions, which are mandatory under the contribution formula, generally are based on compensation (subject to the $170,000 limit for 2001 and the $200,000 limit for 2002,[20] but under a "target benefit" plan may be based on a pension formula. The maximum contributions for such plans are the same as those for profit-sharing plans (i.e., $35,000 or 25% of compensation for 2001 and $40,000 or 100% of compensation for 2002.[21] For 2001, the deduction limitation generally is equal to the contributions made pursuant to the plan's formula.[22] Beginning in 2002, the deductible limit will be the same 25% of aggregate compensation that will apply to profit-sharing plans.[23]The deferred vesting rules apply to money purchase pension plans. Forfeitures by terminating participants generally are applied to offset otherwise required contributions.

[3]—Cash or Deferred Plans (401(k) plans)

Section 401(k) of the Internal Revenue Code permits the establishment of a tax-qualified plan under which a participant can elect either to receive the employer's contribution in cash or have it made to the employee's account in the plan. Many law firms have adopted these plans as suitable vehicles for partners', associates' and administrative employees' retirement programs. Participants' elective contributions, which must be 100% vested at all times, are accumulated tax deferred until the participants reaches retirement age or separates from the firm.[24] Elective contributions by highly compensated plan participants

---

[18] I.R.C. §§ 416(a)(1) and 416(b)(1); 26 U.S.C. §§ 416(a)(1) and 416(b)(1).

[19] I.R.C. § 416(c); 26 U.S.C. § 416(c).

[20] See N 14 *supra.*

[21] See N 12 *supra.*

[22] I.R.C. §§ 404(a)(1), 404(a)(8) and 412; 26 U.S.C. §§ 404(a)(1), 404(a)(8) and 412.

[23] I.R.C. § 404(a)(3)(A)(v); 26 U.S.C. § 404(a)(3)(A)(v), as amended by EGTRRA § 616(a)(2)(A).

[24] I.R.C. § 401(k)(2); 26 U.S.C. § 401(k)(2).

may be limited by the average elective deferral made by non-highly compensated participants,[25] and, in any event, may not exceed $10,500 for 2001.[26]

The dollar limit increases to $11,000 in 2002 and in annual $1,000 increments thereafter, reaching $15,000 in 2006.[27] In addition, beginning in 2002, participants at least age 50 are permitted supplementary "catch-up" deferrals, limited to $1,000 in 2002 and increasing in annual $1,000 increments, reaching $5,000 in 2006.[28] Unlike other participant deferrals, these "catch up" deferrals are not taken into account under the annual $40,000 contribution limit.[29] Beginning in 2002, all participant deferrals, including those by partners, are deductible without regard to the deductible limit equal to 25% of aggregate participant compensation limit.[30]To the extent a partner is permitted to vary his or her contributions to any tax qualified plan (e.g., to a profit-sharing plan), the limitation explained above for highly compensated plan participants and the rules of Section 401(k) will apply, even if the plan is not designed as a 401(k) plan.[31] However, a firm's contribution, that "match" a partner's elective deferrals will not themselves be treated as elective deferrals even if charged to the partner's distributive share.[32]

---

[25] I.R.C. § 401(k)(3); 26 U.S.C. § 401(k)(3).

[26] I.R.C. § 402(g)(1); 26 U.S.C. § 402(g)(1).

[27] I.R.C. § 402(g)(1)(B); 26 U.S.C. § 402(g)(1)(B), as amended by EGTRRA § 611(d)(1).

[28] I.R.C. § 414(v); 26 U.S.C. § 414(v), as added by EGTRRA § 631(a).

[29] I.R.C. § 414(v)(3); 26 U.S.C. § 414(v)(3), as added by EGTRRA § 631(a).

[30] I.R.C. § 404(n); 26 U.S.C. 404(n), as added by EGTRRA § 614.

[31] Treas. Reg. § 1.401(k)-1(a); 26 C.F.R. § 1.401(k)-1(a).

[32] I.R.C. § 402(g)(8); 26 U.S.C. § 402(g)(8), as redesignated by EGTRRA § 611(d)(3)(A).

§ 16.04 Defined Benefit Plans

Partners and administrative staff are generally the participants in a law firm's defined benefit plan. Defined benefit plans provide participants with annual retirement benefits established by a pension formula. A law firm's annual tax-deductible contribution is the amount required to fund the benefits[1] and can be greater or less than the firm's deductible contribution to a defined contribution plan. The amount of the contribution must be determined by an actuary.

A defined benefit plan's pension formula typically takes both years of service and compensation into account. For 2001, only the first $170,000 of compensation may be taken into account under the formula.[2] For 2002, the compensation limit is increased to $200,000 and will be further increased periodically for inflation.[3] A "top heavy" plan that concentrates benefits in "key employees" may be required to provide a minimum annual benefit for all participants.[4]

For 2001, a participant's annual benefit from a defined benefit plan generally may not exceed $140,000.[5] For 2002, the limit is increased to $160,000 and will be further increased periodically for inflation,[6] but also is decreased for pension benefits commencing before age 62. Participants in defined benefit plans do not have the option of selecting various investment funds as do participants in most defined contribution plans. Although it will vary from firm to firm, the investments held by a defined benefit plan will generally be more traditional (e.g., blue chip stocks, corporate and government bonds) avoiding the high-yield, more risky investment options available in defined contribution plans. This is due to the fact that the assets of a defined benefit plan must be available to pay the benefits determined by the benefit formula for all eligible beneficiaries, whereas the obligation of a defined contribution plan is limited to the total of plan assets allocated to each participant.

---

[1] I.R.C. §§ 404(a)(1), 401(a)(8) and 412; 26 U.S.C. §§ 404(a)(1), 404(a)(8) and 412.

[2] I.R.C. § 401(a)(17)(A); 26 U.S.C. § 401(a)(17)(A).

[3] I.R.C. § 401(a)(17)(B); 26 U.S.C. § 401(a)(17)(B) as amended by EGTRRA § 611(c).

[4] I.R.C. §§ 416(a)(2) and 416(c); 26 U.S.C. §§ 416(a)(2) and 416(c).

[5] I.R.C. § 415(b)(1)(A); 26 U.S.C. § 415(b)(1)(A).

[6] I.R.C. §§ 415(b)(1)(A); 2(c); 26 U.S.C. §§ 415(b)(1)(A), (2)(c) as amended by EGTRRA § 611(a).

§ 16.05 "Cross Testing" for Nondiscrimination

For defined contribution plans, whether profit-sharing or money purchase pension plans, demonstration of compliance with the requirement that contributions or benefits do not discriminate in favor of partners or highly compensated employees[1] generally is done by "testing" contributions. The contribution rate for partners and highly compensated employees for the year, expressed as a percentage of that year's compensation, must not exceed that for nonhighly compensated employees (or, if the contribution rate for the partners and highly compensated employees is greater, it must be within the "permitted disparity").[2] Similarly, for a defined benefit pension plan, demonstration of compliance with the nondiscrimination requirement generally is done by "testing" benefits. Either the same benefit formula must apply to all plan participants or alternative "proofs" of nondiscriminatory benefits must be applied.[3]

"Cross testing" is also permitted.[4] For a defined contribution plan, employer contributions are converted into equivalent projected pension benefits for the participant. For a defined benefit pension plan, the participant's projected pension benefits are converted into an equivalent employer contribution rate. Cross testing requires determinations by an actuary.

"Cross testing" often can provide partners increased contributions or benefits while minimizing the cost for benefits for non-partner employees. It is commonly applied where the profit-sharing or pension plan covers partners and staff, but excludes associates.

---

[1] I.R.C. § 401(a)(4); 26 U.S.C § 401(a)(4).
[2] Treas. Reg. §§ 1.401(a)(4)-2, 1.401(a)(4)-7.
[3] Treas. Reg. § 1.401(a)(4)-3.
[4] Treas. Reg. § 1.401(a)(4)-8.

§ 16.06 Other Retirement Programs

In addition to unfunded retirement arrangements and qualified retirement plans, there are other programs through which law firm partners may accumulate retirement benefits. These include (1) partner life insurance arrangements, (2) individual retirement savings arrangements, and (3) post-retirement benefits other than pensions.

[1]—Partner Life Insurance Arrangements

There are two approaches to obtaining insurance on partners' lives. Under one approach, partners designate their beneficiary and are charged with the premiums individually. Under the second approach, the firm is the beneficiary and absorbs the aggregate cost of life insurance policy premiums related to the firm's partners collectively. The approach used depends on the objective of the insurance program. In either case, life insurance premiums are not deductible for tax purposes. When the objective of the program is to provide a surviving spouse benefits not otherwise covered by the firm's unfunded partner retirement program, the partner will designate the beneficiary and will be charged with the premium. When the objective of the program is to develop a vehicle that will eventually fund the presently unfunded partner retirement program in its entirety, the firm will be designated as the beneficiary and will absorb the aggregate cost of the life insurance premiums. The firm should consult with its tax advisor if it contemplates adopting either of these programs because there are tax implications. In addition to the nondeductibility of the life insurance premiums, there are complex rules affecting the deductibility of interest expense if the firm leverages the purchase of the insurance through borrowings.[1]

[2]—Individual Retirement Savings Arrangements (IRAs)

Tax-sheltered individual retirement accounts, commonly known as "IRAs," allow individuals a current income tax deduction for a portion of their compensation paid into the IRA, and income tax deferral on the earnings of the plan.[2] For 2001, the maximum deductible IRA contribution is $2,000. After 2001, the IRA contribution limit will increase over seven years, so that it will be $3,000 in 2002 through 2004, $4,000 in 2005 through 2007, and $5,000 thereafter. Self-employed individuals, including law firm partners, may use IRAs. However, the tax deduction for contributions to an IRA is phased out for higher income taxpayers

---

[1] I.R.C. § 264(a); 26 U.S.C. § 264(a).

[2] I.R.C. §§ 219(a) and 408(e)(1); 26 U.S.C. §§ 219(a) and 408(e)(1).

who are active participants in qualified retirement plans.[3] Contributions may be made to an IRA on behalf of a nonworking spouse even if the working spouse is an active participant in a qualified plan. This deduction is subject to the income-based phase-out.

[3]—Post-Retirement Benefits Other Than Pensions

Some law firms may offer their partners and employees health care and other benefits upon their retirement from the firm. These benefits can either be payable for life or some specified period after retirement. Statement of Financial Accounting Standards No. 106, "Employer's Accounting for Postretirement Benefits Other Than Pensions" (FAS 106), issued by the Financial Accounting Standards Board, requires that for accrual basis financial statements, the present value of these benefits be accrued during the years that the partner or employee is providing services to the firm. FAS 106 also sets forth comprehensive requirements as to the information that should be disclosed in the footnotes to the firm's financial statements. As most law firms are on the modified cash basis of accounting, post-retirement benefits other than pensions are accounted for on a pay-as-you-go basis and not recorded as a liability in the firm's statement of net assets. However, if significant post-retirement benefit plans other than pensions exist, firms generally have chosen to follow the disclosure requirements as set forth in FAS 106.

[4]—Roth IRAs

Individuals may make contributions to a Roth IRA. Unlike a regular IRA, contributions to a Roth IRA are not deductible.[4] Instead, the tax advantages are "backloaded," so that interest and dividends earned

---

[3] I.R.C. § 219(g); 26 U.S.C. § 219(g). The Taxpayer Relief Act of 1997 gradually increases the adjusted gross income ("AGI") phase-out limits, as follows:

Tax year beginning in	Single AGI	Joint AGI
1998	$30,000-40,000	$50,000-60,000
1999	$31,000-41,000	$51,000-61,000
2000	$32,000-42,000	$52,000-62,000
2001	$33,000-43,000	$53,000-63,000
2002	$34,000-44,000	$54,000-64,000
2003	$40,000-50,000	$60,000-70,000
2004	$45,000-55,000	$65,000-75,000
2005	$50,000-60,000	$70,000-80,000
2006	$50,000-60,000	$75,000-85,000
2007	$50,000-60,000	$80,000-100,000

[4] IRC § 408A(c)(1); 26 U.S.C. § 408A(c)(1).

on the Roth IRA may not be taxable. The same income-based phase-out provision for a regular IRA applies to the Roth IRA.[5] Unlike regular IRAs, however, individuals are allowed to make contributions to a Roth IRA after they are age 701/2.[6] Contributions to all IRAs are coordinated to prevent an individual from exceeding the statutory contribution limit. [7]

All earnings on a Roth IRA are exempt permanently from taxation provided distributions occur after the account has been held for at least five years and the account holder is at least 591/2 years old, the distribution is on account of death or disability, or the distribution is for the first-time home purchase.[8]

[5]—Education IRAs

Individuals can make after-tax contributions to an Education IRA.[9] This tax-favored vehicle is a savings account dedicated exclusively to the payment of education expenses for the account's designated beneficiary.[10] In 2001, annual nondeductible contributions of up to $500 can be made to an IRA prior to the time that the designated beneficiary attains age 18.[11] The $500 limit is phased out for single individuals with adjusted gross income between $95,000 and $110,000 and for married individuals filing a joint return with adjusted gross income between $150,000 and $160,000.[12] Beginning in 2002, the annual contribution limit is increased from $500 to $2,000 and the income phase-out range for married taxpayers is doubled.

Earnings of an Education IRA are exempt from tax to the extent distributed to pay higher education expenses of the designated beneficiary.[13] However, if distributions are made for purposes other than the qualified higher education expenses of the designated beneficiary, earnings are included in the designated beneficiary's income and subject to a 10% income tax penalty.[14] Unused Education IRA balances may be rolled over to a Roth IRA.

---

[5] IRC § 408A(c)(2)(C); 26 U.S.C. § 408A (c)(2)(C). See also, N. 3 *supra.*

[6] IRC § 408A(c)(4); 26 U.S.C. § 408A(c)(4).

[7] IRC § 408A(c)(2); 26 U.S.C. § 408A(c)(2).

[8] IRC § 408A(d); 26 U.S.C. § 408A(d).

[9] IRC § 530; 26 U.S.C. § 530.

[10] IRC § 530(a); 26 U.S.C. § 530(a).

[11] IRC § 530(b)(1)(A); 26 U.S.C. § 530(b)(1)(A).

[12] IRC § 530(c)(1); 26 U.S.C. § 530(c)(1).

[13] IRC § 530(d)(2)(A); 26 U.S.C. § 530(d)(2)(A).

[14] IRC §§ 530(d)(2)(B) and 530(d)(4)(A); 26 U.S.C. §§ 530(d)(2)(B) and 530(d)(4)(A).

§ 16.07 Financial Disclosures by Law Firms About Their Retirement Programs

Financial disclosures about retirement programs are usually made in the notes to a law firm's financial statements. The extent and content of disclosure depends on whether the programs are (1) unfunded or (2) funded.

[1]—Unfunded Retirement Programs

Unfunded retirement programs of law firms typically represent commitments to make retirement payments to former partners from future profits of the firm. Disclosure of the commitment in the notes to the firm's financial statements[1] usually includes:

(1) A brief description of the retirement arrangement, including the method of calculating payments.

(2) An identification of the maximum amount payable in a single year, if the partnership agreement specifies a "cap."

(3) An estimate of the aggregate amount payable during the forthcoming year.

[2]—Funded Retirement Programs

Statement of Financial Accounting Standards No. 87, "Employer's Accounting for Pensions" (FAS 87), issued by the Financial Accounting Standards Board (the "FASB"), prescribes an employer's accounting for retirement programs and the related financial disclosure in its accrual basis financial statements. Since most law firms use the modified cash basis of accounting, they do not follow the guidance set forth in FAS 87 as to the recognition of assets of liabilities resulting from the firm's retirement plans. Most law firms do, however, observe the financial statement disclosure requirements as set forth in FAS 87. The FASB requirements include disclosure by an employer of the following information for each type of plan:

---

[1] An example of typical note disclosure of commitments to former partners is contained in Chapter 2 *supra*.

	Defined Benefit Plans	Defined Contribution Plans
a. A description of the plan	X	X
b. The amount of cost recognized during the period	X	X
c. A schedule reconciling the funded status of the plan with amounts reported in the employer's statement of financial position (only applicable to accrual basis statements)	X	
d. Rate assumptions used in developing certain pension disclosure information	X	
e. If applicable, information relevant to related-party transactions, alternative methods used, etc.	X	

FAS 87 specifies the detailed components of each of these disclosure requirements, which are quite comprehensive.[2]

---

[2] An example of note disclosure by a firm which sponsors both a defined benefit pension plan and a defined contribution retirement plan is contained in Chapter 2 *supra.*

§ 16.08 Financial Reporting by Retirement and Pension Plans

Retirement arrangements vary from firm to firm. One configuration that has been adopted by a significant number of law firms includes an unfunded retirement arrangement for partners supplemented by: (1) funded defined contribution plans for associates (many firms allow associates to participate in a defined contribution plan on a non-contributory basis), partners and administrative employees, and (2) a funded defined benefit plan for partners and administrative employees. Funded pension and retirement plans which meet certain levels of eligible participants are subject to filing audited financial statements with the Department of Labor and the Internal Revenue Service. Most firms prepare the financial statements of their funded retirement plans on the accrual basis of accounting in conformity with generally accepted accounting principles. Some firms, however, prepare their funded retirement plan financial statements on the cash or modified cash basis of accounting which is a comprehensive basis of accounting different from generally accepted accounting principles. While the accrual basis of accounting is preferred, regulations promulgated by the Department of Labor regarding the filing of financial information for retirement plans permit the cash and modified cash basis of accounting provided that the method is consistently applied.

[1]—Standards of Financial Reporting

Generally accepted accounting principles for financial statements of funded pension and retirement plans have been set forth by the Financial Accounting Standards Board (FASB) and the American Institute of Certified Public Accountants (AICPA). The basic financial statements for all funded retirement plans are a statement of net assets available for benefits and a statement of changes in net assets available for the benefits. In addition, funded defined benefit plans may include a statement of accumulated benefits and a statement of changes in accumulated benefits although frequently such information is disclosed in a footnote to the financial statements. This information is actuarially determined based on the defined benefit formula for eligible employees. Accumulated benefits information is not applicable to defined contribution plans because, in this type of plan, each participant's benefits are based solely on amounts accumulated in individual participant accounts and not on a benefit formula.

[2]—Examples of Financial Information

The following example illustrates condensed financial information for a law firm's defined contribution plan (Figure 16-B).

Some of the unique accounting principles applicable to retirement and pension plans relate to:

- Investments—Investments generally are accounted for at fair value, based on quoted market prices for publicly traded investments or a market value determined by the investment manager, trustee or custodian for investments that are not traded publicly.
- Benefit obligations—The financial statements focus on net assets *available* for benefits: the plan's obligations for benefits payable currently and in the future are not liabilities of the plan. If significant, the current benefit obligation should be presented in the footnotes to the financial statements.
- Investment options of a defined contribution plan—If the participants in a defined contribution plan are permitted to select from a number of investment options for the purpose of investing their contributions to the plan, current authoritative guidance requires that financial information for each investment option be presented in the plan's financial statements. Because a participant is investing in individual investment options and not the plan as a whole, separate financial statement information for each investment option is needed by the participants to make practical decisions on how their funds should be invested.

The following abbreviated example illustrates the funding status of the defined benefit plan (Figure 16-C)

This plan's unfunded status, as disclosed in the illustration (before any assumption about future compensation levels), is as follows:

Actuarial present value of accumulated plan benefits	$ 2,200,000
Net assets available for benefits	2,000,000
Unfunded pension obligation	$(200,000)

Most law firms choose to present the information relating to the actuarial present value of accumulated plan benefits and the related changes in the actuarial present value of accumulated plan benefits for the reporting period in the notes to the financial statements rather than as separate financial statements.

Figure 16-B. Illustration of condensed financial information for a law firm's defined contribution plan.

ABC LAW FIRM PARTNERSHIP
CONDENSED FINANCIAL INFORMATION
DEFINED CONTRIBUTION PLAN

	Equity Fund	Bond Fund	Money Market Fund	Total
NET ASSETS AVAILABLE FOR BENEFITS:				
Investments at fair value	$2,700,000	$1,520,000	$480,000	$4,700,000
Employer/employee contributions receivable	100,000	80,000	20,000	200,000
Receivable for securities sold	200,000			200,000
Payable for securities purchased		(100,000)		(100,000)
Net assets available for benefits	$3,000,000	$1,500,000	$500,000	$5,000,000

	Equity Fund	Bond Fund	Money Market Fund	Total
CHANGES IN NET ASSETS AVAILABLE FOR BENEFITS:				
Investment income	$275,000	$100,000	$ 25,000	$400,000
Employer/employee contributions	300,000	150,000	50,000	500,000
Benefits paid to participants	(150,000)	(40,000)	(10,000)	(200,000)
Administrative expenses	(30,000)	(15,000)	(5,000)	(50,000)
Net increase	395,000	195,000	60,000	650,000
Net assets available for benefits:				
Beginning of year	2,605,000	1,305,000	440,000	4,350,000
End of year	$3,000,000	$1,500,000	$500,000	$5,000,000

Figure 16-C. Illustration of condensed financial information for a law firm's defined benefit plan.

ABC LAW FIRM PARTNERSHIP
CONDENSED FINANCIAL INFORMATION
DEFINED BENEFIT PLAN

NET ASSETS AVAILABLE FOR BENEFITS:	
Investments at fair value	$1,900,000
Employer contributions receivable	100,000
Receivable for securities sold	50,000
Payable for securities purchased	(50,000)
Net assets available for benefits	$2,000,000
CHANGES IN NET ASSETS AVAILABLE FOR BENEFITS:	
Investment income	$ 200,000
Employer contributions	200,000
Benefits paid to participants	(90,000)
Administrative expenses	(10,000)
Net increase	300,000
Net assets available for benefits:	
Beginning of year	1,700,000
End of year	$2,000,000
ACTUARIAL PRESENT VALUE OF ACCUMULATED PLAN BENEFITS:	
Vested Benefits:	
Participants receiving payments	$ 400,000
Other participants	1,500,000
Nonvested benefits	300,000
Total	$2,200,000
CHANGES IN ACTUARIAL PRESENT VALUE OF ACCUMULATED PLAN BENEFITS:	
At beginning of year	1,900,000
Increase (decrease) during the year attributable to:	
Benefits accumulated	300,000
Increase for interest due to the decrease in the discount period	100,000
Changes in actuarial assumptions	(10,000)
Benefits paid	(90,000)
Net increase	300,000
At end of year	$2,200,000

The information generally contained in the footnotes to the financial statements of defined contribution and defined benefit plans is summarized below:

	Defined Contribution Plan	Defined Benefit Plan
1. Description of the plan including plan amendments	X	X
2. Summary of accounting policies	X	X
3. Funding policy		X
4. Investments	X	X
5. Accumulated plan benefits		X
6. Benefit obligations	X	X
7. Participant loans	X	
8. Income tax exemption	X	X

Actual footnote disclosures will depend on the activity and features of the plan. Additional disclosures may be required to highlight unique activity or features of the plan.

§ 16.09 Government Compliance Reporting (Form 5500)

The Employee Retirement Income Security Act of 1974 (ERISA) established certain reporting requirements for tax-qualified or other funded employee retirement plans.[1] Under these requirements, many plans are required to file certain (1) prescribed forms and (2) plan financial statements and schedules with government agencies.

[1]—Annual Report

An "Annual Return/Report of Employee Benefit Plan" (Form 5500) must be filed annually with the Department of Labor and is used by the three agencies responsible for enforcement of employee benefit plans:

- Department of the Treasury (Internal Revenue Service)
- Department of Labor (Office of Pension and Welfare Benefit Programs)
- Pension Benefit Guaranty Corporation

All filers, regardless of size, must file the Form 5500. While the Form 5500 C/R has been eliminated, the distinctions between large plans (100 or more participants at the beginning of the plan year) and small plans (fewer than 100 participants) have been retained. The Form 5500 is used to provide basic identifying information regarding the plan and the plan sponsor. In addition to the Form 5500, there are a number of schedules that may have to be completed based on the type and/or size of plan. Large plans must provide detailed financial information on Schedule H. Small plans must provide only limited financial information on Schedule I.

Financial information may be prepared using either the accrual, cash or modified cash basis of accounting.

[2]—Plan Financial Statements and Schedules

Plans with 100 or more participants (with certain exemptions) also are required to file a copy of the plan's financial statements, financial schedules and an independent accountant's opinion. Financial schedules required to be filed include:

(1) Statement of all assets held for investment at year-end and a schedule of all assets which were both acquired and disposed of during the year;

---

[1] See § 103 of ERISA.

(2) Schedule of transactions with parties in interest (Part III of Schedule G);

(3) Schedule of obligations in default (Part I of Schedule G);

(4) Schedule of leases in default (Part II of Schedule G); and

(5) Schedule of transactions in excess of 5% of current value of plan assets.

The Form 5500 is due within seven months of the plan's year-end (i.e., by July 31 for calendar year plans). Additionally, plans may obtain an automatic extension of up to two and a half months by filing Form 5558 before the regular due date.

[3]—Examples of Financial Information

Figure 16-D Illustrates an example of a condensed summary of assets and liabilities of a law firm's retirement and pension plans as reported on "Annual Return/Report of Employee Benefit Plan" (Form 5500).

Figure 16-E Illustrates an example of a condensed summary of income, expenses and changes in net assets of a law firm's retirement and pension plans as reported on "Annual Return/Report of Employee Benefit Plan" (Form 5500).

Only the summary headings are presented in the illustrations. The actual Form 5500 requires a detailed breakdown of the components of several of these summary headings.

The difference of $100,000 and $50,000 between the net assets presented in the condensed financial statements (see Figures 16-B and 16-C) and the condensed Form 5500 information (see Figure 16-D) relates to current benefit obligations to participants. As prescribed in the current authoritative guidance, benefit obligations to participants as of the financial statement date are not included in the determination of net assets available for benefits in the financial statements. Currently payable benefit obligations to participants are, however, treated as liabilities and thus included in the calculation of net assets available for benefits on the Form 5500.

Figure 16-D. Illustration of a condensed summary of assets and liabilities of a law firm's retirement and pension plans as reported on "Annual Return/Report of Employee Benefit Plan" (Form 5500).

ABC LAW FIRM PARTNERSHIP
RETIREMENT AND PENSION PLAN ASSETS
AND LIABILITIES
(Form 5500 Format - Condensed)

	Line Item on Form	Defined Contribution Plan	Defined Benefit Plan
	Assets		
(a)	Non-interest bearing cash		
(b)	Receivables	$400,000	$150,000
(c)	General investments	4,700,000	1,900,000
(d)	Employer-related investments		
(e)	Buildings and other depreciable property		
(f)	Total assets	5,100,000	2,050,000
	Liabilities		
(g)	Benefits payable	(100,000)	(50,000)
(h)	Other payables	(100,000)	(50,000)
(i)	Acquisition indebtedness		
(j)	Other liabilities		
(k)	Total Liabilities	(200,000)	(100,000)
(l)	Net assets	$4,900,000	$1,950,000

Figure 16-E. Illustration of a condensed summary of income, expenses and changes in net assets of a law firm's retirement and pension plans as reported on "Annual Return/Report of Employee Benefit Plan" (Form 5500).

ABC LAW FIRM PARTNERSHIP
RETIREMENT AND PENSION PLAN INCOME,
EXPENSES AND CHANGES IN NET ASSETS
(Form 5500 Format - Condensed)

	Line Item on Form	Defined Benefit Plan	Defined Contribution Plan
	Income		
(a)	Contributions	$500,000	$200,000
(b)	Earnings on investments	430,000	205,000
(b)	Net realized gain (loss)	20,000	5,000
(b)	Unrealized appreciation (depreciation)	(50,000)	(10,000)
(c)	Other income		
(d)	Total income	900,000	400,000
	Expenses		
(e)	Benefit payments	(300,000)	(140,000)
(f)	Interest expense		
(g)	Administrative expenses	(50,000)	(10,000)
(h)	Total expenses	(350,000)	(150,000)
(i)	Net income	550,000	250,000
(j)	Transfers to (from) the plan		
(k)	Net assets at beginning of year	4,350,000	1,700,000
(l)	Net assets at end of year	$4,900,000	$1,950,000

§ 16.10 Professional Tax Advice

Ordinarily, it is advisable for the firm to consult a professional tax advisor with respect to the development and implementation of a comprehensive retirement program. Because of the variety of retirement arrangements and plans presently available and the continuing changes in tax rules affecting these matters, such consultation becomes especially critical.

CHAPTER 17

Tax Planning

Chapter Contents

§ 17.01 Tax Planning for Law Firms

"Anyone may so arrange his affairs that his taxes shall be as low as possible; he is not bound to choose that pattern which will best pay the Treasury; there is not even a patriotic duty to increase one's taxes."[1] In his historic 1934 *dicta*, Judge Learned Hand confirmed

---

[1] Helvering v. Gregory, 69 F. 2d 809, 810 (2d Cir. 1934), *aff'd* 293 U.S. 465 (1935).

that everyone has a right to do tax planning to minimize the amount of taxes that he or she has to pay.

The principal objective of tax planning for law firms, therefore, is the lawful reduction of taxes payable by a firm and its partners. This chapter apprises the reader of some of the tax planning opportunities available to law firms. These opportunities are discussed in general terms and are not an all-inclusive list of items to consider when planning the affairs of a law firm.

The discussions in this chapter generally, are based on the tax rules in effect during calendar year 2001. Consequently, these opportunities should not be acted upon without:

(1) advice and comments from the law firm's professional tax advisor, and

(2) consideration of subsequent changes in tax laws and the potential effect of proposed tax legislation.

A discussion of tax planning ideas would not be complete without mentioning the Internal Revenue Service's activity in this area. During 1988, in California, the IRS started a project focusing on attorneys who had not filed tax returns. At the time, there was a perception within the IRS that up to 10% of practicing attorneys were not filing tax returns. To learn more about attorneys and law firms, the IRS organized agents into market segment teams for research and development, case examinations, and production of audit technique guides. Their combined efforts led to the April 1993 release of the *Market Segment Specialization Program-Attorneys,*[2] or MSSP for short. The MSSP is designed to identify industry-specific information needed to develop a cadre of IRS agents capable of examining sole-practitioner attorneys or law firms in general.

The MSSP is a primer on ways to identify and examine noncomplying attorneys. It provides specific guidelines on conducting examinations and what to look for during the examination. It includes discussions of income and expense items and, in the eyes of the IRS, the tax treatment of each. It also discusses client-disbursement accounting and withholding tax issues. The MSSP is helpful, because it highlights what the IRS considers important with respect to law firms and how tax planning for certain items might be viewed by the IRS. Any tax planning should consider the MSSP. Lastly, the MSSP may be the IRS's way of announcing that it intends to increase its audit activity of attorneys and law firms.

---

[2] Department of the Treasury, I.R.S. Training 3149-103, TPDS 83183A. The MSSP was revised as Training 3149-102 in June 1994.

This chapter focuses on some of the areas where tax planning strategies are needed. The strategies involve a firm making choices from alternative courses of action. Choosing the most tax-advantageous course of action should follow a study of the alternatives, the business advantages and disadvantages of each, and the tax consequences of each. However, do not undertake a course of action merely because it has beneficial tax consequences, if it defeats (or seriously jeopardizes) the business purpose of the activity. From a tax planning perspective, there are three areas where choices may be available to a law firm:

(1) Accounting methods;
(2) Accounting periods; and
(3) Partner profit/loss sharing arrangements.

Each area is discussed in the following sections.

§ 17.02 Accounting Methods

[1]—Alternative Tax Accounting Methods

All entities (partnerships or corporations) must compute their taxable income using of recognized accounting methods.[1]

A newly established law firm must choose an overall method of accounting for tax purposes in its first tax return. (Generally, this method is the same as the method used for financial statement reporting purposes.) However, some law firms choose to follow generally accepted accounting principles, a modified cash method or a modified accrual method of accounting for financial statement reporting purposes and to follow tax rules for tax return purposes. Different accounting methods can produce significantly different net incomes (e.g., the selection of useful lives for leasehold improvements, recognition of work-in-progress, and recognition of fees receivable).

Once a firm elects its overall method of accounting, it must make choices regarding the application of this accounting method to specific situations. Law firms that use an accounting method for financial reporting purposes that is different from the one they use for tax purposes should weigh this decision carefully. It creates a burden on the firm's accounting department to maintain books and records for tax purposes, memoranda records for financial reporting purposes, and formal reconciliations to identify and track the current and cumulative differences between these two records. Different accounting records may also create timing differences in the recognition of income or expenses by the firm's partners. (For example, when leasehold improvements are amortized over thirty-nine years for tax reporting purposes and over the life of the lease for financial statement reporting purposes.) This could result in the recognition of an item of revenue or expense by a group of partners in one year for income distribution purposes and by a different group of partners in another year for income tax purposes. In making its decision, the firm should consider which method produces a result that most clearly reflects equity among partners.

Historically, once a partnership established its accounting method (or a specific application of its accounting method), it had to, in most instances, request permission of the Internal Revenue Service to change to another method.[2] When a taxpayer, without prior permission from the IRS, changed the method of accounting for a *material item*, it was not

---

[1] IRC § 446(c); 26 U.S.C. § 446(c).
[2] IRC § 446(e); 26 U.S.C. § 446(e).

allowed to amend prior years' returns to correct the change, because the change had been consistently applied for five years.[3] Similarly, without permission from the IRS, a taxpayer may not retroactively change from an erroneous method to a permissible method by filing amended returns, even if the period for amending the return for the first year in which the erroneous method was used is still open.[4]

[2]—Financial Statements vs. Tax Reporting

In an age where "materiality" is the measurement of correctness, the obvious question facing a law firm is, "When is an item material for tax purposes?" For financial statement purposes, "material" is generally a function of a law firm's net income or ordinary income, but for tax purposes, a material item is any item which involves the proper time for the inclusion of the item in income or the taking of a deduction.[5] In judging whether an accounting practice for an item involves timing, the relevant question generally is whether the practice permanently changes the amount of the taxpayer's lifetime income.[6] If the practice does *not* permanently affect the taxpayer's lifetime income, but does or could change the taxable year in which income is reported, it involves timing and is, therefore, a method of accounting.[7] A change in the characterization of an item also may constitute a change in the method of accounting if the change has the effect of shifting income from one period to another (e.g., a change in treating client disbursements as a receivable instead of the firm's expense).[8] Once a method of accounting is adopted, it must be consistently applied unless authorization is obtained from the Internal Revenue Service to change the method.[9]

[3]—Changing Tax Methods of Accounting

The IRS has issued two Revenue Procedures for changing an accounting method; one for situations in which the IRS will approve accounting method changes automatically,[10] (discussed below), and one in which the taxpayer must apply for and the IRS must grant permission to change a method of accounting.[11] The taxpayer must submit

---

[3] Ltr. Rul. 9421003 (May 27, 1994).
[4] Rev. Rul. 90-38, 1990-1 C.B. 57.
[5] Treas. Reg. § 1.446-1(e)(2)(ii)(a); 26 C.F.R. § 1.446-1(e)(2)(ii)(a).
[6] See § 3.02 of Rev. Proc. 91-31, 1991-1 C.B. 566.
[7] See § 2.01 of Rev. Proc. 97-27, I.R.B 1997-21, 11.
[8] See § 2.01 of Rev. Proc. 97-27, I.R.B 1997-21, 11.
[9] Treas. Reg. § 1.446-1(e)(2)(i)(a); 26 C.F.R. § 1.446-1(e)(2)(i)(a).
[10] See Rev. Proc. 97-27, I.R.B. 1997-21, 10.
[11] See Rev. Proc. 99-49, I.R.B. 1999-52, (Dec. 14, 1999).

Form 3115 Application for Change in Accounting Method any time prior to the end of the tax year for which the change is to be effective.[12] Any adjustment to income, either positive or negative can be amortized over four years.[13]

In processing an application for change in method of accounting, the IRS will consider whether the firm's present method clearly reflects income and whether the firm's books and records will conform with the proposed new method of accounting. The IRS will also consider the need for consistency in the accounting area in light of the reason for wanting to change the method of accounting when the present method clearly reflects income.[14] Usually, as a condition of approving the change, the IRS will require the firm to spread the "catch up" adjustment over a period of years.[15]

To streamline the approval process, the IRS issued a procedure whereby taxpayers can obtain automatic consents to change specified methods of accounting.[16] The procedure consolidates and supersedes most published automatic consent guidelines for changes in methods of accounting and generally provides simplified uniform procedures to obtain automatic consents.[17] Using the automatic consent procedure, if a law firm wishes to change a method of accounting listed in the Appendix of the procedure, it only has to attach a completed Form 3115 to its timely filed tax return and send a copy of the form to the Internal Revenue Service National Office.[18] The advantage of this method versus the more formal procedure is that the law firm can change its method without waiting to receive approval from the Service. The same four-year spread of the opening adjustment applies under the automatic consent procedure,[19] unless a *de minimis* rule applies, under which the taxpayer can elect a one-year adjustment if the amount is less than $25,000.[20] Many of the specified methods of accounting do not affect law firms. However, the Appendix includes a change in the method of accounting for client disbursements which allows an automatic change

---

[12] See § 5.01 of Rev. Proc. 97-27, I.R.B. 1997-21.

[13] See § 5.01 of Rev. Proc. 97-27, I.R.B. 1997-21.

[14] See § 2.07 of Rev. Proc. 99-49, I.R.B. 1999-52, 16.

[15] See § 5.04 of Rev. Proc. 99-49, I.R.B. 1999-52, 31. The amortization period is generally four years.

[16] See § 1 of Rev. Proc. 99-49, I.R.B. 1999-52, (Dec. 14, 1999).

[17] See N. 15 *supra.*

[18] See § 6.02(2)(a) of Rev. Proc. 99-49, I.R.B. 1999-52, 39.

[19] See § 5.04(1) of Rev. Proc. 99-49, I.R.B. 1999-52, 31.

[20] See § 5.04(3)(a) of Rev. Proc. 99-49, I.R.B. 1999-52, 32.

from expensing amounts paid on behalf of clients in a contingent-fee basis to that of recording them as loans receivable.[21]

The accounting method used in one state generally should be the same method used in other states, except for specific state modifications. Depreciation and unincorporated business taxes, where applicable, are example of specific state modifications that often must be made.

Additionally, there has been an increase in the number of U.S. law firms opening offices in other countries, and foreign law firms opening offices in the U.S. Law firms need to be cognizant that tax accounting rules differ from one country to another and often require different tax treatment for the same item (e.g., depreciation methods, allowable employee fringe benefits, allowable entertainment expenses, etc.). Not complying with the tax rules—for whatever reason—in a particular jurisdiction can lead to unexpected tax assessments (and possibly penalties) and may be embarrassing to the law firm.

Since an accounting method must be chosen for U.S. tax purposes in the first year in which a law firm begins business, a non-U.S. law firm presently using the accrual method of accounting in another country should consider using the cash method of accounting in the U.S. to save or to defer taxes. U.S. firms opening offices in foreign countries may face the opposite decision, because foreign jurisdictions sometimes require the use of accrual accounting for tax purposes.

This section discusses some of the accounting methods where tax planning is needed.

---

[21] See Appendix § 1.01 of Rev. Proc. 99-49, I.R.B. 1999-52, 64. It is interesting to note that the Appendix only allows automatic changes for capitalizing client disbursements and not the other way, i.e., expending operating-type expenses that previously were classified as client disbursements on the balance sheet.

§17.03 Income Recognition

[1]—Billing and Collection Accounting

Bills rendered by law firms to their clients are composed of two elements: (1) a fee for services rendered and (2) a request for reimbursement of disbursements made on behalf of the client or in connection with professional services rendered for the client. From a cash flow standpoint, the collection by the firm of a fee is the same as the collection of a client disbursement. However, from a tax accounting standpoint, there may be a difference. Consider, for example, a law firm that maintains its records using the modified cash basis method of accounting and accounts for client disbursements by flowing them through the balance sheet. Following this accounting practice, income is recorded when fees are collected, but no income is recorded when client disbursements are collected. Consequently, when a law firm renders progress billings for work-in-process, there is a timing advantage from a tax perspective in choosing to include client disbursements in the earlier bills and fees in the later bills. Similarly, when a firm receives partial payments from clients for bills rendered, there is a timing advantage for tax purposes in choosing to apply the earlier payments against client disbursements and the later payments against fees, unless the client has specifically identified the manner in which its payments are to be applied.

[2]—Client Deposits/Deferred Income

Periodically, law firms receive cash deposits from clients or prospective clients. Generally, if cash payments are for legal services to be rendered in the future and are held under a claim of right with no restrictions, they are taxable in the year received.[1] For an accrual basis law firm, it may be possible to defer prepayments for future services until the time of performance, but in no event beyond the end of the year following the year of receipt.[2] However, if advances are

---

[1] See:

Supreme Court: Schlude, 372 U.S. 128/83 S.Ct. 601, 9 L.Ed.2d 633 (1963).

Second Circuit: RCA v. United States, 664 F.2d 881 (2d Cir. 1981).

Tax Court: Frierdich v. Commissioner, 56 T.C.M. 1439, Dec. 45,530(M), T.C. Memo 103 (1989); Gustafson v. Commissioner, 55 T.C.M. 250, Dec. 44,607(M), T.C. Memo 82 (1988).

[2] Rev. Proc. 71-21, 1971-2 C.B. 549.

segregated into trust accounts and available only to the extent of services rendered, they may not be taxable currently.[3]

In *Miele v. Commissioner,* the partners of a law firm placed all retainers into a separate trust account. The client "owned" the cash until an undisputed amount was earned by the firm. The firm then had the right to transfer the undisputed amounts to its own bank account. The court reasoned that to the extent that a retainer was received, and the firm performed services against the retainer, the amount of services rendered should be included in income, regardless of whether it had been billed or transferred into the firm's bank account.[4]

In 1990, the Supreme Court held in *Indianapolis Power & Light* that if a taxpayer does not have "complete dominion" over *deposits* when received, then the amounts received are not taxable, even though the taxpayer has unrestricted use of the funds and does not segregate them into separate trust funds.[5] The Court reasoned that the determination of whether deposits are taxable income at the time of receipt depends on the nature of the rights and obligations a taxpayer assumed when the deposits were made and whether the taxpayer had some guarantee that it would be allowed to keep the money.[6] Another court followed the reasoning in *Indianapolis Power & Light*, but held that because the agreements between the parties did not explicitly provide for unconditional refunds, the taxpayer had complete dominion over the payments (otherwise referred to as deposits) and was not allowed to defer income until the following year.[7] It did not matter that the taxpayer never refused to return a deposit when asked. When a law firm receives an advance that may be in the nature of a deposit, it should review its rights and obligations regarding the advance to determine if it is currently taxable. It is equally important for the firm and its client to document their understanding that deposits are refundable at the client's request.

---

[3] See: Miele v. Commissioner, 72 T.C. 284, Dec. 36,055 (1979). *Contra*: Costello v. Commissioner, 50 T.C.M. 1463, Dec. 42,493, T.C. Memo. 571 (1985) in which payment was taxable when received even though held in trust.

[4] Miele v. Commissioner, 72 T.C. 284 (1979)

[5] See Commissioner v. Indianapolis Power & Light Co., 493 U.S. 203, 110 S.Ct. 589, 107 L.Ed.2d 591 (1990). See also, Oak Industries, Inc. v. Commissioner, 96 T.C. Dec. 47,262 (1991), following *Indianapolis Power & Light.*

[6] See Commissioner v. Indianapolis Power & Light Co., *id.*

[7] Michaelis Nursery Inc. v. Commissioner, T.C. Memo 1995-143 Dec. 50,562.

§ 17.04 Year Expenses Are Deductible

[1]—General Rule

Generally, a law firm's overall method of accounting controls when expenses are deductible. Since the Internal Revenue Code is rather vague in its reference to "the proper taxable year under the method of accounting used in computing taxable income,"[1] taxpayers have to rely on treasury regulations and court cases for guidance.

[a]—Cash Basis Law Firm

A cash basis law firm generally deducts expenditures in the year paid.[2] However, if an expenditure creates an asset which has a useful life that "extends substantially beyond the close of the taxable year," the amount may not be deductible or may be deductible only in part.[3] It is clear that this exception applies to expenditures for equipment or leasehold improvements, because both are for property that last more than one year. Determining if a prepaid item should be deducted currently or deducted pro rata over the period covered by the disbursement is more difficult to categorize for cash basis law firms. Some courts have used a "one-year-rule" to distinguish between currently deductible expenses and capital expenditures having a useful life substantially in excess of one year.[4] Under the one-year-rule an expenditure is a capital expenditure if it creates an asset having a useful life in excess of one year.[5] If an expenditure does not create an asset with a useful life of more than one year, then the expense may be deductible in the year paid. If an expenditure covers a period of one year or less, the criteria for deducting the item might depend on whether the expense was a prepayment versus an expenditure legally due and payable. For example, prepaying rent in a year in which a law firm already paid and expensed twelve payments would probably result in a prepaid rent item which would be deductible over the period covered by the prepayment. Contrast a

---

[1] IRC § 461(a); 26 U.S.C. § 461(a).

[2] Treas. Reg. § 1.461-1(a)(1); 26 C.F.R. § 1.461-1(a)(1).

[3] Treas. Reg. § 1.461-1(a)(1); 26 C.F.R. § 1.461-1(a)(1).

[4] See:

First Circuit: Fall River Gas Appliance Co. v. Commissioner, 349 F.2d 515 (1st Cir. 1965).

Second Circuit: Briarcliff Candy Corp., 475 F.2d 942 (2d Cir. 1973).

Fourth Circuit: Jack's Cookie Co. v. Commissioner, 597 F.2d 395 (4th Cir. 1979).

[5] See Zaninovich v. Commissioner, 616 F.2d 429 (9th Cir. 1980).

calendar-year law firm paying rent that is due in November and covers the entire period of December through November (overlapping tax years). In this situation, eleven months of rent apply to the next year, but are deductible in the current year, because there was a legal and binding obligation to make the rent payment (and there are not more than twelve months of rent deducted in the tax return).

Courts have applied a three-pronged test to determine the deductibility of prepaid items. The criteria are:

1) there must be an actual payment (the payment of a refundable deposit will not support a current deduction),
2) there must be a substantial business reason for making the prepayment other than simply accelerating a tax deduction, and
3) the prepayment must not cause material distortion of taxable income in the year of payment.[6]

Another consideration for deducting an expenditure when paid is the customary business practice at the time of the payment.[7]

No discussion of when expenses are deductible would be complete without some mention of the *Indopco*[8] decision. In *Indopco,* the Supreme Court concluded that certain legal and professional fees incurred in a friendly corporate acquisition were capital expenses and not ordinary and necessary expenses. By itself, this decision did more to confuse the decision-making process and to cloud the bright-line test that had been used to determine if an expenditure was a current deduction or had to be capitalized and amortized over a period of years. For twenty years prior to the *Indopco* decision, one of the important criteria used to determine if an expenditure was deductible currently was whether an expenditure created a separate and distinct asset.[9] As a result of *Indopco,* the analysis changed from an objective test (i.e., creating a separate asset) to a subjective test based on the specific facts and circumstances. In *Indopco,* the Supreme Court clarified that the creation or enhancement of a separate and distinct asset is not a prerequisite to whether an expenditure should be capitalized. Instead, in concluding whether an expenditure is deductible currently, the Court focused on the long-term benefit

---

[6] Grynberg v. Commissioner, 83 T.C. 255; Dec. 41,439 (Aug. 27, 1984).

[7] Rev. Rul. 79-229, 1979-2, C.B. 210.

[8] Indopco, Inc. v. Commissioner, 503 U.S. 79 112 S.Ct. 1039, 117 L.Ed.2d 226 (1992).

[9] Commissioner v. Lincoln Savings and Loan Ass'n, 403 U.S. 345, 91 S.Ct. 1893, 29 L.Ed.2d 519 (1971).

created by the expenditure. The Court muted the test somewhat by acknowledging that the mere presence of an incidental future benefit may not warrant capitalization. The fulcrum soon became how "incidental" or "long-term" is a future benefit. As expected, the IRS tends to view many future benefits as significant, even though many taxpayers view the same benefits as incidental.

Fortunately, law firms do not incur the same type of expenses as commercial corporations. However, law firms incur recruiting costs, advertising expenses, training costs and other expenditures that arguably create long-term benefits. Working with various taxpayer-advocate groups, the IRS clarified the treatment of some expenditures. Several courts also have addressed the capital-versus-expense issue. Listed below are some of the *Indopco*-related rulings or decisions that are applicable to law firms:

- Advertising costs generally are deductible as ordinary and necessary business expenses even though they may have some future effect on business activity.[10]
- Incidental repair costs that may have some future benefit are deductible under the fundamental principles for determining whether an expenditure can be expensed or capitalized.[11]
- Severance payments generally are deductible as ordinary and necessary business expenses, even though the payments may create some future benefits.[12]
- Training costs, including the cost of trainers and routine updates of training materials, generally are deductible as ordinary and necessary business expenses.[13]
- Year-2000 conversion costs paid or incurred to convert or replace Year-2000-compliant software can be deducted, even though the expenditure created a future benefit.[14]
- The charge incurred to cancel a lease of computer equipment that was integrated with a lease of more powerful computer equipment from the same vendor had to be capitalized, in part because of the future benefits to be realized by the new lease.[15]

---

[10] Rev. Rul. 92-80, I.R.B. 1992-39 (Sept. 11, 1992).

[11] Rev. Rul. 94-12, I.R.B. 1994-8, 1 (Feb. 4, 1994).

[12] Rev. Rul. 94-77, I.R.B. 1994-51 (Nov. 30, 1994).

[13] Rev. Rul. 96-62, I.R.B. 1996-53, (Dec. 23, 1996).

[14] Rev. Proc. 97-50, I.R.B. 1997-45 (Oct. 21, 1997) The IRS also stated that Year-2000 costs would not qualify for Section 41 research credits, except in extraordinary circumstances.

[15] U.S. Bancorp v. Commissioner, 111 T.C. No. 10, Dec. 27,342-96 (Sept. 21, 1998).

[b]—Accrual Basis Law Firm

A law firm using the accrual method of accounting for tax purposes generally can deduct items in the taxable year when all the events have occurred that establish the fact of the liability, the amount of the liability can be determined with reasonable accuracy, and "economic performance" has occurred with respect to the liability.[16] Economic performance generally occurs when the activities giving rise to an obligation are actually performed.[17] In certain circumstances, an accrual basis law firm also can adopt the "recurring item exception" whereby a liability is treated as incurred for a taxable year if certain requirements are met.[18]

Regardless of the method of accounting, if an expenditure is determined to have significant long-term benefit, it may be a nondeductible capital expenditure rather than an ordinary and necessary business expense.[19]

[2]—Client Disbursements vs. Firm Expenses

As a law firm grows, the ways it does business change. The changes affect the relationships it has with its clients and, correspondingly, the way it invoices its clients. These changes force their accounting systems to become more sophisticated, so that relevant cost information is available to partners to use in preparing invoices. This accounting evolution has led to confusion about what are law firm expenses and what are client disbursements. The distinction is relevant because firm expenses are deductible for tax purposes, while client disbursements are loans and are not deductible, until proven to be uncollectible.

[a]—Categorizing Disbursements

Historically, law firms have referred to client disbursements as either "soft" or "hard" costs. Soft costs were internally developed costs and hard costs were amounts paid to third parties. These generalizations are no longer valid today, because some cost centers that gave rise to soft costs have been out-sourced (and now are paid to third parties) and some payments to third parties have been acknowledged by the IRS to be law firm expenses.. For purpose of simplifying the discussion in this section, the historic connotation of the terms soft disbursements and

---

[16] Treas. Reg. § 1.461-1(a)(2); C.F.R. § 1.461-1(a)(2).

[17] IRC § 461(h); 26 U.S.C. § 461(h). See also, Treas. Reg. § 1.461-4; 26 C.F.R. § 1.461-4.

[18] Treas. Reg. § 1.461-5; 26 C.F.R. § 1.461-5.

[19] IRC § 263; 26 U.S.C. § 263. See also, INDOPCO Inc. v. Commissioner, 112 S.Ct. 1039, 117 L.Ed.2d 226 (1992).

hard disbursements are used. As a result of case law that specifically refers to litigation costs, this category is carved out of hard disbursements and discussed separately.

[i]—Soft Disbursements

The first category of disbursements concerns allocations of firm expenses such as information retrieval services, word processing costs, internal copying and duplication costs, telephone and facsimile expenses, and internal messenger costs. These costs are often referred to as "soft costs" or "indirect costs." Typically, when these costs are paid, the law firm charges its expense account. As the service is provided, a predetermined billing value associated with these costs is charged to a general ledger account on the balance sheet such as "client disbursements" and the related expense account is credited (e.g., duplicating expense is credited for photocopies, telephone expense is credited for facsimile charges). The effect of this entry is to create income, because expenses are reduced. Realizing that expenses have been reduced for an amount that may be billed to a client is another way of saying that the accounting for this item is on an accrual method (i.e., income is being accrued that reduces the cash basis expense).

Taken to the extreme, it is possible to create taxable income for a cash basis law firm, even though the firm never issues a bill or collects cash.

For example, assume a law firm pays rent of $5,000 a month for a copier. Also assume that the firm charges 10 cents for each copy made and that during the month it made 60,000 copies of client-related documents. The accounting entries to record the month's activities are:

[1] Duplicating Costs	5,000	
Cash		5,000
To pay monthly copier rental		
[2] Unbilled Client Disbursements	6,000	
Duplicating Costs		6,000
To record expense offset for 60,000 copies at 10 cents per copy		
Net taxable income for month =$1,000		

Keeping in mind that no bills were rendered, and, therefore, no cash was received, the firm would have $1,000 in taxable income and the partners would pay tax on that income—arguably, the wrong answer for a cash basis taxpayer. This example demonstrates that a cash basis law firm can unintentionally use an accrual method of accounting for items that are more in the nature of normal operating costs.

If a law firm uses a cash basis method of accounting, it should focus on how it accounts for soft costs, so that it does not inadvertently or unintentionally report soft costs on an accrual basis of accounting.

[ii]—Hard Disbursements

The second category of disbursements is expenditures made by a law firm in connection with specific client matters such as airfares, hotels, taxi services, external duplicating, and external delivery services. These costs are often referred to as "hard costs," "direct costs," or "out-of-pocket expenses." Law firms generally have some discretion on the timing and choice of these expenses. Depending on the specific facts and circumstances, these costs also can be normal business expenses incurred in providing legal services to clients.

Often, law firms track these disbursements by charging a particular client's work-in-progress general ledger account, so that they can determine the actual cost of providing legal services to that client and determine how much profit, if any, it made on a particular matter. The simple action of charging a work-in-progress account makes it appear that the charge is a receivable - an amount that is expected to be reimbursed by that client. In reality, that may or may not be the case. The facts and circumstances that give rise to disbursements and the contractual relationship between the law firm and the client should control the accounting for hard disbursements.

Law firms that do not track disbursements by charging a work-in-progress general ledger account might simply charge an expense account to reflect the fact that certain costs are really the costs of rendering legal services to clients. It should be noted that the IRS disagrees that certain types of client disbursements can be expensed when paid. This point will be discussed in more depth later in this section.

[iii]—Litigation Disbursements

The third category of disbursements relates to general litigation costs that are paid on behalf of particular clients and for which the firm expects to be repaid. Litigation costs are costs which would otherwise be paid directly by a client and include disbursements such as court costs, expert witness fees, medical examination expenses, and deposition costs. In addition to litigation costs incurred in connection with net-fee contracts, a law firm can have contractual agreements with clients that ensure recovery of disbursements in connection with particular client matters (e.g., out-of-pocket expenses in contingency cases). Litigation costs have been held to be loans, and, therefore, are not deductible until proven to be uncollectible.[20] Court cases on point generally concern contingency cases and focus on the understanding that clients would repay attorneys for litigation costs out of gross settlement proceeds of successful cases.[21]

[b]—Distinguishing Firm Expenses from Client Disbursements

Category One costs (i.e., soft disbursements) logically can be treated as firm expenses, because a law firm decides both the particular expense and the preassigned value that will be billed to a client. A law firm basically creates the charge to recover operating costs.

Many law firms, in fact, treat soft costs as firm expenses, because they are "manufactured" amounts based on expenses paid by the firm. Soft costs like telephones, messengers, reprographic, faxes, etc. are operating expenses that a law firm pays and allocates to clients for cost accounting purposes. On a cash basis, these items should be expensed when paid, the same as rent, payroll, professional insurance, etc. are expensed when paid. Those costs (i.e., rent, payroll, etc.) are included in determining an attorney's billing rate and are later "reimbursed" when a client pays the firm's bills.

The central issue is when is an expense paid with the expectation of it being reimbursed. This issue can be traced back to payments that a lawyer made in 1925 in connection with a divorce matter.[22] Since the client had an "unconditional" agreement to reimburse the attorney, the court held that the disbursements were not the attorney's expenses, but

---

[20] See:

Fifth Circuit: Hughes & Luce v Commissioner, 70 F3d 16 (5th Cir Nov 15, 1995).

Sixth Circuit: Milan, Miller, Berger, Brody & Miller, P.C. v. United States, 679 F. Supp. 692 (E.D. Mich. 1988).

Ninth Circuit: Canelo v. Commissioner, 447 F.2d 484 (9th Cir. 1971); Hearn v Commissioner, 309 F2d 431 (9th Cir.Oct. 31, 1962).

Claims Court: Boccardo v. United States, 12 Cl. Ct. 184 (1987).

Tax Court: Boccardo v. Commissioner, T.C. Memo 1993-224 ¶ 47,779 (1993); Sivlerton v Commissioner 36 TCM 817 (June 28, 1977); Pelton & Gunther PC v Commissioner 78 TCM 578 (Oct 8, 1999).

Priv Ltr Rul. 9432002, (Mar 30, 1994).

[21] See:

Fifth Circuit: Burnett v. Commissioner, 356 F.2d 755 (5th Cir. 1966).

Tax Court: Pelton and Gurther P.C. v. Commissioner, T.C. Memo 1999-339 ¶ 23914-97 (Oct. 8. 1999); Herrick v. Commissioner, 63 T.C. 562, Dec. 33,050 (1975).

[22] Henry F. Cochrane v. Commissioner 23 B.T.A. 202 (May 13, 1931).

were loans from the client. In reality there is a very fine line between an amount disbursed for which an attorney "expects" to be reimbursed and an amount that is in the nature of an operating expense. Some attorneys say that they never make a disbursement without intending to be reimbursed, and, therefore, all disbursements are loans. Others disagree with that statement as being too broad and blind to how law firms really operate. Those who disagree draw the imaginary line between soft disbursements and hard disbursements or litigation costs, because of the nature of cost disbursements and the fact that they often are manufactured by a law firm in providing services to its clients.

The IRS may not necessarily agree that soft costs should be expensed when paid. In an IRS Chief Counsel Advice Memorandum, the Chief of the Examination Division was advised that a law firm withdrew a request to deduct reimbursable service charges (i.e., soft costs) when paid, when the Office of Assistant Chief Counsel tentatively formed an adverse position on the change.[23] The basis of the adverse opinion was that reimbursable service charges were amounts that the law firm expected to be reimbursed for and, therefore, were in the nature of loans to clients. The IRS privately acknowledged that this ruling was incorrect and that the taxpayer should have been allowed to expense service charges when paid. Unfortunately, the IRS has not withdrawn the ruling. Consequently, a law firm should be cautious of relying on a ruling that, on its surface, does not "make sense." A law firm also should realize that not all IRS rulings are correct.

Distinguishing between Category Two costs ("hard disbursements") and Category Three costs ("litigation disbursements") depends upon both the contractual relationship between a law firm and its clients and the latitude a firm has with respect to the expenses. If a contractual relationship (like the relationship existing in a contingency case) creates a legal expectation that a law firm will be reimbursed for amounts disbursed, then the disbursements probably should be classified as a receivable and not deductible by the firm. Similarly, if litigation costs, which are considered to be the liability of a client, are paid for by a law firm (such as in the case of a contingent fee arrangement), then these costs should be classified as a receivable. However, when a law firm had a gross-fee contract with its client (a contract in which the client is charged only a professional fee and expenses are absorbed by the law firm), the Court of Appeals held that client disbursements were expenses of the law firm, even though they were of a contingent nature.[24]

---

[23] See Priv. Ltr. Rul. 199937031 (June 21, 1999).

[24] James F. Boccardo v. Commissioner, 95-1 U.S.T.C. ¶ 50,284 (9th Cir. 1995).

It is important to emphasize that most of the cases that have addressed the deduction of client disbursements have involved attorneys who specialize in personal injury matters, who work on a contingent-fee basis, and who advanced funds in connection with litigation.[25] These cases are not representative of the type of matters handled by most law firms. Most law firms do not practice personal injury law and most of the time they do not handle contingent cases. Those firms may or may not have a contractual agreement to be reimbursed for their soft disbursements or hard disbursements and, often, do not collect 100% of their fees and expenses. When there is no contractual agreement to reimburse a law firm, then the law firm has a better position to argue that its soft and hard costs simply are normal operating costs in providing legal services and are not loans.

In non-contingent matters, however, many of the disbursements are subject to considerable, if not complete, discretion of the partner responsible for the matter. Normally, for example, the law firm decides that a particular client-related trip is necessary, what form of transportation should be used, what class of airline ticket should be purchased, or what kind of external delivery service to use; clients just expect to have legal matters resolved. This discretion is important because it is one criterion that distinguishes firm operating expenses from client disbursements—client disbursements are amounts which clients would have paid directly under normal circumstances. For example, in a non-contingent matter, an attorney incurs travel expenses that, in addition to his or her professional time, the attorney expects to be reimbursed for. It is the lawyer who decides that he or she, for example, will take a plane (coach class instead of first class) instead of a train, or a limousine instead of a taxi or a subway. The lawyer decides to stay at a moderately priced hotel, instead of a four-star hotel. Contrast these types of discretionary disbursements that are incurred in providing legal services with those in a contingent fee arrangement in which a client would have paid certain amounts with or without the involvement of an attorney (e.g., court filing fees, expert witnesses, court stenographers). This discretion along with the absolute control over how much to bill a client (or how much to write off) and how to present the charge are what logically distinguishes a deductible firm expense from a nondeductible client receivable.

In a technical advice memo released by the IRS, however, the Service ruled that out-of-pocket payments to third parties on behalf of specific clients were in the nature of advances, and not deductible by the

---

[25] See FN 20 and 21.

law firm until proven to be uncollectible.[26] The IRS did not consider the difference between contingent and non-contingent matters, nor did it discuss the absolute discretion an attorney has for out-of-pocket disbursements. For example, an attorney can incur out-of-pocket disbursements in providing services to a client and never intend to charge the client for the disbursements, but the attorney accounts for them in connection with a specific matter to determine if he or she is making a profit on the engagement. Arguably, these types of payments are expenses of the law firm even though they are disbursements to third parties.

Under the cash method of accounting, a law firm generally can expense Category One and, depending on the facts and circumstances, some Category Two costs when incurred, instead of recording them as client disbursements. Litigation costs, on the other hand, always have to be accounted for as receivables when paid and are deductible by a law firm only when they are proven to be uncollectible.

However, if a firm's accounting method for these items is at variance with the cash method, the method generally cannot be changed without first obtaining permission from the IRS. As mentioned previously, a Form 3115 must be filed with the IRS requesting permission to change accounting methods for tax purposes.[27] If permission is granted, the "opening balance" of the affected item usually cannot be written off immediately, but must be deducted (spread) over a period of not more than four years.[28] If the adjustment is less than $25,0000 a taxpayer can make an election to write off the amount in one year.[29]

After a law firm receives permission to change its accounting method, it has to address some difficult administrative problems, such as how to allocate the change to its partners (especially if partners join or leave the firm), how to distribute the cash collected as a result of the change, and what will be the year of change. These types of questions have caused firms to rethink requesting a change, even if it saves tax dollars.

[3]—Depreciation Accounting

Because of significant changes caused by major tax legislation, depreciation accounting can be difficult and time-consuming to

---

[26] Ltr. Rul. 9432002 (Aug. 12, 1994).

[27] Treas. Reg. § 1.446-1(e)(2)(i); 26 C.F.R. § 1.446-1(e)(2)(i). See § 5.01(1)(a) of Rev. Proc. 97-27, I.R.B. 1997-21, 14 and Rev. Rul. 90-38, 1990-1 C.B. 57. See also, § 17.02 of this chapter for Form 3115 filing requirements.

[28] See § 5.02(3)(a) of Rev. Proc. 97-27, I.R.B. 1997-21, 14.

[29] See § 5.04(3)(a) of Rev. Proc. 99-49, I.R.B. 1999-52 (Dec. 14, 1999).

administer. Without the use of computers, it is difficult to keep track of which assets must be depreciated using specified methods and statutory lives.

[a]—Depreciation of Furniture and Equipment

For tax purposes, the cost of depreciable tangible personal property (i.e., assets such as furniture and fixtures, office equipment, and computers) is recovered through systematic charges to expense over a period of years (referred as the "applicable recovery period").[30] Currently, the prescribed federal tax method for determining this expense is the Modified Accelerated Cost Recovery System (MACRS).[31] For assets placed in service between January 1, 1981 and December 31, 1986, the prescribed method is the Accelerated Cost Recovery System (ACRS).

Under MACRS rules, depreciation of tangible personal property generally is calculated using the double-declining balance method[32] switching to straight-line at the optimal point[33] over an applicable recovery period.[34] With certain exceptions, MACRS assumes that tangible personal property purchased in a particular year is placed in service at the mid-point of that year.[35] Instead of following the standard MACRS rules, a law firm can elect at the time of acquisition to use the straight-line method of depreciation over stipulated longer lives.[36] Under MACRS, one-half year's depreciation is allowed in the year of acquisition and the year of disposition.

Under the ACRS rules, depreciation is calculated using statutory percentages that reflect the 150% declining-balance method, switching automatically to straight-line at the optimal point. Alternatively, at acquisition a taxpayer can elect to use the straight-line method over stipulated longer lives.[37] Under ACRS, depreciation is not allowed in the year of disposition.

Assets used predominately outside the United States are not subject to MACRS and must be depreciated under the alternative system using the straight-line method over stipulated longer lives.[38]

---

[30] ITC § 168(c); 26 U.S.C. § 168(ca)

[31] IRC § 168(a); 26 U.S.C. § 168(a). MACRS must be used on assets placed in service after December 31, 1986.

[32] IRC § 168(b)(1)(A); 26 U.S.C. § 168(b)(1)(A).

[33] IRC § 168(b)(1)(B); 26 U.S.C. § 168(b)(1)(B).

[34] IRC § 168(c)(1); 26 U.S.C. § 168(c)(1).

[35] IRC § 168(d)(1); 26 U.S.C. § 168(d)(1).

[36] IRC § 168(b)(3)(D); 26 U.S.C. § 168(b)(3)(D).

[37] § 168 of the Internal Revenue Code of 1954, as modified by the Economic Recovery Tax Act of 1981 (ERTA).

[38] IRC § 168(g)(1)(A); 26 U.S.C. § 168(g)(1)(A).

Used assets cannot be assigned shorter lives than new assets and must be assigned lives and depreciated under the general MACRS rules.

The main tax advantage of using the standard MACRS or ACRS methods of depreciation rather than straight-line depreciation is the ability to provide rapid write-offs. When MACRS and ACRS were first introduced, not every state adopted them for state tax depreciation purposes. For assets placed in service prior to 1993, many states required an adjustment between the state tax depreciation amount and the method used for federal income tax. Since the early 1990's, however, most states have adopted the federal rule thus eliminating the adjustment for newer assets.

[b]—Accounting for Like-Kind Exchanges

Until recently, no guidance existed on how to depreciate the basis of property acquired in a like-kind exchange or an involuntary conversion. A like-kind exchange is defined as the exchange of property held for productive use in a trade or business or for investment, if such property is exchanged solely for property of like kind which is to be held either for productive use in a trade or business or for investment.[39] Property is acquired in an involuntary conversion when such property is compulsorily or involuntarily converted into property similar or related in service or use to the property so converted.[40] Generally, when property is destroyed and insurance proceeds are received, the recipient of the insurance has two years from the end of the tax year in which the cash was received to purchase a similar asset.[41] If the insurance proceeds are not used within this time frame, any unused portion is taxable.

The basis of property acquired in a transaction to which IRC §§ 1031 or 1033 applies is the same as the property surrendered in the transaction less any cash received plus any gain recognized.

For property placed in service after January 3, 2000, the acquired property is depreciated using the same method over the remaining useful life of the asset but only to the extent that the basis of the property acquired does not exceed the basis of the property given up. To the extent that the basis exceeds that of the property given up, such excess should be depreciated as a new asset.[42] If MACRS property was placed in service prior to January 3, 2000, in a like-kind exchange of, or as a result of an involuntary conversion of MACRS property, taxpayers may

---

[39] IRC § 1031(a), 26 U.S.C. § 1031(a).

[40] IRC § 1033(a)(1); 26 U.S.C. § 1031(a).

[41] IRC § 1033(a)(2); 26 U.S.C. § 1033 (a)(2).

[42] IRS Notice 2000-4, 2000-3 I.R.B. (January 4, 2000) paragraphs 6 and 8.

continue to use the method of depreciation they are currently using, if different than outlined above, (e.g. as newly acquired property) or they may switch their depreciation method to the one outlined in Notice 2000-4. However, if the taxpayer chooses to change its method, it must file a change in method of accounting.[43]

These rules are illustrated in Figure 17-A. The illustration shows three scenarios that demonstrate the accounting for gain or loss when insurance proceeds equal, exceed, or are less than the replacement price or basis in the destroyed property. A single desk is used to illustrate the calculations.

Figure 17-A. Illustration of accounting for gain or loss in an involuntary conversion when insurance proceeds are received

	Equals	Exceeds	Less than
Insurance proceeds	800	1,050	700
Replacement purchase price	800	900	700
Adjusted basis of property destroyed	800	800	800
Gain or (loss)	0	150	(150)
Excess of new basis over old basis	0	250	0

In the first example, the insurance proceeds equal the cost to replace the desk and the basis of the desk destroyed. There is no gain or loss recognized and the new desk is depreciated using the same method over the remaining life of the old desk.[44] If the insurance proceeds exceeded the purchase price, then the excess proceeds would be taxable to the law firm. This is illustrated in the column "Exceeds."[45] That example also illustrates that if the basis of the new property (i.e., its purchase price of $900) exceeds the adjusted basis of the old property, the excess (i.e., $900 less $800) plus the gain recognized (i.e., $1,050 less $900) is treated as a newly acquired asset and is depreciated as if there had been no conversion. The basis of the destroyed asset (i.e., $800) continues to be depreciated using the same method over its remaining life. The third illustration in the column "Less than" shows that the insurance proceeds

[43] IRS Notice 2000-4, 2000-3 I.R.B. paragraph 9.
[44] See § 6 of IRS Notice 2000-4; 2000-3 I.R.B. 1.
[45] Treas. Reg. § 1.1033(b)-1; 26 C.F.R. § 1.1033(b)-1.

and replacement property cost less than the destroyed property. Although there is a loss, there are no special rules mandated for accounting for that loss.[46]

[c]—Depreciation of Leasehold Improvements

Under MACRS, the depreciation deduction for leasehold improvements is calculated using the straight-line method.[47] Nonresidential real property (i.e., office buildings and leasehold improvements) placed in service in the United States after May 12, 1993[48] is recovered over thirty-nine years. Assets used outside of the United States have a forty-year life.[49] Acquisitions during a month are assumed to be placed in service at the mid-point of that month.[50]

The thirty-nine-year life for leasehold improvements can create controversy, because it can result in the write-off of substantial sums at the end of a lease (e.g., over one-third to one-half of an asset's cost at the end of a twenty-year lease). Without a special allocation of leasehold amortization, partners at the end of the lease can enjoy a "windfall" tax benefit that more appropriately may be due to former partners.

[d]—Election to Deduct Certain Depreciable Business Assets

Instead of depreciating tangible property under standard MACRS rules, a law firm may be able to make an annual election to expense[51] some[52] of the cost of certain qualified property.[53] The deduction is limited to taxable income before this deduction,[54] but any excess over the limit can be carried forward to offset future business income.[55]

---

[46] Treas. Reg. § 1.1033(a)-1; 26 C.F.R. § 1.1033(a)-1.
[47] IRC § 168(b)(3)(A); 26 U.S.C. § 168(b)(3)(A).
[48] IRC § 168(c)(1); 26 U.S.C. § 168(c)(1).
[49] IRC § 168(g)(2)(C)(iii); 26 U.S.C. § 168(g)(2)(C)(iii).
[50] IRC § 168(d)(2)(A); 26 U.S.C. § 168(d)(2)(A).
[51] IRC § 179(a); 26 U.S.C. § 179(a).
[52] IRC § 179(b)(1); 26 U.S.C. § 179(b)(1). The maximum amount that may be deducted is phased-in as follows:

Tax Year Beginning in	Maximum Expense Deduction
1996	17,500
1997	18,000
1998	18,500
1999	19,000
2000	20,000
2001 or 2002	24,000
2003 or thereafter	25,000

[53] IRC § 179(d)(1); 26 U.S.C. § 179(d)(1).
[54] IRC § 179(b)(3)(A); 26 U.S.C. § 179(b)(3)(A).
[55] IRC § 179(b)(3)(B)(i); 26 U.S.C. § 179(b)(3)(B)(i).

The maximum expense deduction limit is reduced dollar for dollar for each dollar of cost of qualified property that exceeds $200,000.[56] Therefore, when fully phased in, a law firm will not be entitled to expense any fixed-asset purchases if the total cost of qualified purchases in any given year equals $225,000.

A law firm should consider this provision carefully before electing to expense fixed-asset purchases, because the maximum expense deduction (e.g., for 2001 and 2002 the limitation is $24,000) limitation applies at both the partnership and partner levels. The expense under this provision flows from the partnership through to each partner based on the partners' profit and loss sharing agreement. Even though the limitation is applied at the partnership level, it applies "again" at the partner level for other assets that the partner elected to expense.[57] Therefore, a partner with several sources of "Section 179 expenses" can lose a depreciation deduction if his or her total expense under this provision exceeds $25,000 (2003 and later).

A shorthand method of obtaining some of the benefits of IRC § 179 (without making the annual election discussed above) is to establish a base below which personal property will be expensed. Under this policy, an individual piece of personal property will only be capitalized if its cost exceeds a certain amount. Many law firms use this type of policy because it is administratively unreasonable to capitalize and depreciate every asset just because it has a useful life of more than one year. It also is felt that the IRS-established lives on many assets are unrealistic, especially in a high tech environment where obsolescence is a preordained reality. When establishing a policy like this, some firms establish reasonably low bases such as $100. Other firms are more aggressive and establish fairly high bases such as $5,000.

Depending on the firm's revenue, it would seem to be an easy task to justify some base level. However, in one situation, a taxpayer asked the IRS permission to change its base from $1,000 to $2,000 and was denied permission because taxpayers are not allowed to expense tangible personal property merely because the item has a minimal value.[58]

Unfortunately, there is no provision in the Treasury Regulations that permits law firms or other taxpayers to establish a policy under which low-valued assets can be expensed when purchased, except if § 179 applies. Most of the time, an IRS agent will ignore this shorthand method. Knowing that, if a law firm decides to expense low-valued

---

[56] IRC § 179(b)(2); 26 U.S.C. § 179(b)(2).
[57] IRC § 179(d)(8); 26 U.S.C. § 179(d)(8).
[58] ILM 199952010 (Sep. 29, 1999).

assets without the protection of IRC § 179, it should be reasonable in establishing the base. If the base if too high, the policy will attract more IRS attention and may lead to distortions and disallowances.

[e]—Depreciation Limitations Re: Listed Property

Depreciation deductions for certain types of assets may be limited based on the percentage of qualified business use[59] in any given year. These assets, called "listed property," include passenger automobiles, computers and cellular telephones.[60] Each year, a law firm must analyze the business use of its listed property to determine if the limitations apply. If the qualified business use percentage falls below 50% in any given year, the firm must recapture excess depreciation.[61] Excess depreciation is the excess of the regular MACRS depreciation over the alternative depreciation calculated using the straight-line method over an extended life.[62] This excess amount should be included in gross income in that year.

The definition of listed property includes passenger automobiles, whether purchased or leased. The listed property rules impose a dollar limitation on the depreciation deduction for both the year that the automobile is placed in service and each succeeding year.[63] The effect of the limitation is to extend the recovery period over which a vehicle is depreciated. The dollar limitation for listed property is increased annually for inflation adjustments.[64] Instead of a dollar limitation for leased vehicles, there is a reduction in the lease deduction allowed to a law firm.[65] The reduction is achieved by using standard tables issued annually by the IRS.[66] Basically, the reduction in the lease deduction is meant to substantially equal the limitation placed on automobiles purchased.

The deduction allowed for listed property (whether in the form of depreciation or leased payments) also is limited based on the qualified business-use percentage which generally is the ratio of business

---

[59] IRC § 280F(d)(6)(B); 26 U.S.C. § 280F(d)(6)(B).

[60] IRC § 280F(d)(4)(A); 26 U.S.C. § 280F(d)(4)(A).

[61] IRC § 280F(b)(2)(A); 26 U.S.C. § 280F(b)(2)(A).

[62] IRC § 280F(b)(2)(B); 26 U.S.C. § 280F(b)(2)(B).

[63] IRC § 280F(a)(1)(A); 26 U.S.C. § 280F(a)(1)(A). See also, § 4.02 (2) of Rev. Proc. 2001-19, I.R.B. 732 (Feb. 26, 2001). For automobiles placed in service during 2001, the depreciation limitations will apply to cars costing more than $15,400.

[64] IRC § 280F(d)(7); 26 U.S.C. § 280F(d)(7). See also, § 4.02[1] of Rev. Proc. 99-14, I.R.B. 1999-5, 57.

[65] IRC § 280F(c); 26 U.S.C. § 280F(c).

[66] See § 4.03 of Rev. Proc. 99-14, I.R.B. 1999-5, 58 (Feb. 01, 1999).

usage to total usage. These rules are relevant for law firms that provide automobiles—purchased or leased—for attorneys on temporary assignments domestically or internationally.

[f]—AMT Calculations and Straight-Line Election

Federal tax law also requires a separate depreciation calculation for Alternative Minimum Tax (AMT) purposes. For any asset placed in service after December 31, 1986, a law firm must recompute depreciation under the regular MACRS rules using the alternative method.[67] The amount computed under the AMT rules is compared to the regular MACRS depreciation deduction and this difference, called an AMT depreciation adjustment, flows through to the individual partners based on the firm's profit and loss sharing agreement. The partners include their distributive share of the AMT depreciation adjustment in the calculation of their alternative minimum taxable income (on federal Form 6251) on their personal income tax returns.

The firm can elect to depreciate assets using the alternative method (as opposed to the regular MACRS rules) in calculating its ordinary income. A firm might make this election to increase income, for example, through lower depreciation and to reduce the required AMT depreciation record keeping. The election to use the alternative method is used most often for leasehold improvements because the alternative recovery period of forty years is not significantly different from the MACRS recovery period of thirty-nine years. Making the election allows a law firm to maintain only one set of depreciation schedules and eliminates the need to calculate an AMT depreciation adjustment.

A law firm should carefully consider the effects of this election on the individual partners' taxable income before taking such a course of action.

[4]—Purchase vs. Lease Accounting

When a law firm is considering a major purchase (e.g., a large purchase of personal computers or a purchase of a new phone system), it has to decide if it will buy the assets or lease them. An important consideration in making this decision is how long the firm intends to

---

[67] IRC §§ 56(a)(1)(A)(ii), 168(g); 26 U.S.C. §§ 56(a)(1)(A)(ii), 168(g). Under Section 168(g), the alternative method requires the use of the straight-line method over longer lives. However, for AMT purposes, depreciation is calculated for tangible personal property using the longer lives noted in Section 168(g), and the 150%-declining balance method is used to calculate the AMT depreciation deduction. The straight-line method is used for real property in calculating the AMT depreciation deduction.

use the new equipment. If the intended usage is for only a portion of the equipment's useful life, then leasing may prove to be a better option. If the equipment will be used long after its depreciable life (e.g., some types of furniture and fixtures), then purchase may be the better decision. If the equipment is expected to be technologically obsolete before it is fully depreciated according to tax rules (e.g., computer equipment), then leasing may provide the best option.

Financing also is an important consideration in leasing; if a firm does not have excess capital or has to borrow the money needed to purchase the new equipment, leasing may be a valid option. Also, if a firm is concerned with its debt-to-equity ratio or with reflecting debt on the balance sheet, then leasing may be a viable option.[68]

[a]—Purchase Option and Accounting

If a firm purchases equipment, the cost of the equipment is recovered through depreciation.[69] If the firm uses internally generated cash to buy the equipment, that amount is not available for normal distributions and may cause partners to pay tax on income that is not distributed (sometimes referred to as "phantom income"). Alternatively, if a firm uses bank financing to buy the equipment, then it records a liability on its balance sheet for the amount borrowed. Also, the interest rate charged for bank financing may be higher than the imputed interest rate included in lease payments because lessors generally arrange more attractive financing based on volume or use a lower interest rate as a marketing tool. Ignoring all other valid considerations, if an equipment user is a high-rate taxpayer, it normally is more beneficial to purchase new equipment than lease it, because the owner is entitled to all of the tax benefits. In contrast, in a leasing transaction the lessor only passes on some of the tax benefits (e.g., lower financing cost through lease payments).

[b]—Lease Option

Leasing has gained popularity in recent years because law firms have become more management conscious and realize that owning equipment has many hidden responsibilities and burdens. Leasing removes the responsibilities of ownership and offers a law firm potentially valuable options like the ability to upgrade equipment sooner to new technological standards, spreading lease payments over a period commensurate with the equipment's economic life, relieving the firm of inherent disposal problems, and eliminating phantom income.

---

[68] This topic is discussed in more depth in Chapter 29.

[69] See also, § 17.04[3][a] *supra.*

There are no specific rules in the Internal Revenue Code which provide guidance concerning whether a leasing transaction will be considered a true lease or conditional sale for federal income tax purposes. However, under well established case law, the determination of whether a transaction is a true lease or conditional sale for tax purposes is determined according to the substance of the transaction, not its form.[70] This substantive determination focuses on who has the benefits and burdens of ownership for U.S. income tax purposes.[71] The most important ownership attributes are the upside potential for economic gain and the downside risk of economic loss.[72] The right to possess property throughout its economic useful life is also an important attribute of tax ownership. The Internal Revenue Service set forth certain principles and factors that it considers relevant in determining whether an agreement is a conditional sale or a true lease.[73]

Leases can be "closed-end" or "open-end." A closed-end lease is one in which the option purchase price is determined when the lease is signed. An open-end lease, on the other hand, does not specify a purchase price at signing, rather it refers to the fair market value at the termination of the lease. In a sense, using a closed-end lease takes the guesswork out of leasing and allows more accurate present value analysis.

Maintenance agreements also are considerations that should be evaluated when deciding to lease instead of purchase. If lease payments are constant, but maintenance costs escalate after a period of time, then the lease vs. purchase comparison will have to consider variations in maintenance agreements.

If a law firm leases a computer on a five-year basis and decides in Year Two that it needs a more powerful computer, the rollover fee that it pays to the leasing company for a lease on a more powerful computer must be capitalized and amortized over the period of the new lease.[74]

[i]—True Lease

"True lease" means a leasing transaction in which the form of the transaction will be respected and the lessor will be considered the owner of the property for income tax purposes. In a true lease transaction, the

---

[70] Helvering v. Lazarus & Co., 308 U.S. 252, 60 S.Ct. 209 (1939).

[71] Estate of Jerry Thomas, 84 T.C. 412, Dec. 41,943 (1985).

[72] Swift Dodge v. Commissioner, 692 F.2d 651 (9th Cir. 1982), *rev'g* 76 T.C. 547, Dec. 37,085 (1981).

[73] Rev. Rul. 55-540, 1955-2 C.B. 39.

[74] U.S. Bancorp v. Commissioner, 111 T.C. No. 10 (Sept. 21, 1998).

lessee (e.g., a law firm) is not considered the owner of the property and is allowed to deduct lease payments for income tax purposes. To be classified as a true lease, a leasing transaction must have economic substance and a business purpose apart from its tax benefits.[75] In general, courts have found transactions to have economic substance if the taxpayer had a reasonable opportunity to receive an economic profit (pre-tax) from investing in the transaction.[76] Alternatively, a leasing transaction may be given its intended effect if the transaction has a business purpose.[77] The presence of a fair-market-value purchase option in a lease agreement should not change the transaction from a true lease to a conditional sale.[78]

Further, the fact that a purchase option is fixed at the estimated fair market value of the property at the end of the lease should not by itself cause the lease to be treated as a conditional sale.[79]

Using a true lease with a purchase option at its termination can be a technique to amortize the cost of equipment over a longer period. For example, leasing a phone system over a seven-year period and then exercising the purchase option at termination of the lease will cause the exercise price to be capitalized and depreciated over a period of seven more years. Effectively, the cost of the phone system (including financing) would be spread out over a fourteen-year period and could be a more equitable method of allocating of the costs to the partners who benefited by the system. However, this method would defer the tax benefits that could have been realized if the equipment were purchased and depreciated over only seven years.

[ii]—Purchase vs. Lease Analysis

The amount of expense available as a tax deduction will vary from year-to-year depending on whether the transaction is structured as a purchased or as a lease. An example of the year-by-year results of leasing vs. purchasing a piece of equipment is presented below:

---

[75] Frank Lyon Co. v. United States, 435 U.S. 561, 98 S.Ct. 1291 (1978), and Rice's Toyota World, Inc. v. Commissioner, 81 T.C. 184, Dec. 40,410 (1983), *aff'd in part, rev'd in part* 752 F.2d 89 (4th Cir. 1985).

[76] Wade L. Moser v. Commissioner, 914 F.2d 1040 (8th Cir. 1990).

[77] Frank Lyon Co. v. United States, N. 75 *supra.*

[78] Lockhart Leasing Co. v. Commissioner, 446 F.2d 269 (10th Cir. 1971), *aff'g* 54 T.C. 301, 314-315 Dec. 29,962 (1970).

[79] Frank Lyon Co. v. United States, N. 75 *supra.*

Table 1:	Purchase			Lease
	MACRS depreciation	Interest at 10%	Total	Rent
Year 1	$20,000	$10,000	$30,000	$21,000
Year 2	32,000	8,000	40,000	21,000
Year 3	19,200	6,000	25,200	21,000
Year 4	11,520[80]	4,000	15,520	21,000
Year 5	11,520	2,000	13,520	21,000
Year 6	5,760	-------	5,760	21,000
Year 7	-----------	--------	---------	21,000
	$100,000	$30,000	$130,000	$147,000

Based upon the fact pattern illustrated (which assumes that repayment of debt is on a straight-line basis over five years), purchasing the asset as compared to leasing the asset produced a tax advantage (i.e., higher deductions in the earlier years). However, the faster tax deduction necessitated outside borrowing which may have caused cash flow considerations for WIP and A/R, especially if these assets are tied into existing loan agreements. These considerations, however, are only a couple of factors in the overall economic analysis of this transaction. Another important factor to consider is the different "cash flow" that occurs when a firm purchases rather than leases equipment. This timing difference can be assessed through an analysis that takes into account the "present value" of money. Further analysis may be required if additional alternative approaches involving different fact patterns are available. This analysis becomes more complicated if the leased equipment has a longer life, if a purchase option at the end of the lease is expected to be exercised, or if the leased equipment is an automobile, because deductions for lease payments for certain leased cars are limited.[81] Consequently, in order to properly evaluate tax and other economic advantages and disadvantages underlying lease vs. purchase decisions, it is generally useful to create a financial model which embraces, among other things, "discounted cash flow" or other "present value" techniques.

---

[80] IRC § 168(b)(1)(B); 26 U.S.C. § 168(b)(1)(B) requires that depreciation be calculated under the straight-line method in the first year that it will yield a larger depreciation deduction than the general MACRS method.

[81] IRC § 280F(c), 26 U.S.C. § 208F(c) and § 4.03 Rev. Proc. 98-30, I.R.B. 1998-17, 6 (Apr. 7, 1998). The limitation on deducting lease payments is designed to be substantially equivalent to the limitations on depreciation deductions on certain purchased luxury cars.

[iii]—Conditional Sale

"Conditional Sale" means a leasing transaction in which the form of the transaction is not respected for tax purposes and is considered to be a sale in which the lessee is considered to have purchased the property in exchange for a debt obligation. As a result, the total expected lease payments are capitalized and depreciated over the tax life of the assets. An offsetting entry is made to set up the expected lease payments as a liability. In a conditional sale transaction, the lessee is considered to have more ownership attributes than the lessor. For example, the right of a lessee to possess property throughout its economic useful life is a strong indication that the lessee is the tax owner of the underlying property.[82] Another indication of purchase exists when the rental payments are applied against the purchase price or create an equity interest in the asset. Also, when a lessee is economically compelled to exercise a purchase option (e.g., the option price is nominal in relation to the value of the property, also referred to as a bargain purchase option), the lease would likely be treated as a conditional sale.[83]

[c]—Financial Accounting Considerations

Generally speaking, for financial accounting purposes under FAS 13, leases are classified as either operating leases or capital leases. If a lease meets one or more of the following criteria it will be classified as a capital lease:

(1) The lease transfers ownership of the equipment to the lessee by the end of the lease term.

(2) The lease contains a bargain purchase option.

(3) The lease term is equal to 75% or more of the estimated economic useful life of the lease equipment. However, if the lease term falls within the last 25% of the equipment's estimated economic useful life, this criterion shall not be used.

(4) At the beginning of the lease term, the present value of the minimum lease payments equals or exceeds 90% of the fair market value of the equipment. Generally, a lessee calculates the present value of the minimum lease payments using its incremental cost of borrowing. However if the lease term falls within the last 25% of the equipment's estimated economic useful life this criterion shall not be used.

---

[82] Pacific Gamble Robinson v. Commissioner, 54 T.C.M. 915 Dec. 44,281 (1987).

[83] Oesterreich v. Commissioner, 226 F.2d 798 (9th Cir. 1955), *rev'g* 12 T.C.M. 277, Dec. 19,522 (1953).

If a lease agreement does not meet the criteria for being classified as a capital lease it is an operating lease

[5]—Interest Capitalization on Leasehold Improvements

Prior to the enactment of the Tax Reform Act of 1986, there were various provisions in the Internal Revenue Code that discussed the tax accounting treatment of self-constructed assets (e.g., inventory and fixed assets used in a trade or business). To clarify these provisions and to define what costs should be included in self-constructed assets, Congress drafted a set of provisions, known as the "Uniform Capitalization Rules," which codified the pre-1986 provisions into one Code section.[84] The provision that affects most law firms concerns the interest capitalization rules for self-constructed fixed assets; primarily leasehold improvements that are paid for by the law firm. These assets include items such as actual construction costs, design costs, architectural fees, engineering fees, and consultants' fees in connection with a leasehold improvement project.

Under the interest capitalization rules, a law firm must capitalize interest on some types of direct debt ("traced debt")[85] and indirect debt ("non-traced debt") incurred during the construction period of leasehold improvements.[86] The construction period for leasehold improvements generally begins when physical construction commences[87] (e.g., plumbing, electrical, walls, etc. are physically installed) and ends when the asset is ready to be placed in service.[88]

If a construction project involves separate units such as multiple floors in an office building and the production period of each unit is distinct and independent, then the production period for each unit may end when each unit is placed in service instead of when the entire project is completed.[89]

Interest on traced debt should be capitalized and included in the depreciable basis of the improvement. If the firm does not specifically borrow or if the traced debt does not equal the cost of the leasehold improvement, the firm must capitalize a part of its interest on nontraced

---

[84] IRC § 263A; 26 U.S.C. § 263A.

[85] Treas. Reg. § 1.263A-9(b); 26 C.F.R. § 1.263A-9(b). Traced debt is determined by applying the rules of Temp. Treas. Reg. § 1.163-8T which relate to the allocation of debt to expenditures. IRS Notice 88-99, 1988-2 C.B. 422.

[86] IRC § 263A(f)(3); 26 U.S.C. § 263A(f)(3).

[87] Treas. Reg. § 1.263A-12(c); 26 C.F.R. § 1.263A-12(c) and §1 of IRS Notice 88-99, 1988-2 C.B. 422.

[88] Treas. Reg. § 1.263A-12(d); 26 C.F.R. § 1.263A-12(d).

[89] Treas. Reg. § 1.263A-12(d)(3); 26 C.F.R. § 1.263A-12(d)(3).

debt using the avoided-cost method, without regard to whether such payment was possible.[90] The theory behind the avoided-cost method is that other interest costs could have been reduced if, in the case of leasehold improvements, construction had not occurred and the amount used for construction could have been used to pay off existing debt. The avoided-cost concept is applied using a mechanical formula that can be calculated using various methods.[91]

A *de minimis* rule provides that interest does not have to be capitalized on leasehold improvements when the construction period does not exceed 90 days and the cost of the improvements does not exceed $1,000,000 divided by the number of days in the production period.[92] For example, assume that construction of leasehold improvements on one floor of an office building began June 1 and ended August 15 and cost $25,000. Even though the construction period was less than 90 days (i.e., 76 days), interest would have to be capitalized because the cost of the improvements ($25,000) exceeds the *de minimis* amount ($1,000,000 divided by 76 day construction period, or $13,158).

For tax purposes, depending on the year the improvement is placed in service, capitalized interest is amortizable over the statutory life of the leasehold improvement (i.e., thirty-nine years).

[6]—Charitable Contributions as Business Expenses

From time to time, law firms are asked to make donations to various charitable or civic organizations. In some situations, the intention is strictly donative. In others, the firm feels pressured because of a business relationship with the organization, a business relationship with a board member, or a business relationship with another important contributor to the organization.

Charitable contributions retain their character and flow through the partnership directly to the partners as itemized deductions. A partner whose adjusted gross income exceeds an applicable amount[93] is

---

[90] Treas. Reg. § 1.263A-9(a)(1); 26 C.F.R. § 1.263A-9(a)(1).

[91] See § VI of IRS Notice 88-99, 1988-2 C.B. 426.

[92] Treas. Reg. § 1.263-A-9(f); 26 C.F.R. § 1.263A-9(f).

[93] IRC § 68(b); 26 U.S.C. § 68(b). See also, § 3.06; Rev. Proc. 2001-13 I.R.B. 200113 (Jan.. 16, 2001). *The applicable amount is adjusted annually for inflation. For 2001, the applicable amount is $132,950, except in the case of a married person filing a separate return the applicable amount is $66,475.* IRC § 68(f); 26 U.S.C. § 68(f) phases out this limitation for tax years beginning after December 31, 2005, as follows

- For tax years beginning in calendar years 2006 and 2007, the limitation is 2/3 of IRC § 68(b) amount
- For tax years beginning in calendar years 2008 and 2009, the limitation is 1/3 of IRC § 68(b) amount

required to reduce the amount of certain itemized deductions by 3% of the excess of adjusted gross income ("three-percent rule") over the applicable amount.[94] In no event may the reduction be more than 80% of the allowable itemized deductions.[95]

Sometimes, because of the circumstances leading to a law firm's making a contribution, the item is more in the nature of a business expense than a contribution. In these situations, it may be possible to reclassify the amount as an ordinary and necessary business expense.[96] As business expenses, these amounts are used to calculate partnership ordinary income and are not reported to partners as contributions. As a result, they reduce adjusted gross income on the partners' returns and, in many cases, minimize the loss of itemized deductions under the three-percent rule.

Obviously, not all contributions are subject to reclassification. To qualify, a contribution must bear a *direct* relationship to the business and must be made with a *reasonable expectation* of a financial return commensurate with the amount of the expense.[97]

Contributions made with a true donative intent cannot be reclassified.

[7]—Valuing Property Received in Exchange for Services Rendered

Occasionally, clients are unable to pay for legal services in cash; as a result, a law firm may accept stock, restricted stock, or other property as payment for services performed. For example, a law firm may receive options or preferred stock of a closely held company that has no readily ascertainable value and is only exercisable or redeemable upon successful completion of a legal matter.

The Code provides that if the beneficial interest in the property received is transferable or is not subject to a substantial risk of forfeiture, the fair market value of the property is taxable at the time of receipt.[98] However, if a law firm, in connection with the performance of services, receives property that is subject to "substantial risk of forfeiture" within the meaning of the Code,[99] then it would not be subject

---

[94] IRC § 68(a)(1); 26 U.S.C. § 68(a)(1).

[95] IRC § 68(a)(2); 26 U.S.C. § 68(a)(2).

[96] Treas. Reg. § 1.170A-1(c)(5); 26 C.F.R. § 1.170A-1(c)(5).

[97] See: S. Marquis v. Commissioner, 49 T.C. 695, Dec. 28,893 (1968) and Ltr. Rul. 8145020 (July 30, 1981).

[98] IRC § 83(a); 26 U.S.C. § 83(a). The regulations [Treas. Reg. § 1.83-3(d); 26 C.F.R. § 1.83-3(d)] provide that transferability means the property would not be subject to a substantial risk of forfeiture in the hands of the transferee. Accordingly, risk of forfeiture is the governing factor.

[99] IRC § 83(c)(1); 26 U.S.C. § 83(c)(1).

to tax on the property when received. If risk of forfeiture exists, income is not recognized by the firm until risk of forfeiture lapses.[100] The amount of income to be recognized then is the fair market value of the property on the date the substantial risk of forfeiture lapses.

A law firm can elect to include in gross income the fair market value of the property in the year it is received, even though it is subject to a substantial risk of forfeiture.[101] A law firm may wish to consider this election if it anticipates an increase in individual income tax rates in future years or anticipates that property will appreciate before substantial risk of forfeiture lapses. If an election is made with respect to investment-type property (e.g., stocks or bonds), any appreciation or loss in value after the Section 83 election is made is subject to the preferential capital gains tax rates. The election must be made within thirty days of receipt of the property.[102]

[8]—Purchasing vs. Developing Computer Software

Few developments have so profoundly affected business efficiency as computers. First, mammoth computers that consumed full-sized rooms provided management with a means to modernize their production facilities or accounting and finance departments. These computers generally were very expensive and often came bundled with special-purpose software. Software sometimes was sold as a loss leader designed to entice a buyer into purchasing a computer worth millions of dollars. Alternatively, computer manufacturers would modify basic software programs to meet a customer's specific needs. Bundling was done for two reasons: first, for investment tax credit purposes, and, second, to allow a computer manufacturer to control the hardware and software market.

As early as 1951 and continuing through the 1960s, the Justice Department attacked IBM for monopolistic practices because, among other reasons, it would not unbundle its software. After years of squabbling and litigation, IBM relented and began unbundling its software and making its computer architecture available so that other software companies could write programs for IBM computers.

During the 1960s and 1970s, most of the computer budgets were weighted in favor of hardware purchases rather than software acquisitions. Software maintenance costs were high, however, because they funded armies of programmers who wrote and maintained computer code. Today, because of tremendous improvements made in hardware

---

[100] Treas. Reg. § 1.83-1(a)(1); 26 C.F.R. § 1.83-1(a)(1).

[101] IRC § 83(b); 26 U.S.C. § 83(b).

[102] IRC § 83(b)(2); 26 U.S.C. § 83(b)(2).

technology, computers are significantly more powerful and a fraction of their ancestors' cost. Software too has changed and today is geometrically more complex and expensive because the hardware allows for more sophisticated computer code written in high-level computer languages. Clearly, the tables have turned.

Law firms generally did not make the same evolution from manual systems to computer systems that corporations made. While corporations invested large sums of money in computerized manufacturing systems or integrated computerized inventory systems, law firms continued using books, papers, and typewriters to practice law. Law firms had no need for computers because they had accounting departments that recorded receipts and took care of the books. Years after large corporations harnessed the power of computers, law firms began using them, and then only slowly. First, computers were introduced into the internal accounting system, then into other administrative functions, including secretarial word processing. To some, the final straw came when associates started to use computers at their desks for writing briefs or sending e-mail. Today, one can look back and see that most law firms have evolved (or are continuing to evolve) into technologically efficient businesses.

Now, computers are sold at almost giveaway prices, while accounting systems for law firms, docket tracking systems, and payroll systems cost millions of dollars. With the introduction of very powerful computer operating systems, complex, integrated computer programs, and wide-area networks, law firms often do not have the in-house resources to implement and modify software applications. Running with skeleton computer staffs who are not trained in the nuances of sophisticated computer applications, law firms often buy packaged software applications from one vendor and then engage a software consultant to install or to modify the software. In the vernacular, times have changed. However, the rules concerning when to capitalize or expense software costs remain much the same as they were years ago.

Why would a book written for modern attorneys cover the "ancient" history of computers and how hardware and software have changed during the last forty years? The reason is to place in perspective the differences between "the then and the now" and how the IRS has reacted to the evolution. In 1969, when big, expensive computers were in vogue, the IRS issued a revenue procedure giving guidelines on how to account for software costs; should they be capitalized or expensed?

This section will focus on accounting for software costs from a tax perspective. It will include a discussion of accounting for purchased software, developed or customized software, and modifications. This section also will discuss accounting for software training, because it is associated with this topic.

[a]—Purchased Software

As previously mentioned, a 1969 revenue procedure was issued by the IRS to give guidance on how to account for computer software costs.[103] Overall, the revenue procedure said that the IRS would not "disturb" (i.e., make an adjustment for) the method of accounting used by a taxpayer, as long as the method was consistently applied to the same type of software costs. Section four of the revenue procedure described purchased software as software that is bundled with hardware or whose cost is separately stated (i.e., off-the-shelf software or software purchased from a vendor) and is treated by a taxpayer as an intangible asset. For software purchased after August 10, 1993, Congress reduced the depreciation period from a five-year life or shorter life if proven to a thirty-six month life.[104]

Following the revenue procedure, most law firms that purchase commercially available software realized that software is an intangible asset and is recoverable through amortization. Included in this category are commercially available electronic spreadsheet programs, database programs, word processing programs, general ledger programs, etc. Although these types of programs are relatively inexpensive, the IRS generally takes the position that, regardless of the amount, all purchased software should be capitalized and amortized over a thirty-six-month period.

While accounting for the cost of purchased software seems intuitive, accounting for its installation or modification is not as clear. This subject will be developed further in this section.

[b]—Costs to Develop Software

How should a law firm account for software development costs? The 1969 revenue procedure said that the cost of developing software so closely resembled research and experimental expenditures as to warrant accounting treatment similar to those costs.[105] Generally, if a law firm develops software internally using its own employees, the costs of development are deductible.[106] The IRS said that it would not disturb a taxpayer's treatment of software development costs if:

---

[103] Rev. Proc. 69-21, 1969-2 C.B. 303.

[104] IRC §§ 167(f) and 197(e)(3); 26 U.S.C. §§ 167(f) and 197(e)(3).

[105] See § 3.01, Rev. Proc. 69-21, 1969-2 C.B. 303.

[106] IRC § 174(a); 26 U.S.C. § 174(a) and § 3 of Rev. Proc. 69-21, 1969-2 C.B. 303. The preamble to final Treasury regulations issued under IRC § 263A on August 6, 1993, p. 20, states that the IRS "has no present intention to changing its ad.

- All of the costs attributable to the software development project are consistently treated as current expenses,[107] or
- All of the costs attributable to the software development project are consistently treated as capital expenditures that are amortized over a period of five years.[108]

In this statement, the IRS said that a taxpayer had to look to its method of accounting to determine the accounting for current software development expenditures. The important point is that all costs attributed to a software project have to be treated consistently. Therefore, if a law firm's method of accounting is to capitalize development costs, then all costs, including salaries paid to employees who worked on the project, should be capitalized. The opposite is also true; if a firm's method of accounting is to expense development costs, than all costs associated with a project should be expensed, including amounts paid to independent consultants.

When computers and software were less complicated and intimidating, a law firm usually used its own employees to make software changes or to develop its own internal applications. By expensing or capitalizing their salaries, the firm probably created its method of accounting for all future similar costs. The fact that computer programs are more expensive today or that software consultants are used today in place of employees does not change the method of accounting. Any change in the treatment of such costs is a change in accounting requiring approval from the IRS before the change can be made.[109]

Seldom are decisions so obvious. More frequently, a law firm purchasing new software that is complex or requires a long installation or modification period (e.g., a new general ledger package) might engage an outside consultant to work with its employees to scope out and to complete the project. In some cases, a firm might buy/license the software from a vendor, engage a consultant to install the application, and engage a second consultant to modify the installed software.

In a 1986 private letter ruling, the IRS reviewed a similar fact pattern.[110] The facts are worth reviewing. A manufacturer wanted to establish an integrated information system. It intended to purchase six software applications and to develop others necessary to complete the system. Because of tight timetables, specific expertise required, and

---

[107] See § 3.01.1, Rev. Proc. 69-21, 1969-2 C.B. 303.

[108] See § 3.01.2, Rev. Proc. 69-21, 1969-2 C.B. 303.

[109] See § 6.01, Rev. Proc. 69-21, 1969-2 C.B. 303

[110] Priv. Ltr. Rul. 8632053, (May 16, 1986).

other factors, management decided to use outside consultants in conjunction with its own personnel to develop the management information system. To implement the system, multiple projects were identified, each with its own project definition phase, general design phase, detailed design phase, and implementation phase. Each phase included numerous steps and progressed in a methodical manner.

The manufacturer compensated the consultants on an hourly basis. The consultants did not provide any guarantees or warranties for the success of performance of the management information system. The consultants were compensated for their time, regardless of the outcome, and bore no risk in the project. Because the consultants assumed no risk, the IRS held that the amounts paid to the consultants were costs incurred in developing software and, accordingly, were deductible currently. The ruling demonstrates that when consultants are used to supplement employees, they are performing the same function that employees would perform given the time and talent. If salaries paid to the employees are expensed, then the method of accounting suggests that the amounts paid to consultants should be expensed.

There are situations when commercial software is not available to do what a law firm wants done. For example, a boutique patent firm might want a special document-handling system or a detailed billing system to track patent renewal fees. Realizing that software is not commercially available, a law firm might decide to develop its own software or to engage a software consultant who can write the code they need. Once again, the firm is faced with a question of whether it should expense or capitalize the development costs.

In a private letter ruling, the IRS addressed this question and gave guidance.[111] In the ruling, a taxpayer outgrew its existing software and wanted to acquire a new system that would handle all of its locations. It decided to engage software Consultant A to develop the new software system under a contract for a fee not to exceed a specific amount. The contract also included language to the effect that if the software did not work as desired, then Consultant A could be held liable up to the amount that it was paid by the taxpayer. Once Consultant A started the project, it became obvious that Consultant A would not be able to complete the project based on the terms of the original contract. Presumably, Consultant A realized that the project was bigger than originally thought and that it needed more time and money. The taxpayer and Consultant A renegotiated the contract so that, from that point on, Consultant A would be working under a time-plus-expense, open-end

[111] Priv. Ltr. Rul. 8614004 (Nov. 25, 1985).

job order. The taxpayer also hired new employees to work with and oversee Consultant A. This effectively transferred the risk of completion and usability from Consultant A to the taxpayer. As expected, the system took substantially longer to complete and cost in excess of the original contract price.

During the design and implementation of the new software, the taxpayer realized that it needed new hardware to run the new software, so it purchased a new computer. Until the new software was ready, it needed to use its existing software on the new hardware. Consequently, the taxpayer hired Consultant B to convert its existing software to the new hardware. Consultant B was hired on a time-plus-expense basis and the taxpayer bore the risk of converting the existing software to the new computer.

In weaving its way through the 1969 revenue procedure, the IRS focused on the accounting method in place and who bore the risk of development. Equating the software development costs as akin to research and experimental expenditures, the IRS commented that the provisions allowing a taxpayer to expense research and experimental expenditures apply not only to the taxpayer, but also to costs incurred on its behalf by another person or organization (e.g., a software consultant).[112] In deciding if payments to Consultant A were software development costs (i.e., current expenses) or purchased software (i.e., capitalize), the IRS focused on who bore the risk of development. It repeated that under the original contract, Consultant A bore the risk of development up to a certain amount and that the taxpayer knew from day one that that amount was the most that it would pay for the software under the original contract. The IRS held that after the contract was modified the amount paid up to the specific amount of the original contract was purchased software because the consultant assumed the risk of development. Payments to A in excess of original amount became contract research and were deductible when paid or incurred. With respect to the amount paid to Consultant B, the IRS held that the taxpayer bore the risk of developing the software and, therefore, the amounts were currently deductible.

As mentioned, a law firm's accounting method for software development plays a critical role in deciding if software costs should be expensed or capitalized. One clear indication of an accounting method is how a law firm accounts for employees who work on software development projects or who assist independent consultants with

---

[112] Treas. Reg. § 1.174-2(a)(2); 26 C.F.R. § 1.174-2(a)(2). See also, Priv. Ltr. Rul. 8614004 (Nov. 25, 1985).

software projects. Following the old saying that "you can't have it both ways," a law firm has to be consistent in its treatment of all development costs — those incurred internally and those paid to independent consultants. Referring again to research and experimental costs, the IRS held that a taxpayer has to be consistent from year to year in its accounting method for the same type of expenditure, unless it requests permission to change its accounting method.[113] The IRS also looked to consistency in a situation in which a corporation purchased a replacement computer and wanted to capitalize software costs for the new computer. Focusing on the fact that the corporation expensed software costs during the five-year period during which the original computer was used, the IRS held that the new software costs could not be capitalized without prior approval of the Commissioner.[114] To capitalize the costs would be a change in accounting from its present accounting method of expensing such costs.

Returning to the distinction between installation and modification, it is important to recall the few guidelines mentioned previously that the IRS has published. If analysis of installation is begun at a purely clinical and technical level, installation of software can be compared to the installation of a piece of manufacturing equipment. If installation requires minimal efforts (e.g., uncrating and plugging the machine into an electrical outlet), then installation costs are probably expensed, especially if the installation is done by company employees or service technicians working under a service contract. However, if installation requires considerable effort, then the cost should be added to the cost of the equipment and depreciated over the life of the equipment. The same concept applies to software. Since many software applications today are easily installed through setup procedures contained on CD-ROMs or computer diskettes, there is little or no extra cost involved in installing software. In more complex applications such as general ledger systems or time and billing systems that have to be integrated into other systems, it is less clear when installation ends and modifications begin. One criterion is when a system is in a state of readiness and capable of being used. This, by the way, is the same criterion used to determine when an asset is placed in service. Many law firms argue that installation ends and modifications (i.e., expenses) begin when the program runs the way the programmer intended. Others argue that a program is unusable until it is modified to do everything on someone's "wish list." Which is

---

[113] Treas. Reg. § 1.174-3(a); 26 C.F.R. § 1.174-3(a). See also, Rev. Rul. 68-144, 1968-1 C.B. 85.

[114] Rev. Rul. 71-248, 1971-1 C.B. 55 (Jan 1, 1971).

correct? The answer lies in the specific facts and circumstances for each law firm, but will depend on the method of accounting that a law firm uses to account for software modifications or maintenance. Most law firms prefer to consider modifications made by their employees or independent consultants as expense items, rather than capitalizing them.

How are these principles applied to the costs incurred to address the "year 2000" problem? One school of thought suggests that costs incurred to distinguish between the years 2000 and 1900 are capital expenditures because they benefit future periods. In advice to IRS agents, the Service said that it would not disturb the accounting method used by a taxpayer to account for costs to develop new software to replace its existing software, to purchase or lease new software to replace its existing software, or to develop or purchase software tools to assist in converting existing software to be year 2000 complaint.[115] Citing the 1969 revenue procedure, the IRS essentially said that taxpayers have to be consistent in applying their accounting methods. If software development costs had been expensed in the past, then they should be expensed in the future even though year-2000-related costs benefit future periods. It also advised that taxpayers wishing to change their accounting methods for software development costs could follow automatic change procedures.[116]

To sum up this subsection, the treatment of software development expenditures depends on a law firm's consistent application of its method of accounting and whether the firm bears the risk of development. In evaluating an accounting method, it is necessary to look back to the method that was in effect during previous years. Often, development costs in previous years were expensed because they were not large or because a law firm used its own employees to make software modifications or to write new programs. The magnitude of current software costs does not control. However, if a law firm wishes to capitalize development costs (including salaries of employees involved in software development projects) instead of expensing them, the firm can request permission from the IRS to change their method of accounting.

[c]—Training Costs

Early generations of software were fairly easy to learn. Many people used a commercially available help guide or a computerized tutorial to

---

[115] See § 2 of Rev. Proc. 97-50, I.R.B. 1997-45, (Oct. 21, 1997).

[116] See: § 5 of Rev. Proc. 97-50, I.R.B. 1997-45, (Oct. 21, 1997); Rev. Proc. 98-60, I.R.B. 1998-51, 17 (Dec. 10, 1998).

learn how to use the programs. The technological advances made in computer hardware have allowed software developers to build more "bells and whistles" into newer software, thereby making the applications more complex and more difficult to learn. Drop-down menus and built-in help capabilities often are not enough to train people to use the newer generations of software. It is common today for a law firm to hire an outside consultant to train its accounting department in the use of a new accounting system or to teach word processing professionals or lawyers to use new word processing software or new operating systems. Often these training costs are significant and nonrecurring. Law firms wishing to manage the bottom line sometimes argue that, under *Indopco,* training costs benefit future periods and should be amortized over the period benefited. The IRS noted that *Indopco* did not change the fundamental legal principle for determining if a particular expenditure is a current deduction or must be capitalized. Except in unusual circumstances, the IRS ruled that amounts paid for training, including the cost of trainers or routine updates of training materials, are generally deductible as business expenses in the year paid, even though they may have some future benefit.[117] What are unusual circumstances? Courts held in the case of the Atomic Energy Commission that the cost of training a new work force had to be capitalized because substantial training was required before a license was issued to operate a nuclear facility.[118] The difficulty with such decisions is that if training is considered so unusual as to be capitalized, then there may be no amortization of the amount capitalized as long as the trained work force is required. While current-year training of new employees is deductible, the company has an asset in the original trained work force for which it cannot demonstrate a useful life, except possibly the life of the nuclear license in the case of the Atomic Energy Commission. While computer training might be more expensive today, in concept, it is no different from the periodic training of employees to do their jobs using the tools currently in place by a company. Those are ordinary and necessary business expenses, not amounts that should be capitalized.

[9]—Prepaid Rent

As year end approaches, law firms that have had profitable years often try to find deductions to lower the partnership's taxable income

---

[117] Rev. Rul 96-62, 1996-2, C.B. 9 (Dec. 23, 1996).

[118] Madison Gas and Electric Co. v. Commissioner, 633 F2d 512, 80-2 U.S.T.C. ¶ 9754 (CA-7, 1980) and Cleveland Electric Illuminating Co. v. Commissioner, 7 Cl. 220 (1985).

(i.e., ordinary income). The reasoning is simple, the lower the firm's income the less taxes the partners pay. One expense category that garners attention is rent, because it is one of the largest expense items.

Putting aside for the moment the hoped-for tax-saving advantage behind paying rent in advance, there are other reasons that law firms might pay rent in advance. These include times when a lessor insists on payment of the last year's rent (or some other period at the end of the lease term) as a form of security deposit, when a cash-short lessor offers a sizable discount for paying rent in advance, or when a cash-flush lessee negotiates an advance payment to get better terms or more space. But even where such non-tax reasons are present, firms hope that advance payment will pass muster as an ordinary and necessary business expenses for tax purposes.

If the only business purpose of paying rent in advance is to gain a tax advantage, the chances of having the IRS agree that the payment is deductible in the year paid are very small. Courts have consistently held that a cash-basis taxpayer generally may not deduct prepaid rent in the year paid because the payment is not an ordinary and necessary business expense for that year. Instead, taxpayers must deduct prepaid rent ratably over the term of the lease.[119] The exception to this rule is if a payment was actually made there is a substantial business reason for making the prepayment and the prepayment does not cause a material distortion in the taxpayer's taxable income in the year of prepayment.[120] The courts have been reserved in finding that taxpayers have satisfied this three-pronged test.[121]

These tests can be very subjective. Better lease terms are a business purpose, but proving it may require the landlord or other lessor to testify.[122] Satisfying the non-distortion test means that, in any event, an advance payment will not be allowed if it accelerates a deduction that "materially distorts" a firm's taxable income. Unfortunately, the IRS and several courts have taken the position that an expense taken in the wrong year results in a distortion of income for that year and is considered to be material.[123] Another obstacle put in front of taxpayers to prevent them from deducting prepaid rent is an Internal Revenue Code provision that there must be economic performance before an expenditure can be expensed.[124] Economic performance is deemed to

---

[119] Treas. Reg. § 1.162-11(a); Howe v. Commissioner. T.C. Memo, 2000-291.

[120] Howe v. Commissioner, *supra* N. 119, Grynberg v. Commissioner, 83 T.C. 255 (1984).

[121] Grynberg v. Commissioner, *supra* N. 120.

[122] Howe v. Commissioner, *supra* N. 119.

[123] Treas. Reg. § 1.461-1(a)(3); 26 C.F.R. § 461-1(a)(3).

[124] IRC § 461(h)(1); 26 U.S.C. § 461(h)(1).

occur when rental space is actually used or a legally binding provision makes the tenant liable to the landlord before the day the first rental payment is due.

[10]—Establishing and Maintaining a Web Site

Based on limited observations, it appears that every law firm in the United States of any size has a web site. Thus we have new and often sizable costs. A bare bones web site can cost less than a thousand dollars to create, but many large firms spend hundreds of thousands of dollars developing web sites. Maintaining webs sites is not cheap (some firms with several hundred lawyers have a separate web page for each lawyer). Setting up a web page involves (a) developing the content, (b) translating the desired content into web site software, and (c) putting the software on a server. The tax treatment of each follows:

[a]—Developing Web Site Content

For a law firm, a web site is an advertising medium, used primarily to attract clients and secondarily as a recruiting device. As a general rule, advertising is deductible in the year the expense is paid or accrued.[125] This is true even though it is clear that much advertising has a benefit beyond the current year, particularly goodwill and image advertising. There is no tax authority yet on how to account for artistic preliminaries (e.g., writing, photographing, art work, editing) that go into creating a web site whose purpose is advertising and whose benefit extends beyond the year incurred (although it seems clear that consulting fees to determine whether a web site will be developed and its scope are currently deductible)[126].

The closest analogy to the artistic development stage is the preparation and printing of trade catalogs. The IRS takes the position that these costs must be capitalized and deducted over the life of the catalog.[127] The courts are mixed on the question. Two cases hold that the cost of preparing and printing catalogs with a useful life of several years is deductible when incurred.[128] A third holds that such costs must be capitalized.[129] In view of the lack of specific guidance and

---

[125] Treas. Reg. § 1.162-1(a).

[126] The IRS and the courts have consistently held that investigatory expenses are currently deductible. TAM 7906011; Appeal of Schlosser Bros., Inc., 2 B.T.A. (1925).

[127] Rev. Rul. 68-360, 1968-2 CB 197.

[128] Sheldon & Co. v. Commissioner, 54-2 USTC ¶ 9526, 214 F2d 655 (6th Cir. 1954), Harper & McIntire Co. 57-1 USTC ¶ 9627, 151 F. Supp. 588 (D.C. Cir. 1957).

[129] Best Lock Corp. v. Commissioner, 31 TC 1217 (1959).

that the courts are two to one for the immediate write-off of catalogs, law firms have plenty of authority to deduct these costs currently if they want to, but they should recognize that the IRS might question the deduction (see below). We believe that, in any event, the cost of the development could be bundled with the cost of the software and deducted over 36 months, as discussed below.

The IRS Industry Specialization Program (ISP) recently considered web site design costs. In internal documents, which were made public, the IRS discusses whether web site design is an advertising expense. The catalog analogy is not mentioned. The IRS recognizes that advertising expenses generally are deductible currently even though they may have some future effect on business activity.[130] The initial design costs of a web site, however, might be treated differently. The IRS stated that "design costs more closely resemble nonrecurring promotional or advertising expenditures that result in benefits to the taxpayer which extend beyond the year in which the expenditures are incurred; such expenditures are a capital investment and are not currently deductible."[131] When the IRS tested its theory that package design costs should be capitalized in *RJR Nabisco v. Commissioner,* however, it lost.[132] Tax Court held that these costs were deductible currently. Undeterred by the loss, the IRS has nonacquiesced on *Nabisco*[133] and has stated in the recently released ISP document that web site design is very similar to the package design issue in the food and beverage industry. Thus, law firms should be prepared for the possibility that IRS will take the position on examination that web site development costs are not deductible currently.

The Financial Accounting Standards Board's Emerging Issues Task Force has reached a final consensus on accounting for web site development costs for financial statement purposes. Treating web site development costs differently for book and tax purposes will flag the issue for examining agents. In general, the financial statement rules are:

- Costs incurred during the planning stage - Expense;
- Costs incurred for activities during the web application and infrastructure development stage - Capitalize;
- Costs incurred to create initial graphics for the web site - Capitalize;
- Costs incurred to update graphics (unless, under SOP 98-1, additional functionality is probable) - Expense;

---

[130] Rev. Rul. 92-80, 1992-2, C.B. 97.

[131] Rev. Rul. 89-23, 1989-1, C.B. 85.

[132] RJR Nabisco v. Commissioner, T.C. Memo 1998-252.

[133] AOD/CC 1999-012.

• Costs incurred during the operation stage (unless, under SOP 98-1, additional functionality is probable) - Expense.

[b]—Creating Web Site Software

In a previous section, the tax accounting rules for the creation of software a law firm will use internally (e.g., accounting systems, case control and communications) were discussed. Although a web site is an advertising and recruiting medium aimed at potential clients and recruits, the tax accounting rules for software development costs for the site are the same as for internal-use software. If a law firm does not have talent in-house to write software for the web site, it may have to hire outside consultants to do the work. If the consultants do their work under a turn-key approach and assume the risk of getting the site up and running, then it is probable that the law firm should capitalize those costs as purchased software and amortize them over a thirty-six month period. If, however, a law firm assumes the risks of programming the site or if it uses its own programmers, then the expenditures might be software development costs that, depending on the law firm's method of accounting, may be deductible currently. If the costs of writing the initial software for the site are significant, the IRS may take the position that the costs are more similar to the package design costs and should be capitalized.

[c]—Maintaining a Web Site

Maintaining and updating a law firm web site devoted to attracting clients and recruits is deductible advertising expense.[134]

[d]—Cost of the Server

Law firms may lease server capacity rather than buy the hardware. Lease costs for any hardware under a true operating lease are deductible currently, but lease costs under a capital lease must be allocated between interest expense and depreciation. Any service charges for hardware are deductible currently.

[11]—Real Estate Operations

Most law firms rent their offices rather than own them. Lawyers generally have been reluctant to permit the chores involved in maintaining real estate to disturb the firm's primary role of client service or

---

[134] Treas. Reg. § 1.162-1(a).

have been unwilling to assume the risks of ownership. In periods of declining property values due to recession and the allure of sharing in potential gains from the recovery of office property values, law firms are reexamining this decision. Ownership of the firm's office carries certain rewards and risks, some of which are tax related.

The objective of investing in real estate should be to realize a profit. A law firm that is considering a potential real estate investment should evaluate each alternative based on an extensive analysis of the pretax economics. Tax advantages should be reviewed only as a means of enhancing investment yield, not as an end in themselves. It is never advisable to permit tax advantages to override fundamental and other investment considerations.

[a]—Potential Benefits

There are numerous potential benefits of owning the firm's offices, including the following:

[i]—Depreciation Deduction

The depreciable basis of the office building includes expenditures made from borrowed funds providing the owners with tax deductions (primarily as depreciation) for which there is no cash outlay during the early years of the real estate investment project. The depreciable life of an office building that is placed in service in the United States after May 13, 1993, is thirty-nine years.[135] For buildings outside the United States, the depreciable life is forty years.[136]

[ii]—Leverage Using Debt

The use of debt allows investors to increase the size of the project, enhancing the economic rate of return in the early years of the real estate investment project (as long as the expenses of ownership are not in excess of the fair value of rent that the firm would otherwise be required to pay for comparable office space).

[iii]—Appreciation Income Deferral

Income from appreciation in the value of the real estate is not taxed until the real estate is sold. (Of course, there is no guarantee that the property will appreciate—it could lose value in poor economic times.)

---

[135] IRC § 168(c)(1); 26 U.S.C. § 168(c)(1).
[136] IRC § 168(g)(2)(C)(iii); 26 U.S.C. § 168(g)(2)(C)(iii).

[iv]—Capital Gains Tax Rate[137]

When real estate is sold at a profit, the difference between the sales proceeds and the adjusted basis (cost minus accumulated depreciation) is taxable gain.[138] To the extent of straight-line depreciation taken on the building, and any excess of selling price over original cost, the partners may enjoy the benefit of turning ordinary depreciation deductions into capital gains.[139] This benefit only exists in years when the capital gains tax rate is lower than the ordinary income tax rate.

[b]—Potential Risks and Other Matters

Some of the potential risks and other matters which a firm should consider, before purchasing an office building to house its law offices, include: (1) costs involved, (2) building operation, (3) partnership issues with respect to ownership of the building, and (4) the alternative minimum tax.

[i]—Cost Considerations

Leasing office space usually involves the payment of rent (plus an occupancy tax in some instances). Owning an office building involves financing the project and repaying the mortgage plus interest, the payment of real estate taxes, and the payment of operating expenses (including utilities, cleaning and maintenance services, insurance, etc.).

[ii]—Operating Considerations

Operating the office building involves hiring a supervisor and staff or management company to run the building on a day-to-day basis and to interface with other tenants, if any.

[iii]—Partnership Considerations

Ownership by the firm of the office building which houses the firm's law office raises a series of issues relating to equity among the firm's partners. These issues include:

(1) Should the building be owned by the firm or by a separate real estate entity?

---

[137] Beginning after May 6, 1997, the maximum capital gains tax rate on the excess of net long-term capital gains over net short-term capital losses is 20% for all but those in the 15% bracket. Effective for 2000, a rate of 18% applies to assets held more than five years.

[138] IRC § 1001(a); 26 U.S.C. § 1001(a).

[139] IRC § 1250(a)(1)(A); 26 U.S.C. § 1250(a)(1)(A).

(2) Should all of the firm's partners participate in the ownership of the real estate partnership or should participation be on a voluntary basis? (How are shares to be determined?)

(3) When a partner retires, dies, or withdraws from the firm, how is the former partner's share of the real estate investment handled?

(4) What rent will be charged to the firm by the real estate entity? (If a market rate is to be used, how will it be determined?)

(5) What profit-sharing formula will be used to distribute gain or loss, if, at a future date, the firm decides to move its offices and sell the office building?

[iv]—Alternative Minimum Tax

For alternative minimum tax purposes, the building has to be depreciated over the straight-line method[140] using the alternative depreciation system life of forty years.[141]

[c]—Landlord Concessions

In difficult economic times, landlords use a variety of lease inducements to keep tenants in their buildings as well as to lure new tenants to sign leases. Some of these inducements include deferred rental agreements (including rent holidays), contributions toward leasehold improvements, paying off a tenant's existing lease, and reimbursing moving expenses.

[i]—Deferred Rental Agreements and Rent Holidays

Two common landlord concessions are deferred rental agreements and "rent holidays." Generally, deferred rental agreements are leases for tangible property which have terms under which rent allocable to one calendar year is not payable until after the close of the succeeding calendar year or there are rent escalations during the term of the lease. For tax purposes, the major difference between these two concessions is that under a deferred rental agreement, rental payments are leveled, so that there is a rent deduction each year, even if no rent is paid. When a provision in a lease qualifies as a rent holiday, however, a rent deduction is allowed only when the rent is actually paid.

A deferred rental agreement is a lease in which all or a portion of the rent allocated in the lease is not payable until after the year succeeding the year to which the rent is allocated. With respect to a deferred rental

---

140 IRC § 56(a)(1)(A); 26 U.S.C. § 56(a)(1)(A).

141 IRC § 168(g)(2)(C)(iii); 26 U.S.C. § 168(g)(2)(C)(iii).

agreement, a law firm is allowed (1) annual rent deductions for the amount allocated to the period by the lease, adjusted to its present value,[142] and (2) an interest expense deduction.[143] These rules are commonly referred to as the "economic accrual principles."

A rent holiday provides "free" rent or greatly reduced rent for a period of months, not to exceed twenty-four months. Stated differently, little or no rent expense is allocated in the lease to this period. Qualifying as a rent holiday depends on many factors including the term of the lease, the number of months of free or substantially reduced rent, and the escalation clauses for future rent payments in relation to the market conditions at the time the rent holiday is negotiated. If the lease is for over fourteen years and three months, or is a sale-leaseback, it is important to prove that the rent holiday was not negotiated with a tax avoidance motive.[144] Documentation of the intentions of the parties and evidence of market conditions at the time a lease is negotiated can provide strong support that a deferral agreement qualifies as a rent holiday.

Under the cash basis method of accounting, used by most law firms in preparing their tax returns, a law firm does not recognize any rent deductions until after the rent holiday expires.

Rent is not always paid in cash; sometimes, law firms pay rent indirectly. If a law firm agrees to pay a portion of the landlord's real estate taxes or maintenance expenses of the property (which may include janitor service, water, heat, fire insurance premiums, or the cost of repairs to buildings), the payments are a form of rental payments. In cities where there is an occupancy tax return, these "payments in kind" can be a form of rent subject to the occupancy tax.

[ii]—Contributions Toward Leasehold Improvements

A very common arrangement between a landlord and a law firm is for the landlord to construct and pay for leasehold improvements that meet the law firm's specifications. Normally, the landlord capitalizes the cost of leasehold improvements and is entitled to deduct depreciation or amortization costs over a period of thirty-nine years. Although the law firm receives the benefits of these improvements, it is not taxed on the value of the improvements. It follows that the law firm does not have a capital investment in the improvements, so it cannot amortize them.

Three common methods lessors use to pay for leasehold improvements are depositing money into a construction trust account, paying

---

[142] IRC § 467(b)(1); 26 U.S.C. § 467(b)(1).
[143] IRC § 467(a)(2); 26 U.S.C. § 467(a)(2).
[144] IRC § 467(b)(4); 26 U.S.C. § 467(b)(4).

a law firm's construction contractors directly, or reimbursing a law firm for amounts that it paid for customized leasehold improvements. Depending on the terms of the lease, these "buildout" allowances can catch unwary law firms off-guard and may cause a significant tax issue. If a lease doesn't clearly document that the lessor owns all leasehold improvements paid for through the buildout allowance, then the tenant may realize taxable income when the improvements are paid for. In an IRS industry coordinated issue paper on tenant allowances to retail store operators, the Service concluded that amounts received from a landlord for improvements are considered to be an "accession of wealth" and taxable to the retail store.[145] The pivotal fact in deciding if the tenant realizes taxable income is whether the tenant or landlord owns the improvements. If the tenant does not own the improvements, then it does not recognize income.[146] However, if the tenant owns the improvements, then it has to recognize taxable income for the leasehold improvements paid for by the lessor. If the improvements are nonresidential real property, then the law firm has to recover the capitalized amounts over a thirty-nine year period. A horrendous answer by anyone's standards.

Realizing the scope of the controversy and how it affects small business owners, Congress changed the law for leases entered into after August 5, 1997. From that date on, a landlord can pay for qualified construction or leasehold improvements in connection with a short-term lease on retail space without the lessee incurring the harsh tax result.[147] The new law allows a lessee to receive cash or rent reductions from a lessor under a short-term lease of retail space[148] for the purpose of constructing or improving qualified long-term property for use in the lessee's trade or business, but only to the extent that such amount does not exceed the amount expended by the lessee for construction.[149] A short-term lease is defined as a lease for occupancy or use of retail space for fifteen years or less.[150] However, options to renew are

---

[145] Internal Revenue Service Industry Specialization Program Coordinated Issue Paper dated October 8, 1996.

[146] Elder-Beerman v. Commissioner, U.S. BankrCt Sohio No. 95-33643 (Mar. 20, 1997).

[147] Tax Relief Act of 1997 enacting I.R.C. § 110.

[148] I.R.C. § 110(a)(1); 26 U.S.C. § 110(a)(1).

[149] I.R.C. § 110(a)(2); 26 U.S.C. § 110(a)(2).

[150] I.R.C. § 110(c)(2); 26 U.S.C. § 110(c)(2).

included in the lease term.[151] Retail space is defined as property leases, occupied, or otherwise used by a lessee in its trade or business of selling tangible personal property or services to the general public.[152] As a result of this provision, law firms will be able to negotiate and sign leases with build out allowances without the fear of being taxed on landlord-provided improvements.

The cost incurred by a tenant to make its own leasehold improvements is capitalized and amortized over their applicable recovery period, usually thirty-nine years, without regard to the lease term.[153]

[iii]—Cancellation of an Existing Lease

Another incentive offered by landlords is to pay off a law firm's existing lease, so that it is canceled. This can be accomplished in the following ways: (1) the future landlord can reimburse the prospective law firm tenant for payments made relating to the law firm's existing lease, or (2) the future landlord can pay the law firm's existing landlord directly for the remaining lease payments. The general rule regarding the payment made for cancellation of a lease is that if the law firm pays a cancellation fee to its existing landlord, the payment is deductible as a business expense.[154] If, however, the new landlord pays the law firm for the cancellation expenses and the law firm pays the same to the existing landlord, the law firm has taxable income[155] and business deductions for canceling the lease.

[iv]—Reimbursements for Moving Expenses

Occasionally a new landlord will offer to pay for or reimburse a law firm's moving expenses to entice the law firm to move into the new landlord's building. In this situation, the law firm has taxable income equal to the cost of the move and a corresponding deduction.

[d]—Passive Activity vs. Normal Operations

Many law firms find themselves leasing (or in some cases, owning) more office space than is required by the size of their practice. As a practical solution to this problem, these firms will sublet (or lease) their extra office space until the space is needed for their practice. This transaction is a passive activity and creates an interesting tax consequence that may have an impact on the individual partners or shareholders of the firm.

---

[151] I.R.C. §§ 110(c)(2) and 168(i)(3)(A); 26 U.S.C. §§ 110(c)(2) and 168(i)(3)(A).
[152] I.R.C. § 110(c)(3); 26 U.S.C. § 110(c)(3).
[153] IRC § 168(i)(8); 26 U.S.C. § 168(i)(8).
[154] Rev. Rul. 69-511, 1969-2 C.B. 23.
[155] IRC § 61(a); 26 U.S.C. § 61(a).

A passive activity is defined as an activity which involves the conduct of any trade or business in which a taxpayer does not materially participate.[156] Generally, rental activities are automatically considered to be passive activities.[157] A partnership which conducts activities that are considered passive activities cannot offset ordinary income or losses with passive activity income or losses. The passive income or loss generated by a partnership must flow through to the individual partners who must accumulate all of their individual passive income and losses in computing their taxable income.

Following the general passive activity loss rules, one could expect that a law firm subletting (or leasing) some of its office space would have to report this income or loss separately from the income generated from the practice of law. However, if the activities constitute an "appropriate economic unit" under the facts and circumstances test,[158] the law firm may be able to combine rental and business activities, so that the rental activity will not be subject to the passive activity loss rules. However, once activities are grouped, they may not be regrouped in subsequent taxable years.[159] One *major* qualification is that the law firm must own the building or the lease, and not a related entity such as another partnership owned by some or all of the law firm partners.

Law firms operating as corporations, whether S Corporations or C Corporations, are subject to essentially the same rules.

---

[156] IRC § 469(c)(1); 26 U.S.C. § 469(c)(1).

[157] IRC § 469(c)(2); 26 U.S.C. § 469(c)(2).

[158] Treas. Reg. §§ 1.469-4(c)(2) and 1.469(d)(1); 26 C.F.R. § 1.469(c)(2) and 1.469-4(d)(1).

[159] Treas. Reg. § 1.469-4(e)(i); 26 C.F.R. § 1.469-4(e)(1).

§ 17.05 Accounting Periods

Generally, law firms must compute their income for tax purposes using a fixed accounting period of twelve months.[1]

[1]—Fiscal Year vs. Calendar Year

Prior to the Tax Reform Act of 1986 (TRA'86), law firms operating as partnerships, S Corporations, or Personal Service Corporations had some latitude in selecting a fiscal or calendar year accounting period. The TRA'86 revoked that latitude by requiring, as a general rule, that law firm partnerships have the same year-end as the majority interest of their partners (the "required year").[2] Since most partners are individuals having calendar years for income tax purposes, the required year for most law firms is the calendar year. If partners have a fiscal year-end (e.g., the year-end of an individual in the UK is 5 April), then they would not have to use a calendar year-end in the U.S. for their partnership. For law firms operating as S Corporations or Personal Service Corporations, the required year or permitted year is always the calendar year.[3]

One exception to the general rule allowed a partnership, S Corporation, or Personal Service Corporation to retain or change to a fiscal year if it could demonstrate a valid business purpose (i.e., a "natural business year").[4] A valid business purpose did not include deferral of income for partners or shareholders.[5]

If a law firm partnership or S Corporation could not demonstrate a natural business year, but wanted to retain its fiscal year (e.g., June 30) it could make a one-time election (not now available),[6] or it could change to a new fiscal year one resulting in a deferral of three months or less.[7] In either case, however, the law firm would have to make required payments.[8] This one-time election is referred to as a "Section 444 Election." Personal Service Corporations also could elect to retain their fiscal years, however, they were subject to deduction limitations.[9]

---

[1] IRC § 441(b); 26 U.S.C. § 441(b).

[2] IRC § 706(b)(1)(B); 26 U.S.C. § 706(b)(1)(B).

[3] IRC §§ 441(i) and 1378(b); 26 U.S.C. §§ 441(i) and 1378(b).

[4] IRC §§ 441(i) and 706(b)(1)(C); 26 U.S.C. §§ 441(i) and 706(b)(1)(C).

[5] IRC §§ 441(i), 706(b)(1)(C) and 1378(b); 26 U.S.C. §§ 441(i), 706(b)(1)(C) and 1378(b).

[6] IRC § 444(b)(3); 26 U.S.C. § 444(b)(3).

[7] IRC § 444(b)(3); 26 U.S.C. § 444(b)(3).

[8] IRC § 444(c)(1); 26 U.S.C. § 444(c)(1).

[9] IRC §§ 280H(a) and 444(c)(2); 26 U.S.C. §§ 280H(a) and 444(c)(2).

A newly organized law firm is eligible to make the election, but the fiscal year must end on September 30 or later.[10]

[a]—Natural Business Year

Conceptually, a natural business year is the end of a normal business cycle. To remove subjectivity, the Internal Revenue Service created an objective, mathematical calculation that focuses on the income stream of a law firm. Using this approach, a law firm must pass a "25% test" to demonstrate its natural business year.[11] The 25% test is met if a law firm receives 25% of its gross receipts during the last two months of the proposed fiscal year and in each of the two prior corresponding twelve-month periods. A law firm may periodically have to demonstrate that it is still in compliance with the 25% test.[12]

If a law firm previously using a calendar year can pass the 25% test, it can request permission from the Internal Revenue Service to change to a fiscal year that will result in a deferral of less than three months.

If the Internal Revenue Service concludes that the 25% test is not achieving its purpose (i.e., defining a natural business year), it may consider specific facts and circumstances (including potential tax consequences) in identifying a natural business year.[13] Ordinarily, factors considered to be "issues of convenience for the taxpayer" (e.g., use of a particular year for financial statement purposes, hiring patterns, admission of new partners, promotion of associates, or effective date of pay raises) will *not* be sufficient business reasons.[14]

[b]—Section 444 Election

As mentioned, if a law firm partnership or S Corporation made a Section 444 election, it had to agree to make required payments. A law firm organized as a Personal Service Corporation does not make required payments, but is subject to minimum distribution requirements which have a similar effect on any tax deferral benefits.[15]

A required payment is a non-interest-bearing deposit[16] that is paid by a partnership or S Corporation to the Internal Revenue Service on or before May 15 following the calendar year in which the fiscal year

---

[10] IRC § 444(b)(1); 26 U.S.C. § 444(b)(1).
[11] See § 4.01 of Notice 2001-35, 2001-23 IRB 1314.
[12] See § 5.04 of Notice 2001-35, 2001-23 IRB 1314.
[13] Rev. Rul. 87-57, 1987-2 C.B. 117.
[14] *Id.*
[15] IRC § 280H(a); 26 U.S.C. § 280H(a).
[16] IRC § 7519(f)(3); 26 U.S.C. § 7519(f)(3).

begins.[17] The deposit is calculated at the highest individual tax rate plus 1%[18] (prior to 2001, the rate was 40.6%;[19] after 2000, the rate is 40.1%) on deferred base-year income[20] and is reported to the IRS on Form 8752.[21] Deferred base-year income is the product of base-year income (ordinary taxable income for the prior fiscal year) multiplied by the deferral-period percentage (the number of months from the end of the firm's previous taxable year to December 31, divided by twelve).[22] For a partnership, base-year income is the firm's ordinary taxable income earned during the tax year immediately preceding its current tax year adjusted for certain partner-specific items (e.g., guaranteed payments, interest income, charitable contributions, Keogh contributions).[23]

For an S Corporation, base-year income is the aggregate of a company's ordinary income items and any separately stated items for the immediately preceding year.[24] The S Corporation calculation is similar to a partnership's, except that a special adjustment is made for compensation paid to shareholders during the deferral period, that is, from the end of the taxable year through December 31.[25]

The required payment is fully refundable if the law firm elects to terminate its fiscal year end.[26] If the amount of the required payment decreases because of a reduction in income from the previous year, part of the required payment is refundable.[27]

[c]—Advantages of a Fiscal Year

There are three primary advantages of a law firm maintaining a fiscal year-end:

[i]—Deferral of Income

The first, and most important advantage, is the deferral of income resulting from the firm's year not coinciding with the individual

---

[17] Temp. Treas. Reg. § 1.7519-2T(a)(4)(ii); 26 C.F.R. § 1.7519-2T(a)(4)(ii).

[18] For year beginning before 2001, the rate is 40.6%. For years beginning after 2000, the rate 40.1% for 2001, 39.6% for 2002 and 2003, 38.6% for 2004 and 2005, and 36% for 2006 and thereafter. IRC § 1(2); 26 U.S.C. § 1(2).

[19] IRS Ann. 94-5, I.R.B. 1994-2, 39.

[20] IRC § 7519(b); 26 U.S.C. § 7519(b).

[21] IRS Announcement 90-112; I.R.B. 1990-40, 37.

[22] IRC § 7519(d); 26 U.S.C. § 7519(d).

[23] IRC §§ 702(a) and 7519(d)(2)(A); 26 U.S.C. §§ 702(a) and 7519(d)(2)(A).

[24] IRC §§ 1366(a) and 7519(d)(2)(B); 26 U.S.C. §§ 1366(a) and 7519(d)(2)(B).

[25] IRC § 280H(a); 26 U.S.C. § 280H(a).

[26] IRC § 7519(c)(2); 26 U.S.C. § 7519(c)(2).

[27] IRC § 7519(c)(1); 26 U.S.C. § 7519(c)(1).

partners' years. When a firm ends its accounting period within the tax year of the partners, income generated by the firm between the end of its year and the end of the partners' years is deferred until the next reporting year of the partners.[28] Partners of a firm that can demonstrate a natural business year benefit the most from the deferral, because they do not make a required payment. To a lesser extent, firms that elected a fiscal year and have been paying the required payment will benefit if the actual income earned by the firm during the deferral period is greater than the base upon which the required payment is calculated. They also benefit on the deferral of state taxes, because no state has a rule similar to the required payment federal rule. For federal income tax purposes, the deferral benefit was adversely affected by the current estimated tax payment requirements for partners. The deferral benefit still exists for most state income tax purposes.

[ii]—Ease of Administration

The second advantage of maintaining a fiscal year is that the tax return processing function will not conflict with other year-end administrative functions. For example, the firm can prepare the partners' Schedule K-1s before December 31 and not interfere with processing other year-end items, such as W-2 Forms and 1099 Forms.

[iii]—Accuracy of Tax Estimates

A third advantage of maintaining a fiscal year-end is that the firm will have a more accurate estimate of its fiscal year-end income which the partners can use to calculate the remaining estimated tax payments which are due after the end of the firm's fiscal year.

[d]—Disadvantages of a Fiscal Year

There are two principal disadvantages to a law firm maintaining a fiscal year-end.

[i]—Prepayment of Taxes

One significant disadvantage for firms retaining a fiscal year and not meeting the natural business year test is that they have to make required payments; in effect, they are prepaying their federal income

---

[28] For example, assuming the partnership year-end is September 30, 19X0, the income earned by the partnership between October 1 and December 31, 20X0, will not be subject to tax until the partner's year-end in 20X1.

taxes. Also, the required payments are made using a rate 1% higher than the highest individual marginal tax rate. This disadvantage may become significant if the deposit the firm pays is higher than the total tax that would have been paid by the individual partners if they paid their own income taxes on the deferred income. This situation could exist because the deposit is based on a higher marginal rate and does not consider deductions, exemptions, or credits that individual partners might otherwise be entitled to. State tax advantages continue, however, because states do not have similar payment requirements.

This disadvantage is exacerbated if the actual deferral-period income is less than the base that was used to calculate the required payment. If deferral-period income continues to be less than the base-year income, then a firm should increase its deferral-period income, or consider switching to a calendar year.

[ii]—No Interest on Deposit

A second disadvantage is that the required deposit does not earn interest.

[e]—Termination of Fiscal Year Election

A law firm can elect to terminate its fiscal year election without obtaining consent from the Internal Revenue Service.[29] The firm is entitled to a full refund of the required deposit which it can distribute tax free to the partners.[30] A refund is payable on the later of April 15 of the applicable calendar year or ninety days after the date on which the refund claim is filed.[31] The Code provides that no interest is payable on a refund.[32] The IRS has held that no interest is payable on a refund even if the refund is made eight months late.[33]

One consequence of terminating a fiscal-year election is that the individual partners (or S Corporation Shareholders) will report more than twelve months of income in their individual tax returns, because they are not entitled to spread the terminated short-year income over a four-year period.[34]

---

[29] Treas. Reg. § 1.444-1T(a)(5); 26 C.F.R. § 1.144-1T(a)(5). A short-period return is required. The firm should write "Section 444 Election Terminated" on the top of the first page of the short-period return.

[30] See N. 25 *supra* and Notice 89-41, 1989-1 C.B. 681, dated April 10, 1989, for procedural guidance on obtaining a refund of the required balance.

[31] IRC § 7519(c)(3); 26 U.S.C. § 7519(c)(3).

[32] IRC § 7519(f)(3); 26 U.S.C. § 7519(f)(3).

[33] Ltr. Rul. 9430001 (July 29, 1994).

[34] Treas. Reg. § 1.444-1T(a)(5)(iii); 26 C.F.R. § 1.144-1T(a)(5)(iii).

Another consequence of changing year-ends is that a law firm may wish to change the year of its pension plans to conform to the firm's year-end. In this situation, the plan may be subject to retesting and could have excess contributions in the year of change.

A law firm should carefully consider the tax as well as administrative impact of terminating a fiscal-year election before pursuing this course of action.

[f]—Change in Accounting Period

Unless a fiscal year-end is being terminated, once a law firm establishes its accounting period, prior permission of the Internal Revenue Service is required, in most cases, to change to another period.[35] Application to change an accounting period is made by filing Form 1128 with the IRS.[36] The change is not effective until written permission is received from the IRS.

[2]—Timing of Qualified Pension Plan Contribution Deduction

As a general rule, under the cash method of accounting, a deduction is allowable only in the year in which an otherwise deductible item is paid.[37] An exception to the general rule permits a deduction in the current year for payments of a law firm's contribution to a qualified pension plan, if the contribution is paid by the due date of the tax return (including extensions) and certain other requirements are met.[38] However, if the pension plan is a money purchase plan or a defined benefit plan, the contribution must be made within eight and a half months of the end of the plan year in order to meet the minimum funding requirements[39] and to avoid a possible excise tax.[40]

When a cash basis accounting law firm wants to obtain a current tax advantage for this delayed payment and also wishes to maintain symmetry between its tax return and its accounting records, it should consider accruing its unpaid pension plan contribution as an expense in the current annual accounting period. Of course, the maximum pension plan deduction with respect to any taxable year is subject to certain limitations under the Internal Revenue Code, which may affect the utilization of this technique.[41]

---

[35] Treas. Reg. § 1.706-1T(b); 26 C.F.R. § 1.706-1T(b) and IRC § 442; 26 U.S.C. § 442.

[36] Treas. Reg. § 1.442-1(b)(1); 26 C.F.R. § 1.442-1(b)(1).

[37] Treas. Reg. § 1.446-1(c)(1)(i); 26 C.F.R. § 1.446-1(c)(1)(i).

[38] IRC § 404(a)(6); 26 U.S.C. § 404(a)(6).

[39] IRC § 412(c)(10); 26 U.S.C. § 412(c)(10).

[40] IRC § 4971(a); 26 U.S.C. § 4971(a).

[41] IRC § 404; 26 U.S.C. § 404.

§ 17.06 Partner Profit/Loss Sharing Arrangements

[1]—Sharing Firm Income

All law firms have a method of allocating current year's profits or losses to partners or members regardless of the way the firm is organized. Partnerships and professional corporations generally have a profit or loss sharing agreement to allocate current results. For tax purposes, a partner's share of income, gain, loss, deductions, or credits usually is controlled by the agreement.[1] These agreements can be less rigid than partnership agreements of commercial or investment entities, so that law firms can exercise discretion in compensating partners for exemplary or extraordinary work done throughout the year. Partnership agreements may be modified for a particular year after the close of that tax year, but not later than the date (not including any extension of time) for filing the partnership return for that year.[2] This section discusses some of the ways that profits or losses are shared by various types of partners.

[a]—Apportioning Income

Normally, law firms allocate income to its equity partners based on some systematic method. That method might be a tradition allocation using partnership income-sharing percentages or a percentage based on ownership units. In addition to the normal allocations based on some percentage method, law firms might have a bonus pool that is allocated based on performance. Another method of allocating income is to have a compensation committee determine partners' shares based on some other criteria. Suffice to say that there are many ways of apportioning income to equity partners.[3]

[b]—Guaranteed Payments

Guaranteed payments often are used to compensate active non-equity partners and inactive retired partners. An amount paid to a partner is a guaranteed payment if it is determined without regard to the income of the partnership.[4] Guaranteed payments sometimes are

---

[1] IRC § 704(a); 26 U.S.C. § 704(a).

[2] IRC § 761(c); 26 U.S.C. § 761(c).

[3] Chapter 24 discusses the allocation methods in more detail and in the context of the autocratic approach, the democratic approach, the formula approach, the lockstep approach, the modified lockstep approach and the committee approach See § 24.03 *infra*.

[4] IRC § 707(c); 26 U.S.C. § 707(c).

used to ensure a first-year partner (i.e., a new partner or a lateral-admission partner) a fixed and determinable cash flow. Some firms pay "salaries" to active partners based on their seniority; these amounts also may qualify as guaranteed payments.

Properly constructed guaranteed payments are deductible from firm profits for federal income tax purposes in the year paid (assuming the firm uses a cash method of accounting). Unlike a share of firm profits, which depends on the character of the income to the partnership, guaranteed payments always constitute ordinary income.

Guaranteed payments also are an effective method of compensating a partner who agrees to a foreign assignment, because they allow the overseas partners to have foreign-source income which is needed to claim an Internal Revenue Code Section 911 exclusion. Guaranteed payments (whether paid to nonresident alien partners or to U.S. partners on foreign assignment), however, decrease the foreign-source income of the other partners and can limit their utilization of foreign tax credits. Paying foreign-assignment partners too much in the form of guaranteed payments can upset the parity between partners by reducing the foreign-assignee's worldwide tax liability and increasing the U.S. partners' liabilities.

On the state level, most states (and local jurisdictions) view guaranteed payments as allocations of partnership income instead of deductions from firm profits. Where applicable, partners must allocate guaranteed payments to various states based on the firm's business-allocation percentages. This requirement to allocate income throughout the country has been a point of irritation (and litigation) for partners receiving guaranteed payments, because they have to file tax returns in the same jurisdictions (i.e., state and local) as active partners even though they only practice law in one office.[5]

On the local level, guaranteed payments generally are not considered deductions of the firm.[6] Accordingly, a law firm is required to add them back for purposes of calculating unincorporated business income tax.

[2]—Active Partners

For purposes of this section active partners are individuals who share in the current year's profits either through allocations of income (i.e., equity partners) or through fixed distributions (i.e., non-equity partners. Each will be discussed in the following sections.

---

[5] See Heffron v. Chu. 144 A.D.2d 729, 535 N.Y.S.2d 141 (3d Dept. 1988) and Weil v. Chu, 120 A.D.2d 781, 501 N.Y.S.2d 515 (3d Dept. 1986).

[6] For example, the New York City unincorporated business tax.

[a]—Equity Partners

An equity partner (also referred to as an "percentage partner") has a share in some portion of the current year's profits and a vote in firm matters. An equity partner is considered to be the owner and reaps the rewards when business is good and suffers the consequences when it isn't.

Generally, an equity partner's share in the profits of a firm is determined annually when a law firm amends its partnership agreement to incorporate an updated schedule of partners' profit-sharing percentages. The schedule usually is not modified during the course of the year, except to accommodate the death, retirement or withdrawal of a partner, or admission of a new partner. Instead of incorporating partners' profit-sharing percentages in the partnership agreement, some firms empower an executive compensation committee to determine compensation of each partner based on performance during the year. Another approach to compensating partners is to share profits up to a specified limit and to allocate the remaining profits (i.e., a bonus pool) based on the current year's performance. Flexible allocation approaches have also been used to more closely match each partner's compensation with that partner's efforts and results.

Some items of income, deductions, or credits can be apportioned using special allocation percentages, provided the allocations have substantial economic effect.[7] Achieving equity among partners is a law firm's usual objective for adopting special allocation procedures. Examples of special allocations include:

(1) *Change in accounting period:* Allocation of any "transitional adjustment" (the opening adjustment) solely among the partners in the partnership during the year of change.

(2) *Collection of fees:* Allocation based on percentages in effect during the year in which the fees were earned, for example, contingent fees.

Equity partners in LLPs or LLCs normally share profits that same as partners in a general partnership, even though they may be referred to as members instead of partners. Shareholders of personal service corporations normally are remunerated based on methods similar to partnerships, except their shares are referred to as salaries and dividends, if applicable.

---

[7] Treas. Reg § 1.704-1(b)(2); 26 C.F.R. § 1.704-1(b)(2).

[b]—Salaried-Equity Partner

A salaried-equity partner is a hybrid between the equity partner described above and a non-equity partner discussed in the next section. A salaried-equity partner normally would not have an ownership percentage or any voting rights. The only indicia of equity ownership is the fact that a salaried-equity partner would receive an allocation of current year profits based upon notional shares in the firm. These notional shares approximate the number of actual shares a partner would own if he or she were a full equity partner. In some jurisdictions, such as the UK, the earnings paid to the salaried-equity partner are deducted as an expense when arriving at the firm's distributable income. In the U.S., since the partner's share is determined with respect to the firm's income, it may not qualify as a guaranteed payment and, therefore, is more in the nature of a share of ordinary income. Consequently, amounts allocated to salaried-equity partners is reported as ordinary income on Schedule K-1, regardless of when they are paid.

For a U.S.-based partner, the designation of being a salaried-equity partner has little or no negative tax effect. That may not be the case for a similarly designated salary equity partner who is a non-resident alien. If, for example, a non-resident salaried-equity partner in the U.K. is allocated effectively connected income from the U.S., then the firm would be required to withhold income tax on his share of the effectively connected income.[8]

[c]—Non-Equity Partners

Non-equity partners are those who do not have a vote in partnership matters or a percentage interest in the current year's profits. They generally receive fixed distributions or guaranteed payments that are based upon negotiated agreements, as opposed to a share of the current year's profits.

Law firms can be creative in the designations that they give to non-equity partners.[9] Sometimes they are called "fixed distribution" partners, "junior" partners, "salaried" partner (as contrasted with salaried-equity partners), "contract" partners, "non-percentage" partners, or "of counsels."

Contrary to the term "non-equity," these partners may have equity in a firm resulting in accumulated, but undistributed profits or contributed capital. Sometimes, firms have non-equity partners make small capital contributions, so that they are considered to be "at risk" for

[8] See IRC § 1446; 26 U.S.C. § 1446.

[9] Dawson 672 N.E.2d 589, 592 (N.Y. 1996).

international tax reasons (e.g., is a person has capital, they may be a partner for Belgian income tax purposes, even though they don't share profits).

For tax purposes, non-equity partners are partners and each should receive a Schedule K-1 showing their guaranteed payment. Non-equity partners must include these amounts in their personal tax returns (or corporate return of a PC partner) for the taxable year within which the partnership year ends if the firm uses a cash method of accounting for tax purposes.[10] Generally, amounts paid to active non-equity partners who are individuals and not PC partners are subject to self-employment taxes. One exception is payments to active fixed-distribution partners who are nonresident alien partners.[11]

[3]—Retired Partners

Compensation arrangements for retired partners vary greatly. Some firms continue paying retiring partners a share in the firm's current year's profits, but at a reduced rate. Other firms pay retired partners fixed amounts (adjusted for changes in the cost of living) from unfunded deferred compensation agreements. Still other firms pay retired partners their share of "pipeline" income as it is received by the firm. Another variation is to pay retired partners based on "phantom shares" (the retirement payment is based on nonvoting "as-if-shares" applied against current year's profits.) Retirement payments to retired partners may qualify for exclusion from federal self-employment tax.[12] To be excluded, each of the following five criteria must be met.

(1) The retirement plan must be written.

(2) The retired partner did not render *any* services to the firm during the taxable year.

(3) No obligation exists from the other partners to the retired partner, except with respect to retirement payments.

(4) The retired partner's share of the capital of the partnership has been paid to him in full.

(5) The periodic retirement income payments must continue for the retired partner's lifetime.

[4]—Former Partners

Some law firm partnership agreements have provisions which call for an allocated share of partnership income to be assigned to former

---

[10] Treas. Reg § 1.707-1(c); 26 C.F.R. § 1.707-1(c).

[11] IRC § 1402(b); 26 U.S.C. § 1402(b).

[12] IRC § 1402(a)(10); 26 U.S.C. § 1402(a)(10).

partners (i.e., partners who have withdrawn from the firm) for a year or more subsequent to their withdrawal. Generally, the allocation of a share of taxable income to former partners directly reduces taxable income allocable to the active partners. However, there may be instances when the distributable share of income of former partners is paid to former partners in installments over a period of years, possibly to enforce noncompete agreements. In these instances, the firm may choose (or may be required) to spread the allocation of taxable income to these former partners over the period of years during which the cash is distributed to them. This will, in turn, have a reciprocal effect on the cash flow and taxable income of the active partners (i.e., it will increase the active partners' cash flow and taxable income in the early years when the former partners' distributions are held back and it will decrease the active partners' cash flow and taxable income in the later years when the former partners' distributions are paid). Instead of paying former partners a share of income, law firms frequently negotiate liquidation agreements which provide for payments not dependent on the firm's income. If these payments qualify as guaranteed payments, they can be deducted on the firm's federal income tax return.[13] It is important to refer to the partnership agreement to determine the nature of these payments.

Law firm agreements usually provide that no value is assigned to goodwill, because the future income of the firm is principally dependent on the energy level of the active partners and only in small part on the historical value of the firm's name. However, if the agreement provides that a withdrawing partner is entitled to be paid for a share of the firm's goodwill, then part of the payment may be nondeductible.[14] If the agreement is silent with respect to the distribution of goodwill or specifically states that goodwill is not distributable, then the liquidating payment will be a guaranteed payment.[15]

[5]—Reasonable Compensation for PC Shareholders

The "members" (or "shareholders") of C corporation law firms (PCs or personal service corporations) are careful to make their corporate status clear on business cards, letterheads, formal documents, and firm signatures. However, when it comes to introducing themselves, they often introduce themselves as "partners." Consequently, they are regarded as such by clients and friends and are treated as partners within their PCs.

---

[13] IRC § 736(a)(2); 26 U.S.C. § 736(a)(2).

[14] IRC § 736(b)(2); 26 U.S.C. § 736(b)(2).

[15] See Tolmach v. Commissioner, T.C. Memo 1991-538 ¶ 47,713 (Oct. 29, 1991).

The main difference between a member and a partner is that a member is an employee. The main downside of employee status is that the firm can deduct salary only to the extent it is "reasonable." Law firms that pay out most of their earnings as members' salaries sometimes worry that the IRS "excess comp" weapon will be used against them and that the IRS could allege that part of such salary is nondeductible dividends rather than compensation for services.[16] Despite the potential danger, it is common practice for PCs to have a last-minute year-end "fire drill" to zero out the firm's taxable income via year-end bonuses. And despite the IRS interest in the area, which is discussed below, very few of these bonuses are questioned by the IRS or by state revenue authorities. However, there is risk, and forewarned is forearmed.

A 1994 IRS field service advice released in 2000 determined that on the facts of the case the IRS (1) should go forward with Tax Court litigation and (2) was likely to win.[17] The main facts are summarized, as follows:

> A C corporation law firm paid its shareholder-employees a modest base salary plus a year-end bonus, which was in proportion to each shareholder-employee's stock in the firm. Each spring, the Review Committee evaluated each shareholder and determined how many shares each shareholder-employee would be entitled to buy (or required to sell) to achieve the desired bonus allocation at year-end. After ratification by all the shareholders, the shareholder-employees bought or sold shares as appropriate. Associates were not included in the bonus plan. The firm had not paid dividends the past two years.

This, in substance, is the process that many law firms operating as partnerships, LLPs, LLCs and S Corporations go through annually without incurring tax at the entity level on profit distributions that are proportionate to the partners' (or shareholders') capital accounts, units, or shares. The IRS makes much of the fact that distributions in the field service advice were in proportion to shareholdings. While that may be true, there are those who would argue that the IRS has put the cart before the horse.

---

[16] IRC §162(a)(1) provides that deductions for ordinary and necessary business expenses include a reasonable allowance for salaries or other compensation for personal services actually rendered. See generally Reg. §1.162-7.

[17] FSA 1994-16 (November 23, 1994), 2000 TNT 179-42.

In a typical situation, desired compensation is determined first and then shareholdings are adjusted to produce the desired result. Making this clear in a PC's procedures may be a mitigating factor in an IRS exam.

If a PC law firm were held to the same standards as regular corporations, a court might find that at least some of the compensation paid by a PC that distributes all or most of its annual net income as salary and bonus is a nondeductible dividend.

The test, as set forth in the regulations[18] and in court decisions[19] is two-pronged: (1) is the compensation reasonable in amount and (2) does it have the characteristics of a dividend. The first is more important than the second, but the second cannot be ignored — i.e., even though compensation is "reasonable" in amount, it may still be classified as a dividend if it has dividend characteristics.

The courts have viewed the following as indicating that distributions are dividends rather than compensation:

(1) salary and bonuses relate directly to the taxpayer's ability to pay them;

(2) the taxpayer consistently has "negligible" taxable income, and salary and bonuses apparently are used to absorb it;

(3) the taxpayer does not pay dividends;

(4) salary and bonuses are made in the proportion to stockholdings; and

(5) end-of-the-year bonuses are paid only to employees who are shareholders.[20]

The most obvious possibility is to set compensation independently of shareholdings and then adjust shareholdings. This would entail, for example, a new partner having no shares his or her first year and being allowed (required) to buy shares proportionate to his or her first-year income percentage at the beginning of the second year. The field service advice quoted above concedes the significance of this, stating that "the key issue [is] whether the petitioner will be able to convert dividends into compensation by tying the amount of stock ownership to the employee's value to the firm." In addition, it would seem prudent to pay out as large a proportion of income as monthly salary as possible rather than as year-end bonus. Including associates in the bonus pool also would be a plus.

---

[18] Reg. §1.162-7(b)(1) suggests, but does not specify the second prong.

[19] Nor-Cal Adjusters v. Com., 503 F.2d 359 (9th Cir. 1974), *aff'g* 30 TCM 837 (1971), T.C. Memo. 1971-200.

[20] For example, see *Nor-Cal Adjusters v. Commissioner, supra* N. 17.

The field service advice is not the law; it is merely an opinion from the IRS headquarters that the facts are good enough to litigate in the Tax Court. Of course, the IRS loses lots of cases that they consider "good enough to litigate," including a taxpayer victory in the Tax Court that makes interesting findings on interesting facts:

> Mr. Ashare was the sole shareholder and sole lawyer-employee of a PC (the other employee was a secretary). In 1989 he settled a class action suit against the City of Detroit - representing pensioners - and earned a contingent fee of $12.6 million. He had worked on the case almost exclusively for many years. The PC never paid a dividend and, with the exception of 1990, for many years paid all its income to Ashare as salary. The IRS contested the deductibility of the amounts paid in 1990 ($1,690,834), 1991 ($2 million) and 1992 ($4.65 million). The PC settled on the basis that, of these amounts, $126,553, $52,958, and $47,404 respectively were nondeductible dividends. In 1993, the PC paid Ashare salary of $1,750,000, $1,061,971 of it on December 30, and the next day, in return for a promissory note, borrowed $816,756 from Ashare. This generated a loss carry back to 1990, which generated a tax refund. The IRS contended that none of $1,750,000 paid in 1993 was deductible. The PC received no fees under the contingent arrangement after 1993, but was obligated to do considerable follow-up work.

The Court held that, since Ashare earned the $12.6 million fee for the PC, that under his compensation agreement with the PC he was to be paid all the fees he generated less expenses (an arrangement that the Court determined was reasonable in the circumstances), and that since his salary during 1989-1993 was less than that, the $1,750,000 salary paid in 1993 was reasonable. This despite that the PC had received all of the fee in earlier years. The Court noted that it is settled that an employee can be compensated for services performed in prior years,[21] that compensation also can be justified by services to be rendered in the future,[22] and the fact that $916,756 of the $1,750,000 the PC paid

---

[21] IRC §162(a)(1); Lucas v. Ox Fibre Brush Co., 281 U.S. 115, 119 (1930), *aff'g* 32 F(2d) 42, *rev'd* 8 BTA 422 (1927); Alpha Med., Inc. v. Commissioner, 172 F.3d 942, 945 (6th Cir. 1999), revg. 47 TCM 893 (1997), T.C. Memo. 1997-464; Reg. §1.162-7(a).

[22] The following are among the Court's citations to support that "[a] deduction for compensation is not allowed to the extent that the compensation is paid for something other than services rendered by the payee/employee *primarily* in or before the year of payment. (Emphasis added.) IRC § 162(a)(1).

Ashare in 1993 had been borrowed from Ashare did not compromise deductibility, differentiating this (favorably) from paying compensation with a promissory note rather than cash.

This decision is in line with other cases that are liberal in determining reasonable compensation where the employee-shareholder is the dominant factor in the success of a service business.[23] However, distributing the lion's share of the profit for the year via a post-Christmas bonus may be a red flag to the revenue authorities. As we said earlier, it is cosmetically correct to pay as much of the shareholder-employees' annual salary as possible in regular, identical, payments throughout the year. The difficulty is managing cash flows throughout the year to be able to make the requisite payments.

---

[23] Eduardo Catalano, Inc., Pension Trust, et al. v. Commissioner, 38 TCM 763 (1979), TC Memo. 1979-183

§ 17.07—Operations in Multiple States and Cities

Law firms with offices located in several cities or states must choose an appropriate method of determining income (and each partner's share thereof) for each taxing jurisdiction.

[1]—Income Allocation Methods

Generally, states specify how income will be allocated. One method of allocating income is to account for income and expenses by office. This method is commonly referred to as the "separate accounting" or the "separate books and records" method. Creating and utilizing this type of system is often time-consuming and expensive. It involves developing procedures for capturing and allocating individual items of fee revenue, direct expenses, and indirect expenses. This system also has to be able to accommodate transfers between offices for inter-office work and accept charge-backs when less than 100% of a receivable is collected. In addition, if expenses (e.g., home office accounting costs, tax preparation fees for the firm) are paid by one office but benefit all offices, this method should be capable of allocating overhead items in a rational manner.

In the absence of separate books and records, the method used most frequently to apportion income and expenses among offices is the three-factor apportionment formula. This method takes into account the relationship of certain activity in each state to the total. Normally, the activities measured are property (e.g., depreciable tangible property and real property—including leasehold improvements), revenue and payroll. Changing the numerator of the three-factor formula for property, revenue and payroll for a particular state results in the business allocation factor to that state. Unfortunately, there are no uniform definitions for income or expenses comprising the three-factor formula. There is a growing tendency among states to double weight the sales factor, which increases the business allocation factor in those states having a sales factor greater than the property or payroll factors. Some states use gross assets instead of depreciated assets and others force sales to be attributed to the home state if a firm does not file a return in a state to which it allocates income. Each variation of the standard three-factor formula causes inconsistencies among different states' formulas and can result in a law firm allocating more or less than 100% of its income to appropriate states.

[2]—Determining Presence and Nexus

Each state's rules for determining nexus—business contact or presence in a state—vary, and depend on the amount and type of contact a law firm partnership has with a particular state. Many states consider a law firm to be doing business in a state if it provides professional services within that state (e.g., handles a matter like a trial in that state). If a firm is considered to be doing business in a state it has nexus with that state and should allocate some of its income to that state. Unlike sellers of tangible property, which generally have to have an office in a state to be subject to that state's taxes, law firms only have to render professional services within a state to be judged to have nexus in a state. There are few, if any, states which have established *de minimis* rules that permit a law firm to escape taxation when it provides professional services within a state. If a law firm is determined to be doing business in a state, its partners may be responsible for filing their own nonresident personal income tax returns in that state. For convenience, some states allow nonresident partners to be included in a combined or group nonresident income tax return.

[3]—Sales Taxes on Library and Equipment Purchases

Law firms should be aware that states and cities are becoming more aggressive in identifying firms that may be doing business in their jurisdictions. The purpose of the attention is to determine if law firms should be on the sales or use tax rolls (or, as mentioned earlier, if its partners should be filing tax returns in the state).

Several states have conducted sales and compensating use tax examinations of law firms to determine if they should self-assess use tax on information services, supplies, computer equipment, furniture, equipment, etc. that may have been purchased from out-of-state vendors. In the event of an assessment for sales or use tax on prior years' purchases, law firms may not be able to charge their clients for the tax where the disbursement related to a client matter, because the matter which gave rise to the tax may have been previously billed. Also, some sales or use tax assessments may need to be capitalized in the year paid if they relate to capital expenditures that were capitalized in a prior year.

For example, a patent law firm pays an out-of-state company for a computer-based search report that the firm uses in a legal opinion. Assuming the search company had no nexus in the state in which the law firm is located, it probably would not have charged sales or use tax on the report. Some states consider the report an information service which is subject to sales or use tax. Several years later when the matter is closed, the firm could be audited by the state or city and assessed use tax. More than likely, it is too late to bill the client, so the assessment becomes the law firm's expense.

Tracking purchases that might be subject to sales or use tax can be an irritant; however, firms should be aware that, with proper accounting, costs that relate to purchases on behalf of clients can be billed to the clients. Sales and use taxes should be viewed from the perspective that they are part of the cost of doing business in some cities and states.

[4]—Sales Taxes on Professional Services

A few state legislatures have considered imposing a sales tax on professional services. Three states enacted legislation, only to have it subsequently repealed.[1] This is an area to watch for further developments.

[5]—Personal Property Tax

Another way that various jurisdictions are raising revenue is through personal property taxes. Generally, items such as furniture and equipment, software, and some leasehold improvements are subject to personal property tax. The depreciable lives and methods required to be used to calculate depreciation often differ from the methods used for federal income tax purposes.

Law firms should periodically perform physical inventories of their personal property and reconcile the results to their personal property tax returns to ensure that they are not paying tax on previously retired or sold assets.

---

[1] Florida and Massachusetts would have subjected all professional services to sales tax. Tax preparation services rendered between 1991 and 1996 were subject to Connecticut sales tax. Effective June 30, 1996, this provision was repealed.

CHAPTER 18

Business Expenses and Fringe Benefits

Chapter Contents

---

§ 18.01 Partner and Employee Business Expense Deductions

This Chapter discusses partner and employee business expense deductions. In its simplest form, tax planning and deciding on business-related deductions is arranging one's affairs so that a person pays taxes only to the extent required by law. Judge Learned Hand's 1947 comment on tax planning is an apt way to begin this section:

> "Over and over again courts have said that there is nothing sinister in so arranging one's affairs as to keep taxes as low as possible. Everybody does so, rich or poor; and all do right, for nobody owes any public duty to pay more than the law demands: taxes are enforced extractions, not voluntary contributions. To demand more in the name of morals is mere cant."[1]

Some of the more important types of partner and employee business expense deductions are discussed in this section.

[1]—Travel, Meal and Entertainment Deductions

Travel and entertainment costs incurred by lawyers and administrative staff of a law firm must be "ordinary and necessary" and either directly related to or (in the case of meals and entertainment) associated with the active conduct of a trade or business before they are deductible in part or in full.[2]

[a]—Travel Expenses

These amounts represent ordinary, necessary and reasonable expenses incurred while traveling away from home (generally overnight) solely or primarily for business reasons.[3] Travel expenses include transportation, meals, lodging, and incidental costs, but do not include amounts which are lavish or extravagant under the circumstances.[4]

A law firm may deduct reimbursements to partners and associates for business travel if the amount of each expenditure, the date of the travel, the destination of each trip and the business purpose of the trips are properly documented.[5] If a law firm expects an individual partner to absorb his or her own properly documented travel expenses, the partner can deduct those expenses on Form 1040, Schedule E, Part II (i.e., personal income tax return).[6]

---

[1] Commissioner v. Newman, 159 F.2d 848 (2d Cir. 1947).

[2] IRC § 274(a)(1)(A); 26 U.S.C. § 274(a)(1)(A).

[3] IRC § 162(a)(2); 26 U.S.C. § 162(a)(2).

[4] IRC §§ 162(a)(2) and 274(k)(1)(A); 26 U.S.C. §§ 162(a)(2) and 274 (k)(1)(A).

[5] Treas. Regs. § 1.274-5(b)(2); 26 C.F.R. § 1.274-5(b)(2). See also, Treas. Reg. § 1.274-5(c)(2); 26 C.F.R. § 1.274-5(c)(2).

[6] Frederick S. Klein v. Commissioner, 25 T.C. 1045 (1956). See also: Laurie G. Johnson, T.C. Memo 1984-598, 49 T.C.M. 81; Ltr. Rul. 9330004 (Apr. 14, 1993), Ltr. Rul. 9330001 (Apr 13, 1993), and Ltr. Rul. 9316003 (Dec. 23, 1992).

Generally, commutation costs between home and the firm's office are not deductible,[7] unless the reimbursements qualify as a *de minimis* fringe benefit.[8]

If a law firm allows an attorney to remain out of town on Saturday night (assuming no work is done on Saturday or Sunday) in order to obtain lower airfares, the reimbursement for the extra night is deductible by the firm.[9]

A growing trend is for law firms to implement a business expense reimbursement program under which a company credit card is issued to each partner and associate. There are several benefits associated with issuing a company credit card. First, the firm can establish a standard policy requiring all firm-related charges to be on the credit card. This eliminates, or at least reduces, cash vouchers and provides better internal control. Second, the firm can obtain a master listing of charges by partners and associates and can use the statistics to negotiate better rates at hotels, airlines, and restaurants. Third, it allows the firm to implement a semi-monthly or monthly reimbursement policy that reimburses the person only when the expense report is submitted. This feature alone brings structure to a reimbursement policy and teeth to a position that reimbursement won't be made unless there is the proper documentation. Using an expense report and reimbursement policy eliminates the daily cash reimbursements that require a law firm to keep large amounts of cash on hand and can cause a potential security risk. And fourth, using a credit card procedure transfers the payment responsibility to the partner and associate and reduces the firm's paperwork. Credit card receipts can be adequate substantiation for business expense purposes.[10]

It is important to distinguish between the types of travel expenses that can be reimbursed tax-free under an accountable plan (accountable plans are discussed later in this chapter). The following sections distinguish travel that is temporary, indefinite or infrequent.

[i]—Temporary vs. Indefinite Travel

In today's business environment, many partners and associates spend considerable time traveling on both in-town and out-of-town assignments. Historically, an associate or partner traveling to a work

---

[7] Treas. Reg. § 1.162-2(e); 26 C.F.R. § 162-2(e).

[8] IRC § 132(a)(4); 26 U.S.C. § 132(a)(4).

[9] Ltr. Rul. 9237014 (June 10, 1992).

[10] Treas. Reg. § 1.274-5(c)(2)(iii); 26 C.F.R. § 1.274-5(c)(2)(iii). See also, Lt.r. Rul. 9805007 (Feb. 2, 1998) and Ltr. Rul. 9706018 (Aug. 21, 1996).

location other than his or her usual place of business, could only claim a deduction if he or she went to his or her office first and then went to a client's office or other work location. In that situation, a deduction could be claimed based upon the mileage between the office and the alternative work location[11] or based upon the actual cost (taxi fare, train fare, subway fare, etc.).

It is well settled that expenses incurred by a partner or associate when traveling either out of town[12] or in the same geographical area as the taxpayer's principal place of business[13] are reimbursable.[14] The criterion the IRS uses for expense reimbursement purposes is whether an assignment at a work location is temporary or indefinite.[15]The ruling explains three situations where travel expenses between a taxpayer's residence and a work location are deductible. They are:

1. A taxpayer may deduct daily transportation expenses incurred in going between the taxpayer's residence and a "temporary" work location outside the metropolitan area where the taxpayer lives and normally works.
2. If a taxpayer has one or more regular work locations away from the his or her residence, the taxpayer may deduct daily transportation expenses incurred in going between the residence and a temporary work location in the same trade or business, regardless of the distance.
3. If a taxpayer's residence is his or her principal place of business, he or she may deduct daily transportation expenses incurred in going between the residence and another work location in the same trade or business, regardless of whether the other work location is the regular work location or a temporary one and regardless of the distance traveled.

The Chief Counsel of the Internal Revenue Service issued a series of advisories for determining whether a work location is temporary. If the assignment at a work location is realistically expected to last for one year or less (and, in fact, does), the assignment is temporary in the absence of facts and circumstances indicating otherwise.[16] If assignment at a work location is realistically expected to last for more than one year, or there is no realistic expectation that the employment will last for one

---

[11] CCA 200027047, May 10, 2000, Example 3.
[12] IRC § 162(a)(2), 26 USC § 162(a)(2).
[13] See Rev. Rul. 99-7; I.R.B. 1999-5, 4, January 15, 1999.
[14] IRC § 162(a)(2), 26 USC § 162(a)(2).
[15] Rev. Rul. 99-7, *supra* N. 13.
[16] CCA 199948019, September 3, 1999; Example 1.

year or less, the employment is not temporary, regardless of whether it actually lasts less than one year.[17] If a work location is reasonably expected to be temporary (i.e., less than one year), but at some later date the expectation changes, the date the expectation changes is the date that the employment ceases to be temporary.[18]

If a partner or associate is assigned to a work location other than his or her regularly assigned office for an indefinite period of time, the assignment will not be considered temporary.[19] It does not matter that the assignment actually lasts for less than one year.[20]

A partner or associate may be responsible for overseeing more than one matter concurrently. If so, each matter must be evaluated individually to determine whether it is temporary or indefinite. As long as a project reasonably is expected to be completed within one year, it will be temporary.[21] It does not matter how many actual days are spent at the client site. The key for determining deductibility is the date the taxpayer is assigned to the project and the date that his or her involvement terminates.[22] Therefore, if an associate spends a few days per month at a client site, but the length of the engagement is expected to last more than one year, work at that location is considered indefinite.[23]

These rules may cause some accounting and policy concerns for a law firm, because a law firm will have to carefully monitor periods of assignment and, depending on the facts, will have to treat seemingly the same expense reimbursements differently. If a law firm has a policy of reimbursing transportation expenses (e.g., cab fares, train tickets, or mileage reimbursements) for associates assigned to client matters, the firm will have to be able to track the duration of each assignment to comply with the rules. For example, assume a person is assigned to a trial that is expected to last one year or more and that the assignment is not temporary under the IRS rules. In that situation, all travel reimbursements would be taxable to the associate and the law firm would have to withhold taxes if it reimbursed any travel expenses. Alternatively, assume that an assignment is expected to be for eight months, but seven months into the assignment the scope changes, so that it is extended by six months. The point at which the scope changes (i.e., seven months into the assignment) the nature of the assignment changes

---

[17] CCA 199948019, September 3, 1999; Example 1.
[18] CCA 200018052, March 10, 2000; Scenario 5.
[19] CCA 199948019, September 3, 1999, Example 2.
[20] CCA 200018052, March 10, 2000; Scenario 6.
[21] CCA 199948019, September 3, 1999, Example 1.
[22] CCA 200018052, March 10, 2000, Scenario 5.
[23] CCA 200018052, March 10, 2000, Scenario 4.

from one that was temporary to one that is indefinite. When the assignment changes to one that is indefinite, the law firm must begin withholding taxes on any travel reimbursements to any individual affected by the change. Even though the temporary and indefinite rules also apply to partner expense reimbursements, the withholding rules obviously do not apply, because there is no withholding on a payment to a partner. If a reimbursement is taxable, it should be reported to a partner as a guaranteed payment on Schedule K-1.

In the perspective of law firm administrators and accounting departments, application of these rules to the specific facts and circumstances of each associate (or partner) may be a nightmare. In the example above, assume that two associates were assigned to the project, only one was assigned from day one and the other was assigned in the sixth month of the project. When the scope changed in the seventh month by extending the project by six months, the project became indefinite for the first associate, but was still temporary for the second associate because the assignment was still expected to last for less than one year. Extending the application of this rule to all associates and partners will make administering the policy very difficult and almost impractical.

The rules become more onerous and difficult to follow when there is a break in assignments. Consider, for example, an assignment that is temporary, because it begins and ends within a twelve-month time period. Within a matter of weeks after the assignment finishes, however, an associate or partner unexpectedly is reassigned to the same work location for a period of time that when added to the initial period extends beyond one year. How long must a break in assignment periods be before the two prongs of the assignment are added together to cause the total assignment to be longer than one year? Currently, there is no definitive IRS guidance on how long a break must be between assignments at the same work location. Obviously, the longer the break, the greater the chance that the work assignment will retain its temporary status. The IRS has stated that a break of one year will be significant enough, so that a second assignment of less than one year will be considered temporary.[24] However, according to the IRS, a break of only two or three weeks is inconsequential and will not restart the temporary "clock" running.[25]

The IRS softened the one-year rule by saying that a break could be considered significant if the associate or partner is absent from the work location for seven months.[26] For example, assume that on

---

[24] CCA 200018052, Scenario 7, March 10, 2000.
[25] CCA 200026025, May 3, 2000, Example 1.
[26] CCA 200026025, May 31, 2000, Example 2.

August 31 an associate completes an eight-month assignment at a client location and on April 1 of the next year is reassigned to the same location for an anticipated period of one-year or less. The new assignment would probably be considered temporary because it started seven months after the first assignment ended.[27] This assumes that during the interim period, the associate did not perform any services at that client location.

An associate's job classification or the nature of the duties performed will have no impact in determining whether the work location is temporary or indefinite.[28] The focus is on each associate's or partner's assignment at a work location, irrespective of the length of the actual project. For example, if a particular associate expects to work on a matter at a particular location for only six months, but the project is expected to last more than one year, the associate's assignment would be temporary.[29] It makes no difference if the associate's tasks change with relation to the particular job, it is the length of the associate's involvement in the project which determines if travel expense reimbursements are taxable or tax free.

These rules are mandatory and cannot be dismissed by simply asserting that the accounting system is not capable of handling the subtle differences between a temporary and an indefinite assignment.[30] The IRS also has stated that an employer cannot rely on self-serving statements from associates that their travel expense reimbursements are tax free.[31] The law firm must require substantiation from an associate before it can reimburse a travel expense without withholding taxes.

[ii]—Infrequent Work Locations

It is common for an employee to perform services at a particular location on a recurring, but infrequent or sporadic basis for a period of more than one year. It would be impractical or unreasonable to focus solely on the expectation of the total span of employment at a particular location by applying the one-year limitation used to determine temporary status for deduction purposes. In these cases, the taxpayer should look at the realistic expectation surrounding the infrequent or sporadic nature of the employment to determine if the time spent at the client location can be considered temporary.[32] The IRS has not issued

---

[27] CCA 200026015, May 31, 2000, Example 4.
[28] CCA 200027047, May 10, 2000, Example 4.
[29] CCA 200018052, March 19,2000, Scenario 7.
[30] CCA 1999 48018.
[31] CCA 1999 48018.
[32] CCA 200026025, May 31, 2000, Example 5.

any specific guidelines to determine when an assignment is so infrequent or sporadic that it may be treated as if it were temporary under the one-year limitation. However, the IRS Chief Counsel's office has indicated that thirty-five whole or partial days in a given year would qualify the location as temporary for deduction purposes.[33] This means, for example, that if an assignment is expected to last fifteen months, but that an associate is expected to work at that location for only thirty-five days during the year, that the assignment will be considered infrequent and any travel expense reimbursements will be tax-free.

Considering the nature of assignments and responsibilities, it is probable that an assignment for an associate at a particular work location might be indefinite, but for the partner it might be infrequent.

[b]—Business Meals

These expenses represent the cost of food or beverages consumed with guests in an atmosphere conducive to a business discussion or meeting. "Meals" include food or beverage costs incurred in entertaining clients at the law firm's office, at a restaurant, or in attending a business convention or reception, business meeting, or business luncheon at a business club.[34]

An occasional luncheon meeting between lawyers in the same firm to discuss operations of the firm might be considered an ordinary and necessary business expense.[35] However, when firm meetings take place over lunch more than on an occasional basis (e.g., daily) the meals are considered personal in nature and not business-related.[36]

[c]—Entertainment Expenses

The term "entertainment" includes any activity that is of a type generally considered to constitute entertainment, amusement or recreation, such as entertaining at country clubs, theaters, nightclubs, golf or athletic clubs, and sporting events.[37] Entertainment expenses must be ordinary and necessary and either be directly related to or associated with the active conduct of a law firm's business before they are deductible.[38] Under present law, "associated entertainment" includes

---

[33] CCA 200026025, May 31, 2000, Example 5.

[34] IRC § 274(e)(1); 26 U.S.C. § 274(e)(1). See also, Treas. Reg. § 1.274-2(f)(2)(i); 26 C.F.R. § 1.274-2(f)(2)(i).

[35] Wells v. Commissioner, 626 F.2d 868 (9th Cir. 1980), *aff'g* T.C. Memo 1977-419, 36 T.C.M. 1698 (9th Cir. 1977). See also, Treas. Reg. § 1.132-6(e)(1); 26 C.F.R. § 1.132-6(e)(1).

[36] Moss v. Commissioner, 758 F.2d 211 (7th Cir. 1985).

[37] Treas. Reg. § 1.274-2(b); 26 C.F.R. § 1.274-2(b).

[38] See N. 2 *supra*.

entertainment and business meals that satisfy all the following requirements:[39]

1. Before or at the time of the entertainment, the law firm had more than a general expectation of deriving income or other specific business benefits (other than goodwill) at some indefinite future time.
2. Either directly before or after the entertainment activity, a law firm representative and the person being entertained actively engaged in a business meeting, negotiation, discussion or other bona fide business transaction for the purpose of deriving income or other specific business benefit.
3. The principal purpose for the combined business/entertainment activity was the transaction of business.

Occasionally, expenditures are meant to be nothing more than goodwill. If an expenditure for meals or entertainment occurs under circumstances where there is little or no possibility of conducting business affairs or carrying on business negotiations or discussions, the expenditure will be considered nondeductible goodwill.

For various business reasons, law firms rent "skyboxes" at sports arenas or entertainment/convention centers. A skybox is a private luxury box that is separate from other seating and is available at a price higher than other seating. The purpose of entertaining in a skybox is to provide a more private environment in which a law firm can entertain clients, solicit potential clients, or entertain employees. Normally there are two costs associated with renting a skybox; the annual rent for the skybox itself and the annual cost of each seat in the skybox. The costs associated with skyboxes may not be insignificant. Realizing the preferential nature of a skybox and the high associated costs, Congress chose to limit the deductions associated with a skybox. If a skybox is used for more than one event during the period covered by its lease, then the deduction is limited to the sum of the face value of a non-luxury box seat tickets for the number of seats in the box.[40] Consequently, if a law firm pays a flat amount for the lease of a skybox and the cost of each ticket for each event during the lease period of the box, its deductible cost would be limited to the number of seats available times the face value of non-luxury box tickets. Presumably non-luxury box tickets would be "box seat" tickets. The effect of this rule is to eliminate a deduction for the box itself.

---

[39] Treas. Reg. § 1.274-2(a)(1); 26 C.F.R. § 1.274-2(a)(1).
[40] IRC § 274(l)(2); 26 U.S.C. § 274(l)(2).

To eliminate deductions associated with buying tickets through scalpers, the law provides that only the face value of a ticket for an activity considered to be for entertainment, amusement, or recreation is allowable as a deduction.[41] Consequently, if a law firm rents a skybox for a single event or a group of seats for client entertainment purposes, the entertainment deduction is limited to the sum of the face values of the tickets purchased. Depending on business reason for purchasing the tickets, the deduction may be further limited by the expense limitation that is discussed in the next section.

[d]—Limitation on Meal and Entertainment Deductions

Since the 1960s, Congress has believed that the tax laws did not focus sufficiently on the personal-consumption element of deductible meal and entertainment expenses and unfairly permitted taxpayers who could arrange business settings for personal consumption to receive, in effect, a federal tax subsidy for such consumption.[42] As a result, Congress passed legislation to disallow expenses that are considered "lavish or extravagant under the circumstances"[43] and then reduced by 50%—referred to as the "50% haircut"—the amount of meal and entertainment expenses that law firms can deduct on their federal income tax returns.[44] The 50% haircut applies to meal and entertainment expenses incurred in years beginning after December 31, 1993. (The previous disallowed amount was 20%, which applied from 1987 through 1993.)

Expenses subject to the 50% haircut are business meals, including meals while away from home overnight on a business trip, meal expense at a business luncheon club[45] or at a convention, and client entertainment expenses, including sports and theater tickets. Included in the 50% haircut are taxes and tips in connection with business meals (but not the cost of a taxis to get to the business meals), cover charges for admission, and other related expenses (e.g., parking at a restaurant, theater or sports arena).

It is important to note that when a firm deducts client disbursements as firm expenses, the 50% haircut applies when expenses are *incurred* and not when the firm is reimbursed.

---

[41] IRC § 274(1)(1)(A); 26 U.S.C. § 274(1)(1)(A).

[42] General Explanation of the Tax Reform Act of 1986, p. 61, prepared by the Staff of the Joint Committee on Taxation.

[43] IRC § 274(k)(1)(A); 26 U.S.C. § 274(k)(1)(A).

[44] IRC § 274(n); 26 U.S.C. § 274(n).

[45] Luncheon club due are not deductible at all. See § 18.01[1][h], *infra*.

The 50% haircut provisions are not as straightforward as they seem. As with other provisions of the Internal Revenue Code, the 50% haircut provision has to be applied based on specific facts and circumstances using court cases, regulations and IRS rulings. Law firms faced with escalating non-deductible meal and entertainment expenses have been trying to aggressively and legitimately interpret available authoritative material to reduce the 50% haircut. One way of reducing the 50% haircut is to focus more closely on exceptions to the disallowance rule (these are discussed in the following section.)

If an expenditure is not incurred for the benefit of an employee, the first inquiry which needs to be made is whether such expenditure is discriminatory. For example, if a holiday party is open to all employees regardless of their position in the firm, the cost of the party would be fully deductible. However, if it were only open to partners or only to attorneys, then such a function may be non-deductible.[46] However, if the type of activity is discriminatory, but such type of activity is infrequent in nature and not excessive in value, it may be fully deductible as a *de minimis* fringe benefit.[47] "Frequency" and "value" have not been defined under the current version of IRC § 132.[48]

[e]—Exceptions to the 50% Haircut

The law provides specific exceptions from the 50% haircut that law firms should consider when planning their meal and entertainment activities.[49] Some exceptions that apply to law firms are:

1. Expenses for goods, services, and facilities to the extent that the expenses are treated as compensation to an employee and subject to the normal payroll withholding taxes (e.g., health clubs).
2. Expenses paid or incurred by a law firm in connection with the performance of services by the firm (e.g., client meals and entertainment charge back to clients). This exception applies, for example, to reimbursements of clients disbursements, if the law firm considers client disbursements as loans made on behalf of clients.[50] Firms that treat client disbursements as their expenses (i.e., they expense disbursements when made and income reimbursements in income when received - assuming cash basis) would not meet this exception.

---

[46] IRC § 274(e)(4); 26 U.S.C. § 274(e)(4) 1.274-2(f)(2)(v); 26 AFR 1.274-2(f)(2)(v).
[47] IRC § 274(n)(2)(B), 26 U.S.C. § 274(n)(2)(B).
[48] See § 18.03 *infra*.
[49] IRC § 274(n)(2); 26 U.S.C. § 274(n)(2).
[50] See § 17.04[2], *supra*.

3. Expenses for recreational, social or similar activities primarily for the benefit of employees who are not highly compensated employees.[51] For this purpose, a partner or shareholder owning less than a 10% interest in the law firm is not considered to be a shareholder or owner, so by default, those individuals are considered employees for this purpose.

Point three above applies often to law firms and is worth taking a closer look at. It provides for a full deduction for expenses for recreational or social activities that are primarily for employees. For example, expenses incurred for employee benefit programs such as expenses for:

- An annual Christmas or holiday party, annual picnics, or summer outings, or
- Maintaining a swimming pool, baseball diamond, bowling alley, or golf course

would not be subject to the 50% haircut, as long as the expenses are primarily for the benefit of employees.[52] However, any expenditure that is made under circumstances that discriminate in favor of shareholders, owners, or other highly compensated individuals probably will not be considered to have been made for the benefit of employees in general and will not meet the 50% haircut exception. Depending on the fact, an expense that clearly discriminates in favor of owners or shareholders may not be deductible at all.

Other types of meal and entertainment expenditures that may be excluded from the 50% haircut are award dinners, meetings, conventions, employee recognition meals and/or entertainment, project "wrap-up" meals or entertainment, staff mentoring/counseling meals and team building. No attempt is made here to define these terms, because there has been very little judicial guidance on any of them.[53]

Included in the employee benefit classification would be expenses to enhance employee productivity or to improve employee morale, such as attending a baseball game, provided that no business was discussed at the game.[54] Note that this requirement seems at odds with the general requirement of a substantial business purpose, but

---

[51] Highly compensated is defined in IRC § 414(q); 26 U.S.C. § 414(q).

[52] Treas. Reg. § 1.274-2(f)(2)(v); 26 C.F.R. § 1.274-2(f)(2)(v).

[53] IRC § 274(e)(4); 26 U.S.C. § 274(e)(4) 1.274-2(f)(2)(v); 26 AFR 1.274-2(f)(2)(v).

here, the business purpose is the morale of the employee. By extension, this exception might be a viable way to avoid the 50% haircut for lunches or cocktail parties to reward associates for jobs well done.

There is an old saying about not mixing business with pleasure. In one fact pattern, the mixture was very detrimental, because too much business was discussed at a morale building event and caused the entire deduction to be disallowed.[55]

Another exception to the 50% haircut is for food or beverages that are excludible from an employee's gross income as a result of IRC Section 132(a)(4) - *de minimis* fringe benefit.[56] For example, if an attorney must work overtime to comply with the wishes of a client or partners, the meal that he or she orders may qualify for a 100% deduction either as a *de minimus* occasional fringe benefit or as a meal furnished for the convenience of an employer.[57] If, a meal was furnished at lunch for compensatory reasons (e.g., so that the employee can leave early), however, or if there were restaurants in the area that were open and at which the associate could get a fast lunch, then neither Sections 119 nor 132 may shield the lunch from inclusion in the associate's income.

Perhaps the most obvious solution to avoid the 50% haircut is to pass the meal and entertainment expenses on to clients. This may be easier said than done, however. When Congress enacted the meal and entertainment limitation, it allowed a service provider (e.g., a law firm or accounting firm) to pass on the limitation to its client as long as the service provider provided the client with the required substantiation.[58] The substantiation requirements include adequate records or sufficient evidence corroborating the amount of the expense, the time and place of travel, entertainment, amusement, recreation, or use of a facility or property, the business purpose of the expense, and the business relationship of the person entertained to the person providing the entertainment.[59] Applying this requirement literally, a law firm would have to, in effect, give the client sufficient documentation to enable the client to meet the substantiation requirements. The best way to meet the requirements would be to give the client the original receipts supporting

---

[54] Treas. Reg. § 1.274-2(f)(2)(v); 26 C.F.R. § 1.274-2(f)(2)(v); TAM 8029034 (1980); Miami Roofing and Sheet Metal, Inc. v. Commissioner, No. 8111 (T.C.M. 1947).

[55] TAM 200030001 (April 6, 2000).

[56] See ^ 18.03, *infra,* for a discussion of *de minimus* fringe benefits.

[57] IRC § 119, 26 U.S.C. § 119.

[58] Treas. Reg. § 1.274-5T(h)(3); 26 C.F.R. ¶ 1.274-5T (h)(3).

[59] I.R.C. § 274(d); 26 U.S.C. § 274(d), and Treas. Reg. §§ 1,274-5T(c) and 1.274-5T(h); 26 C.F.R. §§ 1.274-5T(c) and 1.274-5T(h) See also § 18.01[2], *supra*.

the meal or entertainment. In the alternative, the law firm should show on the face of the bill those details required for substantiation (i.e., who was entertained, where the entertainment took place, what was discussed, the relationship of the parties, etc.). Simply submitting a bill that lists the dollar amount of the meals or entertainment and not listing the rest of the required substantiation may not give the client sufficient information to alert the client to the fact that it has to take the haircut. If the substantiation is not given to the client, the haircut probably stays with the service provider.[60]

[f]—Mileage Reimbursements

Generally, mileage reimbursements to partners or employees for use of their personal cars while performing firm business are not includible in the individual's gross income.[61] Reimbursement can be made at a standard rate per mile.[62] The mileage rule is expanded because the substantiation rules are applied without regard to who owns the vehicle.[63] The individual must substantiate the mileage driven through adequate records or by sufficient evidence corroborating his or her statement.[64] To meet the "adequate records" requirement, the regulations state that an individual should maintain an account book, diary, log, statement of expense, trip sheets, or similar record and documentary evidence which, in combination, are sufficient to establish each element of an expenditure or use.[65]

An alternative to a mileage reimbursement plan is a Fixed and Variable Reimbursement (FAVR) allowance plan that places the burden of recordkeeping on the law firm. A FAVR allowance reimburses employees a fixed amount at specified intervals and variable amounts at specified intervals based on the projected operating costs associated with an employee's business use of an automobile.[66] Therefore, a FAVR allowance is not based on the actual miles driven by the employee, but on a formula used to derive a close approximation of the total costs associated with operating an automobile. In periods of rapidly rising

---

[60] See ¶ 20 of Ltr. Rul. 9720005 (Jan 31, 1997).

[61] IRC § 62(a)(2)(A); 26 U.S.C. § 62(a)(2)(A).

[62] The rate per mile changes as the cost of owning and maintaining a car changes. The optional mileage allowance for 2001 is 34.5 cents per mile. See §§ 2 and 11 of Rev. Proc. 2000-48, I.R.B. 2000-49 Nov. 16,2000).

[63] Reg. § 1.62-2(e)(2) and Treas. Reg. § 1.274-5(g)(2)(iii); 26 C.F.R. §§ 1.62-2(e)(2) and 1.274-5(g)(2)(iii).

[64] Treas. Reg. § 1.274-5(c)(1); 26 C.F.R. § 1.274-5(c)(1).

[65] Treas. Reg. § 1.274-5(c)(2)(i); 26 C.F.R. § 1.274-5(c)(2)(i).

[66] See § 8 of Rev. Proc. 2000-48, I.R.B. 2000-49 (Nov. 16, 2000).

costs to operate cars, a FAVR allowance will allow a law firm to reimburse its employees more than the standard-rate-per-mile method. When this procedure is used, however, the business use percentage for the car will be deemed to be not greater than 75%.

Amounts paid under the standard-rate-per-mile method or the FAVR method do not have to be reported to the employee on Form W-2. However, if a law firm gives a monthly car allowance and does not require accounting of its use, the amount is taxable to the employee. The employee must claim his or her own tax deduction on Form 2106 for the business use of the car; the deduction is subject to the 2% floor for miscellaneous itemized deductions.

[g]—Unreimbursed Partner Expenses

Law firms differ on their policies concerning partner expenses—either practice development expenses or client expenses. Some firms allow partners to charge all such expenses to the firm on the theory that the expenses were incurred to service existing clients or to generate new business. Other firms provide an allowance based on partnership units or the partner's need (e.g., business developer). When the allowance method is used, the firm should have procedures in place to review the propriety of items charged and to verify that they are proper business expenses. When a firm allows a partner to charge business expenses to the firm, the partner is not allowed to deduct the expenses on his or her personal tax return.[67]

Some firms do not allow partners to charge any practice development or entertainment expense to the firm. When this is a firm's policy, *albeit* unwritten but understood and practiced, a partner can deduct unreimbursed business-related expenses against partnership income on Form 1040, Schedule E.[68] However, tax return preparation fees to prepare a partner's tax returns are deductible only as itemized deductions and not against partnership income, whether or not reimbursed.[69]

[h]—Club Dues

Partners in law firms have long been members of country clubs or luncheon clubs. The dues for these clubs are not deductible by a law firm or its partners or shareholders. The prohibition on deducting club dues applies to all business, social, athletic, luncheon, country, hotel, airline, and sports clubs.

---

[67] Magruder v. Commissioner, 57 T.C.M. 117, T.C. Memo 1989-169 (1989).

[68] See N. 6 *supra.*

[69] Ltr Rul. 9126014 (March 29, 1991).

Regulations clarify the disallowance rule by providing that the purposes and activities of a club, and not its name, determine whether it is organized for business, recreation, or social purposes.[70] Absent a showing that a principal purpose of an organization is to conduct entertainment activities for members or guests, professional organizations (e.g., accounting or bar associations), trade associations (including business leagues, chambers of commerce, boards or trade, and real estate boards), and civic or public service organizations (e.g., Kiwanis, Lions and Rotary) are *not* subject to the allowance rules.[71]

Meal and entertainment expenses incurred in connection with business at these clubs remains deductible subject to other limits (e.g., 50% haircut).

[i]—Duplicate Housing Costs

As previously mentioned, travel expenses are not deductible unless the expenses are incurred while away from home overnight on business.[72] In today's mobile environment it is not uncommon for a partner or associate to be assigned to a matter for an extended period of time in a city located a significant distance from his or her home office. For convenience and cost factors, the person might rent an apartment in the distant city and live there while working in that area. Since everyone is assumed by the IRS to have one home, the question is which location is "home" for tax purposes? The answer to this question may have significant ramifications. The taxpayer will not be able to deduct any expenses associated with his or her tax home.[73]

Generally, a taxpayer's home is considered to be located at the taxpayer's regular or principal place of business. Normally, an associate's principal place of business is the office of the law firm to which he or she is assigned. If, however, a taxpayer has no regular or principal place of business, then the taxpayer's home is his or her abode in a real and substantial sense (i.e. where the taxpayer maintains certain personal and business connections).[74] If neither criteria applies, then the taxpayer is considered to be an itinerant whose home is wherever the taxpayer happens to work.

The factors to consider in determining which place of business is the principal place, are the total time ordinarily spent by an associate or partner at each location, the degree of business activity conducted

---

[70] Treas. Reg. § 1.274-2(a)(2)(iii)(a); 26 C.F.R. § 1.274-2(a)(2)(iii)(a).

[71] Treas. Reg. § 1.274-2(a)(2)(iii)(b); 26 C.F.R. § 1.274-2(a)(2)(iii)(b).

[72] IRC § 162(a)(2), 26 USC § 162(a)(2); Commissioner v. Flowers, 326 U.S. 465 (1946).

[73] IRC §§ 162, 262; 26 USC §§ 162, 262.

[74] Rev. Rul. 93-86 1993-2 C.B. 71.

at each location, and whether the financial return (i.e., the salary earned by an associate) at each location is significant or insignificant. This is considered the objective test.[75] An associate in this situation, is considered to be away from home when he or she is working at an out-of-town location. Any business-travel expenses in connection with work at that location are deductible.[76] A partner generally is governed by the same rules, except that it is more difficult to identify where the partner's financial return is located because a partner's income is allocated based on where the firm's profits are earned.

These rules can be difficult to apply in a situation, for example, where an attorney has extended assignments in two non-contiguous localities. In this type of situation, the person probably thinks that his or her tax home is where his or her family lives and where he or she maintains most of his or her possessions. The fact that a partner or associate designates an abode as his or her tax home is not decisive. A Court considered the situation in which a taxpayer maintained two homes near different business locations in distant cities.[77] He spent four days per week at location X, and earned approximately 83% of his annual revenue at that location. The other three days of the week, he resided with his family at location Y, near a second place of business. His revenue from work at location Y accounted for the remaining 17% of his income. On his tax returns, he deducted the expenses incurred at location X because he considered location Y his tax home. Applying the objective test, the Court reasoned that he spent more time in location X, had greater business activity in location X, and earned more money in location X. The Court held that location X was his tax home and, accordingly, he could not deduct any of the expenses associated with location X.

Some courts[78] have taken a more comprehensive view of where a taxpayer's home is for tax purposes. These courts have looked at the purpose of the Code provision[79] in order to mitigate the burden upon someone forced to maintain two residences and to incur duplicate living expenses because of the requirements of his or her business. It has always been a fundamental principle of taxation that a person's taxable income should not include the cost of producing that income.[80]

---

[75] Markey v. Commissioner, 490 F2d 1249.

[76] Rev. Rul. 54-147, 1954-1 C.B. 51, See also IRC § 162(a)(2), 26 USC § 162(a)(2).

[77] Robertson v. Commission, 190 F3d 392 (5th Cir. 1999).

[78] See Mitchell v. Commissioner, 78 TCM 355 (1999) and Andrews v. Commissioner, U.S. Court of Appeals, 1st Cir. 90-2165(1991).

[79] IRC § 162(a)(2); 26 U.S.C. § 162(a)(2).

[80] Hantzis v. Commissioner, 638 F2d 248 (1st Cir. 1981.

The guiding policy must be that the taxpayer is expected to locate his or her home for tax purposes at his or her major post of duty.[81] These courts,[82] have not denounced the objective tests, rather they have acknowledged that, in deciding what living expenses are deductible, other factors may be considered or even found determinative under appropriate circumstances.[83] Some of these other factors include whether business reasons were a predominate factor in the duplicate living expenses, where the taxpayer is registered to vote, where the taxpayer has registered his or her automobile, and where the taxpayer maintains his or her bank accounts.[84]

Proper application of these principles can make it easier to staff matters at geographically distant locations, because duplicate living expenses can be reimbursed without the threat of withholding taxes. In the case of a partner, if the principles are applied, then duplicate housing expenses can be reimbursed under an accountable plan as an ordinary and necessary business expense without having to be reported on Schedule K-1 as a guaranteed payment. It should be noted, however, that just because duplicate living expenses are deductible, does not insulate a person from filing tax returns in more than one state. Depending on the rules in each state, it is possible for a person to be considered a resident in two states at the same time. Careful tax planning is needed to maximize the benefit of reimbursing duplicate housing expenses, while at the same time avoiding duplicate resident status for state tax purposes.

[2]—Reimbursement "Accounting"—Substantiation Requirements

Law firms typically reimburse partners, associates and supervisory administrative staff for travel expenses and business meals related to firm or client matters. Some firms also reimburse certain business entertainment expenses. In order for travel and entertainment expense reimbursements to be excluded from employee wages subject to withholding tax,[85] there must be an "adequate accounting" by the employee to the employer for these expenses. To qualify as an adequate accounting, the employee must submit a properly supported expense report and the employer's procedures for approval of reimbursements must be adequate. Four elements of each expenditure must be

---

[81] See *Andrews v. Commisioner, supra* N. 78.

[82] See *Mitchell v. Commissioner* and *Andrews v. Commisioner, supra* N. 78.

[83] See *Andrews, supra* N. 78.

[84] See *Mitchell v. Commissioner, supra* N. 78.

[85] Treas. Reg. § 31.3401(a)-1(b)(2); 26 C.F.R. § 31.3401(a)-1(b)(2).

substantiated with specificity.[86] They are: (1) cost, (2) time and place, (3) business relationship, and (4) business purpose.

[a]—Cost

Each expenditure should be recorded separately on the expense report. For each expenditure of $75[87] or more, documentary evidence (e.g., a receipted bill) must be attached.[88] However, a firm's internal policy may require a threshold lower than the IRS's (e.g., a firm may require receipts for all expenses regardless of amount).

[b]—Time and Place

Appropriate identification of the destination and the date of departure and return from each trip should be recorded on the expense report to substantiate travel expenses. The date and place of each business meal or entertainment activity should be recorded on the expense report to substantiate these expenses.

[c]—Business Relationship

The names, occupations, and titles of guests at business meals or entertainment activities should be recorded, together with enough other information to establish their business relationship.

[d]—Business Purpose

The business purpose of each trip should be recorded to support travel expenses. For business meals and entertainment expenses the record should indicate: (1) the business reason or the nature of the business benefit realized or expected to be gained, and (2) the nature of the business discussion preceding or following the activity. As previously mentioned, descriptions are very important, particularly in situations where a full deduction (i.e., without a 50% haircut) is sought by the firm. For example, if a partner takes an associate to lunch to reward him or her for preparing a good brief, a simple explanation of staff lunch will not suffice, the partner will have to specify why the lunch took place, e.g., to congratulate or to reward in order to claim a full deduction as an employee achievement award.

As an alternative to collecting receipts for an adequate accounting, a law firm could use a per diem allowance for ordinary and necessary

---

[86] IRC § 274(d); 26 U.S.C. § 274(d).

[87] Treas. Reg. § 1.274-5T(c)(2)(iii)(B).

[88] Treas. Reg. § 1.274-5(c)(2)(iii)(B); 26 C.F.R. § 1.274-5(c)(iii)(B).

expenses paid or incurred while traveling away from home.[89] Under the per diem method, fixed amounts are set for lodging, meals, and incidental expenses while traveling within the continental United States. As long as the set amounts are not exceeded, a law firm is not required to collect receipts and can consider the alternative procedures as meeting the substantiation requirements.[90] The general rule is that the amount of the expense that is deemed substantiated for each calendar day is equal to the lesser of the per diem allowance for such day or the amount computed at the federal per diem rate for the locality of travel for such day.[91] Under an optional high-low substantiation method, per diem rates are keyed to the high-cost and low-cost locality as determined by the IRS.[92] For 2001, the per diem for travel to a high-cost locality is $201 and for all other locations it is $124.[93] The per diem allowance method does not cover a situation in which an employer provides a per diem for lodging, but not for meals and incidentals (i.e., meals and incidentals are reimbursed based on actual receipts, if required).

[e]—Accountable Plan

Generally, a partner or associate will report his or her business expenses to the firm in an expense report and receive reimbursement for those expenses. Assuming an expense is deductible as an ordinary and necessary business expense, the partner or associate will not recognize income when he or she is reimbursed and the firm will claim a deduction for the same amount or will post it to a receivable account (e.g., client disbursement). Under Treasury Department regulations, a law firm can claim a deduction for those expenses and the associate or partner can avoid income recognition, only if the reimbursement is under an accountable plan.[94] An accountable plan must meet three requirements:

1. An expense must be incurred in a business context in connection with the performance of services as a partner or associate of the firm.[95]

---

[89] Rev. Proc. 2000-39, 2000-41, IRB 340 (Sept 26, 2000).

[90] See § 2.04 of Rev. Proc. 2000-39, 2000-41, IRB 340.

[91] See § 4.01 of Rev. Proc. 2000-39, 2000-41, IRB 340.

[92] See § 5 of Rev. Proc. 2000-39, 2000-41, IRB 340.

[93] See § 5.02 of Rev. Proc. 2000-39, I.R.B. 2000-41 (September 26, 2000).

[94] Treas. Reg. § 1.62-2; 26 C.F.R. § 1.62-2; see also CCA199948016, September 3, 1999.

[95] Treas. Reg. § 1.62-2(d); 26 C.F.R. § 1.62-2(d); see also CCA 199948016. September 3, 1999.

2. Each expense reimbursed under an accountable plan must be substantiated within a reasonable period of time. The substantiation requirements will differ depending on the expense type. However, for transportation expenses, the elements are amount, time, use and business purpose.[96]

3. The partner or associate must return any reimbursed amounts in excess of actual expenses within a reasonable time.[97]

Regardless of whether a law firm has an accountable plan, reimbursements must be for valid business expenses. If an expense is paid under a non-accountable plan (i.e., an advance not requiring substantiation), it is taxable income to the employee and the law firm must withhold income and FICA taxes when the reimbursement is made.[98]

[3]—Expense Reimbursement Policy Statement

To safeguard travel and entertainment deductions, the firm should disseminate an expense reimbursement policy statement.

Figure 18-A illustrates a format for a law firm's expense reimbursement policy statement.

[4]—Expense Reports

A law firm's accounting procedures should include: (1) a requirement for timely submission of documented expense reports for all reimbursed expenses (including receipts for expenses in excess of $75)[99] and (2) a system of hierarchical approval of all expense reports, including those submitted by partners.

Figure 18-B illustrates a format for a law firm's expense reimbursement report.

---

[96] Treas. Reg. § 1.62-2(e); 26 C.F.R. § 1.62-2(e); see also CCA 199948016, September 3, 1999.

[97] Treas. Reg. § 1.62-2(f); 26 C.F.R. § 1.62-2(f); see also CCA 199948016, September 3, 1999.

[98] Treas. Reg. § 1.62-2(c)(5); 26 C.F.R. § 1.62-2(c)(5); see also CCA199948018.

[99] See N.96 supra.

Figure 18-A. Illustration of an expense reimbursement policy statement for a law firm.

ABC LAW FIRM PARTNERSHIP
EXPENSE REIMBURSEMENT POLICY STATEMENT

TO: All Professional Staff

FROM: Management Committee

There are four overriding principles with respect to reimbursable expenses incurred by professional staff. They are:

1. *Nature of expenses:* First and foremost, any expenditure incurred must be necessary and reasonable, both as to the nature of the item and as to the amount involved. In this regard, you should exercise careful judgment in weighing the types of expenditures and the costs involved.

2. *Client Charges:* All expenses incurred which are directly related to and necessary for serving a client must be charged to that client. Considerable care must be taken in determining those expenditures that are charged to a client. A good rule of thumb to use is to ask yourself whether you could justify each and every expenditure charged to the client if requested to do so by such client.

3. *Documentation:* All reimbursable expenditures must be fully described and supported on your expense report in conformity with IRS requirements. Each entry must contain a clear description of both the business reason for the expenditure and the names of any other persons involved. Receipts are expected for all expenditures, but those expenditures in excess of $75 must be accompanied by appropriate original receipts.

4. *Approval:* All expense reports must be approved by the partner designated to review them.

Figure 18-B. Illustration of an expense reimbursement report for a law firm.

ABC LAW FIRM PARTNERSHIP
EXPENSE REIMBURSEMENT REPORT

NAME:________________________ PERIOD COVERED ____________________

Date	Business Matter	Details of Expense	Code #	M&E Limit*	Amount Chargeable to Clients	Firm
6-5-200X	Departure Lunch	Lunch with J. Jones, associate, as a reward for preparing an outstanding brief	999-005	N		$100
6-22-200X	Client X - Litigation	Plane to Houston	640-001	N	$250	
6-24-200X	Client X - Litigation	Lunch outside courtroom with Jane Joe of X Corporation to discuss progress of case	999-009	Y	$ 75	
		Totals			$325	$100

PREPARER'S SIGNATURE:____

APPROVER'S SIGNATURE:____

*Meal & Entertainment Expenses subject to the 50% limitation.

§ 18.02 Employee Relocation Costs

In multi-office law firms, temporary or permanent transfers of partners, associates, and administrative employee are inevitable and commonplace occurrences. Without proper tax planning, relocating an employee or partner can create unexpected tax results. This section highlights some of the areas to be aware of in relocating an individual.

[1]—Expenses for a Temporary Transfer

It is typical for a firm to take an ordinary and necessary business expense deduction to send an employee from one office to another for an overnight trip or for a week. But, what about sending an associate from New York to Washington D.C. for ten months? When is the trip a temporary transfer and not a permanent move? After years of litigation which never seemed to adequately define "temporary" versus "indefinite," Congress changed the law so that travel expenses while "temporarily away from home during any period of employment" will be deductible if the period is realistically expected to last one year or less.[1] In providing guidance on how to implement the new law, the IRS applies the one-year test to a *single* location[2]—seemingly more generous than the Internal Revenue Code.

If an assignment is temporary, the cost of transferring an attorney to another business location is deductible by the firm as an ordinary and necessary business expense[3] and is not taxable to that person. A transferee may also be reimbursed for or deduct subsistence expenses which include local commuting, lodging, meals and laundry while temporarily away from home.[4] The simplest way to reimburse an employee for temporary away-from-home expenses is through the employee's expense report. This way, the employee does not have to report the income or corresponding expenses. However, if family members accompany the transferee, their expenses are not deductible by either the firm or the employee.[5] Unlike moving expenses defined below, partner expenses are treated the same as other associates/ employees.

---

[1] IRC § 162(a); 26 U.S.C. § 162(a).

[2] Rev. Rul. 93-86, 1993-40 I.R.B. 1 (Nov. 24, 1993).

[3] IRC § 162(a)(2); 26 U.S.C. § 162(a)(2).

[4] Treas. Reg. § 1.162-2(a); 26 C.F.R. § 1.162-2(a)

[5] Treas. Reg. § 1.162-2(c); 26 U.S.C. § 1.162-2(c).

[2]—Moving Expenses for a Permanent Transfer

If a transfer is indefinite or permanent (i.e., out of town for over one year),[6] the Internal Revenue Code allows an employee or partner to take a deduction for (1) the direct cost of moving household goods and personal effects from a former residence to a new residence,[7] and (2) the cost of traveling from the old home to the new home, including lodging costs, but not meals while *en route.*[8] Disbursements for pre-move house-hunting trips, meals while moving, house-selling expenses, and temporary quarters at a new job site are not deductible. Employees who use their cars for moving and other expense purposes can use an optional standard mileage rate in computing deductible costs.[9]

The reporting requirements for qualified moving expense reimbursement are quite simple.[10] The law allows an employee to exclude from gross income amounts paid directly or reimbursed by an employer for moving expenses that would otherwise be deductible. The reporting requirements are similar to those required to reimburse an associate for a normal business lunch. However, if a law firm reimburses or pays other non-excludable items (e.g., house-hunting trips, meals en route, etc.), then the payments are not deductible by a law firm, unless, in the case of an employee, the payments are classified as "compensation" and are subject to the normal payroll taxes.[11]

The Code does not classify partners are employees for purposes of the qualified moving expense reimbursement fringe benefit. Consequently, reimbursed qualified moving expenses for a partner must be reported to the affected partner as a guaranteed payment. In this situation, the partner has to include the reimbursement in gross income. However, the reimbursed qualified moving expenses can be added to other unreimbursed qualified moving expenses and taken as a deduction on Form 3903 to arrive at gross income on the partner's personal income tax return.[12] It should be noted that non-excludable payments for partners must be reported as guaranteed payments on Schedule K-1 and are not deductible on a partner's personal tax return.

---

[6] IRC § 162(a); 26 U.S.C. § 162(a).

[7] IRC § 217(b)(1)(A); 26 U.S.C. § 217(b)(1)(A).

[8] IRC § 217(b)(1)(B); 26 U.S.C. § 217(b)(1)(B).

[9] The applicable standard mileage rate in connection with a relocation for business purposes is 12¢ per mile. See § 7.02 of Rev. Proc. 2000-48, 2000-49 I.R.B. 570.

[10] IRC § 132(a)(6); 26 U.S.C. § 132(a)(6).

[11] IRC § 82; 26 U.S.C. § 82.

[12] IRC § 62(a)(15); 26 U.S.C. § 62(a)(15).

[3]—Purchase of Transferee's Home

To lessen the distress and burden of selling a house in connection with a relocation, a law firm occasionally makes an arrangement with a relocation service company to offer to buy the transferee's home for an appraised value.

If a law firm engages a relocation company and that company purchases the associate's home for a calculated fair market value and assumes the responsibilities of ownership (e.g., real estate taxes, assessments, utility charges, insurance, mortgage payments), then the employee does not realize income when those items are paid by the relocation company.[13] When an employee sells the house to a relocation company, there is no compensation income for the amount of real estate commission paid or accrued.[14] Likewise, when the house is sold by the relocation company, the employee does not recognize income for real estate sales commission.[15]

When a law firm buys the house directly from an employee either because of firm policy or in connection with a previously negotiated agreement, any gain or loss the firm incurs on the ultimate sale of the house will be capital in nature.[16] If a law firm contracts with an independent relocation service company to buy the house from the employee and resell it, without having the normal responsibilities of ownership transferred to the relocation company, the IRS has held that the ultimate gain or loss is a capital transaction of the law firm.[17] The reasoning behind the IRS's conclusion is that the relocation firm was deemed to be an agent of the law firm and, therefore, the economic substance should be the same as if the law firm bought the house directly from the employee.

However, if a law firm could successfully argue that a relocation company is not its agent, then the firm would not be considered the owner of the house. It might be difficult to sustain this argument, especially if any gain or loss realized by the relocation service is passed on to the law firm. When the gain on the sale of a home to a third party was paid to the relocated employee, a court held that the relocated employee retained the benefits and burdens of ownership, that the relocation company was not an agent of the employer, that

---

[13] Ltr. Rul. 9620026 (May 17, 1996).

[14] Ltr. Rul. 9552040 (Sept. 29, 1995) and Ltr. Rul. 8425069 (Mar. 20, 1984).

[15] Rev. Rul. 72-339, 1972-2 C.B. 31 and Ltr. Rul. 8425069 (Mar. 20, 1984).

[16] Azar Nut Co. v. Commissioner, 931 F.2d 314 (5th Cir. 1991). See also, Rev. Rul. 82-204, 1982-2 C.B. 192.

[17] Ltr. Rul. 9036003, (May 31, 1990).

the agreement between the relocation company and the employee was an executory sales contract, that the employer did not obtain actual or beneficial ownership of the employee's residence, and that the employer could deduct amounts paid to the relocation company as ordinary and necessary business expenses.[18]

With respect to partners, amounts paid to a relocation company probably are taxable to the partner, who would take a deduction on Schedule E as an unreimbursed expense, to the extent deductible.

If a law firm reimburses an associate or partner directly or pays commissions for selling a home or other closing costs on behalf of the associate or partner, the commissions or closing costs are taxable benefits. The appropriate tax treatment for the costs incurred in selling and buying a home is a reduction in the sales price of the home sold and an increase in the basis of the home purchased.[19]

---

[18] See Amdahl Corp. v. Commissioner, 108 T.C. 507 (1997).

[19] Committee Reports for § 13213 of the Revenue Reconciliation Act of 1993.

§ 18.03 Employee Fringe Benefits

[1]—In General

Statutory fringe benefits are those benefits that have been exempted from income taxation by law to encourage employers to provide these benefits to their employees. Law firms generally are permitted to deduct the cost of providing such benefits and employees generally are permitted to exclude from income the value of contributions and benefits under statutory fringe benefit plans.[1] Fringe benefits typically conferred on lawyers and administrative employees of a law firm include partial or full subsidization of the cost of coverage for:

(1) Disability insurance;
(2) Group-term life insurance;
(3) Medical insurance; and
(4) Company eating facilities.

Certain criteria must be met in order to qualify the cost of a particular fringe benefit for exemption from income taxation. In addition, there are limitations on the amount of tax-free income that is available under each type of fringe benefit.[2] The firm's professional tax advisor should be consulted to determine the criteria for qualification and the maximum excludable income for the firm's fringe benefit programs.

The fringe benefit regulations can have a significant impact on law firms; they can also be beneficial to employees. If a benefit qualifies, the law firm is allowed a deduction and the employee or partner does not have to include it in his or her taxable income. Depending on the fringe benefit, partners are considered employees and enjoy the same benefits tax-free.[3] The significant aspects of the regulations are reviewed in this section.

[2]—Parking, Transit Passes and Vanpooling

Fringe benefits for parking, transit passes and vanpooling have taken a roller coaster ride to arrive at today's qualified transportation fringe benefits. Initially, parking and transit passes were covered by

---

[1] See, e.g.: IRC §§ 101(b), 106, 120, 125, 127, 129 and 132; 26 U.S.C. §§ 101(b), 106, 120, 125, 127, 129 and 132.

[2] See, e.g.: IRC §§ 101(b)(2)(A), 127(a)(2), 129(a)(2), 132(f)(2) and 132(g); 26 U.S.C. §§ 101(b)(2)(A), 127(a)(2), 129(a)(2), 132(f)(2) and 132(g).

[3] Treas. Reg. § 1.132-1(b)(2)(ii) provides that partners are considered employees for purposes of the working condition fringe benefit rules and Treas. Reg. § 1.132-1(b)(4) provides that any recipient of a *de minimis* fringe benefit is an employee.

different subsections of the Internal Revenue Code and vanpooling was not considered. Also, partners and shareholders owning 2% or more of S corporations were covered by original legislation. Once these benefits were grouped under the same Internal Revenue Code section, they were limited to employees. This section reviews the evolution of parking, transit passes and vanpooling, who is eligible for the fringe benefits, when eligibility occurred and what limits currently are in place.

[a]—Evolution of Benefits: Moratorium to Present Day

In the 1970s, the IRS aggressively applied a United States Supreme Court decision holding that Internal Revenue Code Section 61 "is broad enough to include in taxable income any economic or financial benefit conferred on the employee as compensation, whatever the form or mode by which it is effected."[4] Armed with support, the IRS targeted what, at that time, were considered to be inconsequential benefits that were not material enough to warrant attention. Some of the benefits targeted for taxation at the individual level were reserved parking spaces in which employees (often officers or key personnel) had their names on cement blocks, the value of lunch rooms provided to employees, free coffee or rolls, and employer-owned automobiles. Often, corporations were forced to pay the employees' tax on these benefits and associated withholding taxes to avoid having to report additional taxable income retroactively to employees, some of whom may have switched jobs before the examinations started. Congressmen were deluged with complaints about these adjustments and decided that legislation was needed to prevent the IRS from continuing to tax fringe benefits.

In 1978, Congress passed a moratorium prohibiting the Treasury Department from issuing any fringe benefit regulations prior to 1980.[5] The moratorium was extended several times[6] until passage of The Tax Reform Act of 1984 ("TRA of 1984" or "the Act")[7] In the TRA of 1984 Congress addressed which fringe benefits should be taxable and which should be exempt.

---

[4] Commissioner v. Smith, 324 U.S. 177, 181, 65 S.Ct. 591, 89 L.Ed. 830 (1945).

[5] See Pub. L. No. 95-427, § 1, effective Oct. 7, 1978.

[6] Pub. L. No. 96-167 extended the moratorium through May 31, 1981 and the Economic Recovery Tax Act of 1981 (Pub. L. No. 97-34) extended the moratorium through December 31, 1983. In Ann. 85-4, 1984-4 I.R.B. 31, Treasury voluntarily announced that it would not issue any regulations or rulings altering the tax treatment of nonstatutory fringe benefits prior to January 1, 1985.

[7] The Tax Reform Act of 1984 is part of the Deficit Reduction Act of 1984 (Pub. L. No. 98-369).

The TRA of 1984 clarified that any fringe benefit not qualifying for exclusion under the Act or another specific Internal Revenue Code Section is includible in a recipient's gross income to the extent that the value of the benefit exceeds the amount paid by the recipient. The legislation stated that if a fringe benefit is taxable, then it is subject to the normal withholding taxes. Two of the fringe benefits[8] created by the Act are important to law firms: working condition fringe[9] and *de minimis* fringe.[10] Initially, parking was a working condition fringe benefit and transit passes were *de minimis* fringes. Various changes that are discussed later in this section were made to each benefit, until 1992 when Congress restructured Code Section 132 and included parking and transit passes in a new category, qualified transportation fringe.[11] The Act raised the limits on these benefits, but crafted new rules to insure that the benefits would truly be benefits and not alternatives. Under the law an employee will not have to pick up income merely because he or she has the choice of taking the benefit or a cash reimbursement.[12]

Although the 1992 legislation unified transportation fringe benefits, it also created some administrative headaches. Whereas partners and 2% shareholders of S corporations were eligible for parking benefits when they were classified as working condition fringe benefits, the new law covered only employees. Also, under the 1992 legislation, if a law firm paid a benefit even $1 higher than the amount stipulated, then the entire amount paid was taxable instead of the incremental amount. Merely offering employees cash in lieu of a non-cash benefit—which was required by some states—created yet another problem with the 1992 law because the cash option caused the entire benefit to be taxable, even to those who opted for the non-cash benefit.

In 1997 and 1998, Congress revisited the qualified transportation benefits and ultimately conformed them so that the same rules applied to all transportation benefits and the cash-in-lieu rules were in parity with state laws.

---

[8] In addition to the two fringe benefits discussed in this section, the Tax Reform Act of 1984 included legislation creating fringe benefits for no-additional-cost services, qualified employee discounts, athletic facilities, and qualified tuition reductions. See I.R.C. § 132(b), (c); 26 U.S.C. §132(b), (c).

[9] IRC § 132(a)(3); 26 U.S.C. § 132(a)(3).

[10] IRC § 132(a)(4); 26 U.S.C. § 132(a)(4). See also, discussion of overtime meals and cab fares at § 1706[3][d] *infra*, and other *de minimis* fringe benefits at § 17.06[3][j] *infra*.

[11] IRC § 132(a)(5); 26 U.S.C. § 132(a)(5).

[12] IRC § 132(f)(4); 26 U.S.C. § 132(f)(4).

The evolution of the parking and transit pass rules is discussed in more detail in the following sections.

[b]—Parking

[i]—Qualified Parking Benefit—Current Law

Employees are permitted to exclude up to $180 per month (indexed for inflation) from income for qualified parking benefits.[13] Qualified parking is defined as parking provided to an employee on or near the business premises of the employer or on or near a location from which the employee commutes to work.[14] Qualified parking does not include parking on or near the employee's residence. Therefore, an employee living and working in the same city would not be able to claim the exclusion for his or her residential parking garage. Partners are not eligible for the qualified parking benefit.

[ii]—Qualified Parking Benefit—Historic Perspective

As previously mentioned, the parking benefit has caused confusion, because partners were originally eligible for the benefit, but lost the benefit when it became a qualified fringe benefit. For purposes of the original commuter parking benefit, an employee was defined to be an individual currently employed by the employer[15] and any partner who performed services for the partnership.[16] Independent contractors, however, were specifically excluded from the January 1985 definition of employee,[17] and so were excluded from tax-free parking, even though independent contractors were exempt from tax on parking benefits under prior law.

Unlike some Code sections that prohibit an employer from discriminating in favor of highly paid employees or partners, the parking fringe benefit allowed discrimination. Consequently, a law firm could provide tax-free parking to its partners and not provide any parking to its associates. However, the tax-free parking benefit could not be given as an offset to compensation. There was no dollar limit on the commuter parking benefit when it was classified as a working condition fringe benefit.

---

[13] IRC § 132(f)(1)(C); 26 U.S.C. § 132(f)(1)(C).

[14] IRC § 132(f)(5)(B); 26 U.S.C. § 132(f)(5)(B).

[15] Treas. Reg. §§ 1.132-5(a)(1) and 1.132-1(b)(2)(i); 26 C.F.R. §§ 1.132-5(a)(1) and 1.132-1(b)(2)(i).

[16] Treas. Reg. §§ 1.132-5(a)(1) and 1.132-1(b)(2)(ii); 26 C.F.R. §§ 1.132-5(a)(1) and 1.132-1(b)(2)(ii).

[17] Treas. Reg. §§ 1.132-5(a)(1) and 1.132-1(b)(2); 26 C.F.R. §§ 1.132-5(a)(1) and 1.132-1(b)(2).

The Energy Policy Act of 1992[18] substantially changed the parking benefit by redesignating it from the working condition fringe benefit category to the *de minimis* fringe benefit category. Under the law, Congress consolidated various fringe benefits, including parking, into a new fringe benefit category, Qualified Transportation Fringe.[19] Under the law, partners were excluded from the tax-free benefit and a limit was placed on the amount qualifying for tax-free treatment. The *de minimis* qualified parking benefit was limited to $155 per month, but was indexed for inflation.[20] Another important aspect of the 1992 change was that it eliminated the cliff provisions under which one dollar over the limit caused the entire amount to be taxable. Now, only the amount in excess of the limit is taxable.

The law also created parity in the valuation rules that apply to determining the value of the *de minimis* qualified transportation fringe and the amount considered to be includible in income.[21] Consequently, the value of parking includes taxes and other fees that a person would have to pay based on an arm's length transaction. The value of the parking is the amount subject to the fringe benefit limitation, not the actual amount paid or the subjective valuation placed on it by the employee or the law firm. If a person has a parking space in a building reserved in his or her name, the value of the parking for fringe benefit purposes is the right of access on any given day, even though the parking space is not actually used.

The 1992 change also included a prohibition on paying cash in lieu of transportation fringe benefits. That prohibition existed from January 1, 1993 through December 31, 1997.

In 1990, Congress passed legislation that was intended to respond to an environmental issue, but caused a conflict between state law and the federal law as those laws applied to parking fringe benefits. Congress wanted to respond to global warming concerns of the loss of ozone caused by pollutants, so it enacted the Clean Air Amendments Act of 1990 that was designed to reduce air pollution and to encourage mass transportation. It required certain employers with more than 100 employees in targeted states[22] to implement alternative commuting strategies to reduce air pollution. The responsibility for designing

---

[18] Pub. L. No. 102-486.

[19] IRC §§ 132(a)(5) and 132(f)(1)(C); 26 U.S.C. §§ 132(a)(5) and 132(f)(1)(C).

[20] IRC §§ 132(f)(2) and 132(f)(6); 26 U.S.C. §§ 132(f)(2) and 132(f)(6).

[21] Treas. Reg. § 1.61-21(b); 26 C.F.R. § 1.61-21(b).

[22] Targeted states included California, Connecticut, Delaware, Illinois, Indiana, Maryland, New Jersey, New York, Pennsylvania, Texas, and Wisconsin. See ¶ 640 of *Employer's Guide to Fringe Benefit Rules* (Thompson Pub. Group).

alternative commuting strategies fell on each state. Depending on the state, the task was formidable. Law firms employing more than 100 employees in New York City, for example, with its highly developed transit system consisting of commuter trains, subways, buses and water ferries had little trouble implementing transit inducements. Law firms in California, on the other hand, faced a significant challenge in designing an alternative commuting strategy, because of the lack of a developed mass transit system. Employers in California had to be creative to comply with the law. Some instituted ridesharing or vanpooling, some started satellite parking coupled with transit buses, and others instituted flexible work schedules that paid a cash incentive to arrive at the office before 6:00 a.m. This last option created a conflict with federal law because federal law said that if cash was offered in lieu of the fringe benefit, then the entire parking fringe was includible in income, even if the employee elected the parking benefit.

Realizing the inadvertent conflict that it created when it passed the Clean Air Amendments Act, Congress changed the law, effective January 1, 1998, to allow employees to choose between receiving taxable compensation and a qualified parking benefit.[23] Under the law, employees electing to receive cash in lieu of qualified parking are subject to the normal payroll withholding on the cash, and other employees electing to receive the qualified parking benefit are not taxable on the benefit.

[c]—Transit Passes and Vanpooling

[i]—Transit Passes and Vanpooling—Current Law

As part of its qualified transportation fringe benefit, Congress chose to allow an exclusion for transit passes vanpooling.[24] For 2001, an employee is allowed to exclude from gross income up to $65 per month, ($100 in 2002) for transit passes and vanpooling expenses.[25] A transit pass is any token, pass, farecard, voucher or similar item entitling a person to transportation on a mass transit facility.[26] A vanpool is defined as a highway vehicle that has seating capacity for at least six adults (excluding the driver) and meets two mileage requirements. The first requirement is that at least 80% of the vehicle's mileage use must be for transporting employees between their residences and their place of

---

[23] IRC § 132(f)(4); 26 U.S.C. § 132(f)(4).

[24] IRC § 132(f)(1)(A),(B); 26 U.S.C. § 132(f)(1)(A),(B).

[25] IRC § 132(f)(1)(A),(B); 26 U.S.C. § 132(f)(1)(A),(B).

[26] IRC § 132(f)(5)(A); 26 U.S.C. § 132(f)(5)(A).

employment. The second requirement is that, on average, the number of employees transported each trip must be at least one-half of the adult seating capacity of the vehicle.[27]

[ii]—Transit Passes and Vanpooling—Historic Perspective

The vanpooling and transit pass provisions were enacted to encourage use of mass transportation in congested metropolitan areas, the TRA of 1984 created a transit pass *de minimis* fringe benefit. Originally, transit passes could be sold to employees at a discount of up to $15 per month. Instead of transit passes, a law firm could give employees $15 in tokens or fare cards which enabled employees to travel on a transit system. Like the parking benefit, the transit benefit had a cliff provision so that if more than the limit (i.e., $15) was paid, then the entire benefit became taxable. After significant public pressure to increase the limit, the IRS, in a proposed regulation, increased the transit pass limit to $21,[28] effective July 1, 1991. The increase was made under the authority of legislative history. At that time, use of vanpools was added to the *de minimis* fringe benefit category.[29]

A major change to the transit pass fringe benefit occurred with the passage of the Energy Policy Act of 1992. The Act increased the statutory exclusion for transit passes to $60 and indexed it for inflation. It also eliminated the cliff provision, replacing it with a provision that only the amount paid in excess of the limit would be includible in an employee's gross income and subject to the normal payroll withholding taxes. The 1992 Act also created an exclusion for vanpooling. When Congress changed the law in 1997, eliminating the prohibition of paying cash in lieu of a parking benefit, it knocked the taxation of qualified transportation fringe benefits out of sync because transit passes and vanpooling were still subject to the cash-in-lieu prohibition. As the law stood, it was okay for a law firm to offer some employees cash to come to work early without affecting the tax-free parking benefits enjoyed by other employees, but it was not acceptable to offer cash in lieu of transit passes or vanpools. Merely by offering the cash-in-lieu option for transit passes or vanpools caused the entire amount to be includible in employees' income.

As if realizing the confusion it created, Congress reacted in 1998 by retroactively amending the law to extend the more liberal rule (i.e.,

---

[27] IRC § 132(f)(5)(B); 26 U.S.C. § 132(f)(5)(A).

[28] Proposed fringe benefit regulations increase the limit from $15 to $21.

[29] See the Energy Policy Act of 1992 (Pub. L. No. 102-486).

cash or benefit) to transit passes and vanpools, thereby bringing all qualified transportation benefits back into parity.[30]

[3]—Working Condition Fringe Benefits

A working condition fringe is any property or service provided by an employer to its employees to the extent that the costs of the property or services would qualify as ordinary and necessary business expenses under IRC §§ 162 or 167.[31] If a benefit qualifies as a working condition fringe, a law firm can deduct the cost of the benefit and does not have to include it in an employee's gross income.[32]

For purposes of the working condition fringe benefit, "employee" includes any partner performing services for the employer, any individual currently employed by the firm, any director of the firm and any independent contractor who performs services for the firm.[33] Additionally, the non-discrimination rules applicable to other types of fringe benefits do not apply to working condition fringes.[34]

The regulations give several examples of working condition fringes: The value or use by an employee of a company car or airplane for business purposes;[35] Fringe benefits provided by an employer for the safety of its employees, in circumstances where such expenses would be considered ordinary and necessary;[36] Outplacement services provided to terminated employees provided that the employee does not have an option to receive severance pay or increased severance pay in lieu of outplacement services.[37] There are a variety of other benefits enumerated in the regulations, however they do not apply to law firms.

Any exclusion is only available to the extent that the benefit was for business purposes. Said differently, any personal component would be taxable to the employee. For example, if for other than security reasons, a firm provides chauffeur services valued at $30,000 per year to a partner, and 30% of the chauffeur's time is spent driving the recipient for personal reasons, only $ 21,000 (70% of $30,000) is excludable from income, the remaining $9,000 is fully taxable.[38]

---

[30] Transportation Equity Act for the 21st Century (Pub. L. No. 105-178) enacted June 9, 1998 and applied retroactively to taxable years beginning on or after January 1, 1998.

[31] IRC § 132(d); 26 U.S.C. § 132(d).

[32] IRC § 132(a)(5); 26 U.S.C. § 132(a)(5).

[33] Treas. Reg. § 1.132-1(b)(2)(i)-(iv); 26 C.F.R. § 1.132-1(b)(2)(i)-(iv).

[34] Treas. Reg. § 1.132-5(q); 26 C.F.R. § 1.132-5(q).

[35] Treas. Reg. § 1.132-5(b); 26 C.F.R. § 1.132-5(b).

[36] Treas. Reg. § 1.132-5(m); 26 C.F.R. § 1.132-5(m).

[37] Rev. Rul. 92-69, 1992-2 C.B. 51

[38] Treas. Reg. § 1.132-5(b)(3)(ii) 26 C.F.R. § 1.132-5(b)(3)(3)(ii).

[4]—De Minimis Fringe Benefits

Most reasonable people consider materiality when deciding if something is important. Materiality normally is considered in the context of the value of something or the number of times something occurs. If something is material in the tax context, then it should have special rules, otherwise, it's not worth worrying about. This is the concept behind the catchall fringe benefit known as *de minimis* fringe benefits. Congress described a *de minimis* fringe as being any property or service the value of which is (after taking into account the frequency with which similar fringes are provided by the employer to the employer's) so small as to make accounting for it unreasonable or administratively impracticable.[39]

The definition sounds simple, but it is fraught with ambiguities that need explanations before any law firm can comfortably offer *de minimis* fringe benefits to its employees and know that neither the law firm nor its employees will have tax problems in the future.

Unlike some fringe benefits, partners do qualify for exclusion from gross income for *de minimis* fringe benefits, because the term "employee' includes any recipient of the fringe benefit[40]

This section will discuss the application of *de minimis* fringe benefits in the context of law firms.

[a]—Employee-Measured Frequency

As the term suggests, frequency is simply how often a similar fringe is provided by a law firm to employees.[41] Interestingly, the regulations say that if an employer provides a free lunch each day to one employee, but not to another employee, then the free lunch is not a *de minimis* fringe benefit, even though the free lunch with respect to the entire work staff may be infrequent.[42]

Notwithstanding that example, the regulations go on to say that when it is administratively difficult to determine the frequency with respect to a particular individual, frequency is determined by reference to the frequency with which the employer provides the fringes to the work-force as a whole.[43] The challenge is identifying a situation in which it is administratively difficult to determine the frequency with respect to one individual. Since computers are so pervasive within law firms and

---

[39] I.R.C. § 132(e)(1); 26 U.S.C. § 132(e)(1).

[40] Treas. Reg. § 1.132-1(b)(4); 26 C.F.R. § 1.132-1(b)(4).

[41] Treas. Reg. § 1.132-6(b)(1); 26 C.F.R. § 1.132-6(b)(1).

[42] Treas. Reg. § 1.132-6(b)(1); 26 C.F.R. § 1.132-6(b)(1).

[43] Treas. Reg. § 1.132-6(b)(2); 26 C.F.R. § 1.132-6(b)(2).

accounting software is so sophisticated, it is difficult to envisage a situation in which a law firm would not be able to track how often an associate or support staff received a benefit of little value, such as an overtime meal. As long as it is possible to track these costs, the test for frequency will be at the individual level and not at the workforce level.

If it is not unreasonable or administratively impractical to account for the value of a benefit provided to an employee, then the value of the benefit has to be included in the employee's gross income (and subject to the normal payroll taxes).[44] Generally, the frequency test is administered on an individual-by-individual basis and not on an average of eligible employees.[45] Again, the regulations give an example that giving a cash fringe benefit is never excludable as a *de minimis* fringe benefit.[46] Unless otherwise allowed, giving a cash-equivalent fringe benefit generally is not excludable from an employee's income, even though the same property or service could have been a *de minimis* fringe benefit.[47] For example, if a law firm gave an employee cash to buy a theater ticket, the cash would be taxable to the employee, even though the theater ticket would have been a *de minimis* fringe benefit if the firm had given the ticket instead of the money.

[b]—Overtime Meals and Cab Fares

The most common *de minimis* fringe benefit is one that excludes occasional meal money and local transportation from an employee's gross income. It also is the most contentious; because the benefit must be provided on an, occasional basis.[48] Whether a benefit is provided to an employee on an occasional depends upon the frequency, i.e., the availability of the benefit and regularity with which the benefit is provided to an employee.[49] Accordingly, meals, meal money or transportation fare, or a combination of such benefits provided to an employee on a regular or routine basis, are not provided on an occasional basis.[50] These benefits also must be provided enable the employee to work overtime.[51] In the case of meals or meal money, the meal must be consumed during the overtime period to qualify for the

---

[44] Treas. Reg. § 1.132-6(c); 26 C.F.R. § 1.132-6(c).
[45] Ltr. Rul. 9148001 (Feb. 15, 1991).
[46] Treas. Reg. § 1.132-6(c); 26 C.F.R. § 1.132-6(c).
[47] Treas. Reg. § 1.132-6(c); 26 C.F.R. § 1.132-6(c).
[48] Treas. Reg. § 1.132-6(d)(2)(i)(A); 26 C.F.R. § 132-6(d)(2)(i)(A).
[49] Treas. Reg. § 1.132-6(d)(2)(i)(A); 26 C.F.R. § 132-6(d)(2)(i)(A).
[50] Treas. Reg. § 1.132-6(d)(2)(i)(A); 26 C.F.R. § 1.132-6(d)(2)(i)(A).
[51] Treas. Reg. § 1.132-6(d)(2)(i)(C); 26 C.F.R. § 132-6(d)(2)(i)(C).

exclusion[52].Providing meals based on the number of hours worked (e.g., $1.00 per hour for each hour over eight hours or $10 for dinner after working a ten-hour day) does not qualify for this exclusion, unless it meets the other tests.[53]

It is important for some law firms to realize that the *de minimis* fringe benefit for occasional overtime meals also applied to local transportation, i.e., taxicabs or limousines. While this generally only applies to large metropolitan areas, it may be the most expensive *de minimis* fringe benefit. It also is unclear if local transportation means taking an employee from the firm's office to a place where he or she can get public transportation home or does it include taking the person all the way home - something akin to commuting home. Obviously, the definition of local transportation depends on the particular facts and circumstance for each law firm.

The rules sound simple enough to administer, but they are not. The most difficult issue is the definition of the word "occasional." Firms in which associates work overtime almost every evening (either because of firm-related demands or the need to get adequate charge time) will find it difficult to argue that the meals and local transportation furnished to associates are occasional and, therefore, excludible from the associates' gross income. There continues to be no guidance on defining "occasional." Shortly after the final regulations were issued, the authors of the regulations published an article in which they stated that based on "an informal poll of the persons . . . responsible for regulations and ruling in this area" it was felt that "more than once a week" should be viewed as "occasional."[54] This would suggest that when a law firm considers vacation and other time off, occasional might be less than 50 times a year.[55] Another important consideration is that the occasional test applies to both overtime meals and local transportation. So, if an attorney did not meet the occasional test with respect to meals, no matter how infrequently he or she used local transportation to go home after working overtime, none of the local transportation would be occasional. One taints the other.

In a technical advice memorandum, the IRS concluded that employees who were entitled to meal allowances on a routine basis for overtime work were taxable on the fringe benefit, because the meals were not occasional - they were negotiated as past of a union

---

[52] Treas. Reg. § 1.132-6(d)(2)(i)(C); 26 C.F.R. § 132-6(d)(2)(i)(C).
[53] Treas. Reg. § 1.132-6(d)(2)(i)(C); 26 C.F.R. § 1.132-6(d)(2)(i)(C).
[54] See Special Report 45 Tax Notes 743, (Nov. 6, 1989)
[55] See Special Report 45 Tax Notes 743, (Nov. 6, 1989)

contract and were automatically paid.[56] If an overtime meal qualifies as a *de minimis* fringe benefit, then it is not subject to the 50% haircut.[57]

There is one last point to be made regarding the application of the *de minimis* regulations. If because of either the value or frequency of a benefit exceeds occasional, then all of the benefits are taxable to the employee - not just those in excess of something that would have been occasional. For example, if an employee consumes 150 meals during the year and takes a car home half of the time, those benefits may not be occasional. If not, then all of the meals and transportation would be taxable.[58] The regulations place an onerous burden on law firms' accounting departments to track the number and frequency of overtime meals and cab fares for each employee to determine if the benefits are excludable or includible in employee gross income.

[c]—Special Rule for Employer-Provided Transportation

Under certain circumstances the cost of employer-provided transportation may be substantially excluded from an employee's wages. If a law firm provides transportation to an employee for use in commuting to or from work because of *unusual circumstances* and *unsafe conditions*, the value of the benefit is deemed to be $1.50 per one-way commute, regardless of the actual cost.[59] This exemption is not available to highly compensated individuals, i.e., "control employees."[60] Both criteria—unusual circumstances and unsafe conditions—are dependent on the particular facts and circumstances of each employee. For example, assume that an employee who normally works from 9:00 a.m. until 5:00 p.m. is asked to change his or her work schedule temporarily to midnight until 8:00 a.m. If the firm has a car pick up the employee for the midnight shift, it could exclude the actual cost of the car from the employee's gross income and instead, include $1.50 for the one-way commute. The law firm can deduct the actual cost incurred, but the employee is taxed only on $1,50.

If on the other hand, an employee (not a control employee) normally works from 9:00 a.m. until 5:00 p.m. and is asked occasionally (e.g., once every two weeks) to work overtime, the law firm

---

[56] See N. 57 *supra.*

[57] I.R.C. § 274(n)(2); 26 U.S.C. § 274(n)(2).

[58] Treas. Reg. § 1.132-6(d)(4); 26 C.F.R. § 132-6(d)(4).

[59] Treas. Reg. § 1.132-6(d)(2)(iii)(A); 26 C.F.R. § 1.132-6(d)(2)(iii)(A).

[60] A control employee is a person earning over the amount allowed under Treas. Reg. § 1.61-21(f)(5), adjusted for inflation or a 1% owner. For 2001, the base limit is $155,000. See 2000-66, I.R.B. 2000-52, 600 (Dec. 23, 2000).

could send the person home in a car and exclude the cost from the employee's gross income on the basis that benefit was occasional. The difference between this example and the previous one is that the person's regular schedule was temporarily changed and that for one leg of the transportation was unsafe to commute in the normal manner.

[d]—Special Valuation Rule Re: Unsafe Travel Conditions

At first glance this rule seems very similar to the employer-provided transportation *de minimis* fringe benefit discussed in the previous section. In fact, there is a similarity, but only in amount and not for the same reason.

Many law firms have administrative employees (e.g., typists, proofreaders) who normally and continuously work the night shift (e.g., 5:00 p.m. to midnight or midnight to 7 a.m.). For safety reasons, these employees are allowed to take a cab to or from work when unsafe conditions exist. Since this benefit is provided every day it is not considered to be "unusual" and, accordingly, does not qualify as a *de minimis* fringe benefit[61]. To avoid having night-shift employees taxed on a benefit that originates from a concern for their safety, the Treasury Department created a special valuation rule that values this benefit at $1.50.[62]

Under the special-valuation rule, the excess cost of a one-way commute over $1.50 is exempt from gross wages provided certain conditions are met. The more important of these conditions are that the transportation is provided solely because of unsafe conditions, the law firm has a written policy concerning unsafe conditions, the employee is paid on an hourly basis, the employee is paid one and a half times the regular rate for overtime, and his or her compensation does not exceed a specified amount which is indexed for inflation.[63]

[e]—Other *De Minimis* Fringe Benefits

There is no complete list of *de minimis* fringe benefits that are excludable from a person's gross income. However, Treasury regulations give examples, including:

---

[61] See Chapter 18.03[3][c], *supra*.

[62] Treas. Reg. § 1.61-21(k)(3); 26 C.F.R. § 1.61-21(k)(3).

[63] Other conditions to qualify for the exemption are that an employee is not claimed as exempt from the minimum wage and maximum hour provisions of the Fair Labor Standards Act of 1938, that the employer maintains a written plan stating that the transportation is provided to secure against unsafe conditions, and that the employee cannot use the transportation for any personal purposes. Treas. Reg. § 1.61(k)-21; 26 C.F.R. § 1.61-21(k)-21.

- occasional typing of personal letters by a company secretary,
- occasional use of copying machines for personal purposes,
- occasional cocktail parties, group meals, or picnics for employees and their guests,
- traditional birthday or holiday gifts of property (but not cash) with a low fair market value,
- occasional theater or sporting event tickets,
- coffee, doughnuts, and soft drinks,
- local personal telephone calls, and
- flowers, fruits, books or similar property provided to employees under special circumstances (e.g., on account of illness, outstanding performance, family crisis, or wedding).[64]

In each case, the general rule—the value or frequency is so small as to make accounting of the benefit unreasonable or administratively impractical—must be applied to determine if a benefit is *de minimis.* Associates and partners can enjoy these fringe benefits without adverse tax consequences.

Some of the benefits on Treasury's list need no explanation (i.e., coffee, doughnuts and soft drinks), however, some are not so obvious. For example, nothing explains what group meals are or how many employees have to be present to qualify as a *de minimis* fringe benefit. The same vagueness exists for occasional cocktail parties. When one considers that these events can be expensive and obviously not difficult to account for administratively, a level of concern is raised if the IRS does not view these expenses as *de minimis*.

Some fringe benefits clearly are not *de minimis.* For example, season ticket to sporting events or theatrical performances are not *de minimis* fringe benefits.[65] Likewise, the commuting use of an employer-provided car more than once a month or membership in a country club, regardless of usage and not *de minimis.*[66]

The amount of any *de minimis* fringe benefit is not subject to the nondiscrimination tests.[67] Thus a *de minimis* fringe benefit may be excludable for an employee's gross income is provided exclusively to highly compensated employees.[68] Since partners are considered employees for *de minimis* fringe benefit purposes, this rule would seem to include partners in the nondiscrimination rule.

---

[64] Treas. Reg. § 1.132-6(e)(1); 26 C.F.R. § 1.132-6(e)(1).

[65] Treas. Reg. § 132-6(e)(2); 26 C.F.R. § 132-6(e)(2).

[66] Treas. Reg. § 132-6(e)(2); 26 C.F.R. § 132-6(e)(2).

[67] Treas. Reg. § 132-6(f); 26 C.F.R. § 132-6(f).

[68] Treas. Reg. § 132-6(f); 26 C.F.R. § 132-6(f).

[5]—Employee Cafeterias

On-premises cafeterias are provided to law firm employees and partners as a fringe benefit to provide a meal at a reasonable price and as an inducement to remain on the premises instead of going to distant restaurants. Cafeterias can be owned and operated by a law firm, owned by the law firm and operated by a food service company, or owned by someone else (e.g., another tenant in the building) with costs shared by a law firm. However owned and operated, cafeterias often are subsidized in some fashion (e.g., an owner provides office space, heat, light, electricity, and absorbs part of the cost of food or the cost to prepare and serve the food). The tax results of subsidizing a cafeteria depend upon the amount of the subsidy, the amount charged for food, the revenue collected annually, and various forms of discrimination. Following is an example that presents general assumptions and variations of facts to demonstrate how different the tax results can be to employees and to law firms.

General Assumption—A law firm owns a cafeteria in its building that is open to all employees and partners. The firm subsidizes heat, light, electricity and office space.

1. Revenue equals direct costs. The value of meals provided to employees at an employer-operated cafeteria is excludable from an employee's gross income as a *de minimis* fringe benefit only if on an annual basis, the revenue from the cafeteria equals or exceeds the direct operating costs.[69] Direct operating costs include the cost of the food, labor to prepare the food, and labor to serve food.[70] Only the labor costs incurred primarily on the premises (i.e., in the law firm's cafeteria) are included in the cost of labor.[71] For purposes of this test, a law firm is allowed to exclude from the calculation the cost and revenue of each employee meal that is excludable from an employee's income under the convenience of the employer test.[72] If a law firm charges non-employees a greater amount for food than it charges employees (e.g., food from a firm's cafeteria is served to clients in a conference room and the client is charged for the food at a marked-up amount), then the actual cost of the food and revenue (i.e., the amount charged the client) must be disregarded for purposes of this test.[73]

---

[69] I.R.C. § 132(e)(2); 26 U.S.C. § 132(e)(2) and Treas. Reg. § 1.132-7(a)(1); 26 C.F.R. § 1.132-7(a)(1).

[70] Treas. Reg. § 1.132-7(b)(1); 26 C.F.R. § 1.132-7(b)(1).

[71] Treas. Reg. § 1.132-7(b)(1); 26 C.F.R. § 1.132-7(b)(1).

[72] Treas. Reg. § 1.132-7(a)(2)(iv); 26 C.F.R. § 1.132-7(a)(2)(iv).

[73] Treas. Reg. § 1.132-7(a)(2)(iv); 26 C.F.R. § 1.132-7(a)(2)(iv).

If revenue from the cafeteria equals or exceeds the cost of operating the facility, then the subsidy, if any, qualifies as a *de minimis* fringe benefit and is not subject to the 50% haircut.[74]

2. **Food priced at fair market value.** If cafeteria users pay the fair market value for the food, the subsidy is not includible in an employees' or partners' gross incomes nor is it subject to the 50% haircut.[75]

3. **Food priced at less than fair market value.** Annual cafeteria revenue does not equal direct operating costs. Employee and partner pay less than the fair market value of the food. The difference between the fair market value of the food and the amount paid by the employee is includible in his or her gross income, unless the convenience of the employer rule applies (see variation 5 below). The difference between the fair market value of the food and the amount paid by the partner is either nondeductible by the firm or is reportable as a guaranteed payment. The direct cost subsidy (difference between the direct cost of the food and the amount collected) is subject to the 50% haircut.

4. **Cafeteria discriminates and revenue equals direct costs.** A cafeteria can discriminate in favor of highly compensated associates or partners in many ways. For example, assume highly compensated individuals are charged less than the fair market value while the amount charged other employees is enough to allow annual revenue to equal direct costs. Although the mathematical test of the *de minimis* fringe benefit is met, the discrimination test is not, so the highly compensated non-partners' gross income will include the difference between the fair market value of the food and the amount they paid for it. The partner's portion would not be deductible by the firm, unless it was reported as a guaranteed payment. The non-highly compensated employees, however, would meet the *de minimis* requirements and would be able to exclude from gross income any benefits of the firm's subsidy. The direct cost subsidy for the highly compensated non-partner would be subject to the 50% haircut.

5. **Convenience of the employer test.** The value of meals furnished to an employee are excludable from an employee's gross income if the meals are furnished in the law firm's office and are furnished for the convenience of the law firm.[76] Meals furnished at no cost

---

[74] I.R.C. §§ 132(e)(2) and 274(n)(2)(B); 26 U.S.C. §§ 132(e)(2) and 274(n)(2)(B).

[75] Treas. Reg. § 1.61-21(b)(1); 26 C.F.R. § 1.61-21(b)(1), and IRC § 274(n); 26 U.S.C. § 274(n), and General Explanation of the Tax Reform Act of 1986 prepared by the Staff of the Joint Committee on Taxation, page 67.

[76] I.R.C. § 119(a); 26 U.S.C. § 119(a).

to the employee will be regarded as furnished for the convenience of the employer if they are provided for a substantial non-compensatory business reason.[77] Meeting the non-compensatory standard may be difficult for law firms and will depend on the specific facts and circumstances, not merely the law firm's representation.[78] Non-compensatory business reasons include (1) an employee has to be available for emergencies during work hours[79] (e.g., experience can demonstrate that emergencies occur or have occurred that cause employees to be called back to work during their normal lunch period), (2) because of the employer's business, an employee's meal period is restricted and he or she cannot be expected to eat elsewhere in a short period of time[80] (e.g., the employer's peak work load occurs during the normal lunch period), or (3) an employee cannot otherwise get lunch within a reasonable period of time (e.g., insufficient eating facilities in the vicinity).[81] Another example would be meals served on the employer's premises to employees whose working overtime hours coincide with a time when many eating establishments are closed.[82] Meals furnished to or to attract prospective employees are considered to be furnished for compensatory reasons.[83] The fact that an employer stipulates that the meal is furnished for non-compensatory reasons is not persuasive.[84] If meals are excluded from an employee's income under the convenience of the employer test, they are *de minimis* fringe benefits and are not subject to the 50% haircut.[85]

Since partners are not employees, they do not qualify under the convenience of the employer test.

If a law firm cannot meet the convenience of the employer test, then the value of the employees' meals are includible in the employees' gross income. If the meal amounts are reported in the firm's tax return as wages (and reported on W-2s to the employees), then they are not subject to the 50% haircut.[86] If a tax return is filed based on the

---

[77] Treas. Reg. 1.119(a)(2); 26 C.F.R. § 1.119(a)(2).

[78] Treas. Reg. § 1.119(a)(2)(i); 26 C.F.R. § 1.119(a)(2)(i).

[79] Treas. Reg. § 1.119(a)(2)(ii)(a); 26 C.F.R. § 1.119(a)(2)(ii)(a).

[80] Treas. Reg. § 1.119(a)(2)(ii)(b); 26 C.F.R. § 1.119(a)(2)(ii)(b).

[81] Treas. Reg. § 1.119(a)(2)(ii)(c); 26 C.F.R. § 1.119(a)(2)(ii)(c).

[82] Rev. Rul. 74-411, 1971-2 C.B. 103.

[83] Treas. Reg. § 1.119(a)(2)(iii); 26 C.F.R. § 1.119(a)(2)(iii).

[84] See California Hotel & Casino v. Commissioner, T.C. Memo 1997-445 (Sept. 30, 1997). See also, Ltr. Rul. 9602001 (Sep. 15, 1995) and Ltr. Rul. 9148001 (Feb. 15, 1991).

[85] I.R.C. § 132(e)(2); 26 U.S.C. § 132(e)(2) as amended by the Taxpayer Relief Act of 1997.

[86] I.R.C. §§ 274(n)(2)(A) and 274(e)(2); 26 U.S.C. §§ 274(n)(2)(A) and 274(e)(2).

position that meals are provided at the convenience of the employer and later upon audit the IRS determines that the convenience of the employer test is not met, then the value of the meals associated with the employees is includible in the employees' gross incomes and continues to be subject to the meal and entertainment limitation.[87] This means that if a firm gambles that it will be able to meet the convenience of the employer test and fails, both the employees are subject to tax on the meals (a tax that the law firm normally pays) and the law firm is subject to a 50% haircut on the same amount.

If a law firm provides meals for a charge (e.g., in a firm cafeteria) and the employee has a choice of purchasing or not purchasing a meal, then the meal is not furnished at the convenience of the law firm. Likewise, if a firm gives a certificate for an overtime meal, but that meal can be eaten anytime (e.g., the next day for lunch), then the value of the certificate is taxable when given to the employee. Thus, if an employee has a choice of accepting the meal or obtaining a meal somewhere else or at some other time, the meal is not furnished at the convenience of the employer.[88]

[6]—Dependent Life Insurance

Law firms sometimes provide a nominal amount of group-term life insurance for dependents of employees as a fringe benefit. However, Treasury regulations specifically state that employer-provided group life insurance on the life of a spouse or child is not an excludable fringe benefit.[89] Treasury recanted its position by allowing law firms to provide an incidental amount of insurance—face amount less than $2,000—as a *de minimis* fringe benefit if certain conditions are met.[90]

[7]—Educational Assistance Program

Continuing legal education (CLE) is a requirement for most professionals. Often, law firms offer in-house legal training programs to attorneys or allow them to attend programs sponsored by other organizations to obtain the necessary CLE. Law firms can deduct the cost of continuing legal education courses for attorneys or support staff if the courses maintain or improve skills or meet the requirement of existing law to remain in good standing with the bar.[91] However, if the

---

[87] I.R.C. §§ 274(n)(2)(A) and 274(e)(1); 26 U.S.C. §§ 274(n)(2)(A) and 274(e)(1).

[88] Treas. Reg. § 1.119(a)(3); 26 C.F.R. § 1.119(a)(3).

[89] Treas. Reg. § 1.132-6(e)(2); 26 C.F.R. § 1.132-6(e)(2).

[90] IRS Notice 89-110, 1989-2 C.B. 447.

[91] Treas. Reg. § 1.162-5(a); 26 C.F.R. § 1.162-5(a).

education is to meet the minimum educational requirements or to qualify a person for a new trade or business (i.e., law school, bar exam fees, etc.), the educational expenses are not deductible as a business expense.[92] Deciding what is a qualified business expense and what is not has been the subject of many court cases.

To lessen the complexity of deciding what is deductible, Congress enacted legislation—educational assistance programs—that allows a law firm to deduct non-business-related educational expenses that increase the educational level of employees. Educational assistance expenses are defined as those incurred for courses of instruction or the education of an employee and include expenses such as tuition, books and supplies.[93] They do not include job-related education to maintain or improve existing skills. The maximum annual exclusion from an employee's gross income under Section 127 is $5,250.[94] To qualify as an educational assistance reimbursement plan under Section 127, the plan must be in writing and for the exclusive benefit of employees.[95] Also, benefits under the plan must be only for educational assistance of the employees[96] and not discriminate in favor of "highly compensated" employees.[97] In addition, not more than 5% of the amounts paid by the firm can be for the benefit of shareholders or owners (e.g., partners).[98] Lastly, the plan must be communicated to the eligible employees.[99] A plan can provide educational assistance benefits for former employees who terminated their employment voluntarily, involuntarily or as a result of disability.[100] An educational assistance plan also can be used in connection with an employer's downsizing efforts to retrain terminated employees.[101] If the plan qualifies, the firm should file a Form 5500, as appropriate. Failure to follow the requirements may disqualify a plan, causing any paid benefits to be taxable to employee recipients. Failure to file the appropriate forms may lead to IRS penalties.

As a result of the Economic Growth and Tax Relief Reconciliation Act of 2001, graduate-level courses beginning after December 31, 2001[102] are excluded from income under Section 127. This is a change

---

[92] Treas. Reg. § 1.162-5(b); 26 C.F.R. § 1.162-5(b).
[93] IRC § 127(c)(1); 26 U.S.C. § 127(c)(1).
[94] IRC § 127(a)(2); 26 U.S.C. § 127(a)(2).
[95] IRC § 127(b)(1); 26 U.S.C. § 127(b)(1).
[96] IRC § 127(b)(4); 26 U.S.C. § 127(b)(4).
[97] IRC § 127(b)(2); 26 U.S.C. § 127(b)(2).
[98] IRC § 127(b)(3); 26 U.S.C. § 127(b)(3).
[99] IRC § 127(b)(6); 26 U.S.C. § 127(b)(6).
[100] Rev. Rul. 96-41, I.R.B. 1996-45 (Nov. 4, 1996).
[101] Rev. Rul. 96-41, N. 91.3 *supra.*
[102] IRC § 411(a) of the Economic Growth & Tax Relief Reconciliation Act of 2001.

from prior law. Prior versions of the law did not include any graduate-level courses. As a result, law firms can now deduct the cost of law school tuition paid on behalf of its employees and probably the cost of bar review courses. If the payment is made for a course that was taken prior to the associate or employee joining the firm no exclusion is available, unless a common law relationship existed prior to the beginning of the course. Section 127 probably does not cover bar exams, so any reimbursement of those costs taxable to the associates.

The expansion of Section 127 to include graduate-level courses will expire on December 31, 2010 as part of the 2001 act's Sunset Provision.

[8]—Annual Physical Examination

Another fringe benefit often provided by law firms is an annual physical examination for partners, senior associates, or key administrative staff. The examination can be provided by a group of doctors that specialize in executive physicals or it can be done by a person's own doctor. It is irrelevant if the costs can be paid directly by the attorney or employee and reimbursed by the firm or paid directly by the firm.

The tax treatment of this benefit for associates, administrative staff and partners is quite different. A law firm can deduct the amount paid for employees' (i.e., associates or administrative staff) physical examinations, because they are not "medical diagnostic procedures"[103] and are not subject to the discrimination tests for self-insured medical expense reimbursement plans. Accordingly, when the firm pays for an employee's annual physical examination, the amount is excludable from the associate's gross income.

The tax result for a partner is different, because partners are self-employed individuals and not employees.[104] As a result, partners are not eligible for benefits under Internal Revenue Code Section 105. Consequently, if a law firm pays for the annual physical examination of one of its partners, the partnership cannot deduct the cost of the exam, except as a guaranteed payment to the specific partner. The partner has gross income in the amount of the examination and a corresponding medical expense that is subject to the normal medical expense limitations.[105]

---

[103] Treas. Reg. § 1.105-11(g)(1); 26 C.F.R. § 1.105-11(g)(1).

[104] IRC §§ 105(g) and 401(c)(1); 26 U.S.C. §§ 105(g) and 401(c)(1).

[105] IRC § 213; 26 U.S.C. § 213.

[9]—Employer-Provided Retirement Planning Services

Retirement planning is a very important to most career-minded working men and women. As discussed in Chapter 16, there have been important changes in the types of plans available to working men and women. Most of the time, law firms sponsor defined contribution plans for their employees, although they tend to have non-contributory plans for associates. Regardless, associates and support staff tend to participate in these plans. Generally, the plans grow and become a large asset of the employee. Realizing this, Congress enacted a qualified employer-provided retirement planning services fringe benefit that allows law firms to pay for retirement planning advice or information provided by a qualified retirement planning counselor.[106] The retirement planning extends to an employee's spouse. This benefit is available for tax years beginning after December 31, 2001 and allows an employer to pay retirement planning costs without having the benefit included in an employee's income. The exclusion will apply to certain advice given regarding the plan such as advice and information regarding retirement income planning and how the plan fits within the employees overall retirement income plan. The exclusion does not apply to any related services such as accounting, brokerage, legal and tax preparation fees.

The retirement planning benefit does not appear that the benefit applies to partners, because they are not considered employees for purposes of this provision.

This provision may be available for a limited time only, because it is set to expire on December 31, 2010 in as part of the 2001 Act's sunset provisions.

[10]—Summary—Tax Effects of Fringe Benefits

This section summarized the tax effects for partners and non-partners (i.e., associates, other timekeepers and support staff) of fringe benefits covered above. Figure 18-C in the following section presents an executive summary of the benefits and their related tax effects for partners or non-partners.

---

[106] IRC § 132(a)(7); 26 U.S.C. § 132(a)(7) enacted as part of The Economic Growth and Tax Relief Reconciliation Act of 2001

§ 18.04 Self-Employed Accident and Health Insurance Deduction

Historically, partners have been allowed to deduct a percentage of the amounts they paid for accident and health insurance premiums when calculating their federal adjusted gross income. The Health Insurance Portability and Accountability Act allows a deduction for self-employed health insurance as follows:

Years Beginning:	Applicable Percentage
2001 through 2002	45%
2003	50%
2004	60%
2005	70%
2006 and thereafter	80%[1]

The insurance coverage includes a partner's spouse and dependents. This "above-the-line" deduction is permitted only if the partner is not eligible to participate as an employee in any subsidized health plan maintained by some other employer, or in a subsidized plan maintained by the spouse's employer.[2]

Health insurance premiums not deducted in calculating adjusted gross income can be treated as a medical expense on a partner's return.[3] However, medical expenses can be deductible as itemized deductions only to the extent they exceed 7.5% of adjusted gross income.

---

[1] IRC § 162(1)(1); 26 U.S.C. § 162(1)(1).
[2] IRC § 162(1)(2)(B); 26 U.S.C. § 162(1)(2)(B).
[3] IRC § 213(a); 26 U.S.C. § 213(a).

Figure 18-C. Summary of fringe benefits and related tax effects for law firm partners and non-partners.

SUMMARY OF FRINGE BENEFITS TAX EFFECTS

	For Partner		For Non-Partner	
Fringe Benefit	Taxable	Non-Taxable	Taxable	Non-Taxable
• Transit passes and parking	X			X
• Employee cafeterias:				
—Revenue equals direct cost		X		X
—Food priced at fair market value		X		X
—Food priced at less than fair market value	X		X	
—Cafeteria discriminates and revenue equals direct cost	X			X
—Convenience of the employer test	X			X
• Occasional meals and cab fares for overtime		X		X
• Routine meals and cab fares for overtime	X		X	
• Employer-provided transportation for unusual or unsafe conditions	X		X[4]	X
• Employer-provided transportation for unsafe travel conditions	X		X	X[5]
• Incidental amount of dependent life insurance		X		X
• Educational Assistance programs		X		X
• Annual physical examinations	X			X
• Other *de minimis* fringes		X		X[6]

Accident and health insurance premiums paid by a law firm for its partners are guaranteed payments under Internal Revenue Code Section 707(c) if paid for services rendered in the capacity of a partner and are not calculated based on the firm's income. As guaranteed payments, the amounts are includable in the partners' gross income and are deductible to the extent allowed under Code Sections 162(1) and 213(a).[7]

---

[4] Highly compensated individuals are taxable on this benefit. See § 17.06[3][e] *supra.*

[5] Normally only night-shift support staff are eligible for the special fringe benefit of $1.50 per one way.

[6] Other fringes have to meet the general definition of de minimis to be non-taxable

[7] Rev. Rul. 91-26, I.R.B. 1991-15 (April 15, 1991).

§ 18.05 Home Office Deduction

After years of litigation and legislation, it is very difficult for a self-employed attorney who has an office in which he regularly meets clients, to claim a home office deduction. During those years, the most contentious point of disagreement concerned the definition of principal place of business. In 1993, the Supreme Court interpreted principal to mean the most important or significant place for the business.[1] In 1997, Congress addressed and clarified principal place of business controversy.[2] For taxable years beginning after December 31, 1998, Congress expanded the definition of principal place of business to include a home office if it is used to conduct administrative or management activities of the taxpayer's trade or business and there is no fixed location of the trade or business where the taxpayer conducts substantial administrative or management activities of the trade or business.[3]

It is important to note that while the Tax Relief Act of 1997 relaxed the provisions under which a person could claim a home office deduction, it did not change the exclusive use requirement. If for example, an attorney claims a home office deduction for his or her den and that room is used even part of the time by other family members (e.g., children working on a computer in the den, home financial matters are conducted in the den, or the family watches television in the den) then the exclusive use rule may be violated.[4] As a result, it is very difficult, if not impossible, for an attorney who has an office for meeting clients to claim a home-office tax deductions.

---

[1] Soliman v. Commissioner, 506 U.S. 168, 113 S.Ct. 701, 121 L.Ed.2d 634 (1993).

[2] § 932(a) of the Taxpayer Relief Act of 1997.

[3] I.R.C. § 280A(c)(1); 26 U.S.C. § 280A(c)(1).

[4] Cook v. Commissioner, T.C.M. 1997-378 (1997).

CHAPTER 19

Law Firm Structures

Chapter Contents

---

§ 19.01 Expanding Sphere of Operations

As a law firm expands its sphere of operations and considers peripheral activities (e.g., trust companies, real estate operations, etc.), additional organizational and operational decisions sometimes are needed. Law firms around the world are faced with the same basic issue; growth or no growth. Many firms opt for growth and focus their planning on expansion within the United States or internationally. Included in the decision matrix are considerations of what structure a firm should use, where it should practice law, how it will grow, and what other lines of business it should consider.

This Chapter discusses many of the growth considerations facing law firms from a tax perspective. Each decision may affect the manner in which the firm or its partners are taxed. The areas discussed include:

(1) Forms of doing business,
(2) Operations in multiple states and cities,
(3) Mergers and acquisitions,
(4) U.S. firms operating outside the United States,
(5) Non-U.S. Firms operating in the United States,
(6) Affiliation with other law firms,
(7) Multidisciplinary practice,
(8) Jurisdictional objections to firm structure.

§ 19.02 Forms of Doing Business

The basic decision facing a law firm is the form of business it will use to practice law. Traditionally, the form of choice has been that of a partnership—when two or more attorneys agree to practice law in an unincorporated business, to share profits or losses, and to be personally liable for all business debts. For various legal, ethical, economic, and practical reasons, some law firms have opted to do business in the corporate form—either as a professional service corporation ("PC") or as S Corporations. Limited liability companies and limited liability partnerships also are popular because of interest (if not the immediate need) in limiting the personal liabilities of partners.

This section highlights some of the important elements of each form of business, criteria for electing S Corporation Status, guidelines for incorporating a partnership, and application of check-the-box regulations.

[1]—Partnership Structure

From a tax perspective, depending on the size and practice area of a law firm, operating as a partnership provides the greatest operational flexibility. Partnerships can have an unlimited number of partners of different classes to meet their business needs (e.g., equity partners, salaried partners, of counsel).

Items of income, gains, losses, deductions, and credits that pass directly to partners based on their allocable shares[1] and special allocations are subject to tax at the partner level and generally not at the partnership level. If a partner is an individual, his or her share of firm profits are subject to individual income taxes. If the partner is a professional corporation, the corporation is subject to tax on its share of firm profits.

Operating in a partnership structure, a law firm might have local or city taxes that are assessed against the firm. For example, if a partnership operates in New York City, it is subject to an unincorporated business tax. If a firm does business in Philadelphia, there is a business profits tax that is assessed against the firm. There are similar taxes in Columbus, St. Louis, Detroit, Cleveland and others cities throughout the United States. In addition, there can be privilege type taxes that are assessed against the gross receipts or turnover of a law firm. Examples of these can be found in Washington D.C. and Los Angeles.

---

[1] IRC § 704(b); 26 U.S.C. § 704(b).

Partnerships that use the cash method of accounting for tax purposes, do not have to make year-end distributions other than for guaranteed payments so the administration of a partnership tends to be easier than that of a corporation. If a firm uses an accrual method of accounting, then guaranteed payments do not have to distributed before the end of the year. All current-year partnership profits are taxable to its partners in the year earned by the partnership, even if the profits are not distributed until the following year. A partner's allocable share of partnership income generally is subject to self-employment tax[2] although half of the self-employment tax is allowed as a deduction in calculating adjusted gross income.[3] Because partnerships are pass-through entities, partners generally have to file state tax returns (and pay tax) in each state or city in which their partnership does business. There is an exception to this rule for partners who operate as professional corporations. That is because a PC generally pays all distributions to it employee/owners before the end of the year and takes a deduction for the salary. If the PC partner worked only in Florida or Texas (where there is personal income tax), then its income would be zero, even if it had to file a tax return in a state in which its partnership did business. Unless the state is New York, which adds back income paid to corporate officers, the PC would escape state tax on its income.

If a law firm is large and operates internationally, then a partnership structure can be cumbersome and restricting. It can be cumbersome because each partner may have to file personal tax returns in each country in which the firm does business. Depending on the facts, this multiple filings can cause incremental double taxes. The administration and cost of global filings can make a partnership structure less desirous than say a corporate structure, if allowed. Operating as a global partnership can be restricting because it is common that non-Americans dislike the idea of filing U.S. tax returns - which is what they would have to do if they were an equity partner of a U.S. law firm.

With respect to mergers or acquisitions, operating in a partnership form provides greater flexibility. For example, it is easier and less expensive to liquidate a partnership because the only tax that applies is at the individual partner level.

---

[2] IRC § 1402(a); 26 U.S.C. § 1402(a). Self-employment tax is comprised of two taxes: (1) old age, survivor and disability insurance (OASDI) and (2) hospital insurance (HI). For 1999 and 2000, the OASDI tax rate is 12.40% (IRC § 1401(a); 26 U.S.C. § 1401(a) on the first $72,600 and $76,200 of self-employment income) and the HI tax is 2.90% (IRC § 1401(b); 26 U.S.C. § 1401(b)) on *all* self-employment income (the cap on HI income was removed for years beginning after December 31, 1993). See also, Social Security Admin. News Release October 19, 1999.

[3] IRC § 164(f)(1); 26 U.S.C. § 164(f)(1).

[2]—Corporate Structure

The most common reason to do business as a corporation is to limit liabilities resulting from non-malpractice-related matters. For this reason, partners in partnerships sometimes elect (if a partnership allows such an election) to be corporate partners (i.e., personal service corporations) instead of remaining individual partners.

Law firms electing to operate as corporations normally do so as a professional corporation (PC) also referred to as a qualified personal service corporation. A PC can have an unlimited number of shareholders, unless the entity elects S Corporation status.[4] To operate as a qualified personal service corporation, substantially all of the activities of the corporation must involve the practice of law. In addition, substantially all of the stock must be held directly or indirectly by employees performing legal services for the corporation[5]. The substantially all test is satisfied if a shareholder spends at least 95% of his or her time practicing law[6] Income earned by a corporation is subject to the normal corporate income tax rates, which, at the federal level, currently are lower than the highest individual rates.[7]

Like a partnership, a corporation may have to file a tax return in every state in which it does business. Since a corporation files its own state tax returns, officers/shareholders are not required to file tax returns in each state in which the corporation does business. Instead employee/owners are required to apportion their income to the states in which they did business on a days-in-days-out basis.

Instead of being partners, PC owners are employees/shareholders of the corporation. Salaries paid to employees/shareholders are subject to the normal payroll withholding tax requirements, including FICA and FUTA. Self-employment taxes do not apply. PCs also can deduct the cost of certain fringe benefits provided to their employees/shareholders, such as qualified transportation fringe benefits, qualified moving expenses and cafeteria plans, which are fringe benefit plans that allow participants to choose between taxable and nontaxable benefits. When the PC operates as an S Corporation, however, the fringe benefit rules applicable to partners, rather than corporate rules, apply to any shareholder owning more than 2% of the stock.[8]

---

[4] See discussion in § 19.02[3][c] *infra.*

[5] IRC § 448(d)(2); 26 U.S.C. § 448(d)(2).

[6] Reg. § 1.448-1T(e)(4); 26 C.F.R. § 1.448-1T(e)(4).

[7] IRC § §§ 1 and 11(b); 26 U.S.C. §§ 1 and 11(b), as amended by § 205 of the Economic Growth and Tax Relief Reconciliation Act of 2001. For 2001, a corporation's taxable income between $75,000 and $10,000,000 is taxed at 34%. For individuals filing a joint return, taxable income over $297,350 is taxed at 39.1%.

[8] IRC § 1372; 26 U.S.C. § 1372.

If distributions other than salaries are made to shareholders, they are considered dividends and are subject to a second level of tax—individual taxes. To avoid a corporate level tax, PCs try to make year-end compensation payments to minimize the income that is subject to federal and state corporate income taxes. The year-end distributions tend to cause more administrative effort and complexity than found under the partnership form. A PC operating as an S-Corporation must be careful to distribute profits to the partners in accordance with the ownership percentages of the shareholders, otherwise there is a risk of inadvertently terminating the firm's S election by violating the one class of stock requirement. If the election is terminated, the firm will be subject to corporate level tax and the partners will run the risk of the IRS determining that they have received excess compensation and having such compensation recategorized as a dividend.

Operating as a PC can complicate possible mergers or combinations, unless the other party is a corporation. Additionally, liquidating a PC can be more complicated and expensive, because there can be taxes at both the corporate and individual levels.

In situations where a PC operating as a C Corporation pays out all or most of its income as compensation and bonuses and no dividends are paid, there is a risk that the IRS will attempt to disallow a portion of the deduction as unreasonable compensation. Conversely, if the PC accumulates some of its earnings in order to make investments unrelated to its business, there is a risk that the IRS will attempt to subject the corporation to the accumulated earnings tax.

In the international environment, it might better administratively to operate as a corporation, but the laws of each country need to be considered because not all countries or bar associations allow lawyers to practice in corporate structures.

[3]—LLC or LLP Structure

In response to the desire to limit personal liability, two new forms of business organization have evolved which combine the flexibility of the partnership structure with the limited liability aspect of a corporation. The new structures are the limited liability company (LLC) and the limited liability partnership (LLP). The purpose of these entities is to limit a partner's/owner's personal liability to his or her own acts of negligence, malpractice or misdeeds and to protect them from another's negligence. For federal income tax purposes, these entities are treated as partnerships (i.e., the entity files a partnership tax return and its owners/partners received Schedule K-1s). Some states, e.g., New York and California, impose a tax or filing fee on LLPs and LLCs doing business within its borders.

Some complications exist at the state level, because not all states have enacted legislation authorizing the LLP structure e.g., Illinois. Some LLC legislation does not include LLP legislation.

Most state statutes are flexible enough to allow a law firm to tailor the terms of its LLC agreement to the needs of the firm (e.g., centralization of management or circumstances under which the business will be continued). Firms operating in more than one state have to be aware of possible inconsistencies and cognizant of changes in state LLC laws.

Large professional service partnerships had been concerned that the switch to an LLC would prevent them from maintaining the use of the cash basis of accounting. This is due to the fact that an LLC may have members who have an interest in profits, but who may not exercise any management control. This could potentially result in the LLC being classified as a tax shelter if more than 35% of the losses are allocated to these non-equity partners. A tax shelter is precluded from using the cash method of accounting. The Service has ruled, however, that a law firm partnership with equity and non-equity partners will not be precluded from forming an LLC and retaining the cash method of accounting.[9]

LLPs or LLCs that operate internationally face a hurdle of being able to practice law using the same structure, because not all countries understand the nuances of LLPs or LLCs. In France, for example, an LLP may be viewed as a partnership, but an LLC probably will be viewed as a corporation. In other countries, such as Australia, an LLP may not be allowed to operate at all. As more countries begin to understand more about LLPs and LLCs, there may be more acceptance of these structures so that law firms can operate transparently throughout the world.

[4]—Electing S Corporation Status

Prior to the advent of LLPs and LLCs some firms elected S Corporation status to maintain the benefits of flow-through taxation and limited personal liability.

A professional service corporation with no more than seventy-five stockholders can elect S Corporation status providing that all of the shareholders are individuals, estates, or certain types of trusts and are not non-resident aliens.[10] To avoid the seventy-five stockholder limit, it

---

[9] Ltr. Rul. 9426030 (July 1, 1994).

[10] IRC § 1361(b)(1); 26 U.S.C. § 1361(b)(1). For taxable years beginning before 1997, the maximum number of shareholders was thirty-five.

is possible to form a partnership of S Corporations with each S Corporation having no more than seventy-five stockholders[11] In addition, the electing corporation can only have one class of stock.[12] All shareholders must consent to the election,[13] which can be made any time during the preceding taxable year or no later than the fifteenth (15th) day of the third month of the start of the taxable year in which the election is effective.[14]

Operating as an S Corporation is similar to operating as a partnership, because income "passes through" the entity directly to the employees/shareholders who then report it on their own personal income tax returns.[15] Instead of receiving a distributive share of partnership income, employees/shareholders receive a combination of salaries and non-deductible "dividends." The salaries are subject to the normal payroll withholding requirements for both federal and state income tax purposes as well as social security taxes and unemployment taxes. The withholding reduces or minimizes the need for officers/shareholders to make quarterly estimated income tax payments. In an effort to minimize FICA and FUTA taxes, some firms have taken a reduced salary and an increased "dividend." The dividend is not subject to payroll taxes. While this can be a reasonable planning technique when properly used, some taxpayers have gotten greedy and paid a price. If the salary payments are not reasonable with respect to the income of the S Corporation earnings, the IRS will recategorize the "dividend" as wages and assess FICA and FUTA taxes.[16]

The distinction between wages and ordinary income can be important for state tax purposes. To the extent that a shareholder receives wages, he will pay state taxes in his state of residence and any states where he or she physically provides services. The ordinary income portion will, subject to the firm's business-allocation percentage, be subject to state taxes. However, if a shareholder allocates too much of his or her income to wages to avoid potentially higher state taxes, the state tax authorities can challenge the partners salary under their own version of the excess

---

[11] Rev. Rul. 94-43, I.R.B. 1994-27, 8 (July 5, 1994).

[12] IRC § 1361(b)(1)(D); 26 U.S.C. § 1361(b)(1)(D).

[13] IRC § 1362(a)(2); 26 U.S.C. § 1362(a)(2).

[14] IRC § 1362(b)(1); 26 U.S.C. § 1362(b)(1).

[15] IRC § 1366(a)(1); 26 U.S.C. § 1366(a)(1).

[16] See *Radtke v. Commissioner*, 712 F.Supp. 143 (1989) where partner in a sole proprietorship law firm declared that all of his income was in the form of a dividend. IRS reasoned that $0 compensation was not reasonable and assessed FUTA and FICA taxes. See also *Spicer Accounting, Inc., v. United States*, 918 F.2d 90 (9th Cir. 1990).

compensation rules. These rules in essence recategorize salary payments as ordinary income and subject the excess to tax based upon state allocation-percentage. Aside from the employment tax issue outlined above, the IRS will not care whether the shareholders compensation is treated as wages or ordinary income, because it is subject to U.S. income tax either way.

An electing S Corporation is not subject to the normal corporate federal income tax and does not file a corporate Form 1120. Instead, an S Corporation files a Form 1120S. An S Corporation, like a partnership, reports its items of income, gain, loss, deductions, and credits to its owners/stockholders.

In a situation where an existing PC has been operating as a C Corporation and wishes to elect to become an S Corporation, a corporate level tax may be imposed on "built-in-gains" and any accumulated earnings and profits of the corporation measured as of the effective date of the election. When the PC uses the cash method of accounting, its receivables and unbilled work will represent built-in-gains and can be taxed at the corporate level in the S Corporation's years during which the receivables and unbilled work are collected. Careful planning is needed to ameliorate the otherwise harsh results of this rule.

Not all states recognize S Corporation status. For those that do not, the corporation would have to file a regular corporate income tax return and pay applicable corporate income taxes.

The same issue exists internationally; most countries would tax an s Corporation as a regular corporation.

[5]—Incorporating a Partnership

For various reasons, a law firm practicing as a partnership might wish to incorporate. There are three alternative methods that a firm can use to incorporate:[17]

1. The partnership can transfer its assets to a PC in exchange for stock of the PC and the PC's assumption of the partnership's liabilities, if any. The partnership can then distribute the stock of the PC in liquidation to its partners.
2. The partnership can liquidate and distribute its assets and liabilities to its partners, who then contribute the same to the PC in exchange for stock of the PC. The partnership then liquidates.

[17] Rev. Rul. 84-111, 1984-2 C.B. 351.

3. The partners can contribute their interests in the partnership to the PC in exchange for stock of the PC. The partnership then liquidates.

In each of these scenarios, the partnership assets and liabilities are transferred to a corporation and the partnership dissolves. Generally, incorporation can be accomplished without adverse tax consequences if the partners of the discontinuing partnership are in control of the new corporation after the merger and partnership property is transferred solely in exchange for stock or securities of the corporation.[18] Control for tax purposes means that the transferring partners must own immediately after the transfer stock possessing at least 80% of the total combined voting power of all classes of stock entitled to vote and at least 80% of the total number of shares of all other classes of stock of the corporation.[19] However, if the amount of liabilities transferred exceeds the basis of the assets transferred, gain is recognized to the extent of the excess.[20] For purposes of this rule, when the partnership used the cash method of accounting, any liabilities which have not yet given rise to a deduction (i.e., accrued expenses) are ignored.

Any partner receiving stock solely in exchange for services will be taxed on the receipt of the shares.[21]

[6]—Choosing Between a Corporate Structure and a Partnership Structure

Most, but not all, U.S. law firms choose to operate as partnerships. Occasionally, a new firm will choose a corporate structure when it begins business or an existing law firm may decide to change its structure from a partnership to a corporation. Likewise, a law firm organized as a corporation may decide to change to a partnership structure on the belief that it would be easier to merge with another partnership. A well thought out decision should consider the relevant advantages and disadvantages of the structures prior to incorporation or restructuring as a partnership.

[a]—Advantages of Corporate Form Over Partnership Form

As previously mentioned, law firms must elect to operate as either a partnership or a corporation This section discussed some of the advantages of operating as a corporation.

---

[18] IRC § 351(a); 26 U.S.C. § 351(a).

[19] Treas. Reg. § 1.351-1(a)(1); 26 C.F.R. § 1.351-1(a)(1).

[20] IRC § 357(c)(1); 26 U.S.C. § 357(c)(1).

[21] IRC § 351(d)(1); 26 C.F.R. § 351(d)(1).

1. An employee/owner is taxed on what he or she receives during the year. A partner, however, is taxed on a share of the firm's income, including phantom income (i.e., the excess of taxable income over cash received during the year),

2. An employee/owner files tax returns where he or she render services, which generally is the state in which his or her office is located and the state in which her or she is resident, if different. A partner, however, has to file tax returns in any state in which the partnership conducted business, although electing to file composite returns mitigates this issue.

3. An employee/owners only pays FICA and FUTA and not self-employment tax. Partners pay self-employment tax.

4. An employee/owner is subject to normal payroll tax withholding, so his or her quarterly estimated tax payments often are eliminated or minimized. A partner, however, does not have payroll tax withholding and has to make quarterly estimated tax payments.

5. An employee/owner (other than one owning 2% or more of an S Corporation) can participate in employer-funded qualified pension plans (i.e., defined contribution plans and defined benefit plans). A partner is not allowed to participate in employer-funded plans.

6. An employee/owner can participate in all fringe benefit plans[22] of the law firm, but a partner is not allowed to participate in qualified moving expense fringe benefit, the qualified transportation fringe benefit, or the qualified retirement planning fringe benefit.

7. An employee/owner can participate in d a dependent care assistance program,[23] but a partner cannot.

8. An employee/owner can participate in cafeteria plans in which participants can choose among benefits of the plans (e.g., pre-tax medical insurance, pre-tax dental insurance, pre-tax life insurance). Partners are not allowed to participate in cafeteria plans.

9. An employee/owner's personal liability in a corporation is limited to his or her investment in the company stock. A partner in a general partnership has unlimited liability for act of the partnership and a partner in an LLP or an LLC has liability limited to the amount his or her capital in the firm. In some cases, lenders require personal liability for some debts, even if the debt would otherwise be limited because of the firm's structure.

10. An employee/owner is able to participate in a medical expense reimbursement[24] plan that provides annual physical exams,

---

[22] I.R.C. § 132; 26 U.S.C. § 132.
[23] I.R.C. § 129; 26 U.S.C. § 129.
[24] I.R.C. § 105; 26 U.S.C. § 105.

but a partner is not allowed to participate in such a plan without being taxed on the benefit.

11. There is less of a record-keeping burden in determining the basis of shares of stock than there is in determining the basis of a partnership interest (i.e., inside and outside basis).

12. An employee/ owner has a smaller chance of a tax audit for an employee who reports W-2 income than there is for a partner who may have significant adjustments to his partnership ordinary income. This is particularly true for law firms with more than 100 partners who must file the partners K-1's electronically for tax years beginning on January 1, 2000 and thereafter.

[b]—Disadvantages of Corporate Form Over Partnership Form

Although there are advantages for being an employee/owner over those for being a partner, there are disadvantages as well. Some of them are:

1. An employee/owner cannot deduct his or her unreimbursed business expenses "above the line." He or she must treat such expenses as an itemized deduction subject to the 2% AGI floor and potentially other limitations on itemized deduction.
2. An employee/owner generally is limited to predetermined compensation and a bonus that can be tied to the person's ownership in the corporation. A partner, however, has more flexibility in allocating and apportioning income among partners because similar "ownership" measurements and tests do not apply.
3. The employee/owner cannot take a deduction for one-half of self-employment taxes paid
4. An employee/owner cannot claim a deduction above the line for any portion of his or her medical insurance premiums, but a partner can.
5. Upon audit, an employee/owner who receives significant compensation runs a risk of having the IRS assert constructive dividends for excess compensation resulting in a second layer of federal tax. A partner is not subject to excess compensation issues.
6. An employee/owner of a law firm has a more difficult task of valuing his or her stock in a corporation, unless the corporation's stock is exchanged at par value. if that is the case, there can be hidden issues of goodwill. A partner generally does not have a problem valuing his or her interest in a partnership because it is accounted for through normal capital accounting procedures.

The observations made in this section about the advantages and disadvantages of being an employee/owner versus a partner are relevant for any firm beginning business, any firm considering a change in structure or any firm considering a merger with another firm structured differently. Careful consideration and weight should be given to these factors and others before a final decision is made.

[7]—Check-the-Box Regulations

The Treasury Department has recognized that occasionally state or non-US restrictions do not allow a partnership or LLC to operate as such for local tax and/or regulatory purposes. This often requires a partnership to be treated as a corporation in those jurisdictions and income earned in those jurisdictions would not be included in the firm's partnership tax return. Depending upon the type of entity required and/or selected in such jurisdictions Treasury has provided relief through the "check-the-box regulations.[25] The "check-the-box" regulations allow law firms practicing as LLCs or as corporations in various state and non-U.S. locations to be taxed as partnerships, for federal purposes. Under the regulation's, an LLC (or other "eligible corporation") is taxed as a partnership if it has two or more owners,[26] and is ignored for tax purposes - a so-called "tax nothing or disregarded entity" - if it has one owner. This often is referred to a single member LLC[27]—e.g., a lawyer practicing as a sole practitioner. By making an election, the owners of an LLC can choose to have their income taxed as if they were operating a partnership.[28]

Check-the-box applies to eligible corporations.[29] Generally, one judicial entity (the traditional corporation) in each country is identified in the regulations as a *per se* corporation[30] All other judicial entities can choose to be treated as either corporations or partnerships (or ignored, if they are single-owner) for U.S. tax purposes. In Germany, for example, the *AG* (the vehicle for public companies) is on the *per se* list, while the *GmbH* (the typical legal form of German subsidiaries of U.S. multinationals) is not, and therefore is an "eligible entity."

---

[25] Reg. § 301.7701-3(a); 26 C.F.R. 301.7701-3(a).

[26] Reg. § 301.7701-3(b)(1)(i).

[27] Reg. § 301.7701-3(b)(1)(ii).

[28] Reg. § 301.7701-3(c)(1)(I). The election is made by filing Form 8832 within 75 days after or 12 months before the selected effective date.

[29] Reg. § 301.7701-3(a)

[30] Reg. § 301.7701-2(b)(8)

In the U.S., if an LLC is treated as a partnership for federal income tax rules, then all states except Texas treat an LLC as a partnership for state tax purposes.[31]

Like an S Corporation or a limited partnership, an LLC offers both limited liability to its owners (called "members") and a single level of taxation at the member level. However, the LLC does not impose the restrictions on shareholders that an S Corporation does and does not require a general partner as a limited partnership.

---

[31] CCH EXP, MC IT GUIDE ¶65, Limited Liability Companies.

§ 19.03 Structures of U.S. Firm Operating Outside the United States

There is a belief that has developed during the late 1990s that suggests that there will be only about ten international law firms in the world within ten to fifteen years. The belief is founded on the perception that clients will reduce the number of law firms that provide legal services to them and will demand global service from those law firms on their short lists. This belief has fueled growth plans for some U.S. law firms and has spurred international growth plans.

There are many factors that need to be considered when deciding on a structure for operating outside the United States. Some of these include how the foreign partners will view their association with the U.S. firm in various structures, how local regulations will control the practice of law in the foreign jurisdiction, what bar restrictions will prohibit a firm from practicing law in a particular country, and liability issues.

The ultimate decision on what form of business to use in non-U.S. offices will depend on many factors and the type of practice to be established. The factors often are fluid and need to be updated with each decision tree. This section discusses some of the important structural considerations in connection with global expansion.[1]

[1]—Branch Structure

In establishing a non-U.S. presence, U.S. law firms generally will operate in the foreign location as a branch of the U.S. firm. Some foreign countries, however, do not recognize the partnership form of business and will treat the U.S. branch as a corporation for local tax purposes (e.g., Czech Republic, Russia, Hungary). Other times, a law firm will set up a separate corporation to do business when tax or regulatory conditions make it more advantageous to operate through a corporate structure.

In some circumstances, it is possible to form a corporation and then, using the check-the-box regulations, elect to have the entity treated as a partnership for U.S. tax purposes[2] unless the entity is on the *per se* list.[3]

---

[1] See Chapter 20 for a discussion of tax considerations for law firms practicing in the international arena.

[2] Treas. Reg. § 301.7701-3(a); 26 C.F.R. § 301.7701-3(a).

[3] Treas. Reg. § 301.7701-2(b)(8); 26 C.F.R. § 301-7701-2(b)(8).

If a firm has one or more offices in foreign countries and wants to admit a foreign national without subjecting him or her to U.S. taxation, the firm might consider forming a local partnership (if allowed) and admitting the foreign national to that partnership. The U.S. firm could be the local firm's general partner, so that it maintained control of the local office and was able to share its profits with other partners of the firm. For financial accounting and tax purposes, the local office would be a branch office of the U.S. firm, but the foreign national partner, only being a partner of the local firm, would not have any U.S. filing requirements, because he or she is not a partner of the U.S. firm.

If a foreign national partner became an equity partner of a U.S. firm, he or she would be subject to the same U.S. reporting requirements (and state tax filing requirements) as their American partners. The profits of the foreign partnership would be distributable to both the foreign partner and the U.S. partnership (as general partner) based on their allocable partnership shares. The U.S. partnership could then distribute its share of foreign profits to U.S. partners.

If a firm operates as one global firm through branch offices, every equity partner is required to file a U.S. tax return. Conversely, all U.S. partners may be required to file returns in most, if not all, of the jurisdictions where the firm conducts its international business. The amount of income upon which a non-resident partner is taxed in the U.S. is based upon the percentage of global profits derived in the U.S. This is known as effectively connected income. Non-resident partners are subject to withholding by the firm on their effectively connected income and must file U.S. tax returns to get refunds of amounts withheld that exceed their U.S. tax liability.

US partners are taxed on 100% of their global income. As mentioned above, U.S. partners will most likely have to file income tax returns in various foreign jurisdiction. However some jurisdictions provide for the filing of composite returns (e.g., Belgium or in some cases England) and others require an entity level tax (e.g., Czech Republic, Hungary, Turkey and Hong Kong). Those jurisdictions that have an entity level tax do so either because they do not recognize the partnership as a form of business or because they impose a branch tax.

[2]—Hybrid Global Partnership

A hybrid global partnership is a structure consisting of one or more partnerships that effectively operate as a single global firm, but locally operate as distinct legal entities. An example of a hybrid global partnership is the U.K.'s multinational partnership (MNP), which allows solicitors to share profits with U.S. partners, while not actually being in partnership with them. Under U.K. rules the MNP allows solicitors to partner with some U.S. partners while maintaining a position that it is a separate partnership. As long as the U.S. firm controls the MNP and shares profits with the MNP, however, the IRS probably will view the MNP as a branch office.

The actual structure used in a particular country may be influenced by non-tax and non-accounting factors such as local bar rules or other regulatory restrictions. Regardless of the actual structure a firm uses, it must be aware of the tax rules, bar rules, and any other legal requirements to doing business in every jurisdiction that it intends to enter.

[3]—Umbrella Structure

During the past several years, there has been a growing trend among large law firms to expand through merger into other markets, rather then building practices through more traditional means. As firms expand across national and continental borders, they sometimes consider structures that are not traditional structures for law firms. One such structure that is eliciting the focus of law firm management is the umbrella structure. Large, multinational law firms have viewed the umbrella structure as a way to resolve some of their more difficult organizational and administrative problems.

Umbrella structures have been in existence for over twenty-five years and have been used mainly by public accounting firms. One of the main purposes of an umbrella structure is to allow an organization to enjoy the benefits of a global partnership while restricting the jurisdictions in which its partners have to file tax returns.

An umbrella structure can take different forms. Conceptually, the underlying principle is to have a group of member law firms operate under the advise and consent of a corporate entity. Each member firm operates in a particular country or region and has agreements in place with the corporate entity under which they agree to follow a common standard to grow the network of member firms. One of the biggest benefits to using an umbrella structure firm is that each partner only files tax returns within his or her country or region of residence.

An alternative to using a corporate entity is to have contractual agreements between member firms, but those agreements can make it easier to argue that the network is global firm.

The governance entity (i.e., the corporate entity) and cost sharing agreements between the member firms and the governance entity or service corporation provide for the sharing of common expenses between the member firms. There are significant limitations placed upon the member firms and the governance entity, neither one can be used to share profits or exercise control over the group. The governance entity can do no more than advise the member firms. If the profit sharing or control elements are present, the firm will open itself up to scrutiny from the IRS.

Some have criticized an umbrella structure by saying that the IRS would not approve it and that members of the network will have to file tax returns throughout the world. They reason that it looks and operates too much like a global partnership Like many structural decisions, the merits or those for and against an umbrella structure should be viewed academically and practically. Most importantly, a law firm's specific facts and circumstances should be considered when evaluating the merits and viability of an umbrella structure.

§ 19.04 Non U.S. Firms Operating in the United States

Several non-U.S. law firms subscribe to the idea that there will fewer international law firms in the future and that those that survive will have to have vibrant offices in England/Europe, Southeast Asia and the United States.

Foreign law firms have shown an interest in opening offices in the U.S. to serve existing clients doing business in the U.S. Opening an office in the United States, however, can cause unexpected tax filing requirements for foreign partners. This section reviews some of the important structural matters that need to be considered before opening an office in the U.S.

Several structures are available to a foreign firm practicing law in the U.S. The advantages or disadvantages of a U.S. branch of the foreign partnership versus a professional service corporation should be considered.

A local branch of a foreign partnership will be treated as a partnership for U.S. income tax purposes. Although the operations are described as a branch, the "branch tax" would not apply, because it is only imposed on branches of foreign corporations.[1] For U.S. income tax purposes, a partnership is a transparent entity that is not subject to U.S. income taxes, although all of its partners must file U.S. and state income tax returns. Unless a person is a citizen of the U.S., a resident of the U.S. or a "green card" holder, a foreign partner is subject to tax in the U.S. only on his or her effectively connected net income. Generally, effectively connected income is income earned in the United States.

Income tax treaties often help in easing the filing requirements for non-resident aliens. If a provision of a U.S. treaty with a foreign government regarding the filing requirements of non-resident partners conflicts with U.S. law, the treaty can be relied on, with disclosure, to avoid the requirement. Many treaties contain a so-called "waters-edge election" which can be used to account for income that is subject to tax in the U.S. Under this election, income is allocated to the office that a person is assigned to instead of where the work was done. Administratively, this method is easier to apply because many law firms use the same method to allocate its income to individual offices. By making this election, a firm reports income attributable to people assigned to offices in the United States, regardless of where they worked. For example, if a lawyer is assigned to a Chicago office and works twenty-five percent of his or her time outside of the United States, then all of fee income

---

[1] IRC § 884(a); 26 U.S.C. § 884(a).

(less expenses) of that person would be sourced to the U.S. for tax purposes. If a corporation is formed to undertake the U.S. activities, it will be required to the file a corporate income tax return, Form 1120. In addition, the firm will have to file Form 5472, Information Return of a 25% Foreign-Owned U.S. Corporation or a Foreign Corporation Engaged in a U.S. Trade or Business. Form 5472 requires disclosure of the identity of the corporation's owner and any financial transactions between the corporation and the foreign related party. Unlike a partnership, the corporate entity will be subject to a corporate tax rate of up to 35%.[2]The corporation may have a percentage of its interest deduction (if any) disallowed if the non-U.S. firm loans money to the corporation or guarantees any debts of the corporation.[3] If the firm earns any capital gains on firm investments such gains will be taxed at the regular corporate tax rate rather than the preferential individual capital gains rates.[4]

Any distributions to the foreign partnership will be subject to a dividend-withholding tax to the extent the corporation is considered to have earnings and profits for U.S. tax purposes. The withholding tax rate is 30% or such lesser rate as may be provided by a tax treaty. The dividend-withholding tax imposes a second layer of taxation that is not present when operating as a partnership. The advantage of the U.S. corporation is that it eliminates the burden associated with non-resident partners filing individual non-resident U.S. tax returns. Whether it is efficient for the firm to organize its U.S. operation as a corporation depends, in part, upon a balancing of the following factors:

(1) projected U.S. office revenues and exposure to possible dividend withholding tax; and

(2) the desire to avoid the administrative burden associated with filing U.S. income tax returns for members of the firm.

---

[2] IRC § 11(b); 26 U.S.C. § 11(b). The corporation tax rate of 34% applies to taxable income that exceeds $75,000 but is less than $10 million. If taxable income exceeds $10 million the tax rate is 35%.

[3] IRC § 163(j); 26 U.S.C. § 163(j).

[4] IRC § 1(h); 26 U.S.C. § 1(h).

19.05 Operations in Multiple States and Cities

Law firms with offices located in several cities or states must choose an appropriate method of determining income (and each partner's share thereof) for each taxing jurisdiction.

[1]—Income Allocation Methods

Generally, states specify how income will be allocated. One method of allocating income is to account for income and expenses by office. This method is commonly referred to as the "separate accounting" or the "separate-books-and-records" method. Creating and utilizing this type of system is often time-consuming and expensive. It involves developing procedures for capturing and allocating individual items of fee revenue, direct expenses, and indirect expenses. This system also has to be able to accommodate transfers between offices for inter-office work and accept charge-backs when less than 100% of a receivable is collected. In addition, if expenses (e.g., home office accounting costs, tax preparation fees for the firm) are paid by one office but benefit all offices, this method should be capable of allocating overhead items in a rational manner.

In the absence of separate books and records, the method used most frequently to apportion income and expenses among offices is the three-factor apportionment formula. This method takes into account the relationship of certain activity in each state to the total. Normally, the activities measured are property (e.g., depreciable tangible property and real property—including leasehold improvements), revenue and payroll. Unfortunately, there are no uniform definitions for income or expenses comprising the three-factor formula. There is a growing tendency among states to double weight the sales factor, which increases the business allocation factor in those states having a sales factor greater than the property or payroll factors. Some states use gross assets instead of depreciated assets and others force sales to be attributed to the home state if a firm does not file a return in a state to which it allocates income. Each variation of the standard three-factor formula causes inconsistencies among different states' formulas and can result in a law firm allocating more or less than 100% of its income to appropriate states.

[2]—Determining Presence and Nexus

Each state's rules for determining nexus—business contact or presence in a state—vary, and depend on the amount and type of contact a law firm partnership has with a particular state. Many states consider a law firm to be doing business in a state if it provides professional services within that state. (e.g., handles a matter like a trial in that state). If a firm is considered to be doing business in a state it has nexus with that state and should allocate some of its income to that state. Unlike sellers of tangible property, which generally have to have an office in a state to be subject to that state's taxes, law firms only have to render professional services within a state to be judged to have nexus in the state. There are few, if any, states which have established *de minimis* rules that permit a law firm to escape taxation when it provides professional services within a state. If a law firm is determined to be doing business in a state, its partners may be responsible for filing their own nonresident personal income tax returns in that state. For convenience, some states allow nonresident partners to be included in a combined or group nonresident income tax return.

[3]—Sales Taxes on Library and Equipment Purchases

Law firms should be aware that states and cities are becoming more aggressive in identifying firms that may be doing business in their jurisdictions. The purpose of the attention is to determine if law firms should be on the sales or use tax rolls (or, as mentioned earlier, if its partners should be filing tax returns in the state).

Several states have conducted sales and compensating use tax examinations of law firms to determine if they should self-assess use tax on information services, supplies, computer equipment, furniture, equipment, etc. that may have been purchased from out-of-state vendors. In the event of an assessment for sales or use tax on prior years' purchases, law firms may not be able to charge their clients for the tax where the disbursement related to a client matter, because the matter which gave rise to the tax may have been previously billed. Also, some sales or use tax assessments may need to be capitalized in the year paid if they relate to capital expenditures that were capitalized in a prior year.

For example, a patent law firm pays an out-of-state company for a computer-based search report that the firm uses in a legal opinion. Assuming the search company had no nexus in the state in which the law firm is located, it probably would not have charged sales or use tax on the report. Some states consider the report an information service which is subject to sales or use tax. Several years later when the matter is closed, the firm could be audited by the state or city and assessed use tax. More than likely, it is too late to bill the client, so the assessment becomes the law firm's expense.

Tracking purchases that might be subject to sales or use tax can be an irritant; however, firms should be aware that, with proper accounting, costs that relate to purchases on behalf of clients can be billed to the clients. Sales and use taxes should be viewed from the perspective that they are part of the cost of doing business in some cities and states.

[4]—Sales Taxes on Professional Services

A few state legislatures have considered imposing a sales tax on professional services. Three states enacted legislation, only to have it subsequently repealed.[1] This is an area to watch for further developments.

[5]—Personal Property Tax

Another way that various jurisdictions are raising revenue is through personal property taxes. Generally, items such as furniture and equipment, software, and some leasehold improvements are subject to personal property tax. The depreciable lives and methods required to be used to calculate depreciation often differ from the methods used for federal income tax purposes.

Law firms should periodically perform physical inventories of their personal property and reconcile the results to their personal property tax returns to ensure that they are not paying tax on previously retired or sold assets.

---

[1] Florida and Massachusetts would have subjected all professional services to sales tax and Connecticut would have taxed tax preparation services.

§19.06 Merger Considerations

There are myriad reasons why law firms consider merging. Some of the more common are to provide better client service, to increase or establish a market presence in a particular city, to expand into new specialties, to reduce redundant administrative expenses and overhead, and to compete more effectively by increasing the size of the firm.

The term "merger" has many connotations. Lawyers use the term generically to refer to the combination of two or more law practices. From a tax perspective, a merger implies the combination of a smaller firm into a larger one and the subsequent disappearance of the smaller firm.

Depending on the structures of the merging firms, there may be tax consequences associated with a merger. In addition, if the merging entities use different methods of accounting (e.g., modified-cash method vs. accrual method or expensing client disbursements versus capitalizing them as receivables), the accounting methods that must be used by the continuing entity need to be determined. If the discontinuing entity is on a fiscal year-end, its partners/shareholders may have a problem with bunching of taxable income in the year of the merger, that is, more than twelve months of income would be included in the partners'/shareholders' individual income tax returns.

In addition to focusing on economic and business-related issues, law firms should analyze the prospective merger from a tax perspective to avoid or mitigate possible adverse tax consequences.

Some of the tax results from four types of merger scenarios are discussed in the following paragraphs.

[1]—Partnership Merges into Partnership

Frequently, one partnership transfers its assets and liabilities to another partnership. The Internal Revenue Code provides that in the case of a merger or consolidation of two or more partnerships, the resulting partnership shall be construed to be the continuation of the merging partnership whose members own more than 50% of the capital and profits of the resulting partnership.[1] The taxable year of the discontinuing partnership is considered terminated. Also, the discontinuing partnership must file its final federal and state income tax returns as of the date of the merger.[2]In this type of merger, the transferred assets retain the same tax basis. The tax accounting methods to be used by the resulting partnership are those of the partnership which is construed as continuing.

---

[1] IRC § 708(b)(2)(A); 26 U.S.C. § 708(b)(2)(A).

[2] IRC § 706(c); 26 U.S.C. § 706(c).

If the members of the merging partnership do not have more than a 50% interest in either the capital or profits of the resulting partnership, all merged partnerships are terminated.[3]

The Treasury department's amendment to the IRC § 708 regulations prescribes two distinct forms which a merger can take; the assets-over form and the assets-up form.[4] In an assets-over merger, the terminated partnership contributes all of its assets and liabilities to the successor partnership in exchange for an interest in the successor partnership. Immediately thereafter, the terminating partnership distributes interests in the successor partnership to its partners in liquidation of their partnership interests in the terminated partnership.[5]

An assets-up merger occurs when the terminating partnership transfers the assets up to the partners who then contribute the assets to the successor partnership in exchange for a partnership interest.[6]

[2]—Partnership Merges into PC

The three methods used to incorporate a partnership[7]can be used to merge a partnership into a PC. Generally, no gain or loss is recognized if a partnership transfers its assets and liabilities to a PC solely in exchange for stock, if immediately after the exchange the contributing partners are in control of the PC.[8] Control is defined as the ownership of stock possessing at least 80% of the total combined voting power of all classes of stock entitled to vote and at least 80% of the total number of shares of all other classes of stock of the PC.[9] If, however, Code Section 351 applies, but liabilities exceed the basis of the assets transferred to the PC, then some gain will be recognized[10].

Frequently, when a partnership "merges" into a PC the partners do not attain the requisite 80% control of the continuing entity. As a result, the nonrecognition of income provisions of Code Section 351 do not apply, so the transaction is considered to be a sale or exchange for tax purposes. Gain may be recognized to the extent that the fair market value of the assets transferred and liabilities assumed exceed their tax basis. Said differently, gain is equal to the difference between the value of the stock received and the net assets transferred. For a law

---

[3] Treas. Reg. § 1.708-1(c)(1); 26 C.F.R §1.708-1(c)(1)
[4] Treas. Reg. § 1.708-1(c)(3); 26 C.F.R § 1.708-1(c)(3).
[5] Treas. Reg. § 1.708-1(c)(3)(i); 26 C.F.R §1.708-1(c)(i).
[6] Treas. Reg. § 1.708-1(c)(3)(ii); 26 C.F.R §1.708-1(c)(ii).
[7] See § 19.02 [5]*supra.*
[8] IRC § 351(a); 26 U.S.C. § 351(a).
[9] IRC § 368(c); 26 U.S.C. § 368(c).
[10] IRC § 357(c); 26 U.S.C. § 357(c).

firm using the cash method of accounting, the assets transferred include those assets recorded on the partnership's balance sheet (e.g., furniture, fixtures, equipment, leasehold improvements, cash, client disbursements, prepaid assets, investments and miscellaneous assets) plus the fair market value of other unrecorded assets, such as accounts receivable and work-in-process, which presumably have a zero tax basis.

Liabilities generally include all liabilities shown on the balance sheet.

If accounts receivable, work-in-process, and other zero-basis assets are left in the partnership, then other tax issues must be addressed, such as lack of continuing business activities and *de facto* liquidation.

[3]—PC Merges into PC

A merger of a PC into a PC can qualify as a statutory merger under Section 368(a)(1) of the Internal Revenue Code, so that there would be no gain recognized on the merger, except to the extent that money or property is exchanged for stock.

[4]—PC Merges into Partnership

There is no easy way to "merge" a PC into a partnership. This type of transaction will usually be construed as a liquidation of the PC and will cause tax consequences at both the corporate and shareholder levels.

If a PC liquidates and contributes *all* of its assets and liabilities to a partnership, its shareholders become partners in the partnership and the corporation will recognize gain equal to the excess of the fair market value of its assets over the PC's adjusted basis in those assets. For a cash basis law firm, assets such as accounts receivable, work-in-process, and client lists (all presumably with a tax basis of zero) must be valued at market. In addition, the shareholders would recognize gain on the difference between the net value of the property distributed and their basis in the stock of the PC.

If, instead, the PC itself became a partner in the partnership and continued doing business as a PC partner until all the shareholders retired, the tax problems could be lessened. However, stockholders in a merged PC normally want to be partners in the partnership.

To avoid recognition of gain on the transfer of zero-basis assets such as accounts receivable and work-in-process, a PC might consider retaining those assets until collected and then distributing the proceeds to the PC shareholders. Depending on how long it takes to collect the receivables, this alternative may be technically more difficult to structure and support, particularly if the PC is not considered to be an operating business. If the PC is construed as not doing business, there would be a *de facto* liquidation and distribution that would result in the same tax consequence as discussed in the preceding paragraphs.

[5]—Tax Accounting for Merger-Related Costs

At some point during the merger process, it will be necessary to account for the merger-related costs. For purposes of this section, merger-related costs are expenditures that are incurred during the process to identify a law firm with which to merge, to do due diligence with respect to that firm, to negotiate the deal, and to close the deal through completion of the required documents. Depending on the type of merger, these costs can be significant, especially if the costs were incurred in connection with a merger of international law firms. The accounting treatment of merger-related costs for financial statement purposes may differ from the tax accounting principles discussed in this section.

The most difficult task in accounting for merger-related costs from a tax perspective is categorizing them. Merger-related costs may be ordinary and necessary business expenses deductible under IRC Section 162, deferred expenses that are start-up costs under IRC Section 195, or capitalized costs under IRC Section 263. Unfortunately, there are no bright-line tests that make categorization any easier. Misclassifying these costs, however, can have a significant effect on a firm's ordinary income because Section 162 costs are deductible currently, Section 195 costs are amortizable over no less than sixty months, and Section 263 costs generally are not deductible.

To qualify as an ordinary and necessary business expense, a merger-related expenditure first must be incurred in the expansion of an existing business (e.g., merger with another existing law firm), and not be a cost that is in the nature of a capital item. Although a detailed discussion of the difference between ordinary and necessary costs and those that are capital in nature is beyond the scope of this section, a simple example may illustrate the distinction. Costs incurred by a law firm to identify merger targets in another city are probably ordinary and necessary business expenses, because the investigation was broad-based and did not focus specifically on a single firm. However, costs incurred to perform due diligence with respect to a specific target after the partners or shareholders of each firm voted their intention to merge are probably capital costs if the merger takes place. There may be a wide gulf between the time when the preliminary investigatory costs are incurred and the time when the deal closes. The categorization of costs during that time period depends on the facts and circumstances at the time the costs are incurred.

The other category of merger-related costs is referred to as Section 195 costs or "start-up" costs. Congress enacted IRC Section 195 [11] as a means of ending contentious litigation over the deductibility of costs incurred during the process of acquiring a business. Essentially, the Code section carved out a category of costs defined as "start-up expenditures" and provided that these costs would be amortized over a period of not less than sixty months. Eligible start-up expenditures are investigatory expenses or start-up costs related to the creation or acquisition of a new trade or business, which would be currently deductible if incurred in the operation or expansion of an existing trade or business. The House and Senate Committee reports explained that eligible investigatory costs are those "incurred in reviewing a prospective business *prior to reaching a final decision* to acquire or to enter that business.[12] The challenge is distinguishing between investigatory expenses, which are eligible for deferral under Section 195, and acquisition costs, which must be capitalized.

Legislative history and rulings from the Internal Revenue Service give guidance on how to distinguish costs by creating a "whether" and "which" test.[13] Simply stated, the whether and which test provides that expenses that relate to a decision *whether* to purchase or merge with a new business and "which" business to purchase are investigatory costs and are subject to deferral under Section 195 as start-up expenditures. Once a law firm votes to acquire a business, costs incurred after that point for appraisal of assets, an in-depth review of the target's books and records, and drafting documents are capital in nature.

Section 195 defuses potential arguments about whether an expenditure is currently deductible or if it can be recognized over a period of at least sixty months. Understanding what costs qualify for favorable treatment rather than being capital in nature is very fact intensive and requires a complete understanding of the circumstances in which the expenditures are incurred.

It is important to note that Section 195 only applies when a law firm is considering acquiring a business that is not an existing law firm. If a law firm is targeting an existing law firm, then costs associated with the merger or acquisition are not eligible for deferral under Section 195 and are either currently deductible as ordinary and necessary expenses or are capital in nature.

---

[11] Miscellaneous Revenue Act of 1980.

[12] See pp. 10 and 11 of the House Report and pp. 11 and 12 of the Senate Report.

[13] *Id.*, See also: Rev. Rul. 99-23, I.R.B. 1999-20,17 (May 17, 1999); Rev. Rul. 77-254, 1977-2 C.B. 63.

§ 19.07 Law Firm Affiliation

Very few law firms have the resources to operate in every state or in every country where their clients have offices or need legal assistance. Additionally, not all firms have adopted the philosophy that a merger will solve all of their problems. Many times the need to have legal representation or legal resources where a law firm does not practice requires a law firm to engage a local attorney to do the work. While seeking one-off relationships may be desirable to some firms, this may not allow proper time to explore the qualifications and competencies of the assisting lawyers.

A growing trend in the legal profession is to form professional associations or affiliations, either nationally or globally. Operating through affiliations is one way to continue providing client service, while not incurring the costs associated with opening a new office to respond to the need or merging with another firm. Forming an affiliation allows member firms to interview each other to understand the capabilities, quality control, and culture of the other firm. Once established, an affiliation provides member firms with the ability to have a trusted professional in another city assisting his or her client. It also provides each participating firm the ability to generate additional revenue by handling matters for other affiliated firms. Some firms use this type of arrangement as a trial marriage prior to entering into merger discussions. If the affiliation works, then merger talks might be the next step. If not, unnecessary time and expense have not been incurred.

Before entering into an affiliation, firm management needs to know that there are risks associated with entering into an affiliation that each firm needs to be aware of. Not all may be as it seems. Some unscrupulous attorneys may use the affiliation as a chance to "steal" clients or may try to generate work from their affiliate rather than reciprocate.

Perhaps the biggest benefit of a well-planned affiliation is that it allows small to mid-size firms to grow with their clients, rather than losing the client when they expand into new markets. For example, if Firm A, a Denver mid-size law firm with offices in Colorado and Montana needs legal advice on Minnesota law for one of its clients, a partner in firm A can pick up the phone and call his affiliate in Minnesota. Firm A did not have to start interviewing suitable attorneys in Minnesota. Accordingly the client does not undergo any undue delay and the partner in Firm A has the piece of mind knowing that an attorney meeting his standards in the other jurisdiction will service his client. The client is satisfied and the affiliate has received additional work.

Other benefits inherent in an affiliation are the ability to have periodic conferences to keep other offices up to date on important issues in a particular locality, so that clients with offices in those locality are being adequately serviced. The affiliated firms can advertise as such, thereby increasing their own marketability. An international affiliation allows member firms to exchange staff and creates expertise in new specialties. Other types of affiliations which could be formed, could focus on niche-specialty areas—for example a patent firm may want to form an affiliation with a tax boutique firm to bolster its current practice. Member firms may also be able to use their expanded resources to develop training programs to educate non-clients and perhaps increase their existing client base. Firm websites can list affiliated firms so that users can understand the breadth of services available to them.

§ 19.08 Multidisciplinary Practice

There are few topics that elicit as many unbridled reactions or emotions as a discussion of the place of multidisciplinary practices in the United States. Some commentators believe that these firms will be a reality in time, while others will do everything they can to stop them from taking hold in the U.S.

By definition, in a multidisciplinary practices (or MDPs), lawyers practice as part of an organization with other professionals, such as certified public accountants, real estate consultants, and architects, with shared ownership. In practice, MDPs take many forms, in part to conform to rules regarding the practice of law in various countries and jurisdictions, and in part to achieve the goals of the parties.

Europe is ten years ahead of the United States in implementing MDPs. MDPs in Europe and elsewhere have taken the form of the Big Five accounting firms acquiring or establishing strategic alliances with quality - sometimes quite big - law firms. As a result of these transformations, all Big Five now style themselves as professional service firms.

These acquisitions and alliances are intended to serve clients more efficiently with "one-stop shopping." In theory, all the services needed to complete complex financial transactions can be handled by one professional organization. Obviously the downside is that not all one-stop-shopping provides the highest quality service and the most knowledgeable professionals-something that all clients want and need. The fact that Europe has taken the lead on implementing MNPs allows American law firms to benefit from European experiences - good or bad.

The laws on MDPs in the various countries vary widely. For example, Germany has long permitted lawyers and tax accountants to practice together. The United Kingdom, on the other hand, has an absolute ban on MDPs. Although, this has not prevented the Big Five from achieving much the substance of MDPs with major UK law firms through contractual arrangements and strategic alliances.

In the United States, the states and the District of Columbia set their individual rules for the practice - fifty-one sets of rules. The American Bar Association has had serious debates on the subject for several years and several years ago voted down a subcommittee report that would have opened the door for MDPs in the U.S. The subcommittee is reconsidering its proposal and may address the issue again. At this point, its recommendation has not cast in stone.

If the ABA approves MDPs, then states have to weigh in on one side or the other. If states take act, it is likely that MDP legislation will not be uniform from state-to-state.

New York State recently enacted MDP legislation. It allows lawyers to conduct or own non-legal businesses and to engage in contractual relationships that include allocation of costs. This permits strategic alliances, but does not permit non-lawyer ownership. Other bar associations are edging toward MDPs, but require at least majority ownership by lawyers.

A likely beneficiary will be boutique, specialty firms. For example, a firm specializing in environmental law might join with environmental consultants and engineers.

A major argument for MDP is that the substance will be achieved via contractual arrangements and strategic alliances even if rules prohibiting MDPs are left on the books. For example, one of the Big Five recently completed a strategic alliance with a firm specializing in tax work in Washington, D.C., albeit the rules in Washington D.C. are more liberal than other jurisdictions.

In pure MDPs, firms may be restricted by conflict of interest rules. For example, if a lawyer handles the public offering for a new security, the accounting division of the firm would not be able to perform any of the auditing functions. Or, if the accounting arm represents a client, will the law firm be prohibited from representing another company because of that relationship? Another issue is how to handle firm management. For example, if the managing partner in an MDP is a CPA, how much input could he or she have in the management of the legal practice? Does the issue change if the managing partner is an attorney who has not practiced law, but rather spent his career with a large accounting firm?

These are a smattering of the issues that must be addressed before the MDP can become a fully integrated concept. For now, the profession is in a wait-and-see mode.

CHAPTER 20

Global Operations

Chapter Contents

---

§ 20.01 Globalization of Law Firms

Multinational companies are expanding nationally and internationally - often by merger and acquisition. The incentive is survival. In many industries, the size needed to compete (and, therefore, to survive) is much larger than it used to be. to And these far-larger and far-more-global companies are demanding worldwide service from their service providers. This has put pressure on the service providers to provide critical mass, not just outposts, in many locations around the world. Clients increasingly expect their law firms to provide seamless service around the world. Traditionally, many firms have relied on alliances with quality local firms to supply quality legal services to their clients abroad, but, more and more, firms are merging with foreign firms so that they can, in effect, supply these services themselves. The major law firms also are responding by sending larger numbers of partners and associates abroad to beef-up existing branches or to add American expertise to merger partners. That there is a need for global expansion, and rewards if it is done right is the good news. But ill-conceived and ill-executed domestic expansion has been disastrous for many U.S. firms. Foreign expansion has all the risks of domestic expansion, plus additional risks and considerations. For example some risks are:

1. Communications can be expensive and frustrating. In many major cities, getting telephone service takes far longer, is far more expensive, and is far less reliable than what we are used to in the United States. Communications also will be hampered by time-zone differences. The East Coast of the U.S. is five hours behind London and six hours behind the rest of Western Europe. U.S. and Pacific Rim offices have little or no overlap of regular daytime office hours. It is a rare U.S. lawyer who is not handicapped if he/she does not type well enough and is not computer literate enough to compose and send e-mail messages. If he/she has frequent communications with colleagues in distant time zones, the handicap is more serious.
2. Language will be a consideration if the branch is not in a country whose first language is English. English is widely spoken in many countries as a second language, and it is true that English-only American tourists can get along pretty well in the major cities in which an American law firm is likely to open a branch. But American lawyers will not be able to communicate with some clients is they don't speak the local language and, in any event, will be hampered professionally and socially. Depending on the type of practice a firm has, it is likely that it will be necessary to have a good number of bilingual secretaries and support staff if they, too, must communicate with the U.S. home office.

---

[1] See Chapter 20.02[2] and [18] for discussion of registering to do business in another country and bar restrictions.

3. Local customs and labor laws should be determined before you invest too much time and money investigating establishing a branch. For example, many countries have far more public holidays than the U.S., mandatory vacations of five or six weeks, severe limits on hours that can be worked each week, and severe restrictions on staff reductions. Workplace customs also should be investigated.

4. Restrictions on the practice of law should also be investigated.[1]

This chapter discusses considerations for:

- U.S.-based law firms doing business outside of the United States,
- Non-U.S.-based law firms doing business in the United States,
- Tax considerations for partners and associates on assignments outside the United States,
- Foreign tax credits,
- Moving expenses,
- Withholding taxes,
- Social security liability, and
- Totalization agreements

§ 20.02 U.S.-Based Law Firms Practicing Outside the United States

When a law firm decides to open an office outside of the United States, it will need to consider many factors before making important decisions. Many of the decisions facing a law firm are discussed in this section.

[1]—Location

If one asks a real estate consultant for the three most important factors in deciding where to buy or rent, the consultant will often say, "Location, location, location." Many law firms have found out the hard way that location is very important and can have a significant effect on the successfulness of an office. Lawyers should have office space near clients' offices or easily accessible to them through public transportation or good roadways. Location also identifies the firm's culture and image. Having the wrong address can send the wrong message and may effect a firm's reputation before it even begins business. When unfamiliar with a city, it is wise to note the locations of expected clients or competitors and to use a real estate consultant to learn more about various parts of a city and to focus on available space.

[2]—Registering for Business

We learn a lot from hindsight. It's interesting to learn how law firms went about registering to do business in foreign countries. Some firms, especially in the early formation of international law firms, were awkward in the manner in which they opened foreign offices. In one case, an associate from Brussels spent weekends in Prague and became familiar with the yet-unannounced Government plans to begin privatization. Realizing the opportunity, the associate began taking "vacations" (i.e., holidays) in Prague and met with local people to position himself and his firm for the eventual announcement. Eventually, he "moved" to Prague to pursue his business develop efforts in earnest. He was able to develop the market and brought in many new clients to his firm. The only thing that he forgot to do was to register to do business. When the tax office caught up with him (and his firm) there were many anxious and costly months to unravel the tax issues and to register the firm as a "good citizen."

The example may seem far-fetched, but it happened. The reason that it happened is that the firm's administration was not charged with the responsibility of opening offices. In fact, they didn't even know that they had an office in Prague.

Contrast the Prague story to one in which a firm was opening an office in Hong Kong. In that case, the administrative staff in the United

States, at the direction of the management committee, went to Hong Kong and worked with qualified consultants (i.e., real estate consultants, accountants, and local lawyers) to set up the office. Once the office was physically ready, the administrative staff notified the lawyers that they could move in.

The moral of these stories is that work should be done by those who are qualified. It is wiser to be coordinated and to register with the local law society, the local municipality the tax office and others, if necessary, so that lawyers are not bothered by distractions. By registering before a firm begins operations, a firm makes a good impression with the government and can identify issues before they arise. It may cost more in the beginning to be methodical, but the payoff is realized when lawyers can focus on client matters, instead of responding to suspicious and arrogant tax or regulatory agents who are trying to reconstruct the past.

[3]—Structure

Before registering to do business in a foreign county, a U.S. law firm needs to decide on the structure to use in that country. As noted in Chapter 19, there are various structures to choose from including operating through branches of the U.S. partnership, separate local partnerships, and local corporations. Depending on tax and business considerations, local bar rules, and other regulatory restrictions, international law firms can have complicated structures that use different forms throughout the world.

[4]—Accounting Methods

U.S. law firms are used to sophisticated general ledger systems that track global income by office. It may come as a rude awaking to unwary controllers or chief financial officers to learn that the U.S. accounting methods are not universal. The reality is that each country has its own set of accounting rules, some of which are unique for tax purposes and some for regulatory purposes. For example, in the U.K. depreciation is not allowed; instead capital allowances can be taken, but not for leasehold improvements. Also, in the U.K., most meal expenses are not deductible, whereas in the U.S. half generally are. In Germany, as in other countries, the classification and lives of furniture, fixtures and office equipment are different than those used in the United States.

It is important to identify accounting method differences and have computer systems available to track those differences. For example, since depreciation methods vary throughout the world, the basis that a law firm has in its assets will vary. As a result, when assets are sold the gain or loss will differ. Without a computer to calculate the difference, a controller will find it virtually impossible to make the proper calculations and may end up paying more taxes than are necessary.

It is important to review foreign accounting procedures when an office is opened to ensure that proper tax determinations are made for items of income and expense that are reported in local tax returns, or other statutory filings.

[5]—Value Added Taxes

U.S.-based law firms understand and are used to paying sales taxes on items they buy for the business (e.g., sales tax on furniture, computers, stationery, supplies, etc). Many countries have something called value added tax ("VAT") or consumption tax that is not familiar to American law firms and can be an unexpected reality of operating in a foreign country. Generally, VAT is an amount that is added to the cost of an item and borne by the consumer. The concept behind value added tax is that every link in the chain from original production through distribution to consumption adds a fixed percentage to the cost of the item, so that the consumer pays the government the accumulated tax.

The application of value added tax is confusing to American law firms, because they do not know when to assess VAT and when not to. If something is zero-rated, then no VAT is assessed. If an item is not zero-rated (i.e., law firm services in most countries), then VAT is assessed, unless an exception applies. One exception in some countries is if the work originated based on instructions from America. But that exception does not always apply.

Deciding when VAT should be added to legal service fees is complicated in some countries based on the determination of what kind of lawyer provided legal assistance. In Belgium for example, if the firm has more than fifty percent of its partners registered with the A Bar, then VAT is not added to a bill sent by a Belgian office. If, however, less than fifty percent of the partners are in the A Bar (i.e., they are in the B Bar), then VAT must be added to an invoice, unless the services are for export or otherwise exempt.

Law firms that have to add VAT to their bills can claim a credit for VAT that they pay on items that they purchase (i.e., supplies, rent, services, etc.), if they are registered with the VAT authority. If, however, a firm does not have to add VAT to their bills (e.g., the Belgian A Bar example), then they cannot reclaim the VAT.

If a firm can reclaim VAT, then the VAT charges and credits generally will wash over a period of time, so there is no net cost to the firm. If they cannot reclaim VAT, then any VAT they pay on purchases is an increased cost of doing business.

If some countries, VAT can be an unexpected source of revenue. For example, in Japan where there is a consumption tax, there is a consumption tax credit for each partner. Regardless of the credit, consumption taxes have to be added to invoices to Japanese clients. If the accumulated credits for all the partners who file tax returns in Japan exceed the consumption tax collected from clients, the law firm does not have to pay the withheld consumption taxes to the government. Ergo, the law firm has unexpected income.

It is easy to understand why American law firms are confused about value added taxes or consumption taxes. Clearly they are confusing. It is best to engage a qualified consultant to advise a law firm on the application of these taxes, so that a firm doesn't accidentally end up in a situation where it has unintentionally violated the law and is subject to VAT and penalties.

[6]—Foreign Tax Credit

A foreign tax credit is the ability to get credit in the country of residence for a tax paid to another jurisdiction. Foreign taxes can be applied against either a law firm or its partners. If a country taxes the entity, then foreign tax is assessed against the firm; whereas, if the entity is viewed as a pass-through, then foreign tax is assessed against each equity partner.

The issue of foreign taxes for an American law firm practicing outside the U.S. is to know how whom the foreign tax is assessed against and how to mitigate the tax. If the tax is assessed against the firm, then conceptually it flows through to each partner who can claim a foreign tax credit on his or her personal tax return (assuming the partner is an individual).[1] If the tax is assessed against the individual partner, then that person often has to file a foreign tax return reporting his or her share of taxable income allocated to a particular jurisdiction.

Some of the countries that assess tax against individual partners include the United Kingdom, France, Belgium, Italy (depending on the firm's Italian structure), Germany, and Japan. Countries such as Hong Kong and Singapore assess tax against the branch, but the tax is allocated to each partner. Countries such as Hungary, Turkey, Russia, Mexico, Czech Republic and Poland tax the entity directly.

The importance of realizing the tax structure of the country in which a law firm will operate is that law firm management can judge if the foreign tax will be greater than or less than the U.S. tax that

---

[1] See § 20.05, *infra,* for a discussion of foreign tax credits.

will be assessed against the same income. Since a U.S. citizen or "green card" holder is subject to tax on his or her worldwide income, it is important to know if foreign taxes will he higher or lower than U.S. taxes. If the foreign taxes are higher, there is a greater likelihood that the partner will not be able to claim a credit for the full amount of the foreign taxes in his or her U.S. tax return. If that is the case, then the firm might try to do some planning of where work should be done for the foreign office. For example, since the tax rate in Turkey is high, if might make sense to have work done in Saudi Arabia or Hong Kong where the tax rates are lower. By netting the ultimate tax paid on all foreign income, it might be easier for a U.S. partner to claim a full credit.

[7]—Allocation of Income

A significant problem of operating branches throughout the world is how to allocate income to various jurisdictions. Should income be allocated where the work is done, where the attorney is assigned, where the client is, where the bill is rendered, etc.? Unfortunately, there is no definitive answer, because the laws in many countries differ, making it difficult to develop a consistent and practical allocation method[2] Sometimes, law firms allocate income to the locations where the work is done and make adjustments to comply with local jurisdictions, where necessary. This method is consistent with the one generally required for purposes of calculating foreign tax credits in the U.S. It is more common, however, for law firms to allocate income to the office that the attorney who did the work is assigned. The method chosen can affect the allocation of income to different taxing jurisdictions. Most jurisdictions are "comfortable" (or at least accepting) of either method, as long as the method is applied consistently.

For foreign tax credit purposes, however, if a law firm has more U.S.-based lawyers working outside the U.S. than non-U.S.-based lawyers working in the U.S., the wisest method is to source income where the work was done. Understandably, this might mean that there are two different methods of allocating income for general tax purposes and foreign tax credit purposes, but the difference can pay off by allowing U.S.-based partners to claim more foreign tax credits.

With respect to allocating income among the partners, it may be possible to allocate foreign-source income to the foreign partners if

---

[2] Some developing countries like Indonesia use a "force of attraction" rule, which sources income to the country based on the location of the payer.

the allocation has "substantial economic effect."[3] The advantage of this allocation will depend on the composition of the partners (U.S. vs. foreign). For example, if a foreign partner's share of firm profits is determined solely on the basis of profits generated by the foreign office or foreign partnership, the foreign partner would be relieved of all U.S. tax filing requirements, since the foreign partner would technically have no U.S.-source income. However, such an allocation method would reduce the foreign-source income allocable to the U.S. partners and may limit their utilization of foreign taxes as credits on their U.S. returns.

[8]—Allocation/Apportionment of Expenses

Most firms can readily identify direct costs that are allocable to foreign branches. However, in determining the U.S.- and foreign-source income of a U.S. partnership with branch operations, certain expenses must be allocated and apportioned under Internal Revenue Code Section 861. As a general rule, interest and certain overhead costs must be allocated or apportioned between domestic and foreign sources as provided in the regulations. Following more traditional accounting practices, some firms allocate other forms of home office overhead, such as costs associated with the accounting department, management expenses, the annual audit fee, pension costs, etc. While these accounting allocations may be appropriate, not all foreign countries concur and may not allow deductions for all overhead allocations. In addition, some foreign countries require significant documentation to support overhead expense allocations.

[9]—Foreign Currency Translation

For financial reporting purposes, the translation of foreign books of account into U.S. dollars may result in a translation gain or loss. Accounting rules require that all elements of financial statements should be translated using a current exchange rate.[4] For balance sheet items, the exchange rate is the rate as of the balance sheet date. For the profit-and-loss statements, an appropriately weighted average exchange rate for the year may be used. The translation adjustments resulting from translating the branch's functional currency into U.S. dollars are not included in determining net income, but are reported separately and accumulated in a separate component of equity.

---

[3] IRC § 704(b)(2); 26 U.S.C. § 704(b)(2). See also, Treas. Reg. § 1.704-1(b)(5) Ex. 10; 26 C.F.R. § 1.704-1(b)(5) Ex. 10.

[4] Financing Accounting Standards Board Statement No. 52, "Foreign Currency Translation," ¶ 12 (1981).

The functional currency of the local branch or partnership is generally the local currency in which the firm transacts its business. In most case, the functional currency of a U.S. branch operating in a foreign jurisdiction will be the U.S. dollar if it conducts its transactions in U.S. dollars and maintains its books of account in U.S. dollars.

[10]—Foreign Currency Transactions

An exchange gain or loss may be triggered under Internal Revenue Code Section 987 on the transfer of property. A transfer to or from a branch would be determined daily. If on any day contributions (or distributions) exceed distributions (or contributions), the excess is treated as a transfer of property. The amount of the Section 987 gain or loss is determined using the spot rate for translating transfers into the taxpayer's functional currency.

Most U.S. law firms do not follow Section 987. Generally, when property is transferred to a foreign branch it is recorded at the U.S. dollar amount and when property is returned to the U.S., it is recorded based on the converted value into U.S. dollars. The effect of this "shorthand" method is that any gain or loss from fluctuations in foreign currency on property transfers is left in the branch accounts and isn't recognized until the branch is closed.

[11]—Guaranteed Payments

Guaranteed payments represent amounts paid to a partner for services or for the use of capital if the payments are determined without regard to partnership income.[5] Law firms often pay foreign assignee partners guaranteed payments to create sufficient foreign-source income to allow the partner to claim an Internal Revenue Code Section 911 exclusion or to maximize treaty benefits (e.g., U.S./French treaty). The problem faced by many U.S. law firms is the proper way to structure a guaranteed payment. Treasury regulations give the following example:

> Partner C in the CD partnership is to receive 30 percent of partnership income as determined before taking into account any guaranteed payments, but not less than $10,000. The income of partnership is $60,000, and C is entitled to $18,000 (30 percent of $60,000) as his distributive share. *No part of this amount is a guaranteed payment.*[6] [Emphasis added]

---

[5] IRC § 707(c); 26 U.S.C. § 707(c).

[6] Treas. Reg. § 1.707-1(c) Example (2); 26 C.F.R. § 1.707-1(c).

The reasoning behind the conclusion is that there was no guaranteed payment is that Partner C would have received 30% of the profit without the guarantee. Thirty percent was more than the amount of the guarantee. A guarantee is supposed to without regard to the income of the firm.[7] The regulation changes the facts so that the partnership made $20,000 instead of $30,000 and concludes that the guarantee in that case would be $4,000 (i.e., the difference between the $10,000 and his share of profits - 30% of $20,000).[8]

There are several valid ways to structure guarantees. The easiest was is to reduce the partner's percentage share of income and substitute the value of the lost percentage with a fixed guarantee that is not tied to income. Then the partner can be given a guaranteed payment in addition to his or her percentage share of income. If the person ultimately receives less than he or she would have as a full equity partner, then it is possible to give a performance bonus (not a bonus based on the firm's income) or to make up the difference in future guaranteed payments. There is a concern that if the total amount paid to a guaranteed payment partner over an extended period of time equals what the person otherwise would have made as an equity partner, then the IRS may attack the substance of the guarantee. There is no evidence that this has ever happened.

Guaranteed payments should be agreed in advance of the time when they are earned and should be documented in the form or a written agreement.

In establishing a foreign practice, consideration should be given to the local tax treatment of guaranteed payments. Most foreign countries do not recognize guaranteed payments, so they may be treated differently for tax purposes by a foreign country.

[12]—Tax Equalization/Protection

A U.S. firm may want to consider a tax equalization or protection plan for U.S. partners or employees who are temporarily assigned to foreign offices. A tax equalization plan keeps the individual "whole"; the objective is that the individual pays the same amount of tax as if he or she were not on a foreign assignment. Any additional tax cost is paid by the U.S. firm and any tax savings is retained by the firm. This program is based on a hypothetical U.S. tax and requires a gross-up calculation. A tax protection plan provides coverage to the assignee only if the total tax paid exceeds his or her U.S. tax. Any tax savings are retained by the assignee.[9]

---

[7] See FN 5, *supra*.

[8] Treas. Reg. § 1.707-1(c) Example (2); 26 C.F.R. § 1.707-1(c).

[9] See § 20.04[3], *infra*, for a more detailed discussion of equalization and protection plans.

[13]—Treaty Protection

Tax planning should be considered prior to the commencement of a foreign assignment. A review of the relevant treaty may result in significant tax savings for the assignee. Many of the treaties concluded by the U.S. provide an exemption from foreign tax if the U.S. assignee spends fewer than 183 days in the aggregate in the foreign country during the tax year. Planning opportunities generally arise in the year of arrival and departure. Note that foreign tax years may not necessarily coincide with the calendar year observed in the U.S.

[14]—Social Security Totalization Agreements

Social Security Totalization Agreements provide that an employee or self-employed person is required to pay social security tax to only one country on earned income and provides that the individual does not lose benefits as a result of payments made to different countries as a result of a foreign assignment or employment.[10]

[15]—Filing Requirements—Partnership and Partners

In most foreign jurisdictions, a U.S. firm is required to file some type of tax return. If the country recognizes a flow-through entity, then the firm would file something like a partnership return. If the country does not recognize a flow-through entity, then the firm might be required to file something that resembles a corporate tax return. Sometime, like in the case of Japan, the entity itself does not file a return; instead, each partner reports his or her share of income from that jurisdiction. The firm's books and records are used only for audit purposes.

Whatever return is filed normally reports income earned from the country in which the return is filed. Rarely, is it necessary to disclose global income to a foreign country, although in the case of allocating income to residents and non-residents, Germany tax officials may request global income to verify that allocations to German-based partners are appropriate. This is normally done when projected income is less than expected and the partners request a reduction in their quarterly assessments. The same disclosure could be required by other countries.

It is wise to engage competent tax assistance when preparing foreign tax returns or when working with foreign tax inspectors.

If a U.S. firm admits non-American partners resident in another country to the firm, they are considered to be non-resident aliens

---

[10] See § 20.10, *infra,* for a more detailed discussion of totalization agreements.

(NRA) for U.S. income tax purposes. A NRA partner is considered to be engaged in a trade or business in the U.S.[11] and, therefore, will have effectively connected income, unless her or she receives a guaranteed payment. Regulations provide that every NRA who is engaged in trade or business in the U.S. at any time during the taxable year is required to file a return on Form 1040NR.[12] In a controversial private letter ruling, the Internal Revenue Service ruled that only a resident partner of a foreign law firm had to file a U.S. income tax return, because the other partners were residents of a foreign country with which the United States had a treaty.[13] It should be understood that private rulings cannot be relied on by other taxpayers, although they do express the IRS's views given a particular set of facts and circumstances. The ruling mentioned was going to be withdrawn. However, before it could be withdrawn, the Treasury Department released a new model treaty interpretation of paragraph 1 of Article 14 covering independent personal services.[14] The interpretation said that, "a partner would be taxable solely in his state of residence if he performed all his activities there." Stated differently, the interpretation meant that if a non-resident foreign partner is a resident in a treaty country and did not provide independent personal services in a fixed place of business in the United States, then that partner did not have to file a U.S. income tax return. The interpretation does not apply to other forms of income allocated to a non-resident partner (e.g., interest or dividends), to interest paid on capital accounts, or to income from other than the partner's independent personal services. The model treaty wording surprised technicians within Treasury who did not agree with the interpretation and recommended that the OECD form a subcommittee to opine on the taxation of non-residents so that there would be a uniform position. Newer treaties negotiated after the model treaty interpretation was released do not contain similar language under Article 14.

One of the issues in the private ruling is the definition of a "fixed place of business," because without a fixed place of business, there may not be a permanent establishment. The OECD issued draft changes to the model tax treaty in which it focused on the definition[15]

---

[11] IRC § 875(1); 26 U.S.C. § 875(1).

[12] Treas. Reg. § 1.6012-1(b)(1); 26 C.F.R. § 1.6012-1(b)(1).

[13] Priv. Ltr. Rul. 93310112 (May 5, 1993).

[14] United States Treasury Department Technical Explanation for the Model Income Tax Convention released September 20, 1996.

[15] See Draft Contents of the 2002 Update to the Model Tax Convention, issued by OECD 2 October 2001.

which suggests that any new model treaties will broadly define "fixed place of business." Any clarification in the term may mean a non-resident partner that has access to any space in his or her firm's U.S. office space will be considered to have a fixed place of business, thereby, further weakening the position of the private ruling.

These developments suggests that the private ruling and model treaty interpretation are not viable and that law firms should not rely on them when deciding if non-resident partners should file U.S. tax returns.

[16]—Withholding on Distributions

If a partnership has effectively connected taxable income and any portion is allocable to a non-resident alien partner, the partnership must withhold U.S. tax at a rate one percent higher than the higher U.S. tax rate.[16] A revenue procedure provides guidance as to the withholding requirements applicable to partnerships with foreign partners.[17] Generally, a partnership must make estimated tax payments for each non-resident equity partner on or before the fifteenth day of the fourth, sixth, ninth and twelfth months of the partnership's taxable year for U.S. income tax purposes, using Form 8813, Partnership Withholding Tax Payment. A partnership's failure to withhold may subject it to penalties.[18]

Forms 8804, Annual Return for Partnership Withholding Tax, and 8805, Foreign Partner's Information Statement of IRC § 1446 Withholding, are to be used to pay and report Section 1446 withholding tax based on effectively connected income allocable to foreign partners, without regard to distributions. Form 8804 is used to report the total liability under Section 1446 to show the amount of effectively connected taxable income and the tax payments allocable to the non-resident alien partner for the partnership's tax year. These forms are to be filed on or before the fifteenth day of the fourth month following the close of the tax year of the partnership.[19] The non-resident alien partner claims the withholding tax as a credit on the individual income tax return which the partner is required to file.[20]

---

[16] IRC § 1446(a)(1); 26 U.S.C. § 1446(a)(1). For years beginning before 2001, the applicable tax rate is 39.6%. For 2001 the rate is 39.1% and for 2002 and 2003 the rate is 38.6%. For 2004 and 2005 the rate is 37.6%. For 2006 and thereafter, the rate is 35%. IRC §§ 1 and 1446 as amended by § 205 of The Economic Growth and Tax Relief Reconciliation Act of 2001.

[17] Rev. Proc. 89-31, 1989-1 C.B. 895 and Rev. Proc. 92-66, 1992-2 C.B. 428.

[18] IRC §§ 6662, 6663 or 6672; 26 U.S.C. §§ 6662, 6663 or 6672.

[19] IRS Ann. 90-6, 1990-3 I.R.B. 36, and IRS Pub. 515, rev. Nov. 1993.

[20] See § 9.01 of Rev. Proc. 89-31, 1989-1, C.B. 895.

[17]—Certification of Filing (Form 6166)

A U.S. law firm does not have to open an office in a foreign country to be doing business outside the United States. Most double tax treaties that the U.S. is a party to view independent personal services (which includes the practice of law by partners) as services that are taxable where services are rendered. Normally that means that if services are provided in a country that country has a right to tax income earned as a result of those services.

Most countries realize that non-residents will not willingly file tax returns and pay tax on services rendered outside of their country. To ensure that a country collects is just due of tax for work done within its boundaries, many countries assess withholding tax against payments on account of services rendered. Procedurally, the withholding tax is collected by the payer at the time that payment of an invoice is made. So, for example, if legal services are rendered to a client in Spain, the client is supposed to withhold Spanish tax from the invoice when it is paid. The American law firm, therefore, receives the net amount. The withholding rates generally range from 20% to 30% and is in lieu of filing a tax return.

Unfortunately, the withholding is applied against the gross fee and it is blind to where the work was performed. Remembering that a country can tax work done within its boarders, it seems incorrect that the withholding would apply to the gross amount, especially when little or no work may have been done in the country. Countries like Spain, Italy and Indonesia assess withholding under a claim of right doctrine which suggests that regardless of where the work was done, they have a right to withhold tax on the gross fee - and do. It doesn't take too much withholding before a law firm's gross margin evaporates.

To avoid withholding issues, the Treasury Department negotiated double tax treaties to, among other objectives, identify which country has a right to tax income. Most treaties, however, only focus on individuals and corporations as those eligible for treaty benefits. American law firms ask what about partnerships and quickly learn that they are not covered by treaties - only their partners are.

With respect to income earned by law firms (i.e., personal services), treaties generally say that the income will not be taxed by the country in which the work was done, but by the country in which the individual or corporation is resident. Procedurally, a personal must show that he or she (or it if a corporation) is eligible for treaty benefits such as avoiding withholding. To do that an individual or corporation must obtain an IRS Certification (i.e., Form 6166) from the IRS in Philadelphia.

The IRS will issue a Certification only to a resident and only if the resident has filed a tax return. To most law firms, these requirements seem easy enough to meet. Many unsuspecting law firms, however, eventually learn that the IRS will not issue a Certification solely to a law firm, because most law firms are partnerships and that partnerships are not covered by the treaty. As a result, the IRS requires that each partner in a partnership be certified. This means that each partner has to sign a power of attorney authorizing the IRS to verify that he or she has filed a personal income tax return for the same period that certification is requested for. This requirement often is a contentious matter for attorneys who often resist signing powers of attorney.

The next requirement for Certification is that the partner be a resident. Most Americans who pay U.S. taxes feel that they are residents of the U.S., even if they happen to be on assignment in another country. Unfortunately, the IRS does not interpret the word "resident" in a very broad manner. Its interpretation is that a resident is one who is working and living in the U.S. That means that the IRS will not certify a U.S. partner on assignment outside the U.S. If the IRS knows that to be the case, they will issue a partial Certification and exclude the non-resident partner. For U.S. firms operating throughout the world, this seems harsh and unfair, but it is the current policy.

Law firms should be aware of the Certification process and seek competent tax assistance when faced with the situation in which the IRS intends to issue a partial Certification, which means that the firm will not be able to avoid some withholding.

One last point on Certifications. If there is no treaty with a country (e.g., Hong Kong, Brazil, Argentina), then a Certification will not be effective in avoiding withholding taxes. In those situations, a law firm would have to pass the foreign tax paid onto its partners who would try to claim a foreign tax credit on their personal returns for the withheld tax.

[18]—Bar Restrictions

All U.S. law firms are subject to bar and regulatory rules in the states in which they practice. In the United States and many parts of Europe, law firms can be authorized to practice law (albeit only U.S. law) by simply registering with the local bar. Not all countries believe in reciprocity. Some countries (e.g., Australia, Brazil, Argentina, parts of Canada, Chile, Columbia, Greece, India, Indonesia, Korea, Philippines, Thailand, Taiwan, Venezuela, India) do not allow Americans to practice law or to share income with practicing lawyers in their countries. Some countries (e.g., Czech Republic, Hungary, Turkey) also require that local practice be owned by a local national lawyer. Other countries (e.g., United Kingdom, Italy, Spain, Belgium, Switzerland, Japan, Mexico, Hong Kong, Singapore, Russia) allow American to practice U.S. law, sometimes are registered foreign lawyers or its equivalent.

This laundry list demonstrates that an American law firm cannot simply open an office wherever it wants to. Local bar rules can be very stringent and restrictive. It is very important to understanding bar rules before a firm begins business in another country. Beginning business can be as simple as flying into a country to visit a prospective client and occasionally returning on client matters.

It is interesting to note that local bar associations generally are not the ones who are monitoring U.S. firm's presence in their countries. It is normally the local lawyer who may feel threatened or wants to protect his or her turf who will report a violation to the bar association. Sometimes, violations can be dealt with swiftly; other times, they can be distractions, irritations and problems. Understanding the rules and complying with them is the best answer to avoid issues.

§ 20.03 Non-U.S.-Based Law Firms Practicing in the United States

Foreign law firms have shown an interest in opening offices in the U.S. to serve existing clients doing business in the U.S. and to obtain new U.S.-based clients. Unlike opening offices in other parts of the world, opening an office in the United States can cause unexpected filing requirements for foreign partners. This section reviews some of the important matters that need to be considered before opening an office in the U.S.

[1]—Structure

Choosing the appropriate structure for U.S. operations is of paramount importance. If a branch structure is chosen, non-resident partners will have to file U.S. tax returns (something they loath doing). Choosing some other structure (e.g., an umbrella structure or a hybrid partnership structure) may be an appropriate, depending on how the law firm intends to do business. For example, if there is global control and profit sharing exercised at a central point, the structure could be viewed as a partnership, regardless of how it is organized. Choosing a corporate structure is yet another alternative.[1]

[2]—Accounting Methods

Once in the United States, a law firm must use an allowable accounting method,[2] regardless of the accounting method used in a foreign country. The accounting method used in the United States does not have to be the same as that used in another country; for example, a firm may decide to use the cash method to determine U.S. taxable income of the branch, even though the accrual method is used in the foreign country.[3] Even if the overall method of accounting for U.S. tax purposes is the same as that used in the home country, there may be differences in application. For example, in the U.K. a law firm uses the accrual method of accounting, but it is not the same as the U.S. accrual method. In the U.K., the accrual method is described as a "full and fair" accounting method. In application, this means that WIP is valued for income tax purposes at cost (e.g., salary, heat, light, operating costs, etc.), so there is no accrual of profits. In the U.S., however, accrual accounting theoretically would include 100% of the WIP (including profit) or none of the WIP on the basis that no bills have been rendered.

---

[1] These structures are discussed in Chapter 19.

[2] See discussion of accounting methods in Chapter 17.02, *supra*.

[3] IRC § 446(a); 26 U.S.C. § 446(a).

[3]—Allocation of Income

A branch of a foreign partnership operating in the United States will create a permanent establishment in the United States.[4] Business profits attributable to a permanent establishment generally are treated as effectively connected to a U.S. trade or business and are subject to U.S. tax.[5] Foreign partnerships have the same problem allocating income as U.S. partnerships operating in a foreign country.

It may be possible to structure the partnership agreement to allocate U.S.-source income to those partners who perform work in the U.S., thereby reducing or eliminating the U.S. taxable income of the remaining partners. Making a specific allocation of U.S. profits to U,S,-based partners, however, is akin to the "eat-what-you-kill" concept and means that the U.S.-based partners can be allocated only U.S.-source income and no income from other sources.[6] Overall, allocations of U.S.-source income in a disproportionate manner must have substantial economic effect.[7]

In what has been viewed as an unusual private letter ruling, the IRS allowed an alternative allocation which lead to an unexpected tax filing result. Following a provision of the U.S./German income tax treaty, a partnership organized under the law of the Federal Republic of Germany was allowed to execute an agreement with a U.S.-resident partner whereby all of its U.S. branch income was allocated to the U.S.-resident partner.[8] In addition, the U.S.-resident partner was taxable only on his distributive share of partnership income (presumably from the U.S. operation and not German-source) and its non-U.S. partners were not taxable in the U.S. on their distributive shares. It is questionable if the IRS would rule the same today if asked the same question.

Another way to allocate U.S.-source income is to pay a guaranteed payment,[9] which is allocated to the country where the work is done (e.g., assuming a foreign partner spends 80% of his or her time working in the U.S., then 80% of a guaranteed payment would be allocated to the U.S.)[10]

---

[4] Rev. Rul. 65-263, 1965-2 C.B. 561.

[5] IRC § 864(c)(2); 26 U.S.C. § 864(c)(2).

[6] See Example 10(ii) Treas. Reg. § 1.704-1(b)(5); 26 C.F.R. 26 § 1.704-1(b)(5).

[7] IRC § 704(b)(2); 26 U.S.C. § 704(b)(2).

[8] Ltr. Rul. 9331012 (May 5, 1993).

[9] See Chapters 17.06[1][b] and 20.02[11], *supra,* for more discussions of guaranteed payments.

[10] IRC § 861(a)(3); 26 U.S.C. § 861(a)(3).

[4]—Allocation and Apportionment of Expenses

In determining the U.S.- and foreign-source income of a U.S. branch of a foreign partnership, certain expenses must be allocated and apportioned under the principles of Internal Revenue Code Sections 861 and 882. As a general rule, interest and certain overhead costs must be allocated or apportioned between domestic and foreign sources as provided in the regulations. To properly compute U.S.-based income, home office overhead charges might be charged to the U.S. accounts.

[5]—Treaty Considerations

Planning opportunities exist under the various treaties concluded by the U.S.; specifically, the provisions on "residence," "independent personal services" and "dependent personal services."

A foreign partner temporarily in the U.S. may be considered a non-resident even when his or her stay is longer than 183 days under certain "tie-breaker" treaty provisions, if the foreign partner's "vital economic interests" remain in the foreign place of residence.

Opportunities for the allocation of work between the foreign office and the U.S. office may provide a possible reduction of the firm's exposure to U.S. income tax through a split billing arrangement or accurate internal accounting records. For example, under Article 14 of the German treaty, work performed in Germany from the liaison efforts of the U.S. office will be taxable only in Germany if performed by a German resident. If, however, the German resident is a partner in the international firm, then Germany may tax the resident only on his or her share of the German-source income on the assumption that the person is filing a U.S. return and returns for other countries in which the firm does business. Depending on the specific treaties, this approach is taken by other countries like Belgium or Singapore.[11]

[6]—Filing Requirements—Partnership and Partners

The U.S. branch of a foreign partnership is treated as a U.S. partnership with respect to its effectively connected U.S. income and is required to file a U.S. Partnership Return of Income (Form 1065). If the U.S. entity is a corporation, it must file Form 5472, Information Return of a 25% Foreign-Owned U.S. Corporation or a Foreign Corporation Engaged in a U.S. Trade or Business.

---

[11] "Convention Between the United States of America and the Federal Republic of Germany for the Avoidance of Double Taxation and the Prevention of Fiscal Evaluation With Respect to Taxes on Income and Capital and Certain Other Taxes," U.S.-Germany, Art. 14, (CCH) Tax Treaties § 3249.29 (Aug. 21, 1991).

If there is substantial economic effect, partnership income can be specifically allocated to the partners who are subject to U.S. income tax on their allocable share of partnership income[12] or they can be paid guaranteed payments.[13] Regulations require that each partner file a U.S. income tax return (either Form 1040 for a resident partner or a Form 1040NR for a non-resident partner)[14] reporting his or her allocable portion of partnership income earned in the U.S., if any. In addition to a federal tax return, partners in a U.S. partnership generally are subject to state income tax returns for every state in which the firm does business.

In a controversial private letter ruling, the Internal Revenue Service ruled that only a resident partner of a foreign law firm had to file a U.S. income tax return, because the other partners were residents of a foreign country with which the United States had a treaty.[15] This ruling probably would not be issued today by the IRS and should not be relied on in any case.[16]

[7]—Employee Considerations

The foreign firm may consider treating its foreign partners on assignment to the U.S. as employees, rather than as equity partners. Salaries are deductible from effectively connected U.S. income, while a partnership distribution is nondeductible. These employees would be required to file either a Form 1040 or Form 1040NR depending on their residency status for U.S. income tax purposes. To be considered employees, the foreign partners should resign from the firm before moving to the U.S. Resignation needs to be more than in name only. If a person continues sharing profits globally or having a vote in partnership matters, the IRS may not agree that payments are salary payments, and instead consider the person a partner. Careful planning should be done to avoid a reclassification situation.

[8]—Withholding on Distributions

The distribution of effectively connected U.S. income to a nonresident alien individual partner will cause the partnership to pay a withholding tax equal to the top individual tax rate[17] times the amount

---

[12] IRC § 704(b); 26 U.S.C. § 704(b).

[13] IRC § 707(c); 26 U.S.C. § 707(c).

[14] Treas. Reg. § 1.6012-1(b)(i); 26 C.F.R. § 1.6012-1(b)(i).

[15] Priv. Ltr. Rul. 93310112 (May 5, 1993).

[16] See § 20.02[15], *supra*, for a more detailed discussion of the filing requirements for a non-resident alien equity partner.

[17] The rates are 39.1% for 2001, 38.6% for 2002, and declining in stages to 35% in 2006.

allocated to individual partners.[18] Internal Revenue Code Section 1446 permits these partners to credit this withholding tax against any income tax liability they may have on their individual returns.[19]

---

[18] IRC §§ 1 and 1446(b)(2); 26 U.S.C. §§ 1 and 1446(b)(2).

[19] IRC § 1446(d)(1); 26 U.S.C. § 1446(d)(1). See also § 20.02[16], *supra,* for more discussion of withholding on distributions.

§ 20.04 United States Partners and Associates Assigned to Foreign Countries

[1]—Tax Planning for Lawyers Assigned Abroad

Transferring lawyers to offices in foreign countries for tours of duty is very expensive. An associate that a firm pays $180,000 in Washington, D.C. can cost double that when he or she is assigned to a high-cost city in Europe or Asia (most foreign assignments by U.S. law firms are to such locations). While overseas assignments are expensive, they are less expensive if there is proper tax and compensation planning in advance of assignments.

This section discusses only the tax (and compensation, as it relates to tax) aspects of a foreign assignment, but selecting the right person and treating that person fairly when he or she returns to the U.S. are other key elements of foreign assignments that can make or break the success of an offshore office. Briefly, there is nothing more expensive than an overseas assignment that doesn't work out because the wrong person was selected. And there is nothing that makes it more difficult to get associates (or partners, for that matter) to accept foreign tours than the perception that their careers will suffer as a result.

Basic U.S. draw or salary is only the starting point of a firm's out-of-pocket cost of sending partners and associates to foreign offices. Other costs can include:

1. cost-of-living adjustment or overseas premium,
2. housing allowance,
3. moving expense reimbursement (including house-selling assistance if a home is sold),
4. school fees,
5. home leave (and associated travel costs), and
6. language lessons, if applicable.

Virtually all foreign offices of U.S. law firms are in major cities, but there will be additional costs if lawyers are assigned to true hardship posts, which involve premium pay and perhaps a second home in an area that provides reasonable creature comforts, security, and proper schools for the spouse and children.

[2]—Tax Policy for Lawyers Assigned Abroad

Most of the additional items listed in the preceding paragraph are U.S. taxable income to the employee or a partner. The principal exceptions are that, on assignments that qualify for the foreign earned income exclusion,[1] both

1. compensation for services rendered of up to $78,000 in 2001 and $80,000 thereafter (adjusted for a cost of living adjustment beginning in 2008)[2] and
2. housing costs over a base amount,

are excluded from taxable income.[3] In general, an assignment of a year or more qualifies for both exclusions. They are elective and can be elected separately. A partner's income does not qualify for either exclusion unless (1) the partner's share of foreign-source income from all non-U.S. operations is sufficient to cover the exclusion (2) the partner is compensated by a guaranteed payment or (3) a combination of both.[4] Because of interplay with the foreign tax credit in high-tax foreign countries, whether or not either exclusion should be elected should be determined on a case-by-case basis. All of these details are discussed in this section.

[3]—Protection vs. Equalization

Firms generally reimburse lawyers on foreign tours for the additional income tax generated by the various allowances under one of two approaches. Under a "tax protection plan," the partner or employee is reimbursed for taxes (U.S. and foreign) in excess of what he/she would have paid had he or she not been transferred. If the taxes in the foreign location are less than would have been paid in the U.S., the transferee keeps the difference. Under a "tax equalization plan," the assignee is made whole, but the firm keeps any tax saving generated by the transfer. As a general rule, a transfer will not generate a tax saving unless:

1. the transferee is on the low end of the lawyer pay scale,
2. taxable reimbursements are modest, and
3. the locale is low-tax, like Hong Kong.

---

[1] IRC § 911(a); 26 U.S.C § 911(a).

[2] IRC § 911(a)(1); 26 U.S.C § 911(a)(1).

[3] IRC § 911(a)(2). 26 U.S.C § 911(a)(2).

[4] T. B. Foster, CA-2, 64-1 ¶9362, 329 F2d 717; E. L. Carey, CtCl, 70-1 USTC ¶9455, 427 F2d 763.

To keep the assignee whole, a tax equalization plan might also take into account (1) the state and local taxes the transferee would have paid had he or she stayed home and (2) the transferee's outside income (this is especially important in the case of a working spouse's income). If the transfer is to a high-tax country, taking high outside income into account can make a transfer prohibitively expensive. Fortunately, countries often do not tax the foreign-source investment income of short-term assignees, unless it is remitted.

Some firms, for cost and administrative reasons, opt not to protect or equalize associates. Instead, using ballpark estimates (and intelligence about what comparable law firms are doing), they give associates a flat amount and put the onus on the associates to manage their personal tax matters.

Most employers use the tax equalization approach. One reason is that it is fairer and makes it easier to transfer employees from one jurisdiction to another. Regarding fairness, it eliminates one employee getting a windfall while an employee in different circumstances or assigned to a different country does not.

The hypothetical U.S. tax the transferee would have paid, absent a transfer, is computed using either actual or assumed deductions (a percentage of gross income).

The following example, Figure 20-A, illustrates reimbursement amounts calculated under a tax equalization plan

Figure 20-A. Illustration of reimbursement amounts calculated under a tax equalization plan.

	U.S. Hypothetical	Foreign Assignment
Salary	$180,000	$180,000
Cost of living adjustment/Overseas premium		30,000
Housing allowance		60,000
Education allowance		30,000
Home leave		20,000
Income (before deductions)	$180,000	$320,000
U.S. Tax (with earned income exclusion elected, say)	$ 25,000	$ 85,000
Less hypothetical U.S. tax		(25,000)
Tax to be reimbursed		60,000
Gross-up of reimbursement		40,000
Total tax reimbursement		$100,000
Income (before deductions) (above)	180,000	320,000
Total out-of-pocket cost to law firm	$180,000	420,000
Less U.S. salary		(180,000)
Additional cost of foreign assignment		$240,000

[4]—United States Taxation of U.S. Citizens Residing Abroad

The United States taxes the worldwide income of both its residents and its citizens.[5] Thus, a citizen of a foreign country who becomes a resident of the U.S. is taxed on his or her worldwide income as long as U.S. residency is maintained. Similarly, a U.S. citizen is taxed on his or her worldwide income even though he or she is a resident of a foreign country. Typically, other countries do not tax citizens who are resident in another country on their worldwide income. This is why many of the best tennis payers in the world are residents of no-tax venues like Monaco or Bermuda, but none of them are Americans.

Americans resident in a foreign country also are subject to that country's income tax. All foreign countries tax the income a lawyer earns while on a tour-of-duty in a branch office. Generally, associates are subject to tax in a particular country based on the salary earned in that country. A partner, however, may be subject to tax on a remittance basis (e.g., United Kingdom or Singapore) or based on the partner's share on income sourced to that country (e.g., Belgium or Germany).

The rules vary on the taxation an assignee's investment income from sources outside the country. The basic tax policies (and rates) of the countries that host most U.S. lawyers on assignments to their firms' foreign offices are discussed in this chapter.

As noted, double taxation for U.S. lawyers working abroad is mitigated or eliminated by the U.S. foreign tax credit[6] and, alternatively, by foreign income taxes can be taken as itemized deductions.[7] Double taxation of personal-service income earned abroad also can be mitigated by the foreign earned income exclusion and the exclusion for excess housing costs. The foreign tax credit limitation is complicated, and there are precise requirements for qualifying (and staying qualified) for the earned income and excess housing costs exclusions. These topics are discussed in the following sections.

[5]—Foreign Income Exclusions

A lawyer transferred abroad can qualify for both the earned income exclusion and the excess housing costs exclusion by satisfying either (1) the bona fide residence test or (2) the physical-presence test.[8] In both cases, the exclusions reduce gross income; that is, by reducing income they eliminate income in the taxpayer's highest bracket first.

---

[5] IRC § 61(a); 26 U.S.C. § 61(a).

[6] IRC § 901(a); 26 U.S.C. § 901(a).

[7] IRC § 164(a)(3); 26 U.S.C. § 164(a)(3).

[8] IRC § 911(d)(1); 26 U.S.C. § 911(d)(1).

The exclusions can be elected separately.[9] The housing exclusion amount is housing expense (as defined) less a base amount and is limited to the taxpayer's foreign earned income (after deducting the earned income exclusion amount). An election can be made on a timely filed return or on an amended return.[10] Also, subject to restrictions, an election can be made on a late return.[11] An election remains in effect until revoked. Revocation is made on a statement filed with the tax return for the year for which it is to be effective. This can be on an amended return filed within the three-year statute of limitations. Once revoked, another election cannot be made until the sixth year following the first year for which the revocation is effective, unless the IRS acquiesces.

The regulations are liberal in describing facts that the IRS may take into account in reaching a favorable decision.[12] These include:

1. a period of U.S. residence,
2. a move from a foreign country to another foreign country that has different tax rates,
3. a substantial change in a country's tax laws, and
4. a change of employer.

A 1996 Private Letter Ruling states that the IRS granted consent when a taxpayer changed employers and transferred from England to Hong Kong, satisfying both the change-of-tax-rate and the change-of-employer circumstances of the regulations.[13] The four facts listed in the regulations are not exclusive. Other facts that might generate IRS approval are a substantial pay increase (as in making partner) and getting married.

[a]—Foreign Earned Income

Foreign earned income is income from foreign sources earned by an individual for services rendered while he or she is a qualified individual (as described below). Income received in the year following the year in which the services generating it were rendered is foreign earned income in the earlier year. Income received in the second succeeding year does not qualify.

---

[9] IRC § 911(a); 26 U.S.C. § 911(a). The earned income exclusion limitation is $78,000 for 2001 and $80,000 thereafter (subject to an inflation adjustment beginning in 2008). IRC § 911(b)(2)(D); 26 U.S.C. § 911(b)(2)(D).

[10] Treas. Reg. § 1.911-7(a)(2)(i)(A) and (B); 26 C.F.R. § 1.911-7(a)(2)(i)(A) and (B).

[11] Treas. Reg. § 1.911-7(a)(2)(i)(C) and (D); 26 C.F.R. § 1.911-7(a)(2)(i)(C) and (D).

[12] Treas. Reg. § 1.911-7(b)(2); 26 C.F.R. § 1.911-7(b)(2).

[13] IRS Letter Ruling 9625060, March 28, 1996.

[b]—Qualifying for the Exclusions

To be a qualified individual, a taxpayer must (1) satisfy either (a) the bona fide residence test or (b) the physical-presence test and (2) maintain his or her tax home in a foreign country. The tax home need not be in the same country as the country in which the taxpayer has his or her bona fide residence. For example, a lawyer working out of offices in both Paris and London might have a tax home in Paris (because it is the source of more than half of his income) and his bona fide residence in London (because he has his home and other indicia of residence there). Similarly, the tax home need not be in the country where the lawyer accumulates most of the foreign-country days to satisfy the physical-presence test.

An important planning point is that one test can be used one year and the other test the next year. For example, the physical-presence test often works best the first and last years and the bona fide residence test might be best in the intervening years (if, for example, there were too many days in the United States to satisfy the physical-presence test).

[c]—Bona Fide Residence

To satisfy this test, the taxpayer must be a U.S. citizen and a bona fide resident of a foreign country or countries for a period that includes an uninterrupted period that includes an entire taxable year. (A U.S. resident who is not a citizen may qualify under the terms of some income tax treaties.) The period of bona fide residence can begin and end with partial taxable years, as long as they are tacked onto intervening tax years that are periods of uninterrupted bona fide foreign residency. For example, if a lawyer establishes his residency in London on November 1, 2001 and maintains his residency there through March 31, 2003, he would have 61 qualifying days in 2001, 365 qualifying days in 2002, and 91 qualifying days in 2003.[14]

A transferee to a foreign city can establish residency from the first day if the transfer is for an extended period of time and a home is established. The regulations provide that, to the extent practical, bona fide residence shall be determined using the principles of section 871 and the attendant regulations. An alien is a resident if he or she is not a mere transient or sojourner.[15] Whether he or she is a transient depends on the length and nature of his or her stay. Case law indicates that getting involved in the community is particularly

---

[14] Treas. Reg. § 1.911-3(d)(3); 26 C.F.R. § 1.911-3(d)(3).

[15] Treas. Reg. § 1.871-2(b); 26 C.F.R. § 1.871-2(b).

important if the taxpayer's family does not accompany him.[16] Since 1985, the Section 871 regulations have provided that residency of aliens is determined under the objective rules of section 7701(b) - which provides, in general, that an alien who is in the United States for a specified number of days during the current and preceding two the years is a resident. However, Reg. § 1.871-2(c) provides that, for the purpose of determining whether an individual qualifies as a bona fide foreign resident under section 911(d)(1)(A), the more subjective rules of Reg. § 1.871-2(b) continue to apply. Unless a transferee obviously is treating his foreign location as his home, relying on bona fide residency for the section 911 exclusions involves risk.

Bona fide residency in a foreign country for an uninterrupted period can be maintained despite temporary trips to the United States or elsewhere on business or vacation.[17] In fact, a lawyer on an extended tour who obviously satisfies the residency test - i.e., who has established a home, whose family is with him or her, whose children are in local schools, and who has other close ties to the community - should be able to spend considerable time in the United States without jeopardizing his or her foreign residency. In fact, the major advantage of bona fide residence over physical presence is that the taxpayer can spend more time in the United States than the average of 35 days a year permitted by the physical-presence test. The courts have not dealt with year-after-year presence in the United States of, say, eight weeks, but the Tax Court held that spending five months in the United States did not interrupt a taxpayer's otherwise continuous long-term foreign residency.[18]

[d]—Physical Presence

An assignee satisfies this test if he or she has been physically present in a foreign country or countries for at least 330 full days during any period of twelve consecutive months.[19] The 12-month period can begin on any day and ends on the day before the same day 12 months later - e.g., beginning January 12, 2002 and ending January 11, 2003 for an assignee who arrives in London to begin his tour the morning of January 11, 2002. A full day starts and ends at midnight. An assignee who is traveling between two foreign locations is not docked a foreign day if he or she is outside any foreign

---

[16] *N.C. Fuller,* CA-6, 53-1 USTC ¶9405, 204 F 2d 592.

[17] Treas. Reg. § 911-2(d)(5); 26 C.F.R. § 911-2(d)(5) and Treas. Reg. § 1.911-2(c); 26 C.F.R. § 911-2(c).

[18] Hack v. Commissioner, 33 T.C. 1089 (1960).

[19] IRC § 911(d)(1)(B); 26 U.S.C. § 911(d)(1)(B); Treas. Reg. § 1.911-2(a)(1)(ii); 26 C.F.R. § 1.911-2(a)(1)(ii).

country for less than 24 hours. A foreign country is any sovereign country other than the United States and includes that country's territorial waters and air space. If, in travelling between two foreign locations, an assignee spends less than 24 hours in the United States, the time in the U.S. is treated as time spent traveling over areas not within any country.[20]

To get credit for January 12, 2002, the newly arrived lawyer must be in a foreign country 330 days during the period January 12, 2002 through January 11, 2003 - i.e., if he's not in a foreign country for 36-or-more days during this period, at least some days will be lost. However, later on, for example, 60 consecutive days in the United States - January 1, 2003 through March 1, 2003 - could pass muster (assuming that other absences didn't interfere):

> January 12, 2002 through January 11, 2003 - 365 days less 11 days = 354 days
> February 1, 2002 through January 31, 2003 - 365 days less 31 days = 334 days
> February 1, 2003 through January 31, 2004 - 365 days less 29 days = 336 days

This favorable result is despite that any 12-month period that included 36-or-more days in the period January 1, 2002 through March 1, 2002 would not pass muster - the taxpayer, not the IRS, selects the test periods.

Assignees who plan to rely on the physical-presence test to qualify for the section 911 exclusions should keep records to support their days of presence in foreign countries. Considering the subjectivity of the residence test, an assignee always should try to meet the physical presence test unless doing so is a business restriction.

[e]—Tax Home Requirement

The tax home of a qualified individual must be in a foreign country.[21] An individual shall not, however, be considered to have a tax home in a foreign country for any period for which the individual's abode is in the United States.[22]

---

[20] Treas. Reg. § 1.911(d); 26 C.F.R. § 1.911(d).

[21] IRC § 911(d)(1); 26 U.S.C. § 911(d)(1); Treas. Reg. § 1.911-2(b); 26 C.F.R. § 1.911-2(b).

[22] IRC § 911(d)(1); 26 U.S.C. § 911(d)(1); Treas. Reg. § 1.911-2(b); 26 C.F.R. § 1.911-2(b).

The requirement that a taxpayer not have an abode in the United States was added to § 911 in 1978. The House Ways and Means Committee report on this legislation discussed abode as follows:

> "[A] taxpayer is ineligible for the deduction for excess foreign living costs for any period for which his abode is in the United States. For example, a taxpayer who lives in Detroit, Michigan, but commutes daily to work in Windsor, Ontario, would ordinarily have his tax home in Windsor, but nevertheless would be ineligible for the deduction for excess foreign living costs."

Based on the law relating to section 162, it is clear that London would be the tax home of a lawyer assigned to his or her firm's London office for a period of at least one year and who in fact worked principally out of that office during that period.[23] Thus the crucial point is whether the assignee had any "abode" in the United States during that period.

> "'Abode' has been variously defined as one's home, habitation, residence, domicile or place of dwelling.[24] Black's Law Dictionary 7 (5th ed. 1979). While an exact definition of abode depends upon the context in which the word is used, it clearly does not mean one's principal place of business. Thus, abode has a domestic rather than a vocational meaning, and stands in contrast to 'tax home'. . . ."

The two cases most in point deal with similar facts and provide a taxpayer-friendly standard.[25] Both involve U.S. citizens who were pilots for Japan Airlines. Each was based in Japan, flew routes to both the U.S. and Asia, had a wife and children who lived in the U.S., had minimal contact with Japanese society or culture, and, literally, lived out of suitcases. They lived in a hotel owned by the airline two miles from the Narita airport, 43 miles from Tokyo. When they made flights, they checked out of the hotel and left their belongings there in storage. When they checked back in they would reclaim their stored items. On these facts, it was determined that both were bona fide residents of Japan for Section 911 purposes and that neither had an abode in the United States. The Court in *Jones* quoted the language stated above from the House Ways and Means Committee report on the 1978 legislation.

---

[23] See Chapter 18.02[1], *supra,* for discussion of away-from-home expenses.

[24] G.H. Jones, CA-5, 91-1 USTC ¶50,174, 927 F2d 849; J.S. Cobb, 62 TCM 408, Dec. 47,535(M) , TC Memo. 1991-376.

[25] FN 2 *supra* and J.S. Cobb, 62 TCM 408. Dec. 47,535(M), TC Memo. 1991-376.

Thus a lawyer assigned to his or her firm's London office for at least a year and who lives in the area will not have an abode in the United States. If the London office is the lawyer's principal place of business, London will be his or her tax home.

[f]—Maximizing the Exclusion

In the year of transfer and the year of return, the exclusion is prorated on a daily basis. Thus, in 2002, when the annual exclusion is $80,000, the exclusion is computed as follow:

$$\frac{\text{Qualifying days, say 60} \times \$80{,}000}{365} = \underline{\underline{\$13{,}151}}$$

Because of the mechanics of the physical-presence test, it is possible to have the qualifying days start before the assignee leaves the United States. For example, Carol's first full day in London after flying from the U.S. is July 1, 2002. The 330th day is May 26, 2003. While on assignment, if she is continually in a foreign country (the UK or otherwise) for that period, she can count back to the first day of the 12-month period - May 27, 2002 - and have her 12-month period start then, rather than July 1, the first day of 24-hour physical presence. (She will have been present in a foreign country or countries 330 days during the 12-month period.) Thus, there are 221 qualifying days in 2002, and her exclusion for 2002 is $48,438, computed as follows:

$$\frac{221 \times \$80{,}000}{365} = \underline{\underline{\$48{,}438}}$$

Had the qualifying period begun July 1, 2002, there would have been 184 qualifying days in 2002 and the exclusion would have been $40,329, $8,109 less than computed above. With a combined federal, state and city rate for a New Yorker of, say, 43%, some $3,500 is saved by this effortless planning. Any days in the period July 1, 2002 through May 26, 2003 that she is not in a foreign country will draw the beginning date forward a day from May 27, 2002 (assuming that none of the days brought into the new 12-month period in 2003 are spent out of a foreign country).

[g]—Housing Exclusion

The housing exclusion is in addition to the foreign earned income exclusion and is elected separately. It permits the exclusion of the housing-cost amount, which is actual foreign housing costs (as defined) in excess of a base amount."[26] The base amount is equal to 16% of the salary of a U.S. government employee at grade level GS-14, step 1. Effective for 2000, and continuing until it is adjusted, this salary is $63,567, and 16% is $10,171. The GS-14, step 1 salary is determined on January 1 of the calendar year in which the assignee's tax year begins. The base amount is determined on a daily basis. Thus, for 2001, it is $10,171 multiplied by the fraction determined by dividing (1) the number of qualifying days in the taxable year by (2) the number of days in the taxable year.[27] If the election is made, it applies to the taxpayer's' entire housing-cost amount.

The amount that can be excluded is the excess of:

1 The foreign earned income of the taxpayer for the taxable year, over

2. The amount of such income excluded from gross income as "foreign earned income."

3 Thus, for example, if an assignee has foreign earned income of $200,000 in 2002 (a year when the exclusion amount is $80,000) and he elects to exclude foreign earned income, the housing exclusion is limited to $120,000. Thus, if both exclusions are elected, the foreign earned income exemption is computed first. If any of the assignee's foreign earned income is other than "employer provided amounts," the portion of the housing amount attributable to the other amount is taken as a deduction from gross income rather than an exclusion. As will be discussed, all of an employee's foreign earned income will be employer provided amounts, unless he or she also has self-employment income.

Housing expenses include:

1. Rent, the fair rental value of housing provided by the employer,
2. Utilities (other than telephone charges),
3. Real and personal property insurance,
4. Occupancy taxes (other than those described following as non-deductible),
5. Non-refundable fees paid for securing a leasehold,
6. Rental of furniture and accessories,
7. Household repairs, and
8. Residential parking.[28]

---

[26] Treas. Reg. § 1.911-4(a); 26 C.F.R. § 1.911-4(a).
[27] Treas. Reg. § 1.911-4(a); 26 C.F.R. § 1.911-4(a).
[28] Treas. Reg. § 1.911-4(b)(1); 26 C.F.R. § 1.911-4(b)(1).

Housing expenses do not include:

1. The cost of buying a house, improvements, and other costs that are capital expenses;
2. The cost of purchased furniture or accessories or domestic labor (maids, gardeners, etc.);
3. Amortized payments of principal on debt secured by a mortgage on the taxpayer's housing;
4. Depreciation of housing owned by the taxpayer, or amortization or depreciation of capital improvements made to housing leased by the taxpayer;
5. Interest and taxes deductible under section 163 or 164 or other amounts deductible under section 216 (relating to the deduction of interest and taxes by tenants (owners) of cooperative apartments);
6. The expense of more than one foreign household (except when justified by adverse living conditions - discussed following);
7. Expenses excluded from income under section 119 (meals and lodging furnished for the convenience of the employer);
8. Expenses claimed as deductible moving expenses under section 217; or
9. The cost of a pay television subscription[29]

[h]—"Reasonable" Housing Expenses

Housing expenses must be reasonable. Expenses are not reasonable to the extent that they are lavish or extravagant under the circumstances.[30] There is no official guidance; but there is little probability that the IRS will contend that housing expense is lavish or extravagant in the circumstances. There is no recorded instance of the IRS attacking housing expenses as lavish or extravagant, nor is there any recorded instance of the IRS successfully attacking travel and entertainment expenses on that basis.[31] The apparent enforcement approach is to permit housing appropriate to taxpayers' income, even if it is lavish or extravagant.

---

[29] Treas. Reg. § 1.911-4(b)(2); 26 C.F.R. § 1.911-4(b)(2).

[30] Treas. Reg. §1.911-4(b)(4); 26 C.F.R. §1.911-4(b)(4).

[31] "Lavish or extravagant under the circumstances" entered the Internal Revenue Code lexicon in 1962 with the amendment of section 162(a)(2) (§4(b), Revenue Act of 1962), relating to the deductibility of meals and lodging expense. The term was added to section 911, effective January 1, 1982, when it was amended to provide for the exclusion of the "housing cost amount."

[i]—Housing Amount

The housing exclusion is an all-or-nothing election.[32] It is applied before the earned income exclusion in reducing foreign earned income.[33] Housing expenses are excluded to the extent they relate to employer-provided amounts.[34] These include all amounts paid in cash or in kind, and include salary, bonus, and all allowances. Housing expenses are limited to foreign earned income.[35] Any excess can be carried forward to the next year (but only to the next year). Unless a taxpayer is self-employed, all of his or her foreign earned income will be employer-provided amounts. A guaranteed payment to a partner is an employer provided amount. Figure 20-B illustrates the interplay of a housing exclusion and a foreign earned income exclusion.

Example: Jones is an associate and a bona fide resident of France throughout 2000. His salary for the year is $250,000 - not including employer-provided housing having a fair rental value of $50,000. Thus, his foreign earned income for the year is $300,000. In addition, he has $10,000 of qualifying housing expenses, so his total housing expense is $60,000. He elects the foreign earned income exclusion - $76,000 in 2000. The base housing amount is $10,171 (GS-14, step one salary of $63,567 X 16% = $10,171 X 366/366 = $10,171).

Figure 20-B. Illustration of housing exclusion and foreign earned income exclusion.

Foreign earned income	$300,000
Housing cost amount($60,000 less $10,171)	(49,829)
Foreign earned income after housing cost amount	250,171
Foreign earned income exclusion (smaller of $76,000 or $250,171)	(76,000)
Adjusted gross income (assuming no other income)	$174,171

[32] IRC § 911(c)(1)(A); 26 U.S.C. § 911(c)(1)(A); Treas. Reg. § 1.911-4(d)(1); 26 C.F.R. § 1.911-4(d)(1).

[33] Treas. Reg. § 1.911-4(d)(1) and Treas. Reg. § 1.911-3(d)(2)(i); 26 C.F.R. § 1.911-4(d)(1) and § 1.911-3(d)(2)(i).

[34] Treas. Reg. § 1.911-4(d)(1); 26 C.F.R. § 1.911-4(d)(1).

[35] Treas. Reg. § 1.911-4(d)(2); 26 C.F.R. § 1.911-4(d)(2).

In the illustration, Jones' foreign earned income exclusion is $76,000 and his housing cost amount is $49,829 ($60,000 less $10,171). In this case, both are excluded in full, because the combined amount - $125,829 - is less than total foreign earned income ($300,000).

If Jones had been a partner, with the same income as above received as a "guaranteed payment" from his U.S. firm, the answer would have been the same.

If Jones had been a partner, and the above income was his share of the income of the Paris branch office (and thus self-employment income), the earned income exclusion would remain $76,000. But, rather than being excluded, his housing cost amount - $49,829 - would be a deduction from gross income (i.e., an "above the line" deduction, not an itemized deduction). If, because of the limitation, some housing cost amount is not deductible, it carries forward to the next year and can be deducted to the extent there is excess foreign earned income (i.e., foreign earned income that is not absorbed by that year's earned income exclusion and housing cost amount.[36] An important difference between the housing exclusion and the housing deduction is that the housing exclusion reduces foreign earned income before it is reduced by the foreign earned income exclusion. For the deduction, the order is reversed. Foreign earned income is first reduced by the foreign earned income exclusion, and the housing deduction is limited to the remainder. There is no carryover of housing amount in excess of foreign earned income, but, considering that the exclusion gets first crack at foreign earned income, an excess exclusion is unlikely.

[j]—Qualified Second Household

If an assignee maintains a second household outside the United States for his or her spouse and children because the living conditions at the assigned location are dangerous, unhealthy or otherwise adverse, the expense of both households qualifies for the housing expense exclusion or deduction.[37]

[k]—Separate Exclusions for Husband and Wife

Many of those considered by their firms for foreign assignments are married to someone who also has a career. Often, this conflict is resolved by arranging - one way or another - for both spouses to end up on tours of the same length to the same place. In this case, each

---

[36] IRC § 911(c)(3); 26 C.F.R. § 911(c)(3).

[37] IRC § 911(c)(2)(B); 26 C.F.R. § 911(c)(2)(B).

qualifies for the foreign earned income exclusion of $80,000 in 2002 and following. This can be taken on a joint return, but only to the extent that each has foreign earned income. For example, if one spouse has foreign earned income of $200,000 and the other has $50,000, the total exclusion is $130,000 ($80,000 plus $50,000). If they file separately, they can allocate housing expense as they choose, but each would have to reduce his or her share by a full base amount. On a joint return, there would be only one base amount.

§ 20.05 Foreign Tax Credit

[1]—Overview

The United States taxes the worldwide income of its citizens and residents. To prevent (or mitigate) double taxation, U.S. citizens and residents can elect to take a credit against their U.S. tax for the foreign tax they pay on foreign source income. This limitation is computed by multiplying total U.S. tax by the ratio that foreign source gross income bears to total gross income. In the case of U.S. assignees to foreign branch offices, salary received for services rendered abroad is foreign source income.

If a partner receives a guaranteed payment for services rendered abroad, that, too, is foreign source income for U.S. income tax purposes, as is income identified as earned by the foreign practice.

If all of the partners of the firm are treated as earning a proportionate share of the firm's income from all sources, (i.e., domestic and foreign), the partners working in the foreign branch will have foreign source income only in the ratio that the firm's foreign source gross income bears to total gross income. If the firm's has little foreign source income, a foreign-based partner could have paid more foreign taxes than he or she can claim as a credit on a U.S. personal income tax return. When foreign taxes are limited, an individual is said to be in an "excess credit position," which means that foreign taxes have to be carried back two years and forward five years.[1] As an alternative, each year taxpayers can choose to take foreign taxes as a credit or as an itemized deduction. However, the rules for application of the credits can be confusing. For example, if in Year one a person has excess credits and carries those credits into Year two, the election to deduct Year two's taxes is effective only with respect to Year two's taxes and does not change the excess credits from Year one. Consequently, Year one's excess credit carry over to Year 3.

Taxpayers will choose to take foreign income taxes as a deduction only where they have foreign taxes far in excess of the foreign tax credit limitation. These choices can be changed on a timely filed amended return.

The concept of foreign tax credits is not limited to the United States. For example, the United Kingdom and Germany allow foreign tax credits against their taxes, although in the case of Germany, credits are only allowed for taxes paid to a country with which Germany does not have a double tax treaty.

---

[1] IRC § 904(c); 26 C.F.R. § 904(c)

[2]—Foreign Tax Credits Versus Foreign Income Exclusions

Foreign tax credits cannot be taken on income that has been excluded under section 911. If a taxpayer is assigned to a high-tax country, it may be beneficial to forgo the exclusion. The alternative minimum tax - "AMT" - also must be considered. The AMT, designed originally to insure that high-income taxpayers did not use high deductions to avoid paying their "fair share" of income tax, now snares many who do not fit the targeted profile. This is mainly because statutory thresholds have not kept pace with inflation. Whether foreign tax credits or income exclusions are most beneficial often is not clear-cut, without doing tax calculations that compare results with and without exclusions.

§ 20.06 Moving Expenses

As previously discussed, relocating employees or partners have special tax considerations.[1] Moving associates or partners in connection with foreign assignments have special rules and require special considerations. Two important considerations that apply to reimbursements for foreign transfers are the sourcing of the payment for tax purposes and the application of the payment.

The first consideration is how should moving costs be sourced for tax purposes? A moving expense from the U.S. to a foreign assignment is sourced foreign. A moving expense from a foreign assignment back to the U.S. not foreign source income, unless it is guaranteed by the law firm, in writing, before the tour begins, whether or not the assignee stays with the firm when the tour is over.[2] This is important, because income does not qualify for the Section 911 exclusions unless it is foreign source, nor does it increase the foreign tax credit limitation.

The second consideration is that moving expense reimbursements apply entirely to the year of the move if the taxpayer qualifies for the foreign income exclusion for at least 120 days during that year. If not, the reimbursement is allocated on the basis of the number of qualifying days in the year of the move to total days in that year, with the balance allocated to the next year. The 120-day rule applies in reverse for the year the taxpayer returns to the United States.

In a non-leap year, assuming that there are no non-U.S. days when the physical presence is used, the following arrival and departure dates will put the taxpayers within the 120-day limit in the year of arrival and year of departure:[3]

	Physical presence	Bona fide residence
Arrival date: On or after	October 7	September 2
Departure date: On or before	March 27	May 1

---

[1] See Chapter 28.02, *infra,* for a discussion of relocation costs and moving expenses.

[2] Reg. § 1.911-3(e)(5)(i).

[3] Reg. § 1.911-3(e)(5)(ii).

For example, assume that Bill Smith's first qualifying day is November 1, 2003. He has 61 qualifying days in 2003. He received a taxable moving expense reimbursement of $20,000, which must be reported as income in 2003. But only $3,342 is treated as attributable to services performed in 2003:

$$\frac{\text{61 qualifying days in the year of move}}{365} \times \$20{,}000 = \$3{,}342$$

The balance, $16,658, is treated as attributable to services rendered in 2004.

§ 20.07 United States Principal Residence

One of the most important decisions a homeowner has to make when transferring temporarily to a foreign country is whether to sell or retain his or her U.S. home. Tax considerations are important, but fluctuating values and mortgage rates mean that a seller might be priced out of comparable housing in the same or comparable location. And, of course, the additional costs of brokers' fees, closing costs, etc. out and back in can be considerable. Another reason for retaining a current residence is the extraordinary appreciation that many homeowners have realized in recent years.

The taxation of gain on the sale of a principal residence changed dramatically in 1997. Prior to that, taxpayers could rollover the gain on the sale of a principal residence to the extent that the proceeds were reinvested in a new principal residence within two years.[1] The residence had to be the principal residence at the time it was sold. Apropos for those on foreign assignments, the reinvestment period was tolled while the taxpayer's tax home was outside the United States, to permit a reinvestment period of up to four years.[2]

Effective for sales after May 6, 1997, there no longer is rollover. Instead, gain of $500,000 for joint returns and $250,000 for single returns is excluded if the house was a principal residence for a total of two years during the five-year period preceding the sale of the residence.[3] Thus, the residence no longer must be a principal residence at the time it is sold. Moreover, the sale of a subsequent principal residence - say, an apartment in London - also qualifies if its sale follows the earlier sale by more than two years.[4]

In defining "principal residence," intent makes less difference than under the old rules, in that the proposed regulations provide that "use" requires "occupancy."[5] The old regulations did not. The proposed regulations state that absences of two months on vacation do not break residency,[6] but provide that a break of one year while a professor is on a foreign sabbatical does break residency.[7] This seems determinative that whether of not the residence of a lawyer who was abroad for several years is a principal residence is essentially, a mathematical computation.

---

[1] IRC § 1034(a); 26 U.S.C. § 1034(a).
[2] IRC § 1034(k); 26 U.S.C. § 1034(k).
[3] IRC § 121(a); 26 U.S.C. § 121(a).
[4] IRC§ 121(b)(3)(A); 26 U.S.C. § 121(b)(3)(A).
[5] Prop. Treas. Reg. § 1.121(c); 26 U.S.C. § 1.121(c).
[6] Prop. Treas. Reg. § 1.121(f) Example 5; 26 C.F.R.. § 1.121(f).
[7] Prop. Treas. Reg. §1.121(f) Example 4; 26 C.F.R. §1.121(f).

By negating all factors except occupancy, the new rules make it easier for assignees to take the position that they are no longer residents for state and local income tax purpose without jeopardizing their U.S. home's status as a principal residence.

§ 20.08 Withholding Tax

U.S. employers of employees based abroad must continue to withhold on wages. However, the amount of the withholding can be reduced to the amount that is expected to be due taking into account exclusions for foreign earned income if it is reasonable to assume that the employee will qualify for the exclusions.[1] This must be verified by the employee to the employer in writing[2] Similarly, U.S. withholding can be reduced for the effect of anticipated foreign tax credits. Moreover, a U.S. employer is not required to withhold U.S. income tax if it is required to withhold foreign income tax.[3]

---

[1] Treas. Reg. § 31.3401(a)(8)(A)-1(a)(1)(i); 26 C.F.R. § 31.3401(a)(8)(A)-1(a)(1)(i).

[2] Treas. Reg. § 31.3401(a)(8)(A)-1(a)-1(A)(1)(ii); 26 C.F.R. § 31.3401(a)(8)(A)-1(a)-1(A)(1)(ii).

[3] Treas. Reg. § 31.3401(a)(8)(A)-1(b)-1(A)(1); 26 C.F.R. § 31.3401(a)(8)(A)-1(b)-1(A)(1).

§ 20.09 Social Security Liability

A U.S. citizen (or resident) who is an employee of an "American employer" (a U.S. individual, corporation or partnership) will pay U.S. social security taxes even though employed abroad[1] and even though the income is excluded from his/her gross income under Section 911.[2] For this purpose, a U.S. partnership is one at least two-thirds of whose partners are U.S. residents.[3]

Partners who are U.S. citizens or residents are subject to self-employment tax on their worldwide earned income. The Code provides that the Section 911 exclusion does not apply to self-employment tax.[4]

As a general rule, it is advantageous for a U.S. person on a temporary tour abroad to pay U.S. employment taxes rather than host country employment taxes. In almost all cases, foreign employment taxes are higher than U.S. employment taxes (Hong Kong, which has no social security tax, is an exception). In addition, employment taxes paid to the host country for a short period may not generate any payments at retirement (and in any event will be subject to currency risk). Moreover, being out of the U.S. system may reduce payments received at retirement.

However, where a lawyer is assigned to a foreign office for a year or more, the host country always has the right to subject wages and self-employment income earned within its jurisdiction to social security tax,[5] unless a totalization agreement applies. And, as noted, if a U.S. citizen or resident works abroad for an American employer, the income also will be subject to U.S. social security tax.

---

[1] IRC § 3121(b); 26 U.S.C. § 3121(b).

[2] Section 911 excludes only taxes imposed by subtitle A of the Internal Revenue Code. Section 3121 is in subtitle C - Employment Taxes.

[3] IRC § 3121(h); 26 U.S.C. § 3121(h).

[4] IRC § 1402(a)(11); 26 U.S.C. § 1402(a)(11).

[5] Statutory exemptions from income tax for de minimis amounts earned on certain short assignments, such as the U.S. 's $3,000 exemptions under IRC § 861(a)(3) in certain circumstances, may or may not be exempt from employment taxes.

§ 20.10 Totalization Agreements

[1]—Prevent Double Taxation/Preserve Benefits

Tax totalization agreements eliminate double social security tax contributions when a resident of one country is transferred to another country for a temporary assignment.[1] Tax treaties (which focus on preventing double taxation of income and capital gains) do not limit the right of treaty partners to levy social security taxes in any of the circumstances discussed in this chapter. The U.S. has 18 totalization agreements. These include the UK, France, Germany, and all the other European Union countries except Denmark, plus Canada, Norway, South Korea and Switzerland. Prominent by their absence are Australia and Japan, but they, plus Brazil, are negotiating totalization agreements with the U.S.

Totalization agreements only apply when the individual otherwise would be subject to social security taxes in both counties. To be exempt, the transferee's employer or the self-employed individual must obtain a Certificate of Coverage from the U.S. to present to the host country's social security administration. This can be obtained by writing the Social Security Administration, Office of International Policy, P.O. Box 17741, Baltimore, Maryland 21235.

The term "totalization" connotes the other purpose of the agreements - the totalization of benefits. If a person has accumulated coverage under two systems, but under either system he or she lacks the years of coverage to get benefits, the individual can elect to combine the years of coverage and receive a pro-rata benefit from each country. For example, an individual who has six years of coverage in the U.S. (enough to qualify for benefits) and 10 years in the other country (where it takes 12 to qualify for benefits) can elect to be credited with 16 years in each country, and get 6/16th of the U.S. benefit and 10/16th of the other country's benefit. These agreements in most cases provide considerably more double taxation protection to associates than to partners.

[2]—Five-Year Limit for Employees

If an employee is sent to a country with which the U.S. has an agreement country and expects to stay for five years or less, he or she (and the U.S. employer) will continue to pay U.S. social security tax

---

[1] Totalization Agreements are entered into under section 233 of the Social Security Act. They do not require approval of two-thirds of the Senate. Rather, they become effective if neither the Senate nor the House objects within 60 session days of an agreement being presented.

(and not pay it in the host country). It is possible that a term longer than five years can be obtained by application to the competent authorities (designated revenue officials). Some agreements provide a one-year limit on extensions and generally authorities do not extend more than 18 months. Often, the authorities will not extend agreements unless there are changed circumstances. As noted, income otherwise subject to U.S. social security tax is not exempt merely because it is excluded from gross income for income tax purposes under Section 911.[2] If an assignment originally expected to last less than five years is extended beyond that point, the host country (rather than the U.S.) is entitled to assess social security tax from the date intention changes, even though less than five years has expired. As will be discussed, in some cases this reliance on intent can provide flexibility as to which country's social security taxes are paid.

[3]—American Employer

Totalization agreements do not apply to employees unless they remain in the employ of the their "American employer" (e.g., working for the branch of their U.S. law firm) or for an affiliated foreign employer if the American employer agrees to pay the employee's social security tax. As noted, a U.S. employer includes a corporation organized under the laws of the United States or any State, a partnership if at least two-thirds of the partners are U.S. residents, and an individual who is a resident of the U.S.

[4]—Foreign Affiliate

As noted, the term American employer includes a "foreign affiliate" of an American employer if the American employer has entered into an agreement with the Internal Revenue Service under Section 3121(l) of the Internal Revenue Code to pay Social Security taxes for U.S. citizens and residents employed by the affiliate. This election covers all eligible employees and cannot be revoked. An "affiliated employer" is (1) a corporation in which the American employer has at least a 10% interest in its voting stock or (if not a corporation) (2) an entity in which the American employer has at least a 10% profit interest. The employee must be "transferred" by his or her American employer. Thus, a U.S. resident who is hired abroad by an American employer for service abroad does not qualify. If the American employer has entered into agreement under section 3121(l), payments made by the American employer into a tax-qualified pension or profit-sharing plan on behalf of

---

[2] See § 20.09, *supra,* for a discussion of social security liability.

the employee working for a foreign affiliate will be treated as if the employee continued to work for the American employer.[3]

[5]—Rules for Partners

If a partner is sent to a country with which the U.S. has an agreement, then under the typical agreement he or she is covered only so long as he or she does not become a resident of the host country. Residency criteria vary, but, on average, a partner would be at risk if the tour were for two years or more (as discussed later in this section, 24 consecutive months would be more than enough to make a foreign national a U.S. resident in most instances). Most agreements speak only of residency, but the agreements with France and Belgium provide a 24-month limit for self-employed persons, while the German agreement provides a five-year limit (in none of these agreements is residency a factor). Residency is determined under the rules of the host country. The agreements do not define residency, and there is no tie-breaker provision to prevent an assignee from being considered a resident of both the home and host countries. However, totalization agreements provide that a covered individual cannot be taxed in both countries. Compensating a U.S. partner assigned abroad via a guaranteed payment would not achieve employee status for totalization agreement purposes.[4] On the other hand, the partner's affiliation (foreign or U.S.) does not affect his or her totalization eligibility - i.e., a partner does not have to be transferred to a related partnership - he or she must merely set up business in the other country. If a person is regarded as self-employed under the rules of one country and an employee under the rules of the other, many treaties provide that transferees will be subject to the coverage laws only of the country where the employee resides.[5]

If a transferred employee works abroad for his or her U.S. employer, he or she has no choice but to stay in the U.S. system and forgo the host country system, unless the tour is expected to last more than five years (in which case the totalization agreement provides that the employee will be under the host country system and not the U.S. system). If the stay is expected to be for less than five years, and a certificate of coverage is not obtained from the U.S. (or obtained and not submitted to the host country authorities), the transferee will remain in the U.S. system and also be subject to the host country system. As a practical matter, there appears to be little risk in a transferee on an "open ended" assignment taking the position that his or her assignment is expected to

---

[3] Treas. Reg. § 1.406-1; 26 C.F.R. § 1.406-1.
[4] Prop. Treas. Reg. § 1.1402(a)-2(g); § 1.1402(a)-2(g).
[5] E.g., Article 4 (3) of the U.S. agreement with the UK.

be for less than or more than five years, depending on whether he or she wishes to be in the U.S. system or in the foreign system. if there is contrary documentation, such as an employment contract, the employee should not indulge in this flexibility. Social security administrators very rarely question the bona fides of an applicant's expectations, but the host country may well notice if a firm has a pattern of four-year tours becoming six-year tours.

CHAPTER 21

Risk Management

Chapter Contents

---

§ 21.01 Overview

A generation ago, law firms thought of risk in the context of malpractice exposure—the risk of being sued for doing a poor job of "lawyering." Today, mentioning "risk" to a managing partner of a law firm brings to mind a myriad of areas in which a law firm's actions can bring about adverse consequences.

There is nothing more sacred—or prized—to a lawyer than his or her reputation. Likewise, there is nothing more important to a law firm than the cumulative reputations of its lawyers. It is that cumulative reputation that speaks to the level of service that clients can expect. Although it takes years to establish a good reputation, it can take very little time to tarnish that reputation because risk was not properly managed.

The importance of risk management is illustrated by the efforts of the American Bar Association and state bar associations and the many books and articles on the subject.[1] This chapter discusses risk management in

---

[1] See, for example, Fortune and O'Roark, "Risk Management for Lawyers," 45 S.C.L. Rev. 617 (Summer 1994).

the context of modern-day law firms and draws on the literature on the risk management, the PricewaterhouseCoopers Law Firm Survey, and on our experience. Many firms have gone past the single person shop into regional, national, or international law firms and now face many of the risks that are addressed in the following sections. The chapter identifies many of those risks and addresses steps to minimize them, including the creation of a risk management team.

§ 21.02 Risk Management Team

Managing risk begins by realizing that a law firm can be subject to many different risks. The next step is assigning qualified personal to deal with those risks. In theory, risk is best controlled by each partner. In reality, however, it is the actions of each engagement partner that can cause risk to become an issue.

Many law firms have management committees or boards that are vested with the day-to-day responsibilities of running the firm and managing practice economics such as chargeable hours, billings, collections, and expenses. Depending on the size of the firm and how it wants to respond to risk management issues, the management committee can either handle risk management issues directly or it can use its oversight function by delegating the function to a partner. In general, law firms are committing far more resources to risk management now than ever before.[1]

[1]—Risk Management Partner

The focal point of any effective risk management program is the person responsible for managing risk. In the majority of cases, this person is a partner who is often a member of the management committee or reports directly to it. These jobs take time and cannot be done properly (and certainly not enthusiastically) unless the partner or partners involved are kept whole financially.[2]

It is the risk management partner's job to identify areas of risk, lead a risk management steering committee, establish policies and procedures to guard against those risks, and monitor compliance with the policies and procedures. The risk management partner should be astute enough to recognize risk exposure and strong enough in character or demeanor to be able to enforce the rules. Having the responsibility but no enforcement clout translates into an environment in which following policies is at the whim of partners or associates, who may not have any interest or incentive to comply. That latitude can be a recipe for trouble.

[2]—Partners and Practice Groups

Unless a law firm is small, it is difficult, if not impossible, for one person to administer a risk management program. Normally, a risk

---

[1] Harned, "Risk Management Key to Avoiding Pitfalls," Legal Mgmt, Vol. 17 No. 4, p. 61 (July/August 1998). at 61; "Executive Summary Risk Management At Large Law Firms,", pp. 1021, 1024 (PLI/NY 1998).

[2] Jacques, *Organizing Your Practice For Success and Avoiding Malpractice Claims* p. 1 (John Weil & Co. 1999), See Harned, N.1 *supra* at 65. at 697.

management steering committee is formed to work with the risk management partner. When a firm has multiple branch offices, it is common to appoint risk management partners in charge of the larger offices and, depending on the size of the practice, appoint A steering committee to work on local risk management issues. This is especially true of non-US-based offices that may have many professional or cultural differences between the way law is practiced in one country verses the way it is practiced in the United States. Together, branch risk management teams, the home-office steering committee and the global risk management partner must take ownership of the risk management policies and procedures that they establish.

Ownership includes the responsibility of monitoring their policies to ensure compliance. Through conscientious monitoring, the steering committee should be able to determine how often established policies and procedures are by-passed, why they were by-passed, and who authorized the exception. Depending on the findings, the steering committee should recommend changes in the policies and procedures so that they are current with new business risks. For example, in the last decade, risk management policies and procedures had to be modified to encompass electronic mail.

Another important responsibility that the risk management partner and steering committee have is to devise procedures that partners and associates must follow in the event that a troublesome practice matter (i.e., a claim) arises. This precaution is simple damage control so that a bad situation does not get worse.

§ 21.03 Policies and Procedures Manual

The risk management partner along with the steering committee is responsible for developing realistic and workable risk management policies and procedures manual. An effective way to establish policies and procedures is to develop a questionnaire for each department, each practice group and each office to identify what procedures are in use, and what needs to be changed or monitored without disturbing the efficiency of the workflow. The questionnaire should be completed by a representative group of partners, associates and support staff. It is important to interview all levels because one level, such as a partner, might discuss what they think is happening only to have the support staff contradict the statement by describing the situation from their perspective.

Following completion of the questionnaires, the steering committee should conduct selected interviews to clarify points made in the questionnaire and to solicit risk management suggestions for formulating policies and procedures.

Depending on the size of the firm, the interview process should include members of practice groups and individuals from other offices, especially non-US offices. It is likely that non-US office personnel will discuss risk management issues that are unique to their countries and that could never be anticipated without first-hand knowledge.

Based on the interviews, the steering committee should formulate a list of policies and procedures. It also is valuable to prepare a risk matrix that lists the types of risk that were identified and categorizes them based on severity. After sufficient discussion, the steering committee should draft the risk management policies and procedures. After drafting, the risk management policies and procedures should be distributed to the management committee (if any), to the managing partner, executive officer (if any), chief financial officer, executor director (if any), controller, managing partners of each office, managing partners of each practice group, and general counsel. Each person should have the opportunity to comment on the proposed policies and procedures before they are issued.

When the policies and procedures are approved, they should be distributed (in paper copy or electronically) to every member of the firm. Depending on the topic, copies of the policies should be displayed in the firm's lunchroom on bulletin boards. Again, depending on the topic, the steering committee should give presentations to selected groups within the firm to make sure that they are aware of the policies and procedures. At the same time, the steering committee needs to explain the possible repercussions for not abiding by the policies and procedures. Not all policies and procedures have the same risk potential, so the repercussions need to be tailored to the severity of the infraction. The point being communicated is that management is concerned with managing its risk and has approved policies and procedures to do just that. Those firm members or employees who will not follow the policies and procedures are unnecessarily subjecting the firm to risk and need to understand that a penalty is associated with that type of indifference or behavior.

When the policies and procedures are implemented, they should be identified as short-term action plans—those action plans that yield immediate benefits—and long-term action plans—those that require more time to implement and to align with best practices.

Periodically, the steering committee needs to monitor compliance with the policies and procedures and can use the firm's internal auditors for this function (more will be discussed on this subject later in the chapter). Based on the results of monitoring compliance, the steering committee should consider changes to the policies and procedures. This process should be repeated periodically, but more so when the policies and procedures are first introduced.

If something should happen that creates risk for the firm or that was not anticipated when the policies and procedures were created, the steering committee needs to formulate changes to the policies to ward off similar risks in the future.

§ 21.04 Risks to be Managed

The first step in establishing an effective risk management system is to identify the areas in which there are risks and then formulating policies and procedures to avoid the risks. Acknowledging that there hundreds of risks facing law firms, for purposes of this chapter, the risks are categorized as

1. Performance risks,
2. Operational risks,
3. Financial and accounting risks,
4. Trust account risks, and
5. Employee risks.

Each of these risks is discussed in this section. Strategies to manage these risks are discussed later in this chapter.[1]

[1]—Performance Risks

Performance risks arise from situations in which legal services were provided negligently or poorly. Performance risks can lead to malpractice claims that, if successful, can destroy a firm and ruin its partners or owners financially and professionally. The cost of these claims goes far beyond the direct, immediate dollar cost; the disruption, lost time, and the effect on a firm's morale and reputation can take a heavy toll on the future operation of the firm.

Performance risks can be categorized into three areas: professional conduct, client base variables, and partner composition. Each will be discussed in this section.

[a]—Professional Conduct

Broadly speaking, professional conduct considers the ways in which attorneys practice law, i.e., do business. In terms of malpractice claims, this area generates more litigation against a law firm than most other risk areas.

Some professional conduct risks that can lead to malpractice claims are:

1. Inaccurate or incomplete legal advice - in the rush to complete a project within a real or perceived limited time frame, an attorney may not spend enough time on a matter to make sure that he or she has the correct answer and that the advice is complete.

---

[1] See § 21.05 *infra*.

2. Not qualified to accept assignment - When evaluations and advancement are tied to hours, an attorney may accept an assignment for which he or she is not qualified or may not seek the assistance of someone who is qualified.

3. Uncontrolled growth - Firms that experience rapid growth through mergers or lateral admissions are more likely to be divided into discrete, increasingly narrow practice specialties, giving rise to the "cottage industry" practice model (lack of strong central control) and making it more difficult to avoid conflicts.[2]

4. International expansion - Firms that have expanded internationally may experience different professional standards or practices in the way business is conducted.

5. Inadequate supervision - Inadequate supervision normally applies to associates, but can apply to lateral admissions when partners are autonomous and don't work with other partners.

6. Conflicts - Accepting client assignments without checking to determine if there are client conflicts.

It is interesting to note that more malpractice is committed by attorneys with at least ten years experience than by those with less experience (the lowest malpractice rate of all is for lawyers just out of law school).[3] This is noted to dispel the notion that a firm's risk management procedures can be relaxed for those at the top. Another statistic is that a sizable percentage of negligence is due to administrative errors, and that a sizable percentage of these are for missing deadlines and failure to calendar properly.[4]

[b]—Client Base Vulnerability

This risk refers to the vulnerability that a firm faces when its client base is concentrated in a practice area that is particularly vulnerable to a business cycle. For example, the merger and acquisition legal practice and real estate practice are more vulnerable to a significant downturn in the economy than the litigation practice. Another good example is the rise and fall of the dot-com practice - when the economy was strong, dot-com euphoria permeated the economy and was as much a blessing for law firms that rendered services to those companies as it was a curse to those firms that lost valued associates or

---

[2] Davis, "The Long-Term Implications of the Kaye Scholer Case For Law Firm Management - Risk Management Comes of Age," 35 S. Tex. L. Rev. 667, 667 (1994).

[3] Fortney, "Law Firm Risk Management and Peer Review," 51 Con. Fin. L. Q. Rep. 98, 103, fns. 61, 62 (Spring 1997).

[4] *Id.* at 98.

partners to dot-com companies. When the dot-com environment collapsed, some law firms suffered because they lost the revenue stream and had excess associate capacity which lead to layoffs.

Client base vulnerability also refers to the vulnerability a firm faces when its practice is heavily dependent on a very few clients - the key-client syndrome. Losing a dominant client can be devastating to a firm. This can occur because of poor work, the loss of a key contact (at either the client or the law firm), the expansion of the client's in-house legal department, or the client's merger or acquisition by another company, among other things. In a merger of equals, who gets the legal work can depend on something akin to a coin toss: one company gets to pick the accounting firm and the other gets to pick the law firm. Clients also are lost when a client that had used many law firms decides to consolidate the work into fewer law firms, maybe as few one. Small firms are particularly vulnerable to this pullback because they are likely to lack the breadth of expertise or the size to handle all of the work.

[c]—Partnership Composition

One normally would not think that the partner composition of a law firm would be a risk worth talking about. The reality is that some firms have found out the hard way that partner composition makes a difference. There have been times when major law firms experienced so much internal strife that the firm ultimately decided to dissolve instead of resolving the strife. This can happen because younger partners are unhappy that senior partners are allocated a larger share of profits than they are and decide to have a "palace coup" to oust some or all of the senior partners. It also can happen when a block of partners wants to pursue a strategic business plan and other partners disagree. Friction within a partnership can occur after a merger when two groups of partners join together and one side or the other finds out that pre-merger shared information was more hype than reality.

[d]—Business Dealings With Clients/Directorships

Generally, it is a bad idea to have business dealings with a client.[5] It is a basic tenant that a lawyer has a fiduciary duty in his or her dealings with a client. Observance of that duty can be challenged when that obligation appears to conflict with the actions of a law firm or one of its partners in a business deal with a client. It is not unusual, for example, for a partner of a law firm to be the lead outside

---

[5] See Fortune and O'Roark, "Risk Management For Lawyers," 45 S.C.L. Rev. 617 pp. 621, 622, 640 and N. 25 (1994). See also "Executive Summary Risk Management At Large Law Firms," (PLI/NY 1998). See N. 3 *supra* at 104 and N. 73 at 106.

counsel for a client. When that lawyer is also to be a member of the client's board of directors, there can be conflict of interests; if not in reality, at least in appearance. While "wearing two hats" can create opportunities for a law firm, it also can raise allegations of impropriety and conflicts of interest. More and more, society is focusing on the appearance of impropriety, even in the absence of actual impropriety. The risk is real. Any attack against a partner—in which the firm is accused through association—will tarnish the firm's reputation.

Not-for-profit boards involve less—but still substantial—risk. Although they do not have shareholder suits, they are more likely than for-profit organizations to have poor financial controls or lack good oversight, and may be more susceptible to defalcations or accounting irregularities. When this happens, a board member, who is also the not-for-profit's outside counsel, is (along with his or her firm) a likely target for allegations or damages.

For these reasons, larger firms generally discourage partners from wearing two hats with the same client.

[2]—Operational Risks

[a]—Office Security

Office security starts at the front door or in the reception area. The risk is that someone who should not have access to the office gets access. Without a building pass, firm-provided security tag, or access key, a firm can unknowingly expose itself to a risk to its assets or to the personal assets of its partners or employees. It is not uncommon for thieves to pose as repair men or as professionals and to walk into a law firm (or follow someone through security doors) where they steal wallets, purses or computers. If they can do that without getting caught, one has to wonder if they can steal confidential files as easily. The physical integrity of a law office, therefore, is vital.

[b]—Confidentiality

A cornerstone of the attorney-client relationship is confidentiality.[6] It is absolute—except where certain criminal acts can be forestalled by the attorney's disclosure[7]—and nothing can destroy trust faster than a lawyer violating this trust. Whatever information anyone in a firm—lawyers or otherwise—learn about client matters is confidential. Through the years, there have been stories about secretaries or

---

[6] See Fortune and O'Roark, "Risk Management For Lawyers," 45 S.C.L. Rev. 617, p. 652 (1994). See, for example, Bravin, "ABA Endorses Expanding the Reasons For Breaching Client Confidentiality," Wall Street Journal, http://www.wsj.com (Aug. 7, 2001).

other support staff, sharing insider information with roommates, relatives, or friends to profit illegally from confidential information. Leaks can happen when confidential information is discussed in elevators, lavatories, on the street, in restaurants, are bars or over cell phones. Leaks can be innocent and unintentional, but they happen and that's the risk. The consequences to the individual and to the firm can be dire if there are breaches—including jail for the perpetrators in the case of insider trading. Unlike most areas of malpractice vulnerability, confidentiality is an area where service employees, such as mail room personnel, telephone operators, and food service employees, can get a firm into just as much trouble as the lawyers. A good risk management program needs to address these risks.

[c]—Client Files

Access to client files represents a significant risk within a law firm. Files that are loose on an associate's desk or left unattended at a secretary's station can be invitations to those who want improper access to them. The fact that "nothing ever happened before" is not a good reason to ignore the potential risk. Client files contain very confidential information that should never be accessible by those who do not have a reason to have access.

Another issue of leaving files "all over the place" is the risk that a file will get lost. Everyone has seen the professional's office that seems to be stacked to the ceiling with papers. Can anyone really remember what is in any pile, let alone what is in the office? If an important file is buried in someone's office and it is needed, the risk is that it won't be found. How much exposure this causes obviously depends on the specific facts. The point is that the exposure would not exist if files were controlled property.

Another common risk for law firms is that a lawyer has his or her own file on a matter. If there are notes in a personal file that do not make it into the master client file, some piece of information may be missed by a person working with the file. This risk also is manageable if addressed.

When transferring a confidential file from an attorney's office or secretary's station to another attorney or to the file room, security is lost when it is put in the interoffice mail instead of being hand carried to the destination. No matter how good interoffice mail procedures are, the inevitable can happen and the file could be lost or misplaced.

At times, files are sealed by court order so that no one is allowed to read them or, more importantly, disclose information in them. In a

---

[7] See Fortune, N. 6 *supra,* at 647.

highly publicized story, a well known New York law firm did not adequately marked a file to show that it was sealed by the court. A partner who apparently did not know anything about the case or the news stories that had been on television or in the newspapers made a statement about one of the companies involved in the sealed matter. The comment created significant embarrassment to the firm and its partner. The court was not happy with the disclosure nor was the firm pleased with the bad press that it received.

It is not uncommon for an attorney to take a file home to work on it in the evening or on a weekend. By taking a file out of the office, the risk that confidential information will be compromised rises. For example, an attorney might read a document while traveling on a plane, train or bus and be unaware that someone might be reading over his or her shoulder or be capable of reading upside down when seated across from him or her. In cities where commuting on public transportation such as in Chicago, Washington D.C. or New York is commonplace, this risk is magnified.

Once at home, security can be compromised by not securing client files. For example, if a person has a roommate (as younger attorneys are prone to do), what is to stop the roommate from reading the file? Or if the roommate has a friend visiting and the friend asks the attorney innocently, "What are you working on," saying anything can be too much. Even letting the roommate know the name of the client can compromise the file, especially when "innocent" comments are made later that allow the roommate or someone else to connect the comment to the work the attorney was doing earlier in the day.

Because of the nature of client files, they deserve the attention of the risk management partner and should have procedures and policies in place to minimize the risks.

[d]—Procedures and Using Calendars

An American Bar Association study found that 21% of malpractice claims were for administrative errors, and that 40% of these were for failure to calendar properly.[8] Other studies indicate that as many as half of all malpractice claims are due to missed deadlines.[9] Thus, from one-fourth to perhaps one half of all claims could be eliminated if things were done when they were supposed to.

Using "personal" calendars can be beneficial until something that is entered the personal calendar never makes it to the master office calendar and something is missed.

---

[8] See Fortune, N. 6 *supra,* at 624.

[9] See Fortune, N. 6 *supra,* at 624.

Allowing different groups to use different procedures or calendars ultimately leads to the same potential risk that something like an important due date will "slip through the cracks" and be missed.

[e]—Information Technology

One of the most important focuses of a risk management program must be the information technology area because everything a lawyer does is affected by information technology. Computer risks and corrective procedures were discussed in a previous chapter; this section will highlight those areas not discussed previously.[10]

This section illustrates that everyone in a law office with access to a computer is in a position to make a costly risk management mistake when he or she transmits a document electronically.

[i]—Electronic Word Processing and Transmission

There probably isn't a law firm in the United States that doesn't use electronic wording processing to prepare documents. Other that the use of a telephone, there may not be another piece of equipment that is used so pervasively in law firms. Given the significant usage, a risk management plan must be aware of how technology can create risks. Some risks are:

- Computer files can be copied onto diskettes without the firm's knowledge,
- Computer files can be lost when a computer freezes or a hard disk crashes,
- Current computer files can be overridden by other files when there are too many versions of the same document and there is no standard naming policy,
- There are insufficient backups of a workstation or the network,
- Network access within the firm is not restricted so anyone on the network has access to everything on the network, and
- Network firewalls to protect against unauthorized access are insufficient.

Sending word-processing documents to clients through e-mail have their own risks. Consider, for example, when a letter is sent to a client via the Internet and it was not protected from changes. The recipient could easily make a change by adding or deleting the word "not" and

---

[10] See Chapter 13 for a discussion issues relating to automated accounting records.

the meaning would be very different. If the document is on the firm's computer-generated letterhead, the risk could be enormous. Another example is not removing historic codes that track modifications. Image the embarrassment of a client who might look at those codes and learn that the letter was sent to a rival or competitor and "modified" so that it appeared to be original work for the recipient.

[ii]—Discretion

Potentially one of the biggest risks in electronic mail is the ability to communicate so effectively. While fast communication clearly is an advantage, it also is a risk. Consider, for example, the associate who intends to provide a responsive service by responding to a client's e-mail. Normally, an associate would not think of sending a letter to a client without a senior associate's or partner's approval, but e-mail is different. E-mail is perceived as informal. it's quick and more efficient. but it also is a formal trail. So, in the desire to respond to a client when a reviewer is not around, an associate sends an e-mail and either communicates an incorrect response or make a typo that changes the intent of the response. Using proper discretion, the associate might not have sent the e-mail.

If you burn a piece of paper or put a document through the shredder, it no longer exists. If you "delete" verbiage on your computer screen, it disappears, but it still exists. A computer expert with a discovery subpoena can retrieve deleted material. This has been demonstrated in litigation, with dire consequences for those who thought that they had destroyed notes, comments, first drafts, private letters, etc. Discretion suggests that something that one does not want discovered should not be entered into a computer file or especially said in an e-mail.

[iii]—Computer Vulnerability

Computers are the focus of any would-be thief or hackers, because of their value—either hardware or data. valuable information is on the firm's computer. information from confidential client information, to personnel hiring practices, to partner compensation, to competitor intelligence is on the firm's computer. All of that information is vulnerable to inappropriate access or loss.

If computer files are stored on a diskette, little harm is done if the diskette is dropped, if the temperature goes to 100 degrees, if there is a power outage, or a power surge. But all of these incidents can cripple or destroy a computer or worse, the information stored on the computer. These occurrences can be triggered by a flood in the basement, an explosion on the other side of the city, or a five-state grid failure.

There is little risk that a team of thieves will distract a lawyer so that they can steal his or her file satchel for its intrinsic value as it goes through carry-on X-ray at the airport, or that someone will lift a file from a lawyer's desk for its value as waste paper. But a laptop is vulnerable because of its value and the ease of converting it into cash. And bear in mind that far more confidential information might be in a laptop than in a hard copy file.

Because of the many and diverse computer vulnerabilities facing law firms, they often have special computer vulnerability studies done so that they can assess their risks and develop procedures to respond to them.

[iv]—Incompatibility

Law firms often complain about the cost of computer equipment and wonder why they have to spent so much on technology. When personal computers began to emerge as viable tools to increase efficiency, many law firms searched for ways to implement the new technology, but at the least cost. Some firms kept the cost down by installing software that ultimately was not able to do what the firms needed done or was incompatible with the software used by their clients.

Firms that installed top-of-the-line word processing software later were shocked to find out that newer versions of the same software were not compatible with older versions. In order to maintain compatibility, firms had to replace older software, even though the older software continued to do what it was originally purchased for.

The built-in obsolesces that has contributed to economic growth through replacement products has migrated into the computer world, especially in operating systems. It seems that every four or five years, hardware or software vendors change something so dramatically that the new version no longer works with an earlier version or may work "most of the time" with an earlier version. Consider operating systems. Firms that were using the Microsoft Windows 3.1 operating system were satisfied with the versatility and efficiency of the software. When Microsoft introduced Windows 95, parts of it did not work with Windows 3.1. The problem was realized when a firm bought new computers with Windows 95 on them. They then had to upgrade existing computers so that they would be compatible. Firms that tried to avoid the conversion issue simply did not adopt a newer version. For example, many firms did not convert from Windows 95 to Windows 98. They elected, instead, to convert to Windows NT and programs that were written for that platform, but that meant converting all computers in the firm. That conversion process is expensive. It seems, in fact, that each conversion is more expensive than the last one—all because of compatibility issues. There may not be practical and affordable answers to compatibility issues, but the risk management plan must consider compatibility for the simple reason that incompatibility issues can stop a firm dead in its tracks.

[f]—Branch Office Operations

Branch offices appear to generate a disproportionate number of malpractice claims.[11] The reasons have not been documented, but they no doubt include the following:

- Less careful monitoring of client intake (including conflicts, screening of clients for undesirable traits, and realistic assessment of whether there is the expertise and depth to handle the work).
- Less depth of technical expertise for second-partner review.
- Less effective monitoring of other aspects of quality control.
- Conflicting cultures if the branch was acquired rather than staffed by home office transfers. In practice, branches often include many lateral hires, even if the branch was originally colonized by main office partners and associates.

Law firms that focus on international markets can choose between opening their own offices or forming correspondence type relationships with other firms. In whatever configuration, foreign branches or foreign affiliations pose the same risks to quality control of domestic branches (discussed above), with higher degree of risk for a number of reasons:

- There are varying degrees of true culture conflicts,
- Conflicts will be harder to monitor and they take longer to resolve,
- Client intake (for issues other than conflicts) will be harder to monitor,
- Non-American lawyers tend to be less concerned about some of the risks that U.S. law firms focus on and, therefore, are less inclined to follow pre-established risk management policies

[3]—Financial and Accounting Risks

Risks of impropriety are foremost in the minds of those responsible for risk management. When there defalcations, for example, they

---

[11] See Executive Summary Risk Management At Large Law Firms, N. 5 *supra,* at 1025.

occur in the financial area. A law firm's risk management program has to anticipate the possible risks and develop appropriate measurements to prevent or to minimize those risks.

[a]—Accounting Software Risks

A law firm cannot function effectively and efficiently without a good accounting system. An accounting system is a generic term that identifies more than the computer system that is used to account for the day-to-day financial transactions of a law firm. It includes the firm's general ledger, the accounting department that records transactions into the general ledger, the billing and collections departments, the accounts payable department, and other specialty departments that keep track of firm assets or expenditures. Perhaps most importantly, an accounting system includes the in-place procedures that ensure the smooth and accurate flow of information from one department to another. The amalgamation of accounting procedures with the various systems is what determines the quality of an accounting system. The ultimate test of an accounting system is its ability to track all financial aspects of a law firm, so that management can effectively manage.

Many law firms today are reorganizing into practice groups or specialty groups. The challenge for the accounting system is to be able to account for transactions based on the new structure. The risk is that it can't. All to often, management changes the firm's structure so that it is responsive to client's needs, but the accounting system does not change. As a result, the accounting system can no longer identify profits (or losses) based on management's needs. Thus, management may not know if a particular practice group is making money and, if it is, what its gross margin is. Without addressing this inadequacy, the firm faces a risk that management cannot manage and will not be able to identify which business segments are profitable and which that are not.

The risks associated with having a poor accounting system or one that does not function efficiently include:

1. Inability to account for transactions in the form or detail that is needed by management,
2. Inaccurate accounting for day-to-day transactions,
3. Slow flow of information from one department to another,
4. Loss of financial information,
5. Lengthy delay in closing the general ledger and the preparation of financial statements,
6. Inability to perform timely reconciliations (e.g., reconcile checkbooks or interoffice accounts).

Keeping in mind these risks (and many others), consider a firm that has merged with another firm or has expanded its operations outside of the United States. The number of accounting-related risks associated with such an expansion increases geometrically. After a merger, for example, the acquired law firm's accounting system must be integrated into the accounting system of the acquiring (or continuing) firm. The acquired or merged firm may have processed daily transactions very differently, so its accounting system has to be changed to adapt to the continuing firm's procedures. The accounting system integration process is further complicated if the merged firm is in another country. It is very probable that the merged firm's accounting system was established to account for transactions based on local regulatory and tax reporting requirements that are very different from those of the continuing firm. If these requirements exist, they will continue, escalating the difficulty of establishing a combined accounting system that is able to deliver the financial information that management needs.

A firm that expands its practice beyond the borders of the country in which it has historically practiced law faces risks that are similar to those encountered in a merger environment. There can be, however, one big difference. In a merger, there are often two firms with established accounting systems that need to be integrated. In an expansion where, for example, a US-based firm opens an office in Europe, there generally is not an established accounting system. This means that the firm has to hire local employees who are not familiar with its accounting system and often are given very little guidance from the home office. As firms further increase their presence outside of the United States (or the countries in which their home offices are located), accounting-system risks likely will be reduced, because the firms have become more familiar with the accounting risks associated with operating overseas offices and probably have established procedures to address those risks. In that case, it might be possible to clone the procedures that are used in an established non-US office and adapt them to the new office.

[b]—Accounting Department Procedural Risks

The accounting department of any business serves a vital role because it is responsible for recording and tracking the daily financial activities of the organization. Ultimately, the accounting department is responsible for determining the financial results - did the business make a profit or loss.

Realizing that the number one focus within a law firm is the practice of law, accounting departments are viewed as "backroom support" and sometimes do not have the same type of attention that line lawyers do.

When assessing risk with a law firm, however, all backroom support functions should be incorporated into the risk assessment, so that appropriate risk management procedures are developed for the accounting department. This section reviews risks associated with accounting department functions and safeguarding assets.

[i]—Accounting Department Risks

As previously mentioned, accounting departments are responsible for tracking the daily transactions of a law firm. Depending on the size of the law firm, the accounting department can be as small as a part-time bookkeeper or as large as hundreds of people. Most firms have their own accounting staff, but some have begun to outsource the function to companies that specialize in backroom support for law firms. The common theme for all accounting departments is tracking time spent by timekeepers, recording cash receipts, making disbursements, keeping the general ledger, and preparing management financial information. Some accounting departments also do payroll functions and run the computer operations.

This section reviews some of the areas of risk associated with the accounting department. Three risks that affects all areas within an accounting department are turnover, training, and segregation of duties. Regardless for the causes of turnover (e.g., pay issues, personal chemistry issues, management issues, work conditions, competency, etc), any break in the continuity of the accounting function can be disruptive and can cause risks. With respect to training, it should be obvious that inadequate training or the lack of proper supervision will cause risks and may lead to undetected errors. Segregation of duties often depends on the size of the accounting department, so that the more segregation of duties there is, the less risk. Unfortunately, the antithesis is true. Other risks within an accounting department area:

- Time and Billing—

  1. New timekeepers are not be entered in the system timely
  2. Changes in billing rates are not be entered timely
  3. Incorrect client matters are entered and not timely reconciled
  4. Timekeepers do not enter adequate descriptions of work performed
  5. The system does not allow enough space for sufficient descriptions of work
  6. Daily diaries are lost or not filed in time
  7. Cutoffs are missed
  8. Timekeepers charge the wrong client matters and the errors are not discovered before a bill is prepared

9. Program accepts time entries without verifying reasonableness of entry

- General Ledger ("GL")—

1. Access to GL is not limited
2. GL software does not allow electronic analysis of accountings
3. Standard GL accounts are not used by branch offices
4. All branch offices use the same GL software
5. GL is not designed for practice group accounting
6. GL is not designed for departmental cost accounting
7. GL account titles are vague or misleading
8. Too few GL accounts so that account titles are meaningless
9. GL software is not integrated with time and billing system, accounts payable system, etc.

- Work-in-progress ("WIP") and Accounts Receivable -

1. WIP is not billed timely or charges are not for good time (i.e., time that can never be billed)
2. Collection efforts are not performed timely and past due or disputed receivables are not followed up
3. Partial payments on account are not applied properly
4. Receipts that are unmatched with receivables are not reconciled promptly
5. Collection efforts not performed or not done timely
6. Charge-offs not approved
7. Client disbursements are not identified to a matter on a timely basis
8. Differences in client disbursements postings are not reconciled timely
9. Chargeable client disbursements are incorrectly recorded as firm expenses

- Disbursements and Accounts Payable—

1. Invoices not reviewed for appropriateness or approved
2. Invoices prepared with incorrect amounts
3. Duplicate payments are made
4. Invoices not processed timely
5. Invoices not classified correctly
6. Insufficient supporting documentation for invoices
7. Check amounts disagree with invoices

8. Checks are issued before verification that work was done or purchase was received
9. Bogus vendors are listed in the system and paid

As mentioned, these are some of the risks associated with accounting department functions. The list is not all inclusive and will vary with the size of the accounting department and internal controls that are in place.

[ii]—Safeguard of Assets

In the macro view, safeguarding assets means establishing risk management policies that will protect the assets of the firm. In the micro view, safeguarding assets means that each person must focus on the assets in his or her custody and ensure that they are not misused or lost. This book has previously discussed risks associated with loss of assets by embezzlement, fraud and theft,[12] so the discussion in this section is limited to a list of the type of risks associated with safeguarding assets.

- Examples of asset risks—
  1. Insurance is less than needed to replace assets
  2. Personal computers, fax machines, copiers, etc. can be stolen
  3. Checks can be forged or stolen
  4. Cash can be stolen or diverted through theft or deception
  5. Assets may become technology obsolete and expensive to replace
  6. Unauthorized purchases
  7. Purchases not in accordance with policies and procedures
  8. Assets purchased are not controlled when received
  9. Assets may not be recorded timely or correctly

One of the most common ways to divert funds is through expense reports. Given the opportunity and the inspiration, some people will try to steal from the firm by submitting false expense reports for travel or entertainment. They may create expenses that never existed, change amounts on receipts, or charge airline tickets and then return the ticket for a refund. It is not the purpose of this chapter to identify the hundreds of ways that people cheat on expense reports, except

---

[12] See Chapter 7 for a discussion of controls to reduce the likelihood of loss by embezzlement, fraud, and theft.

to say that a risk management plan has to be designed to protect firm assets and expense reports are a significant risk.

[4]—Trust Account Risks

For various reasons, lawyers often hold money (or other valuables) for clients. Sometimes the money is held in contemplation of a purchase or sale, such as escrow funds for the purchase of a business. Sometimes money is held pending distribution, such as the distribution of money in a class-action suit or distribution of an estate. Other times money is held pending the settlement of a dispute. Whatever the reasons, money in trust accounts normally is not the law firm's, so the firm has a fiduciary responsibility to protect and to account for the money. The risks associated with trust assets include:

1. Assets are not accounted for properly
2. Distribution of the trust assets is not controlled properly
3. Too few checks and balances exist for trust checking accounts, so checks can be changed during reconciliation of the bank account
4. If trust accounts are controlled by lawyers and not by firm management, there is a higher probability of impropriety, especially that lawyers will "borrow" against trust assets

[5]—Employee Risks

The category of employee risks encompasses risks emanating from the employer/employee relationship. Discussed in this section are payroll and human resources risks and workplace risks.

[a]—Payroll and Human Resources Risk

The most important asset that a law firm has is its employee base—its attorneys and other employees. Collectively, a law firm is like a sports franchise in which every person is important. As a result, there are risks associated with each employee, albeit the risks are more magnified and pronounced the more important a person's position. Some of the risks associated with employees are:

1. Individual hired does not meet the firm's hiring criteria
2. Individual lied on job application
3. Individual's compensation and benefits are incorrect
4. Hiring procedures violate laws and regulations
5. Inadequate review and evaluation procedures to document performance
6. Unauthorized alterations to payroll records

7. Incorrect payroll amounts
8. Withholding exemptions exceed limit
9. Time reports are not reconciled to payroll
10. Payroll not processed timely
11. Payroll not approved
12. Payroll expense not recorded timely or recorded incorrectly
13. Payroll issued to unauthorized or nonexistent employees
14. Inadequate training

[b]—Workplace Rules Risk

Violating workplace rules is not malpractice per se, but violations can cost millions of dollars, hurt moral, and generate terrible publicity. Most violations are of the Equal Opportunity Employment Act and the Americans with Disabilities Act.[13] Both vastly alter the employer-employee relationship that existed a generation ago. The basics should be well known to everyone who works at a law firm. They include:

1. The Civil Rights Act of 1964, which prohibits employment discrimination on the basis of race, color, religion, sex, or national origin.
2. The Age Discrimination in Employment Act of 1967, which protects workers who are age 40 or older.
3. The Americans with Disabilities Act of 1990, which prohibits employment discrimination against qualified individuals with disabilities. The Act requires employers to make reasonable accommodations for disabled employees, but does not require that productivity goals be reduced.[14]

Discrimination includes harassment and a hostile work environment.[15] Harassment and a hostile environment can be initiated (and, when it occurs, often is initiated) by an employee's peers. Thus, a firm is just as much at risk with the behavior of low-level employees as it is with the senior partner.

In law offices, the risks in this area are mainly (1) sexual harassment—in most cases a male in a power position making advances on

---

[13] Glater, "New Guards to Lessen Liability," New York Times, http://www.nytimes.com (Aug. 8, 2001). See Fortney, N.Note 3 *supra,* 51 Con. Fin. L. Q. at 102.

[14] See Fortney, N. 3 *supra,* 51 Con. Fin. L.Q. at 106 (N. 50). See U.S. Equal Opportunity Employment Commission Web Site - Federal Laws Prohibiting Job Discrimination Questions and Answers, Titles I and V of the Americans with Disabilities Act, Reasonable Accommodation, http://www.eeoc.gov.

[15] See *Id.*, (U.S. Equal Opportunity Employment Commission Web Site) under Sex Discrimination.

a female in a subordinate position—and (2) minority and female lawyers alleging that discrimination held back their advancement. Foul language also has been alleged to constitute a hostile environment,[16] and some companies have made foul language a cause for termination. A growing allegation is that minorities are handicapped, because they do not have powerful mentors in the firm.[17]

Being lawyers, most partners are aware of discrimination in general, but may choose to not focus on specific instances in which some type of discrimination takes place. Sometimes they ignore a situation in hopes that it was an aberration. Other times, they may be impervious to the affect that a comment or action will have on employees. A good risk management plan has to focus on employee/employer interaction so that appropriate procedures are developed to avoid workplace risks.

---

[16] E.g., June Hironaka v. United States Postal Service, March 27, 2001, U.S. Equal Opportunity Appeal No. 01976665. See Note 14 *supra.*

[17] Glater, "Few Minorities Rising to Law Partner," New York Times, http://www.nytimes.com (Aug. 7, 2001).

§ 21.05 Strategies to Manage Risks

[1]—Policy Manual

One of the most important cornerstones to risk management is an up-to-date policy manual that includes policies and procedures for each department in which risks are discussed.. It should address important policies and procedures that the risk management partner or firm management have identified that are vital in managing the risks the firm faces.

Procedures are an absolute necessity, but they don't help if they aren't enforced. Firm policies and office information should be in a manual that each new employee - professional staff or otherwise - is required to read.[1] And they won't be enforced unless firm's management has the will and the power to enforce them. An understandable byproduct of firms becoming far larger and consisting of discrete, highly specialized practice specialties is that top management has far less control over the matters that cause risk to the firm.

The policy manual should include specific policies concerning the areas of risk and stipulate normal operating procedures that should be followed. It also should identify at what level procedures can be modified and by whom.

[2]—Quality Control

One of the best ways to manage risk for a law firm is to have an effective system of quality control in place. In the broadest sense, quality control is a system that establishes standards on how new matters are accepted, how services are rendered, what kind of supporting material is retained, how advice is given, and how the system ultimately insures that established procedures are followed. This section will discuss quality control aspects in more detail.

[a]—Accepting New Client Matters

Without clients, there would be no quality control issues to address. It seems logical, therefore, that a discussion of quality control begins with accepting new clients or new matters from existing clients.

---

[1] See Davis, "The Long-Term Implications of the Kaye Scholer Case For Law Firm Management - Risk Management Comes of Age," 35 S. Tex. L. Rev. 667, at 699 (2. Preparation of Policy Manuals, Training Programs, Checklists, Computer Systems, and Disaster Recovery Plans) (1994).

[i]—Checklists

A law firm should have standard procedures that are followed when deciding to accept a new client. Often the procedures are in the form of a standard checklist that is completed as part of the client-evaluation process. The checklist should include background information about the prospective client, its credit worthiness (i.e., ability and willingness to pay for legal services), its reputation and integrity, what services the prospective client needs, what timetables the client has, and why the firm should have it as a client.

As part of the evaluation phase, conflict checks must be performed. An important part of an effective quality control system is to use a computer program for conflict checking that is capable of ferreting out complex international relationships of a large corporation that have many subsidiaries in many countries. Another aspect of conflict checking is determining if the acceptance of the prospective client will cause a conflict for a non-client that the firm would like to have as a client. If acceptance of a small client will cause a conflict with a larger non-client that the firm is pursuing, then the business decision may be made not to accept the smaller client.

Bar associations throughout the world have different definitions for what constitutes a conflict. Larger firms that operate in the international arena should consider the different definitions when establishing their conflict standards. Depending on how a firm is structured, it will have to adopt a standard that is compatible with each jurisdiction in which it practices. The implication of adopting a uniform standard is that it will be overly conservative for a branch office where the conflict rules are not as severe. This may put that branch at a competitive disadvantage with a local firm for new client matters.

The firm should decide if it is qualified in the area of law needed to represent the client or if it needs to engage other specialists.

Once the checklist and conflict checking are completed, the prospective-client partner should sign off the documents with a recommendation to accept or to reject the proposed client. If the decision is made to accept the client, the paperwork should be routed to a reviewing partner or committee that should review the checklist and decide if the firm should accept or reject it as a client.

If the decision is made not to accept the prospective-client, a refusal letter should be sent to the business or individual that clearly states that the firm is refusing to represent the party. The letter should not state specific reasons for the refusal and should not comment on the merits of the prospective client's legal position. It should advise the client to seek another attorney. Any documents taken to aid in the investigation should be returned and a receipt obtained. (Taking documents should be avoided if possible, as it suggests an attorney-client relationship and also makes possible the allegation confidential information was used improperly.) It is wise to ask for a signed copy of the refusal letter.

[ii]—Engagement Agreement

When a firm decides to accept a new client or a new matter from an existing client, it should document the scope and terms of the representation through an engagement agreement that is signed by a representative of the law firm and the new client. The agreement also should state the fee (or how it will be calculated) and the billing arrangements. Most importantly, the agreement should define clearly the scope of the representation - what is included and potentially what is not included. This will be useful if the client alleges negligence in matters outside the scope of the engagement as stated in the agreement.

[b]—Performing the Engagement

The manner in which the engagement is performed can make a significant difference in limiting risk associated with the engagement. If the work is done professionally and completely, the probability of having a malpractice issue is reduced. Areas of concern are assigning and supervising attorneys, issuing findings, and second-partner review.

[i]—Assigning and Supervising Timekeepers

Lawyers are presumed to be experts in any work they undertake, and are held to that standard in malpractice litigation. After a law firm has decided to accept a new client or a new matter from an existing client, it must determine if it can staff the assignment with associates who are capable of doing the work and have the time to do the work.

If associates are not familiar with the area of law relative to the client matter, then the firm should do something to train the attorneys. One method would be to conduct internal CLE programs using associates or partners who are familiar with the area of law or, if the firm is small or lacks internal resources, it should find qualified CLE programs offered by competent third parties.

In addition to having trained associates who will do the work, the firm must have senior associates or partners who are capable of supervising the attorneys. It is important to demonstrate that not only did the firm assign competent attorneys to do the work, but it had an established procedure to review and supervise the attorneys.

[ii]—Documentation and Opinion Letter

A physical file (as opposed to a computer file) should be created for every client matter and should contain supporting material that is complete and accurate. Just as lawyers are very familiar with organized and referenced case files, every client matter file should be subject to the same level of thoroughness. Documentation should include cases read with summaries of their relevance, printouts of legal cites including the law or applicable regulations, articles or treatises that are relevant and anything else that was considered in reaching a conclusion. For example, all notes from meetings, telephone conversations or e-mails should be included in the file.

To facilitate review, the risk management partner should establish standards regarding how correspondence is prepared. There should be a standard template that is used for all memoranda, letters, faxes and notes so that all correspondence looks the same and presents the same image to clients. Depending on the document, there also should be a standard template that specifies how a document should be formatted and structured. In certain situations, such as very important documents, a professional editor should review the documents, so that they read and communicate professionally.

Just before a matter is closed, the file should be reviewed by an experienced associate or partner to verify that all open points were addressed and cleared. When the matter is finished, a closing letter should be sent to the client stating that the representation is completed and that no further work will be performed. This will forestall claims by a client that the attorney continued to represent him and that the attorney is negligent for not pursuing matters after the date of the closing letter.

[iii]—Second-Partner Review

The old saying that "two heads are better than one" emphasizes the point that having two sets of eyes look at the same matter will lessen the chance that a particular matter will become a risk management issue sometime in the future. Conceptually, two qualified and responsible attorneys reviewing the same document or discussing a conclusion of law and a recommendation to a client will increase the level of confidence that the business is being conducted professionally and that technical advice is sound. Clients should understand that a second-partner review is part of the process to achieve a high-quality work product and that they will be billed for it. Lack of this level of back-up is a reason for many malpractice claims against small firms.

To effectively manage risk, a second-partner review procedure should be in place for:

(1) Any formal legal opinions;

(2) Any due diligence and investigatory reports;

(3) Any advice on major transactions;

(4) Any high risk matters—especially those involving multiple conflicting practices;

(5) Any letter or opinion relying on complicated facts or containing advice on complicated or unsettled areas of law.

[3]—Operational Safeguards

Operational safeguards begin with the phone operator, the receptionist, the mailroom clerk, or anyone else who has initial contact with clients or visitors. Employees need to understand that visitors listen to what is being said in public spaces, so they need to be aware of casual conversations or comments that are made in lobbies, hallways or lavatories of the law firm. Procedures to limit risk management should include caveats or warnings about what not to say in public areas where the comments may be heard.

Other operational safeguards include protecting the physical plant, protecting client files, maintaining internal controls and using calendars and checklists.

[a]—Physical Plant

An effective risk management program must safeguard assets and, in the event that the physical plant is not functional, provide adequate backup so that a law firm can continue doing business.

Safeguarding assets means protecting assets from physical harm including theft or damage. For example, a law firm's risk management plan would ensure that there is adequate insurance to cover damage from fire, water, weather, vandalism and terrorism. The insurance should ensure the replacement of lost or damaged assets with comparable equipment, so that attorneys can continue business. After the World Trade Center disaster, law firms, as well as other businesses, realized first-hand the importance of having adequate insurance in force from financially sound companies.

Another aspect of insurance is business continuation insurance. Law firms are not immune to problems that prevent them from continuing to function smoothly. All if takes is a fire in the building, an electrical outage, a watermain break, or a sealed off security area to disrupt a business. Often the disruptions are minimal, but they can be much longer than that, as seen in New York after the events of September 11, 2001. Some law firms thought that $1 million of business interruption insurance was sufficient only to find that it was a small fraction of the actual loss from not being able to conduct business.

When business is critical, law firms should have contingency plans that allow them to continue doing business even if their primary work spaces are not accessible. For example, what some firms in New York did as part of their contingency plans was to have alternative office space in other parts of the city and to have duplicate computer records maintained outside the city. Those firms who planned for a disaster were prepared to operate out of alternative space soon after the events of September 11, 2001. Those that did not have contingency plans were not able to reopen for many days and some of them had to borrow space in clients' offices until alternative plans could be developed.

Insurance is only one aspect of a risk management plan and it generally is only effective after the damage has already occurred. Safeguarding physical assets includes having sufficient controls over firm-owned assets to know where they are and that they are being used correctly. Law firms, for example may have hundreds of personal computers, some of which are not covered by insurance because the cost of the machine is less than the deductible. Because of the size of personal computers, they need to be safeguarded by locking them in a drawer or in cabinet or by attaching a security cable to the computer so that it can't be moved without removing the cable. In addition, the firm should have an inventory control number on each computer and should periodically inventory the computers to verify that they are accounted for. The same procedures can be used for other assets such as facsimile machines, copying machines, telephones, or kitchen equipment.

Another computer-related risk to guard against is a computer virus, which can infect a machine from a diskette or from the Internet. A good virus protection program should be standard issue for the firm's network and each computer that is allowed to connect to it.[2]

Other assets have to be protected too. For example, blank checks should be secured in a locked location with limited access. That may seem like common sense, and it is. In fact, most ideas regarding safeguarding assets are common sense and can be developed by any intelligent person if he or she thinks about them. More often than not, the loss of office assets (or personal assets of employees) results in carelessness because a person didn't take the time to protect the property.

There is a direct connection between safeguarding assets and having an effective system of internal controls to prevent the loss of assets.[3] For example, safeguarding assets from purchase-related fraud

---

[2] See Chapter 13 for more risk management type comments on computer security.

[3] See § 21.05[3][c] for a discussion of internal controls.

would segregate the function of placing purchase orders from the function of receiving the assets and paying for them.

[b]—Client Files

Client files are very important because they are confidential documents that have to be protected and safeguarded. As a result, paper files should always be secured in a safe place every night. Often, especially in larger cases, client files are secured in a locked case room with access limited to those who are working on the case.

The risk management partner needs to develop a policy with respect to client files so that confidentiality can be maintained. A sign-out system for files is one way to protect access to files. Files and notes should not be left unattended on desks or in conference rooms. When confidentiality is paramount, such as in a merger or acquisition, the use of code names may be a way to maintain a higher level of confidentiality.

In an age of high technology, the risk management policies need to consider computer files too. Very little is done today within a law firm that is not done on or through a computer; for example, word processing, telephone messaging, Internet, electronic mail, computerized spreadsheets, Blackberries, Palm pilots, wireless computing, electronic research, etc. These tools are used in concert to provide integrated legal services. While these tools have been the reason for the substantial and sustained economic growth experienced during the 1990s, they also are the Achilles' heels of a risk management system. These tools represent a risk, because they cannot be secured like paper. For example, even though an attorney locks his or her computer in a case room overnight, it could be that word processing files or scanned documents were on the network and saved to a server for damage recovery purposes. As long as a document is on the server, there is a very high probability that there is a backup—one that some attorneys or computer technicians would be able to access. That of course means that discovery is easier, because computer records exist somewhere within a law firm's archives (on site or offsite) that can be accessed.

Destruction of files, notes or superseded documents also should be included in a risk management program. A destruction policy is best applied on a systematic basis to all documents to avoid allegations that the policy may have been selectively used to destroy sensitive documents.

[c]—Internal Controls

Volumes have been written on internal controls; what are they and how they work. A lengthy discussion of internal controls is beyond the scope of this chapter, but some comments are necessary.

In the abstract, internal controls are procedures to ensure that policies will be followed. If used properly, they are safeguards to protect the firm from risks. A simple example is the requirement that the person who reconciles a bank account is not the same person who draws the checks. The reason should be obvious—to eliminate the possibility that someone will draw a check payable to himself or herself and then change the name on the check after it clears the bank.

Internal controls can be designed around any area of a law firm. They often are implemented in areas of greatest risk or exposure where exceptions could cause a material effect on income or a embarrassment to the firm. In the accounting area, internal controls generally would focus on ensuring segregation of duties so that one person does not perform two functions that inherently should be separate. Areas of concern include cash and bank accounts, purchasing, accounts payable, payroll, client disbursements, and partner accounts. Internal controls developed in these area are designed based on an assessment of operational and financial process controls with the intent of reducing risk to the law firm.

[d]—Using Calendars and Checklists

As previously mentioned, An American Bar Association study found that a large percentage of malpractice claims were caused by administrative errors such the failure to calendar a due date properly.[4] Lawyers and their staffs are busy people, and should have foolproof procedures to see that nothing is overlooked. There are software programs for calendaring that will keep track of due dates and can be used effectively if given good input. Because proper use of calendars—and follow-up —is an absolute must, dual calendaring is in wide use and is strongly recommended. In some firms, there is a third, central, calendar. This is worthwhile backup. At a minimum, a calendar should be kept by both the lawyer and his or her secretary or administrative assistant.

Mention was made of using a checklist for accepting a new client.[5] In any risk management program, checklists should be a requirement in the preparation of documents and in many procedures. They keep vital steps from being overlooked and they are a permanent paper trail to support that things were done when they were supposed to. A partial list of areas where checklists are useful and in wide use include:

- Preparation of wills and trusts;
- Preparation of tax returns;

---

[4] See § 21.04[2][d].

[5] See § 21.05[2][a].

- Preparation of contracts;
- Preparation of real estate closing documents and leases;
- Depositions;
- Other matters—For example, in preparing opinion letters, the checklist would provide for both the preparer and the second-partner reviewer to sign off.

The types of checklists that should be used will vary with each practice and with the size of the firm. In a smaller firm where very few people are expected to do many functions, checklists can be used as a confirmation that everything was considered.

[4]—Internal Auditor

An internal auditor is a person who works for a law firm and does a review similar to what an independent auditor would do. The internal auditor has been used in corporations for decades, but only recently has been introduced in law firms, and then, only in the largest law firms. The purpose of using an internal auditor is to allow a specific person to focus on areas of interest to the audit committee or management committee. The person should not report to the chief financial officer or other financial people who have line functions to ensure that the auditor is independent of those supervisors. By reporting directly to the audit committee or management committee, the internal auditor has a direct line reporting responsibility to partners who need to hear unvarnished results.

An internal auditor often is used in connection with an independent auditor and can perform some of the detailed testing that the independent accountant would have performed. Internal auditors are particularly effective in reviewing procedures used in branch offices to determine if they are consistent with firm policies, and if not, to identify the scope of variance. They also can be used effectively to identify and address areas of low risk in a law firm, such as making surprise petty cash counts, reviewing trust accounts, reviewing bank reconciliations, etc.

Internal auditors can be used to evaluate the adequacy and effectiveness of internal controls by testing the controls. Often they can identify new control issues and formulate action plans to limit risk.

[5]—Independent Audit or Review

Another part of a comprehensive risk management program is to have an independent audit or review of the firm. A review generally is very limited in scope and does not provide any meaningful level of assurance.

Although there are general questions concerning procedures, a review is not designed to confirm that the policies are being followed.

An audit, on the other hand, is designed to understand procedures and to develop audit plans to test the procedures. As a result, the level of confidence obtained through an audit is higher than through a review. The scope of an audit can be tailored to the needs of a law firm. So, for example, a law firm could have an audit plan written to audit the payroll process, even though that process would not have otherwise been subject to a detailed audit.

An audit is not designed to detect fraud. The mere fact that an audit is done rises the level of awareness within a law firm and might be a deterrent.

[6]—Peer Review

A peer review is a review of how the firm's risk management policies are being followed. Peer reviews are not widely used presently, but the use is growing, especially as firms' awareness of risk management issues increases. When peer reviews are used, their scopes vary, but generally are formalized programs that expand as exceptions are found. In other words, when there are more deviations from firm risk management policies, the review is expanded to learn if there were any significant exceptions. Peer reviews often are conducted by firm partners and may involve the use of outside risk management consultants if confidentiality issues can be addressed and resolved.

[7]—Malpractice Insurance

The last defense in a risk management program is good malpractice insurance. Every lawyer practicing law should have malpractice insurance and treat the insurance company as an active partner in risk management program. Insurers can play an important role in risk management by assessing risks and making suggestions that will reduce risk and typically require risk-reducing procedures to be in place.

A critical element of malpractice coverage is how lateral hires are covered. Professional liability insurance covers a law firm and the lawyers named on the policy application for claims made and reported during the policy period. When a malpractice claim is made against a lawyer who has left the firm, the policy will defend the claim and pay the claim when necessary. The lawyer may or may not be covered under his or her former firm's policy - but may be covered under a personal policy. This can raise questions such as who will defend whom, who will pay costs, who will pay the claim, and who will pay the deductible. It is vital that a firm understand the terms of its insurance coverage.

CHAPTER 22

Financial Modeling

Chapter Contents

---

§ 22.01 Financial Modeling for Law Firms

Law firms use financial models to assist in decision-making when choosing from among two or more alternative strategies. A successful financial model presents a clear and meaningful comparison of the projected financial results of the alternative strategies being considered.

The principal advantage gained from using a financial model is the ability to quickly produce and compare a series of financial projections based upon alternative actions. The typical financial model is designed to respond in financial terms to "what if" style questions. (For example: "*What* is the impact on net income *if* billing rates are increased by 5%?").

Most financial models involve a multitude of assumptions, input data and calculations. They are typically repetitively produced using variations of the original assumptions. For these reasons, financial models are typically constructed using general business spreadsheet software.

Some basic strategic challenges faced by law firm management which could benefit from the use of a financial model include: (1) deciding which revenue and expense factors would have the most meaningful impact on improving a firm's profitability; (2) assessing whether controlled internal growth vs. a merger or acquisition would create more wealth for a firm's partners over the long-term; and (3) determining whether leasing vs. purchasing an office building would provide more economic benefits to a firm and its partners.

This chapter discusses financial models that address these three issues. It also identifies several other financial models of interest to law firm management. In addition, it describes the three basic steps involved in financial modeling: (1) creating a financial model; (2) using a financial model; and (3) interpreting the results.

§ 22.02 Types of Financial Models

Law firms can make use of many types of financial models used by businesses. These include (1) traditional five- to ten-year models for evaluating growth and other strategic issues and (2) three- to five-year models for evaluating current plans such as technology-related investments and other tactical issues.

Three types of financial models that are particularly relevant to law firm decision making are: (1) long-range profit-planning models; (2) merger and acquisition accounting models; and (3) office occupancy cost models. Each type of model uses a different set of variables (i.e., input data and assumptions) and a different calculation methodology.

[1]—Long-Range Profit-Planning Models

Long-range planning models usually focus on alternative strategies for improving a firm's profits. The components of these models typically include:

(1) Estimated growth rate;
(2) Staffing plan projections;
(3) Revenue projections;
(4) Compensation cost projections;
(5) Operating expense projections; and
(6) Net income projections.

The foundation for this type of financial model is often the growth rate estimate, which should be projected in conjunction with the firm's strategic planning (see Chapter 12). It helps determine the staffing plan projection which, in turn, drives the revenue, compensation cost, and operating expense projections. These latter three components generate the net income projection, which represents the "bottom line" of the exercise.

Sometimes, equity partner leverage (i.e., the ratio of all non-equity partner lawyers-to-equity partners) is the focus of the profit-planning model which results in the growth rate being driven by lawyer staffing plan projections. In other cases, the profit-planning model may be driven in reverse—for example, when net income goals are defined and growth rate requirements become the result.[1]

---

[1] Chapter 12 *infra*, "Long-Range Planning," details a step-by-step program for developing a long-range profit planning model. Figures 12-D and 12-E, in that chapter, illustrate examples of output from this financial model under two alternative scenarios.

[2]—Merger and Acquisition Accounting Models

Merger and acquisition accounting models usually focus on alternative strategies for increasing partners' income by expanding the firm's size. The components of these models often include:

(1) Lead firm's results of operations;
(2) Target firm's results of operations;
(3) Merger adjustments;
(4) *Pro forma* operating results of the merged firm; and
(5) Projected operating results of the merged firm.

The key components of this type of financial model are the assumptions underlying the projected results of the merged firm. They include assumptions about revenue, expenses, and the number of equity partners who will survive the merger. Interposing these projection assumptions, together with the merger adjustments, on the results of operations of the lead firm and the target firm, gives rise to the projected results of operations of the merged firm. These projected results represent the purpose of the exercise.[2]

[3]—Office-Occupancy Cost Models

Office occupancy cost models usually focus on alternative strategies for minimizing the firm's occupancy costs. The components of these models often include:

(1) Occupancy expense projections;
(2) Tax-benefit projections;
(3) Cash-flow projections (year-by-year); and
(4) Discounted-cash-flow projections.

The unique aspects of this type of financial model include: (1) occupancy expense projections, which can be based on either a lease or purchase assumption; (2) tax benefit projections which relate to the individual partners rather than to the partnership; and (3) cash-flow projections that are determined first on a year-by-year basis and then on a discounted-cash-flow basis. The discounted cash flow projection represents the net result of the exercise, which can be justifiably compared to an alternative scenario—even though the two cash-flow streams are entirely different in duration and magnitude.

---

[2] Chapter 23 *infra*, "Merger and Acquisition Accounting," details a step-by-step program for developing a merger and acquisition accounting model. It also includes illustrative examples of output from this financial model under alternative scenarios.

Details of a step-by-step program for developing an office occupancy cost model are shown in succeeding sections of this chapter. Illustrative examples of output from this financial model under alternative scenarios also is presented.

[4]—Other Financial Models

Financial models can provide useful information for law firm management involved in a variety of other decision-making situations, for example: developing budgets, evaluating alternative billing rate structures, opening new offices, developing new practice areas, creating lawyer compensation models, planning property and equipment purchases, projecting partner cash distribution schedules, appraising partner retirement programs, assessing the state and federal income tax impact of incorporating the partnership, and other issues.

The following sections of this chapter demonstrate a long-range financial-planning model concerning the purchase or lease of additional office space. Although the illustrations are tailored to a real estate model, it should be noted that the same methodology can be used (with some tailoring) for other financial modeling, such as the decision to purchase or lease computers, office equipment, etc. Each model must be tailored to account for factors that are unique to the item being modeled. For example, not included in the real estate lease vs. purchase model is the residual value of the purchased property sometime in the future. Since real estate historically has appreciated over a long period of time, considering the residual value of the building might make a material difference in the lease vs. purchase decision. If a model considers leasing vs. purchasing computers, however, there would be little or no residual value at the end of a short period of time. To accurately model a lease vs. purchase computer decision, the lack of residual value should be considered in addition to the cost of disposal at the end of the computers' useful lives.

§ 22.03 Creating an Office-Occupancy Cost Model

Creating a financial model involves three basic steps:

(1) Analyzing the decision-making process;
(2) Developing input data, assumptions and statistics; and
(3) Processing calculations.

Each of these steps will be discussed in the paragraphs that follow. For purposes of illustration, the following discussion will contain a description of the steps involved in creating an office-occupancy cost model. The three basic steps are the same for all financial models; however, the detailed components of each step are unique to the individual model.

[1]—Analyzing the Decision-Making Process

If a law firm decides to significantly expand its law offices, management must seek to minimize the impact of this decision on the size of the firm's occupancy costs. Options that management may consider include a lease option and a purchase option.

[a]—Lease Option

The firm may choose to lease some additional space in the building which houses its present law offices or it may choose to move to a new location and lease entirely new or renovated office premises. In either event, an inflationary economy will probably force the firm to pay a higher rent per square foot for the new space compared to the cost of its present space.

[b]—Purchase Option

The firm may choose to purchase a new or renovated building to house its law offices. Purchase of a building usually involves financing a significant portion of the investment.

The economic structure of each of these two options is quite different and the possible variations under each option are numerous. Faced with the challenge of choosing the option with the most advantages, prudent law firm management may have a financial model developed to assist them in the decision-making process. To achieve management's objective, the model must have the following components:

(1) Occupancy-expense projections on two separate schedules (one for the lease option and one for the purchase option);

(2) Tax-benefit projections (for each of the two options) quantifying the estimated federal and state income tax impact on the firm's individual partners (since partnerships are not taxed as entities) or on the corporation; and

(3) Cash-flow projections (for each of the two options) detailing the estimated source and use of the partnership's funds related to the lease/purchase decision and combining the net result with the estimated income tax benefit to be achieved by the firm's partners from this activity.

In addition to year-by-year cash-flow projections, it will be necessary to calculate a discounted-cash-flow for each financial model in order to give effect to the impact that the time value of money has on the disproportionate annual cash flows generated by each model.

[2]—Developing Input Data, Assumptions and Statistics

To present the occupancy-expense projections, tax-benefit projections and cash-flow projections, a series of modules for each of these three components of the financial model must be developed. Each module must contain: (1) basic input data, (2) assumptions and (3) a statistical means to convert the input data and assumptions into an annual cost. Modules for an office-occupancy cost model include: rent expense, purchase cost and depreciation, financing arrangements and interest, other occupancy expenses, income taxes and other factors which are not quantified.

[a]—Rent Expense

In addition to the annual rent cost and lease period under the existing lease, input data relating to the proposed lease period and proposed cost per square foot of new leases are needed. Assumptions should be developed regarding exercise of lease renewal options and the timing for the lease of additional space. Square feet can function as the statistic to be used to convert the input data and assumptions into an annual cost. For this purpose, it will be necessary to determine the firm's year-by-year space requirements in terms of square feet during the period to be covered by the financial model.

[b]—Purchase Cost and Depreciation

Under the purchase option, input data regarding the estimated purchase price of the property is needed, together with a procedure for allocating the price between the cost of the land vs. the cost of the building. Assumptions should be developed regarding the method of depreciation, depreciable life, and salvage value of the building. The building's estimated depreciable life can serve as the key statistic in converting the input data and assumptions into an annual cost.

[c]—Financing Arrangements and Interest

In most cases, the law firm will obtain a bank loan to finance a significant portion of the purchase price for the property. In addition to the basic input data (i.e., the purchase price for the property), assumptions are needed for the percentage of the purchase price to be financed, an estimated interest rate, and the repayment period for the loan (in years). The interest rate and the repayment period can serve as the key statistics in converting the input data and assumptions into an annual cost.

[d]—Other Occupancy Expenses

These expenses will vary considerably with the terms and conditions of lease agreements and property purchase agreements. Once a building is purchased, other occupancy expenses could include real estate taxes, utilities, maintenance, and similar costs. When office space is leased, other occupancy expenses could include occupancy taxes and escalation costs (i.e., the tenant's proportionate share of increases in the landlord's real estate taxes, utilities, maintenance, and similar costs). A practical method of estimating the impact of other occupancy expenses is to handle them in the aggregate. Under this procedure, all other operating expenses are assumed to represent input data for a single cost, which is assumed to vary with the number of square feet occupied. Other occupancy expenses are then converted to a cost per square foot. Square feet of space to be occupied each year can then be used as the statistic to convert the input data and assumptions into an annual cost. Obviously, if a particular occupancy expense is particularly significant and does not vary with square feet of occupied space, a separate methodology can be developed for converting this expense into an annual cost.

[e]—Income Taxes

The current year's federal income tax rate (and relevant state or city income tax rates) and, to the extent available, information about future rates should be assembled. A composite federal tax rate and a composite state/city tax rate should be developed for the current year. In the case of a partnership, an assumption will have to be made whether each composite rate is representative of the tax rate applicable to the partners as a group. In the case of a corporation, the tax rates in effect for each taxing jurisdiction can be used. In addition, an assumption will have to be made as to changes (if any) in future income tax rates over the period to be covered by the financial model. The tax rates developed for each year are used for determining the estimated annual tax benefit covered by the financial model.

[f]—Factors Not Quantified

Practical considerations may create situations where certain factors are not reflected in the results of a financial model. For example, an office-occupancy cost model may not reflect the estimated impact of property appreciation over time and the potential gain which might be realized if the property were to be sold for a profit. This is obviously a key factor to be considered when purchasing property. However, it is usually difficult and risky to project future profit, which depends on the outcome of uncertain future events. (In certain instances, a sensitivity analysis might be prepared to evaluate potential outcomes.)

How these nonquantified factors are dealt with depends on their importance in the ultimate decision-making process. Potential solutions include: (1) not building the model, (2) disclosure as part of the model and (3) dismissal as immaterial in the circumstances. How to handle these situations will be a judgment call each time a financial model is prepared. When in doubt about the importance of a particular non-quantified factor, it is usually a good practice to disclose that it has not been considered. The ultimate decision-maker can then make the final call as to how its absence influences the final decision.

[3]—Processing Calculations

Processing calculations in a financial model occur at three separate levels: (1) module level (for example: depreciation computations), (2) component level (for example: occupancy-expense projections), and (3) summary level (for example: discounted-cash-flow comparisons). Each higher level of calculations depends upon the results of lower-level calculations.

Some examples of the calculations contained in the modules and components comprising an office-occupancy cost model are discussed below.

[a]—Occupancy-Expense Calculations (Lease Option)

There are three elements (or modules) which comprise occupancy-expense calculations under a lease option: (1) rent expense under the current lease, (2) rent expense for added office space, and (3) other occupancy expenses. For illustration purposes, it has been assumed that a law firm will continue to occupy its present office space for the next thirty years under a present lease which contains two renewal options (each for ten years) and a new lease for the last ten years at a rent increased by 50% during these latter years. It has also been assumed that other occupancy expenses would gradually increase over the thirty-year period based on an estimated rate of inflation. Finally, rent expense for added space has been calculated based on a separate lease for the difference between footage of the present office space and the firm's estimated office space requirements over the thirty-year period.

Figure 22-A illustrates a calculation of the incremental rent expense for the law firm's additional office space.

ABC LAW FIRM
INCREMENTAL RENT EXPENSE CALCULATION

	Projections			
	Years 1 to 10	Years 11 to 20	Years 21 to 30	Total
SIZE OF OFFICE SPACE				
(in square feet)				
Requirements	60,000	60,000	64,000	
Present office	40,000	40,000	40,000	
Increase	20,000	20,000	24,000	
PRICE OF OFFICE SPACE				
(per square foot)				
First 10 years	$ 25			
Next 20 years		$ 30	$ 30	
INCREMENTAL RENT EXPENSE				
(in 000's)				
Rent expense (annual)	$ 500	$ 600	$ 700	
Number of years	10	10	10	
Rent expense (aggregate)	$5,000	$6,000	$7,000	$18,000

---

[b]—Occupancy-Expense Calculations (Purchase Option)

There are three elements (or modules) that comprise occupancy expense under a purchase option: (1) depreciation, (2) interest expense and (3) other occupancy expenses. For illustration purposes, it has been assumed that a law firm will purchase property containing an office building and finance the full amount of the purchase cost through a bank loan. (Mortgagors typically do not lend 100% of property purchase costs; however, the full financing approach has been used in order to illustrate the impact of both debt and equity financing of the purchase.) It has also been assumed that the firm's purchase cost of the property is allocable 85% to the building and 15% to the land and that the firm will depreciate the building on a straight-line basis over thirty years. Finally, other occupancy expenses have been assumed to gradually increase over the thirty-year period based on an estimated rate of inflation.

Depreciation is a very important element of financial modeling, because an asset may be depreciated over a different life for financial statement purposes, than for tax purposes. In the illustrations in this chapter, the building is depreciated over a thirty-year period, even though the life for tax purposes is thirty-nine years.[1] If the modeling is done for financial statement purposes, it is important to note that the building will be depreciated nine more years for tax purposes, after it is fully depreciated for book purposes.

Figure 22-B illustrates calculations of depreciation and interest expense related to the law firm's purchase of a building to satisfy its office space requirements.

ABC LAW FIRM
DEPRECIATION AND INTEREST
EXPENSE CALCULATIONS
($ in thousands)

	Projections			
	Years 1 to 10	Years 11 to 20	Years 21 to 30	Total
DEPRECIATION CALCULATION				
Property purchase price				$21,000
Less-allocation to land (15%)				3,000
Building cost				$18,000
Straight-line depreciation (30-year life)	$6,000	$6,000	$6,000	$18,000
INTEREST CALCULATION				
Bank loan-beginning of year	$21,000	$10,500	—	
Bank loan-end of year	10,500	—	—	
Repayments (over 20 years)	$10,500	$10,500	—	$21,000
Average outstanding bank loan	$15,800	$5,200	—	
Interest rate	10%	10%	—	
Interest expense (10 years)	$15,800	$5,200	—	$21,000

---

[1] IRC § 168(c); 26 U.S.C. § 168(c).

[c]—Tax-Benefit Calculations

There are generally two elements comprising tax benefits in office-occupancy cost models: (1) federal income tax benefits and (2) state and local income tax benefits. For illustration purposes, a 30% federal income tax rate and a 5% state income tax rate have been assumed. (These are purely arbitrary rates.) The state tax rate of 5% is an incremental rate. It is based on a statutory state tax rate of 7% reduced by 30% to give effect to the tax benefit of deducting state income taxes from federal taxable income.

[d]—Cash-Flow Calculations

Net cash flow in the office-occupancy cost model represents the difference between (1) calculated occupancy expenses of the partnership and (2) calculated tax benefits of the partners (as previously described). The tax benefits to a corporation are not shown.

§ 22.04 Using an Office-Occupancy Cost Model

Using a financial model involves three presentations: (1) a base case; (2) alternative scenarios; and (3) comparison of base case vs. alternative scenarios. Each of these presentations will be discussed in the paragraphs that follow.

[1]—Base Case

In terms of financial modeling, the base case is that projection (or series of calculations) which portrays the facts and assumptions related to a potential business decision without giving effect to variations in the assumptions which might occur as a result of negotiations, more precise data, or better insight into future events. For example, in a long-range profit-planning model, the base case might be a five-year projection of the law firm's income based on the current year's actual profit and loss statement adjusted solely for inflation, or based on an assumption that growth and other trends will continue as they have in the past few years (i.e., a "status quo" approach).

For purposes of illustrating the office-occupancy cost model, two base cases have been selected: (1) a lease-option projection and (2) a purchase-option projection.

[a]—Lease-Option Projection

The base case lease-option projection is composed of three parts: (1) an occupancy-expense projection, (2) a tax-benefit projection and (3) a cash-flow projection. Each of these component parts was discussed previously.

Figure 22-C illustrates the base case lease-option projection.

ABC LAW FIRM
LEASE-OPTION PROJECTION
BASE CASE
($ in thousands)

	Input Data Assumptions	Projected Results Years 1 to 10	Years 11 to 20	Years 21 to 30	Total
OCCUPANCY-EXPENSE PROJECTION					
Rent expense (current lease)	Per lease	$ 10,000	$ 10,000	$ 15,000	$ 35,000
Rent expense (added space)	Fig. 22-A	5,000	6,000	7,000	18,000
Other occupancy expenses	Estimate	3,000	4,500	6,000	13,500
Partnership occupancy expenses	A	$ 18,000	$ 20,500	$ 28,000	$ 66,500
TAX-BENEFIT PROJECTION					
Federal Tax	30%	$ 5,400	$ 6,200	$ 8,400	$ 20,000
State Tax	5%	900	1,000	1,400	3,300
Partners' tax benefit	B	$ 6,300	$ 7,200	$ 9,800	$ 23,300
CASH-FLOW PROJECTION					
Partnership occupancy expenses	A	$(18,000)	$(20,500)	$(28,000)	$(66,500)
Partners' tax benefit	B	6,300	7,200	9,800	23,300
Net cash flow		$(11,700)	$(13,300)	$(18,200)	$(43,200)

[b]—Purchase-Option Projection

The base case purchase-option projection is composed of three parts: (1) an occupancy-expense projection, (2) a tax-benefit projection and (3) a cash-flow projection. Each of these component parts was discussed previously.

Figure 22-D illustrates the base case purchase option projection.

ABC LAW FIRM
PURCHASE-OPTION PROJECTION
BASE CASE
($ in thousands)

	Input Data Assumptions	Projected Results Years 1 to 10	Years 11 to 20	Years 21 to 30	Total
OCCUPANCY-COST PROJECTION					
Depreciation	Fig. 22-B	$ 6,000	$ 6,000	$ 6,000	$ 18,000
Interest expense	Fig. 22-B	15,800	5,200	—	21,000
Other occupancy expenses	Estimate	4,000	6,000	8,000	18,000
Partnership occupancy expenses		$25,800	$17,200	$14,000	$ 57,000
TAX-BENEFIT PROJECTION					
Federal Tax	30%	$ 7,700	$ 5,200	$4,200	$ 17,100
State Tax	5%	1,300	900	700	2,900
Partners' tax benefit	B	$ 9,000	$ 6,100	$4,900	$ 20,000
CASH-FLOW PROJECTION					
Loan principal repayments	Fig. 22-B	$(10,500)	$(10,500)	—	$(21,000)
Interest expense	Fig. 22-B	(15,800)	(5,200)	—	(21,000)
Other occupancy expenses	Estimate	(4,000)	(6,000)	(8,000)	(18,000)
Partnership cash flow		(30,300)	(21,700)	(8,000)	(60,000)
Partners' tax benefit	B	9,000	6,100	4,900	20,000
Net cash flow		$(21,300)	$(15,600)	$(3,100)	$(40,000)

[2]—Alternative Scenarios

Processing alternative scenarios achieves the ultimate purpose underlying the creation of a financial model. This is accomplished by changing one or more of the assumptions in a financial model's base case and by processing the revised data and preparing a new report. Changes in assumptions might occur as a result of negotiation, more precise data, or better insight into future events (or possibly to merely test the potential impact of a given factor on the model results).

For example, changes in assumptions in an office-occupancy cost model might arise from: (1) a variation in purchase price for the property or (2) a variation in the interest rate for the bank loan to be obtained to finance the property.

[a]—Purchase Price Variation

The office-occupancy cost model, previously illustrated, assumed that the property would be purchased for $21 million, of which $18 million was allocated to the cost of the building and $3 million to the cost of the land. After viewing the results produced by the financial model based on this asking price for the property and after scrutinizing other information and facts about the property, the firm's partners may decide to make an offer for the property at a lesser amount.

Scenario B in Figure 22-E illustrates the cumulative impact of changing the assumed purchase price for the property to $18 million, of which $15 million is allocated to the cost of the building.

[b]—Interest Rate Variation

The office-occupancy cost model, previously illustrated, assumed that the bank loan obtained to finance the purchase of the property would carry an interest rate of ten percent. However, the firm's partners may be able to obtain a reduced interest rate on the bank loan, as a result of negotiation or because of changes in economic conditions.

Scenario C in Figure 22-E illustrates the cumulative impact of changing the assumed interest rate on the bank loan to 9 percent.

ABC LAW FIRM
PURCHASE-OPTION PROJECTION UNDER
THREE ALTERNATIVE SCENARIOS
($ in thousands)

	Alternative Scenarios		
	A	B	C
KEY ASSUMPTIONS:			
Property purchase price	$21,000	$18,000	$21,000
Interest rate for loan	10%	10%	9%
	Projected Results over 30 years		
OCCUPANCY-COST PROJECTIONS:			
Depreciation	$18,000	$15,000	$18,000
Interest expense	21,000	18,000	18,900
Other occupancy expenses	18,000	18,000	18,000
Partnership occupancy expenses	$57,000	$51,000	$54,900
TAX-BENEFIT PROJECTIONS:			
Federal tax	$17,100	$15,300	$16,500
State tax	2,900	2,600	2,700
Partners' tax benefit	$20,000	$17,900	$19,200
CASH-FLOW PROJECTION:			
Loan principal repayments	$(21,000)	$(18,000)	$(21,000)
Interest expense payments	(21,000)	(18,000)	(18,900)
Other occupancy expenses	(18,000)	(18,000)	(18,000)
Partnership cash flow	(60,000)	(54,000)	(57,900)
Partners' tax benefit	20,000	17,900	19,200
Net cash flow	$(40,000)	$(36,100)	$(38,700)

[3]—Comparison of Base Case vs. Alternative Scenarios

The bottom line in a financial model is a comparison between the base case and one or more alternative scenarios. The purpose of this comparison is to identify the scenario which provides the optimum benefit. For example, in an office-occupancy cost model, the optimum benefit would usually be provided by the scenario which produces the least cost (all other factors being equal).

There are two methods of making this comparison: (1) a year-by-year cash-flow comparison and (2) a discounted-cash-flow comparison.

[a]—Year-by-Year Cash-Flow Comparison

As its title implies, this method simply compares cash flow under the base case and under each alternative scenario on a year-by-year basis and in the aggregate.

[b]—Discounted-Cash-Flow Comparison

This method has an advantage over the year-by-year method because it takes into account the time value of money.

Both methods are illustrated in Figure 22-F.

ABC LAW FIRM
LEASE VS. PURCHASE CASH FLOW ANALYSIS
COMPARISON OF FOUR SCENARIOS
($ in thousands)

	Purchase Scenarios			Lease Scenario
	Alternative A	Alternative B	Alternative C	Alternative D
YEAR-BY-YEAR CASH FLOW	(Fig. 18-D)	(Fig. 18-E)	(Fig. 18-E)	(Fig. 18-C)
Years 1 to 10	$(21,300)	$(18,600)	$(20,200)	$(11,700)
Years 11 to 20	(15,600)	(14,100)	(15,400)	(13,300)
Years 21 to 30	(3,100)	(3,400)	(3,100)	(18,200)
Regular cash flow	$(40,000)	$(36,100)	$(38,700)	$(43,200)
DISCOUNTED-CASH FLOW				
Discounted cash flow at 8%	$(19,600)	$(17,400)	$(18,800)	$(14,600)

§ 22.05 Interpreting the Results

As can be seen from Figure 22-F, purchasing the building (under each of three purchase alternatives A-B-C) clearly is less costly in the aggregate compared to leasing the office space (alternative D) over the thirty-year period. However, note that there is a decided difference in the timing of the outlay of funds for the purchase versus the lease of the office space. Leasing the space calls for a markedly smaller outlay of funds in the early years versus the later years, while purchasing the property calls for a heavy outlay of funds in the early years versus less spending in the later years.

The discounted cash flow calculation information presents a clearer picture than the year-by-year cash flow analysis. It takes into account the time value of money impact of the differing cash flows and presents a net result for comparative purposes. Figure 22-F shows that the lease option (alternative D) clearly is less expensive than the purchase options (alternatives A-B-C) under the discounted cash flow method.

One final note: the potential appreciation of the property over time is an advantage of the purchase options which has not been quantified in the financial model. It should be taken into consideration in the decision-making process—if not objectively, at least subjectively.

CHAPTER 23

Merger and Acquisition Accounting

Chapter Contents

---

§ 23.01 Articulate a Strategy for Growth

Sustaining growth through changing economic conditions is the result of vision, hard work and realistic action plans. Growth also can occur as a result of economic developments affecting a law firm's clients. While it is great to be lucky and to benefit from clients' growth, it is nicer to know that growth happened because it was planned.

Sometimes, a law firm is forced into a situation where it has to consider a merger just to maintain its client base. For example, if a major client moves to another city and wants to continue using the same law firm, that firm has to consider opening an office in the other city or merging with another firm, to properly service the client. The need to grow can be caused by the expansion or diversification of a client that forces a law firm to become proficient in a new specialized area of the law. Growth also can be fueled by the perception that a law firm practice has to be global in order to survive in the future and that requires offices in major cities throughout the world. Whatever the reason, firm management has to be cognizant of where they are today, where they want to be tomorrow, and how they are going to get there.

During the 1980s and 1990s, corporations experienced unprecedented growth through mergers and combinations. The larger corporate clients became, the more pressure they put on law firms to grow. Some firms responded to that pressure by sending attorneys from existing offices to new locations where they opened offices. Other firms, realizing that starting an office from scratch was time-consuming and expensive (especially without an existing block of business), focused instead on merging with existing, compatible firms in new locations. Mergers or acquisitions of parts of other law firms became the most common and efficient ways for law firms to expand into new markets, to obtain the necessary new specialties, and to provide the legal coverage expected by their clients.

One of the most important measurements of a merger is the synergy that is created as a result of the combination. Synergy represents the partners' joint actions that, when taken together, increase their collective effectiveness. It results in the whole being greater than the sum of the parts. A successful merger is one that creates synergy in an area that allows the combined firm to grow faster than either predecessor firm would have grown on its own.

The first step in the merger process is articulating the strategy of growth and having the partners agree to that strategy. Does the firm want to grow by merging with a firm that is roughly its same size? Does the firm want to acquire a smaller firm and cloak the transaction as a "merger"? Or, does the firm want to "cherry pick" a key lawyer from another firm, a specialty group in another firm, or a branch office of another firm? Each of these strategies (and others) has been the *modus operandi* of acquiring firms.

By analyzing the strategies for growth and by articulating the plans for carrying out those strategies, a law firm becomes focused and better able to identify the best merger candidate. Merging with a recognized firm may sound nice, but if the merger does not meet the strategic objectives of both firms, it can be disastrous. Merging with a smaller firm or one that is not as well known but that meets the articulated strategic objectives can be a dynamic opportunity that creates a level of synergy not achievable by either firm on its own.

§ 23.02 Merger Action Plans

Once the decision is made to merge, a firm needs to develop an action plan that it can follow throughout the process. The action plan should include:

(1) Forming a merger team;
(2) Identifying the strategic considerations;
(3) Identifying target firms;
(4) Evaluating the deal;
(5) Closing the deal; and
(6) Implementing the deal.

Each of these action plans will be discussed in this chapter. At the end of this chapter there will be a discussion of some deal breakers that derailed merger talks.

§ 23.03 Form a Merger Team

The merger team is a group of partners or shareholders and administrative personnel who "have a need to know" about merger talks and who will participate in the evaluation process. The better organized the team, the better it performs its mission and the better impression it makes on the other law firm. The merger team should consist of people such as the managing partner, senior partner, finance partner, tax partner, practice leader, executive director, and director of finance. Depending on the skills of the team members, it may be worthwhile to have an independent consultant work with the team to facilitate the process. The size of the team depends on the size of the firm and how it operates, but usually it will be as small as practical. In general, the team should consider its task confidential to avoid office rumors that often take on exaggerated lives with incorrect information. The fewer people involved and the more closely guarded the status of the process, the easier it will be to evaluate the proposed merger and to prepare a recommendation to the partnership or shareholders. Each person on the team should have a primary assignment and should report to the committee as a whole. Also, each member should have a counterpart in the other firm so that communication and coordination between firms is facilitated.

It is not uncommon for a managing partner to begin talks with another firm before anyone on the management committee or executive committee knows anything about the exploratory talks. Depending on the charge that has been given the managing partner by the management committee, this independent action may circumvent sound merger principles. For example, if a managing partner or key shareholder conducts his or her own discussions with a target firm, and concludes that a merger with that firm would be beneficial, it may be embarrassing for the individual and the firm if a decision is made later not to merge with that firm. Instead of the "lone ranger" approach, a firm should determine strategic considerations against which it will measure any merger candidate. Once that is done and a list of possible firms is developed, it is reasonable that the managing partner will make an overture to one of those firms, not one that he or she chooses based solely on personal knowledge.

§ 23.04 Strategic Considerations

Once the strategy for growth is articulated and accepted, it is necessary to develop a list of strategic considerations that will be used to identify the right merger candidate. There are many strategic considerations that could be evaluated by a law firm contemplating a merger or acquisition. Nine considerations that should be analyzed include:

(1) Financial measurements;
(2) Firm name and governance;
(3) Partner/Shareholder considerations;
(4) Practice areas and client strategies;
(5) Personnel considerations;
(6) Geographic strategies;
(7) Accounting considerations;
(8) Tax considerations; and
(9) Operational considerations.

The list is not meant to be comprehensive, nor is it designed to rank the criteria. Each firm needs to compose and order its own list based upon factors most relevant to its articulated growth strategy.

[1]—Financial Measurements

Since the objective of most law firm mergers is to create synergy that will allow the new firm to increase partner profits, the first financial factor the merger team should focus on is the composition of the other firm's net operating income.

[a]—Gross Fees

A merger team needs to consider the source of the gross fees and whether any client or industry/practice group generates more than a reasonable percentage of the gross fees. This is important because if, for example, 35% of a firm's gross fees are earned from a few clients, then the commitment of those clients to remain with the new firm after the merger is critical. It is equally important to verify that there will not be a conflict with any of those clients.

The merger team needs to understand what is included in gross income and be able to contrast that understanding with what is included in its firm's gross income. The merger team should determine:

(1) Whether income includes only cash-basis income or whether it includes income calculated under a full accrual method or a modified accrual method;

(2) The likelihood of full realization of work-in-process ("WIP") and accounts receivable ("A/R") if the accrual method is used;

(3) Whether gross income includes an offset for client disbursements that might be reported differently by the other firm;

(4) Whether gross income includes any valuation reserves for WIP or A/R; and

(5) Whether gross income includes the amortization of an "opening" adjustment caused by a change in accounting methods or change in the firm's year-end.

These and other similar issues should be addressed by the merger team to ensure that the gross receipts of a target firm will be comparable to its own. All analysis should be done using both firms' managements' latest financial statements.

Another measurement that the merger team should consider is the amount of gross fees by partner and by lawyer. These measurements are important because they give an overview of the "financial health" of a target firm. If a target firm's gross fees per partner are less than the merger team's, there should be some analysis to determine if the lower number is an aberration or if there is something endemic to the way the firm is run. Factoring in hourly charge rates, hours worked, and leverage of associates to partners may explain variances.

The merger team should analyze hours worked in the context of the firm's culture or commonly accepted practices in that area. If fewer hours are worked by associates as a result of a "quality of life" issue, then a merger team should evaluate whether adjusting the hours worked will bring about a mass exodus, causing the loss of talented associates. If fewer hours are worked by partners, then the merger team should evaluate why that is and whether something can be done to increase hours without negatively affecting partners whom they want to retain.

A merger team should realize that in different parts of the country and in the world, for that matter, different forces influence the way in which a law firm conducts business. In France, for example, it might be illegal to work on certain days, so the number of hours will be affected. In the UK, it is common to book fewer hours than are booked in New York, although each hour normally is charged out at a higher billing rate. New York law firms tend to work longer hours and have higher billing rates than in other parts of the United States. Merger teams should be aware of these and other factors, because it may be impossible to obtain parity in all locations. Factoring those realizations into the strategic considerations means that a merger team does not have to waste time analyzing variables that are accepted as normal. However, knowing the cause of gross income variances allows a merger team to address important revenue recognition policies and to develop economic models that can test planned utilization levels, leverage, chargeable hours per lawyer, billing rates, realization percentages, and profit-per-partner targets for the new firm. Often realizing these cultural or practice differences is the first step in working to reasonable and rational resolutions.

[b]—Gross Operating Expenses

There is a certain irony in the fact that most law firms have more expense accounts than income accounts. Fortunately, the numbers in the income accounts normally are larger than the numbers in the expense accounts. The observation about the number of accounts is important because it means that there are accounts that should be analyzed before "signing off" on the merger.

The objective in analyzing gross operating expenses is the same as that in analyzing gross fee income. A merger team needs to understand what expenses the other firm generates, and if those expenses are comparable to its own. Even though a target firm's expenses are less in absolute amounts, they may be higher when analyzed based on the average operating expense per attorney or some other factor. Obviously, there can be a myriad of reasons to explain differences. For example, the target firm's benefit plans or health plans for its attorneys may be more generous, expatriate programs may cover more costs, or office space may be more expensive. Likewise, differences can be caused by application of different depreciation methods, different methods of accounting for client disbursements, different accounting methods for software development costs, and different salary structures. The differences themselves are not as important as understanding why they exist, so that adjustments can be made after a merger, where appropriate, to ensure better economics among partners.

The merger team also needs to focus on outstanding commitments and contingencies such as real estate leases, pension plans, debt covenants, pending or threatened lawsuits, guarantees, unfunded partner retirement benefits, etc. Based on the type of law practiced, the merger team also should consider the related levels of professional liability and other insurance for the new firm.

[c]—Net Operating Income

Perhaps nothing is more revealing than the bottom line. Several lawyer-oriented publications track net income per lawyer or partner and use it as the unofficial tool to measure the profitability of law firms. Many law firms use those rankings to measure the success of their own practices, even though many of them acknowledge flaws in the measurement criteria. If a firm relies on industry-published statistics, it is very important to verify the accuracy of the statistics with the merger candidate, because differences can exist from simply reporting one income or expense item differently than the way others in the professional report the same information.

Examination of various ratios based on net operating income is an excellent first step in comparing firms, albeit from a very high level. Income per partner can be an important consideration in determining the income sharing percentages to be assigned to each partner in the new firm. However, the merger team needs to dig down to determine the substance behind the numbers.

[2]—Firm Name and Governance

Two very important considerations that should be addressed early in the evaluation process are the name of the new firm and how it will be governed. These considerations are important, because they are subjective and personal factors that can distract partners from focusing on the real economic and strategic reasons for the merger, particularly with respect to international mergers.

[a]—Firm Name

Picking a name for a new entity requires sensitivity and diplomacy, because there is nothing more "personal" to a law firm than its name and reputation. To a law firm merging into another firm, the loss of its name can be traumatic and emotional. Partners or members who feel that they are losing their name may feel that they are "selling out" to the other firm and may not develop the same level of loyalty they had to their old firm. Selection of a name, therefore, must be thoroughly discussed, so that there are not lingering animosities after the merger. In most situations, early discussion and selection of a new name is advisable.

However, when two firms are comparable in size and there is a fear that announcing the new name will distract the merger process, it might be advisable to delay the announcement. That way, partners or shareholders of each firm focus primarily on the benefits to be derived from the merger and are not negatively distracted by the name. Once they have accepted the merger concept, announcing the name will have less significance.

Normally, the name of the new entity is some combination of the names of both firms, because of the reputations and goodwill associated with the existing names. Firms with long names often truncate several trailing names, so that the combined name is not too long or difficult to say. In some cases, some part of the smaller firm's name is tacked onto the end of the name of the larger firm and used that way in the local markets where the smaller firm practices. After some transition period, the name of the smaller firm may be dropped for simplicity. Larger firms might consider using a consultant to prepare a list of two or three possible names and might survey key clients or members of the business community for their reactions to the possible name.

It is important to develop a marketing and branding strategy for the new name so that clients begin to associate with the new name and cease using the name of either merged firm.

[b]—Governance

Law firms govern themselves in a variety of ways. Regardless of structure (e.g., partnership or corporation), governance tends to be centralized or decentralized.

Firms using the centralized form of governance tend to have management committees that make all major decisions and set the strategic goals and objectives of the firm. Some firms refine centralized management to a point where one person assumes only administrative responsibilities and essentially functions as the chairman and president by making all the major decisions. In that form of governance, a management committee is there to advise the chairman and, often, professional, non-lawyer managers are engaged to assist the chairman in running the firm. The theory behind this form of governance is that a law firm cannot be a democracy of partners, because too many partners or shareholders are distracted by management considerations (i.e., too much non-chargeable time) and, consequently, there are too many opinions on how to conduct business. This form of management tends to mirror corporate America management structures with a chairman of the board, president, executive vice-president, etc. Law firms that practice as professional corporations have the same structure as corporate America, but do not necessarily opt for a non-democratic form of management.

On the opposite end of the spectrum, firms that use committees to govern tend to have more partners or shareholders involved in management. Sometimes, there are conflicting strategies that result from different committees approaching the same issue from different directions. When this happens, more meetings and discussion have to take place to resolve differences. The committee approach may also create fiefdoms in which partners or shareholders measure their importance by the committee that they chair. The committee structure tends to work better for smaller law firms, but may become cumbersome for larger firms, especially international firms. However, in the traditional sense of the term, a partnership is one in which all partners have a say in management and generally voice their opinions. Nowhere is this form of governance more pronounced than in the United Kingdom.

The merger team needs to consider the different governance structures and decide which type of governance will be required in the new firm. Depending on the size of the target firm, this evaluation should take place early in the merger process.

[3]—Partner/Shareholder Considerations

Merger teams should never lose sight of the ultimate reality—that regardless of other altruistic reasons, law firms are in business to make money. The first and foremost consideration in any merger should be its effect on the partners or shareholders, because the firm exists primarily for their benefit. They are both the owners of the law firm and its principal work force. In assessing whether a merger will work, a merger team should consider the skills, experience, and age of the partners or shareholders in the other firm. During this process, it is very important to identify the "rainmakers" in the other firm and to formulate strategies to retain them.

At the same time, a merger team might identify non-performing partners. If this happens, the merger team has to evaluate the extent of the problem and whether it is something that should be dealt with before or after the merger.

Because the partner or shareholder group is so important to the well being of the new firm, special focus should be given to:

(1) Partner classifications—a single class or special classes of partners or shareholders;

(2) Development of a system of rewards, compensation policies and benefits;

(3) Development of a career track for associates and formulation of admission policies;

(4) Uniform retirement policies and early or normal withdrawal policies;

(5) Performance evaluation criteria and counseling non-performers;

(6) Matrix expectations, including chargeable time, practice development, and administrative responsibilities;

(7) Identification of partner authority and responsibilities;

(8) Slotting partners of both firms into a common grid for practice and compensation purposes;

(9) Retention strategy for rainmakers; and

(10) Timely and forthright communication with partners or shareholders.

In addition to focusing on the retention of existing partners or shareholders, the merger team should be cognizant of the risk of defection by some partners or shareholders, especially "rainmakers." It should also be sensitive to the early retirement of some partners or key associates who might not be happy with the proposed merger. It is important to work with partners who are in charge of practice areas or industries, so that they cooperate and work to make a smooth transition, instead of being parochial about their areas and resistant to changes brought on by the merger. A merger team should never lose sight of the fact that partners have egos that sometimes can distort reality and get in the way of rational business decisions.

[4]—Practice Areas and Client Strategies

Practice areas and client strategy considerations focus on the differences in the ways that law firms operate and whether there are endemic differences that will prevent a merger.

[a]—Practice Areas

A law firm's practice is its lifeblood and its principal source of revenue. Therefore, it demands keen attention. In assessing the risks and rewards of a proposed merger, a merger team should consider the practice area of the other law firm, and assess how effectively that practice can be merged with its own.

Attention should be given to how the other firm's practice is organized. Common ways of organizing a law practice are by industry, specialty or practice group, geography, or some combination of the three. Depending on the size of the firm or its practice area, it might have substructures within categories.

The merger team also should consider the tenure and influence of partners who lead practice groups or industries and whether they will be supporters of or obstructionists to the merger. It could happen that partners in charge of key practice areas are not in favor of a merger, because they might lose their in-charge position. If those partners are influential enough, they can make the evaluation process more difficult by not cooperating or by acting in such a way that partners in the other firm feel that they are not welcome and will be subservient to them. If taken to an extreme, this type of behavior could derail the merger.

Some considerations that the merger team should address in this area are:

(1) The length of time the other firm has practiced under its existing practice structure;

(2) The willingness of partners in the other firm to accept a different practice structure;

(3) How partners in the other firm would be slotted into the new practice structure;

(4) If one or more unique or specialized practice areas require a practice structure that will differ from that chosen for the rest of the practice; and

(5) The proposed practice structure of the new firm—by practice lines, industry specialties, or some other method.

The merger team has to evaluate what organizational changes will be necessary to meld the practice areas into one accepted methodology. Identifying the organizational differences in each firm's practice area is important because incompatible methods may require more analysis and modifications to combine them effectively. Also, forcing one firm to adopt the practice structure of the other firm may cause confusion, friction, and lost billable hours.

[b]—Client Strategies

Client strategy considerations require focus on both the industries in which clients are grouped and the clients themselves.

A merger creates the perfect opportunity to exercise selectivity over the type of specialties that the new law firm wants to practice and over the types of clients that the firm wants. When law firms are small and growing, they tend to accept a diverse group of clients often with no common connections. As firms develop specialties in various industries or areas of the law, they have less time to devote to clients that fall outside their practice concentrations. The more they specialize in one area of the law, the less time they can devote to another specialty practice. Likewise, clients that once demanded significant time and attention often change and might start their own in-house legal departments, thereby needing less outside counsel. For various reasons, a law firm's client list might be unfocused. In addition, the firm may be trying to be all things to all clients. A merger is the perfect time to inventory the client list and to decide selectively which specialties the firm will practice and which clients it no longer wishes to serve.

A merger team should consider selectivity and synergy when evaluating a merger. Areas to address are:

(1) The number of practice areas of the other firm and the depth of coverage and expertise in those areas;
(2) Which specialties of the other firm are compatible with or complementary to the firm's existing specialties;
(3) What synergies can be realized in leveraging specialties from one firm with specialties in the other firm;
(4) What new specialties will be created in the new firm and these specialties' growth potential;
(5) Evaluation of specialties that will not be on target and how they should be discontinued;
(6) The impact the merger might have on existing clients, especially important clients;
(7) The percentage of the firm's revenue from its top ten clients and whether those clients will continue to be clients of the merger firm;
(8) The ability of the new firm to attract new clients and to develop new specialties; and
(9) What conflicts might be created as a result of the merger.

A careful evaluation of practice areas, specialties and client base will give the merger team a better perspective of what effect the merger will have on the existing business of each firm. If the merger does not create an identifiable increase in the level of synergy, then it could be that the practices are too different to merge or that significant changes should be made (e.g., selectively resigning from certain clients) to one or both practices before a merger vote is taken.

[5]—Personnel Considerations

The single most important asset of a law firm is its professional staff. Without them, partners cannot leverage their time or talents. Without competent and intelligent associates at all levels, partners could not be assured that research is complete and comprehensive, and that briefs communicate in an effective manner. Because of their importance, a merger team should focus on associates' skills, experience levels, and areas of specialization. In addition, it is relevant to consider the effect that a merger will have on high performing associates or non-equity attorneys who fill important niches within the other firm. Turnover of these key attorneys can alter the intended benefits of a merger and impede the synergistic opportunities.

Differences in pay and benefit packages for associates may be an issue because associates tend to discuss such matters. Focusing on personnel matters before a merger will allow a merger team to develop a strategy to retain key associates and to reduce turnover. At the opposite end of the spectrum, the merger team should critically review whether some associates should be counseled about the viability of their careers in the new firm. Some of the factors that the merger team will want to focus on include:

(1) Associate lawyer staff size, promotion policies, and recruiting strategies of the new firm;

(2) A retention policy for valued associates and dismissal strategy for non-performers;

(3) A methodology for merging two staffs into a common structure with the understanding that some associates will be valued at a higher level, and some may be classified lower;

(4) The difference in chargeable hour expectations of both firms, with a focus on obtaining the best common denominator;

(5) Compensation models for the new firm and transition policies, if any, to equalize associates performing similar jobs in the same office or in different offices (especially between the United States and non-U.S. offices);

(6) Fringe benefits (e.g., vacations, personal days, overtime meals, medical plans, 401(k) plans, personal computers, etc.) for the new firm;

(7) Rotation, assignment and continuing education policies; and

(8) Transfer or expatriate policies, if applicable.

As important as these considerations are, their importance is magnified when the proposed merger candidate is a law firm in another country. Law firms in other countries, such as the U.K., have very different policies for associates, especially in the areas of compensation, chargeable hour expectation, billing rates, and benefit plans. These factors create a more challenging task for the merger team and may require a longer transition period to create parity throughout the firm.

[6]—Geographic Strategies

Geographic strategy suggests that, for whatever reason, a firm is not satisfied with the location in which it is practicing law or feels that it has to operate in other geographic locations. Maybe the city or area of the country in which it has an important part of its practice is not growing or major corporate clients have moved or merged, so the firm wants to open an office in a faster growing city. A firm might aspire to dominate a geographic market and believe that it needs multiple offices in larger cities within its chosen geographic area. Maybe a firm believes that it has to be located in a specific geographic area to broaden its areas of specialization. And, there is the "domino" theory, in which the first law firm to merge becomes an inducement to a string of other firms that feel that they have to merge to remain competitive with their peer firms.

Geographic strategies become geometrically more difficult and more relevant as the geographic distance increases. A local or regional merger, for example, has the least geographic considerations, because a firm normally is quite familiar with the area in which it currently practices. Also, many of the economic considerations, culture and business mores are the same within regions.

Expanding into new regions through the merger process introduces a new set of geographic considerations. For example, a New York or Washington D.C. firm that merges with a firm in California will have to contend with a different time zone, and may have to contend with a different business climate (maybe more casual), lifestyle differences that focus more on "quality of life" issues, and differences in management philosophies. Successful transcontinental mergers have dealt with these and other geographic considerations.

The most challenging geographic merger is the international merger. The geographic considerations in this type of merger are much more formidable to deal with because of the differences in cultures, time zones, business mores, regulatory requirements, accounting principles, tax compliance requirements, and general business philosophies. All of these considerations are present in a merger with a law firm in the U.K. And yet, a merger with a firm in London is easier for a U.S. firm than a merger with a law firm in Tokyo, Moscow, or Mexico City because of language, cultural, and regulatory differences. To balance that statement, one should not forget what George Bernard Shaw once said that Americans and British are "two peoples separated by a common language." As humorous as that might sound, suffice to say that mergers with firms in locations throughout the world are possible and can be done. Several U.S. and U.K. firms have demonstrated that international mergers can be done and be done effectively.

Whatever the geographic considerations, the business strategy has to determine whether expansion will benefit the firm in terms of practice area, client, and industry strategy, particularly in the case of an international merger.

If the geographic strategy focuses on domination of a current geographic market, the same evaluation must be made of how the practice area, client, and industry strategies will be affected. Careful consideration of key differences is a must before embarking on the journey.

[7]—Accounting Considerations

Accounting practices are one of the last factors to be evaluated when considering a merger. The review often takes place later in the evaluation process because law firms are very protective of their financial information. Its placement in the process should not be construed as indicative of accounting considerations being any less important. On the contrary, a review of the financial information is extremely important and may, in fact, be very challenging. The merger team must become familiar enough with the other firm's financial statements so that it can identify adjustments that will be needed to make the financial statements compatible with its own and can determine the true value of all of the assets.

Comparability is important so that each firm can be evaluated based on the same criteria. Comparability, however, may be more demanding than what meets the eye. For example, two firms may have accounts on their balance sheets called "Client Disbursements." One firm might post all disbursements made in connection with client service to client disbursements, whereas, the other firm may only post the traditional "hard costs" to client disbursements. Both firms use the same account title, but record very different information. The merger team needs to realize that there may be a difference in accounting methods and must be capable of measuring the financial impact of bringing the two statements into parity. In order for the merger team to be able to evaluate accounting and financial information furnished by each of the two former firms, this information must be reclassified and adjusted, so that it is based upon comparable accounting policies and comparable asset valuation procedures.

The merger team also has to evaluate whether the assets are worth what they are listed at on the balance sheet. The most obvious assets for valuation assessment are work-in-process (WIP) and accounts receivable (A/R). Larger firms generally have established procedures for when WIP or A/R should be reserved or written off, whereas, smaller firms might review the realization of WIP and A/R on a case-by-case basis. A similar analysis of leasehold improvements must be made, so that the amortization basis used by each firm is the same.

Other assets and liabilities that the merger team needs to evaluate are prepaid assets, depreciation methods, investments, accounting methods for software development costs, unrecorded assets, contingent liabilities, contingent tax matters (e.g., unincorporated business tax, where applicable), lease commitments (for both office space and equipment), unrecorded liabilities, unfunded employee retirement plans, unfunded deferred compensation partner plans, accounting for retainers, and unamortized opening adjustments from accounting method changes.

[8]—Tax Considerations

Just as comparability of accounting information is important in assessing the two former firms' financial statements, comparability of tax information is important in assessing the relative tax positions of the two former firms. There are two categories of tax considerations that a merger team should review. The first category includes the tax changes that will result when the merger is consummated and the second category includes tax changes that will result after the firms begin operating as a single firm.

The first category is sometimes overlooked because it focuses on the "disappearing" firm's tax problems. When a firm merges into another firm, under U.S. tax rules, it must file a final tax return as of the date of the merger. If the firm has an unamortized opening adjustment from a change in accounting methods, the entire unamortized balance must be included in the firm's final tax return. Tax matters are more complex if a firm is on a fiscal year-end for tax purposes and merges with a firm on a date other than its year-end. Its partners, who are assumed to be on a calendar year-end, will have to pick up more than twelve months of income in their next tax returns. If the firm was on a fiscal year-end and had to pay a required payment, then the payment can be refunded, but the refund process can be slow and may overlap with an estimated tax payment date, causing a duplication of tax payment. Potentially, the biggest surprise comes when a firm is using an incorrect method of accounting (e.g., for client disbursements) and has to change the method before merging with the new firm. The change can cause an unexpected increase in phantom income on the final tax return. The merger team should be aware of these potential issues so that they are thoroughly discussed before the merger.

In mergers between law firms located in different countries, there may not be a "disappearing" firm issue. In England, for example, there are schemes to keep the existing firm in existence, although the practicality of doing so can create an administrative nightmare for the home-office accounting staff.

The second category of tax considerations includes changes that have to be made after the firms merge. This category includes:

(1) Tax accounting methods (e.g., cash vs. accrual, accelerated vs. straight-line depreciation, etc.), tax accounting periods (e.g.,

calendar vs. fiscal year) and tax accounting entities (e.g., partnership vs. professional corporation) for the new firm;

(2) Differences (if any) to be established between financial reporting policies and tax accounting policies for the new firm;

(3) U.S. Partnership Return of Income data gathering procedures to be developed by the new firm;

(4) State and local tax issue positions to be taken by the new firm; and

(5) The impact of IRC Section 704(c) on both firms.

The last point needs some commentary. For tax purposes, Section 704(c) of the Internal Revenue Code requires partnerships that contribute assets to a new partnership to track the assets so that income associated with those assets flows to the contributing partner. Since most U.S. law firms use the cash method of accounting, they do not have a tax basis in any of the WIP or A/R that is on the financial statements. As a result, when the assets are transferred in a merger, the tax basis is zero. When the WIP or A/R is collected, it creates income to the merged firm. The issue is which legacy group of partners should be taxed on the income. When a merger is between two U.S.-based firms, the issue is more theoretical than practical, because the income is all from U.S. sources and will be taxed to one partner or another. But, when the merger is between a U.S. firm and a non-U.S. firm, the issue is very important because of the way the income is sourced. In a merger with a German firm, for example, receipt of German A/R will create German-source income. Without Section 704(c), that income would be apportioned to all global partners. With 704(c), however, those receipts will be allocated only to the German partners. Realizing and discussing this type of unique tax treatment during negotiations can lesson tensions after a merger.

As formidable as the tax considerations can be when both firms are, for example, U.S. law firms, the challenge is greater when analyzing potential tax differences between a U.S. firm and a non-U.S. firm. For example, a merger of a U.S. firm into a U.K. firm may create an opportunity to change the year-end of the U.S. firm while allowing it to continue a cash-method of accounting. Such a merger also raises issues of worldwide tax filing requirements, U.S. withholding on effectively connected income allocable to the non-U.S. partners, and an assortment of other tax complications. A merger of a U.K. firm into a U.S. firm includes those considerations mentioned before plus the possible loss of a beneficial tax year (i.e., a 30 April year-end might have to change to a 31 December year-end) and an increase in taxable income caused by discontinuing the separate firm.

A merger between a U.S. firm and a German firm can create benefits for the German partner. Most German law firms (as other European law firms) use the accrual method of accounting. When a German law firm merges with a U.S. law firm, it is possible to change the German firm's accounting method for tax purposes to a cash basis method of accounting, regardless of the accounting method used for financial statement purposes. When the change from accrual to cash is made, the German partners can obtain a tax benefit by the change in the form of a negative adjustment (in the U.S. it would be referred to as a Section 481 adjustment) that literally reverses the accrued income existing on the date of the merger. If the entire negative adjustment is allocated to the German partners, they can experience a potentially significant reduction in their German taxable income.

If there are any major tax claims pending or threatened against one of the former firms, or if an aggressive filing position has been taken on a major controversial tax issue by one of the former firms, the manner of absorbing the cost of these potential claims should be dealt with up front, in a manner which results in fairness among partners. Appropriate communications to the effected partners or shareholders should be made.

[9]—Operational Considerations

Operational considerations are a catchall category to address other considerations on which a merger team should focus. Included in this category is the legal form of the entity that will practice law, technology platforms, support and administrative staffs, office facilities, and other operating costs.

[a]—Form of Entity

In the vast majority of mergers, the form of entity is not a major consideration. Often a partnership merges with another partnership and continues doing business as a partnership. Alternatively, a professional corporation mergers with another professional corporation and continues operating as a professional corporation. These mergers require little or no analysis. When a partnership merges with a professional corporation, or vice versa, more consideration and analysis needs to be given to the structure under which the continuing firm will practice law. Merger teams need to focus on the differences between the two structures and be sensitive to them. In addition to tax matters,[1] there are these important differences between a partnership and a professional corporation:

---

[1] See Chapter 19 *supra* for a discussion of tax matters.

(1) The extent of personal liability a partner is willing to accept is an issue;

(2) In a partnership, partners are self-employed, whereas in a professional corporation, shareholders are employees;

(3) In a partnership, there are very few fringe benefits that can be absorbed by the firm, whereas, in a professional corporation, many fringe benefits can be paid for by the corporation;

(4) A partner often has phantom income, whereas any phantom income in a professional corporation is absorbed by the corporation;

(5) There is only one level of tax in a partnership (i.e., at the partner level), whereas in a professional corporation there can be two levels of tax (i.e., at the corporate level and at the shareholder/employee level); and

(6) Regulatory restrictions at a state level on the practice of law may vary between a partnership and a professional corporation.

The form of entity takes on special importance when there is a merger between law firms located in different countries because of regulatory restrictions or tax considerations. For example, if a French firm merges into a U.S. firm, the French firm may lose its right to practice law in France. If a law firm in Hungary, the Czech Republic or Turkey merges into a U.S. firm, then local regulatory rules prohibit ownership of the local firm by those who are not nationals of those countries. Likewise, if a U.K. firm merges into a U.S. firm, there are restrictions placed by the Law Society on solicitors sharing profits with lawyers who are not registered foreign lawyers. Suffice it to say that international mergers require sophisticated analysis to overcome regulatory restrictions and to avoid unwanted tax consequences.

[b]—Information Technology

A merger team needs to identify differences in technology used by the target firm and what changes or improvements will be required in the new firm. Broadly speaking, technology includes computer systems and networks, computer software, voicemail and phone systems, copiers, fax machines, and communication devices. Fortunately, most of these systems can be modified to work together in an efficient manner in a merged firm. Computer systems, including software, however, can be an issue, because not all computer systems or platforms are compatible. Replacing an existing system or installing a new computer network can be a very expensive proposition. One should not lose sight of or underestimate the importance of focusing on technology issues during the merger evaluation process. Since most lawyers rely on technology, they need a seamless solution that will allow lawyers from predecessor firms to communicate with each other and to share documents. If lawyers cannot function in an efficient manner using current technology, they will be less productive and the firm's profits will suffer. As innocuous as computers might be, inefficient or nonfunctioning systems can be an *Achilles heel* of rendering distinguished client service.

Consequently, a merger team must consider the compatibility of both firms' computer systems and networks and estimate the costs of modifying them so that they work together, or the cost of replacing one or both systems. When analyzing the cost of converting one firm's computer system to another, the merger team should consider a special allocation of those costs back to the partners or shareholders of the other firm. Alternatively, the merger team might recommend that the new firm absorb the conversion cost as an inducement for the target firm to merge.

Firms that try to save costs by ignoring incompatibility may find that using incompatible computer platforms can create degradation that impairs the free movement of information between or within firms. Because of the specialized nature of technology, it is often advisable for a merger team to bring in a qualified consultant who can analyze differences, propose solutions and estimate costs.

[c]—Office Space and Operating Costs

One anticipated result of a merger is cost savings through economies of scale. While it is true that mergers can create opportunities to eliminate duplicate costs over a longer period of time, the reality is that a merger creates extra unbudgeted, operating expenses. For example, when two firms have an office in the same city, the merger team needs to consider possible options: continue operating two offices, relocate everyone from one office to the other (co-locate), or lease new space for everyone. Operating two offices challenges a merger's effectiveness, unless practice groups can be brought together in one location or the other. Relocating everyone from one space to another assumes that there is sufficient space in the other facility to handle the larger group. Alternatively, leasing new space and moving everyone into it will allow co-location, but have many undesirable costs. Depending on the economic conditions in that city, landlords may allow a buildout or decoration allowance to offset office space construction. Additionally, there may be moving expenses, abandonment expenses for old leasehold improvements, and possibly lease termination costs and commissions. From a positive standpoint, moving into new space allows a new firm to respond to high occupancy costs by resizing attorneys' offices. It also allows synergies to be realized sooner through integration of professional staffs.

In addition to office space, the merger team should consider possible cost savings from back office operations. Instead of having two accounting departments, two billing departments, two computer departments, etc. the new firm should be able to combine many of these functions and then selectively use downsized satellite operations in branch offices.

A merger team should review space considerations and operating costs to determine the needs of the new firm and whether eliminating duplicate or redundant expenses can reduce costs.

§ 23.05 Target Identification

Once the strategy considerations are listed, it is time to prioritize them and to identify a list of firms that meet those considerations. Some firms perform these tasks using internal resources, while others engage outside consultants to insure confidentiality. Information on most firms can be readily obtained from various law-firm-related publications, through electronic searches of public databases, and through law firms' home pages on the Internet. The Internet is a valuable source because it often tells a reader what a particular law firm is most proud of and how it views itself. These insights are invaluable in preparing a *dossier* on each firm. Each *dossier* should follow the same format so that target firms can be compared on the same basis. The lists should evaluate each firm based on strategic considerations previously discussed, including practice/industry specialties, geographic locations, number of partners and attorneys, measurement of the financial success of the firm (i.e., revenue per partner, revenue per lawyer, etc.), reputation of the firm, and other relevant criteria.

This is where prioritizing becomes so important. If a firm is methodical, it will follow its prioritized list and criteria as closely as possible. Assuming that the firm obtains accurate information about each target, the list should identify the top two or three firms that truly meet its criteria. If, however, a firm deviates from its list or ignores the priorities that it assigned to a particular area and opts instead, for example, for a firm because of its reputation, it may find later that a methodical approach would have been better. Too often, firms with "great" reputations lose their edge and begin losing key partners and clients. Merging with a firm that is going through a metamorphosis without being aware of the change means that a healthy firm may unintentionally inherit one or more critical problems. Solving those problems after a merger may be divisive and distracting to a point where it would have been better not to merge.

§ 23.06 Evaluate the Deal

Once a merger team has evaluated the key strategic considerations that can influence the success of the merger, it is time to make a basic decision: Is the firm more interested in acquiring part of the target's business than it is in merging with the target?

When merger talks begin between two firms, it is often the intention that if everything goes well, the firms will merge. Along the way, however, it may happen that one firm discovers through the strategic evaluation process that the target firm has a problem that it would rather not inherit. The problem could be potential liability in a matter yet to be litigated or a block of business or a group of partners that the firm does not want. Whatever the reason, there should be a conscious focus on what is really wanted from the target firm. If the answer is that the firm only wants a group of partners in a particular specialty, then that is the way the deal needs to be evaluated. Of course, that also means that some difficult discussions need to take place between the acquiring firm and the target firm.

If the decision is made to continue merger talks, then it is necessary to evaluate the specific deal from the following perspectives:

(1) Strategic considerations;
(2) Financial due diligence; and
(3) Financial projections.

[1]—Strategic Considerations

Everyday, decision-makers chose among alternatives when making decisions. Disciplined decision-makers obtain as many facts as are available before making decisions. They are not impetuous and they try to leave emotions out of the decision-making process. "Good" decisions, therefore, generally are the product of a process that collects relevant data, digests that data, and chooses the best alternatives.

So too, when a law firm is considering a merger, it should use a logical process when deciding on its merger candidate. Earlier in this chapter, considerable attention was given to developing a list of strategic considerations that should be used in making a merger decision. The philosophy behind the list is to allow a law firm to focus on what is most important for its growth and the best way to achieve that growth. It also allows the firm to weigh each criterion so that the most important ones are considered earlier in the merger process. In concept, developing the strategic considerations becomes a self-analysis of the "culture" or ethos of the firm, so that a firm knows what is important and what is not. By developing the list and articulating it to partners or shareholders and to a target firm, a law firm essentially communicates the skeleton of a mission statement that is understandable internally and externally.

Seldom will all the strategic considerations align perfectly. More than likely, a law firm will have to compromise or modify one or more criteria. It is important, however, that key criteria not be compromised, for to do so may substantially alter the decision tree and lead to the wrong result.

In evaluating successful mergers, it is common to see a correlation between the attention that was given to early identification of strategic considerations and the actual evaluation criteria used for the specific deal. The more closely a law firm follows a methodical approach and avoids the "temptations of the moment," the more likely the merger will be successful. A firm that deviates from the strategic considerations because it intuitively knows that a particular firm is the "best" candidate or approaches a merger for merger's sake, finds either difficulty in closing the deal or impediments to implementing the deal.

For practical reasons, law firms should engage outside consultants to assist in this process. Consultants are independent advisors who are not inclined to rubber stamp a deal, especially when the strategic criteria do not match. More is said on this point at the end of this section.

[2]—Financial Due Diligence

It is necessary to prepare *pro forma* financial statements to see what the financial position and results of combined operations will look like. The *pro forma* calculations generally are done using prior-year's financial information. Presentation of a *pro forma* statement of income and expenses involves collecting and developing four types of financial information:

(1) Lead firm's results of operations;
(2) Target firm's results of operations;
(3) Merger adjustments; and
(4) *Pro forma* operating results of the merged firm.

Collection and development of the financial information underlying the *pro forma* income statement is discussed below. For purposes of this discussion, one firm has been designated the "Lead Firm" (Firm A) and the other firm has been designated the "Target Firm" (Firm B). The combined firm, after the merger, has been designated the "New Firm" (Firm ABC). Development of the *pro forma* information will involve (1) "reclassifying" each of the individual firm's financial statements to make them comparable to the other firm's, and (2) "adjusting" the combined data to give effect to merger assumptions.

[a]—Lead Firm's Results of Operations

Financial statements produced by two firms engaged in merger discussions may not be comparable. For example, one firm might use the cash basis method of accounting while the other firm uses the accrual basis method of accounting (or, in the U.K., full accrual method of accounting that is "fair and true"). To make the financial statements comparable, one firm's statements must be reclassified to conform to the accounting method of the other. This exercise is accomplished by converting the cash basis firm to the accrual basis and by converting the accrual basis firm to the cash basis. In a typical situation, this would involve accruing some portion of WIP and A/R and recording prepaid assets, accounts payable, and accrued liabilities.

For illustrative purposes, it is assumed that Firm A will reclassify its cash basis financial statements to the accrual basis, which is used by Firm B, as set forth in the following example:

FIRM A
MERGER RECLASSIFICATIONS

(Cash Basis converted to Accrual Basis)

	Cash Basis	Reclassification	Accrual Basis
Fee Revenue	$11,500,000	$1,000,000	$12,500,000
Employee Costs	(6,000,000)	—	(6,000,000)
Operating Expenses	(1,400,000)	(100,000)	(1,500,000)
Distributable Income	$4,100,000	$900,000	$5,000,000

[b]—Target Firm's Results of Operations

Financial statements for two firms considering a merger might not be completely comparable if they have been prepared for different periods of time, for example, if one firm's accounting period is a "calendar year" and the other firm uses a "fiscal year."

For illustrative purposes, it is assumed that the two firms wish to merge effective March 31 and that Firm B will reclassify its calendar year financial statements to the fiscal year (March 31) which is used by Firm A, as shown in the following example:

FIRM B
MERGER RECLASSIFICATIONS

(Calendar Year converted to Fiscal Year)

	Calendar Year	Reclassification	Fiscal Year
Fee Revenue	$12,000,000	$500,000	$12,500,000
Employee Costs	(6,200,000)	(200,000)	(6,400,000)
Operating Expenses	(1,500,000)	(100,000)	(1,600,000)
Distributable Income	$4,300,000	$200,000	$4,500,000

[c]—Merger Adjustments

Two firms wishing to merge may decide to organize the new firm in a manner that represents a change from either former firm's organizational structure. For example, the new firm may decide upon a redefinition of certain attorneys as "counsels" rather than "partners" or one firm might be a partnership and the other a professional corporation. While this redefinition does not affect the stature of the attorneys concerned, it can have a financial statement impact. When these attorneys were classified as partners, their compensation was not reflected as an expense of the business and, therefore, it did not reduce the firm's distributable income. Their compensation represented a distribution of profits. When these attorneys are classified as counsel, the firm may decide to reflect their compensation as an expense of the business and it will, therefore, result in a reduction in distributable income.

Some of the adjustments that might be considered to create comparability include client disbursements, recognition of WIP or A/R, prepaid assets, retainers, accrued income or expenses, and valuation issues.

For illustrative purposes, it is assumed that the merger team has determined that five partners of the former firm will be classified as counsel in the new firm, and that their aggregate compensation will be fixed at $500,000 per year (which approximates their share of the former firms' income during the past year).

[d]—*Pro Forma* Operating Results of Merged Firm

Preparation of a *Pro Forma* Statement of Distributable Income for the Merged Firm has two principal purposes; (1) to assist the merger team in evaluating the earning power that each of the two former firms brought to the merger, and (2) to establish a single set of accounting and financial reporting policies for the new merged firm to use in its future operations.

The *pro forma* statement is intended to portray the results of operations of the new firm based on the assumption that the two former firms have been merged for the past year. The *pro forma* statement is compiled from three components: (1) results of operations of the Lead Firm (Firm A), (2) results of operations of the Target Firm (Firm B), and (3) merger adjustments based on assumptions. Each of these components was discussed in previous paragraphs.

Figure 23-A illustrates a *pro forma* statement of distributable income for a new law firm resulting from the merger of two former firms.

It is important to recognize that the apparent increase in income per partner resulting from the merger adjustment is "illusory." This is because the merger adjustment, which decreased distributable income by $500,000 and reduced the number of partners by five, has no economic effect (i.e., the $500,000 which was the five former partners' share of distributable income has now become a $500,000 expense reduction of distributable income). The remaining partners' share of income remains unchanged.

Figure 23-A. Illustration of a pro forma statement of distributable income for a new law firm resulting from the merger of two former law firms.

ABC LAW FIRM
PRO FORMA STATEMENT OF DISTRIBUTABLE INCOME
ASSUMING A MERGER OF TWO FIRMS
($ in thousands)
Results of Operations

	Firm A	Firm B	Merger Adjustments	*Pro Forma* Combined
FEE REVENUES:				
Reported Revenues	$11,500	$12,000		$23,500
Revenue Reclassification	1,000	500		1,500
Revenue Adjustment			—	—
EXPENSES:				
Reported Expenses	(7,400)	(7,700)		(15,100)
Expense Reclassification	(100)	(300)		(400)
Expense Adjustment			$(500)	(500)
Distributable Income	$5,000	$4,500	$(500)	$9,000
NUMBER OF PARTNERS:				
Firm A Partners	23		(3)	20
Firm B Partners		22	(2)	20
Total Partners	23	22	(5)	40
INCOME PER PARTNER:				
Firm A Partners	$ 217			
Firm B Partners		$ 205		
Firm ABC Partners				$ 225

---

[3]—Financial Projections

Once the merger team is satisfied that they have developed a *pro forma* income statement for the "base year" of the merger, it is time to make some projections of what the merged firm's results of operations would be under a series of assumptions. The assumptions needed to make these projections should be realistic and should portray the potential benefits and risks, which have come to the attention of the merger team during negotiations.

Components of the projections include: (1) revenues, (2) expenses, (3) distributable income, (4) number of partners, and (5) income per partner. Steps for compiling and using these projections include:

(1) Developing base case projections;
(2) Creating alternative projections; and
(3) Comparing base case with alternative projections.

Each of these steps will be discussed below.

[a]—Developing Base Case Projections

Base case projections frequently start with the *pro forma* income statement and project results for a period of years assuming no changes except for the impact of inflation. Figure 19-B illustrates a base case income projection for a new law firm created from a merger.

[b]—Creating Alternative Projections

Alternative projections should deal with the merger team's realistic assumptions of the benefits and risks of the merger. For illustrative purposes, it is assumed that the merger team has five expectations. Some of the other assumptions that might be considered are a modification to the capital structure, a change in the method of financing the firm, the possible creation of a new benefit plan for partners and support staff, or a decrease in the days outstanding for A/R.

[i]—Synergy Assumption

The merger team might logically expect that the partners from both former firms will work together to generate additional work from their existing clients (e.g., Firm B's tax partner may obtain tax work from Firm A's real estate partner's clients). For illustrative purposes, it is assumed that this synergy will increase fee revenue by 5% in each of the first two years after the merger and that the services will be provided by improving partner and associate utilization without additional cost. This latter assumption is optimistic.

[ii]—Client Conflicts Assumption

The merger team might recognize the risk that certain clients may not remain with the merged firm because of real or perceived conflicts; for example, if Firm A was representing the plaintiff and Firm B was representing the defendant in a litigation case prior to the merger and this case continued after the merger. (For illustrative purposes it is assumed that this will reduce revenues by 5% in the first year after the merger and that this reduction will be sustained in future years.)

Figure 23-B. Illustration of "base case" projections of distributable income for a new law firm created from a merger.

ABC LAW FIRM
DISTRIBUTABLE INCOME PROJECTIONSBASE CASE
($ in thousands)

	Pro Forma		Projections	
	Year 1	Year 2	Year 3	Year 4
KEY ASSUMPTIONS:				
(cumulative)				
A-Billing rate increase	—	5%	10%	15%
B-Expense inflation Factor	—	5%	10%	15%
C-Number of partners	40	42	44	46
PROJECTIONS:				
D-Fee Revenue	$25,000	$26,250	$27,500	$28,750
E-Expenses	(16,000)	(16,800)	(17,600)	(18,400)
Distributable Income	$ 9,000	$ 9,450	$ 9,900	$10,350
Partners	40	42	44	46
Income per partner	$ 225	$ 225	$ 225	$ 225

[iii]—Economies of Scale Assumption

Parties to a merger typically expect to eliminate some duplicative operating expenses. This occurs sometimes, but not always. (For illustrative purposes, it is assumed that both firms in a merger had offices in New York and Chicago and that the merger team has decided that the offices in both cities can and will be consolidated, thereby reducing duplicative rent and other operating costs by $500,000 and reducing duplicative salary costs for office administration by $300,000. This aggregate reduction of $800,000 results in a 5% reduction in the firm's overall expenses.)

[iv]—Compatibility of Rates Assumption

The merger team might decide to increase one former firm's billing rates for attorneys (and possibly also increase billing rates for word processing and reprographics services) to the level of the other firm and to increase one firm's compensation levels for associate lawyers to the level of the other firm. (For illustrative purposes, it is assumed that this will increase fee revenues by 10% and expenses by 5% in the first year after the merger and that these increases will be sustained in future years.)

[v]—Merger Costs Assumption

The merger team should expect that there would be merger costs to be absorbed, usually in the first year after the merger. (For illustrative purposes, it is assumed that moving costs, office-remodeling costs, and other merger costs will increase the new firm's expenses by 5% on a one-time-only basis during the first year after the merger.)

For illustrative purposes, the assumptions discussed in the previous paragraphs can be summarized as follows:

	Cumulative Projected Increase (Decrease)		
	Year 2	Year 3	Year 4
Fee Revenues:			
Inflation impact	5%	10%	15%
Synergism assumption	5%	10%	10%
Client conflicts assumption	(5%)	(5%)	(5%)
Compatibility of rates assumption	10%	10%	10%
Total Revenue increase	15%	25%	30%
Expenses:			
Inflation impact	(5%)	(10%)	(15%)
Economies of scale assumption	5%	5%	5%
Compatibility of rates assumption	(5%)	(5%)	(5%)
Merger costs assumption	(5%)	—	—
Total expense increase	(10%)	(10%)	(15%)

Figure 23-C illustrates an alternative projection of distributable income for the merged firm, after giving effect to the assumptions discussed in the previous paragraphs.

Figure 23-C. Illustration of "alternative case" projection of distributable income for a law firm created from a merger.

ABC LAW FIRM
DISTRIBUTABLE INCOME PROJECTIONS
BASE CASE
($ in thousands)

	Pro Forma Year 1	Projections Year 2	Year 3	Year 4
KEY ASSUMPTIONS:				
(cumulative)				
A-Fee revenue increase	—	15%	25%	30%
B-Expense increase	—	0%	10%	15%
C-Number of partners	40	42	44	46
PROJECTIONS:				
D-Fee Revenue	$25,000	$28,750	$31,250	$32,500
E-Expenses	(16,000)	(17,600)	(17,600)	(18,400)
Distributable Income	$9,000	$11,150	$13,650	$14,100
Partners	40	42	44	46
Income per partner	$225	$265	$310	$307

[c]—Comparing Base Case with Alternative Projections

The merger team will want to create a series of alternative projections or computer models to explore the impact of those potential benefits and risks of the merger that they consider to be significant.

Once the projection process has been completed, the merger team will find it useful to compare the various alternative projections with the base case to view the expected impact of the various scenarios that they have considered. Although a four-year comparison is shown below, it should be understood that more than four years could be projected. However, the further the projection, the less reliable the results. A comparison of the "base case projection" versus the "alternative projection" previously illustrated is summarized below:

	Income Per Partner	
	Base Case Projection (Fig. 19-B)	Alternative Projection (Fig. 19-C)
Year 1	$225	$225
Year 2	$225	$265
Year 3	$225	$310
Year 4	$225	$307

One way of reviewing this comparison is to consider the "base case projection" as the firms' potential results if they merely became associated but did not merge, and to consider the "alternative projection" as the firms' potential results if a merger was consummated.

Some observations that can be drawn from this comparison are:

(1) The merger expectation assumptions underlying the alternative projection have yielded an improvement in per partner income in Years 2, 3 and 4; and

(2) The improvement in income per partner resulting from the merger levels off in Year 4.

[4]—Communication and Focus

A lot has been said in this chapter about the nuts and bolts of evaluating a merger. An equally important, if not the most important, consideration is the communication and focus of the negotiating team and its consultants.

Nothing causes more confusion or problems than bad communication. Bad communication results from many factors, including

(1) A merger team that does not operate as a cohesive, focused group,

(2) Poor flow of information within the merger team,

(3) Poor flow of information or inadequate flow of information to its advisors,

(4) Misunderstood responsibilities of team members,

(5) Multiple and conflicting communications with the target firm

(6) Inability to understand accounting schedules

(7) Misunderstood or undocumented timetables,

(8) Unreasonable expectations,

(9) Language barriers or the meanings of selected words;

(10) "Chemistry" or personality conflicts between team members within the firm, with merger team members from the target firm, or with advisors.

That list is not all encompassing; surely everyone can think of one or more reasons why bad communications arise. Ultimately, the chairman or partner-in-charge of the negotiating team is the person who sets the stage for a viable and effective merger team or a team that will stumble because of its own inability to communicate effectively. The chairman must take charge and make sure that each person on the team understands his or her role and that information is free flowing, so that everyone is "on the same page." Nothing is more frustrating or counterproductive than to be asked to review a document only to find out that the document has been superseded twice. Likewise, "private" conversations within the group or between firms can cause problems. For example, when members who are responsible for a particular area find out that the chairman of the team had a private conversation (or worse yet an agreement) on a topic that the chairman may not have understood.

Sometimes communication issues arise because of cost considerations. For example, if a law firm engages an advisor to work with it on a merger evaluation and, as a result of expanded scope (e.g., preparation of multiple schedules and analysis), the advisor's cost mushroom. Instead of keeping information from the advisor to keep costs down, it is better to discuss the expanded scope and the resulting costs. Alternatively, it is better to negotiate the advisor's fees the same as a law firm's client would negotiate with a law firm whose fees seem out-of-line. Withholding information is counterproductive and causes bad communication.

Inadequate communication will distract the focus of the team and may lead to a situation in which discussion of small points prevents the team from focusing on the big picture.

Good communication, on the other hand, facilitates sharing of thoughts - thoughts that may lead to ideas and ideas that may lead to a better answer. There is an old saying that two heads are better than one. This is very true in a merger environment where so many different disciplines, experiences and levels of expertise come together to solve a problem. Fluid communication can make the difference between a successful merger and one that is weighed down with problems.

§23.07 Close the Deal

After two law firms complete their evaluations of the deal and decide that it is in their best interests to combine practices, it is necessary to negotiate those items needed to close the deal and to document those agreements. Before closing the deal, both firms have to agree on:

(1) Structure of the new firm;
(2) Management and governance of the new firm;
(3) Transition period for full implementation;
(4) Documents and protecting the name.

Each of these topics is discussed below.

[1]—Structure of the New Firm

As merger talks progress, the structure of the new firm begins to take shape. For example, it will be obvious if the firm intends to operate as a partnership rather than a professional corporation. However, if the target firm is a professional corporation, then this topic will require attention and negotiation because of the potentially troublesome tax effects of liquidating a professional corporation.

Structure means more than just the legal form under which the firm will practice law. It implies how the new firm will acknowledge the admission of the target firm and integrate its members into the fold. Will it be recognized as a merger of equals or a takeover of the target? Each has its own connotation and that connotation permeates the professional environment. Generally, management's goal is to integrate the target firm by recognizing the values that it brings to the new firm and by strategically placing some of its former partners on visible or sensitive committees, such as the executive committee or management committee. These decisions should be part of the negotiations so that the operating structure of the firm is discussed during this stage.

Another structural issue concerns the way the practice will be organized. For example, if one firm is organized by industry groups and the other by practice units, there will have to be a workable integration plan that will avoid undue anxiety about a different operating structure. One approach would be to integrate groups as new matters arose so that there is a transition to a new system. Another approach would be to have both firms continue operating without change until co-location is implemented, at which time the new practice structure would be introduced.

[2]—Governance of the New Firm

Before the deal can be closed, there has to be agreement on how the new firm will be governed. If the merger is between a small firm and a larger firm, simply adding a partner or shareholder to the acquiring firm's management group may be all that is necessary. When two small firms or midsize firms merge, it may be necessary to expand the size of the management group to include representation from each firm and, possibly, from each office or practice group. Mergers of large firms, especially mergers of international law firms, may challenge the effectiveness of either firm's existing management committee and require an entirely new governance structure. Suffice it to say that with any merger some change will be needed in the governance of the new firm.

Philosophically, an important question should be addressed; what client responsibilities should members of the governance committee have? Historically, client-service partners or shareholders viewed management jobs as just another responsibility. Depending on the size of the firm, that philosophy still has merit. However, the management challenges created by mergers of large firms demonstrate that managing an international law firm may be a fulltime job. Consequently, it is becoming more common for a managing partner to shed client responsibilities and to focus full time on running the global law firm business. An extension of this philosophy is that very few partners should be involved in the daily management of the firm. Instead of using line partners, professional non-lawyer executives could assume key management functions and work directly with the managing partner on day-to-day matters.

In closing the deal, agreement must be reached on governance matters, including:

(1) Identifying the management team for the new firm and naming the senior partner or president and other key members;

(2) Deciding if there will be separate management teams for each firm, with some umbrella management structure superimposed over the firms (this assumes mergers of two large firms in different parts of the country or in different countries);

(3) Deciding if there will be senior partners/executive vice presidents for each operating office, or if practice group leaders or industry leaders will work directly with the management committee in running the practice;

(4) Deciding if there will be committees, who will be assigned to those committees, and what, if any, responsibilities and authority these committees will have;

(5) Deciding who will be in charge of administrative support services and where those services will be rendered;

(6) Creating a merger document or prospectus for partners or shareholders that addresses these matters and explains the pros and cons of the proposed merger; and

(7) Drafting a new partnership agreement or shareholders' agreement.

It is very important to make governance appointments that include representatives from each predecessor firm. To do otherwise might send the wrong message to partners or shareholders and staff of the target firm and may be the cause of discontent within the new firm. It is vitally important for the partners or shareholders to be supportive of the new governance structure, so that lawyers can focus on what they do best—practice law.

[3]—Transition Period for Full Implementation

Under the best conditions, a merger can take place as of a point in time by simply combining the firms and operating as one firm from that point forward. Unless otherwise specified, all contingencies that exist for either firm will become contingencies for the new firm and all partners or shareholders will share accordingly. When conditions are less than perfect, firms might consider a transition period during which certain matters can be resolved. During the transition period, the firms would operate as one firm and would convey the image of a single firm to clients. Transition periods might be considered when:

(1) A large variance between partner compensation systems argues in favor of having the less profitable firm implement procedures to increase profits per partner before sharing in a new partner compensation system;

(2) A contingency needs to be resolved before partner profit sharing can be implemented;

(3) Significantly different employee compensation systems or benefit plans need a transitional period to bring them more in line with an agreed upon standard; or

(4) Significant structural, governance, or statutory issues exist and time is needed to resolve these matters.

The merger documents should specify the transition period and authorize a shorter transition period if conditions change.

[4]—Documents and Protecting the Name

The final step in closing the deal is signing the documents. The number of documents depends on what the parties agree to. In all mergers there should be a merger document that partners or shareholders of both firms sign. The merger document should identify all major points, especially those that required additional negotiating. If there are transition periods, there should be separate documents for each agreement. For example, if there is a transition period during which one firm has to improve partner earnings to bring them into parity with the other firm's, or if there is a transition period for balancing associate compensation packages, an agreement should spell out what is expected to be accomplished during a specific period of time. Basically, each agreement documents the intent of the parties to the merger.

Another important document is an agreement that protects the new firm name. The new firm does not want its name used without its permission and should have an agreement that stipulates just that. In addition, the new firm does not want dissenters to the merger resigning and reusing the name of one of the firms. Having a document in place to restrict the use of either predecessor firm's name is a form of insurance to make sure that neither name is reused.

§ 23.08 Implement the Deal

Once the deal is closed, it must be implemented. During the implementation phase, attention to detail is a must. The speed of implementation is not as important as the manner in which the implementation is done. Following a methodical and logical approach will yield better results than the philosophy of "full steam ahead and we'll fix problems later." A law firm's mission is to render quality legal services, therefore, the merger must be implemented as seamlessly as possible to avoid disruption in the delivery of those services. This section identifies and discusses some of the more important implementation steps, as follows:

(1) Communication;
(2) Timetables;
(3) Co-location;
(4) The best practices;
(5) Accounting policies;
(6) Accounting and reporting systems; and
(7) Monitoring results.

[1]—Communication

Communication is the means of letting people know what is happening and why. Insufficient or ineffective communication can be worse than no communication at all. It follows, therefore, that one of the most important aspects of implementing a deal is communicating it to those effected by the deal. The process begins with the merger team communicating with each other and with the merger team of the other firm. Jointly, they should develop communiqués that clearly express the purpose of the merger, information about both firms, management of the new firm, structure and governance, etc. Depending upon the audience, communication can be in the form of presentations to both firms via teleconference or videoconference and through periodic written internal documents and periodic press releases. Use of Intranets and Web sites have become popular ways of disseminating information.

As the merger is implemented, there should be a formal method of communicating information to partners or shareholders, associates, support staff, clients, and the news media. Since partners or shareholders are the owners, it is important to communicate with them more frequently than other groups. They have to understand more about the merger and be able to explain how it will affect employees. They should guard against saying too little, because rumors start when the sharing of information is inadequate. Obviously, there are matters that must be kept confidential within the partner or shareholder group, but those can be identified as "confidential and private," with the understanding that they will not be discussed with the staff. Management should not lose sight of the fact that partners are intelligent human beings who need information to understand and to accept change.

Depending on the size of the firm and its practice structure, information can be disseminated through practice or industry group meetings. Using this forum encourages the formation of camaraderie and allows groups to hear the information at the same time.

[2]—Timetables

The firm should develop realistic timetables to implement the merger. The old saying, "First things first" is relevant during the implementation stage, because certain events must occur before other ones can begin. It is a good idea to develop a list of tasks to accomplish and assign completion dates for each. In a more complex merger, perhaps using a project manager computer program might be a viable tool. Another viable alternative is engaging an accelerated transition consulting team that specializes in implementing the final 10% of a merger—the part that often consumes scarce management time. In other less complicated mergers, simply keeping a "to do" list will suffice.

A note of caution about aggressive timetables is in order. Management will be judged internally and externally by the way in which the merger is implemented. If the timetable is aggressive and causes confusion or wastes time because, for example, computer programs are rolled out before they have been properly tested and debugged, then management appears to be out of control. Dealing with aggressive timetables can create problems that result in lost time, because timekeepers are distracted from practicing law (i.e., they do not charge as many hours). In addition, costs to fix problems can be substantial.

[3]—Co-location

No merger can be successful if both firms continue practicing law as if they were separate firms. At some point, the new firm should move lawyers from one office to another to begin the process of co-location. Co-location allows teams or groups to begin practicing together and facilitates synergy. Co-location can be more challenging when predecessor firms have offices in the same city and neither office has enough space to absorb the staff from the other office.

Jockeying people within offices and staggering moves between offices is one practical alternative. Another alternative is to find new office space, but this can be more expensive when lease commitments and other factors are considered. Law firms in different geographic locations should consider transferring lawyers from one office of one predecessor firm to an office of the other firm to encourage integration of the professional staff.

Another aspect of co-location is the physical environment. The physical plant includes office space, computer capabilities, telephone systems, and support staff. Office space involves the location of the office, size of each lawyer's office, and the office decor. Computer capabilities include the type of computers and operating systems, the computer network, platform and wiring, word processing software, remote computer access, and miscellaneous software applications. Each aspect of co-locating should be planned to minimize distractions and to ensure a smooth implementation. Because the process of planning for co-location can be a drain on a firm's internal resources, the firm should consider outsourcing this function to a company that specializes in this area.

Another very important aspect of co-location is the placement of the accounting department and backroom support functions. Assuming that each predecessor firm had these departments, the new firm probably does not need to maintain two complete departments. The new firm might, for example, move most important accounting and financial support functions to one office to benefit from the economies of scale. But then there is the question, "Which office?" Normally, these functions are done in the same office where the continuing firm's accounting and financial support functions were performed. In a transcontinental merger or a merger of comparably sized firms, that decision will depend on a number of factors, including available space, cost of operating in a particular location (e.g., rent and payroll), age and efficiency of equipment at each location, knowledge and quality of workforce at each location, and sophistication of software systems.

In an international merger, the decision about where important accounting, financial support and administrative functions should be located becomes more relevant, because the window of opportunity for establishing contact with the other office may be limited. For example, in a merger of a German law firm with a Los Angeles-based law firm, there is no time during the normal workday (i.e., 0900 hours to 1700 hours) when administrative staff in Germany are in the office at the same time as their counterparts in Los Angeles. There are two practical solutions; first, change the work scheduled of staff in both locations so that there are common hours during which they can communicate, or, second, change the location where these important functions are performed. Since most international firms will have at least a New York or Washington D.C. office, there should be some consideration in the example given of moving the accounting and financial support functions from the West Coast to one of the East Coast locations. That will give both the German and California offices sufficient time to coordinate with those departments. There are obvious cost and personnel considerations in such a transfer, but the idea highlights the complex co-location issues that surface in an international merger.

[4]—Choose the Best Practices

One advantage of a merger is the opportunity to identity the best practices of each firm and to implement those practices in the new firm. Early in the implementation stage, the designated team should review each practice to determine which the new firm should use. Departments that should be reviewed include personnel, recruiting, client conflicts, billing and collections, payables, practice support, accounting and financial, partner accounts, document services, secretarial services, management information services, library services, telecommunications, reprographics and facilities.

The purpose of choosing the best practices, as opposed to only those practices used by the continuing firm, is to harmonize practices and to demonstrate the willingness to adopt procedures followed by the predecessor firms. Combining the best practices of each firm softens the transition and makes the implementation process more collegial.

[5]—Accounting Policies

A very important part of the implementation process is agreeing on the accounting policies that will be used by the new firm. The importance of this step increases with the size of the merger. For example, in a merger of small or midsize partnerships or professional corporations, there probably are few accounting policies that need modifying. Generally, the accounts of the target firm are added to the accounts of the lead firm (Firm A) and the lead firm's accounting policies survive. However, there may be minor differences in accounting for client disbursements, operating leases, partner benefits, retainers, software development costs, etc. that need special attention. It also is common for firms of this size to continue using the modified cash basis method of accounting.

In mergers of large firms, especially mergers of international law firms, a great deal of attention must be given to new or revised accounting policies. For example, considering the overall method of accounting, it is common in the United States for a law firm to use the cash basis method of accounting for tax and financial statement purposes. Law firms wishing to track the true economics of their practices, however, might consider adopting the accrual method of accounting for financial management purposes, while maintaining the cash basis for tax purposes. In the United Kingdom, however, it is common for the accounts to be drawn up on the "true and fair" accrual method for financial management and tax return purposes. This accrual method differs from that used in the United States, because it accrues only the cost element of fee income, not the profit element, as would be the case under U.S. accounting principles.

Focusing next on the accounting methods for individual accounts, the new law firm, for example, might amortize leasehold improvements over the remaining life of each lease for financial management purposes, rather than over the thirty-nine-year period required for U.S. income tax purposes or over some entirely different method in another country. Each accounting policy should be reviewed to verify that it is consistent with the goals and objectives of the new firm.

Assuming that management relies on some system of accounting in order to generate management reports, it is important to have standardized accounting policies to generate those reports. Management reporting refers to accounting information that is given to the management or executive committee and is used to evaluate the financial health of the firm. Often, the policies might mirror generally acceptable accounting principles (GAAP), but may not when U.S. GAAP is compared to GAAP used in another country. As a result, management reporting may differ from financial statement reporting because of the accounting policies employed. The mission of management reporting is to achieve comparability in the way operating income is determined, so that income allocations to partners or shareholders are consistent. When the accounting systems used by two law firms are very different, it is necessary to implement an accounting system that tracks the income and expenses on the same basis—even if those policies are not used for tax reporting purposes or financial statement purposes.

For management reporting purposes, comparability of accounting policies must be obtained for WIP and A/R, client disbursements, prepaid assets, depreciable property, property that is subject to amortization, intangible assets, investments, goodwill, retainers, accrued liabilities, contingencies, operating leases, capital leases, partner loans, guaranteed payments, and capital accounts. This list will expand or contract depending on the size of the merger.

[6]—Accounting and Reporting Systems

In connection with determining accounting policies, the new firm has to select the accounting and reporting systems it will use. Included in this category are the accounting software, billing software, time-entry software, client tracking and conflict software, and other applications that will be used to accumulate and generate financial information for the new firm. In addition to the software applications, the new firm has to modify or create new accounting controls, data security controls, and internal control procedures.

Implementing these modified or new systems is complicated by size of the firm and the distance between offices. It is important that each office have direct access to these systems so that data can be entered remotely and reports generated locally. This is particularly important in the case of an international merger because of differences in time zones, need for local books and records under local accounting rules, and tax requirements. All of these issues should be considered when implementing the merger.

[7]—Monitor Results

The last stage of implementation is monitoring the results. Difficult decisions will be made in every merger and procedures will be adopted that may not have universal support. Since it is impossible to insure that everything will work perfectly after implementation, it is important to monitor results and to make changes when necessary. The firm needs a flexible implementation plan, so that it can adapt to changing circumstances. The need for monitoring argues in favor of a transition period for major changes, so that there is time to evaluate the implementation properly and to make appropriate adjustments. If major changes are staged in phases, then monitoring can take place and allow for smoother implementation.

§ 23.09 "Roadblocks" and Deal Breakers

It would be trite to say, "Not all mergers work." In fact, it might be more correct to say, "Only a few merger attempts work." There are many reasons why merger talks collapse. Some are within the control of the negotiating teams, others are not. Listed below are some of the more common "roadblocks" and deal breakers.

[1]—Independent Consultant

We have all heard the saying, "An attorney who represents himself/herself has a fool for a client." There is some reality to this saying, especially when reason takes a backseat to personalities. A firm may have addressed many of the strategic considerations and dealt effectively with most of the differences between itself and another firm, only to get to a point in the negotiations process when, for no apparently good reason, one firm takes an unyielding position that derails the merger.

To avoid this type of roadblock, a firm should consider using an independent consultant, who understands law firm issues from accounting, tax, and management perspectives and who can focus on and negotiate substantive and sensitive issues. The consultant can discuss these issues in private with the firm before trying to negotiate a satisfactory resolution that both sides can accept.

[2]—Firm Name

It is not surprising that naming the new firm can be a challenge and sometimes a deal breaker. That is why it is important to focus on the new name early in the process. Choosing a name takes on added importance when a partnership mergers with a professional corporation because of the inherent differences in the two entities. Other difficult situations exist when the two firms are roughly equal in size, when one or both firms have been practicing under their existing names for a long time, or when the reputation of one firm is thought to be superior to the other's. Deciding on a naming convention is never easy and often results in some combination of the names of the two previous firms. Merger negotiations have been terminated at very late stages, because an appropriate "first name" compromise could not be reached.

One way to avoid this roadblock is to engage a consultant who will independently research each firm's history and prepare a list of possible names. Putting the responsibility on a consultant can deflect emotional reactions that might surface when this important, but sensitive, subject is discussed. As mentioned earlier, another strategy might be to delay announcing the new name until late in the merger process so that partners or shareholders support the merger idea and do not allow a name to overshadow the expected benefits of the merger.

[3]—Governance

Governance is one of the recurring issues that complicate the merger process. Failure to reach agreement regarding who is in charge and how the new firm will be run have been reasons for failed mergers. In the merger of a smaller firm with a larger firm, governance can be an issue if the larger firm assumes that, because of its size, its governance structure will continue after the merger. If the larger firm does not listen to the other firm's management and does not try to incorporate some of its talent into the new firm's governance, irreconcilable differences may be created. Two firms of comparable size might face a harder challenge agreeing on management assignments, including senior partner, because each firm might view its management team as superior. If they run parallel management teams to avoid the tough decision, they duplicate overhead and create a recipe for lower profits and more problems. To avoid resistance to the merger, the new firm might divide equally key management positions between partners or shareholders of the predecessor firms to balance the scales and win support from each firm. Consideration of the other firm's views and attempts to develop alternative governance structures that involve partners from both firms can be ways to construct a smooth transition to the new firm.

[4]—Compensation and Benefits

Compensation deal breakers involve both associates and partners.

[a]—Associate Compensation Packages

One of the merging firms might have a superior compensation and firm-paid benefits package for its associates. If the differences are economically material, then bringing one firm's associates into parity might be difficult and expensive and may ultimately be a deal breaker. There are very practical problems with combining firms with diametrically different compensation philosophies. The reality is that associates talk with their peers about sensitive subjects such as compensation. If the two systems are not brought into parity shortly after co-location, associates will compare notes and soon the issue will be public. This issue is prevalent in global mergers, because U.S. firms generally have higher pay scales than other countries, such as the U.K.

It is one thing to bring compensation systems into parity and another to decide who pays for the adjustment. The firm paying more might feel that it has already paid its fair share and may insist that the other firm's partners absorb the one-time special charge. When faced with the financial adjustment, that firm may decide that a merger costs more than the benefits justify and break off merger discussions.

To avoid a broken deal, the firms might consider a transition period, during which time compensation adjustments are made to lower-paid associates. As part of the adjustment, key associates might be given greater bonuses as an inducement to remain with the firm during the transition phase.

[b]—Partner Compensation

Partners are not immune from comparing their earnings with the earnings of partners in other firms. Partners who merge into a new firm expect to earn at least their prior level of income, and hope to earn substantially more. As a result of changing from a lock-step system to a merit-based system or *vice versa*, it is possible that some partners will not be satisfied. If too many partners are dissatisfied, the merger will not advance past the negotiation stage.

Partners' compensation is determined based on the accounting methods employed. If, as a result of the merger, accounting methods change and income goes down, there could be disgruntled partners who question retrospectively the wisdom of a merger. This situation can be identified during the due diligence *pro forma* calculations, so that workable solutions are proposed before the imbalance becomes a deal breaker. It should be noted, however, that significant costs can be incurred in mergers of large firms and that it is conceivable that the first-year profits will suffer as a result.

[5]—Capitalization

All law firms need money to operate. Some firms generate the money through cash flow, while others rely on borrowing or permanent capital. When law firms with different capital philosophies discuss a merger, capital becomes an issue; how much and from where. The thought of having to borrow money to contribute capital may not be palatable for some partners and may be the reason why merger talks break down. This also is true for a merger of a professional corporation and a partnership, because shareholders of a professional firm expect to have current earnings paid out to avoid a corporate level tax.

The capitalization issue may arise from banks. In challenging economic times, banks scrutinize the capitalization of their borrowers, especially law firms and other professional firms whose assets are primarily receivables. As a result of the merger, two firms that had not had a capitalization might find that they do now.

A merger of a U.K. firm and a U.S. firm can make capital issues more important because U.K. firms include some portion of WIP and A/R in capital. As a result, they have paid tax on WIP and A/R included in capital, whereas U.S. firms generally have not paid tax on WIP and A/R. If the U.K. firm changes to the accounting method of the U.S. firm, the U.K. partners will feel that they have lost their capital (because WIP and A/R are not recognized on a cash basis) and some of their earnings. This is a significant issue and one that has scuttled more than one transatlantic merger.

If capital issues are not discussed and explained to partners in both firms, these issues can become deal breakers.

[6]—Conflicts and Risk Management

Large competing companies do not like to be represented by the same law firm and, in many cases, the same law firm is stopped from representing competing companies because of conflicts. If two law firms discuss merger possibilities and later discover that each represents major competitors, a decision has to be made to withdraw from one client, to defer the merger until the conflict is resolved, or to terminate merger discussions. This potential deal breaker should be identified early in the merger process.

Likewise, one of the firms may be exposed to significant financial risk from contingent liabilities. These can include the uninsured portion of professional liability claims, letters of credit securing lease obligations, unfunded partner retirement benefits, and guarantees of partner obligations. Early in the process, firms should agree upon the treatment of amounts ultimately paid by the new firm under these preexisting contingencies. In addition, the firms should identify how these risks arose (including potential partner and/or client problems) and procedures to reduce exposure for contingencies in the new firm.

§ 23.10 Assessing the Benefits and Risks of a Merger

There are many financial and non-financial factors to be considered in assessing the benefits and risks of a merger. Some of these factors have been touched upon in the preceding sections. Of course, an overriding factor to be considered in the merger of any two law firms is the compatibility of the partners in the firms that are being merged and the synergy that is created as a result of the combination. All other factors pale in comparison to these important issues.

CHAPTER 24

Partners' Compensation

Chapter Contents

§ 24.01 Law Firm Partners' Compensation: An Overview

At the outset, it should be recognized that partner compensation decisions for small law firms can be made very quickly at a short annual meeting of all the firm's partners. Typically, the smaller the partnership, the swifter the decision-making process. However, at larger firms, partner compensation decisions become more complex—more voices need to be heard and more criteria need to be evaluated. Consequently, the entire process becomes more time-consuming.

This chapter addresses the issues faced by medium, large, and mega law firm partnerships and corporations in their quest to assure a fair and equitable distribution of their firm's profits among its partners and shareholders.

There is no "perfect" plan for compensating a law firm's partners. A mechanical formula based solely on productivity and practice development is not the total solution. A partner compensation plan also should consider a breadth of criteria, including recognition of those partners who have gained the respect of their fellow partners and their clients. It should also acknowledge individual partner's successes in developing associates into partners, recruiting new associates, sharing in the firm's management activities, creating partner synergism, and similar characteristics.

For partnerships and corporations alike, the plan a firm chooses should be based on a proper blend of: (1) theoretical general purpose goals, (2) pragmatic firm-oriented objectives and (3) a workable system.

[1]—General Goals of Partner Compensation Plans

General purpose goals of successful partner compensation plans include: (1) rewarding quality partner performance; (2) recognizing "Star" or "Fast Track" partners; (3) retaining the best partners; (4) recruiting highly rated new partners; and (5) assuring fair treatment among partners. Each of these goals will be discussed in the paragraphs that follow.

[a]—Rewarding Quality Partner Performance

A partner compensation plan that is designed to reward quality performance gains the respect of all the firm's partners. It should be geared to long-term performance, not merely year-to-year variations. However, a compensation plan must provide short-term rewards to retain partners and to motivate them.

[b]—Recognizing "Star" or "Fast Track" Partners

Each partner is unique and develops his or her skills in different ways and at different times. Partners who were clerks for judges at some time in their careers may bring different experiences to the partnership than partners who tracked the normal progression. Younger partners with more developed skills or more dedication to the practice often are acknowledged as being "stars" or they are said to be on a "fast track." Either of these designations are a short-hand way of saying that the young partner is valuable to the firm and that the firm can expect much from them now and in the future. Said differently, these are the people that law firms do not want to loose. A compensation plan, therefore, should recognize that some young partners will outperform other partners and must "be taken care of." The reward system should be geared to deal with this disparity.

[c]—Retaining the Best Partners

The focus of the plan should be to encourage the firm's best partners to remain with the firm (i.e., a "golden handcuffs" approach). The compensation plan should contain enough financial incentives to make the best performing partner want to stay with the firm, instead of leaving the firm. Rewarding the best performing partners may cause problems for the compensation committee because other partners who consider themselves to be "best performing" may not be rewarded based on their expectations and may leave the firm over what they consider preferential treatment. These are difficult considerations that must be addressed in a compensation plan.

[d]—Recruiting Highly Rated New Partners

An objective measure of the plan's usefulness will be its ability to attract new partners to the firm from the senior associate ranks and to attract lateral partners from other firms. As previously mentioned in other sections of this book, there is no longer a stigma associated with a partner leaving his or her firm for a better opportunity with another firm. However, recruiting these highly rated lateral partners can cause considerable consternation within the partnership ranks because of the way that firm profits are allocated. Firms that are successful in enticing highly rated lateral partners generally discuss the need for the new partners with the partnership, so that they obtain approval (or, at least, an assurance of support) from the other partners. The key is maintaining open communications in the firm.

[e]—Assuring Fair Treatment Among Partners

It is particularly important that the plan be viewed as fair and equitable by all (or at least a sizable majority) of the firm's partners. This promotes harmony and a positive working environment. If the plan's compensation incentives are properly balanced between rewarding new business achievers (the "rainmaker" and "stars" partners) and rewarding hard workers (the "client service" partners), it will promote teamwork among the partners and encourage an equitable distribution of work among the partners.

[2]—Specific Objectives of Partner Compensation Plans

In addition to the general-purpose goals, most firms will want to gear their partner compensation plans to achieve specific firm-oriented objectives. These objectives can relate to long-range plans or to short-term needs. For example, the firm may want to offer special rewards to encourage industry specialization or branch office growth, or it may want to accelerate retirement by older partners to make room for new partners. These objectives should be worked into the partner compensation plan adopted by the firm.

[3]—Components of Partner Compensation Plans

Partner compensation plans range from simple straightforward calculations to highly complex formulas. Successful plans are not necessarily complex. Rather, they are well-constructed systems that are based upon thoughtful consideration by a knowledgeable group of the firm's partners, taking into account input from all of the firm's partners. Partner compensation plans have five key components:

(1) Measuring partners' performance;
(2) Evaluating partners' performance;
(3) Ranking partners' performance;
(4) Choosing a partnership definition of "profits";
(5) Developing a partnership profit-sharing formula;
(6) Comparing partners' compensation under alternative scenarios; and
(7) Assessing and addressing partner compensation trends.

Each of these components will be discussed in the following sections of this chapter.

§ 24.02 Measuring Partners' Performance

The first step in a partner's performance-based compensation plan is to develop a system for measuring each partner's performance.

Some would assume that it is not necessary to measure performance in a lockstep environment. That is not necessarily the case. In a highly publicized merger between a U.K.-based law firm and one in the U.S., performance ultimately was used to decide which partners "earned" the right to continue being equity partners. Those who had not performed as expected for their lockstep position lost their equity status and were made guaranteed payment partners. Performance matters in any environment.

Measuring performance involves selecting the appropriate: (1) performance measurement criteria, (2) performance measurement programs and (3) performance measurement reports.

[1]—Performance Measurement Criteria

Each partnership must decide how it will determine outstanding performance (i.e., performance that exceeds that which is expected of a partner). Criteria must be selected to establish benchmarks against which each partner's performance can be measured. Once the criteria are identified, the partnership must decide how much weight to assign to each criterion. The criteria commonly used to measure partner performance include: (1) professional competence, (2) practice development, (3) productivity and (4) profitability.

[a]—Professional Competence

A partner's professional competence generally is the most important element in measuring partner performance and usually is the most difficult element to measure, because it cannot be measured on a statistical basis. However, in many cases it is self-evident. In all but the largest law firm partnerships, each partner has a wealth of knowledge about the professional competence of his or her fellow partners, including the respect and admiration they command from their peers, clients and staff. Professional competence is not just technical proficiency in the practice of law; it also includes leadership ability, the successful development of associates into partners (i.e., mentoring), strengthening the cohesiveness of the partnership, promoting the firm's image, and similar attributes.

[b]—Practice Development

Clients are the lifeblood of any law firm and the need to attract new clients (and retain existing ones) is essential for the short- or long-term success of a law firm. In some firms, a partner's ability to generate new business is considered to be a particularly important element in measuring partner performance. This ability can be measured in terms of fees generated from new clients and fees generated from new business for existing clients. New business generators ("rainmakers") are particularly important in firms that depend on non-recurring transactional business or litigation. This criterion is less important in firms handling recurring corporate and tax work. However, not evaluating this criteria even in a firm that has recurring work can lead to complacency, which can erode any business-development skills a person might have and leave them ill prepared for a competitive proposal opportunity. The loss of this competency can have a disastrous effect on the firm, particularly in a downward economy when generating new business may mean the continuation or dissolution of the firm.

[c]—Productivity

A partners' productivity can be measured by determining a partner's: (1) chargeable hours related to client matters and (2) non-chargeable hours related to those firm matters, which the partnership has recognized as important partner responsibilities (e.g., management committee activities, risk management partner, recruiting, etc.). Another measure of a partner's productivity is his or her pyramid of responsibility (i.e., the number of associates' chargeable hours for which the partner is responsible). This element can be measured by how well a partner has leveraged the hours spent on client matters by assigning less important tasks to associates.

[d]—Profitability

The bottom line measurement of success for a law firm is its profitability. Consequently, the profitability of each partner must be a factor in measuring his or her performance. Generally, a partner's ability to carry out profitable work can be measured using three criteria: (1) fees billed to clients, (2) realization of fees billed and (3) speed of collection of fees billed. In the new-style economy, however, profitability goes beyond the simple measurement of dollars that flow into the firm, because law firms conduct business quite differently in this environment. It is more common now to use what heretofore were considered to be unconventional billing arrangements to generate a larger share of the firm's net income. Some unconventional methods include the use of fixed fees for certain matters, invoicing work at lower rates with the agreement that large contingent bonuses will be paid at the successful completion of a matter, charging out new associates at no profit margin so that only salary is covered, or accepting shares of stock in exchange for services. Each of these billing arrangements can bring profit to the firm and must be evaluated in terms of the overall expected benefit to the firm.

[2]—Performance Measurement Programs

Measuring a partner's performance requires compilation of a certain amount of statistical data. It would be wrong, however, to measure a partner's performance solely on statistical information. Consequently, performance measurement programs should be designed to: (1) collect "subjective" information about a partner's professional competence and (2) compile "objective" statistics about a partner's practice development, productivity, and profitability.

Oral or written comments about partners' professional competence are usually restricted to "partner only" communications. The statistical compilations are usually prepared by the firm's administrator or chief financial officer with the controller and submitted to the firm's partner compensation committee.

Figure 24-A illustrates an example of a statistical compilation of certain law firm partner performance measurement criteria.

ABC LAW FIRM
PARTNERS' PERFORMANCE STATISTICS

	Partner X	Partner Y	Partner Z
PRACTICE DEVELOPMENT:			
New client revenues	$1,000,000	$400,000	$ —
New business for existing clients	500,000	300,000	100,000
Total	$1,500,000	$700,000	$100,000
PRODUCTIVITY:			
Chargeable hours (client matters)	1,500	1,300	2,000
Non-chargeable hours (firm matters)	300	650	100
Associate vs. partner leverage	2.0	1.5	1.0
PROFITABILITY:			
Fees billed to clients	$600,000	$500,000	$400,000
Realization of fees billed	111%	90%	83%
Speed of fee collections (months)	5.0	7.0	5.7

[3]—Performance Measurement Reports

Each partner's performance can be rated in one of three ways: (1) oral comments by the other partners, (2) secret ballot or (3) a written performance measurement report. In order to generate written performance reports, the firm must create a hierarchical reporting structure (e.g., partners who are department heads or practice group leaders prepare reports on partners in their respective departments or groups, the managing partner prepares reports on the department heads, etc.). Smaller firms tend to discuss partner performance, rather than following the longer process of writing comments on evaluation forms.

If the firm chooses to use a written performance report, the form of report should be clear, concise, and complete. The report should identify only those criteria that the firm believes are particularly relevant to the conduct of its business and operating philosophy and, consequently, deserve to be measured.

A straightforward rating system should be selected. Ratings are useful for organizing heterogeneous statistical data into a homogeneous summary. However, it is important that all ratings be supplemented with brief written commentary to avoid misleading implications. For example, a partner may be rated poorly regarding fee collections, when in fact his or her inability to collect a fee resulted from a client going bankrupt *after* the matter was turned over to the partner by a retiring partner. Written comments are most important when they have the potential to negatively impact a partner's standing in the firm.

Figure 24-B illustrates an example of a summary of three partner performance measurement reports, together with ratings for three hypothetical partners. The illustration is purposely brief. It is intended solely to illustrate concepts. Many firms will want to choose a more comprehensive, thought-provoking format and/or different measurement criteria.

Figure 24-B. Illustration of concepts, which may be embodied in law firm partner performance measurement reports.

ABC LAW FIRM
PARTNERS' PERFORMANCE MEASUREMENT REPORTS
SUMMARY OF SELECTED CONCEPTS

	Partner X	Partner Y	Partner Z
PROFESSIONAL COMPETENCE:			
Client Matters	A	A	B
Firm Matters	A	B	B
The Bar	B	A	B
PRACTICE DEVELOPMENT:			
New Clients	A	B	C
New Business for Existing Clients	A	B	C
Public Relations	B	A	B
PRODUCTIVITY:			
Chargeable hours (client matters)	B	C	A
Non-chargeable hours (firm matters)	B	A	C
Associate vs. partner leverage	A	B	C
PROFITABILITY:			
Fees billed to clients	A	B	C
Realization of fees billed	A	B	C
Speed of fee collections	A	C	B

COMMENTS:
Partner X ____________________
Partner Y ____________________
Partner Z ____________________

(RATINGS:
A = ABOVE AVERAGE B = AVERAGE C = BELOW AVERAGE)

§ 24.03 Evaluating Partners' Performance

As stated previously, there can be quite a difference between the ways that small and large firms evaluate partner performance. This section reviews six of the more common compensation approaches, including:

(1) The Autocratic Approach;
(2) The Democratic Approach;
(3) The Formula Approach;
(4) The Lockstep Approach;
(5) The Modified Lockstep Approach; and
(6) The Committee Approach.

While each of these approaches continues to be used by a number of firms, over the past several years the committee approach has gained momentum, particularly at larger firms.

[1]—The Autocratic Approach

The autocratic approach is the most direct and efficient approach. However, it does not always satisfy the majority's view. Under this approach, the firm's managing partner assigns compensation to each partner. This approach may be used by firms in which the managing partner knows each partner's contribution to the practice and each partner accepts the autocratic style of management. The managing partner: (1) may or may not consult with other partners, (2) may or may not utilize partner performance reports and (3) may or may not provide for an appeal process. This approach tends to run its course when partners reject the autocratic style and argue for more democracy within the firm.

[2]—The Democratic Approach

The democratic approach is theoretically the fairest approach, because it takes into account the views of all of the firm's partners. However, it can become cumbersome, particularly for larger firms. It usually does not involve the use of partner performance reports. Instead, it uses either an oral or written ballot (often a secret ballot) with each partner assigning shares to all of the other partners, excluding himself or herself. The results of the balloting are then tabulated and averaged. Secret ballot tabulations are commonly carried out by the firm's administrator or its independent accountants. A summary of the results of this process is illustrated below:

	Shares Assigned to			
	Partner	Partner	Partner	
Balloting Partner	X	Y	Z	Total
Partner X	—	55	45	100
Partner Y	55	—	45	100
Partner Z	65	35	—	100
Average of 3 ballots	40	30	30	100

[3]—The Formula Approach

Theoretically, the formula approach is the most objective method of determining a partner's compensation. It has the advantage of being 100% objective, but it is limited by the statistics that a firm's accounting system can generate with precision. Fortunately, with high-speed computers and enough administrative staff, it is possible to generate computer reports that allow the calculations required by the formula method.

Measurements usually include financial statistics such as responsible billings, new business development and fees collected. The formula also might include subjective criteria such as quality of work performed, community activities, contributions to the firm, and teamwork. These measures are weighted according to a predefined formula to calculate an overall evaluation score.

The formula approach can be illustrated by the following example. Assume the partners get 85% of the net collections of amounts that they billed their clients. Net collections would be cash collected less direct client service expenses such as associates' salaries attributable to those matters. In addition, a partner might share in 15% of the net collections on client matters that they brought to the firm. Firm expenses (i.e., those not specifically associated with a client matters, but more in the nature of overhead costs) are subtracted from the income that is not allocated to specific partners and become the firm's profit or loss that is apportioned to all equity partners. That amount can be apportioned based on each partner's profit-sharing ratio.

The advantages of a formula-based system is that its is relatively easy to administer and doesn't require much subjectivity or evaluation of performance. Individuals are rewarded based on predetermined quantitative criteria and everyone knowing where they stand. This system quickly penalizes slackers who "retire at their desks."

The disadvantages, however, may outweigh the advantages. Because one's compensation is weighed so heavily to fee income that he or she is responsible for, a partner may hoard work even if another partner is more qualified to do the work. If associate time flows to the group to which the associate is assigned, then there is little reason to use associates in other groups, even if they are more qualified. The focus shifts from accomplishing firm goals and providing the best client service to improving one's statistics. If for some reason, a partner has to take personal time (i.e., personal injury or family emergency), then that person's compensation can be dramatically affected, because the person cannot generate fee income during his or her absence. Also, depending on the measurement criteria, the formula approach may fail to reward certain types of contributions. If administrative functions (i.e., recruiting, management committees, time spent counseling associates, writing articles or delivering speeches, working on bar association activities, etc.) are not considered in the measurement criteria, partners tend to avoid firm-related assignments that are vital to a well managed firm. Firms that use this method and realize some of shortfalls often create exceptions to supplement unusual situations.

Once the formula approach is ensconced in a law firm's culture, it is difficult to change to another approach unless there is a very convincing reason. Even so, few firms are using the formula approach because it does not reward performance.

[4]—The Lockstep Approach

The lockstep approach is the simplest approach to dividing partnership profits, because it is based solely on the seniority of each partner. Under this approach, each partner receives the same amount of compensation as those who have been with the firm for a similar length of time. Modifications are usually made for lateral partners and for situations where health or other factors have significantly reduced a partner's effectiveness. The system works best with a very homogenous partner group.

The lockstep approach can be illustrated in the following example. Assume that units are assigned in the following manner:

Years as partner or age	Units assigned
New partner	5 units
Second year	6 units
Third year	7 units
Fourth year	8 units
Fifth year	9 units
Sixth through age 65	10 units
66 years old	9 units
67 years old	8 units
68 years old	7 units
69 years old	6 units
70 years old	5 units
Older than 70 years	3 units

A pure lockstep approach seems to work where three elements are present:

(1) The firm is very profitable - firm management is able to exact high levels of high quality work from the partners, because partners' shares are high,

(2) The firm is well established with a solid base of long-term blue-chip clients - the firm rather than individual partners controls most of the work, and

(3) The firm has every indication of continuing in business indefinitely with its present level (or better) of profitability.

Overall, a lockstep system is easier to administer. As stated, it rewards senior partners for past contributions and recognizes the value of experience more than possibly performance. If partners accept the lockstep system, discussions and bickering about performance-related issues are avoided and the atmosphere is more collegial and client focused. Additionally, partners tend to share work more with those partners or associates more qualified to do the work, because there is no financial incentive to hoard the work for themselves.

Disadvantages to the lockstep system include the failure to reward individual performance within each experience level and the risk of losing partners unwilling to wait for future rewards. Depending on the firm's culture, it can be harder to motivate partners under the lockstep system, because their compensate is preordained. Recruiting lateral partners is more difficult under the lockstep approach, because new partners do not really fit in well and other partners who have been in the queue can be frustrated if a lateral partner is admitted at a higher level. The test of a lockstep system occurs in recessionary periods when it takes hard work to generate fee income. When younger partners are the ones doing the hard work, but the older partners are getting a larger share of the pie simply because of seniority, younger partners tend to consider other options that will pay them for their hard work.

[5]—The Modified Lockstep Approach

The modified lockstep approach was created out of necessity, because the pure lockstep system had identifiable limitations. Under a modified lockstep system, the level a person achieves is not necessarily tied to the number of years the person has been a partner. Although the same tiers might exist, a person's progression through those tiers can be tied to a combination of years-of-service and performance. For example, in the tiers identified in the lockstep approach above, most new partners would probably start at the first level with five units. However, if a new partner showed remarkable and unique skills, that person could start at level two and be awarded six units. During succeeding years as a partner, it would be common for partners to advance through the tiers, but it would not be guaranteed. Years as a partner would still be a factor, but advancement also would depend on firm management's assessment of the partner's current and prospective worth to the firm. "Stars" would be moved to new levels faster than those regarded as average. In addition, a pre-determined percentage of the firm's profits would be reserved for year-end bonuses, which would be awarded for exceptional work during the year. As will be discussed, it is vital that the partners know what it takes to get to the next level and what the decision makers base their decisions on. Also, admitting lateral partners into the firm at appropriate levels is easier in the modified lockstep approach than it is in a pure lockstep system.

[a]—Advancement to the Next Level

Under a modified lockstep approach, advancing to the next level should not be automatic. The levels should be broad enough so that it requires a challenge and personal effort to make the jump. Getting to the next level should be something worth working for both in terms of money and prestige within the firm. "Stars" won't be happy if promotion leaves them only marginally better off than average-performing peers.

Advancement also should be predicated on sustained performance over two or three years (not for a one-shot success, which is the primary role the bonus). The corollary of broad levels is that promotion or demotion should be based on sustained performance. A partner generally would be expected to remain at a level for more than one year and that promotion to the next level would be based on more than one year's performance.

Under the modified approach, it is consistent to have demotion as well as it is to have advancement. So, if a person is at a level and is no longer performing at the expectations of that level, this system allows for the person to be lowered to a level at which his or her performance is acceptable.

[b]—Bonus Pool

Many firms allocate a substantial portion of their profits to a bonus pool to be distributed at year-end at the discretion of firm management. This complements the policy of broad compensation levels based on sustained performance over more than one year. It permits one-shot efforts to be adequately recognized - winning a big case or bringing in a big client - and it permits rising "stars" to be recognized without advancing them to the next level. Bonuses should be large enough to be regarded as something special in terms of both money and recognition.

[c]—Modified Lockstep Example

Building on the previous lockstep example, units under a modified lockstep approach could be allocated for a ten-partner firm two ways: first, units awarded for seniority and second, units awarded for performance vis-à-vis that expected of a partner at his or her experience level, as follows:

- Outstanding performance — 5 Units
- Above expected performance — 3 Units
- Expected performance — 1 Unit
- Below expected performance — 0 Units
- First-year partner — 0 Units

Partner	Seniority Units	Total Units	Performance Units
A-New partner (not rated)	5	0	5
B-Second-year partner rated Outstanding	6	5	11
C-Third-year partner rates As Expected	7	1	8
D-Fifth-year partner rated As Expected	9	1	10
E-Sixth-year partner rated As Expected	10	1	11
F-Sixth-year partner rated Above Expected	10	3	13
G-Sixth-year partner rated Outstanding	10	5	15
H-Sixth-year partner rated Below Expected	10	0	10
I-67-year old partner rated As Expected	8	1	9
J-70-year old partner rated Above Expected	5	3	8
Total			100

If the firm has budgeted net income of $5,500,000 for the year - and reserves $500,000 for merit bonuses at year-end - each unit is expected to be worth $50,000 (i.e., $5,500,000 divided by 100 units). Some firms pay out profits as they become available, while others have conservatively computed monthly "draws" based on units, with the balance paid after the end of the year. In this case, for example, $36,000 per unit might be paid out during the year in monthly installments of $3,000.

[6]—The Committee Approach

The committee approach is effective in larger firms, because it takes into account the views of a cross section of the firm's partners and it does not create a burden on the entire partnership. It involves the selection of a partners-compensation committee, typically composed of from three to five members. The committee may be selected by the firm's managing partner, by its executive committee, or by a ballot of the partners. Membership on the compensation committee may be continual, changed every year, or systematically rotated over a selected period (for example, three years).

While selection of the committee members may be carried out in a fairly democratic manner, the composition of the committee is usually required to be weighted toward the firm's more senior partners. A summary of the results of this process is illustrated below:

	Number of Partners		Percentage of Partners	
	Total Partnership	Compensation Committee	Total Partnership	Compensation Committee
Senior Partners	5	2	20%	40%
Experienced Partners	10	2	40%	40%
Newer Partners	10	1	40%	20%
	25	5	100%	100%

The compensation committee is charged with evaluating the firm's partners and assigning a level of compensation to each partner. Their deliberations may be based solely on their instincts, they may refer to partner performance statistics, or they may be guided by partner performance reports. Partners' performance may be evaluated based on measurement against firm standards or against individual goals established for each partner. Compensation committees, however, should have as much statistical information as possible. This hopefully includes at least the following for each partner:

- Chargeable hours, billings, and collections compared to budget;

- Utilization of associates and other partners (i.e., the size and profitability of the partner's pyramid);
- New-client business brought to the firm during the year;
- New projects from existing clients generated during the year;
- Time devoted to non-chargeable matters compared to budget.

As a result of its evaluation process, the committee will usually produce a partner performance evaluation summary. These evaluation summaries assign to each partner: (1) an experience level and (2) a performance rating within the experience level.

Figure 24-C illustrates an example of partners' performance evaluation summary indicating the dispersion of twenty-five partners' evaluations:

ABC LAW FIRM
PARTNERS' PERFORMANCE EVALUATION SUMMARY

		Experience Level		
	Totals	Senior Partners	Experienced Partners	Newer Partners
PERFORMANCE RATING				
Above Average	5	1	3	1
Average	15	3	5	7
Below Average	5	1	2	2
	25	5	10	10

§ 24.04 Ranking Partners' Performance

Correlating partners' performance evaluations with partner compensation schedules requires compilation of a partner-ranking summary.

Partner-ranking summaries consider both (1) the current year's partner performance evaluation and (2) the partner's sustained performance over the past several years. These rankings recognize that some partners achieve their full potential faster than others. Developing partner ranking summaries involves three steps. They are:

(1) Assigning rating factors;
(2) Creating a ratings matrix; and
(3) Preparing a point schedule.

Each of these steps will be discussed in the paragraphs that follow.

[1]—Assigning Rating Factors

The purpose of assigning factors to each rating category is to: (1) weight the individual classifications in each category and (2) weigh each of the rating categories vs. the other categories. For example, in the following illustration, "performance rating" factors have been assigned a higher weight than "experience rating" factors.

Performance Rating	Factor	Experience Rating	Factor
Above Average	4	Senior Partners	3
Average	3	Experienced Partners	2
Below Average	2	Newer Partners	1

[2]—Creating a Ratings Matrix

The purpose of creating a ratings matrix is to correlate the performance rating factors with the experience rating factors. For example: A senior partner (factor = 3) with an above average rating (factor = 4) would receive a total of 12 points (3x4), as indicated in the following matrix:

	Experience Rating		
Performance Rating	Senior Partners	Experienced Partners	Newer Partners
Above Average	12	8	4
Average	9	6	3
Below Average	6	4	2

[3]—Preparing a Point Schedule

The final step in developing a partner-ranking summary involves: (1) assigning a point value to each partner's combined experience/performance ratings based upon the assigned factors as set forth in the ratings matrix, (2) converting the point values to profit-sharing percentages, and (3) summarizing the results in a partner-ranking summary.

Figure 24-D illustrates an example of a partner-ranking summary, including a point schedule and a profit-sharing percentage schedule.

ABC LAW FIRM
PARTNERS' RANKING SUMMARY

	Cumulative			
Partner	Experience Rating	Performance Rating	Points Assigned	Profit-Sharing Percentage Assigned
A	Senior	Above	12	18%
B	Senior	Average	9	14
C	Experienced	Above	8	12
D	Experienced	Above	8	12
E	Experienced	Average	6	9
F	Experienced	Average	6	9
G	Experienced	Average	6	9
H	Experienced	Below	4	6
I	Newer	Above	4	6
K	Newer	Average	3	5
			66	100%

§ 24.05 Choosing a Partnership Definition of "Profits"

Critical to the allocation of income among partners in a law firm is the selection of a clear definition of what the partners consider to be the firm's "profits."

Law firms have adopted a variety of partner profit-sharing approaches. These approaches produce different results, because they use different accounting methods to measure the firm's profits.

[1]—Types of Accounting Methods

Accounting methods fall into three general classifications:

(1) Cash basis accounting method;
(2) Accrual basis accounting method; and
(3) Hybrid accounting methods.

Each of these methods will be discussed in the following paragraphs.

[a]—Cash Basis Accounting Method

Under the cash basis method of accounting, revenue is recognized when cash is received and expenses are recognized when cash is paid. Most U.S.-based law firms adopt a modified cash basis method of accounting to conform, in major respects, to their method of reporting for tax purposes. The usual modification involves the capitalization and depreciation of property, equipment, and leasehold improvements.

Many law firms that use the modified cash basis method of accounting for financial reporting purposes and for tax purposes also use this method for partner profit-sharing purposes.

The principal advantage of using the modified cash basis method of accounting for partner profit-sharing purposes is its simplicity and clarity. Its principal disadvantage is that it does not provide the partners with any share of the firm's unbilled and uncollected fees. In a firm where partners are partners for long periods of time, the disparities caused by using the cash method of accounting for financial statement purposes tend to average themselves out. But, in a firm that has significant partner turnover either through withdrawing partners or admission of lateral partners, the cash method tends to distort the true economics of a partner's interest. The distortions and inequities of the cash method are more prevalent and obvious in a merger situation between a U.S.-based law firm and one form another country. Larger firms with significant international operations are finding it more judicious to use the accrual method of accounting for financial statement purposes and the cash method for U.S. tax purposes.

[b]—Accrual Basis Accounting Method

Under the accrual basis method of accounting, revenue is recognized when income is earned and expenses are recognized when obligations are incurred. Most law firms that adopt the accrual basis of accounting in preparing their financial statements usually adopt the method completely; however, a few firms have adopted a modified accrual basis, which involves the accrual of uncollected fees but not the accrual of unbilled fees.

Most law firms that use the accrual basis method of accounting for financial statement purposes and partner profit-sharing purposes do not use this method for tax purposes. They use the modified cash basis method for tax purposes. This creates a difference between book income and taxable income.

The principal advantage of using the accrual basis method of accounting for partner profit-sharing purposes is its inherent fairness (i.e., its ability to allocate to the partners their full share of the firm's earnings whether the firm's fees have been collected or remain uncollected or unbilled). Its principal disadvantage is the dampening effect that it has on the partners' willingness to bill and collect fees promptly. Fees are billed and collected more promptly when partners' profit-sharing is directly linked to cash basis income. Another disadvantage to using the accrual basis method for partner profit-sharing purposes is that it results in a difference between individual partner's book income and taxable income, which must be explained to each partner.

[c]—Hybrid Accounting Methods

Some law firms have adopted hybrid methods of accounting for partner profit-sharing purposes. These hybrid methods typically represent a combination of the modified cash basis method of accounting together with a pragmatic recognition of a portion of the difference between cash basis income and accrual basis income. The additional amount recognized is usually based on the amount of fees receivable and unbilled fees that are collected within a "spillover" period subsequent to the firm's year-end.

Typically, the reason that a firm adopts a hybrid method is an attempt to combine the best elements of the cash basis method (i.e., simplicity) and the accrual basis method (i.e., fairness).

[2]—Comparison of Allocable Partnership "Profits" under Alternative Accounting Methods

A law firm's cumulative "profits" over the life cycle of the partnership will be the same no matter which of the three alternative accounting methods is chosen by the firm. The key difference between these alternative accounting methods is the time frame during which these "profits" are reported and the partnership sharing arrangements that exist during each time frame.

For example, during a given year, a law firm's "profits" could differ significantly under each of the three alternative accounting methods, as illustrated in Figure 24-E.

Figure 24-E. Illustration of allocable partnership "Profits" under Alternative Accounting Methods.

ABC LAW FIRM
ALLOCABLE PARTNERSHIP "PROFITS"
UNDER ALTERNATIVE ACCOUNTING METHODS

	Accounting Method		
	Cash Basis	Accrual Basis	Hybrid
BASE FOR ALLOCATING PARTNERSHIP "PROFITS":			
Net Income (Cash Basis)	$2,500,000	$2,500,000	$2,500,000
Unbilled & Uncollected Fees:			
End of Year		1,300,000*	
Beginning of Year		(800,000)	
Collection of Unbilled & Uncollected Fees During First Two Months Subsequent to:			
End of Year			800,000*
Beginning of Year			(600,000)
Allocable Partnership "Profits"	$2,500,000	$3,000,000	$2,700,000
BASE FOR ALLOCATING CURRENT YEAR'S CASH BASIS NET INCOME:			
Allocable Base for Applying Current Year's Profit-Sharing Percentages	$2,500,000	$1,700,000	$1,900,000
Allocable Base for Applying Prior Year's Profit-Sharing Percentages	—	800,000	600,000
Allocable Current Year's Cash Basis Net Income	$2,500,000	$2,500,000	$2,500,000

*Represents base for commitment to allocate future year's cash basis net income using historical profit-sharing percentages.

§ 24.06 Developing a Partnership Profit-Sharing Formula

Once the compensation committee has ranked each partner's performance and a partnership definition of "profits" has been determined, it is time to develop a partnership profit-sharing formula. The typical formula is structured by considering three elements:

(1) Allocation Base;
(2) Allocation Concepts; and
(3) Allocation Programs.

Each of these will be discussed in the paragraphs, which follow.

[1]—Allocation Base

The typical allocation base used for allocating partnership profits is the firm's net income on a cash basis. In some cases, an accrual basis or a hybrid basis (described in the previous section) is used. Some firms also make certain adjustments to the allocation base in an attempt to achieve a greater degree of equity among partners. Some of the more common revenue additions and expense elimination adjustments include:

[a]—Revenue Additions to the Allocation Base

There are two types of revenue additions: income that is allocated to all partners and income that is specifically allocated to certain partners.

Revenue that is allocated to all partners includes fee income and income earned by specific partners, but is attributable to the firm because of the partnership relationship. This type of income includes directors' fees, teaching stipends, executors' fees, etc. Even though one partner earned the fee, most partnership agreements contain provisions that the income belongs to the firm because the partner is acting as a partner on behalf of his or her other partners.

Revenue additions that are specially allocated to partners might result from very unusual situations or be for very large amounts. A firm that normally does not do contingent work might, for example, allocation a large contingent fee only to the partners who were partners in the year in which the work was done. Or, if a law firm was granted a change in accounting by the IRS and had to amortize an opening adjustment over a period of four years, they might specifically allocate the yearly amortization only to those partners who were partners in the year the change was granted. These adjustments or allocations are usually defined or identified in a firm's partnership agreement.

[b]—Expense Eliminations from the Allocation Base

These adjustments usually result from policy decisions made by the partnership's executive committee. They typically consist of expenses that the firm has decided should be allocated to partners on a specific identification basis, because individual partners can control the amount of expense incurred on their behalf. These expense eliminations sometimes include contributions to Keogh plans and individual partner retirement plans, investment counsel fees related to individual retirement plans, secretarial bonuses, charitable contributions, and similar items. Mechanically, these expenses are charged directly to the specifically identified partners' accounts. This action has the effect of increasing the amount of "profits" allocable to all of the partners.

[2]—Allocation Concepts

Developing a partnership profit-sharing formula involves a series of conceptual decisions. The principal issues to be faced include:

[a]—Prospective vs. Retrospective Allocations

In most law firms, partner-income-allocation percentages are adopted at or near the end of the year. However, in some firms, these percentages are applied to income earned in the next succeeding year on a prospective basis. In other firms, these percentages are applied to income earned during the latest year completed on a retrospective basis.

[b]—Fixed vs. Percentage-Share Allocations

In some law firms, partners are assigned fixed dollar amounts of compensation, whereas in other firms partners are assigned a percentage share of the firm's income for the year. Some firms distinguish between equity partners (i.e., percentage partners) and non-equity partners (i.e., fixed-income partners). Other firms assign each partner both a fixed dollar amount (a "draw") plus a percentage of the firm's income in excess of the total fixed payments. There are various other combinations of these themes in use.

[c]—Profit-Sharing vs. Return on Capital Allocations

In some law firms, partners are allocated interest on their capital accounts. The aggregate of these interest charges is deducted from the firm's income before the application of profit-sharing percentages. The purpose of this interest on capital allocation is to recognize that some of the firm's partners (usually the more senior partners) are financing the firm's operations. This return on capital allocation is usually found where the partnership has chosen to finance its operations with partners' capital rather than borrowed funds and where there is an imbalance in capital investments by the partners (i.e., those partnerships where partner profit-sharing percentages are not close to being in line with partner capital investment percentages).

[3]—Allocation Programs

Each law firm has certain unique partner compensation objectives which are often part of an overall partner deployment program. These program objectives must be addressed in developing a partner profit-sharing formula. These objectives fall into several categories, including: (1) retired partner programs, (2) new partner programs, (3) foreign service and branch office programs and (4) bonus pool programs.

[a]—Retired Partner Programs

Some law firms contemplate a transition period of gradual reduction in activity and profit participation (during which the partner is an "active" partner), with a residual lifetime profit-participation income commencing at the close of the period. In other firms, retired partners, deceased partners' estates, and withdrawn partners are paid fixed sums for a stated period after retirement, death, or withdrawal. There are many other variations on these themes. In most cases, the amounts to be paid to former partners are deducted from the firm's net income before profit participation by the firm's active partners. Prudent firms set an annual "cap" on aggregate distributions to former partners (e.g., 5% or 10% of net income).

[b]—New Partner Programs

Some law firms provide fixed sum compensation to new partners during the first one or two years after their admission. Other firms provide new partners with a guaranteed minimum income during this period. When these situations occur, the new partner sums are deducted from the firm's net income before profit participation by the firm's active partners.

[c]—Foreign Service and Branch Office Programs

Law firms that second partners from a U.S.-based office to a non-U.S.-based office often provide foreign-assignment packages to cover unusual costs such as cost-of-living differentials, housing, education (for children), home-leave allowances, etc. These foreign-assignment costs are referred to in this chapter as supplemental compensation. These costs are considered to be expenses of the firm (i.e., expenses of doing business outside of the U.S.), so they are deducted from the firm's net income before apportioning profit to the firm's active partners. For income tax reporting purposes, foreign-assignment costs should be reported as guaranteed payments on Schedule K-1.

[d]—Bonus Pool Programs

Some law firms adopt prospective partner profit-sharing programs that provide for partners' income allocations which total less than the aggregate amount of the firm's income (e.g., 90%). The rest of the income (e.g., 10%) is held back and allocated from a bonus pool determined retrospectively.

§ 24.07 Comparing Partners' Compensation under Alternative Scenarios

Applying each law firm's partnership profit-sharing formula to facts and circumstances can be a complex and time-consuming exercise. In addition, assuming that the firm's compensation committee has discretionary authority to reallocate selected sources of income to more fairly allocate income, it may wish to see this data arrayed using several alternative assumptions. For these reasons, the chief financial officers frequently use personal computers or, in large firms, custom-designed software to calculate the results of alternative solutions. The process consists of three steps: (1) developing input data, (2) calculating partners' compensation, (3) considering alternative allocations.

[1]—Developing Input Data

Computer programs won't run without data. Consequently, the first step is to address a series of questions relating to the facts and circumstances surrounding each partner's participation in the profit-sharing allocation. For purposes of illustrating the effect on partners' compensation using alternative scenarios, this section considers two scenarios in which income has been allocated by the compensation committee. The specific changes will be discussed below. Both scenarios consider Partner A: a senior partner and Partner J: a newer partner. Important factors to addressed are:

	Senior Partner A	Newer Partner J
1-Profit-Sharing Percentage	18%	6%
2-Allocation Base Adjustments:		
a-Trustee fees, executor fees or directors' fees received separately	Yes (*)	No
b-Income from specified real estate and other ventures	No	No
c-Partner retirement plan contributions	Yes	Yes
d-Secretarial bonuses or similar items	No	No
3-Special Allocations:		
a-Interest on capital	Yes	No
b-Retired partner	No	No
c-New partner guarantee	No	Yes
d-Foreign service supplement	Yes	No
e-Bonus pool participation	Yes	Discretionary

(*) The compensation committee has the authority to allocate all or none of the trustee fees to the partner who earned them.

[2]—Calculating Partners' Compensation

Calculating partners' compensation consists of three steps:

Step 1—Determining allocable partnership "profits."
Step 2—Apportioning profits based on: (a) identified "special allocations;" and (b) assigned "profit-sharing percentages."
Step 3—Applying specific adjustments to allocated partnership "profits" to arrive at allocated "net income."

Assume that the firm's cash-basis profits are $2,500,000, that Partner A earned $70,000 of trustee fees and that the compensation committee (or management committee) has set aside a bonus pool of $250,000 that is to be allocated based on the discretion of the compensation committee. It should be noted that the compensation committee (within the authority given it by the partnership agreement) could have made other allocation changes to redistribute income.

In the first scenario, the compensation committee allocated 100% of the trustee fees to the specific partner who earned them and granted a bonus of $86,000 to Partner A, who also was specifically allocated a foreign service supplement - for a foreign assignment - and interest on his capital account. The compensation for Partner A totaled $414,000 and compensation for Partner J was $138,000. Figure 24-F shows the composition and calculation of each partner's income.

Figure 24-F. Calculation of individual partner's compensation under alternative #1.

ABC LAW FIRM
PARTNERS' COMPENSATION UNDER
ALTERNATIVE #1

	Total Firm	Partner A	Partner J
PARTNERS' RANKING			
Experience Rating		Senior Partner	Newer Partner
Performance Rating		Above Average	Above Average
Points		12	4
Profit-Sharing Percentage		18%	6%
PARTNERSHIP "PROFITS" ALLOCATION BASE			
Cash Basis Net Income	$2,500,000		
Trustees Fees Received Separately	100,000		
Allocable Partnership "Profits" (Step 1)	$2,600,000		
PARTNERSHIP "PROFITS" ALLOCATION			
Retired Partners	$ 150,000		
Newer Partners' Guarantee	30,000		$ 12,000
Foreign Service Supplements	20,000	$ 5,000	
Interest on Capital	50,000	15,000	
Bonus Pool	250,000	86,000	
Profit-Sharing	2,100,000	378,000 (18%)	126,000 (6%)
Allocated Partnership "Profits" (Step 2)	2,600,000	484,000	138,000
Trustees Fees Received Separately	(100,000)	(70,000)	
Allocated Cash Basis Net Income (Step 3)	$2,500,000	$414,000	$138,000

[3]—Considering Alternative Allocations

After the initial calculations are done, the compensation committee normally would review them to determine that each partner is being treated fairly. Depending on the partnership agreement, the compensation committee might have latitude to make changes that it feels will more fairly apportion partnership income. For purposes of this illustration, it is assumed the compensation committee has discretion to change the allocation of the trustee fees and the bonus pool.

Using the example in the first scenario, assume that the compensation committee did not feel that Partner J's compensation sufficiently rewarded her for the outstanding work during the year. It decided to make some adjustments to shift income to Partner J. In the second scenario, it is assumed that the compensation committee decided to allocate only 50% of the trustee fees to the partners who earned them and to allocate the rest to all of the partners of the firm (that suggests that Partner A shares not only in a specific piece of the trustee fees, i.e., 50%, but also is apportioned 18% of the reallocated amount). The committee also decided to reduce Partner A's bonus by $20,000 and to allocate it to Partner J. These two changes will apportion more income to Partner J, because she gets a bonus under this scenario that she did not get under the first scenario. She also gets 6% of the trustee fees that were reallocated to all of the partners. Figure 24-G shows the adjustments and that Partner A's income was reduced to $420,000 and Partner J's income was increased to $155,000.

These scenarios are very basic, but demonstrate the ability that a compensation committee has in rewarding partners.

Figure 24-G. Illustration of a calculation of individual partner's compensation under alternative #2

ABC LAW FIRM
PARTNERS' COMPENSATION UNDER
ALTERNATIVE #2

	Total Firm	Partner A	Partner J
PARTNERS' RANKING			
Experience Rating		Senior Partner	Newer Partner
Performance Rating		Above Average	Above Average
Points		12	4
Profit-Sharing Percentage		18%	6%
PARTNERSHIP "PROFITS" ALLOCATION BASE			
Cash Basis Net Income	$2,500,000		
Trustees Fees Received Separately	50,000		
Allocable Partnership "Profits" (Step 1)	$2,550,000		
PARTNERSHIP "PROFITS" ALLOCATION			
Retired Partners	$ 150,000	—	
Newer Partners' Guarantee	30,000	—	$ 12,000
Foreign Service Supplements	20,000	$ 5,000	—
Interest on Capital	50,000	15,000	—
Bonus Pool	250,000	66,000	20,000
Profit-Sharing	2,050,000	369,000 (18%)	123,000 (6%)
Allocated Partnership "Profits" (Step 2)	2,550,000	455,000	155,000
Trustees Fees Received Separately	(50,000)	(35,000)	
Allocated Cash Basis Net Income (Step 3)	$2,500,000	$420,000	$155,000

§ 24.08 Assessing and Addressing Partner Compensation Trends

Up to this point, the discussion has focused on the development of a partnership compensation program and the implementation of that program. Periodically, the executive committee and compensation committee, if there is one, should review the partner compensation program and decide if it is producing the desired results. If it is not, corrections should be made. How often the compensation program is reviewed depends on the firm. A firm that is aggressively addressing certain issues, such as "stars" withdrawing from the firm, should evaluate the effectiveness of its compensation program annually, whereas, a staid firm with few compensation issues may address the overall only once every five years. This process calls for the identification (or re-identification) of:

(1) Compensation goals;
(2) Present trends; and
(3) Plans for improvement

Each of these items will be addressed in the following paragraphs.

[1]—Compensation Goals

These goals were identified at the outset of this chapter and bear repeating. They are:

(1) Rewarding Quality Partner Performance;
(2) Recognizing "Star" or "Fast Track" Partners;
(3) Retaining the Best Partners;
(4) Recruiting Highly Rated New Partners; and
(5) Reassuring Fair Treatment Among Partners

In all but the largest law firm partnerships, the members of the firm's executive committee will be able to assess whether these goals have been and are being met by reference to individual partner reactions to their compensation adjustments over the past five to ten years.

[2]—Present Trends

Periodically, at five- to ten-year intervals, it is useful to quantify the status of the firm's partner compensation program in terms of experience rating trends and performance rating trends and to compare the results with a model based on the firm's goals or an industry average.

[a]—Experience Rating Trends

Figure 24-H illustrates an example of a law firm's partner compensation program results (actual versus goal comparisons) grouped by experience ratings. The example assumes that: (1) the firm equates its experience ratings with the number of years as a partner (newer partner = one to ten years; experienced partner = eleven to twenty years; senior partner = twenty-one to thirty years) and (2) the firm has adopted a partner retirement goal of age sixty-two (approximately thirty years' experience as a partner), after which the partner is classified as an of counsel and receives a flat retirement benefit ranging from $100,000 to $150,000 annually.

Figure 24-H. Illustration of a law firm's partner compensation trends, classified by experience ratings.

ABC LAW FIRM
PARTNER COMPENSATION TRENDS: ALL PARTNERS
GROUPED BY EXPERIENCE RATINGS

Partner Experience Rating	Partners' Average Compensation		Number of Partners	
	Actual	Goal	Actual	Goal
SENIOR PARTNERS				
Above Average	$475,000	$500,000	6	4
Average	$400,000	$400,000	8	12
Below Average	$350,000	$300,000	4	4
			18	20
EXPERIENCED PARTNERS				
Above Average	$300,000	$350,000	15	12
Average	$250,000	$275,000	25	36
Below Average	$175,000	$200,000	10	12
			50	60
NEWER PARTNERS				
Above Average	$190,000	$200,000	10	4
Average	$140,000	$150,000	16	12
Below Average	$100,000	$100,000	6	4
			32	20
TOTALS				
Senior Partners			18	20
Experienced Partners			50	60
Newer Partners			32	20
			100	100

[b]—Performance Rating Trends

Figure 24-I illustrates an example of a law firm's partner compensation program results (actual vs. goal comparison) grouped by performance ratings. Note that the number of partners rated as above average is in excess of the goal. This can be do to the reality that 31 partners are indeed performing at an above average level, or it might signal a flaw in the evaluation process that creates a form of grade inflation so that average performers are evaluated as above average performers. It is best to critically evaluate the bell curve of partner performance evaluation to confirm that the measurement criteria are correct.

[3]—Plans for Improvement

Once the firm's partner compensation trends have been summarized, it is important that they be assessed in terms of the firm's goals and addressed in terms of plans for improvement. The following paragraphs are examples of how the results of the preceding illustrations could be correlated with two of the firm's goals.

[a]—Rewarding Quality Partner Performance

The results indicate that senior partners with "Above Average" performance ratings are being compensated at a level below the firm's goal and that senior partners with "Below Average" performance ratings are being compensated at a level above the firm's goal. The message for the firm's compensation committee is to investigate the reasons for this anomaly and to develop a program to increase the spread in senior partner compensation levels between "Above Average" and "Below Average" ratings.

[b]—Recognizing "Star" or "Fast Track" Partners

The results indicate that partners at all experience levels with "Above Average" ratings are being compensated at amounts below the firm's goal. Consequently, the firm's goal of recognizing "star" or "fast track" performers is not working. The compensation committee may wish to investigate this situation to determine whether it results from a faulty rating system, an over-aggressive target compensation plan, a fall-off in firm profits, or other reasons. Once the reasons have been identified, a plan of corrective action can be implemented.

Figure 24-I. Illustration of a law firm's partner compensation trends, classified by performance ratings.

ABC LAW FIRM
PARTNER COMPENSATION TRENDS: ALL PARTNERS
GROUPED BY PERFORMANCE RATINGS

Partner Performance Rating	Partners' Average Compensation		Number of Partners	
	Actual	Goal	Actual	Goal
ABOVE AVERAGE				
Senior Partners	$475,000	$500,000	6	4
Experienced Partners	$300,000	$350,000	15	12
Newer Partners	$190,000	$200,000	10	4
			31	20
AVERAGE				
Senior Partners	$400,000	$400,000	8	12
Experienced Partners	$250,000	$275,000	25	36
Newer Partners	$140,000	$150,000	16	12
			49	60
BELOW AVERAGE				
Senior Partners	$350,000	$300,00	4	4
Experienced Partners	$175,000	$200,000	10	12
Newer Partners	$100,000	$100,000	6	4
			20	20
TOTALS				
Above Average			31	20
Average			49	60
Below Average			20	20
			100	100

CHAPTER 25

Capital Structure and Financing

Chapter Contents

---

§ 25.01 Capital Structure of Law Firms: An Overview

What is the ideal capital structure for a law firm? The answer depends on the partners' perspective. Capital structure of a law firm results from the interaction of a series of factors, the most important of which is the partners' collective view of the purpose of the partnership as a financial entity. On the one hand, the partners might view the partnership as a source of funding for their future retirement benefits. On the other hand, the partners might consider that the partnership's purpose is simply to finance the firm's current operations. Obviously, the capital needs of partnerships with these diverse objectives are quite different. The first type of partnership would be heavily funded with equity money, whereas the second partnership would be thinly capitalized and financed principally through external capital (bank borrowings and/or leasing). Figure 25-A illustrates a comparison of capital structures under each of these scenarios.

Figure 25-A. Illustration of alternative capital structures for a law firm.

ABC LAW FIRM
COMPARISON OF ALTERNATIVE CAPITAL STRUCTURES
(Modified cash basis presentation)

	Purpose of Capital Structure	
	Future Retirement Funding	Current Operations Financing
Net assets to be financed:		
Investments	$50,000,000	
Other current assets	25,000,000	$25,000,000
Property and equipment	21,000,000	21,000,000
Payroll tax withholdings	(1,000,000)	(1,000,000)
Net assets	$95,000,000	$45,000,000
Financing vehicle:		
Bank loans	$21,000,000	$35,000,000
Partners' equity	74,000,000	10,000,000
Total financing	$95,000,000	$45,000,000

Dynamic changes have taken place in the law firm environment during the past two decades due to: (1) economic pressures, (2) competitive pressures, and (3) cultural shifts. These changes have caused a reconfiguration in the capital structure of many law firms.

[1]—Economic Considerations

The practice of law has become increasingly expensive. In the early 1980s, law firm offices were under long-term leases, were functionally furnished, and office occupancy and operating costs were reasonable. In today's environment, the space needs of law firms have increased because of the firms' growth in size. Office leases have become more expensive, shorter in duration and heavily escalated. In addition, to support their expanded operations and to remain abreast of modern service delivery approaches, law firms must make sizable investments in technology, including computer hardware and software systems for financial management, word processing, knowledge management, document management, and attorney applications.

Financing of office space is typically done through leasing. However, a few firms have purchased office buildings to house their law offices. These firms have usually financed the major portion of this investment through mortgage loans.

Leasehold improvements, furniture and furnishings, technology equipment (computers, telephone and communication systems, printers, copiers, faxes, etc.), and other major pieces of property and equipment are often too expensive to be financed by partners' equity. As a result, these investments are now more typically financed through borrowings, particularly when a firm moves to a new office location or goes through a sizable office remodeling.

Financing partners' drawings through borrowing is very controversial. Some firms believe that such borrowing is counter-productive, because it removes the partners' incentive to bill and collect fees from clients. Other firms accept the need to borrow to finance partners' drawings during certain interim months, but insist that these borrowings be completely cleared up at least once each year. A few firms have continually borrowed to finance partners' drawings; however, it should be noted that some firms that borrowed heavily to make distributions to partners have generally not survived.

[2]—Competitive Considerations

The practice of law has become increasingly competitive. Diversified services, regional or national expansion, and having multinational capabilities have become more important in providing for the service needs of clients and deflecting competition.

Diversified services require practicing additional types of law, in some cases through mergers with or acquisitions of firms that can add new service dimensions to a firm's traditional practice mix. Diversification requires more lawyers, more support staff, more office space and more office equipment that must be financed, often through borrowings.

Expanding operations regionally or nationally requires opening or acquiring branch offices in cities across a firm's home region, or across the United States. Some firms are content to operate from only one office, viewing expansion as too risky. Other firms have developed strategic plans and are carefully expanding by opening branches in cities where they have a significantly existing client service need on a continuing basis. New branches require lawyers, support staff, space and equipment, which often are financed through additional borrowings.

Having multinational capabilities requires either affiliating with existing firms in other countries, merging with or acquiring such firms (if permitted) or opening branches in foreign countries. In each case, expansion overseas usually calls for a sizable investment. While borrowings might finance some of these costs, partners' equity may be the ultimate source of financing for a significant portion of the investment, particularly in "start-up" situations.

[3]—Cultural Considerations

The practice of law has changed culturally. There have been changes in the composition of partnerships and changes in the composition of partners' equity.

Years ago, partnerships were composed of closely-knit groups of loyal, vertically grown partners. Today, many (but not all) partnerships are an amalgamation of previously independent firms, together with segments of other firms and/or a significant number of lateral partners. During the first year after acquiring another firm or acquiring some lateral partners, law firms may be faced with a shortfall in cash. This is caused by the outlay of cash to pay for the new partners' drawings and the expenses of their support staff during a time frame that usually begins four to six months prior to the collection of fees for services rendered to clients. This phenomenon has been dubbed "the lag effect." Financing the "lag effect" is often considered to be a temporary matter and financed through borrowings; however, in the long run, it represents a need for permanent financing, usually through partners' equity.

In the past, a significant number of firms built up sizable capital reserve accounts with the objective of: (1) protecting against temporary shortfalls and/or (2) providing for some or all of the partners' unfunded retirement benefits. Today, most firms have reduced the size of partners' capital accounts and have encouraged partners to fund their retirement benefits through 401(k) or other defined contribution plans.

§ 25.02 Alternative Financing Methods

Law firms are typically financed by a combination of methods: (1) Equity Financing, (2) Borrowing, and (3) Leasing. Some advantages of each of these methods are summarized in the chart below. Each method is discussed in more detail in the paragraphs that follow.

	Advantage		
	Equity Financing	Borrowing	Leasing
Preserves partners' funds?	No	Yes	Yes
Absent an interest cost for the partnership?	Yes	No	No
Relatively simple in execution?	Yes	No	No
Retains partners' incentives to collect fees?	Yes	No	No

It is important to recognize that while Equity Financing eliminates an interest cost for the partnership, the cost burden is merely shifted to the individual partners who incur interest expense through personal borrowings (or forgo interest income on investments) to finance their capital contributions to the partnership.

[1]—Equity Financing

Partnership equity of a law firm has three principal components: (1) permanent capital, (2) undistributed earnings and (3) equity in unbilled and uncollected fees. The third component of equity (often the largest component) is not apparent when a law firm presents its financial statements using the modified cash basis method of accounting. It becomes apparent when the firm presents its statements using the accrual basis method of accounting. Figure 25-B illustrates the various components of partnership equity under both methods of accounting.

Figure 25-B. Illustration of the components of partnership equity under two alternative methods of accounting.

ABC LAW FIRM
COMPARISON OF PARTNERSHIP EQUITY
UNDER ALTERNATIVE METHODS OF ACCOUNTING

	Methods of Accounting	
	Cash Basis	Accrual Basis
Net assets to be financed:		
Investments	$50,000,000	$ 50,000,000
Unbilled & uncollected fees	—	85,000,000
Other current assets	25,000,000	25,000,000
Property and equipment	21,000,000	21,000,000
Payables	(1,000,000)	(11,000,000)
Net assets	$95,000,000	$170,000,000
Partners' equity:		
Permanent capital	$50,000,000	$ 50,000,000
Undistributed earnings	45,000,000	45,000,000
Equity in unbilled and uncollected fees	—	75,000,000
Partners' equity	$95,000,000	$170,000,000

[a]—Permanent Capital

Permanent capital in a law firm partnership represents amounts contributed to the firm's capital by the partners. These amounts generally must come from the individual partners' after-tax earnings. Balances generally are returned to the partners when they retire, die or withdraw, although some firms have a forfeiture provision under which partners loose part of their capital if they leave the firm to join another law firm.

The total amount of permanent capital varies with the firm's view as to the financial purpose of the partnership entity, as previously discussed. Typically, each partner's contribution to permanent capital is determined by a formula expressed in the firm's partnership agreement, often the partnership profit-sharing formula. These formulas often are modified to accommodate capital funding hardships faced by new partners and phase-out requests of retiring partners. Firms often find it difficult to maintain symmetry between the percentage relationship of partners' capital balances and the partnership's profit-sharing percentages. Some firms allocate imputed interest on balances in partners' permanent capital accounts to mitigate this imbalance.

To be successful in establishing an appropriate relationship among balances in partners' permanent capital accounts, a firm's capital account formula must have three elements: (1) a cumulative target that approximates the partners' profit-sharing percentages, (2) a total balance that maintains an appropriate relationship with the changing size of the firm and (3) an annual contribution that does not create an undue hardship for the firm's partners, particularly the newer ones. An example of a "rollover" formula that contains these elements is illustrated in Figure 25-C. The formula calls for adding to capital each year an amount representing 5% of each partner's share of net income and for removing each year all contributions that are over five-years old. For purposes of brevity, the illustration covers only five years. The formula typically works best when it is spread over ten years.

Figure 25-C. Illustration of a "rollover" formula for allocating partners' permanent capital.

ABC LAW FIRM
PARTNERS' PERMANENT CAPITAL BALANCES
IMPACT OF APPLYING "ROLLOVER" FORMULA

Year	Partner A	Partner B	Partner C	Partner D	Total
1	$ 50,000	$ 50,000			$100,000
2	45,000	45,000	$ 35,000		125,000
3	50,000	50,000	50,000		150,000
4	45,000	45,000	60,000	$ 25,000	175,000
5	40,000	40,000	70,000	50,000	200,000
Cumulative-year 5	230,000	230,000	215,000	75,000	750,000
6	30,000	30,000	45,000	45,000	150,000
1	(50,000)	(50,000)			(100,000)
Cumulative-year 6	$210,000	$210,000	$260,000	$120,000	$800,000

[b]—Undistributed Earnings

Undistributed earnings in a law firm partnership represent the firm's cumulative earnings under the modified cash basis of accounting, after deducting cumulative amounts that have been paid to partners or to retirement plans on behalf of partners. Since most law firms report partnership taxable income on the modified cash basis method of accounting, these undistributed earnings represent taxable income to the partners even though the cash has not been distributed to them. Consequently, the partners have a keen interest in receiving distributions of these earnings promptly.

[c]—Equity in Unbilled and Uncollected Fees

Equity in unbilled and uncollected fees in a law firm partnership represents the difference between undistributed earnings on a modified cash basis method of accounting versus undistributed earnings on the accrual basis method of accounting. This difference consists principally of the realizable value of unbilled and uncollected fees reduced by accrued liabilities, if any. These amounts usually are reported on a pre-tax basis. Partners in some firms view these amounts as representing income deferred until after retirement. Whether an individual partner has any equity interest in these amounts is dependent upon the terms of the firm's partnership agreement.

[2]—Borrowing

The three principal sources for law firm borrowings are: (1) short-term bank loans, (2) long-term bank loans, including capital leases[1] and (3) private placements. Typical characteristics of these loans are summarized below:

	Typical Characteristics		
	Short-term Bank Loans	Long-term Bank Loans	Private Placements
Purpose	Working Capital Financing	Property and Equipment Financing	Property and Equipment Financing
Borrowing	Under $10 million (depending upon firm size)	$10 to $25 million	Over $25 million
Interest Rate	Floating	Floating or Fixed	Fixed
Type of Note	Demand	Term	Term
Term of Note	1 year	5-10 years	Over 10 years

[a]—Short-Term Bank Loans

Short-term bank loans usually are obtained for working capital purposes. Law firms typically use this facility to finance seasonal variations in fee collections from clients. Most law firms find that their monthly cash outflow (i.e., partner distributions, associate compensation, employee salaries, and other operating expenses) is fairly stable throughout the year; however, many law firms typically find that cash inflow (i.e., fee collections) is bunched in the fourth quarter. Consequently, to

[1] See Chapter 29, "Property and Equipment Acquisition," *infra.*

make up for this interim shortfall, they typically borrow during the first three quarters and make repayments during the fourth quarter.

Figure 25-D illustrates the effect of short-term bank loans on a law firm's cash flow.

Figure 25-D. Illustration of the effect of short-term bank loans on the cash flow of a law firm.

ABC LAW FIRM
QUARTERLY CASH-FLOW REPORT
IMPACT OF SHORT-TERM BANK LOANS
($ in thousands)

	Quarter				
	1st	2nd	3rd	4th	Full Year
Fees collected	$ 30,000	$ 30,000	$ 40,000	$100,000	$200,000
Employees and suppliers	(25,000)	(25,000)	(25,000)	(25,000)	(100,000)
Property and equipment purchased		(10,000)		(10,000)	(20,000)
Distributions to partners	(20,000)	(20,000)	(20,000)	(20,000)	(80,000)
Cash flow before loans	(15,000)	(25,000)	(5,000)	45,000	—
Short-term bank loans	20,000	20,000	10,000	(50,000)	—
Cash flow after loans	$ 5,000	$ (5,000)	$ 5,000	$ (5,000)	—

Short-term bank loans often have a number of distinctive features, for example: (1) a demand note rather than a term note, (2) a floating-interest rate rather than a fixed rate, and (3) a revolving credit feature.

[i]—Demand Note

Short-term working capital loans are usually represented by a demand note. These demand note arrangements are either: (1) open-ended or (2) with a specific maturity. Some banks require the law firm to clear their loan balance for a thirty-day period once a year. Other banks are content with only the demand note feature.

[ii]—Floating-Interest Rate

Short-term working capital loans are usually priced at a floating interest rate. Consequently, the law firm assumes an interest rate risk.

[iii]—Revolving Credit

Short-term working capital loans often have a revolving credit feature which permits the law firm to decrease or increase the amount of the loan (up to a maximum) during the loan period. Maximum borrowings may be tied to outstanding billed or unbilled fees or a combination of these factors.

[b]—Long-Term Bank Loans

Long-term bank loans are usually entered into by law firms to finance the acquisition of property and equipment (such as leasehold improvements, new furniture and furnishings, computer equipment). Because a long-term loan involves the uncertain risk of future events, banks often require that the law firm present a strategic plan projecting its capital needs, revenues, expenses, and cash flow.

Figure 25-E illustrates the effect of long-term bank loans on a law firm's cash flow.

Figure 25-E. Illustration of the effect of long-term bank loans on the cash flow of a law firm.

ABC LAW FIRM
SEVEN-YEAR CASH-FLOW REPORT
IMPACT OF LONG-TERM BANK LOANS
($ in thousands)

	Year				
	1	2 & 3	4 & 5	6 & 7	Cumulative
Fees collected	$ 200,000	$ 500,000	$ 500,000	$ 500,000	$1,700,000
Employees and suppliers	(100,000)	(250,000)	(250,000)	(250,000)	(850,000)
Property and equipment purchased	(240,000)				(240,000)
Distributions to partners	(70,000)	(150,000)	(150,000)	(150,000)	(520,000)
Cash flow before loans	(210,000)	100,000	100,000	100,000	90,000
Long-term bank loans	240,000	(80,000)	(80,000)	(80,000)	—
Interest cost	—	(50,000)	(30,000)	(10,000)	(90,000)
Cash flow after loans	$ 30,000	$ (30,000)	$ (10,000)	$ 10,000	—

Long-term bank loans often have a number of distinctive features, for example: (1) a fixed term, (2) interest rate options and (3) multiple bank financing.

[i]—Fixed Note

Long-term bank loans usually are documented by a term note. Typical maximum loan periods range from five to ten years, depending on the bank and the economic conditions prevalent at the time of the loan.

[ii]—Interest Rate Options

Long-term bank loans often are priced with an option to choose either a fixed rate or variable rate of interest. In addition, several banks offer further options including a choice of variable rates pegged to certain indexes (such as a prime rate, a LIBOR rate, a CD rate, a Federal Funds rate, a Eurodollar rate).

[iii]—Multiple Bank Financing

Long-term bank loans of less than $10 million typically are financed by a single bank. Financing of loans in excess of $10 million often involves at least two banks. Sometimes the law firm makes separate arrangements and enters into separate agreements with each of the banks. In other cases, banks form a consortium and enter into a single agreement with the law firm, identifying each bank's relative commitment.

[c]—Private Placements

Private placements of notes payable (typically with insurance companies) usually are entered into by law firms in connection with major construction or reconstruction of office facilities and the concurrent purchase and installation of computer systems.

Figure 25-F illustrates the effect of a private placement of notes payable on a law firm's cash flow.

Private Placements of notes payable often have a number of distinctive features, for example: (1) a fixed term, (2) multiple maturity dates, (3) multiple interest rates and (4) an offering document.

[i]—Term Note

Notes payable that are privately placed usually are represented by fixed-term notes. Maximum loan periods often range between ten and fifteen years.

[ii]—Multiple Maturity Dates

Privately placed notes payable often include more than one series of notes, each series maturing sequentially (e.g., Series One repayable annually during years one to ten and Series Two repayable annually during years eleven to fifteen).

[iii]—Multiple Interest Rates

Each series of privately placed notes payable usually bears a different interest rate, with the higher rates assigned to the series with the greater risk.

Figure 25-F. Illustration of the effect of a private placement of notes payable on the cash flow of a law firm.

ABC LAW FIRM
FIFTEEN-YEAR CASH-FLOW REPORT
IMPACT OF PRIVATE PLACEMENT OF NOTES PAYABLE
($ in thousands)

		Repayment Period			
	Construction Period	Years 1 to 5	Years 6 to 10	Years 11 to 15	Cumulative
Fees collected		$5,000,000	$5,000,000	$5,000,000	$15,000,000
Employees and suppliers		(2,500,000)	(2,500,000)	(2,500,000)	(7,500,000)
Property and equipment constructed	$(600,000)				(600,000)
Distributions to partners		(2,000,000)	(2,150,000)	(2,300,000)	(6,450,000)
Cash flow before financing	(600,000)	500,000	350,000	200,000	450,000
Notes payable-Series One	400,000	(200,000)	(200,000)		—
Notes payable-Series Two	200,000			(200,000)	—
Interest cost	—	(250,000)	(150,000)	(50,000)	(450,000)
Cash flow after financing	—	$50,000	—	$(50,000)	—

[iv]—Offering Document

The process involved in undertaking a private placement of debt includes the preparation of an offering document that contains much of the information found in a public offering document, including the presentation of:

(1) Five years of financial information;
(2) Management's discussion and analysis;
(3) Use of proceeds;
(4) Structure of the firm and its personnel;
(5) Practice area information;
(6) Capitalization table;
(7) Description of the offering; and
(8) Audited financial statements.

The notes issued as a result of these private placements are typically sold to insurance companies, banks or other sophisticated institutional investors for their own account and not with a view toward their resale in a manner that would subject the notes to registration under securities laws.

Figure 25-G illustrates an example of financial and personnel highlights that are likely to be included in the forepart of an offering document for the private placement of notes payable by a law firm.

Figure 25-G. Illustration of a law firm's historical financial and personnel highlights appearing in an offering document for the private placement of debt.

ABC LAW FIRM
FINANCIAL AND PERSONNEL HIGHLIGHTS
($ in millions)

Financial Information	19X8	19X7	19X6	19X5	19X4
Fees	$140	$130	$120	$110	$100
Net Income	56	52	48	44	40
Cash Flow	58	54	50	46	42
Net Assets (cash basis)	14	13	12	11	10
Net Assets (accrual basis)	70	65	60	55	50
Capital Expenditures	10	8	6	4	2
Bank Loans	9	7	5	3	1
Personnel Count					
Partners	140	130	120	110	100
Associates	280	260	240	220	200
Paralegals	70	65	60	55	50
Support Staff	560	520	480	440	400
Fees by Practice Area					
Corporate	$110	$103	$ 96	$ 89	$ 82
Litigation	20	18	16	14	12
Other Services	10	9	8	7	6
Total	$140	$130	$120	$110	$100
Fees by Location					
New York	$113	$106	$ 99	$ 92	$ 85
Washington	18	16	14	12	10
Paris	9	8	7	6	5
Total	$140	$130	$120	$110	$100

In addition to financial highlights, the offering memorandum usually contains a table summarizing the law firm's key operating statistics. The purpose of this table is to shed some light on the factors that affect the law firm's profitability and the trends that the firm has experienced during the past five years.

The acronym "RULES"[2] has historically been used to illustrate the key operating statistics of a law firm and hence a law firm's profitability. Set forth below is a summary of key operating statistics which a law firm might consider including in an offering memorandum.

R—Realization of Billing Rates	• Average Billing Rates for Partners, Associates, and Other Timekeepers • Realization Rates for Unbilled Fees and Fees Receivable
U—Utilization of Attorneys	• Average Billable Hours for Partners, Associates, and Other Timekeepers
L—Leverage of Lawyers	• Ratio of Non-Partner Timekeepers to Equity Partners
E—Expense Control	• Average Associate and Other Timekeepers' Compensation and Average Operating Expenses Per Non-Partner Timekeeper
S—Speed of Billings and Collections	• Number of Months Outstanding for Unbilled Fees and Fees Receivable

Figure 25-H illustrates an example of some key operating statistics that are likely to be included in an offering document for the private placement of notes payable by a law firm.

[d]—Borrowing Agreements

Borrowing agreements range from straightforward letters to formidable documents and typically include provisions focusing on: (1) terms of the loan; (2) representations and warranties of the firm; (3) liability of partners; (4) events of default; and (5) definition of accounting terms.

[i]—Terms of the Loan

This section of a borrowing agreement sets forth the terms of a loan and customarily includes the: (1) amount of the loan, (2) interest rate (fixed or variable), (3) repayment period, (4) prepayment rights and (5) collateral (if any).

---

[2] See Chapter 9, "Management Reporting," *supra* for a discussion of "RULES."

[ii]—Representations and Warranties of the Firm

In addition to the usual legal representations and warranties, this section of a borrowing agreement generally calls for the firm to make certain additional representations which could have financial implications, including: (1) the absence of litigation that could materially adversely affect the firm's business or ability to pay the loan, (2) no material adverse change in the firm's business since the date of its last financial statements and (3) the firm is not in default under any existing loan agreements or leases.

Figure 25-H. Illustration of key operating statistics appearing in an offering document for the private placement of debt by a law firm.

ABC LAW FIRM
KEY OPERATING STATISTICS

	19X8	19X7	19X6	19X5	19X4
Billing Rates (Average)					
Partners	$600	$550	$500	$450	$400
Associates and Other Timekeepers	$300	$274	$250	$224	$220
Realization Rates					
Unbilled Fees	100%	95%	90%	85%	80%
Fees Receivable	100%	99%	98%	97%	96%
Billable Hours (Average)					
Partners	1,800	1,825	1,850	1,875	1,900
Associates	1,900	1,875	1,850	1,825	1,800
Lawyer Leverage					
Ratio of Associates and Other Timekeepers to Partners	2 to 1	2 to 1	2 to 1	2 to 1	2 to 1
Expenses (Per Lawyer) ($ in Thousands)					
Associate and Other Timekeepers' Compensation	$110	$100	$90	$80	$70
Operating Expenses	$125	$120	$115	$110	$105
Billing and Collection Speed (Months)					
Unbilled Fees	2.0	2.5	3.0	3.5	4.0
Fees Receivable	2.0	2.2	2.5	2.7	3.0

[iii]—Liability of Partners

The content of the partner liability section of a borrowing agreement is a very controversial matter and often subject to substantial negotiation. In addition to the partnership's responsibility to repay the loan, most loan agreements also address the responsibility of individual partners to repay the loan. Individual partners' liability could be either:

(1) None;
(2) Joint and several; or
(3) Proportionate.

Partners, of course, prefer to have no individual liability under partnership loans. Lenders prefer to have each partner jointly and severally liable. Partners' individual liability is usually a matter that is intensely discussed during loan negotiations. In some instances, the parties have agreed to a proportional liability concept. Under this concept, each partner is individually liable for his proportionate share of the outstanding loan if a "triggering event" occurs (for example: if more than 25% of the partners withdraw from the partnership). The partner's proportionate share usually is based on a formula (for example: 125% of his or her profit-sharing percentage for the past two years over the total profit-sharing percentage of all partners during that period). The formula also must address the treatment of retired, deceased, withdrawn and fixed-income partners. (Partners who retire or die usually are relieved of liability if no event of default exists. Partners who withdraw may be relieved of liability if the lender consents.) One option that some firms are using to appease the interest of both the partners and lenders is to establish loans between the individual partners and the bank with the capital being contributed directly to the firm. Interest is paid by the partnership, but charged to the individual partner. All covenants are developed and calculated at the firm level and the partners only are liable for their individual loans, yet the firm enjoys a significant capital inflow when all loans are aggregated. For example, assume a fifty-partner firm needed to raise additional capital to upgrade their network, laptop computers and for general working capital needs. Also assume that the partners do not want to provide capital directly and have any liability associated with external debt minimized. On the other hand, the bank wants to establish liability at the partnership level. If the firm entered into a loan agreement, which was supported by loans between the individual partners and the bank, the firm would receive $5,000,000 of capital, the bank would establish liability between the partners and the bank and the partners would minimize the amount of liability of each partner. From an administrative standpoint, the bank agreement is managed at the firm level and all interest is paid by the partnership, but allocated to the respective partners' capital account. As partners retire or resign, their portion of the debt is paid off. Similarly, as partners are admitted, they enter into a loan agreement with the bank and additional capital is provided to the firm.

[iv]—Events of Default

Each loan agreement specifies what constitutes an event of default for purposes of the related loan. Typical events of default include: (1) failure to pay debt principal or interest when due, (2) discovery of a false or materially incorrect representation or warranty, (3) failure to observe covenants or terms of loan agreements, (4) initiation of bankruptcy or liquidation proceedings and (5) failure to satisfy a sizable judgment. When an event of default occurs, the lender usually has the right to demand immediate payment of principal and interest on the loan.

[v]—Definition of Accounting Terms

The section of the borrowing agreement which defines accounting terms is an important section. Clear definitions of accounting terms in the loan agreement help prevent misunderstandings in later years. First and foremost, the agreement should identify and define the accounting method that the firm follows in preparing its financial statements; for example: (1) the modified cash basis, (2) the modified accrual basis, or (3) the full accrual basis. (Only the last is in accordance with generally accepted accounting principles.) Other accounting terms that should be defined include: (1) net income, (2) net assets (variations include: net worth, tangible net worth, accrual net worth), (3) partners' equity (variations include: "partners' capital, partners' permanent capital), (4) cash flow, (5) coverage ratio (variations include: debt-service-coverage ratio, fixed-charge-coverage ratio), (6) partners' withdrawals (variations include: partners' distributions, restricted payments to partners), (7) capital expenditures and (8) capital lease (e.g., if capital lease includes a building lease).

[e]—Documents Provided by Borrower

In addition to executing the loan agreement, most lenders require the firm to provide them with a series of documents either prior to or at closing. Documents commonly requested include: (1) the firm's partnership agreement, (2) the firm's latest annual financial statements, (3) an opinion letter provided by the borrowing firm's counsel with respect to the legal enforceability of the loan agreement, (4) evidence of insurance and (5) the name and percentage interest of each of the firm's partners.

[i]—Partnership Agreement

In addition to providing the firm's partnership agreement, some lenders require the firm to represent that it is the latest agreement and that it includes all amendments through the date of the closing.

[ii]—Historical Financial Statements

Lenders generally require a copy of the firm's latest annual financial statements. Where substantial borrowings are involved, the lender usually requires that the financial statements be audited. For private placements, five years of audited financial statements are usually produced. Frequently, the firm's latest quarterly financial statements also are requested. Financial statements typically include: (1) statement of net assets, (2) statement of revenues and expenses, (3) statement of changes in partners' accounts and (4) statement of cash flows.

[iii]—Opinion of Counsel

Lenders normally require counsel for the borrower to provide a written opinion addressing the legal enforceability of the loan agreement and other matters. The firm usually acts as its own counsel for this purpose.

[iv]—Evidence of Insurance

Lenders commonly require the borrowing firm to provide evidence of a minimum amount of malpractice insurance coverage with an insurer acceptable to the lender.

[v]—Name and Percentage Interest of Each Partner

In addition to the name, address and percentage interest of each partner as of the date of the loan, lenders customarily require the firm to provide this information about new partners whenever they are admitted to the firm and to notify the lender whenever partners cease to be members of the firm.

[f]—Financial Covenants and Ratios

In order to monitor the borrower's continuing ability to repay the loan, most lenders establish a series of financial covenants to be observed by the borrower during the term of the loan. These covenants customarily are memorialized in the loan agreement. In reaction to a small number of highly publicized law firm bankruptcies, a few banks introduced some financial covenants that were cumbersome to administer and oppressive in their requirements. Fortunately, through negotiation during the drafting of loan agreements, most law firm borrowers were able to have these covenants modified to achieve the proper balance of protection for the lender and business operation flexibility for the firm. Financial covenants typically are expressed in the form of either a minimum/maximum or a ratio. It is imperative that the agreement be clear in describing each of the covenants and defining how and when they will be measured. In addition, the firm should ensure that they are comfortable that they can meet the covenants, not only now, but also in the future. Failure to do so will cause management to spend an inordinate amount of time and additional expense in getting the violations cleared or waived. The financial covenants discussed below are commonly found in loan agreements executed by law firms.

[i]—Minimum Capital Requirements

Most loan agreements require the firm to maintain minimum capital at year-end (and sometimes on a quarterly basis). This covenant is expressed in some loan agreements as a minimum dollar amount of partners' capital, which the firm must maintain. In other agreements, it is expressed as a minimum ratio of partners' capital versus debt. Loan agreements often establish two minimum capital requirements: one based on partners' capital on a modified cash basis method of accounting and the second based on partners' capital on a quasi-accrual basis method of accounting. The quasi-accrual basis is typically a formula calculation which combines: (1) partners' capital on a modified cash basis, (2) a percentage of currently aged fees receivable and (3) a percentage of currently aged unbilled fees. Figure 25-I Illustrates two examples of minimum capital requirement calculations.

Figure 25-I. Illustration of minimum capital requirement calculations based on borrowing agreements for loans to law firms.

ABC LAW FIRM
MINIMUM CAPITAL REQUIREMENT CALCULATIONS

	Modified Cash Basis Method of Accounting		Quasi-Accrual Basis Method of Accounting	
	Amount	Ratio of Capital to Debt	Amount	Ratio of Capital to Debt
Partners' Equity in Balance Sheet Assets:				
Permanent Capital	$20,000,000		$ 20,000,000	
Undistributed Earnings	30,000,000		30,000,000	
Partners' Equity in Off-Balance Sheet Assets:				
90% of Fees Receivable under 90 days old			40,000,000	
75% of Unbilled Fees under 90 days old			60,000,000	
Partners' Capital (as calculated)	$50,000,000	1:1	$150,000,000	3:1
Minimum Capital Required	$50,000,000	1:1	$100,000,000	2:1
Debt	$50,000,000		$ 50,000,000	
Covenant Satisfied?		Yes		Yes

[ii]—Minimum Cash Flow Requirements

Some loan agreements require the firm to maintain a certain level of cash flow. For purposes of these loan agreements, cash flow should be defined in the agreement and typically is defined as net income on the modified cash basis method of accounting plus depreciation and amortization.

[iii]—Minimum Coverage Ratio

Frequently loan agreements require the firm to maintain a minimum coverage ratio (sometimes called a fixed-charge-coverage ratio or a debt-service-coverage ratio). The ratio represents the number of times that income (as defined) exceeds coverage (as defined). There is a wide disparity in defining the components of this ratio in loan agreements (and in some accounting texts). It is, therefore, essential that this term be well defined in the loan agreement and that both lender and borrower are comfortable in their understanding of its purpose and method of calculation. Figure 25-J illustrates some examples of minimum-coverage ratio calculations based on the terms of agreements underlying loans to law firms.

Figure 25-J. Illustration of minimum-coverage ratio calculations based on terms of agreements underlying loans to law firms.

ABC LAW FIRM
MINIMUM-COVERAGE RATIO CALCULATIONS
($ in thousands)

	Interest Coverage Ratio	Fixed Charge Coverage Ratio	Debt Service Coverage Ratio	Capital Service Coverage Ratio
Income (as defined):				
Net Income	$55,000	$55,000	$55,000	$55,000
Interest Expense	5,000	5,000	5,000	5,000
Rental Expense		6,000	6,000	6,000
Depreciation & Amortization			4,000	4,000
	$60,000	$66,000	$70,000	$70,000
Coverage (as defined):				
Interest Expense	$ 5,000	$ 5,000	$ 5,000	$ 5,000
Rental Expense		6,000	6,000	6,000
Principal Payments on Loans			3,000	3,000
Partners' Withdrawals				46,000
Capital Expenditures				10,000
	$ 5,000	$11,000	$14,000	$70,000
Coverage Ratio (as calculated)	12 to 1	6 to 1	5 to 1	1 to 1
Minimum-Coverage Ratio	5 to 1	3 to 1	2 to 1	1 to 1
Covenant Satisfied?	Yes	Yes	Yes	Yes

[iv]—Minimum Gross Revenue

Some loan agreements require the firm to maintain a level of gross revenue within a certain percentage of the prior year's revenue. Sometimes, this requirement extends to quarterly reporting periods.

[v]—Minimum Current Ratio

Some loan agreements require the firm to maintain a minimum ratio of current assets to current liabilities (for example, 2:1). Sometimes, the definition of current liabilities includes loan guarantees.

[vi]—Limitations on Additional Borrowings

Most loan agreements contain provisions limiting the amount of additional borrowings that the firm may undertake. Limitations generally are applied to long-term and short-term debt (in the aggregate or individually), liens (with identified exceptions), guarantees (with identified exceptions), and capital leases (in some cases). In rare instances, unfunded vested benefits of pension plans have been included in the borrowing base. Because of the wide diversity in the methods used to determine these limitations, it is important that the relevant terms be well-defined in the loan agreements and that both lender and borrower have a clear understanding of the purpose and method of calculating each limitation. Figure 25-K illustrates some examples of borrowing limitation calculations based on the terms of agreements underlying loans to law firms.

Figure 25-K. Illustration of borrowing limitation calculations based on the terms of agreements underlying loans to law firms.

ABC LAW FIRM
BORROWING LIMITATION CALCULATIONS
($ in thousands)

	Dollar Limitations		Percentage Limitations	
	Aggregate Limitation	Individual Limitations	Based on Net Assets	Based on Cash Flow
Borrowings (as defined):				
Long-Term Debt	$10,000	$10,000	$10,000	$10,000
Short-Term Debt	3,000	3,000	3,000	3,000
Capital Leases		1,000		1,000
	$13,000	$14,000	$13,000	$14,000
Limitations (as defined):				
Long-Term Debt		$10,000		
Short-Term Debt		5,000		
Capital Leases		1,000		
Aggregate Borrowings	$15,000			
50% of Net Assets			$12,000	
75% of Cash Flow				$15,000
	$15,000	$16,000	$12,000	$15,000
Covenant Satisfied?	Yes	Yes	No	Yes

[vii]—Limitations on Partner Distributions

Sometimes loan agreements place limitations on annual amounts that may be distributed to partners. In some cases, the limitation is pegged to net income (for example: distributions may be limited to 100% of cumulative net income or to 95% of current year net income). In other cases, the limitation prohibits distributions to partners to the extent that they would result in a default in the debt/equity ratio requirement.

[viii]—Limitations on Capital Expenditures

Some loan agreements place limitations on the firm's expenditures (for example: capital expenditures limited to expenditures funded by the loan proceeds plus $1 million a year for internally funded expenditures).

[ix]—Minimum Number of Active Partners

Some loan agreements require the firm to maintain a minimum number of partners. In other words, the lender is protecting itself from a certain amount of partners retiring and/or resigning (for whatever reason) during the period covered by the loan as the partners drive the revenue base and hence impact the firm's ability to repay the loan.

[x]—Other Covenants

Some loan agreements prohibit the firm from: (1) merging with another partnership, unless the firm is the successor entity, (2) dissolving the partnership, unless the firm's partners control the successor entity (for example, through an 80% ownership), (3) materially amending the partnership agreement, without the lender's consent or (4) expanding the personal liability of the firm's partners to cover debts to other lenders, unless such liability is also similarly expanded to cover the existing loan.

[g]—Financial Reporting Required by Lenders

As part of their loan monitoring process, most lenders require the firm to provide them with annual and quarterly financial reports.

[i]—Annual Audited Financial Statements

At the end of each year during the period of the loan, lenders usually require the firm to submit a copy of their annual financial statements, including: (1) a statement of net assets, (2) a statement of revenues and expenses, (3) a statement of changes in partners' accounts and (4) a statement of cash flows. These reports are generally due within 120 days after the end of the year; however, due dates vary and under some loan agreements they range from 105 days to 150 days. When borrowings under loan agreements are sizable, lenders usually require these financial statements to be audited. In order to avoid future misunderstandings, it is important that the loan agreement specify the accounting method to be followed in preparing these financial statements (for example: "the modified cash basis method of accounting as used in the firm's historical financial statements").

[ii]—Quarterly Unaudited Financial Reports

Most lenders also require the firm to submit quarterly financial reports. Requirements for quarterly reports vary. Some lenders require the same four financial statements that are required at year-end. Some only require a quarterly statement of revenue and expense compared with the prior year figures and the forecast. Others request more detailed information, such as aging reports of fees receivable and unbilled fees. Lenders usually require these quarterly financial reports to be certified correct by a partner (typically either the firm's managing partner, a member of the firm's executive committee or the chief financial officer). Due dates for these reports are generally either forty-five days or sixty days after the quarter's end.

[h]—Compliance Letters and Waivers

In addition to requiring periodic financial statements, most lenders generally require that the firm provide them with periodic reports evidencing the firm's continuing compliance with the loan covenants. If a violation of a loan covenant occurs, the firm must either cure (i.e., correct) the violation or seek a waiver.

[i]—Management's Compliance Letter

Lenders generally require the firm to provide an annual and/or quarterly compliance letter signed by a partner who is a member of the firm's executive committee and/or the chief financial officer: (1) certifying that to the best of his knowledge and belief no event of default has occurred and is continuing (or providing a description of a default which has occurred and the action being taken to correct it), and (2) presenting computations demonstrating compliance with key covenants contained in the loan agreement. Computations included in this letter frequently include loan specified calculations of current results compared with:

(1) Minimum capital requirements;
(2) Minimum cash flow requirements;
(3) Minimum coverage ratio;
(4) Minimum number of active partners;
(5) Limitations on partner distributions;
(6) Limitations on additional borrowings; and
(7) Limitations on capital leases.

When the loan agreement specifies restrictions on mergers or dissolutions, *pro forma* calculations are also included.

[ii]—Auditors' Negative Assurance Letter

In certain cases (for example: in connection with major bank loans or private placements), the lender may require a special report from the firm's independent auditors. The report issued by the auditors usually is phrased in a negative assurance format. For example: "In connection with our audit, nothing came to our attention that caused us to believe that the Firm failed to comply with the terms, covenants, provisions, or conditions of Section XXX of the Indenture dated XXX with XXX insofar as they relate to accounting matters. However, our audit was not directed primarily toward obtaining knowledge of such noncompliance."

[iii]—Lender's Waiver of Compliance

If a violation of any of the loan covenants occurs, the firm should communicate with the lender. In cases where the violation is temporary or minor, the lender may grant a temporary waiver. Notwithstanding the bank loan officer's willingness to grant the waiver, the firm should recognize that obtaining a written waiver may be a time-consuming process, because it usually must proceed through the bank's formal approval process.

In cases where the violation is a serious matter, in order to return to compliance or risk a demand for full payment of the loan, the firm may be required to take major action (e.g., (1) put pressure on the partners to accelerate billing and collections, (2) withhold partner distributions or (3) issue a capital call to the partners).

[3]—Leasing

Law firms typically finance their office space through leases. Sometimes they also lease large computers and major pieces of office equipment.[3]

[a]—Lease Agreements

Lease agreements range from documents of twenty pages with five exhibits (for leasing existing office space) to documents of two hundred pages with twenty-five exhibits (for leasing space in a major new building where construction is being tailored to tenant specifications). The agreement customarily addresses: (1) operating terms of the lease, (2) economic terms of the lease, (3) partners' liability under the lease and (4) ownership of capital improvements to leased property.

---

[3] A discussion of the decision-making process and an illustration of the financial impact of leasing versus purchasing office space are discussed in Chapter 29 *infra*.

[i]—Operating Terms

Each lease agreement usually contains sections relating to: (1) the premises (space to be occupied in rentable square feet, floors on which the space is located, dimensions of the space, expansion space), (2) landlord's rights and responsibilities (certificate of occupancy, building operations, repairs and maintenance insurance) and (3) tenant's rights and responsibilities (access to the premises, subleases, compliance with laws).

[ii]—Economic Terms

Each lease agreement usually contains sections relating to: (1) base rent and escalations, (2) terms of lease and renewal periods, (3) tenant's share of real estate taxes and operating expenses and (4) financing of leasehold improvements (lessor's property versus tenant's property).

[iii]—Partners' Liability

As is the case in borrowing agreements, the content of the partners' liability section of the lease agreement is controversial and subject to substantial negotiation. In addition to the partnership's responsibility to make the rental payments, the personal responsibility (if any) of the individual partners must be addressed. Partners prefer to have no individual responsibility for obligations of the firm under the lease, and lessors prefer to have each partner jointly and severally liable. In some instances, the parties have agreed to a maximum personal liability concept (e.g., if the lease calls for aggregate rental payments of $20 million, the maximum liability of individual partners is $5 million in the aggregate).

[b]—Financial Conditions and Ratios

Certain lease agreements provide for the exemption from personal liability of active partners and the release from personal liability when a partner withdraws, retires or dies, but only when the partnership is able to meet certain financial conditions or ratios.

[i]—Minimum Net Worth

Under some lease agreements partners are exempted or released from personal liability if the firm's finances meet a minimum net worth or minimum net income test. To avoid future misunderstandings, it is important that definitions of the term "net worth" and the mechanics of their calculation be clearly set forth in the lease agreement.

[ii]—Minimum Coverage Ratio

Under other lease agreements, partners are exempted or released from personal liability if the firm's finances meet a minimum coverage ratio. Because this ratio could be calculated in many ways, details of the components of and methodology for the calculation should be included in the lease agreement. One method of calculating this ratio is as follows:

Coverage (as defined):	
Cash	$ 20,000,000
Fees receivable aged under 1 year	50,000,000
Unbilled fees aged under 1 year	80,000,000
	$150,000,000
Gross Rent (as defined):	
Base rent	$ 45,000,000
Tenant's share of real estate taxes and operating expenses	5,000,000
	$ 50,000,000
Coverage Ratio:	
As calculated	3 to 1
Minimum	2 to 1
Condition satisfied?	Yes

[c]—Compliance Letters

Some lease agreements require the firm to provide an annual compliance letter signed by a partner certifying that the firm is in compliance with financial conditions and/or required ratios specified in the agreement. In circumstances where the lease commitment is substantial in amount, the lessor may also require an auditor's negative assurance letter similar in format to letters issued under loan agreements.

§ 25.03 Developing a Suitable Capital Structure and Financing Plan

What is the ideal capital structure for a law firm? The answer depends on the firm history, culture, and partners' perspective and expectations.

While the ideal capital structure may vary from firm to firm, this section sets forth an illustration of how a law firm might develop a capital structure and financing plan to suit its particular needs. The process consists of three steps:

(1) Understanding financing requirements;
(2) Identifying appropriate financing methods; and
(3) Matching financing requirements with financing methods.

[1]—Understanding Financing Requirements

Before choosing a financing method, it is important for the law firm's financial planning team to understand each component of the firm's financing requirements. Five components have been selected for illustration purposes.

For purposes of illustration, it is assumed that the firm will occupy and need financing to:

(1) Lease the use of several floors in a new office building and will not purchase the property;

(2) Spend substantial sums on leasehold improvements and equipment;

(3) Maintain working capital equivalent to one and one-half months' operating expenses;

(4) Cover approximately four months of unbilled and uncollected fees and disbursements; and

(5) Fund a program providing modest income to retired partners (presumed that partners will fund their own retirement obligation).

[a]—Office Space

As a result of practice growth and/or mergers, a sizable number of law firms have been moving offices to new and larger quarters. A few of these law firms have chosen to purchase a building or a condominium section of a building to house their activities, either because of their size or because they perceived an opportunity to participate in the property's potential appreciation. On the other hand, most law firms have chosen not to purchase their office space, because of either their size, their desire to avoid the risk associated with the rise and fall of real estate values, or their desire to avoid the distractions that operating an office building could have on their law practice.[1]

[b]—Property and Equipment

A law firm's move to a new office building usually involves the outlay of substantial funds for constructing leasehold improvements (unless the landlord undertakes the responsibility for funding all or a portion of the improvements through a work letter) and for the purchase of new furniture, office equipment and computers.

[c]—Working Capital

There is no clear-cut answer to the question, "How much working capital should a law firm maintain?" It usually depends on how much risk the partners are willing to take should the firm experience a temporary shortfall in cash flow from a sudden downturn in the economy, a change in direction in the legal environment, a seasonal slowdown in the firm's collection process, or a breakdown in the firm's billing system. Over the years, more than a few firms have used between two and three months of operating expenses as a "rule of thumb" in deciding how much working capital they plan to maintain to protect against these risks. The rule of thumb, however can be very misleading, especially for a law firm that has multiple domestic or international offices, a number of contingent cases, or significant client disbursements (e.g., patent renewal fees, "Blue Sky" fees, or significant litigation costs).

[d]—Unbilled and Uncollected Fees

For most law firms, the billing and collection cycle for fees and disbursements averages between three and five months.

[e]—Partners' Retirement

Historically, many law firms had unfunded partner retirement programs and consequently paid partners' retirement obligations out of profits. In recent years, some firms have shifted this burden to the individual partners by requiring partners to fund their own retirement obligations through defined contribution plans (e.g., profit-sharing plans or 401(k) plans) or defined contribution plans.

---

[1] See Chapter 29 for an illustration of a lease vs. buy model for non-real estate (computer) equipment.

[2]—Identifying Appropriate Financing Methods

Once the firm's financing requirements are known, it is time to identify an appropriate financing method for each requirement. In the following paragraphs, a specific financing method has been identified for each of the five financing requirements and the reasons for each selection have been described. The purpose of this discussion is to describe how to select a financing method and illustrate one example. Obviously, if financing requirements are different, a different choice of financing methods may be appropriate.

[a]—Using Leases to Finance Office Space

Since the law firm in the illustration has decided not to purchase property to house its office space, the decision to enter a lease to finance the office space is self-evident. It is also a logical choice, because it matches cash outflow (through rent payments) with use of the premises.

[b]—Using Borrowing to Finance Property and Equipment

Partners who gain the benefit of the use of property and equipment should bear the burden of financing the use of these assets. Consequently, borrowing to finance property and equipment spending is a logical choice. While it is not always possible to arrange the repayment of debt to coincide with the useful life of these assets, it is important to keep this objective in mind during debt agreement negotiations.

[c]—Using Partners' Capital to Finance Working Capital

The law firm in the illustration determined to maintain working capital equivalent to two and one-half months' operating expenses as a buffer against sudden unforeseen business risks, based on an industry "rule of thumb."

[d]—Using Partners' Memorandum Equity to Finance Unbilled and Uncollected Fees

Partners' equity in unbilled and uncollected fees is not included in a law firm's financial statements when the firm uses the modified cash basis method of accounting; however, most firms keep track of this information through memorandum records. When unbilled and uncollected fees are financed through partners' memorandum equity, it provides a continuing incentive for partners to bill and collect fees so that cash will become available for partners' distributions. This incentive disappears if borrowings are used to finance these assets (other than on a temporary basis arising from seasonal collection trends).

[e]—Using Partners' Funded Retirement Plans to Finance Partners' Retirement Obligations

Notwithstanding the practices of the past, the logical approach to financing partners' retirement benefits is to require partners to fund these benefits during their working years through contributions to a funded retirement plan for partners. When firms historically have maintained an unfunded program, in fairness to partners who are at or near retirement, the change to a funded program approach should include a phase-in period.

[3]—Matching Financing Requirements with Financing Methods

The final step in developing a suitable capital structure and financing plan is to match the firm's financing requirements with the appropriate financing methods that have been identified as being applicable in the circumstances. This matching process is summarized below, based on the assumptions used in the illustration.

Financing Requirements	Financing Method Selected
1—Office Space	1—Leasing
2—Property & Equipment	2—Borrowing
3—Working Capital Assets	3—Partners' Permanent Capital
4—Unbilled & Uncollected Fees	4—Partners' Memorandum Equity
5—Partners' Retirement Obligations	5—Partners' Funded Retirement Plan

Figure 25-L illustrates the financing impact of financing these assets and other requirements using the financing methods selected.

Once the firm has developed its proposed capital structure and financing plan, it is important to review it in the context of the firm's bank loan agreements to ensure that the ratio of equity-to-debt on both the cash basis and the accrual basis are within the parameters established in the loan agreement. For example, a typical loan agreement between a large law firm and a large bank may indicate that the minimum capital requirements call for an equity versus debt ratio in the range of 1.5:1 to 3:1 (on an accrual basis).

The firm should also review its proposed capital structure and financing plan in the context of the partners' objective to achieve a well-balanced debt-to-equity ratio on an economic basis.

Figure 25-L. Illustration of an example of financing certain assets and other requirements of a law firm using selected financing methods.

ABC LAW FIRM
MATCHING FINANCING REQUIREMENTS WITH
FINANCING METHODS

	Cash Basis	Accrual Basis	Economic Basis
Financing requirements:			
1—Office Space			$120,000,000
2—Property & Equipment	$30,000,000	$30,000,000	30,000,000
3—Working Capital Assets	10,000,000	10,000,000	10,000,000
4—Unbilled & Uncollected Fees		80,000,000	80,000,000
5—Partners' Pension Requirements			60,000,000
	$40,000,000	$120,000,000	$300,000,000
Financing methods:			
1—Lease Obligations			$120,000,000
2—Bank Loans	$30,000,000	$30,000,000	30,000,000
3—Partners' Permanent Capital	10,000,000	10,000,000	10,000,000
4—Partners' Memorandum Equity		80,000,000	80,000,000
5—Partners' Funded Retirement Plan			60,000,000
	$40,000,000	$120,000,000	$300,000,000
Ratio of Equity to Debt	1:3	3:1	1:1

CHAPTER 26

Pricing Strategies

Chapter Contents

---

§ 26.01 Law Firm Pricing Strategies: An Overview

Clients usually receive two types of communications from their lawyers: (1) an oral or written report covering the matter for which they were retained and (2) a bill for services rendered. Preparation of the substantive report involves a significant amount of the lawyers' time and energy. It is also very important for the lawyers to spend time and energy in determining the amount of fees to be billed to clients based on a well-thought-out and supportable pricing strategy.

When formulating a pricing strategy a law firm should refer to, among other things, the guidance provided by the American Bar Association's Model Code of Professional Responsibilities for Lawyers (the "Model Code") and the American Bar Association Formal Opinion 93-379, Billing for Professional Fees, Disbursements and Other Expenses (the "Opinion"). In summary, the Model Code, in particular Canon 2, discusses the factors involved in determining a pricing strategy such as the amount of work involved, the experience, reputation and ability of the lawyer, time limits imposed by the client or circumstances and the results obtained. The Opinion discusses the communication of legal service fees and other charges to clients, costs to be included in the formulation of billing rates, and the billing of legal and other (both third party and in-house) services to clients. Both the Model Code and the Opinion should be carefully considered by a law firm before a pricing strategy is finalized and executed.

This chapter discusses three types of law firm pricing strategies: (1) cost-based pricing using hourly rates, (2) value-based pricing using hourly rates and (3) alternative pricing. While the vast majority of economic relationships with clients are still based on the traditional standard hourly rate-times-hours expended concept, alternative pricing arrangements have begun to gain popularity over the past several years. Driving this trend is increased competition for clients among law firms, the desire among clients to manage their legal costs, and the willingness of law firms to enter into alternative arrangements with clients in exchange for the expectation of receiving a certain volume of work.

§ 26.02 Cost-Based Pricing Using Hourly Rates

Cost-based pricing is a highly structured strategy. Under this strategy, billing rates are a function of costs, thus the appropriate costs must be identified and estimated. Creating a cost-based pricing structure involves understanding: (1) pricing factors, (2) pricing methodology for staff services, (3) pricing methodology for ancillary services and (4) the pricing model.

The methodology employed for developing a cost-based pricing system using hourly rates entails the calculation of hourly cost factors for fee earners. These hourly cost factors are composed of both compensation (including benefits) of the timekeeper and a general overhead allocation. They represent an estimation of the cost to the firm of a particular fee earner performing an hour of work, to ultimately be used in determining the price to be charged to the client for that hour.

[1]—Pricing Factors

There are three principal factors that underlie a cost-based pricing structure. They are: (1) staff mix, (2) compensation and other costs and (3) lawyers' utilization.

[a]—Staff Mix

There are three components underlying staff mix in a cost-based pricing structure:

[i]—Staff Classifications

This component focuses on the various classifications of staff that the law firm has identified as "timekeepers" (i.e., individuals who will be assigned a billing rate). Generally, at a minimum, these classifications include (1) partners, (2) associates, (3) paralegals and (4) certain support personnel (e.g., word processors, litigation support personnel, librarians, and other research personnel). Other staff classifications used include non-equity partners, of counsel, and senior and staff attorneys.

[ii]—Staff Levels

This component focuses on the levels that the firm has identified within each staff classification. For example, partners can be subdivided into groups based on years since admission to the partnership or by level of expertise; associates can be subdivided into groups based on years since graduation from law school, etc.

[iii]—Staff Leverage

This component focuses on the relationship between one staff level and another. For example, a law firm can decide on a staff structure consisting of two associates for each partner and one secretary for every two lawyers.

Figure 26-A illustrates an example of staff mix underlying a law firm's cost-based pricing structure.

[b]—Compensation and Support Costs

There are three types of compensation and support costs underlying a law firm's cost-based pricing structure:

[i]—Imputed Equity Partner Compensation

Equity partners share in the profits of the firm; consequently their compensation is not listed as a "cost" in the financial records of a typical law firm partnership. However because equity partner time is an essential part of each client engagement, it is important to establish a "cost" for such time. To achieve this goal, imputed costs can be developed (e.g., either by reference to (a) notional compensation levels paid to client service attorneys with similar years of experience to the equity partner or group of equity partners in question, or (b) compensation paid to comparable executives) and ascribed to equity partner compensation. Imputed compensation amounts can be developed by the law firm for each level of experience within the equity partner classification.

Figure 26-A. Illustration of staff mix underlying a law firm's cost-based pricing structures (for firms with no non-equity partners).

ABC LAW FIRM
STAFF MIX

Staff Classification	Staff Level	Staff Leverage (Number of Staff)
Equity Partners (based on admission date):		
Seven or more years	1	25
Four through six years	2	50
One through three years	3	60
Associates (based on law school graduation date):		
Seven or more years	1	30
Four through six years	2	90
One through three years	3	145
Paralegals (based on college graduation date):		
Three or more years	1	15
One through two years	2	25
Word processors (based on hire date):		
Three or more years	1	5
One through two years	2	5
		450

[ii]—Associate and Staff Compensation

The law firm can develop compensation amounts for each level of experience within the associate, paralegal, word processor, or other "timekeeper" staff classification. This compensation includes salary, bonus, and fringe benefits.

[iii]—Support Costs

These costs include the salaries of administrative employees, occupancy costs, and other operating expenses. A practical approach to including these costs as a pricing factor is to apportion them among the firm's attorneys using (1) an "average cost per lawyer" factor, or (2) an overhead percentage factor. Using the average cost per lawyer method, for example, if a firm had support costs of $50 million and 400 lawyers, the average cost per lawyer would be $125,000.

Figure 26-B illustrates compensation and support costs underlying a law firm's cost-based pricing structure.

ABC LAW FIRM
COMPENSATION AND SUPPORT COSTS

* Imputed costs.

Staff Classification	Staff Level	Base Compensation	Support Costs	TotalCost
Partner	1	$400,000*	$125,000	$525,000
	2	300,000*	125,000	425,000
	3	250,000*	125,000	375,000
Associate	1	200,000	125,000	325,000
	2	150,000	125,000	275,000
	3	115,000	125,000	240,000
Paralegal	1	50,000	—	50,000
	2	35,000	—	35,000
Word Processors	1	35,000	—	35,000
	2	25,000	—	25,000

---

[c]—Lawyers and Other Timekeepers' Utilization

In order to determine the average billable hours to be included in a cost-based pricing structure, a lawyer utilization rate must be established. For example: assume that 2,000 hours represents 100% utilization (based on forty hours in a week multiplied by fifty work weeks in a year). Based on this assumption, a lawyer logging 1,800 chargeable hours would have a 90% utilization rate (1,800 divided by 2,000).

Figure 26-C illustrates lawyer and staff utilization underlying a law firm's cost-based pricing structure.

ABC LAW FIRM
LAWYER AND STAFF UTILIZATION
(2,000 hours = 100% Utilization)

Staff Classification	Staff Level	Estimated Utilization Percentage	Projected Average Chargeable Hours
Partner	1	90%	1,800
	2	93%	1,860
	3	93%	1,860
Associate	1	93%	1,860
	2	95%	1,900
	3	95%	1,900
Paralegal	1	65%	1,300
	2	65%	1,300
Word Processor	1	50%	1,000
	2	50%	1,000

[2]—Pricing Methodology for Staff Services

Pricing law firm staff services, using a cost-based pricing structure, consists of two steps. They are (1) cost determination and (2) rate setting.

[a]—Cost Determination

This step consists of compiling the hourly costs of providing a law firm's services for a given year. It involves the interaction of (1) compensation and support costs with (2) lawyer's utilization.

[b]—Rate Setting

This step consists of establishing a planned profit margin for the firm (for example, 20%, including imputed partner compensation) and applying this profit margin to the firm's hourly cost rate to arrive at an hourly billing rate. Additionally, when finalizing its hourly billing rates a law firm must consider the rates currently being charged in the marketplace by other law firms for similar staff services.

Figure 26-D illustrates an example of a cost determination and rate setting exercise underlying a law firm's cost-based pricing structure.

ABC LAW FIRM
SUMMARY OF COST-DETERMINATION
AND RATE-SETTING EXERCISE

Staff Classification	Staff Level	Compensation & Support Costs	Projected Average Chargeable Hours	Estimated Cost Per Hour	Projected Billing Rate Per Hour at 120%
Partner	1	$525,000	1,800	$292	$350
	2	$425,000	1,860	228	274
	3	$375,000	1,860	202	242
Associate	1	$325,000	1,860	175	210
	2	$275,000	1,900	145	174
	3	$240,000	1,900	126	151
Paralegal	1	$ 50,000	1,300	38	46
	2	$ 35,000	1,300	27	32
Word Processor	1	$ 35,000	1,000	35	42
	2	$ 25,000	1,000	$ 25	$ 30

[3]—Pricing Methodology for Ancillary Services

Ancillary services in a law firm represent those services provided to the law firm client which are an integral part of the service provided by the lawyer or his staff but are not directly provided by the individual lawyer. They include reproduction, facsimile transmission, and similar services.

Law firms that bill for ancillary services generally choose to do so because they are experiencing a high volume of ancillary services for certain of their clients. Rather than increase lawyers' billing rates to all clients, they believe that it is fairer to bill these ancillary services only to those clients who utilize them. Billing ancillary services involves "unbundling" the cost of these services and then establishing appropriate billing rates for them. As prescribed by the ABA Formal Opinion, specific charges for ancillary services may be agreed to with the client in advance or, in the absence of such an agreement, the lawyer may charge no more than the direct cost associated with the service plus a reasonable allocation of overhead expenses associated with the provision of the service (e.g., salary of photocopy machine operator), with no increment added for profit.

Figure 22-E illustrates a summary compilation of billing rates for ancillary services underlying a law firm's cost-based pricing structure.

ABC LAW FIRM
SUMMARY COMPILATION OF BILLING RATES
FOR ANCILLARY SERVICES

	Reproduction Services	Facsimile Transmission Services
Salaries & Fringe Benefits	$ 80,000	$20,000
Third Party Charges	20,000	5,000
Equipment Costs	12,000	3,000
Occupancy Expenses	8,000	2,000
Total Costs	$120,000	$30,000
Number of Copies Produced	1,000,000	65,000
Billing Rate per Copy	12¢	46¢

[4]—Pricing Model

Once the pricing factors for staff services have been determined and a pricing methodology for ancillary services has been developed, the law firm can then organize this information in an orderly manner in the form of a pricing model. A pricing model provides the firm with a vehicle to illustrate alternative billing scenarios by varying staff mix, compensation and support costs, lawyer's utilization, and profit margin.

Figure 26-F illustrates a pricing model underlying a law firm's cost-based pricing structure.

		Pricing Factors			Per Staff member		Aggregate ($ in Millions)	
Staff Class	Staff Level	# of Staff	Chargeable Hours	Billing Rate	Billings Value	Cost Value	Billing Value	Cost Value
Partner	1	25	1,800	$350	$630,000	$525,000*	$ 15,750	$ 13,125*
	2	50	1,860	$274	$509,640	$425,000*	25,482	21,250*
	3	60	1,860	$242	$450,120	$375,000*	27,007	22,500*
Associate	1	30	1,860	$210	$390,600	$325,000	11,718	9,750
	2	90	1,900	$174	$330,600	$275,000	29,754	24,750
	3	145	1,900	$151	$286,900	$240,000	41,601	34,800
Paralegal	1	15	1,300	$ 46	$ 59,800	$ 50,000	897	750
	2	25	1,300	$ 32	$ 41,600	$ 35,000	1,040	875
Word Processor	1	5	1,000	$ 42	$ 42,000	$ 35,000	210	175
	2	5	1,000	$ 30	$ 30,000	$ 25,000	150	125
Ancillary Services**	—	—	—	—	—	—	150	150
		450					$153,759	$128,250

* Imputed cost.

** Does not include a profit margin.

Based on the information illustrated in this pricing model, the law firm projects the following profit:

	Billing Value	Cost Value	Profit	Approximate Profit Percentage
Pricing Model	$153,844	$128,250	$25,594	17%
Eliminate Imputed Partner Compensation	—	(40,000)	40,000	
Deduct Estimated Unrealizable Portion of Billing Value @ 15%	(23,077)	—	(23,077)	
Projected Operating Results	$130,768	$88,250	$42,518	33%

§ 26.03 Value-Based Pricing Using Hourly Rates

Value-based pricing using hourly rates provides more flexibility than the cost-based version. Under this strategy, billings are rendered based on criteria other than cost. An example of value-based pricing is variable rate structures. Variable rate structures can be designed to increase or decrease an individual lawyer's billing rate to take into account the "perceived value" to the client of the services being provided. For example, a law firm might adopt the following variable rate structure for services provided to a client bank:

Type of Work	Billing Rates
Litigation Work	10% increase
Merger & Acquisition work	10% increase
Corporate Work	Regular rates
Tax Work	Regular rates
Real Estate Closings	10% decrease
Trust & Estate Work	10% decrease

Another example of value-based pricing using hourly rates is for the law firm and client to agree upon the hourly rates of various staff levels at the outset of a particular matter, based on the matter's anticipated complexity, the relevant expertise of the law firm, and the relative importance of the matter to the client.

§ 26.04 Alternative Pricing

As previously described, the most common billing methodology used by law firms is multiplying hourly rates of the persons working on the matter by the hours worked. For many kinds of matters, this hourly-rate method serves well. However, many law firms and their clients are seeking to develop other pricing strategies when they might be advantageous.

This section presents alternative pricing approaches that should be considered in light of concerns about the hourly rate system. It reviews important considerations that surround the use of alternative pricing arrangements. The chart at the end of this section provides a list of alternative pricing methods, including a brief description and summary of the advantages and disadvantages of each method.

[1]—Concerns with the Hourly Rate System

Before the 1960s, law firms billed clients on the basis of an unwritten but clear understanding of what the value of the services was to the client. This was in an era when legal matters were less difficult, complex and time-consuming. Billable hours and rates were later developed as an easier way for firms to make that value judgment as they grew, became more profitable and competitive, and adopted more business-oriented management methods.

Thus, for the past several decades, the vast majority of law firms have relied almost exclusively on separate hourly rates for their timekeepers as their principal billing method. Most firms billed their services at standard hourly rates times the number of hours incurred. In some instances, fees were "written up" or "written down" depending on the nature of the matter and the firm's perception of the quality and value of its services on the matter.

Over this period of time, it has become clear that the hourly rate system, combined with other forces at work in the legal market, is not amenable to cost reduction efforts. Using an hourly rate system increases the incentive of lawyers to devote as many hours as possible to a matter in order to increase firm revenues. Many corporations and their general counsel, in public forums, have repeatedly cited instances in which the hourly rate billing system rewarded inefficiency, penalized productivity, and reduced the value received by the client.

Common problems cited include: overstaffing of projects; having two or more attorneys present at all meetings; billing clients for training brand-new associates and for training replacements; excessive pretrial discovery; time devoted to marginal problems or premature work; engaging in too many internal conferences and strategy sessions; waiting too long to enter into serious settlement discussions; and pressuring associates to generate billable hours as a goal in and of itself.

[2]—Reasons for Adopting Alternative Pricing

There are four principal factors which have promoted the increased consideration and adoption of alternative pricing methods: (1) distorted incentives in hourly rate systems, (2) suitability of alternative pricing, (3) acceptance of alternative pricing and (4) available information on alternative pricing.

[a]—Distorted Incentives in Hourly Rate System

As noted above, there is a widespread perception that the hourly rate system encourages inefficiency, excess hours not desired by the client or warranted by the matter, and expenditures of effort unrelated to the value received. Of course, this assumption, for a number of reasons, is not always correct, including: (1) outside counsel want to provide legal services efficiently because they want satisfied customers and additional work, (2) law firms are increasingly competitive and recognize that they must be responsive to their clients' increasing cost consciousness, and (3) lawyers often feel a professional obligation to do work efficiently and to provide value of their services. Still, the perception is strong and widespread and therefore a major stimulus to the exploration and adoption of other approaches.

[b]—Suitability of Alternative Pricing

There is a growing recognition by both inside and outside counsel that legal services can be differentiated according to their complexity, uniqueness and risk. Over time, types of legal services have a life cycle in which they enter the market as original and valuable and then gradually become more like a commodity. Seeking cost containment and alternative pricing can be viewed in the context of the nature of the service being supplied and the manner in which it should be supplied. The hourly rate system makes more sense for a new or highly valuable "product" or service than it does for a commodity product or service. Some percentage of legal services and tasks is sufficiently routine and predictable that it can be viewed as a commodity-like service which could be subject to lower rates and more fixed pricing than obtained through standard hourly rate pricing.

[c]—Acceptance of Alternative Pricing

Alternative pricing has come to be an acceptable concept to both inside and outside counsel. Many outside counsel face extraordinary cost reduction pressures from inside counsel, leading to greater innovation in development of outside counsel management programs, including the promotion of alternative pricing methods. On the supply side, law firms face unprecedented competition due to the growing numbers of lawyers and law firms, leading to far greater responsiveness to alternative pricing ideas. In some cases, law firms have taken the lead in defining and offering such approaches.

[d]—Available Information on Alternative Pricing

There is a growing body of information, experience and case studies available through national, business and trade press articles, conferences, and general communications within the legal industry, including publications such as the American Bar Association's *Beyond the Billable Hour*. These sources confirm the transition to alternative pricing practices.

[3]—Relationship to Corporate Planning and Budgeting

There is some confusion about the difference between using sound management techniques, such as planning, budgeting and reporting requirements, and negotiating alternative pricing arrangements. In many cases, a corporate client's cost reduction and control objectives will be largely achieved through the adoption and enforcement of agreed upon planning, budgeting and bill reporting requirements. These methods require the client and the law firm to define scope, requirements and expectations. Many corporations have found that managing the process (i.e., defining scope, and managing activities, time, and deliverables) rather than focusing on billing rates, has provided them with sufficient control over costs. In addition, teamwork, including shared staffing arrangements, can also have a great impact on reducing the costs of legal services.

[4]—Types of Alternative Pricing

In general, alternative pricing methods can be grouped under the following categories:

[a]—Hourly Rate Basis

There are several variants on the use of Standard Hourly Rates, including Discounted Hourly Rates, Blended Hourly Rates, Bulk or Volume Hourly Rates, Partner-Based Rates, Capped Rates and Cost-Plus Billing. The focus of these alternatives is cost containment or reduction.

[b]—Results Basis

Several alternative pricing methods emphasize tying the law firm's compensation to the results achieved. Examples include Value Billing, Contingency Billing, Incentive Billing and Use of Legal Work Codes.

[c]—Budget Basis

Several alternative pricing methods emphasize planning, budgeting and predictability through fixed price matter or task billing. These include Phased Billing, Fixed Fee Billing, and Capped Task Billing.

[d]—Relationship Basis

Several pricing methods, such as the Retainer approach, relate to the overall relationship between a law firm and its client. In some cases, such as the temporary outsourcing approach, law firm resources are loaned to the client at an advantageous rate to deepen the relationship with the client.

[e]—Combination Basis

Many combinations using the pricing methods previously discussed and/or other alternatives can be developed to tailor a pricing strategy to a specific situation.

[5]—Advantages and Disadvantages

Figure 22-G provides a definition of seventeen different alternative pricing methods along with a summary of the advantages and disadvantages of each method.

Figure 22-G. Comparison of Pricing Methods.

ALTERNATIVE PRICING METHODS
FOR LEGAL SERVICES

PRICING METHOD	ADVANTAGES	DISADVANTAGES
	Hourly Rate Basis	
Standard Hourly Rates Bills are based on the hours worked by outside counsel staff multiplied by their standard hourly rates.	Identifies standard unit of work Permits comparison of rates among outside counsel Time and billing systems handle well Most familiar to outside counsel and clients	Encourages inefficiency, may prolong work Ignores per hour value of work done Bears little relation to results or value obtained for client Involves time-consuming record-keeping and bill preparation by outside counsel Requires detailed analysis by inside staff

Discounted Hourly Rates Outside counsel reduces its normal hourly billing rates by some percentage.	Lowers cost of hourly-based services Identifies standard unit of work Convenient basis for negotiation Flexible (could vary by type and work)	Requires subjective decisions on discount Involves time-consuming record-keeping and bill preparation by outside counsel Requires detailed analysis by inside staff Neither rewards nor provides incentive for efficiency
Blended Hourly Rates Hourly rates of all attorneys working on a matter are averaged, negotiated and established at the outset of a matter. Blended rates depend on the mix of staff. The result is a single hourly rate used for all attorneys rather than separate hourly rates for each attorney.	Encourages more efficient staffing Avoids charges of high partner rates Permits simpler record-keeping and billing for outside counsel Simplifies budgeting Simplifies bill review	Creates incentive to reduce partner and senior attorney involvement and to delegate work to more junior staff, which may be less efficient and result in more overall required hours May require designating certain lawyers to perform key tasks Conceals individual contributions
Bulk or Volume Hourly Rates Outside counsel offers discounts in standard billing rates due to the volume of work assigned or expected to be assigned over a period of time. Usually the client makes a commitment to a certain minimum level of hours. In some cases, different amounts of hours may trigger different billing rates.	Outside counsel can offer better terms based on a predictable stream of work Routine matters that have similar characteristics (e.g., foreclosures) may be assembled as pools to solicit quotes from outside counsel and obtain the most competitive rates. Pooled matters suggest the opportunity for systems, procedures and automation.	May be difficult to bundle enough similar matters Company policy may prohibit promising future legal work. Can lead to low-quality, minimalist services if not properly supervised

Partner-Based Rates Partners receive an hourly rate substantially greater than their usual rates, but no fees are paid for associates and paralegals.	Creates a disincentive for using associates Focuses on use of experienced lawyers Applies best in staffing specialized matters such as high-level transactions	Encourages partners to perform work that could be handled by more junior staff, thus discouraging leverage where it would be appropriate Mostly useful for small outside counsel Little previous use in legal industry Difficult to accommodate in existing time and billing systems
Capped Rates Outside counsel agrees not to charge more than a certain amount per hour (e.g., $300) for any attorney or more than a certain amount of hours for a task (e.g., 7 hours for closing).	Clarifies acceptable billing limits Relatively easy to administer Helps keep costs down for routine matters	May discourage best lawyers from providing services May lead to lower quality of legal services Requires data and experience to set caps properly
Cost Plus Billing Hourly billing rates are established for partners, associates, and paralegals based on actual costs and then an agreed profit per case would be added to the cost-based hourly reimbursement. The profit could be adjusted depending upon the outcome of a case (e.g., premium for early settlement, successful litigation results).	Provides an incentive for outside counsel to deal with a matter efficiently and in a way that is most beneficial to the client Encourages consideration of the value of services rendered by means of assigning profit per case	Difficult to determine mutually acceptable profit Difficult for outside counsel to calculated actual costs Outside counsel may be reluctant to reveal actual costs May provide inappropriate incentive for early settlement

Results Basis

Value Billing Outside counsel bills based on its determination of the value to the client of the services rendered. Incentive bonuses could be established for resolving cases before a specific period of time or within a specified dollar amount.	Provides incentives for efficiently using resources as well as a focus on results Encourages outside counsel to use their best legal skills Allows outside counsel to escape the confines of hourly billing Rewards performance and results rather than hours worked	Challenge of agreeing to fair fee Obstructs budgeting in advance May be difficult to monitor and direct outside counsel's activities, since fees are tied to results Removes quantifiable measures (hours) that aid in comparisons of quality of work
Contingency Billing Payments to outside counsel depend on the amount collected or saved, or other result obtained (e.g., 25% of amounts collected). For defense cases, a reasonable value would be assigned to a case at the outset to include projected indemnity and legal costs. Outside counsel would obtain a percentage of the savings obtained. Another contingency variation is that a prevailing firm is paid more than 100% of its standard hourly fees, whereas a losing firm is paid less than 100% of its hourly fees.	Common form of billing for certain types of matters (e.g., representing plaintiff in personal injury litigation or workers compensation suits) Outside counsel has incentives for efficiency. No payment without results Can be readily combined with other billing terms	Significant control passes to outside counsel, who determines level of effort based on likely fee. Can appear to permit "windfalls" Requires some degree of risk on part of outside counsel Outside counsel tends to be highly selective of cases Defense contingencies are not permitted in all jurisdictions

Incentive Billing Incentives can be established to reward outside counsel for expediting cases. These include bonuses for early settlement within one month of assignment, disposition by motion within six months, or completion of a trial within one year.	Legal costs are generally lower when a case is resolved expeditiously	Bonuses should be tied to results achieved The willingness of an opponent to settle may have little to do with outside counsel's performance
Use of Legal Work Codes Outside counsel record time using a chart of legal work codes (e.g., phase, task, or activity codes) provided by the client. Different code sets may be used for each area of law. Codes are most likely based on phase (e.g., discovery), task (e.g., deposition), activity (e.g., speaking on the telephone), or some combination of these concepts. Bills for each matter summarize the cost associated with the codes the client wishes to track.	Bills are meaningful in that charges are related to case milestones or activities Information recorded by each timekeeper can be summarized to provide an overall picture of the matter's cost components Clients can compare the effectiveness of different firms' handling of similar matters Firms can achieve heightened awareness of their costs for use in pricing work under alternative arrangements.	It is more difficult to creatively describe a matter if a specific code has to be used. It is easier for a third party to audit work based on standard codes and to compare one firm's charges against industry standards. Some companies, deviating from the standard UTBMS, use customized code sets which are difficult for law firms to maintain. Many clients have generated significant data but have not thought through how they will make use of it. This includes the need for meaningful management reports. Effective use of task-based billing requires an initial investment to revise billing and approval procedures.

Budget Basis		
Phased Billing A budget is negotiated between inside and outside counsel that has phases, either by time (e.g., monthly) or activity (e.g., discovery, motions, trial preparation, trial time, etc.). As bills are submitted, any amounts over the budget for the phase are put in a suspense account. Outside counsel can recoup these fees upon the successful and under-budget completion of subsequent phases. Alternatively, upon completion of the matter, both sides negotiate payment of the amount in the suspense file.	Ties budget to strategy, and disciplines counsel to adhere to the plan in an efficient manner Provides incentives to control costs and eliminates unnecessary work while rewarding successful results and early disposition Can aid in the establishment of ranges for acceptable costs for well-known tasks Fairly simple to administer; involves plan of action and budget Eliminates need to conduct detailed bill reviews to evaluate reasonableness of time charges	Useful mostly with costly litigation or transactions Relies on significant up- front planning Depends on experience with phases and costs Presents difficulties in negotiating final payment May delays cash collections
Fixed Fee Billing Outside counsel charges fixed rates for specified types of matters. Usually, counsel describes tasks that will be included in the fixed fee. Most often used for small, routine or repetitive types of matters (e.g., foreclosure).	Provides financial information useful in deciding whether to assign certain types of work outside vs. handling inside Encourages efficiencies including procedures, systems and automation Makes competitive bidding easier Encourages statistical performance measurements Eliminates need for fee bill reviews	Many matters are not routine and do not lend themselves to fixed fees. May require bulk assignment of similar matters to entice outside counsel to settle on fixed fees Outside counsel may be more likely to staff fixed- fee matters with less capable lawyers. May require extensive discussion for matters that fall outside normal parameters.

Capped Task Billing Outside counsel charges a pre-determined amount for each task (e.g., depositions are capped at $200).	Allows finer comparisons of value among outside counsel since tasks (e.g., take deposition, prepare contract) are identified and priced Forces inside counsel to describe in detail the activities associated with the legal services they are buying	May lose sight of broader objectives in concentration on detail May increase cost (although hourly rate could be reduced)
Relationship Basis		
Temporary Outsourcing Outside counsel attorney works in-house as a member of the department for a set period of time, often "at cost," with the understanding he or she will remain on the "partnership track" at his or her firm.	Fosters closer contacts between client and outside counsel Provides the client with full-time legal service in a specialized area at a reduced fee Gives valuable, company-specific training to the lawyer	Attorney will leave the department after the specified contract period expires. Department may fail to develop a needed specialty in-house
Retainers Outside counsel is paid a fixed amount each month. It deducts its fees and expenses from that amount and bills (or subtracts) the difference.	Allows client to "pick up the phone" and call his lawyer for preventative legal advice with less sensitivity to hourly cost Encourages outside counsel to offer discounts Reduces billing complexity Eases budgeting Deters outside counsel from representing competitors or adversaries	Perceived as cash outgoing without control Work may expand to fill available retainer

Combination Basis		
Combination Rates Different rate structures would be used depending on the stage of the matter. For example, fixed fee to prepare complaint and complete discovery tasks, partner-based for key depositions, value for trial.	Allows for a flexible rate structure which, if applied correctly, could maximize the benefits of each fee arrangement Approaches focus on the value of services performed Matches strength of outside counsel to billing arrangement Explicitly encourages innovative billing	Requires judgment of the in-house attorney which may result in inconsistent application May work for only high-fee cases Requires establishment of criteria for when a given billing arrangement or rate structure applies Rarely produces lower bills than hourly rates May be difficult to monitor

[6]—Considerations in Adopting Alternative Pricing

Law firms that move in the direction of developing alternative pricing approaches need to consider both the implications of those pricing strategies and implementation issues.

[a]—Understanding Implications

Alternative pricing arrangements may change the incentives and encourage the most efficient utilization of the law firm's time in handling a matter. Changing the incentive system, however, may create new distortions, adversely affecting the quality of representation and shifting costs to other areas, such as settlements. Thus, careful consideration of alternative mechanisms is essential before they are adopted widely. Moreover, the effectiveness of different alternatives may vary according to several variables, including the nature of the case and the lawyers handling the matter. Alternative pricing entails special responsibilities for both law firms and their clients. It requires a thorough understanding of the service to be provided, the desired results, and the degree to which the pricing method fosters that result. It also requires close communication between inside and outside counsel.

[b]—Implementation Considerations

From the law firm's perspective, the growing number of lawyers and heightened competition, along with the cost pressures emanating from clients are unprecedented. In such an environment, law firm managers need to establish controls to avoid entering into economic arrangements with clients without fully analyzing all dimensions and their implications. Moreover, law firms need to develop financial information systems to provide the kind of cost data necessary to support sophisticated variable pricing and profitability analysis approaches as well as to support the matter budgeting and management needs of the lawyers. Finally, agreement with the firm's clients regarding the way in which they will be billed is another essential implementation consideration.

§ 26.05 Pricing Goals: Adapting to Competitive and Client Challenges

Law firms should seek to use fee arrangements that provide the best possible result in the most efficient way at a reasonable cost to their clients. A fee arrangement that simply reduces costs without obtaining the best overall results would not be in the client's interest.

At the time of undertaking a matter, the law firm should consider which fee arrangement would be most appropriate considering the characteristics of the matter. This requires an analysis of the facts and issues, total risk and exposure (both monetary and precedent-setting risk), judicial forum, and the company's experience in similar situations. In many instances, alternative pricing arrangements may be appropriate for discrete portions of a matter as opposed to the entire matter.

Most clients will not want to compromise quality in achieving their cost containment goals. To that extent, they will appreciate the efforts of law firms which initiate discussions regarding alternative methods of controlling legal costs, and will review the reasonableness of alternative billing arrangements in situations when circumstances change unexpectedly.

CHAPTER 27

Uniform Task-Based Management System

Chapter Contents

---

§ 27.01 The Internet and Task-Based Management: An Overview

Until the past decade, law firm billing was relatively straightforward. Firms billed their clients in greater or lesser detail, typically providing in-depth narrative descriptions of the tasks and processes underlying their hourly charges. In issuing bills and providing the underlying detail, each firm followed its own approach. In recent years, however, many law firms have found that their clients have become more focused in requesting budgets and additional billing information, or asking that billing data be presented in specific formats.

As a consequence of these trends, many law firms' administrative organizations have been faced with the challenge of complying with a broad range of specialized billing requirements—each unique to one client. This situation already poses a substantial burden to a number of firms.

Task-based budgeting and billing are a significant part of new management techniques instituted in the past five years. Task-based management has its roots in legal fee auditing and initially was a tool for use by clients and insurers to categorize time charges appearing on bills rendered in a standard format. Auditors would manually recategorize time charges appearing on bills in order to reach a better understanding of the work accomplished and corresponding costs.

Soon, more mainstream uses of task-based management became apparent to corporate counsel and law firm attorneys. The focus of task-based management has now shifted substantially away from auditing. Task-based management has become a tool for matter budgeting. Increasingly, corporate counsel strive to minimize surprises and increase the predictability of the cost of legal services. Matter budgeting has been an important vehicle for law firms to communicate and negotiate costs with clients at the outset of a matter.

Some clients have tried to simplify their legal cost management and budgeting by pursuing the strategy of fixed-price financial arrangements. For a law firm, task-based management can provide a databank of historical experience for use in pricing services. In recent years, many firms have accepted sizeable assignments under alternative financial arrangements without assurance that the work will be profitable. This knowledge comes only from an understanding of the firm's cost structure and identification of the detailed tasks to be performed in a matter. Law firms can use task-based management to build work plans based on historic experience.

Clients wishing to streamline administrative processes by receiving and approving bills electronically realized that task-based management could provide the standard invoice format necessary to accomplish this goal. The need, therefore, was for a uniform set of billing and task categories-detailed describers of legal work that would be acceptable to both clients and law firms, and could prevail across American industry, financial services, and commerce. Analogous to the role of norms in other industries and functions, standard billing categories make it possible for law firms to standardize their billing systems and for clients, including corporate law departments, to work with their law firms in a far more efficient manner than has prevailed in the past.

§ 27.02 The Internet and Uniform Task-Based Management System (UTBMS)

With the emergence of the Internet, many opportunities have arisen to leverage intellectual capital and digital information technology into client centered applications. These new Internet-based applications create a new electronic service paradigm and add value to the relationship between the law firm and the client. This new era called collaborative partnerships makes strategies, techniques and practices transparent between law firm and client. Collaborative partnerships come about because stakeholders realize that they have cost and pricing reduction opportunities. The electronic glue that holds these collaborative partnerships is called Uniform Task Based Management System (UTBMS). UTBMS is a digital standard. Digitization is the foundation for all Internet-enabled legal applications. So how do law firms adhere to the digital mode? Through UTBMS as the uniform standard that reflects the legal process. It is a task based management system and is the framework for project management and performance measurement. The UTBMS standard will make it easier, simpler, and cheaper for laws firms, clients, and stakeholders to communicate, integrate applications and continually evolve business processes electronically.

Prior to the issuance of the UTBMS standard, no consensus existed in the industry. The American Bar Association (ABA), the American Corporate Counsel Association (ACCA), a group of prominent West Coast Banks and others released code sets, largely for use in litigation. Beginning in January of 1994, those interested in task-based management began to realize that all constituents should work together to achieve consolidation of myriad code sets into a single industry standard.

[1]—The Process of Developing Industry Standard Codes

A consortium of fifty law firms and law departments, in cooperation with representatives from the Second of Litigation of the American Bar Association (ABA) and the American Corporate Counsel Association (ACCA), developed a uniform set of task-based codes to facilitate the planning, budgeting and billing of legal services. PriceWaterhouseCoopers LLP organized the consortium, coordinated the ABA and ACCA participation, and supported the project.

UTBMS was designed to provide meaningful cost information on legal services and to consolidate myriad code sets used by individual companies and firms.

The consortium has developed four distinct Code Sets:

(1) Litigation;
(2) Bankruptcy;

(3) Project (transactions, administrative filings, etc.); and
(4) General Counseling.[1]

To arrive at this result, consortium members met on several occasions to review existing code sets used by individual companies. The group devoted much effort to the clarification and definition of the codes. A primary concern with some existing code sets was the multitude of ways in which a single time entry could be coded, depending on individual interpretation. The definitions for each Code Set minimize opportunity for multiple interpretation.

[2]—Coding Structure

The UTBMS coding structure consists of two fields: tasks (embedded within phases) and activities. The Code Sets accommodate those who wish to track both tasks and activities. Whereas task codes track time associated with tangible work product accomplished (e.g., motion, deposition), activity codes describe how the work was performed (e.g., communicating, drafting). Not every law firm will use activity codes, but the coding scheme is flexible to meet the needs of those who value activity analysis. Members of the consortium discussed the desirability of coding at a lower level below task. In the interest of simplicity, though, this additional detail may be captured using narrative rather than adding more levels. This experience was borne out by those team members having direct experience with coding time.

Members of the consortium defined unique phases and tasks for each of the four Code Sets listed above. The group also defined eleven optional activity codes, which can be used in combination with any of the distinct Code Sets. This means that the activity codes used with the Litigation Code Set are identical to those used with the Project Code Set—only the phase and task codes change.

[3]—Glossary of Terms

Following is a glossary of terms that will be helpful in understanding UTBMS.

[a]—Coding Set/Coding Scheme

A list of alphanumeric codes and corresponding terms and definitions that describe the universe of legal work in a given area.

---

[1] The Bankruptcy, Project and General Counseling Code Sets have not been finalized at the time of printing and will be included in future updates.

[b]—Area of Law

A label describing a discrete area of legal practice or specialization. Examples include real estate, intellectual property, and environmental. The design of UTBMS assumes that each firm and department will define these as appropriate.

[c]—Matter Type

This designation describes or categorizes a specific legal services project for purposes of analysis and reporting. In most cases, matter types are more detailed than areas of law, though for some specialized areas of law there may not be a more detailed listing of matter types. As with the area of law designations, individual firms and departments are likely to have existing matter types for purposes of categorizing matters.

[d]—Phase

This is the highest level category in the UTBMS coding hierarchy. For litigation, examples are Pre-Trial Pleadings and Motions, and Discovery. Phases represent collections of tasks and activities that occur largely in a sequence during the course of a case or matter. Typically, timekeepers record time at the task level, but phase level time entry is also permitted. Phase level time tracking is useful in smaller cases in which task-level detail is not needed.

[e]—Task

This represents more detail under the phase level in the coding hierarchy. All tasks roll up to a phase. Tasks are intended to capture tangible work product produced or business results achieved. Tasks (or phases) are one of two fields to be recorded by timekeepers.

[f]—Activity

This is a code intended to describe how work is accomplished (e.g., communicating, drafting). Eleven activity codes have been defined for use with all four Code Sets. Activities represent the second field to be recorded (optionally) by timekeepers.

[4]—Sample Time Record

A sample time record using the Litigation Code Set appears below. This time entry contains both the traditional narrative section in addition to the task and activity codes. As timekeepers become increasingly facile with the UTBMS coding structures, it is likely that narrative descriptions will become more succinct and standardized. As with the example below, only the name of the deponent is entered and the time record becomes efficient.

Date	Task	Activity	Narrative	Time
9/1/200X	1,330 Deposition	A109 Prepare for/attend	John Smith	1.10

§ 27.03 Corporate Client Perspective

UTBMS provides clients with more informative and consistent legal bills and advances their interests in establishing matter budgets, achieving a better understanding of outside counsel costs, and comparing the effectiveness of counsel.

There are significant benefits to both law firms and clients in terms of administrative simplicity and cost reduction to be gained from standardization. By collaborating electronically, each party can significantly improve transaction processing performance as well. In addition, the development of standard billing categories permits introduction of billing based on Electronic Data Interchange (EDI). This technology is already widely employed in other areas of commercial activity. By linking the suppliers and consumers of legal services, EDI offers the prospect of "paperless billing" and a new level of administrative and cost efficiency.

Clients typically express three principal needs met by UTBMS: matter budgeting, cost analyses, and streamlined administrative processes.

[1]—Matter Budgeting

Increasingly, matter budgeting is being employed by clients wishing to control costs and by law firms wishing to proactively advise clients of costs up front. Included in the Litigation Code Set is a budgeting form that can be used for a specified timeframe or for the entire matter. This format is easily extended to other areas of law. Departments that focus more on budgeting than bill review as a means to control cost are less likely to use activity codes. Proponents of activity codes typically use this data to analyze billings after the fact.

[2]—Cost Analyses

In some instances clients have wanted to analyze their costs along various dimensions to provide benchmarks for the more systematic evaluation of legal costs. In others, there has been a desire to develop a database of costs on discrete legal activities. Most of these efforts have been part of an overriding effort to manage corporate legal expenses more effectively by considering inside/outside mix, comparative performance by attorneys and firms of discrete activities, and other aspects of cost.

Use of alternative financial arrangements, including fixed fees, is the logical outgrowth of task-based analysis. Today, many law departments seek fixed pricing as a strategy and are building data-banks to help establish fixed fee targets based on historic experience with a volume of similar work.

[3]—Streamlined Administrative Processes

There are significant benefits to both law firms and clients in terms of administrative simplicity and cost reduction to be gained from standardization. The administrative process chain (see Figure 27-A) illustrates the steps from matter planning and budgeting to billing that can be streamlined using the Code Set.

Individual law firms and clients can use the UTBMS infrastructure to develop their own guidelines for analyzing billing data. Once the data is available in electronic format, bill review can be automated, with attorney review on an exception basis (e.g., when over budget, when expenses are more than 10% of fees).

As the technology that supports the attorney desktop matures, budgeting and billing data will be easier to capture and manipulate. All relevant data, including work product, will be organized by matter or project and accessible to all attorneys who are part of the team.

§ 27.04 Law Firm Perspective

UTBMS is a great improvement over its predecessors because numerous attorneys were involved in its design. UTBMS allows law firms to avoid an intolerable proliferation of client-specific coding systems, serves as a vehicle to discuss costs with clients in a proactive manner, and provides valuable information on internal operations.

Figure 27-A. The Administrative Process Chain.

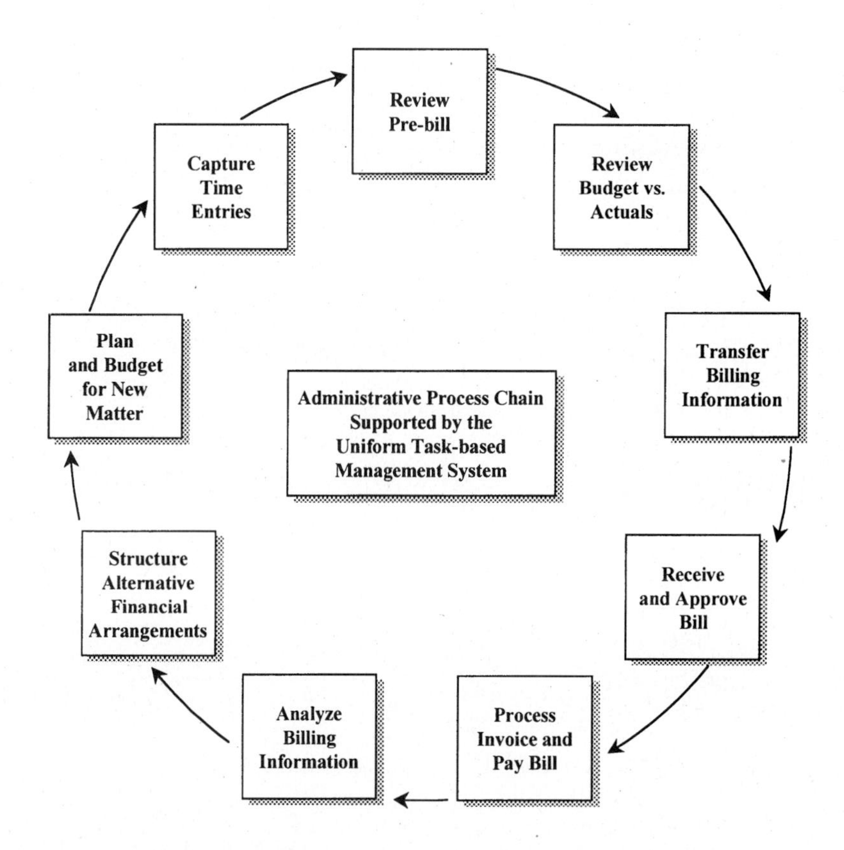

[1]—Addressing Specific Concerns of Law Firm Attorneys

[a]—Administrative Burden

The most significant concern voiced by timekeepers is the level of effort required to record time using UTBMS. For this reason, ease-of-use became a critical success factor in the design of UTBMS. The sample time entry appearing earlier in this chapter illustrates how succinct time entries will become. The universe of UTBMS codes is small and far easier to remember than a host of client-specific codes.

[b]—Micro-management by Clients

Some law firms are concerned that UTBMS will be used as an audit tool. Though some clients have instituted audit programs, many others choose instead to focus on budgeting and streamlined billing processes. The dialogue between corporate counsel and law firm attorneys that occurred during several meetings to discuss UTBMS uncovered the need of law firm partners to make clients realize the cost of legal services before work is undertaken. In several instances, the introduction of task-based budgeting changed the focus of work and the roles assumed by inside counsel without diminishing fees. In fact, fee issues were minimized because the client bought into the law firm's approach.

[c]—Confusion Over Which Code(s) to Use

A primary concern with some existing code sets was the multitude of ways in which a single time entry could be coded, depending on individual interpretation. However, the definitions for each Code Set minimize opportunity for multiple interpretation.

[2]—Adopting a Strategy to Meet Client Needs

Many leading law firms are seizing upon UTBMS as a way to satisfy client requirements by taking the following steps:

[a]—Discussions with Clients

Relationship partners are meeting with clients to explain their firm's capacity to address client concerns about cost. These discussions focus on internal firm controls and procedures and the firm's ability to implement UTBMS concepts for budgeting and billing. Some firms have circulated letters and brochures detailing their proactive approaches to meeting client needs in this area.

[b]—Modifications to Procedures and Systems

Firms are redesigning their timesheets to capture UTBMS data and designing standard reports that serve as task-based budgets and bills.

[c]—Staff Training

Once new client requirements are defined, timekeepers are trained on UTBMS concepts.

[d]—Designing Win-Win Financial Arrangements

Firms are analyzing their data to price work under alternative financial arrangements. To bid successfully on this work, law firms are turning to UTBMS as a mechanism to understand their historic costs for staffing similar matters.

§ 27.05 Guiding Principles In Forming UTBMS

It is important to understand the considerations that went into the development of consensus around a single standard. The guiding principles and assumptions behind the development of UTBMS are detailed below.

[1]—Support of Business Objectives and Processes

Members of the consortium identified a number of business objectives and administrative processes that are supported by the Uniform Task-Based Management System, including planning and budgeting, time entry, status monitoring and reporting, bill preparation, electronic transmission of bills and payments, bill review and analysis, development of alternative financial arrangements, and practice and profitability analysis. Consistently, the group returned to the question: How are we going to use the data to be tracked?

[2]—Simplicity and Ease of Use

Experience of consortium members whose firms and companies have implemented task-based budgeting and billing programs led to a fundamental guiding principle: "keep it simple." Throughout the process of developing UTBMS, consortium members continually returned to this maxim and the results are flexible Code Sets, each with a manageable number of individual tasks.

[3]—Chronology

Another important issue resolved by the consortium is that of chronology. Although the processes of litigation, administrative filings, transactions, and other large matters proceed along a timeline, the group realized that tasks are often performed out of sequence. The UTBMS Code Sets accommodate the need to record time out of sequence, and, at the same time, embrace the logical sequence of steps that occur in various types of matters.

[4]—Suitability for All Size Offices

Currently available technology will be an important asset in the efficient implementation of the coding scheme. Still, the group has assumed that not all law firms will have technology solutions at their disposal to facilitate the capture and analysis of time. Law firms and attorneys can use the codes in a manual fashion.

[5]—Avoidance of Multiple Interpretation

A primary concern with some existing code sets is the multitude of ways in which a single time entry can be coded, depending on individual interpretation. The codes should minimize opportunity for multiple interpretations.

[6]—Flexibility to Track Both Tasks and Activities

Some consortium members valued the ability to analyze work according to categories of activity (e.g., communication, drafting) in addition to task (e.g., deposition). Others emphasized the importance of tracking and analyzing the level of effort expended to complete tangible work product, segments of a case, or defined business objectives. For this group, simply using task codes is sufficient. As an option for those seeking activity detail, UTBMS permits firms and departments to code activities separately from tasks.

[7]—Use of Narrative Time Entries Retained

The design of UTBMS does not envision the elimination of narrative descriptions of time entries. However, the need for this level of detail may be reduced in smaller, less complex matters with successful adoption and implementation of the coding scheme.

[8]—Use of Matter Type Codes to Distinguish and Track Matters

A matter type designation can be used to distinguish among various types of litigation and other matters and to identify alternative dispute resolution matters. Because matter tracking and reporting is specific to every law office, members of the consortium decided not to standardize matter types. Thus, each law department and law firm can develop unique matter type codes.

[9]—Meeting the Requirements of Most Matters

The consortium designed UTBMS to be suitable for use with most matters. However, there may exist cases of such size, complexity, or other unique characteristics that the codes are not sufficiently detailed. The objective was to develop Code Sets for the vast majority of matters and to provide a framework in which more detailed codes can be developed for extraordinary matters.

§ 27.06 Litigation Code Set

The Litigation Code Set enables lawyers to budget and bill by litigation task, aiding client and counsel in understanding, managing and conducting litigation. It is intended to cover all contested matters, including judicial litigation, binding arbitration and regulatory/administrative proceedings.

The Litigation Code Set is grouped into five basic phases or aspects of litigation, plus expenses:

(1) Case Assessment, Development and Administration
(2) Pre-Trial Pleadings and Motions
(3) Discovery
(4) Trial Preparation and Trial
(5) Appeal.

Each phase consists of a number of tasks, such as Written Discovery, Document Production and Depositions. In total, 29 tasks comprise the Litigation Code Set.

All work associated with a task should be included in that category. For example, Depositions (L330) encompasses all time spent on depositions including deposition notices and subpoenas, deposition scheduling and logistics, planning for and preparing to take the depositions and any deposition summaries. The intent is to provide a true picture of the labor cost of each task. (Out-of pocket expenses, such as witness fees and transcripts, are treated under Expenses).

For each billing period, the time charges by an attorney or other professional are recorded by task. The System also allows for accumulation of the time charges, providing a comparison at a glance of the cost of each phase and each task for the month, for a specified budget period, and cumulatively for the litigation. Expenses can also be reported on a period and cumulative basis on request.

For those desiring, a budget can be prepared for each phase, and within that, each task for the whole case and/or by quarter (or other time period). The monthly bills would then compare that month's bill and the cumulative total with the budget.

The System also provides a long form for those wishing to capture the task-based work by specific activity. The activity identifies how the work is being performed (e.g., communicating in firm, researching, drafting, and reviewing). For this purpose, any or all of the eleven activities can be used with any or all of the tasks of the System.

The intention of the Litigation Code Set is to minimize multiple interpretation and options for coding time. It is recognized that not all litigation work will fit neatly in a particular category. Work can overlap tasks, categories may be imprecise, or time may be expended on the truly unusual. Users should categorize the work to its primary purpose. Definitions are provided for guidance. Where uncertainty envelops substantial or repeating work, it is best for client and counsel to agree in advance on the category to be used.

[1]—Phase and Task Codes

L100	*Case Assessment, Development and Administration*
	L110 Fact Investigation/Development
	L120 Analysis/Strategy
	L130 Experts/Consultants
	L140 Document/File Management
	L150 Budgeting
	L160 Settlement/Non-Binding ADR
	L190 Other Case Assessment, Development and Administration
L200	*Pre-Trial Pleadings and Motions*
	L210 Pleadings
	L220 Preliminary Injunctions/Provisional Remedies
	L230 Court Mandated Conferences
	L240 Dispositive Motions
	L250 Other Written Motions and Submissions
	L260 Class Action Certification and Notice
L300	*Discovery*
	L310 Written Discovery
	L320 Document Production
	L330 Depositions
	L340 Expert Discovery
	L350 Discovery Motions
	L390 Other Discovery
L400	*Trial Preparation and Trial*
	L410 Fact Witnesses
	L420 Expert Witnesses
	L430 Written Motions and Submissions
	L440 Other Trial Preparation and Support
	L450 Trial and Hearing Attendance
	L460 Post-Trial Motions and Submissions
	L470 Enforcement
L500	*Appeal*
	L510 Appellate Motions and Submissions
	L520 Appellate Briefs
	L530 Oral Argument

[2]—Activity Codes

The activity codes appearing below are intended for optional use with all four Code Sets.

A100	*Activities*
	A101 Plan and prepare for
	A102 Research
	A103 Draft/revise
	A104 Review/analyze
	A105 Communicate (in firm)
	A106 Communicate (with client)
	A107 Communicate (other outside counsel)
	A108 Communicate (other external)
	A109 Appear for/attend
	A110 Manage data/files
	A111 Other

[3]—Expense Codes

The expense codes appearing below are intended for use with all four Code Sets.

E100	*Expenses*
	E101 Copying
	E102 Outside printing
	E103 Word processing
	E104 Facsimile
	E105 Telephone
	E106 Online research
	E107 Delivery services/messengers
	E108 Postage
	E109 Local travel
	E110 Out-of-town travel
	E111 Meals
	E112 Court fees
	E113 Subpoena fees
	E114 Witness fees
	E115 Deposition transcripts
	E116 Trial transcripts
	E117 Trial exhibits
	E118 Litigation support vendors
	E119 Experts
	E120 Private investigators
	E121 Arbitrators/mediators
	E122 Local counsel
	E123 Other professionals
	E124 Other

[4]—Sample Budget/Bill Format—Litigation

L100	*Case Assessment, Development and Administration*
	L110 Fact Investigation/Development
	L120 Analysis/Strategy
	L130 Experts/Consultants
	L140 Document/File Management
	L150 Budgeting
	L160 Settlement/Non-Binding ADR
	L190 Other Case Assessment, Development and Administration
L200	*Pre-Trial Pleadings and Motions*
	L210 Pleadings
	L220 Preliminary Injunctions/Provisional Remedies
	L230 Court Mandated Conferences
	L240 Dispositive Motions
	L250 Other Written Motions and Submissions
	L260 Class Action Certification and Notice
L300	*Discovery*
	L310 Written Discovery
	L320 Document Production
	L330 Depositions
	L340 Expert Discovery
	L350 Discovery Motions
	L390 Other Discovery

[5]—Definitions

The Litigation Code Set is intended for use in all adversarial matters including litigation, binding arbitrations, and regulatory/administrative proceedings. The following definitions elaborate on the intended scope of each phase and task and should guide attorneys in coding time.

<u>L100 Case Assessment, Development and Administration.</u> Focuses on the case as a whole, the "forest" rather than the "trees."

L110 Fact Investigation/Development. All actions to investigate and understand the facts of a matter. Covers interviews of client personnel and potential witnesses, review of documents to learn the facts of the case (but not for document production, L320), work with an investigator, and all related communications and correspondence.

L120 Analysis/Strategy. The thinking, strategizing, and planning for a case, including discussions, writing, and meetings on case strategy. Also includes initial legal research for case assessment purposes and legal research for developing a basic case strategy. Most legal research will be under the primary task for which the research is conducted, such as research for a summary judgment motion (L240). Once concrete trial preparation begins, use L440 for trial strategy and planning.

L130 Experts/Consultants. Identifying and interviewing experts and consultants (testifying or non-testifying), working with them, and developing expert reports. Does not include preparing for expert depositions (L340) or trial (L420).

L140 Document/File Management. A narrowly defined task that comprises only the processes of creating and populating document and other databases or filing systems. Includes the planning, design, and overall management of this process. Work of outside vendors in building litigation support databases should be an Expense.

L150 Budgeting. Covers developing, negotiating, and revising the budget for a matter.

L160 Settlement/Non-Binding ADR. All activities directed specifically to settlement. Encompasses planning for and participating in settlement discussions, conferences, and hearings and implementing a settlement. Covers pursuing and participating in mediation and other non-binding Alternative Dispute Resolution (ADR) procedures. Also includes pre-litigation demand letters and ensuing discussions.

L190 Other Case Assessment, Development and Administration. Time not attributable to any other overall task. Specific use in a given matter often may be pre-determined jointly by the client and law firm.

L200 Pre-Trial Pleadings and Motions. Covers all pleadings and all pretrial motions and procedures other than discovery.

L210 Pleadings. Developing (researching, drafting, editing, filing) and reviewing complaints, answers, counter-claims and third party complaints. Also embraces motions directed at pleadings such as motions to dismiss, motions to strike, and jurisdictional motions.

L220 Preliminary Injunctions/Provisional Remedies. Developing and discussing strategy for these remedies, preparing motions, affidavits and briefs, reviewing opponent's papers, preparing for and attending a court hearing, preparing witnesses for the hearing, and effectuating the remedy.

L230 Court-Mandated Conferences. Preparing for and attending hearings and conferences required by court order or procedural rules (including Rule 16 sessions) other than settlement conferences (L160).

L240 Dispositive Motions. Developing and discussing strategy for or opposing motions for judgment on the pleadings and motions for complete or partial summary judgment, preparing papers, reviewing opponent's papers, defensive motions (e.g., motion to strike affidavit testimony, Rule 56(f) motion), and preparing for and attending the hearing.

L250 Other Written Motions/Submissions. Developing, responding to, and arguing all motions other than dispositive (L240), pleadings (L210), and discovery (L350), such as motions to consolidate, to bifurcate, to remand, to stay, to compel arbitration, for MDL treatment and for change of venue.

L260 Class Action Certification and Notice. Proceedings unique to class action litigation and derivative suits such as class certification and notice.

L300 Discovery. Includes all work pertaining to discovery according to court or agency rules.

L310 Written Discovery. Developing, responding to, objecting to, and negotiating interrogatories and requests to admit. Includes mandatory meet-and-confer sessions. Also covers mandatory written disclosures as under Rule 26(a).

L320 Document Production. Developing, responding to, objecting to, and negotiating document requests, including the mandatory meet-and-confer sessions to resolve objections. Includes identifying documents for production, reviewing documents for privilege, effecting production, and preparing requested privilege lists. (While a general review of documents produced by other parties falls under this task, coding and entering produced documents into a database is Task L140 and reviewing documents primarily to understand the facts is Task L110).

L330 Depositions. All work concerning depositions, including determining the deponents and the timing and sequence of depositions, preparing deposition notices and subpoenas, communicating with opposing or other party's counsel on scheduling and logistics, planning for and preparing to take the depositions, discussing deposition strategy, preparing witnesses, reviewing documents for deposition preparation, attending depositions, and drafting any deposition summaries.

L340 Expert Discovery. Same as L330, but for expert witnesses.

L350 Discovery Motions. Developing, responding to, and arguing all motions that arise out of the discovery process. Includes the protective order process.

L390 Other Discovery. Less frequently used forms of discovery, such as medical examinations and on-site inspections.

L400 Trial Preparation and Trial. Commences when lawyer and client determine that trial is sufficiently likely and imminent so that the process of actually preparing for trial begins. It continues through the trial and post-trial proceedings in the trial court. Once trial begins, lawyers who appear in court presumptively should bill their court time to L450 Trial and Hearing Attendance. Litigation work outside the courtroom during this phase (e.g., evenings, weekends and the time of other attorneys and support personnel), should continue to be classified using other L400 Tasks.

L410 Fact Witnesses. Preparing for examination and cross-examination of non-expert witnesses.

L420 Expert Witnesses. Preparing for examination and cross-examination of expert witnesses.

L430 Written Motions/Submissions. Developing, responding to and arguing written motions during preparation for trial and trial, such as motions in *limine* and motions to strike proposed evidence. Also includes developing other written pre-trial and trial filings, such as jury instructions, witness lists, proposed findings of fact and conclusions of law, and trial briefs.

L440 Other Trial Preparation and Support. All other time spent in preparing for and supporting a trial, including developing over-all trial strategy, preparing opening and closing arguments, establishing an off-site support office, identifying documents for use at trial, preparing demonstrative materials, etc.

L450 Trial and Hearing Attendance. Appearing at trial, at hearings and at court-mandated conferences, including the pre-trial conferences to prepare for trial. For scheduling conferences that are denominated as "Pre-Trial Conferences," but not directed toward conduct of the trial, use Task L230.

L460 Post-Trial Motions and Submissions. Developing, responding to and arguing all post-verdict matters in the trial court, such as motions for new trial or j.n.o.v., for stay pending appeal, bills of costs, and requests for attorney's fees.

L470 Enforcement. All work performed in enforcing and collecting judgments and asserting or addressing defenses thereto.

L500 Appeal. Covers all work on Appeal or before a reviewing body.

L510 Appellate Motions and Submissions. Developing, responding to and arguing motions and other filings before a reviewing body, such as motions and other filings for stay pending appeal.

L520 Appellate Briefs. Preparing and reviewing appellate briefs.

L530 Oral Argument. Preparing for and arguing an appeal before a reviewing body.

§ 27.07 Bankruptcy Code Set

This Code Set is intended for use on bankruptcy matters. Tasks relating to adversarial matters, such as preference actions, must be captured using the Litigation Code Set.

The Bankruptcy Code Set is derived from the code set published by the U.S. Department of Justice, Executive Office for the United States Trustee.

B100 Administration

B110 Case Administration. Coordination and compliance matters, including preparation of statement of financial affairs; schedules; list of contracts; United States Trustee interim statements and operating reports; contacts with the United States Trustee; general creditor inquiries.

B120 Asset Analysis and Recovery. Identification and review of potential assets including causes of action and non-litigation recoveries.

B130 Asset Disposition. Sales, abandonment and transaction work related to asset disposition.

B140 Relief from Stay/Adequate Protection Proceedings. Matters relating to termination or continuation of automatic stay under § 362 and motions for adequate protection.

B150 Meetings of and Communications with Creditors. Preparing for and attending the conference of creditors, the § 341(a) meeting and other creditors' committee meetings.

B160 Fee/Employment Applications. Preparations of employment and fee applications for self or others; motions to establish interim procedures.

B170 Fee/Employment Objections. Review of and objections to the employment and fee applications of others.

B180 Avoidance Action Analysis. Review of potential avoiding actions under §§ 544-549 of the Code to determine whether adversary proceedings are warranted.

B185 Assumption/Rejection of Leases and Contracts. Analysis of leases and executory contracts and preparation of motions specifically to assume or reject.

B190 Other Contested Matters (excluding assumption/rejection motions). Analysis and preparation of all other motions, opposition to motions and reply memoranda in support of motions.

B195 Non-Working Travel. Non-working travel where the court reimburses at less than full hourly rates.

B200 Operations

B210 Business Operations. Issues related to debtor-in-possession operating in Chapter 11 such as employee, vendor, tenant issues and other similar problems.

B220 Employee Benefits/Pensions. Review issues such as severance, retention, 401(k) coverage and continuance of pension plan.

B230 Financing/Cash Collections. Matters under §§ 361, 363 and 364 including cash collateral and secured claims; loan document analysis.

B240 Tax Issues. Analysis and advice regarding tax-related issues, including the preservation of net operating loss carry forwards.

B250 Real Estate. Review and analysis of real estate-related matters other than B185, including purchase agreements and lease provisions (e.g., common area maintenance clauses).

B260 Board of Directors Matters. Preparation of materials for and attendance at Board of Directors meetings; analysis and advice regarding corporate governance issues and review and preparation of corporate documents (e.g., Articles, Bylaws, employment agreements, compensation plans, etc.).

B300 Claims and Plan

B310 Claims Administration and Objections. Specific claim inquiries; bar date motions; analyses, objections and allowances of claims.

B320 Plan and Disclosure Statement. Formulation, presentation and confirmation; compliance with the plan confirmation order, related orders and rules; disbursement and case closing activities, except those related to the allowance and objections to allowance of claims.

B400 Bankruptcy-Related Advice

B410 General Bankruptcy Advice/Opinions. Analysis, advice and/or opinions regarding potential bankruptcy-related issues, where no bankruptcy cases have been filed.

B240 Restructuring. Analysis, consultation and drafting in connection with the restructuring of agreements, including financing agreements, where no bankruptcy case has been filed.

§ 27.08 Project Code Set

The Project Code Set includes all legal tasks performed for non-litigation matters of a similar task pattern described below. This Code Set applies to all areas of law and can be used for transactions (e.g., real estate, securities, financing, restructuring, mergers and acquisitions), for administrative filings with federal and state agencies, and for stand-alone projects (e.g., establishing an environmental compliance program). All of these assignments share, to a large extent, many of the same underlying process steps.

The Project Code Set is designed to be adaptable to all practice areas and matter types. As such, the phases and tasks defined in these code sets are more general in nature. The Steering Committee concluded that it would not be practicable to develop practice-specific task codes. The group decided instead to develop a standard that specifies the principal categories or types of tasks undertaken on most non-litigation matters (e.g., due diligence, negotiation, documentation), rather than identifying tasks unique to each area of practice (e.g., tenant lease for real estate).

The Project Code Set uses the same list of activity and expense codes presented in the Litigation Code Set.

The following definitions elaborate on the intended scope of each phase and task and should guide attorneys in coding time.

P100 Project Administration. Focuses on administrative aspects of the assignment, including planning, budgeting, and maintenance of documents. Covers developing, negotiating, and revising the administrative plan and the budget for a matter. Also includes developing and communicating project status reports. Time coded here is to be distinguished from strategizing about the project, which is included in the P300 code.

P200 Fact Gathering/Due Diligence. Includes all time spent investigating facts, obtaining documents and completing due diligence and the preparation of related reports and reviews with clients. Also includes coordination with third parties (including other counsel) in connection with the fact investigation, interviews of client and non-client personnel, document review performed for purposes of identifying, understanding and analyzing facts and issues, and all related correspondence.

P210 Corporate Review. This task includes all fact investigation/due diligence from a corporate perspective, such as reviews of corporate structure, reviews of material contracts, reviews of SEC filings, reviews of financing documents, and reviews of industry information.

P220 Tax. This task includes all steps involved in conducting fact investigation/due diligence from a tax perspective.

P230 Environmental. This task includes all fact investigation/due diligence from an environmental perspective.

P240 Real and Personal Property. This task includes all fact investigation/due diligence from a real and personal property perspective.

P250 Employee/Labor. This task includes all fact investigation/due diligence from an employee benefits and labor perspective.

P260 Intellectual Property. This task includes all fact investigation/due diligence from an intellectual property (patent, trademarks, copyrights) perspective.

P270 Regulatory Reviews. This task includes fact investigation/due diligence from a regulatory perspective not covered elsewhere. Includes review of agency filings (e.g., FCC, FTC, and State analogues) by a party to or the subject of the transaction or project. Also includes consumer credit reviews.

P280 Other. This task includes all fact investigation/due diligence not captured more specifically in the P200 codes set forth above.

P300 Structure/Strategy/Analysis. Includes time spent in planning the approach to the deal or project. Tasks include all analysis performed for purposes of developing and reassessing the strategy for the project or transaction, and all steps taken to develop a written outline or description of the structure of a transaction or the strategy for a matter (e.g., term sheets) throughout the life of the matter.

P400 Initial Document Preparation/Filling. This phase includes all tasks undertaken to prepare transaction documents and opinions prior to their being sent to non-client third parties. Also includes all tasks undertaken to file documents (including regulatory filings). All related communications with the client and review of client-generated transaction documentation should be coded here.

P500 Negotiation/Revision/Responses. This phase includes conducting negotiations, revising the initial (P400) transaction documentation as a result of such negotiations, attendance at meetings, and responses thereto (including communications with clients with respect thereto). The review of documents received from non-client third parties should also be coded here.

P600 Completion/Closing. This phase includes all tasks related to transaction pre-closing and closing, project completion or filing acceptance, such as attendance at closing.

P700 Post-Completion/Post-Closing. This phase includes all post-completion or post-closing tasks agreed to at the closing, such as amendments to final documentation and resolution of post-closing issues. Also includes all implementation tasks (e.g., funds held in escrow) and preparation of closing binders (i.e., primarily clerical actions). Would not typically include total or significant restructuring which should be considered a new assignment.

P800 Maintenance and Renewal. This phase includes all tasks related to subsequent maintenance and renewal requirements under the terms of the transaction or project such as monitoring of lease agreements, routine waivers and coordination of UCC requirements.

§ 27.09 Counseling Code Set

The Counseling Code Set is intended to capture time spent by attorneys in preparing and delivering general legal advice for all areas of law (e.g., tax, labor, corporate, regulatory, lobbying). The Counseling Code Set may also be used to capture time over a monthly billing period that is not otherwise attributable to a discrete matter, transaction, project or litigation. Communication between client and counsel about which code set to use at the onset of any matter is advisable.

The Counseling Code Set is designed to be adaptable to all practice areas and matter types. As such, the phases and tasks defined in these code sets are more general in nature. The Steering Committee concluded that it would not be practicable to develop practice-specific task codes. The group decided instead to develop a standard that specifies the principal categories or types of tasks undertaken on most non-litigation matters (e.g., due-diligence, negotiation, documentation), rather than identifying tasks unique to each area of practice (e.g., tenant lease for real estate). Transactional and administrative filing work is covered by the Project Code Set.

The Counseling Code Set uses the same list of activity and expense codes presented in the Litigation Code Set. The following definitions elaborate on the intended scope of each task and should guide attorneys in coding time.

C100 Fact Gathering. This phase includes all initial inquiries, meetings and instructions and the identification and collection of information relevant to the assignment.

C200 Research Law. This phase includes all legal research tasks, including internal meetings and consultants with those with special expertise, and computer and on-line research.

C300 Analysis and Advice. This phase includes all tasks associated with analysis of both the facts and research performed (under C100 and C200) and communicating related opinions or advice to clients. Written communication, meetings, and telephone conversations during which advice is conveyed would all be captured by this phase.

C400 Third Party Communication. This phase includes all discussions with third parties not otherwise covered above, such as communications with regulators or parties to contracts with the client.

CHAPTER 28

Management Information

Chapter Contents

---

§ 28.01 Management Information for Law Firms

In Chapter 9 we discussed management reporting for law firms. Law firm management reports are described in that chapter as being prepared for use by the firm's managing partner or management committee. Management reports highlight key statistics and use graphics to portray results. However, management reports are normally the same set of reports distributed to a limited group of people. Management information is an advanced concept in management reporting.

While there is some overlap in the concept of management reporting and management information, the distinguishing characteristic of management information is that it focuses on getting the right information to the right people at the right time. Management information can go to anyone who needs specific pieces of information on a regular or even irregular basis. Management information can be more effective than management reporting because it focuses the specific needs of the recipient of critical information.

An advance in technology, particularly the new generation of financial systems, facilitates provision of management information in addition to management reports. The management information concept is epitomized in the management inquiry systems currently available.[1]

Benchmarking is an extremely powerful tool to provide vast insights into the practices of world-class law firms. Benchmarking gives management the external perspective that helps law firms take advantage of the best practices in the industry and improve their own performance. From a management information perspective, benchmarking establishes the best starting point for change. It points the way to improvement goals.

---

[1] See § 28.04 *infra*.

§ 28.02 Internal Management Information

[1]—Firm Management

It is important that a law firm have adequate information to manage the practice as a whole. The type, detail and presentation of information varies greatly depending on the firm's operations and culture. Also, depending on the firm's preference, this information might be produced daily, such as a cash collections flash report, weekly, such as an accounts receivable ("A/R") and work-in-process ("WIP") summary, monthly, such as a summary of operating statistics or a statement of revenue, quarterly, such as a detailed revenue and expense variation analysis or annually, such as the firm's financial statements audited by its independent accountant.

Information used to manage the practice must be constantly refined to address changes in the focus and business of the firm. For example, a law firm that recently acquired a significant new litigation matter may want to enhance the management information that it uses to track utilization, or if a firm reorganizes using practice groups, it might refine its management reports to focus on the results of the practice groups. Whatever the case, the ability of a firm to efficiently conduct its operations and make the right business decisions depends on its ability to produce useful and relevant management information.

Firm management information may include but not be limited to:

(1) flash reports;
(2) summary firm operating statistics;
(3) exception reports;
(4) practice area statistics; and
(5) analytical reports.

Following are examples of different types of firm management reports.

Flash reports — These reports are generally prepared on a daily or "flash" basis to highlight a certain key component of a law firm's operations such as cash collections, billings or chargeable hours. These reports may be detailed or summarized depending on the preference of the firm. For example, some firms may list daily cash collections by partner by practice group or department or by client, whereas, other firms may list cash collections in total. Additionally, the firm may include a comparison of the collections to the goal for the day or some other period of time such as a week or month. Many law firm management groups use flash reports to assist in the motivation of the firm's financial goals.

See Figure 28-A for an illustration of a cash collections flash report.

Figure 28-A. Illustration of Cash Collections Flash Report.

ABC LAW FIRM
CASH COLLECTIONS FLASH REPORT
NOVEMBER 15, 19XX

		Collections	
Partner	Client	Fees	Disbursements
Partner A	Client V	$ 50,000	$ 2,000
Partner B	Client W	10,000	500
Partner C	Client X	20,000	1,000
	Client Y	5,000	—
Partner D	Client Z	70,000	3,000
		$155,000	$ 6,500
Collections month to date		$310,000	$20,000
Goal for the month		$750,000	$50,000

Summary firm operating statistics - These reports can take many forms and may be produced weekly or monthly.

On a weekly basis a firm might focus on its aged outstanding A/R and WIP by partner. This information might be used by the management group to ensure that all partners are billing and collecting on a timely basis. The management group might also want to distribute this report to all partners and let "peer pressure" encourage the partners to bill and collect on a timely basis. See Figure 28-B for a sample A/R and WIP report.

Figure 28-B. Illustration of an Aged Outstanding A/R and WIP Report.

ABC LAW FIRM
AGED OUTSTANDING AR/WIP REPORT BY PARTNER
NOVEMBER 15, 20XX

Partner	Total	0-30 days	31-60 days	61-90 days	91-180 days	Over 160 days
Partner A	$100,000	$50,000	$30,000	—	—	$20,000
Partner B	60,000	20,000	30,000	10,000	—	—
Partner C	40,000	30,000	—	—	$10,000	—
Total A/R	$200,000	$100,000	$60,000	$10,000	$10,000	$20,000
WORK-IN-PROGRESS						
Partner A	$150,000	$40,000	$30,000	$20,000	$50,000	$10,000
Partner B	30,000	10,000	20,000	—	—	—
Partner C	80,000	15,000	20,000	5,000	40,000	—
Total WIP	$260,000	$65,000	$70,000	$25,000	$90,000	$10,000
	$460,000	$165,000	$130,000	$35,000	$100,000	$30,000

Many firm's prepare a monthly report which highlights a number of key operating statistics, including a comparison to budget and the prior year. Among other things this report might highlight:

(1) Gross revenue and expenses;
(2) Payments to former partners;
(3) Income available for distribution to partners;
(4) Income distributed to partners;
(5) Gross outstanding AR/WIP;
(6) Partner and associate headcount;
(7) Partner and associate average chargeable hours;
(8) Partner and associate utilization;
(9) Outstanding borrowing; and
(10) Partner capital balances.

The advantage of these "highlights" reports is that it allows management to focus on key data in a summarized and easy-to-read fashion. See Chapter 9, "Management Reporting," for further discussion and an example of a highlights report.

Exception reports — Deviation from established financial goals or targets is a method that the management of a law firm might use to identify potential problems in a lawyer's performance or in the firm's financial record keeping. For example, a weekly exception report might be prepared listing those lawyers with chargeable hours above and below a certain set range for a day, reporting period or year. Management may then inquire of those lawyers as to the reason for the exception or to ensure that the firm's financial systems are properly accounting for attorney time charges. Other items that management might want to include on an exception report would be A/R and WIP realization and aged accounts receivable. See Figure 28-C for a sample exception report.

Figure 28-C. Illustration of a Weekly Exception Report.

ABC LAW FIRM
WEEKLY EXCEPTION REPORT

Daily chargeable hours in excess of 20:

Attorney	Date	Hours Charged
Associate A	November 15	22

AR/WIP Realization > 100% or < 60%

Billing Attorney	Client	Realization %
Partner A	Client X	110%
Partner B	Client Y	50%

Accounts receivable aged greater than 180 days

Partner	Client	Amount
Partner C	Client Z	$10,000

Practice area statistics — Depending on the number of practice areas within the firm, management may want to monitor the performance of these practice areas to ensure the best use of the firm's resources. To accomplish this, management might prepare a report listing the key performance indicators of a particular practice area, which could then be compared to budget, and the firm's other practice areas. These key performance indicators might include individual attorney utilization rates, chargeable hours, cash collections and AR/WIP data. Reports may also be prepared listing the clients of the practice area and the corresponding revenue attributed to those clients compared to the prior year. See Chapter 10, "Profit Center Accounting," for further discussion and illustration of practice area statistics.

Analytical reports — These reports can be used to monitor the trends in a firm's operations through ratio or fluctuation analysis. Analytical procedures can be useful tools by which management can monitor a law firm's performance at a high level and identify potential issues that may

procedures can be useful tools by which management can monitor a law firm's performance at a high level and identify potential issues that may not be apparent from focusing on detailed information. The timely identification of issues gives management the ability to react and address the problem.

As part of their analytical procedures, many firms use ratio analysis to highlight and monitor key statistics such as:

(1) Revenue and expenses per lawyer and partner;
(2) Number of months' revenue in AR/WIP;
(3) AR/WIP realization;
(4) Number of days to bill and collect time charges;
(5) Utilization of attorneys; and
(6) Attorney leverage.

Many law firms also use fluctuation analysis, which focuses on the reasons for changes in financial results when compared to prior year and budget. When researched, the actual reason for the change may be different than what was originally thought and in some cases identify problems in the firm's financial systems or other irregularities. See Chapter 9, "Management Reporting," for further discussion and illustration of various analytical reports.

[2]—Practice/Office Leaders

Practice and office leaders need the practice area subset of information received by firm-wide management, but also need additional targeted information to effectively manage their areas of practice or their office.

The standard information that most practice leaders receive focuses on individual lawyer performance. This includes utilization, billings, collections and origination by lawyer or by partner. The most effective reports highlight or isolate lawyers whose statistics fall outside a predetermined normal range. This type of exception reporting allows practice and office leaders to focus on those lawyers whose statistics are out of line with standards.

Matter reporting is another important aspect of practice and office reporting. The recipients of this information will depend on how the firm is organized. In firms where management is focused at the office level, this information will be useful to office leaders; in firms where management is focused at the practice level, the information will be more useful to practice leaders.

Matter reporting should provide the highlights of specific matters assigned to a practice area or office. This includes outstanding work in progress, outstanding accounts receivable, collections to date, and activities in the current period. To the extent that budget information is available or applicable, this should also be included. The report should highlight matters that are within a certain percentage of their target budget (e.g., 90%) to allow practice leaders to follow matters where the firm might have some financial risk. This type of reporting becomes increasingly important as the number of fixed fee billing arrangements increases. See Figure 28-D for a sample matter report.

Figure 28-D. Illustration of a Matter Report.

ABC LAW FIRM
MATTER STATUS REPORTING

Area of Law: Example

Client/ Matter	Billing Partner	Responsible Partner	Total Outstanding Unbilled Time	Current Period Unbilled Time	Total Fees Billed To Date	Matter Budget	Total Fees Billed as a % of Budget	Total Fees Billed + Unbilled Time as a % of Budget
Client XYZ/ Matter 1	JKL	MNO	$8,000	$4,000	$72,000	$80,000	90%	100%
Client XYZ/ Matter 2	JKL	PQR	$2,500	$2,000	$40,000	$50,000*	80%	85%
Client DEF/ Matter 1	GHI	STU	$10,000	$9,000	$20,000	$100,000	20%	30%
Client DEF/ Matter 2	GHI	STU	$2,000	$1,000	$50,000	N/A	—	—

*Fixed fee billing arrangement

Effective matter reporting requires accurate completion of new matter forms. Matters must be coded by practice area or service area in order to be included in the appropriate practice leader's report.

Matters that are on a fixed fee or other type of fee budget must include that information on the new matter form or through a subsequent procedure that feeds the information into the firm's financial system.

Practice area and office profitability, which is tracked by an increasing number of firms, is also information that can be distributed to the practice and office leaders. The level of distribution may depend on the firm's philosophy on the issue. Some firms keep practice area and office profitability information within the management or executive committee in order to reduce any potential conflicts. Others distribute it more widely.

An effective way to determine component profitability is by using matters as the building blocks. Matter profitability is based on the revenues associated with a matter and the hourly costs associated with the timekeepers who worked on the matter. The resulting report then can provide a variety of statistics, including contribution per full-time equivalent partner and profitability per hour. See Figure 28-E for a sample component profitability report.

Figure 24-E. Illustration of a Component Profitability Report.

ABC LAW FIRM
PROFITABILITY ANALYSIS
JANUARY 1, 19X2 THROUGH JUNE 30, 19X2

Area of Law: Example

	Hours	Billing Value	Direct Cost	Indirect Cost	Contribution
Time Charges					
Partners	200	$49,000	—	$14,000	$35,000
Of Counsel	50	8,500	$ 2,500	3,250	2,750
Senior Associates	200	28,000	8,000	12,000	8,000
Junior Associates	100	11,500	3,500	6,000	2,000
Total	550	97,000	14,000	35,250	47,750
Disbursements and Other Charges					
Cash Disbursements		76	76	—	0
Other Expenses		—	—	—	—
Total		76	76	—	0
Subtotal Billing Value		97,076	14,076	35,250	47,750
Realization Adjustments					
Rate Premiums/Discounts		(500)	—	—	(500)
Unbilled Fees Write-offs		(2,200)	—	—	(2,200)
Billed Fees Write-offs		(1,000)	—	—	(1,000)
Total		(3,700)	—	—	(3,700)
Net Billable		93,376	14,076	35,250	44,050
Carrying Costs					
Unbilled Fees		(550)	—	—	(550)
Unbilled Fees Write-offs		(250)	—	—	(250)
Total		(800)	—	—	(800)
Net Matter Totals		$92,576	$14,076	$35,250	$43,250

Total Contribution per Partner Hour	$216
Key Statistics	
Leverage = Other Attorneys to Partners	1.75
Average Billing Rate/Partner Hour	$245
Average Billing Rate/Associate Hour	$132
Realization Adj. as a % of Billing Value	-3.8%
Carrying Costs as a % of Billing Value	-0.8%

[3]—Partners

Individual partners should receive a different set of management information than firm management or practice and office group leaders. The majority of the information that individual partners receive should focus them on the specific areas that they need to manage and over which they have control. This includes:

(1) Accounts receivable and unbilled time information for the clients which they have originated and have billing responsibility or for which they have management responsibility. These reports should give the partner a quick snapshot of the entire matter, including total fees billed to date, date of the last bill, number of bills outstanding and amount and date of the last collection.

(2) Utilization information for themselves and partners and associates who work on their matters.

(3) Project management information for their matters, including budget to actual on a task basis, if applicable, and percent of budget reached.

See Figure 28-F for a sample project management report.

Figure 28-F. Illustration of a Project Management Report.

	Actual Budgeted Hours	Hours To Date	% of Budget	Budgeted Fees	Actual Fees	% of Budget
Task 1						
Partners	100	80	80%	$25,000	$20,000	80%
Associates	200	220	110%	30,000	33,000	110%
Legal Assistants	50	40	80%	4,000	3,200	80%
Total	350	340	97%	59,000	56,200	95%
Task 2						
Partners	50	10	20%	12,500	2,500	20%
Associates	100	25	25%	15,000	3,750	25%
Legal Assistants	25	0	0	2,000	0	0
Total	175	35	20%	29,500	6,250	22%
Total Project	525	375	71%	$88,500	$62,450	70%

An additional set of information that the partners should receive is a variation on firm management's exception reports. These reports should provide information on such things as significant 90+ day accounts receivable or unbilled time and unusually low or high utilization. The purpose of distributing these reports to all partners is to provide an element of peer pressure. Once partners have a picture of some of the critical issues facing the firm, they can then take the initiative to encourage problem billers or collectors to take action. They will also be aware of lawyers whose utilization may be below normal and consider ways to use those people on their matters, or be willing to take more serious action for people who are consistently low.

Finally, partners should receive overall firm performance data and summary financials in order to keep up-to-date on the firm's performance. This information should be distributed less frequently than the preceding types of information since it is not information upon which they need to take action or an area in which they have any direct control.

Ideally, partners would have on-line desktop access to much of this information through a management inquiry system. This concept is discussed in more detail in Section 4 of this chapter.

§ 28.03 Management Information Requested by Third Parties

What type of information regarding the firm's engagement economics and financial status should be furnished to third parties? Furthermore, in what level of detail should this information be furnished?

These are the questions that management groups of many law firms must ask themselves given the increased level of requests for this type of management information from clients, banks and lessors. Gone are the days when law firms could furnish clients with a one-paragraph bill highlighting services performed. Clients now demand detailed time and expense analyses, sometimes including the breakdown of specific tasks performed by an attorney. Also gone are the days when a bank or lessor would make a business decision regarding a law firm based on a cursory review of the firm's financial statements. Banks and lessors now require detailed financial information including budgets and financial plans as conditions for extending lines of credit, term loans or leases for office space.

In many cases, information produced for the firm's partners and management, such as summary financial statements, billing, accounts receivable and WIP reports and other analysis, can be modified for presentation to third parties.

[1]—Information Requested by Clients

Clients are becoming more aggressive in the type of information that they are requesting from their outside counsel regarding engagement economics. Among the more common requests are:

(1) Detailed time and billing information by matter including time spent by each attorney, either at a particular point in time or as part of a bill;

(2) Detailed analysis of expenses incurred by type and matter; and

(3) Matter budgets with actual time incurred compared to those budgets.

Furnishing this type of information to clients can create several problems for a law firm. While information given to the firm's management may address these items, most law firm financial systems are not geared to produce the information in a "ready to give to the client" form. Therefore the attorney and finance group must spend time and effort to synthesize the information from various reports prepared by the system and re-key it into a client useable format. Additionally, the information will need to be reviewed before it is released to the client. These problems are further compounded by the fact that different clients have different preferences as to how and what information is presented. Finally, by furnishing this information to one client, a law firm is at risk that all of the firm's clients will demand similar analyses.

Another issue faced by some law firms is a client request to furnish, via electronic transfer, detailed time, billing and expense files. The client then performs its own detailed analysis of the data. While this can be advantageous for the client, it creates added concerns for a law firm as control of the data and how it is analyzed and presented is lost. Regardless, the use of electronic transfer of data is becoming more common for law firms

When furnishing management information, such as engagement economics data, to clients, it is important to attempt to standardize, as much as possible, the type of information presented. Many law firms have developed reporting formats geared to the preferences of one or two significant clients. Several major law firms and Fortune 500 corporate law departments have, in conjunction with the American Bar Association and the American Corporate Counsel Association, worked to standardize the reporting of engagement economic data by developing the Uniform Task-Based Management System. This system, among other things, provides for a standard set of tasks to which an attorney may charge their time when performing services for a client.[1]

Most firms expect the level of engagement economic detail requested by clients to increase in the coming years. The management of a law firm must exercise great care in deciding the type and form of information to release and only what is absolutely necessary in the circumstances.

[2]—Information Requested by Banks and Lessors

Banks and lessors have become increasingly sophisticated about law firm operations as a result of the downturn in the legal market place in the late 1980s. While the majority of law firms are still attractive borrowers and lessees, most firms are being subjected to a higher level of scrutiny than in the past when it comes to borrowing and lease agreements. This rigorous screening process currently in place for law firms is not likely to diminish as the legal economy improves. Much of the information requested by banks and lessors is the same as that used by the firm's management group to analyze the firm's operations. However, each bank or lessor has its own set of criteria relating to law firm lending and leasing decisions and, even firm to firm, applies them in a different way.

---

[1] See Chapter 27, *supra,* for a detailed discussion of the Uniform Task-Based Management System.

Information requested by banks and lessors generally focuses on the following:

(1) Historical financial information;
(2) Audited financial statements of the firm;
(3) Client information;
(4) Budgets and business plans;
(5) Headcount and utilization statistics;
(6) Financial ratio analysis; and
(7) Reports regarding the firm's internal control structure (prepared by the firm's independent accountant in conjunction with the firm's annual audit).

Unfortunately, even though the firm may have this data available, it usually is not in a condition that can be given directly to these parties. The conversion of this data to a format agreed upon by the law firm and bank or lessor can be quite time consuming.

When reviewing this information, a bank or lessor might be attempting to answer the following questions:

(1) Historical financial information-

- What has been the average trend in:
- Net income per partner?
- Inflation adjusted income per partner?
- Gross fees per lawyer?
- Operating expenses per lawyer?
- What is the firm's history of bank borrowing?
- What type and amount of payments have been made to former partners?
- What is the type/quality of the firm's assets?
- Does the firm appear to keep cash on hand for contingencies?

(2) Audited financial statements of the firm, including related footnote disclosures-

- What type of opinion did the auditor render?
- What type of commitments does the firm have to its former partners (i.e., income distribution, method of payout to those partners)?
- Does the firm have an unfunded partner retirement plan?
- Has the firm assessed its expected future level of commitment under this unfunded plan?
- What are the firm's current debt and lease commitments?
- What is the level of professional liability insurance?

(3) Client information-

- Is the firm dependent on one or more very large clients?
- How stable is the firm's client base?
- How dependent is the firm on one or two partners for bringing in work?
- Are client relationships "firm" relationships or "individual lawyer" relationships?

(4) Budgets and business plans-

- What type of plan does the firm prepare (i.e., level of sophistication)?
- How does the firm use the plan?
- What is the firm's practice mix?
- What is the outlook for the firm's major practices?
- How integrated are the firms practice groups (i.e., is the firm at risk of a practice group spin-off)?
- What level of revenue growth is planned by the firm and is it realistic?
- What is the firm's expected growth/reduction in the level of expenses and in what areas will this growth/reduction occur?

(5) Headcount and utilization statistics-

- What is the trend in billable hours per partner and per associate?
- Do associates bill more hours than partners do (i.e., is there enough work to keep both partners and associates busy)?
- What is the turnover rate among partners?

(6) Financial ratio analysis-

- What is the firm's billing and receivable realization (i.e., level of write-off of WIP and accounts receivable)?
- What is the firm's net income as a percent of gross fees (e.g., at least 30 to 35 percent)?
- What is the level of permanent contributed capital, including permanent undistributed earnings?
- What is the firm's occupancy expense as a percent of gross fees (e.g., not more than 10%)?
- What is the debt to equity ratio?
- What are the distribution policies of the firm with respect to current profits or accumulated and undistributed profits?

(7) Reports regarding the firm's internal control structure-
- In what areas were control points raised?
- Were any of these points considered to be a material weakness by the independent accountant?

In addition to requesting this information during their due diligence process, banks and lessors may also require quarterly or even monthly updates. In some cases the partners are bound to submit personal financial information. Law firm management must be vigilant to ensure that banks and lessors get only the information that they need to make their business decisions. Furnishing additional information provides little added value but increases risk of the firm's financial information being out of its direct control. Credit and lease agreements should be reviewed in detail by experts inside and outside the firm to ensure that the firm is not bound to unnecessary and cumbersome requirements to provide financial information to these parties.

§ 28.04 Management Inquiry Systems

[1]—What is a Management Inquiry System?

A management inquiry system is a graphical reporting system specifically designed to present summary-level financial information with the option to "drill down" to different levels of detail. For example, from a financial perspective, a management inquiry system allows a user to drill down by office, by practice group, by expense category to see the actual invoice or from a firm management perspective a user can drill down by office, by practice group, by billing lawyer, by client, by matter.

The "drill-down" capability can be described as the key functionality within the financial systems that allows the accountant and financial person to extend their roles back in time towards the source of the data, to the point in time when transactions were originally recorded. In the past, the parties to any transaction (e.g. clients, procurement, and professionals) created simple printed documents with isolated accounting systems. Today's financial reports allow the user to drill-down from a report to get a list of account balances from which the report was generated. This process reveals the transactions from which the summary amounts were produced. With some systems, it is possible to drill-down to the actual journal entries or the original source documents (e.g., copies of invoices that were scanned into the computer) to quickly analyze activity. Drill-down capability brings the following the benefits to law firms:

- Allows administrative management to drill down to pinpoint the exact transaction or account that is being called into question;
- Allows administrative management to analyze data on a transaction level in a time efficient manner;
- Data can be collected from all systems used by the firm and stored in one central location;
- Firm operational data can be built from transaction processes;
- Budgeting, planning and forecasting can be driven from these reports; and
- Allows original transaction sources to be viewed in real-time fashion.

[2]—How Management Inquiry Systems Are Used

A management inquiry system is used most often by a chief operating officer or director of finance as an analysis tool in managing the financial health of a law firm. It gives electronic capabilities that allow a person to quickly determine the answer to a question like,

"Why is this expense category so high?" or "Did we pay a bill this month for consulting?" The financial management inquiry system generally comes standard in most sophisticated general ledger packages.

Some firms believe that members of the management committees also should have the ability to drill down in the general ledger to focus on productivity or profitability—measurements that they use in managing the firm's practice. This capability normally is not standard in most general ledger applications, but can be added through off-the-shelve add-on software or through custom programming.

Since the general ledger is the foundation of any law firm's financial accounting system, it should be more than just a data repository of raw data. The challenges of today's law firm management are driving financial accounting systems to provide reliable financial control, flexible data collection, global processing and readily accessible information. A management inquiry system gives management the electronic tool to meet those challenges.

The law firm's general ledger needs to provide standard accounting and control reports as well as sophisticated, easy-to-use tools that enable users to create any type of financial or management inquiry or report. Today's law firm computerized general ledgers offer management inquiry systems that provide:

- Pull-down menus and dialog boxes to select data
- Multi-currency data for inquiry and reporting
- Report layouts using graphical hierarchies, tree structures, and ledgers
- Drill down to transaction-level detail from all ledgers
- Drill down to third-party applications and journal entry detail
- Cross-service line drilldown to see transaction detail in other complementary products
- Simple or complex online queries

The ability to drill down through various levels of detail is one of the distinguishing features of a management inquiry system. For example, suppose that the head of a practice group sees an upswing in the billable hours in his group. He can first look at individual lawyer statistics to identify particular lawyers who have increased hours, then go one level below that to identify the particular clients and matters that have contributed to the increase.

Figure 28-G illustrates what a screen from a management inquiry system might look like. This example shows billable hours for one month by practice area for the entire firm.

Figure 28-G. Illustration of Billable Hours by Practice Area Screen

Practice Area	Billable Hours	Attorney Hours
Corporate	7,248	178.2
Litigation	8,550	191.7
Tax	1,520	164.5
Trust & Estates	972	156.9
Total	18,290	691.3

Partners leading a practice area can use this information to identify instances where work may need to be spread over more lawyers, and determine, with additional input from the billing partner, whether the upswing in a particular client is short-term or long-term and plan accordingly.

To drill down to the next level of detail, the user would double click the mouse on the corporate practice area. Figure 28-H illustrates the resulting screen, displaying billable hours for all corporate lawyers.

Figure 28-H. Illustration of Billable Hours for Corporate Screen

Attorney or Timekeeper	Attorney/Timekeeper Number	Billable Hours
Jones	0012	260
Roberts	0104	247
Martinez	0075	195
Smith	0145	165
Johnson	0123	192

Another key feature of a management inquiry system is the ability to view data graphically. While graphics can and are often incorporated into management reports, the management inquiry system allows a graphical portrayal on demand. Graphics can help bring certain key points to management's attention in a way that numbers on the page often can not. Figure 28-I illustrates the typical graphic that might be produced on screen-billable hours by practice area.

Figure 28-1. Illustration of Chart of Billable Hours by Practice Area Graphic

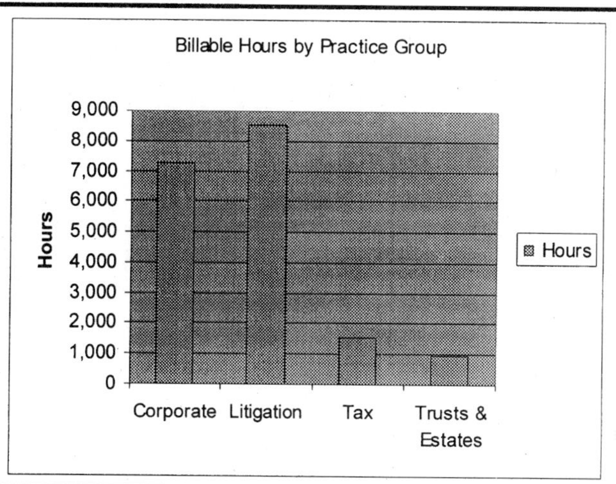

The use of color in graphics can also help highlight particular points. For example, the firm can designate a certain color to show below budget or standard performance and another color for above standard performance (e.g., partners whose billings exceed expectations could be highlighted in yellow while partners whose billings are well below expectation can be highlighted in red).

[3]—Advantages of a Management Inquiry System

There are many advantages to desktop access to information. First, it can replace distribution of hard copy reports, reducing the burden on the firm's administrative staff and limiting waste. It allows the lawyers and managers to access information when they need or want to, including, if they have remote access, when they are away from the office. Remote access can actually increase the likelihood that busy lawyers will review relevant financial information, because they simply need to dial in to the firm, which they are likely doing anyway, rather than carry a set of management reports on the road with them.

A second advantage is that a management inquiry system can give people information in real time rather than monthly or quarterly. For example, if a client calls and wants to know the status of his or her matter, the lawyer can quickly pull up that information and give the client an up-to-date report on billings and work-in-process. Of course the ability to have real-time information requires that processes like time entry are done daily rather than weekly or monthly.

A third advantage of a management inquiry system is the ability for individuals to customize the reports or screens that they see. For example, an individual lawyer may want to create "icons" on his or her desktop for particular clients. A practice manager may want icons for a particular group of lawyers. By creating this personalized reporting format the likelihood of lawyers looking at the information increases.

[4]—Facilitating Project Management

Management inquiry systems can greatly enhance partners' ability to manage clients and matters. This capability is increasingly important as alternative- billing arrangements such as fixed fees, value billing and task-based billing become more common. Firms can improve profitability if they can effectively manage these billing arrangements.

A management inquiry system gives a lawyer managing a matter access to information about the case on an ongoing basis. By preparing a budget at the beginning of the project, that can be updated as the case progresses, the lawyer can see where each person working on the case stands relative to budget. Advanced systems could even alert the lawyer when someone has reached a certain percentage of budget. As task-based budgeting and time recording becomes common practice, the lawyer-manager will be able to compare budget to actual on a task basis (see Chapter 27 for a detailed discussion of task-based billing). Combining that information with an assessment of the degree of completion of the task will help the lawyer keep people on track before budgets are exceeded and firm profitability is affected. It also can be an alert to talk to the client about the budget and negotiate a new arrangement, if circumstances outside the firm's control have had an impact on the budget.

[5]—System Security

Most firms worry about the security issues related to having distributed access to the firm's financial information. These concerns can be allayed through careful planning and administration of the security rights to the management inquiry system and the underlying data.

Ideally, the management inquiry system will be implemented such that the staff level or the role of the user accessing the system governs access to the information. For example, the managing partner of a firm should have access to firm-wide information and all underlying levels of detail. The leader of a practice group or office managing partner should have access only to information on clients and lawyers assigned to their group or office. Finally, billing attorneys should have access to information only on clients and matters for which they are the billing attorney. This last point suggests that management inquiry systems are not intended for management alone. In fact, these systems might be more accurately described as inquiry systems or decision support systems.

It is clear that a management inquiry system can be an important source of management information in today's law firm. It provides timely access to financial data in a dynamic manner that cannot be matched by hard copy reports.

[6]—Distributing Management Information: Law Firm Intranet or Portal

The delivery vehicle of management information is through an Intranet or corporate portal. Today, portals are emerging as the user interface in the web-based world. This is occurring because portals address many of the basic challenges faced in the web-based world. Namely, portals allow the law firm to:

- Manage the confluence of content scattered across information islands, internets and document collections
- Leverage intellectual capital within the law firm by promoting community
- Deliver knowledge in a timely manner
- Increase client intimacy and value
- Orchestrate the plethora of applications, documents and links that embody today's law firm transactions

The leading-edge law firm utilizes a portal as a singular personalized gateway, defines its essence as community and content with its logical extension into legal e-business.

[7]—Defining the Portal

The word portal today is a popular term in the corporate world as well as law firms. Virtually everyone using the Internet integrates portal visits into their online experience. But what does the portal represent within a law firm's intranet? The portal is the single point of access that provides a seamless interface to any and all sources of management information, data, reports, people, or legal applications. It provides the means to search for and locate information, categorizes content, establishes communities of interest, provides access to specialized functions and allows for personalized views. They seek to make the powers of the intranet manageable, simpler to publish and easier to navigate.

The corporate or internal portal plays a role in the knowledge practice of the law firm and are largely responsible for the deployment of a wide range of knowledge—supporting applications already underway on many large law firms intranet. External portals are a key utility in substantiating interaction between the collaboration of client and law firm.

The portal is also the platform for knowledge management and collaboration. Effective collaboration means employees use the knowledge management system and become contributors to it to enhance the content and its value. The capture, analysis and incorporation of knowledge is the foundation of knowledge management. By using this input, organizations can create a customized user experience and improve profit, enhance revenue, retain key talent and expertise and increase customer retention and satisfaction.

§ 28.05 Benchmarking

[1]—Benchmarking: An Overview

Benchmarking is the process of learning from the successes of others and improving one's own performance with that knowledge. In benchmarking you compare your own practices and performance against others in your industry. By using the top industry performers as your comparison group, you can identify ways in which your practices are different and ways to improve those practices.

Benchmarking is just as relevant to law firms as it is to the corporate environment and has, in fact, been used internally by law firm management as a barometer of success. Law firms have long compared their performance to their competitors and peers, often through such published reports as the AMLAW 100. As techniques are refined so that "apples" are compared to "apples," benchmarking improves the quality of the information against which firms can compare their performance.

Benchmarking is meaningful to any management information system, because it focuses management's attention on critical evaluation criteria such as associates' productivity, profits per partner, etc. and measures those criteria against a target population. Evaluating the firm's results without any context is not meaningful, unless the context is the prior-year's results. Benchmarking can help the firm set reasonable goals and develop an action plan for achieving those goals. The process of developing an action plan is as important as setting the benchmark, because it will help the firm determine how it plans to meet its goals.

[2]—Approach to Benchmarking

There are several steps in the benchmarking process. They include:

(1) Determine the evaluation criteria and benchmark population;
(2) Perform the benchmarking study;
(3) Analyze your current performance and identify areas for improvement;
(4) Develop goals related to the benchmarks;
(5) Develop an action plan;
(6) Implement the action plan; and
(7) Evaluate the success.

Each of these steps is described in more detail in the remainder of this section.

[a]—Determine the Evaluation Criteria and Benchmark Population

Defining the scope of the study is an important step, because it will help focus the remainder of the effort. The firm will need to identify the evaluation criteria or functions that it wants to measure against other firms. These criteria can be anything from the level of partner compensation to the productivity of associates. Once the criteria have been identified, the firm will need to identify the key performance variables and measures. For example, key performance measures in the billing process might include:

(1) Age of work-in-process before it is billed;
(2) Time spent on billing or per bill;
(3) Time from distribution of pre-bill to mailing;
(4) Partner satisfaction with billing process;
(5) Client satisfaction with billing process;
(6) Billing staff/lawyer ratio.

These measures will guide the benchmarking study.

[b]—Perform the Benchmarking Study

Often the most difficult part of the benchmarking process is identifying the external sources that can be used to obtain information. Benchmarking information can come from previously published studies and surveys (to the extent that they match the firm's requirements) or it can be based on original work done specifically for or by the firm to address the specific benchmarks identified. A detailed discussion of the sources of benchmarking information can be found in subsection 3 of this Section.

One of the most important aspects of this step is to identify an appropriate comparison group or population. This can include other law that the firm believes are its counterparts. Sometimes, firms chose populations comprised of much larger or more profitable firms because it wants to measure itself against a goal, rather than measure itself against its existing group. Consequently, different comparison groups may be appropriate for different measures of performance. Choosing the right population against which the firm will be benchmarked is critical, because using the wrong population will yield misleading results. Consider for example a situation in which a firm in a large metropolitan area is evaluated against a population consisting of law firms in smaller geographic locations. The size of the firms may be the same, but because the markets are different, the results will be skewed and not meaningful.

The benchmarking process should focus not only on the numerical measures achieved by the comparison group, but also on the specific processes that they have in place that help them achieve their levels of performance.

[c]—Analyze Your Current Performance and Identify Areas for Improvement

To compare the firm's performance to the results of the benchmarking study, the firm will have to analyze its own performance. This step often is referred to as the "as is" assessment or an assessment of the current situation. This step includes determining the firm's own performance on the key measures identified in the first step.

The comparison of firm data to the benchmarking data will help identify areas for improvements by highlighting those measures where the comparison group or groups performed significantly better than the firm.

[d]—Develop Goals Related to the Benchmarks

Once the specific areas for improvement are identified, the firm can begin to develop goals for the future. These goals should include specific performance measure targets. These targets should be aggressive, yet reasonable. Setting aggressive goals will require a thorough understanding of the firm's current situation and also some knowledge about the circumstances that have allowed other firms to perform better on the measurement criteria being considered. If the groups performance is related to circumstances that are significantly different the firm's, it may be difficult to achieve that level without other charges. In the end, it is better to develop goals that require some reach and are achievable given hard work. It also is worth focusing on fewer goals that will truly make a difference and can be reasonable targets, than it is to focus on a number of goals, some of which won't make a difference even if they are achieved.

[e]—Develop an Action Plan

Once the goals are developed, an action plan should be developed that will help the firm achieve the goals. The action plan should outline specific tasks, responsibilities and a timetable. It also should include set evaluation points and subgoals, so that the implementation process is continuous rather than sporadic.

The implementation of the plan is more likely to be successful if those who are responsible for implementing the plan are involved in its development. This involvement can foster a sense of buy-in to the goals and the process.

[f]—Implement the Action Plan

Once the action plan has been developed, it is important to use it as a road map for implementation. Of course, modifications can be made along the way, but the action plan should not simply "sit on the shelf." Firm management is likely to have a large role in the implementation of the action plan.

If firm management receives management information that highlights the key performance measures, it will be better able to monitor and encourage progress. This management information will also help the implementation team assess its own success and understand the impact of its actions on the key performance measures.

[g]—Evaluate the Success

The evaluation process should not be a one-time event. Not only should the project be evaluated during implementation, but it also should be evaluated after completion. Benchmarking is a continuous process and it may be useful to conduct the benchmarking study again. Once the goals have been achieved, it is worth duplicating the same benchmark study to see if there really was progress. If for example, the firm's competitors improved their performance and the repeated benchmark results show that the firm did not advance against the selected population, it means that the goals were not enough or may not have been the right goals. Only when there is progress against the standard, will a firm realize the benefits of a benchmarking exercise

[3]—Sources of Benchmarking Information

One of the most difficult aspects of benchmarking is obtaining reliable data about the population to which the firm will be benchmarked. The difficulty exists because law firms, unlike publicly traded companies, do not release detailed financial information. In fact, most law firms are ultra secretive about their financial information and when it is released for comparative purposes (e.g., to AMLAW 100), sometimes it is suspect. There are several options that firms have when seeking benchmarking information. These include:

(1) published surveys;
(2) surveys conducted as part of the benchmarking project;
(3) best practices data maintained by industry consultants and others; and
(4) benchmarking studies conducted by other firms.

It may be best, or even necessary, to use a combination of these sources in order to get the best and most relevant information for the process that the firm is seeking to improve.

Each of these options, along with the pros and cons of each is discussed in the remainder of this section.

[a]—Published Surveys

There are several surveys of the legal profession that are conducted on a regular basis. Some of these are available to all firms, others are available only to survey participants. There are revenue and profit surveys that are conducted by the legal media. These surveys tend to be less useful for benchmarking purposes, because the information is limited. There also are surveys of law firm financial and operational performance that can be very useful sources of information regarding key performance measures. One such survey is the PricewaterhosueCoopers Law Firm Statistical Survey (which is only available to participants, although participation is open to all firms). Most of these surveys do not release the names of other law firms in their populations, so that confidentiality is maintained. These surveys include information not only on overall revenue and profitability, but also statistics on billing rates, utilization, expenses, staffing levels, cost recovery and other key performance factors. Surveys like the PricewaterhouseCoopers survey typically provide information on the median performance of the group, as well as quartile or decile information that help define the upper and lower ends of the group as well.

The advantage of published surveys is that the information is available and accessible, albeit tightly controlled by the owner of the database. Because it is accumulated and processed by an independent source (e.g., PricewaterhouseCoopers), law firms are more likely to provide accurate information. After all, if accurate information is not given, then the benchmark reports will probably be inaccurate. Another advantage is that the quartile or decile information helps to define the upper end of the group's performance, which is a more aggressive target than a median or average.

A disadvantage, from the perspective of the benchmarking process, is that a law firm will not know the specific makeup of the comparison population and, therefore, may not be measuring the performance of the firms with the best practices in its area of study, let alone in the same geographic area. This disadvantage is easily overcome through up front communication with the owner of the database.

[b]—Surveys Conducted as Part of the Benchmarking Project

Many firms discover that conducting their own targeted surveys is an effective way to supplement available information. Special surveys are particularly important if the benchmarking study is focusing on a strategic issue, such as partner compensation or geographic expansion, which published surveys are less likely to address.

Special surveys also can be used for external evaluation, such as client satisfaction. Client satisfaction surveys are not designed to measure the best practices of the industry. Rather, they are designed to measure client's perceptions about one firm compared to a group. Management can use the results of a client satisfaction survey to learn about clients measure the performance of law firms and what they consider to be important criteria.

Special surveys can be conducted in writing, by telephone, in person or through any combination of these methods. Some topics lend themselves to in-person interviews, because the responses may not be quantitative or easily captured in a written format. In addition, in-person interviews allow the interviewer to ask follow-up questions and to gain a better understanding of the comparison firm's situation.

Special surveys can be conducted by the firm or by an independent party, such as a consultant. The advantage of using an independent party is that people are more likely to provide information to a third party than directly to a competitor. Normally, all firms that participate in the survey will receive a confidential copy of the survey. As a result, the findings are more likely to reflect best practices than a published survey might. Another advantage is that the firm often is able to learn more about the comparison population and how it achieves its level of performance. Unfortunately, the more sensitive the information, the less likely that law firms will disclose it, even to an independent party.

[c]—Best Practices Data Maintained by Industry Consultants and Others

Some industry consultants may have a catalog of best practice information on a variety of topics. While this information may not be published, consultants may be willing to share the benefit of their experience with a law firm client performing its own benchmarking study. Normally, consultants are not at liberty to disclose the identity of the composition of the population or specific firms, but should be able to discuss a firm's evaluation criteria in relation to the group.

The advantage of this approach is that the information is available and can be interpreted by an independent party.

[d]—Benchmarking Studies Conducted by Other Firms

Other firms may have conducted benchmarking studies that are either similar to or encompass aspects of the study that a law firm is envisioning. For example, banks sometimes prepare survey results based on financial statements that are submitted. Another source of survey results is participating in someone else's survey.

The advantage of using such studies is that the information is readily available. A disadvantage is that the comparison group of another firm may not be the one your firm would have chosen.

[4]—Guidelines for Success

Benchmarking can be a tremendous aid to management's decision-making ability. However, the process is time consuming and there are multiple pitfalls, which must be avoided. To help ensure success, the following guidelines should be followed:

(1) The process must be supported by high-level firm management;
(2) Functional experts must participate in the process;
(3) The firm must recognize that time, effort and skills will need to be devoted to the project;
(4) Judgment and insight must be applied to the benchmarking data—interpretation of data is more important than collection of data;
(5) The firm must budget time and money for collection of data from internal sources;
(6) The firm must include concrete action plans and targets; and
(7) Actions should be monitored over time.

Having appropriate management information is one of the most critical components of the process because without that, both firm management and others responsible for the success of the project will not have the information they need to monitor progress and assess the impact of various actions.

CHAPTER 29

Property and Equipment Acquisition: The Lease or Buy Decision

Chapter Contents

---

§ 29.01 Overview of the Issue

The acquisition of property and equipment is necessary for the operation of a law firm. Property and equipment generally includes office space, leasehold improvements, reference materials, furniture, technology equipment (e.g., computers, networks, phone systems, copiers, faxes, software, etc.). With the exception of office space,[1]

---

[1] The acquisition and financial modeling of office space is discussed in Chapter 22, Financial Modeling, *supra.*

most law firms have historically acquired these assets with working capital or through long- or short-term financing. One rationale for the outright purchase of assets is that continued ownership after the financing and depreciation period provides an economic benefit to the firm. This generally holds true for assets that have long useful lives (e.g., office furniture) but not technological equipment. In recent years, however, a number of firms have turned to leasing as an option for the acquisition of high technology assets. Operating leases are more preferential primarily because they are easier and the accounting rules for operating leases do not require the lease commitment of be recorded as a liability on the firm's balance sheet. Rather, the payment is expensed when paid (cash basis) or when due (accrual basis). Nonetheless, both operating and capital leases are used. This trend is a result of a number of factors, including:

- The significant investment needed to provide a sufficient number of computers to remain a viable practice;
- Increasing sophistication of equipment needed (e.g., in the early 1990s, many firms did not have automated phone systems or sophisticated computer networks);
- The rapid advancement in technology equipment causing existing equipment to become obsolete more quickly;
- The reluctance of law firm management to be at risk for losses on obsolete equipment (e.g., computers that were no longer viable for firm use often were offered to employees, donated to charities, etc.).

The decision to purchase or lease assets depends on a number of factors including:

- anticipated useful life of the asset;
- sources and cost of funds;
- lease or financing period;
- tax implications for the partners or shareholders;
- maintenance or other related direct costs of ownership; and
- expected salvage value and means of disposition at the end of usefulness.

As recommended in Chapter 17,[2] it is advisable to develop a financial model taking the above considerations into account to properly evaluate tax and other economic advantages and disadvantages under-

---

[2] See Chapter 17, Tax Planning, § 17.04[4]] *supra.*

Chapter[3] do not take into account specific limitations of the tax code related to the business use of assets or for specific assets such as leased automobiles, but may be modified as necessary to the specific acquisition under consideration. And, while an opportunity cost has been estimated in the development of the model, individual firms will have to assess the specific opportunities at issue to determine appropriate factors in each situation.

---

[3] See § 29.06 *infra.*

§ 29.02 Anticipated Useful Life of Asset

Capitalizable assets are those that have a useful life substantially in excess of one year.[1] For financial statement purposed, when an asset is purchased, its cost typically is depreciated over its useful life, For tax purposes, however, an asset's useful life is not as relevant, because the Internal Revenue Code prescribes depreciable lives based on predetermined categories.[2] Depending on a law firm's specific fact and circumstances, it may be possible to deduct the cost of an asset when it is purchased, subject to certain limitations.[3]

The concept of an asset's useful life must be distinguished from its physical life. As previously discussed, office furniture or equipment and leasehold improvements typically have very long lives. Office computers (i.e., personal computers) on the other hand have physical lives that often may exceed their useful lives - especially from a business perspective. An asset's useful life typically has an inverse relationship to the maturity of technology of its use. That is, the more quickly technology advances, the shorter the useful life becomes.

The longer the useful life, the stronger the argument for purchase and depreciation of the asset, rather than leasing the asset. Continued use after the end of depreciation and financing periods has no cost for the law firm, other than normal maintenance and the ultimate disposition costs.[4]

---

[1] Treas. Reg. § 1.461-1(a)(1); 26 C.F.R. § 1.461-1(a)(1). See also discussion in Chapter 17, Tax Planning § 17.04[1][a] *supra.*

[2] I.R.C. § 168; 26 C.F.R. § 168. See also discussion in Chapter 17, Tax Planning § 17.04[3].

[3] See Chapter 17, Tax Planning § 17.04[3][d] *supra.*

[4] Note however that some jurisdictions, most notably the District of Columbia and Florida, impose a property tax on assets as long as they are in use, regardless of their depreciated or fair market value. The District of Columbia applies the tax rate to the depreciated cost, but not less than 25% of the original purchase price. In such jurisdictions, therefore, there is a continued expense to the firm for fully depreciated assets.

29.03 Sources of Capital

As discussed in Chapter 251,[1] law firm assets are typically financed through a combination of equity financing, borrowing and leasing. Major investments such as for significant leasehold improvements or the upgrade overhaul of firm-wide computer systems generally are too large a drain on working capital to be financed entirely from equity or additional partner investment. This discussion assumes that the decision to seek financing outside the firm has been made and that the choice has been narrowed to leasing or bank loans.

[1]—Purchase Transactions

If a firm decides to seek financing to purchase capital assets, the source of funds will typically be through short- or long-term bank loans or capital leases, which are treated similarly for accounting purposes. The purchased property or equipment is recorded as an asset and the debt incurred is recorded as with an offsetting liability. for the debt incurred and the periodic expenses are is the depreciation of the asset and interest expense.

If a number of smaller purchases are being consolidated into a single note—such as during an upgrade overhaul of a firm's computer network—financial institutions will often offer a period of funds availability at a floating rate, to be converted to a fixed term, fixed rate loan at a specified date.[2]

The various issues related to loan agreements are discussed in Chapter 215.

[2]—Lease Transactions

Statement of Financial Accounting Standards No. 13, Accounting for Leases (SFAS 13) establishes the standards for classifying, accounting for and reporting lease transactions and should be referred to for the fine points of such transactions. In general, the accounting for a lease transaction is dependent may be treated as an operating lease or a capital lease, depending on whether or not, in substance, the lessee or (i.e., the law firm) retains the rewards and obligations of ownership. If so, then the lease is capitalized with the asset and related liability recorded for financial statement purposes. The asset is then amortized to expense over the period of the lease term or the

---

[1] See § 251.02 *supra.*

[2] See § 251.02 *supra.* The various issues related to loan agreements are discussed in Chapter 25.

asset's life. The tax treatment may be different because the life and method of depreciation are governed by tax rules.[3]

Capital leases are treated as financed purchases with appropriate recording of an asset and a liability. If the law firm does not retain the rewards and obligations of ownership not, then the lease is treated as an operating lease, with the monthly cost of the lease recorded as an expense in the period. The relevant expenses are the depreciation of the asset and interest expense. For an operating lease, the rental payment is expensed.

[a]—Capital Leases

While a capital lease is essentially a financed purchase, it can have advantages over outright purchase including:

(1) reduced or known maintenance costs over the term of the lease when such costs are included in the lease agreement;

(2) upgrade incentives to reduce the potential of operating obsolete equipment; and

(3) reduced need to seek general purpose financing and

(4) ability to walk away from the equipment at the end of the lease with no further obligations.

As previously noted, above, a lease which transfers substantially all benefits and risks of ownership to the lessee is classified as a capital lease. According to SFAS No. 13, the existence of any one of the following criteria requires that a lease be treated as a capital lease:

(1) Ownership of the property is transferred to the lessee at the end of the lease term.

(2) The lease includes a bargain -purchase option (;e.g. i.e., an option to purchase the property for $1 at the end of the lease term).a price that virtually assures the exercise of the option.

(3) The lease term is at least seventy-five 75 percent of the economic life of the property.

(4) The present value of the minimum lease payments, net of executory costs (e.g. maintenance, property taxes, insurance, etc.,) represents at least 90 percent of the fair market value of the leased property.

In a manner similar to purchase transactions, a capital lease is recorded at its inception as an asset and a liability. The value of the

---

[3] See Chapter 17, Tax Planning, §§ 17.04[3] and [4].

asset and related liability is the present value of the minimum lease payments during the lease term, net of executory costs. If such a lease meets either of the first two (ownership) criteria, it is amortized over the estimated economic life of the asset. If it meets either of the last two (use) criteria, it is amortized over the term of the lease. During the lease term, payments are allocated between a reduction of liability, executory costs and interest expense to produce a constant periodic rate of interest.

[b]—Operating Leases

A lease which that is not a capital lease is an operating lease. The relevant expense is the periodic rental payment, which may include factors of rental, interest expense and executory costs. It offers many of the advantages of a capital lease, (i.e., reduced or known maintenance costs, upgrade incentives, etc.,) and is usually for a shorter term than capital leases. This is the type of lease that increasingly is becoming increasingly popular for high technology equipment such as desktop computers that were traditionally purchased by law firms.

§ 29.04 Term of Lease or Financing

Financing and leasing allocate the cost of ownership to those who will benefit from the use of the asset. This concept is particularly important to law firms as the individual owners of the firm may change each year as new partners are admitted and others retire or leave. Purchase accounting, however, weights the expense of ownership to the early period of ownership through the nature of MACRS depreciation[1] and the payment of interest. Leasing has the added impact of leveling cash flow over the term of the lease, while financing on a floating rate can produce an uneven cash flow over the term of the note.

The term of financing or leasing is important both in evaluating cash flow as well as the economic benefit of the asset. Care should be taken to avoid financing or leasing assets beyond their useful life. If what would normally be considered an operating lease for financial statement purposes has a lease term in excess of the useful life for tax purposes, then the lease might be considered a capital lease for tax purposes. For example, leasing a digital phone system for a seven-year term might be an operating lease for financial statement purposes but a capital lease for tax purposes, because the depreciable tax life for digital phone systems is five years.

---

[1] See § 25.06 *infra*.

§ 29.05 Maintenance and Related Issues

[1]—Maintenance Costs

Maintenance agreements are often included in a vendor-provided lease and often at very favorable rates. When evaluating third-party leases or financing, it is essential to solicit and evaluate the additional costs of maintenance agreements.

[2]—Asset Tracking

Since law firms do not rely on assets to directly produce revenue as do manufacturing and other enterprises, the structured tracking of assets has been a relatively low priority at many firms. Assets are recorded in the general ledger at the time of acquisition and little further tracking is performed on most assets with the exception of high value items such as art and rugs, and catalogued items as the library collection.

When operating leases are contemplated for multiple, portable components with expected return and upgrade options, however, it is necessary to plan for adequate tracking of these assets, because the law firm has to return the same leased assets at the expiration of the lease. A more formal, bar-coded inventory with periodic inventory updates may be advisable. There are a number of software solutions that integrate directly or indirectly with depreciation systems and law firm general ledgers that should be evaluated in conjunction with undertaking a significant leasing program.

Asset tracking is advisable even if there is no lease involved. Many firms have invested heavily in personal computers, computer networks, and audiovisual equipment. These assets are expensive and, as some firms have found the hard way, they can be difficult to safeguard. Establishing a tracking system the same as would be used for leased assets allows a law firm to maintain better control over its assets, especially for insurance purposes.

[3]—Insurance and Appraisals

Acquisition of significant new assets, or replacement of old, fully depreciated assets may require updating appraisals and property insurance. The insurance provisions of the lease agreement as well as the terms of the firm's business insurance policy must be closely evaluated. It is important to evaluate potential additional costs of increased insurance coverage in the overall cost of ownership model, if applicable.

[4]—Prepayment, Assignment and/or Cancellation

Evaluate carefully the lease clauses relating to prepayment of loans or the ability to cancel leases. What will be the consequences if the firm significantly downsizes or disbands during the term of the agreement? What will be the consequences of upgrading computer hardware before the expiration of a lease? Many standard lease agreements are non-cancelable. When leasing computer equipment, it is advisable to negotiate some provision in the lease that will allow the firm to upgrade computer hardware when existing leased equipment is incapable of efficiently handling the demands of changing technology, e.g., new versions of computer programs that require more greater CPU speeds and more RAM.

29.06 Example Modeling

For practical purposes, only two options—an operating lease and a fixed-rate financed purchase option—are presented here for comparison. The purchase option may be converted to a capital lease for financing purposes if desired. The implications of the Taxpayer Relief Act of 1997 have not been assessed in the development of this model.

This financial model evaluates the viability of leasing 25 desktop computers, which represent one-third of the firm's total desktop computer units. The firm has committed that, to maintain pace with technology, it will replace one-third of all its end-user computers each year, disposing of its oldest computers at that time.

[1]—Model Assumptions

The following assumptions have been made in the example financial model:

(1) **Assets Acquired = 25 desktop computers**
Purchase price of each computer is assumed to be $3,200 for a total current value of $80,000. These computers will be replaced after three years with new computers.

(2) **Debt repayment of lease period = 3 years**
For economic reasons, and to match expense with the benefit of use, the firm has decided to finance the purchase over the term of use. Debt payments are to be made at the end of the period.

(3) **MACRS depreciation period = 5 years**
The Modified Accelerated Cost Recovery System is applied to most tangible depreciable property placed in service after December 31, 1986.[1] Most office equipment, including computers and telephone systems, is classified with a five-year life.[2] For tax purposes, the half-year convention is required,[3] rather than a mid-quarter convention, is used in this example.

(4) **Marginal tax rate for partners = 40.5%**
This rate is purely arbitrary and is based on 36% federal and 4.5% state. The state rate is incremental, based on a 7% statutory rate reduced by 36% to give effect to the tax benefit of deducting state income taxes from federal taxable income. The tax benefit is assumed to be earned ratably throughout the year.

---

[1] IRC § 168; 26 U.S.C. § 168. See also Chapter 17, Tax Planning, § 17.04[3][a].
[2] IRC § 168(e)(3)(B); 26 U.S.C. § 168(e)(3)(B).
[3] IRC § 168(d)(1); 26 U.S.C. § 168(d)(1).

(5) **Interest rate (cost of capital) = 8.75%**
The example rate is fixed although in a particular financing agreement it may fluctuate based on prime plus a factor. Since future fluctuation is unknown, a fixed rate as of the date of the analysis is appropriate.

(6) **Lease terms = 36 months, non-cancelable monthly lease**
Monthly payments of $2,340 are based on a market lease rate quoted concurrent with the interest rate cited above. Payments are made in advance, with the 36th payment made concurrent with the first. At the end of the lease term, the lease could be extended for the same monthly payment on a month-to-month basis, all equipment could be returned and new equipment could be purchased or leased under a new agreement, or the lease equipment could be purchased at fair market value as determined by manufacturers or an independent appraisal. These terms are fairly standard for law firms at the time of this writing.

(7) **Lease Buyout = $0**
This example assumes no lease buyout will be exercised at the end of the lease term, because as the stated assumption goal is that to acquire new, technologically current equipment will be acquired or leased at the end of the lease period.

(8) **Initial fees or downpayment = $0**
No loan origination fees, closing costs, down payments or other initial payments required to secure financing have been assumed for this model as lender policy would vary. A prepayment of the last month's lease has been assumed for the lease (see above).

(9) **Salvage value at the end of debt/leasing period = 10%**
This salvage value is used both for the calculation of the lease rate as well as the estimated sale price of purchased computers after the term of the loan.

(10) **Maintenance costs = $0**
This example assumes a three- year manufacturer's warranty on the equipment. However, if a shorter warranty period is applicable, or if the leasing vendor offers maintenance as a benefit of leasing, the impact of additional maintenance costs must be considered in the analysis.

(11) **Sale gain (loss)**
The gain or loss on the sale of equipment is calculated as the original purchase price less accumulated depreciation less the sale price. For this example, it is assumed that the sale price is equivalent to the salvage value of 10% of the original purchase price.

(12) **Discount rate = 8.5%**

In present -value analysis, the discount rate must be evaluated in light of each situation under consideration. A rule of thumb is to use a weighted -average of cost of capital, although some analyses use an addictive factor to account for opportunity costs. No opportunity costs have been assumed in this rate for ease of demonstration purpose, but they may be relevant and if so should be taken into consideration (i.e., opportunity costs represent the cost of not being able to take advantage of the next best opportunity).

(13) **Disposition costs = $0**

If an asset is purchased, it must be disposed of at some point. There is a cost of disposing of any equipment, especially personal computers (even if they are given away) and that estimated disposition cost should be factored into the purchase vs. lease analysis. For purposes of this example, no disposition costs are included.

[2]—Lease/Buy Model

A purchase -analysis model is developed to calculate the annual book expenses and net after tax cash flow. Figure 29-A illustrates an example of a purchase-analysis model.

Figure 29-A. Illustration of purchase-analysis model.

Purchase	Initial Fees or Downpay-ment	MACRS Depre-ciation	Annual Principal Payment	Interest Expense	Main-tenance	Total Book Expense	Sale Gain <Loss>	Tax Benefit	Net-Cash Flow*
Year 1	—	$16,000	$24,378	$6,038		$22,038		$8,921	$21,495
Year 2	—	25,600	26,600	3,817		29,417		11,908	18,509
Year 3	—	15,360	29,022	1,394		16,754		6,782	23,634
Year 4	—	4,608				4,608	($10,432)	6,088	(14,088)
Year 5									
Total	$ 0	$61,568	$80,000	$11,249	$ 0	$72,817	($10,432)	$33,699	$49,550

* Net-cash flow equals the sum of all cash outlays of the period (e.g., initial payment, payments of principal and interest, maintenance payments, etc.) less related cash receipts (e.g., receipt of salvage value of equipment) less the tax benefit as a result of the accounting treatment of the equipment.

After developing the purchase-analysis model, it is necessary to develop a lease-analysis model, so that the two can be compared. Figure 29-B illustrates a lease-analysis model.

Figure 29-B. Illustration of lease-analysis model

Operating Lease	Initial Fees or Downpayment	Lease Payment	Maintenance	Total Book Expense	Lease <Buyout	Tax Benefit	Net-Cash Flow*
Year 1		$30,420		$30,420		$12,314	$18,106
Year 2		28,080		28,080		11,367	16,713
Year 3		25,740		25,740		10,420	15,320
Year 4							
Year 5							
Total	$ 0	$84,240	$ 0	$84,240	$ 0	$34,101	$50,139

While the purchase model actually results in a slightly lower total after- tax cash flow, a graphical depiction of cumulative cash flows under each arrangement helps clarify the importance of the timing of cash flows. Figure 29-C illustrates a graphical depiction of the cumulative net-cash flows of the lease vs. purchase analysis.

Figure 29-C. Illustration of graphical depiction of cumulative net-cash flows of lease vs. purchase example.

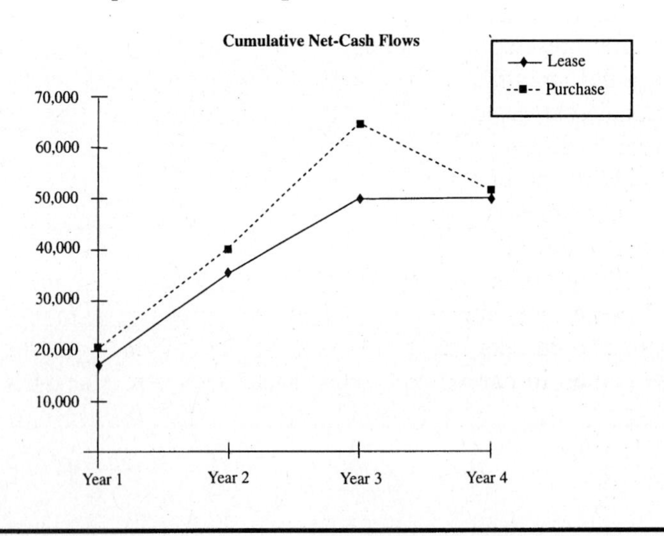

[3]—Analysis of Model

The impact of timing is borne out by a present - value analysis of the net -after—tax -cash flows. The net- + present value is the value today of a series of future payments. It is based on the current discount rate and when payments occur (at the beginning or end of a period). In Figure 29-D illustrates an example of the present-value of net cash flows based on the previous illustrations. The example the analysis below, it is assumed that debt payments are made at the end of the period, while lease payments are made at the beginning of the period. It is also assumed that tax benefits are earned equally throughout a year.

Figure 29-D. Illustration of present-value of net-cash flows.

Present Value of Net Cash Flows

Present Value	Purchase	Lease	Annual Difference
Year 1	$20,537	$17,474	$3,063
Year 2	16,247	14,672	1,575
Year 3	19,062	12,303	6,759
Year 4	(10,440)		(10,440)
Total	$45,406	$44,449	$957

The net present - value analysis shows that in this instance, leasing saves a net amount of $957. These savings do not take into account additional costs as a result of management time, or additional expense required to dispose of purchased equipment, or the additional cost of new equipment under either scenario. While this amount appears small, other factors such as volume (lease rates and finance charges are often reduced as the dollar volume of the transaction increases), discount rate, timing of payments, initial costs, maintenance costs, etc. may have a more significant impact in specific instances. Also, any analysis should take into consideration the opportunity cost of investing in capital in capital equipment as compared to leasing it.

List of Illustrations

Index

[References are to sections]

A

B

E

F

I

K

L

M

O

P

R

S

T

U-V-W-X-Y-Z